ACLS History E-Book Project
Reprint Series

The ACLS History E-Book Project (www.historyebook.org) collaborates with constituent societies of the American Council of Learned Societies, publishers, librarians and historians to create an electronic collection of works of high quality in the field of history. This volume is produced from digital images created for the Project by the Scholarly Publishing Office and the Digital Library Production Service at the University of Michigan, Ann Arbor. The digital reformatting process results in an electronic version of the text that can be both accessed online and used to create new print copies. This book and hundreds of others are available online in the History E-Book Project through subscription.

Many of the works in the History E-Book Project are available in print and can be ordered either directly from their publishers or as part of this series. For information refer to the online Title Record page for each book. Inquiries regarding this series can be directed to info@hebook.org.

ACLS
HISTORY E-BOOK

http://www.historyebook.org

Ira Allen

RECORDS

OF THE

GOVERNOR AND COUNCIL

OF THE

STATE OF VERMONT.

VOLUME II.

EDITED AND PUBLISHED BY AUTHORITY OF THE STATE

BY E. P. WALTON.

MONTPELIER:
STEAM PRESS OF J. & J. M. POLAND.
1874.

CONTENTS OF VOLUME II.

THE THIRD COUNCIL.

OCTOBER 1779 TO OCTOBER 1780.

THOMAS CHITTENDEN, Williston, *Governor*.
BENJAMIN CARPENTER, Guilford, *Lieutenant Governor*.

Councillors:

JOSEPH BOWKER, Rutland,
MOSES ROBINSON, Bennington,
JONAS FAY, Bennington,
TIMOTHY BROWNSON, Sunderland,
PAUL SPOONER, Hartland,
JEREMIAH CLARK, Shaftsbury,
BENJAMIN EMMONS, Woodstock,
IRA ALLEN, Colchester,
JOHN FASSETT, jr., Arlington,
JOHN THROOP, Pomfret,
SAMUEL FLETCHER, Townshend,
THOMAS CHANDLER, jr., Chester.

JOSEPH FAY, *Secretary*.

BIOGRAPHICAL NOTICES.[1]

JOHN FASSETT, JR., was born in Hardwick, Mass., June 3, 1743, and came to Bennington with his father, deacon and captain John Fassett, in 1761; removed to Arlington in 1777, and to Cambridge in 1784. Few men were more constantly in public service than John Fassett, Jr. He was lieutenant in Warner's first regiment in 1775, and captain in Warner's second in 1776. In 1777 he was one of the commissioners of sequestration, and, with Gov. Chittenden and Matthew Lyon, successful in subduing the tories of Arlington. He was elected representative of Arlington in the General Assembly for 1778 and 1779, and for Cambridge in 1787 and '8, 1790 and '91; though in 1779, 1787 and '8, and 1790 and '91 he was also elected Councillor. He served in each office portions of the time. He was a member of the Council in 1779 and until 1795 with the exception of 1786—fifteen years. He was judge of the superior court from its organization in 1778 until 1786—eight years; and chief

[1] For notices of Messrs. Allen, Bowker, Brownson, Chandler, Chittenden, Carpenter, Clark, Emmons, Jonas and Joseph Fay, Robinson, and Spooner, see Vol. I.

judge of Chittenden county court from 1787 until 1794—seven years. The historian of Cambridge, in the *Vt. Historical Magazine*, records Dr. John Fassett as the first physician who settled in the town, coming from Bennington in 1784 and removing to the west after a residence of about forty years in Cambridge. If this was judge John Fassett, he must have been an octogenarian at the time of his migration.—See Hiland Hall's *Early History;* Deming's *Catalogue;* and *Vt. Hist. Magazine*, Vol. II.

JOHN THROOP of Pomfret first appeared in the records of that town as justice of the peace in 1773, when the town was organized. His first appearance in the Vermont State records was as a delegate in the Convention at Windsor, June, 4 1777. He was a delegate in the Conventions of July and December of that year also. His name appears in the roll of the first Council in Ira Allen's *History*, Slade's *State Papers*, and Deming's *Catalogue;* but it does not appear in the records of the Council, whereas that of Moses Robinson does appear in that, and not in the three lists first named. The historian of Pomfret in Z. Thompson's *Gazetteer* (1824) states that "the town was first represented, in 1778, by John Throop." His name does appear in the roll of the second General Assembly, October 1778, but that of John Winchester Dana appears in the journal of the first Assembly, March and June sessions, 1778. Judge Throop was councillor from October 1779 to October 1786; a member of the House in 1787–8; judge of probate 1783–'92; judge of the court of confiscation in Oct. 1779; and of the superior court 1778–'80.—See B. H. Hall's *Eastern Vermont;* Thompson's *Gazetteer;* Deming's *Catalogue;* and *Legislative Directory.*

SAMUEL FLETCHER was born in Grafton, Mass., in 1745; and at seventeen he enlisted and served one year as a soldier in the old French war. On his return he learned the trade of a blacksmith, but removed to Townshend about 1772, and abandoned that trade on marrying a lady who had a fortune ample for that day, a daughter of Col. John Hazeltine, formerly of Upton, Mass., but then of Townshend,—a patriot, and a leading man in the county. At the commencement of the revolutionary war, Mr. Fletcher joined the army and was at the battle of Bunker Hill. In July 1775 the New York Provincial Congress appointed him a lieutenant, but it was found that he was in the continental army at Cambridge as an orderly. In 1776 he returned to Townshend, was elected captain of militia, and in 1777 his entire company volunteered to reinforce the army at Ticonderoga. On that expedition, he with thirteen volunteers attacked a British party of forty men, killed one and took seven prisoners without sustaining any loss to his party. In 1778, having joined his fortunes with the new state of Vermont, he became colonel of a Cumberland county regiment and continued in the military line until he reached and for six years held the highest rank, that of Major General. He was in the battle of Bennington, and served as major in the campaign against Burgoyne until after his surrender.

Townshend was the first town in Cumberland county to send delegates to a Vermont Convention, July 1776—Samuel Fletcher and Josiah Fish being the delegates. They were appointed on the committee "to treat with the inhabitants on the east side of the range of Green Mountains, relative to their associating with this Body;" and the establishment of the state resulted. He was an active member also in the conventions of September and October 1776, and of January 1777 that declared the independence of Vermont; and probably a member of the convention of 1777 which adopted the constitution. He was a member of the first three General Assemblies, and again in 1807; elected Councillor in 1779, and re-elected every year until 1790, and also in 1808 and 1813. He was elected a judge of the superior court in 1782, but refused to serve. From 1788 until 1806 he was sheriff of Windham county, and judge of the county court in 1778, 1783–4, and 1786. He was a member of the Board of War in 1781. He died Sept. 15, 1814. The first person born in Townshend was a daughter to Gen. Fletcher. She married Mr. [probably Ezekiel] Ransom, and was mother of Epaphroditus Ransom, who represented Townshend in the Legislature in 1826–'7, married a belle of Montpelier, Miss Almira Cadwell, and removed to Michigan, of which state he became governor. Gen. Fletcher was a man of enterprise, industry, and skill, and a valuable public officer. He was a fine writer, and for a part of his life kept a full and accurate daily record of public events. His papers were entrusted by his will to his son-in-law, Mr. Ransom, but were unfortunately destroyed in the burning of his house. In person Gen. Fletcher was straight, finely proportioned, but inclined to corpulency—in stature measuring about five feet ten inches; eyes blue, complexion light. He was elegant in manners, bland and refined in deportment, and very particular in his dress. Kind to all, he was generous and hospitable. With all other manly qualities, he was a perfect gentleman.—See Thompson's *Gazetteer; Eastern Vermont;* and Deming's *Catalogue.*

RECORD OF THE GOVERNOR AND COUNCIL

AT THE

SESSION OF THE GENERAL ASSEMBLY AT MANCHESTER,

OCTOBER 1779.[1]

STATE OF VERMONT, Manchester, 14 October 1779.

AT a meeting of Governor, Council, and General Assembly convened at Manchester, date above—Present His Excellency, Thomas Chittenden, Esqr. and the following members of the honble Council vizt :

Joseph Bowker, Esqr.	Jeremiah Clark,
Timo. Brownson,	Ira Allen,
Jonas Fay,	Benjamin Emmons,
Moses Robinson,	Paul Spooner, Esqr.

Voted that a Committee consisting of five members vizt : Jonas Fay, Timo. Brownson, Moses Robinson, Joseph Bowker, & Ira Allen, Esquires, are appointed to join a Committee of the Lower House, who are to receive, sort, & count the votes of the Freemen of this State and Declare those who are appointed to the several offices of Governor, Deputy Governor, Treasurer, and Councillors or assistants[2] for the year ensuing.

Pr. order, JOS. FAY, *Sec'y.*

A committee consisting of six members of the House of Assembly are appointed to Join the above named Committee vizt. John Fassett Jur. Esqr., Amos Robinson, Esqr., Capt. Matthew Lyon, Thomas Chandler, Samuel Fletcher, and Nathan Clark, Esquires.[3]

Having executed the business of their appointment, the following persons are Declared to be choosen, vizt : His Excellency Thomas Chittenden Esqr. Governor; His honor Benjamin Carpenter, Lt. Governor—The

---

[1] The record from this date takes the form of a regular journal more nearly than before.

[2] Sec. seventeen of the Frame of Government made the Councillors justices of the peace for the whole state, and when acting in this capacity they were often, perhaps always, styled "assistants." A heading in the act of 1779, regulating fees, recognized this title, thus: "*Assistants, or Justices Fees.*"

[3] From the *Assembly Journal:*

Resolved that the Council be notified that this Assembly are ready to attend Divine Service, which was accordingly done, and a Sermon Preached by the Reverend Mr. [Benajah] Root.

Hon[ble] Joseph Bowker, Moses Robinson, Jonas Fay, Timothy Brownson, Benjamin Emmons, Paul Spooner, Jeremiah Clark, Sam[l] Fletcher, Ira Allen, John Throop, John Fassett Jur. & Thomas Chandler Jur. Esquires, Councillors—And Ira Allen Esquire, Treasurer.

On this occasion, of course on taking the oath of office, Governor Chittenden delivered a speech, the original of which was found in the office of the Secretary of State, as follows:

A SPEECH OF HIS EXCELLENCY THOMAS CHITTENDEN, ESQ., 14TH OCTOBER 1779.

Gentlemen of the Council and Assembly:

The honor conferred on me by the freemen of this State, in appointing me their chief magistrate, demands a return of my warmest thanks: at the same time, I regret my inabilities to support the character of so important a station. Notwithstanding, as my appointment appears so unanimous, it affords me the highest satisfaction, and is to me a confirmation of their general approbation of my former conduct; therefore, I shall consider it my duty to serve the ensuing year, and by Divine assistance, shall labor to continue an equal, steady firmness, and impartial administration of justice, which has hitherto governed my conduct; relying on the candor and assistance of my council and the Legislature for my support.

Gentlemen:

The Legislature having constitutionally met, I cannot forbear expressing to you my highest satisfaction in the many great and important advantages arising from the due execution and careful administration of the laws, since they took place, and cannot but rejoice when I reflect on the infinite difference between a state of anarchy and that of a well regulated government; the latter of which we daily experience. And I most earnestly recommend to all magistrates, and others in authority under me, together with the freemen over whom I have the honor to preside, to persevere and let their conduct be uniformly just, and upright, and encourage one another to unite in the supporting and maintaining their common rights; which cannot fail to recommend this State to the impartial world. At the same time am unhappy to inform you that, notwithstanding the generous and lenient measures with which the disaffected inhabitants in the lower part of Cumberland County have been indulged,[1] yet they continue in their unjustifiable obstinacy against the authority of this State; I shall, however, recommend the suspension of the laws[2] intended to have been executed on those offenders, at present, in consequence of a letter received from his Excellency John Jay, Esquire, President of Congress, inclosing certain acts passed by that hon-

---

[1] See the proclamation of pardon, *Appendix H*, Vol. I.

[2] The act specially referred to was that of June 1779, "to prevent persons from exercising authority unless lawfully authorised by this State," which, though general in terms, was of course specially aimed against all persons who should attempt to act in the name and by the authority of New York. The penalty for the first offense was a fine not exceeding one hundred pounds; for the second not exceeding forty stripes on the naked body; and for the third, the right ear was to be nailed to a post and cut off, and the forehead was to be branded with the letter C [contumacious ?] with a hot iron.—See Slade's *State Papers*, p. 389.

orable board, relating to a final settlement of all difference subsisting between this and the adjacent States; which I now submit to you for your consideration; a subject of the greatest importance, and demands your most serious attention.[1]

Your agents to Congress have attended, agreeable to their instructions, from time to time. Their proceedings I shall now lay before you for your perusal and approbation; which, I hope, will prove satisfactory. From every circumstance, I think we have the highest reason to believe that from the efforts of our agents and the interposition of Congress, our unhappy disputes with the neighboring States, will soon terminate in a final and happy issue.

With respect to the present situation of the domestic affairs of the State, it is with pleasure that I inform you that the measures pursued by the Board of War, by the assistance of Divine Providence, have proved effectually sufficient to defend our frontiers, against the ravages of the common enemy, while they have been permitted to execute their horrid vengeance on many of the innocent inhabitants of the different parts of the continent; which, in some measure, proves the approbation of Heaven to our Independence, and justifies the measures pursued to support and defend it. As the time for which the troops now in service, are engaged, expires the middle of November next, you will be careful to make such provisions for future defence, as your wisdom shall direct.

Gentlemen of the Assembly:

I shall, from time to time, during the session, digest and communicate to you, such other matters as shall appear to me to require your attention, in a full confidence that the same zeal to promote the common cause, for which the inhabitants of this State have hitherto been distinguished, will be equally conspicuous in your deliberations.

THOMAS CHITTENDEN.

Having Concluded the business of the day adjourned to 8 °Clock To-morrow Morning.

FRIDAY, 15 Oct. 1779.

Met according to Adjournment.

A Committee from the Assembly [having been] appointed to Join a Committee of the Council to prepare an answer to the Governor's speach to said Assembly, viz[t] John Fassett, Jun[r.] Esq[r.], Reuben Jones, Esq[r.] and Nathan Clark, Esq[r.] Voted Jonas Fay & Moses Robinson Esquires a Committee to join the said Committee for the above said purpose. [No answer appears on the journal.]

Voted Jonas Fay, Ira Allen, and Paul Spooner, Esquires, to join a Committee of Assembly to form the outlines of a plan to be pursued for defence before Congress against the Neighboring States in Consequence of a Late Act of that body for that purpose, and make report thereon to this Council.[2]

Adjourned to 8 °Clock Tomorrow.

---

[1] For resolutions of Congress of June 1779, see Vol. I, p. 520; and for resolutions of September 1779, and the consequent action of Vermont, see *Appendix B*.

[2] The committee appointed by the Assembly consisted of the following named gentlemen: Ethan Allen, Reuben Jones, Nathan Clark, and John Fassett. Allen was not a member of the Assembly, however. On other

MANCHESTER, 16 October 1779.

Met according to Adjournment.

Voted His Honor Benjamin Carpenter Esq$^{r.}$ & Benjamin Emmons Esq$^{r.}$ to join a Committee from the Assembly to Examine the Petition of Benjamin Dorchester and make Report.

Having concluded the business of the day,

Adjourned to Monday next 2 ^{o}Clock afternoon.

MONDAY 18 October 1779.

Met according to Adjournment.

Voted that the Committee appointed from the Council to take into Consideration the matter concerning the Estate of Col$^{o.}$ James Rogers, Late of Kent [Londonderry] in this State, (now with the Enemy,) be discharged, & that the Same be laid before the General Assembly for their Determination. P$^{r.}$ order, JOSEPH FAY, *Sec$^{y.}$*

Adjourned to 8 ^{o}Clock Tomorrow.

TUESDAY 19 October 1779.

Met according to Adjournment.

Voted Paul Spooner Esq$^{r.}$ to Join a Committee from the Assembly to Nominate a Board of War.

Voted the Honble Benjamin Emmons & Joseph Bowker Esq$^{rs.}$ to join a Committee from the Assembly to prepare an Act directing the Secretary of State in his office and Duty.[1]

Voted that Ira Allen Esq$^{r.}$ be and he is hereby directed to write a Letter to John Simonds, Commissioner of Sequestration in Andover, to

---

occasions he was appointed on committees when he was not a member. Councillor Fassett served in the House through the October session.

From the *Assembly Journal:*

Resolved that there be a Board of War chosen, to consist of nine persons, five of whom to be a quorum, to conduct the political affairs of the present War in the northern department in this State the ensuing year.

From the peculiar phraseology—"*to conduct the political affairs of the present War,*"—it may be surmised that even then the originator of the resolution contemplated the policy which was adopted a year later, and successfully carried out in the Haldimand correspondence. This phraseology is found in the writings of both Ethan and Ira Allen, who were conspicuous in the subsequent correspondence. The resolution resulted in the appointment of a Board of War.

[1] The committee reported on the 22d and the duties of the Secretary of State were specified by a resolution. He was "to keep a regular office and register all the proceedings of the General Assembly of this State, Charters of Incorporation, Grants of land made within this State, and to receive on file all petitions and remonstrances and grant copies thereof when thereto requested, taking therefor his lawful fees." By the act of Feb. 1779, his fee for affixing the state seal was three shillings; and for recording laws and orders, for military commissions and for justices of the peaces and judges of probate, and for petitions to the Assembly, six shillings each.—See Slade's *State Papers*, p. 318.

request him to make immediate Settlement with the Treasurer of this State. Attest, JOSEPH FAY, *Secy.*

Voted that Ephraim Knap of Arlington, who has lately been under restraint, be & he is hereby Liberated.

Voted Jeremiah Clark & Samuel Fletcher a Committee to Join a Committee of the Assembly to Enquire of Mr. Megreegers Concerning the Estate of Colo. James Rogers.[1]

Voted that the Governor & Council join the House of Representatives in a Committee of both Houses to Confer on the important business of this State.[2]

MANCHESTER 20 Octr. 1779.

Met according to Adjournment.

Voted Samuel Fletcher Esqr to join a Committee from the Assembly to take into consideration the Petition of Mr. Mash, [Daniel Marsh.]

---

[1] Messrs. McGregores in the Assembly journal. The committee learned that Mrs. Rogers had been disabled by losing the use of her limbs, and reported that she with her children be allowed the farm she lived on, with farming and household utensils; which was agreed to. This property had been confiscated, Col. Rogers having joined the enemy.

[2] On this day and succeeding days, the Governor and Council met the House in joint assembly to consider the action of Congress of the preceding September concerning Vermont. For the record and the result, see *Appendix B*.

From the *Assembly Journal*, Oct. 19:

Resolved that a Committee of three to join a Committee from the Council be appointed to nominate eighteen persons nine of whom to be chosen by this Assembly for a Board of War. Members chosen, Mr. Fassett, Mr. I. [Isaac] Clark, and Mr. Aikins, [Edward Aiken of Londonderry.]

Resolved that the Court of Confiscation [Governor and Council] be requested to inform this Assembly whether they have Impowered Major Chandler [Thomas, jr.] to sell lands that have New York title only, or what instructions are in his commission relative to the sale of Fane [Newfane.]

Resolved that there be a Committee appointed to deliver the aforesaid message to the said Court of Confiscation. Members chosen, Mr. Fassett, Mr. Lyon, and Mr. I. Clark.

The Committee appointed to deliver the aforesaid Message to the Court of Confiscation, returned with the following report, viz:

"IN COUNCIL, 19th Octr. 1779.

"This Council having [have] considered the request of the Assembly "relative to Major Chandler, and have no remembrance of authorising "him to sell the New York title by virtue of his Commission. Pr. "order, JOSEPH FAY, *Secy.*"*

Resolved that it is the opinion of this House that the land in Kent [Londonderry] attempted to be sold by Major Thomas Chandler [jr.,] formerly occupied by Colo. James Rogers, is not legally sold.

* This is not in the Council record, that body in this matter having acted as the Court of Confiscation.

Voted that the Governor & Council join the General Assembly Tomorrow Morning at the opening thereof to choose Judges of the Supreme [Superior] Court.

Adjourned to 9 °Clock Tomorrow.[1]

THURSDAY 21t October 1779.

Met according to Adjournment.

Voted Moses Robinson Esqr. to join a Committee of the Assembly to prepare the Powers and Instructions of the Board of War.

Having Taken into Consideration the accounts of Asahel Blanchard, Voted to refer the further consideration thereof to the next session of this Council, & that the same be laid on file.

Voted that in pursuance of a Resolution of the General Assembly Providing for the support of Mrs. Rogers and Family, [it is] ordered that Mrs. Rogers be put into the possession of all and singular the Estate, articles & things contained in said Resolve, thereby to possess the said Estate.

Voted Samuel Fletcher Esqr. a Committee to join a Committee from the House to Take into Consideration the petition of the inhabitants of Westminster.[2]

Adjourned to 8 °Clock Tomorrow.

---

[1] From the *Assembly Journal*, Oct. 20:

The Committee appointed to nominate eighteen persons [for a Board of War,] brought in their report with the following persons nominated for that purpose, viz. Thomas Chittendeu Esqr. Ira Allen Esqr. Joseph Bowker Esqr. Joseph Bradley Esqr. Jonas Fay Esqr. Major Benjamin Wait, Capt. Ebenezer Allen, Benjamin Emmons Esqr. Colo. Samuel Fletcher, Majr. Ebenezer Wood, William Ward, Esqr. Joseph Fay Esqr. Timothy Brownson Esqr. Joshua Webb, Esqr. Capt. Hodges, [Edmond, of Barnard,] Majr. Tyler, [Joseph, of Townshend,] Samuel Robinson Esqr. Jonathan Fassett Esqr.

Resolved to choose by ballot nine persons for a Board of War, when the following persons were accordingly chosen, vizt : His Excellency Thomas Chittenden Esqr. Ira Allen Esqr. Joseph Bowker Esqr. Capt. Ebenr. Allen, Joseph Bradley Esqr. Saml. Fletcher Esqr. Majr. Benja. Wait, Capt. Jonathan Fassett and Timothy Brownson Esqr.

Resolved that the above nine persons are and they are hereby appointed a Board of War for the ensuing year.

[2] From the *Assembly Journal*, Oct. 21:

The Council having joined the house they proceeded to choose Judges of the Supreme [Superior] Court when the following persons were chosen by ballot vizt: the honorable Moses Robinson Esqr. John Shepherdson Esqr. John Fassett, Junr. Esqr. John Throop Esqr. and Paul Spooner Esqr.

His Excellency Thomas Chittenden Esqr. requested to be excused serving in the Board of War—Resolved that he be excused and another chose in his room. Whereupon Samuel Robinson Esqr. was chose by ballot.

Maj. JOHN SHEPARDSON, who was born in 1718 and died in 1798, was in the second company of settlers in Guilford, which in 1772 styled itself "the district of Guilford" in the county of Cumberland and province of New York. Maj. Shepardson was the first clerk, and Capt. John Barney

FRIDAY 22d. October 1779.

Met according to Adjournment.

Voted Moses Robinson Esqr. to join a Committee from the Assembly to prepare a proclamation for a day of public Thanksgiving and prayer.

Resolved that Mr. Daniel Mash [Marsh] be and he is hereby impowered to receive for his use and Benefit all and Singular of that part of the produce of the farm (lately the property of Colo. James Rogers & occupied by the said Mash the last season) which he would have been entitled to Provided the General Assembly had not disannulled the Bargain made by & between the said Mash & Thomas Chandler [jr.] Esqr. in behalf of this State—And that Liberty be given for the Expending the said produce on the premises, said Mash to Quit the premises at or before the first day of April next.

Attest, JOSEPH FAY, *Secy.*

Passed in General [Assembly] & attested by ROSL. HOPKINS, *Clerk.*

Resolved that Jeremiah Clark Esqr. join a Committee from the Assembly to propose a Certain Salary for His Excellency the Governor the preceding and Ensuing year.[1]

Adjourned to 9 oClock Tomorrow.

SATURDAY, 23d October 1779.

Met according to Adjournment.

Resolved that Joseph Fay be & he is hereby appointed Secretary to the Governor & Council for the year Ensuing.

---

supervisor, both of whom were among the earliest adherents to Vermont in that town. The Major was a delegate in the Dorset Convention, Sept. 25 1776; judge of probate under Vermont in 1778, and judge of the superior court in 1778 and '9. A party of Yorkers attempted to arrest Lieut. Gov. Carpenter and Maj. Shepardson in 1782, but failed.—See Thompson's *Gazetteer;* and *Eastern Vermont.*

On this day the General Assembly resolved unanimously to support the independence of the State and grant unappropriated lands.—See *Appendix B.*

[1] From the *Assembly Journal:*

Oct. 23.—The Committee appointed to affix the Governor's Sallary brought in the following report, vizt : "It is our opinion that his Excellency the Governor ought to be paid seven hundred pounds in addition to the three hundred pounds granted to him by the General Assembly in October last for the year past, and that his Excellency ought to have one hundred pounds for the year ensuing as good as money was in the year 1774." Resolved that said Report be accepted.

Oct. 27.—Resolved that the sum of one hundred pound be paid to his Excellency the Governor, the said one hundred pound to be made as good as money was in the year 1774, in addition to his sallary for the ensuing year.

Oct. 25.—Resolved that the Counsellors and Representatives be allowed fifteen dollars pr. day while in service and one dollar pr. mile in coming from their respective places of abode to this place.

Previous to Sept. 1 1777 lawful money or bills of credit equalled gold or silver; Nov. 1 1778 $3.60 in lawful money, and Nov. 1 1779 $16 in lawful money were equal to one silver dollar. The sums in the above resolutions should be measured by this standard.—See Slade's *State Papers*, p. 430.

Resolved that Samuel Fletcher Esq$^{r.}$ join a Committee of the Assembly to propose the Method & price of Granting Land.

Resolved that Major Benjamin Wait be & he is hereby appointed sheriff in & for the county of Cumberland in the Room of John Benjamin for the Time being.

Adjourned to Monday next 10 ^{o}Clock in the Morning.[1]

MONDAY 25 October 1779.

Met according to Adjournment.

Resolved that Joseph Bowker and Moses Robinson Esquires join a Committee from the Assembly to propose & Regulate the setling of the Town of *Bethel*, as also to propose an amendment to the price of Granting.

Resolved that Timothy Brownson and John Throop to join a Committee from the Assembly to Consider the several petitions for Land and which are proper to be granted this present session.[2]

Adjourned to 9 ^{o}Clock Tomorrow.

---

[1] From the *Assembly Journal*, Oct. 23:

The Committee appointed to prepare the power and instructions of the Board of War brought in their report which being read: Resolved that the members of the Board of War be and are hereby impowered to meet and appoint their President and Secretary; which President shall have power to call together the members of said Board with the advice of one or more of the members; and their Secretary shall keep Records of their proceedings;—and they shall have power to examine into the necessity of the defence of the frontiers, and recommend to the Captain General the raising of any number of men (said Board to appoint their officers) for any time not exceeding nine months as they shall judge proper —and also the calling out the militia in such number and proportion as they shall judge necessary—and if necessity call for it, to procure provision, and to store a sufficient quantity for the year ensuing, in order to supply the soldiers that are or may be employed for the security of the frontiers of this State in case that by any means the Continental Commissaries neglect to supply the garrisons there; and shall have power to nominate and appoint a Commissary in order to procure and store such provisions and to draw on the Treasury for the money to defray the charge thereof.

[2] *Report communicated to the Governor and Council by the General Assembly.*

MANCHESTER, October 26, 1779.

To the Honble General Assembly now sitting at Manchester:

Your Committee appointed yesterday to Take into consideration, what petitions for Land there is on file that can be Granted this Sessions beg Leave to Report their Opinion as follows—That the Honble Assembly proceed as soon as may be & Grant to Major Benjamin Wait & his associates the *Isle of Mott* agreeabl to his petition, and to Col$^{o.}$ Danforth Keyes and his associates the Tract of Land called *Royalton*—And to Lt. Jonathan Meachum and his associates the Tract of Land discribed by the name of *Benson*, and to Captain Ebenezer Allen and his associates the Tract of Land called *Fair haven*, as by their several Petitions & Surveys on file may be seen, & no more parcels of Land in this State until their Several bounds can be better ascertained according to the Resolve of the House, Always provided that any Settlers now on

TUESDAY, 26 October 1779.

Met according to Adjournment.

Resolved that Timothy Brownson Esqr. join a Committee from the Assembly to enquire why the Land of Phinehas Hurd Late of Arlington Deceased may not be sold, and examine into the Circumstances of the families of Stephen Fairchilds and Austin Sealey, being read in the Council, was referred to future consideration as mentioned on said petition. [This, except the reference to a petition, and the Committee of the Council, was a resolution of the Assembly. The form of the record is quite irregular.]

Adjourned to 8 oClock Tomorrow.

IN COUNCIL, Manchester, Wednesday 27th Octr. 1779.

Resolved that a Committee of Two be appointed from this Council to join a Committee from the House to examine and assertain the necessary Business to be done at this present Sessions.

Resolved that Timothy Brownson Esqr. join a Committee from the House to devise some proper Measures for appointing of Field & other officers in new regiments or filling up vacancies.

The General Assembly sent two members vizt. Mr. Ithamer Hibbard and John Fassett, Esqr. to request the Governor to Issue his Proclamation for a public Thanksgiving throughout this State on the first Thursday of December Next.

Resolved that Mr. Amos Robinson be & he is hereby requested to call on the Printers to this State and desire him [them] to Complete the Pamphlets Intitled a Vindication by Ethan Allen, and that said Mr. Robinson see them Transmitted to the Governor at Arlington without Delay.[1]

---

either of the aforesaid tracts of Land shall not be molested or dispossessed of his or their Farmes (Provided they pay a proportion of costs) but be admitted as Proprietors.

ETHAN ALLEN, *Chairman of Committee.*

N. B. Each Settler paying his equal part of the cost be entitled to have one hundred acres of Land where he has settled and improved.

E. ALLEN.

The resolution of the House, referred to in the report, provided that no land should be granted until a survey had either been made or approved by the surveyor general. The committee consisted of "Colo. [John] Strong, Brigadier General Allen, and Major [Benjamin] Wait." Allen was not a member of the Assembly.

[1] The brothers, JUDAH PADDOCK SPOONER and ALDEN SPOONER, were the printers, and their office was near Dartmouth college, in the part of Hanover then called Dresden. The Assembly at this session made overtures to induce them to remove their office to Westminster, and the result was that JUDAH PADDOCK SPOONER and TIMOTHY GREEN established the *Vermont Gazette or Green Mountain Post Boy* at Westminster in Feb. 1781, and continued it until 1783, when the office was removed to Windsor, and the *Vermont Journal and Universal Advertiser* was established by GEORGE HOUGH and ALDEN SPOONER, August 7th. In the interim between the suspension of the paper at

Resolved that Edward Harris Esqr. be and he is hereby appointed a Commissioner to dispose of a farm in Wilmington the former property of Phinehas Fairbanks late of said Wilmington, who has gone over to the Enemy, & to pay the Debts due to the Creditters of said Estate, & keep just accounts and Report on oath to this Court of Confiscation as soon as may be. Pr. order, JOSEPH FAY, *Secy.*

Resolved that this Council stand Adjourned to the Second Monday in November next, then to meet in the Council Chamber at Bennington.[1]

Resolved on further consideration that it is necessary to meet again Tomorrow. Therefore Resolved to Adjourn to 8 °Clock Tomorrow morning & that the foregoing Adjournment be held good notwithstanding.[2]

IN GENERAL ASSEMBLY, 27 Oct. 1779.

Whereas the Assembly have Resolved to Grant to Mr. John Payne & his associates the Township of *Bethel* for the sum of one thousand three hundred pounds in addition to what has been already paid, & General Ethan Allen, Colonel Samuel Herrick, Majr. Benjamin Wait, Jonas Fay Esqr. & their associates, whose names are Mentioned in the scedule [schedule] affixed to the petition, the two Islands in Lake Champlain by the name of the *Two Heroes* for the sum of Ten thousand pounds—And to Major Benjamin Wait & his associate the *Isle of Mott* agreeable to his petition—And to Colo. Danforth Keyes and others his associates the Tract of Land called *Royalton*—And to Lieut. Jonathan Meachum & his associates the Tract of Land called *Benson*—And to Capt. Eben-

---

Westminster early in 1783, and the removal of the office to Windsor, ANTHONY HASWELL and DAVID RUSSELL commenced publishing the *Vermont Gazette, or Freeman's Depository*, at Bennington, June 5, 1783. Hence probably the change of the name of the first Vermont newspaper.—See *Thompson's Vermont*, Part II, pp. 171-2.

[1] For description of the Council Chamber, &c., see *Appendix A.*

[2] From the *Assembly Journal*, Oct. 27:

Whereas it has been represented to this Assembly that the transporting of large quantities of provisions out of this State for private uses greatly augments the prices thereof as well as impedes purchasing such provisions as are necessary for the Continental Army and the troops necessary for the defence of this State: therefore Resolved that his Excellency the Governor be requested to issue his proclamation forbidding the exportation of any wheat or wheat flour after this day, except such as is purchased by the Commissary for the use of the army, on penalty of forfeiting the same or the value thereof to the use of this State, except such as is necessary to procure salt and other necessaries for the use of any private family or families, or such as has been bargained away before this day as aforesaid, in either of which case any Assistant [Member of the Council, Assistant Judge] or Justice of the peace of the County may give licence for the exportation of such quantity of any of the foregoing articles as they shall judge necessary for the purpose aforesaid —which proclamation is to continue in force until the next Session of Assembly and no longer. Provided always that His Excellency the Governor and Council shall have it in their power to take off said embargo before that time if it shall be found necessary.

ezer Allen & his associates the Tract of Land called *Fair haven*, as by the several petitions & surveys may be seen,

Resolved that His Excellency the Governor & Council be desired to Carry the above Resolves into Execution under such restrictions and Regulations as they in their Wisdom shall Judge will most Conduce to the best Good of this State & to make out Charters of the Above Tracts of Land Agreeable to the Resolve of the General Assembly.

Passed in General Assembly. Attest, ROSL. HOPKINS, *Clerk.*[1]

THURSDAY October 28 1779.

Met according to Adjournment.

Resolved that His Excellency Thomas Chittenden & Ira Allen Esqr. be & they are hereby appointed a Committee to Receive the money of the proprietors of the *Two Heroes* in Lake Champlain, and also to Erase the names of any proprietor who refuses or neglects to pay the money aforesaid by the 20 day of December next, and to Enter others in their Room that shall appear to pay. Attest, JOSEPH FAY, *Secy.*

Resolved that Benjamin Wait Esqr. Receive the money of the Proprietors of the upper part of Cumberland County, for the Granting fees of the *Two Heroes* in Lake Champlain, and return the money immediately to the Committee appointed to receive the Same; also his honor [Lieut.] Governor Carpenter & Capt. Jesse Burk to receive the money aforesaid of the Proprietors of the Lower part of Cumberland County, & make returns as aforesaid. Attest, JOSEPH FAY, *Secy.*

Voted unanimously that the price of the land known by the name of *Fair Haven*, Granted to Capt. Ebenezer Allen and associates, be one Dollar pr. acre to be paid by the 20 of December next.

Resolved that His Excellency the Governor & Ira Allen Esqr. be a Committee to Receive the money of the proprietors of *Fair haven* & are hereby empowered to Erase any of the names of the Proprietors who refuse or neglect to pay the money as aforesaid, & enter other names in their Room, that may appear to pay the money, paying an equal proportion of the Expence of the proprietors which is not paid on said Right.

By order of Council, JOS. FAY, *Secy.*

Resolved that the price for the Township of *Royalton* be two Dollars pr. acre to be paid by the proprietors of said Town.

Attest, JOSEPH FAY, *Secy.*

THE END OF OCTOBER SESSION 1779.[2]

---

[1] The Assembly journal shows that this resolution was returned by the Governor and Council with the following endorsement, which, however, does not appear in the record of the Council:

"IN COUNCIL Octr. 27th 1779.

"The aforesaid Resolution was read and concurred with except the "township of *Bethel*, which they unanimously decent [dissent] from, and "desire the same may be entered in the Journals of the Assembly.

"Extract from the Minutes, JOS FAY, *Secy.*"

[2] From the *Record of the Board of War*, Oct. 27:

MANCHESTER, October 27th 1779.

Board of War met. Present—Timothy Brownson Esqr., Joseph Bowker Esqr., Samuel Robinson Esqr., Majr. Benjamin Wait, Capt. Ebenr. Allen, Saml Fletcher, Esqr. and Ira Allen Esqr.

Proseeded to the choise of a President & Secretary.

1st. Made choise of Timothy Brownson Esqr. President.

2d. Made choise of Ira Allen Esqr. Secretary.
Members Present were sworn to the faithfull discharge of their office.
Resolved to raise by Enlistment Twenty able bodied effctive men to enter service at Fort Ranger the fifteenth day of November next and to continue in service five months unless sooner discharged.
Resolved that Lieutenant Benjamin Everst take the command of sd. men and have liberty to appoint two Sergeants, two Corporals and one Drummer.
Resolved that said Lieutenant Have Sixty Pounds pr. month, That each sergeant have twenty five pounds pr. month, That each Corporal and Drum have twenty two pounds ten shillings pr. month, That each soldier have twenty pounds pr. month.
Resolved that each Non commissioned officer and soldier have twenty pounds bounty Paid them when they engage.
Resolved that this board stands adjourned without day.

IRA ALLEN, *Secy.*

IN BOARD OF WAR, Manchester, 27th October 1779.

Sir.—I am directed to transmit to you the foregoing resolves and to recommend to your Excellency to carry the same into Execution.

pr. order, IRA ALLEN, *Secy.*

To His Excellency Thomas Chittenden Esqr.

NOTE.—By far the most important and interesting business of the Governor and Council at this session does not appear in its record. In fact, much of the time was spent in joint assembly, in deliberation and debate as to the course to be pursued on the attempt of Congress to decide, indirectly, the question of the state's right to independence; haply to deny it, by a settlement of the respective claims of New York, New Hampshire, and Massachusetts to jurisdiction within its limits. In these deliberations and debates both branches of the government acted in concurrence and for the result both were equally responsible, though *in form*, apparently, the resulting action was by the house of representatives alone. It is fit, therefore, that this important chapter in the history of the State should be inserted in this record of the Governor and Council, and it is therefore embraced in *Appendix B.*

RECORD OF THE GOVERNOR AND COUNCIL

AT AN

ADJOURNED SESSION AT BENNINGTON, NOVEMBER 1779.

BENNINGTON 8 November 1779.

The Governor and Council met according to Adjournment, and proceeded to business.

First took under consideration the petition of Jóab [Joash] Hall and associates for a Certain Gore or Tract of Land, whereupon Resolved to refer the further consideration of the subject until Tomorrow 8 °Clock, to which Time this Council stands Adjourned.

TUESDAY 9 November 1779.

Met according to Adjournment.

This Council having taken into consideration the petition of Doct. Joash Hall, in behalf of himself and associates, bearing date the 31[t] day of December A. D. 1778 and rec[d] on file in the Secretary[s] office the 6 day of January 1779, praying for a Grant of a Certain Gore of Land within this State, &c. Whereupon

Resolved that Ira Allen Esq[r.] the Surveyor General be and he is hereby directed to grant an order of Location & Survey unto the said Joash Hall and Ensign Elihu Lyman, agents for s[d] associates, viz[t.] Beginning at the Northeast Corner of Wallingford, thence Easterly on Shrewsbury South Line to the Southeast Corner thereof being the northwest Corner of Ludlow, thence Southerly on Ludlow west Line to the southwest Corner thereof, & to Extend south in such manner as not to interfere with any former Grant so far as the vacant or unappropriated lands extend, provided always that the vacant Lands does not more than include forty six thousand acres.

By order, JOSEPH FAY, *Sec[y.]*

Resolved that a Committee be appointed to receive the money due from the Proprietors for Granting the following Tracts of Land viz[t]: Two Islands in Lake Champlain by the name of *Two Heroes*, the *Isle of Mott*, *Fair haven*, *Benson*, *Bethel*, & *Royalton*, with full power to Erase the names of any of said proprietors who Neglects or Refuses to pay their respective Grants, and enter others (who will pay,) in their Room. Members choosen, His Excellency Thomas Chittenden Esq[r.], Ira Allen & John Fassett, Jun[r.] Esquires.

Resolved that in each Charter of Incorporation for any Grant of Lands made out and Executed by this Council, a reservation be made therein of all Pine Timber suitable for masts or spars for shipping, to the use of the Freemen of this State forever, which Timber shall be marked by a

Surveyor to be hereafter appointed for that purpose agreeable to the directions of the General Assembly of the representatives of the Freemen of this State.

Resolved that Eight pence L. Money p$^{r.}$ acre be deducted out of the price for Granting the township of *Fair haven*, on account of the reservation of Pine Timber for the use of the Freemen of this State.

Resolved that Each Grantee in the Township of *Benson* pay or cause to be paid unto the Committee viz$^{t.}$ his Excellency Thomas Chittenden Esq$^{r.}$ Ira Allen & John Fassett Ju$^{r.}$ Esquires, one hundred & Twenty Eight pounds, L. money, on or before the 10th day of January next, & that said Committee be and they are hereby impowered to Erase those names who neglect to pay the aforesaid Committee at the aforesaid Time, & put in such persons' names that shall appear to pay said sum.

Adjourned to 8 °Clock Tomorrow.

BENNINGTON 10 Nov$^{r.}$ 1779.

Resolved that every Grantee of the said *Benson*, his Heirs or assigns, shall plant & cultivate Ten acres of Land & build a House at Least Eighteen feet square on the floor, or have one Family settled on Each respective Right or share of Land, within the Term of Two years next after the conclusion of the present War between Great Britain & America, or in two years after the Province of Quebeck shall be United with the free & Independent States of America, on *penalty* of the forfeiture of his Grant or share in s^{d} Township, and the same to revert to the freemen of this State to be by their representatives regranted to such persons as shall appear to Settle & Cultivate the Same.

Adjourned to 8 °Clock Tomorrow.

THURSDAY, 11th Nov$^{r.}$ 1779.

Met according to Adjournment.

Resolved to Grant to Major Benjamin Wait and ninety four others his associates, Eight thousand acres of Land on the *Isle Mott* in Lake Champlain, including three public Rights. Beginning at the south end thereof & extending so far northward as to contain the aforesaid quantity of Eight thousand acres.

Resolved that the said Grant be made out on Condition that the proprietors pay to the Committee appointed for that purpose, on or before the 10th day of January next, thirty six pounds on each Grantee's right or share.

Resolved that the Condition of settlement be the same of the two Islands Granted by the name of the *two Heroes.*

Resolved that a Committee of three be appointed to inquire into the Circumstances of certain Tory Families, viz$^{t.}$ [Stephen] *Fairchilds, Widow* [of Phineas] *Hurd, Austin Sealey & Daniel Burret* [Burritt,] all of Arlington, & see whether they think it is best to sell those farmes formerly their property, or any part thereof, & provide some plan [or place] for said Families, & Report their opinion to the Court of Confiscation as soon as may be. Persons choosen, Capt$^{n.}$ Wallis, [Ebenezer Wallace,] Captain [Matthew] Lyon, and Captain Jonas Galusha.

Adjourned to 8 °Clock Tomorrow.

IN COUNCIL, Friday 12 November 1779.

Met according to Adjournment.

Resolved that the Several Surveyors of this State be directed in Running Town Lines, to allow one chain in thirty for swagg of chain.

Voted Jonas Fay & Joseph Fay Esquires a Committee to prepare the Bills passed by the General Assembly of this State at their last Session, for the press as soon as may be.

This Council having taken into their Consideration the petition of Captain Ebenezer Fisk of Farmington & Col^o. Joab Stafford of New Providence in the State of Massachus^ts Bay & their associates praying for a Grant of Vacant Land in this State, as by their petition on file may appear, whereupon

Resolved that Ira Allen Esqr. the Surveyor General be & he is hereby directed to grant an order of Location & Survey, unto the said Ebenezer Fisk & Joab Stafford & associates to be divided into equal Shares the following tract of Land, vizt. Begining at the Southwesterly Corner of the Township of Granby—then Southerly on the westerly line of a Location heretofore given to Captain Ebenezer Fisk aforesaid & his associates, and Samuel Bishop Esqr. & associates, Captain Beach Tombleson & his associates, to the southwesterly corner thereof, then westerly a parallel Line with the southerly line of said Granby until turning northerly a Parallel line with the westerly line of said Location, until turning easterly a parallel Line with the southerly line of said Granby to the bounds first mentioned will contain twenty three thousand and forty acres of Land and no more.

Attest, JOSEPH FAY, *Sec^y*.

This Council having taken into their consideration the petition of Captain Comfort Sever agent in behalf of the Township of *Royalton* within this State, Praying this Council to defer making out a Charter of Incorporation for said Town of Royalton, agreeable to the request of the General Assembly of this State at their Sessions in October Last until said Inhabitants can have an opportunity to be heard in the Premises by the General Assembly aforesaid at their next Session,

Resolved therefore that a Committee of four be appointed to proceed Immediately to the said Town of Royalton and enquire how many settlers are actually on the premises, when they entered, & how many have made actual Improvements, & are not on the premises, as also to enquire into any other matters of Grievance relating to the matter of the petition, and Report to this Council specially as soon as may be, & that the Facts exhibitted to the said Committee be supported by evidence under oath.

The members choosen—Honble *Benjamin Emmons* and *John Throop, Esquires, Samuel Robinson, Esq^y*. and *Captain Edmond Hodges* & any three of whom are hereby empowered to Act.

Resolved that in the opinion of this Council this business ought to [be] effected at the Expence of the Petitioners. Attest,

JOSEPH FAY, *Sec^y*.

Resolved that a Committee of five be chosen (three of whom to be a quorum) to ascertain bounds of the following Towns vizt. *Pownall, Bennington, Shaftsbury, Arlington, Stamford, Woodford, Glosenbury,* [*Glastenbury,*] *Sunderland,* & to be under the Direction of the Surveyor General of this State & make returns to him as soon as may be. Members chosen, Moses Robinson Esqr., L^t. Joseph Safford, the Honble John Fassett [jr.] Esqr., Samuel Robinson Esqr. & M^r. Simeon Hatheway.

JOS. FAY, *Sec^y*.

Resolved that this Council be & it hereby [is] Adjourned until the 21^t day of December next at one ^oClock P. M. then to meet at Arlington.

Attest, JOSEPH FAY, *Sec^y*.

RECORD OF THE GOVERNOR AND COUNCIL

AT A

SPECIAL SESSION AT ARLINGTON DEC. 8 & 9 1779.

IN COUNCIL, Arlington 8th Decr. 1779.

Present His Excellency the Governor—

Honble Joseph Bowker, Timothy Brownson,
Moses Robinson, Jeremiah Clark &
Jonas Fay, John Fassett Jur Esqrs.

Resolved that the Manuscript entitled "Vermont's appeal to the Candid & Impartial World, containing a Fair Stating" &c. Exhibitted by Stephen R. Bradly, be published and promulgated to the States of America.[1]

DECEMBER 9th 1779.

Resolved that Jonas Fay, Moses Robinson & Stephen R. Bradley Esqrs. be & they are hereby appointed agents to appear at Congress on the first day of February next.

Resolved that Captain Jonathan Fassett be & he is hereby appointed one of the Committee in lieu of Samuel Robinson Esqr., for the purpose of hearing the request of the Inhabitants of Royalton, who at his request is hereby dismissed.

RECORD OF THE GOVERNOR AND COUNCIL

AT AN

ADJOURNED SESSION DEC. 21 1779.

ARLINGTON, 21 December 1779.

The Council met according to Adjournment.

The Committee appointed by the Genl Assembly of this State at their Sessions in October last to receive the money[1] from the several Grantees for the Granting fees of the Township of *Fair haven* take this Method to Notify those Grantees that they shall Continue to receive such monies until the 10 day of January next Inclusive.[2]

Adjourned without day. JOS. FAY, *Secy*.

No record of any meeting of the Governor and Council between the 21st of December 1779 and Jan. 26 1780 has been found; and yet, from an important pamphlet, by Ethan Allen and Jonas Fay, which bore the

[1] See *Appendix D.*

[2] This seems to be both a record of a vote of the Council and the form of a notice to be transmitted to the grantees.

date of January 1 1780, and was "published by order of the Governor and Council of Vermont," it seems that there either must have been a session to order the printing of the document, or an omission of the order in the record of the meetings in December, 1779.—See *Appendix E.*[1]

RECORD OF THE GOVERNOR AND COUNCIL

AT A

SPECIAL SESSION AT MANCHESTER JANUARY 26 1780.

MANCHESTER, 26 Jan$^{y.}$ 1780.
IN COUNCIL, date above.

Present—His Excellency Governor Chittenden.

The Hon^{bles}

Joseph Bowker, Esq$^{r.}$,	John Fassett, jr. Esq$^{r.}$,
Paul Spooner Esq$^{r.}$,	Sam$^{l.}$ Fletcher, Esq$^{r.}$
Benjamin Emmons, Esq$^{r.}$,	

The Proprietors of the Township of *Royalton* having laid before this Council the dispute between them with respect to Granting said Township to the Inhabitants thereof, & a number of non-residents, who by a resolution of Council of the 24 December last was to appear this day & receive the Charter of Incorporation & pay the Granting fees—but as it appears the Inhabitants of said Town did fully understand the Intentions of the resolution aforesaid—Therefore

---

[1] It appears from the following that the Board of War was in session about this time, but no proceedings are recorded:

SUNDERLAND, Dec. 23^{d} 1779.

Debenture of the Board of War.

	£	s	d
Present—Timothy Brownson Esq.	£8	4	0
[Received] TIM$^{O.}$ BROWNSON.			
Maj. Benj. Wait,	28	0	0
[Received] BENJ. WAIT.			
Capt. Ebenezer Allen,	17	4	0
Rec^{d} in full, EBENEZER ALLEN.			
Lieut. Joseph Bradley,	8	4	0
Received in full by a Pay-table order.			
Capt. Joseph Bowker,	20	10	0
Capt. Samuel Robinson,	9	0	0

TIMOTHY BROWNSON, *Pres.*

N. B.—B. Wait paid by J. Bowker.

Resolved to postpone the Making out the Charter of Incorporation of said Town until the Next Session of Assembly in March Next.

Attest, JOSEPH FAY, *Sec'y.*[1]

RECORD OF THE GOVERNOR AND COUNCIL

AT A

SPECIAL SESSION AT ARLINGTON FEB. 1780.

STATE OF VERMONT: IN COUNCIL, Arlington, 29th Feby. 1780.

Present—His Excellency Thomas Chittenden Esqr. Govr.

Honble Joseph Bowker,	Jeremiah Clark &
Moses Robinson,	John Fassett Jr. Esqrs
Jonas Fay,	Joseph Fay, *Secy.*
Timo. Brownson,	

A petition signed Jacob Ruback & others a Committee in behalf of three hundred Inhabitants of the Northern Frontiers of this State, & directed to his Excellency General Washington, praying for relief by Granting Colo. Warners Regiment, or other Troops, to guard said Frontiers, being read & the subject thereof debated on, a vote was called thereon wheather they approve of said petition being sent to General Washington or not, which passed Unanimously in the negative.

Resolved that a copy of this Vote be sent Colo. Warner.

Attest, JOS. FAY, *Secy.*

---

[1] The Board of War met on the 2d of Feb. 1780, as appears by a debenture account, but there is no record of proceedings. It appears however that Capt. Nehemiah Lovewell's company was formed in February 1780, and served in eastern Vermont.—See manuscript *Assembly Journal*, Vol. 2, p. 71; and *Council Journal* and note, *post*, under date of Feb. 15, 1782. The debenture account referred to was as follows:

ARLINGTON, Feb. 2d 1780.

Debenture of the Board of War.

Hon. Timothy Brownson Esq.	£10 4 0
[Recd] TIMTHY BROWNSON.	
Maj. Benj. Wait	37 10 0
[Recd] BENJ. WAIT.	
Lieut. Joseph Bradley	10 4 0
[Recd] JOSEPH BRADLEY.	
Capt. Samuel Robinson	13 10 0
[Recd] SAMUEL ROBINSON.	
Col. Ebenezer Allen	18 12 0
[Recd] EBENEZER ALLEN.	
Capt. Jona. Fassett	9 18 0
[Recd] JONA. FASSETT.	

TIMTHY BROWNSON, *Pres.*

Resolved to choose a committee of three to prepare a draught to lay an Embargo on the Exportation of provision. Members chosen, Jonas Fay, Moses Robinson, and Joseph Bowker Esquires.

Whereas Capt. [William] Fitch, Commissioner of Sequestration for the Township of Paulet, claims a Lot of Land in said Township of Paulet now in the possession of Mabel Benedict, which land is confiscated to the use of this State, & whereas s[d] Fitch refuses to Give a Lease of said Land, Therefore

Resolved that Moses Robinson Commissioner of Sequstration for the Township of Reuport be & he is hereby impowered & required to give a Lease of said Lot of Land unto the said Mabel Benedict for the term of one year, taking proper Measures to secure the pine Timber if any there be in said Lot.

IN COUNCIL, Arlington 29th Feb[y.] 1780.

Whereas it is found that Large quantities of Provisions are continually exported out of this State, which if not immeadiately prevented will render it Impracticable to furnish the troops raised for the defence of the Northern Frontiers, as also prevent the purchasing Commissaries procuring the Necessary provisions in this department for the use of the Army—Therefore

Resolved that any further Exportation of *wheat*, *Rye*, *Indian Corn*, *flour or meal* of any kind, as also *Beef*, *Pork*, or any other Provisions whatever that may be useful for such Supplies, be and are hereby Strictly Prohibited & forbid to be Transported out of this State; also that no provisions of any kind, that may or shall be transported out of the State of New York, contrary to the prohibition of that [State,] be permitted to pass through any part of this State, unless for the use of the Army.—And all *Sheriffs*, *Constables*, *Grand Jurors & Select men* of the respective towns within this State, are hereby authorised and required to Seize any & every of the above Mentioned articles in case they have reason to suspect any person or persons to be carrying them out of this State contrary to the true Intent & meaning of this Resolution, And if need be Command assistants, & make returns to the Next assistant or Justice of the Peace of s[d.] Town the writs of s[d.] Seizure, & unless such person or persons shall satisfy the court before whom the Examination be had, that he or they were not Transporting any of the above mentioned articles out of this State, or that they were for the use of the Army, said articles shall be forfeit, or such person or persons fined not Exceeding forty pounds at the discretion of the court before whom the Tryal shall be had, the one half of the forfeiture to the use of this State, the other half to the person who shall prosecute to effect. This Prohibition to Take place the second day of March next & continue in force thirty days. Attest, JOS. FAY, *Sec[y.]*[1]

---

[1] By an act of the Assembly in March following, the exportation of provisions was forbidden until the 15th of August. This was re-enacted in 1780, and the prohibition continued in force until Feb. 1781.—See Slade's *State Papers*, pp. 396–7.

RECORD OF THE GOVERNOR AND COUNCIL

AT THE

SESSION WITH THE GENERAL ASSEMBLY AT WESTMINSTER MARCH 1780.

The General Assembly met on the 8th, but there is no record of any proceedings of the Governor and Council until the 14th. At the close of the record Secretary FAY left five blank pages "for the purpose of recording the remainder of the journals of Council at the Westminster Session, which by some Mistake in the Transfer of the books from Mr. Tolman to me were not recd." This is dated April 7th 1789, and shows that the journal was not recorded until that time. THOMAS TOLMAN had been deputy secretary, and as such for a time he had possession of the original minutes. The following entries in the Assembly journal show that the Governor and Council met previous to the 14th, and also indicate a portion of its business.

[From the *Assembly Journal.*]

March 9.—His Excellency the Governor made a Speech verbally to this House.

March 10.—The Committee who was appointed to prepare a plan for the defence of the northern frontiers[1] brought in the following Report, viz:

"That it is our opinion that the General Assembly grant or order to be granted [by the Governor and Council] four, five, or six townships of land if it can be found without danger of lapping on the former grants.

"Secondly that his Excellency the Governor be requested to draw on the trustee of the war office (if he find that the avails of the grants before mentioned be not sufficient to procure provisions and the other money that may be necessary to defray the public charges of this State that may accrue,) for Loan office certificates to such amount as he shall find necessary for the supplying the Commissary of purchases—The form of which certificates shall be as follows, viz:

"No. —— CERTIFICATE FOR ————DOLLARS.

I do hereby certify that the State of Vermont is indebted to ————, in the sum of ——— dollars, being for ————, which sum by contract became due to ———— the —— day of ———, for which sum he is to be paid as much money as shall be an equivalent in value to the above mentioned sum by the —— day of———— with the interest at six per cent. pr. annum.

"Thirdly If the provisions cannot be had for money or loan-office certificates as aforesaid, Then his Excellency the Governor is hereby directed to order the Commissary to take the provisions where they can

---

[1] This committee, appointed on the 9th, consisted of Capt. Matthew Lyon, then of Arlington, Ithamer Hibbard of Wells, and Col. William Williams of Wilmington.

be found in the hands of any person over and above the wants of his family, allowing to such person what the selectmen of the town shall judge to be sufficient for the support of such family until the tenth day of September next, paying such person the current price in money or certificates at his election.

"pr. order of Committee, M. LYON, *Chairm.*

The aforesaid Report being read, Resolved that said Report be accepted.

Resolved that the ammunition purchased by the order of this State be disposed of by the Governor and Council as they shall judge necessary for the benefit of this State.

March 11.—The Committee to whom was referred the petition of John Moore, Jonathan Perham and Solomon Harvey and their associates, [agents of the town of Athens,] brought in the following report, viz:[1]

"That in our opinion it would be highly in the interest of this State that the tract of land situate and bounded as returned in the plan annexed to the petition be chartered by this Assembly to the sixty-seven persons whose names are annexed to the petition forthwith upon the following conditions, viz:

"First that if any of the proprietors neglect to pay for their right their names to be erased and others put in their room.

"Secondly That it shall be a condition in the Charter that each one of the proprietors shall begin a settlement on or before the first day of March 1781 on his right and continue to compleat the same.

"Thirdly That one right be reserved to be appropriated for the use of a school and one right for the first Gospel minister that shall be settled in said town, and that said petitioners be allowed corporation priviledges equal to any town in this State; and that said proprietors pay for said tract of land eighteen thousand pounds at or before the delivery of the Charter, which charter shall be made out by the Governor and Council as soon as may be. JOSHUA WEBB, *Chairman.*"

The above Report being read, Resolved that the said Report be accepted and Referred to the Governor and Council to be fully executed.

March 13.—The Committee appointed to examine the several petitions for lands now on file in the Secretary's office, brought in the following report, viz:

"That (in our opinion) we have agreeable to our appointment examined the said petitions severally, and find that there is a large tract of vacant and unappropriated land lying and being in the north part of this State adjoining to the south line of the Province of Quebec and west of Lake Memphremagog and the Green mountains and bounding west on lands heretofore granted by the government of New Hampshire contigious to lake Champlain; That your Committee are of opinion that a part of the said tract sufficient to make six townships of the contents of six miles square each, may, consistent with the interests of this State, be granted by your honors to the following gentlemen petitioners and Company for the several townships hereafter particularly named, viz:

"To Major William Goodrich, Barzilla Hudson, Charles Dibble and Company a township of six miles square as laid down in the plan herewith returned by the name of *Berkshire*—

"To Colo. Roger Enos and Company one like township as returned in said plan by the name of *Enosburgh*—

---

[1] Previous to acting upon this report the resolution of Oct. 20 1779, on land grants, was repealed.

"To Col°. Howel Woodbridge and Jonathan Wells Esqr. and Company one like township as returned in said plan by the name of *Richford*—

"To Doctr. Ezra Stiles,[1] Doctr. Benjamin Gale,[2] and Company one like township returned in said plan by the name of *Montgomery*—

"To the Officers of the Connecticut line, being sixty in number, agreeable to their petition, one like township as returned in said plan by the name of *Wyllis*,[3] [Jay]—

"To Daniel Owen Esqr. and Company one like township as returned in said plan by the name of *Westfield*.

By order of Committee, ETHAN ALLEN, *Chairman*."

Resolutions in detail for these several grants were adopted, and the Governor and Council requested to execute them. Allen was not a member of the Assembly; but, as appears from his charges paid by the State, he was in attendance "by the Desire of the Govr & Council" in June and October 1779, March 1780, and on four occasions in 1782 and '83.

Resolved that this Assembly will join the Governor and Council in a Committee of the whole to take into consideration the exercising the civil laws, and extending their jurisdiction throughout the State, at two o'clock in the afternoon.

March 13, *P. M.*—According to a Resolve passed in the forenoon, this Assembly Resolved themselves into a Committee of the whole with the Governor and Council.

The Committee of the whole having adjourned until to morrow morning nine o'clock, The House proceeded to business.[4]

The record of the Governor and Council is now resumed, as follows:

WESTMINSTER 14 March 1780.

IN COUNCIL, Thursday date above.

Resolved that Samuel Fletcher & his honor [Lieut.] Governor Carpenter join a Committee of the House to prepare a bill Stating fees & fines.

Adjourned to 8 °Clock Tomorrow.[5]

---

[1] Rev. EZRA STILES, D. D., LL.D., of New Haven, Conn. President of Yale College from 1778 until his death, May 12 1795.

[2] BENJAMIN GALE, physician, who was born on Long Island in 1715 and died at Killingworth, Conn., May 21, 1790. He was distinguished for agricultural, medical, and political writings, and was a scientific and practical farmer. An agricultural society in England gave him a medal for an improved drill-plow.

[3] Colonel SAMUEL and Major JOHN P. WYLLIS of Connecticut were officers in the continental army.

[4] Probably the result was the act "repealing a certain paragraph of an act entitled 'An Act making the laws of this State temporary.'"—See Slade's *State Papers*, p. 397.

[5] By a resolution of the Assembly of this date the martial law of the United States was adopted for the time being.

WEDNESDAY 15 March 1780.

Met according to Adjournment.

Resolved, that the conditions of settlement of the Townships of *Berkshire*, *Enosburgh*, *Richford*, *Montgomery*, and *Westfield* be as follows, viz$^{t.}$

That each proprietor of said townships pay to the Treasurer of this State, or a Committee hereafter to be appointed, the sum of Eight pounds L. Money to be made Good as it passed Cur^{r}ent in the year 1774. That the proprietors of *Enosburgh* & *Westfield* make payment to the said Committee on or before the first day of June next, on payment of which *Charters of Incorporation* will be given. And each Proprietor of the above Townships, their Heirs or assigns, shall plant & Cultivate five acres of Land & build a house at Least Eighteen feet square on the floor, or have one family settled on Each respective right or share of Land within the term of four years after the Circumstances of the War will admit of a Settlement with Safety, on penalty of the forfeiture of Each respective Right or share of Land in said Township, and the same to revert to the freemen of this State to be by their representatives regranted to such persons as shall appear to Settle & Cultivate the Same. And said Committee is Impowered to Erase the Names of such proprietors as shall not appear & pay the Money aforesaid & Enter others in their Stead. And that five sixty fifth parts in said Township be reserved for public uses of this State as shall be hereafter discribed in the Charters of Incorporation for said Towns, as also all Pine and oak Timber suitable for a Navy.

Resolved that the Township of Land Granted to the officers of the Connecticut Line [be known] by the Name of *Wyllys*, [now Jay,] that the Conditions of Settlement be as follows, viz$^{t.}$ That Each Proprietor in said Township pay to the Treasurer of this State six pounds L. Money to be made Good as in the year 1774. That settlement be made agreeable to the Terms proposed on the Townships aforesaid, *except* Four years after the present War shall be concluded between Great Britain and America—the same Reservation of public Rights and Timber as in other Towns Granted in this State.

Adjourned to 8°ClockTomorrow.[1]

---

[1] From the *Assembly Journal:*

March 15.—Resolved to reconsider the act that passed the House entitled "An Act for the purpose of impowering the inhabitants of the respective towns in this State to tax themselves on certain occasions"—which Act was sent up for concurrence [to the Governor and Council] and sent back with an amendment; Ordered that said Act with the amendment lie on the table for further consideration. [The record of the Governor and Council does not show this action of that body. The result will appear on the next page.]

March 16.—Resolved that the Governor and Council be and they are hereby requested to obtain a printer to settle within this State for the purpose of printing the Laws, &c., as soon as they shall judge it necessary.

Resolved that the Court of Confiscation be and they are hereby required to order the commissioners for sale of confiscated lands to bring their business to a close so as to make a compleat settlement before the next session of Assembly.

The following message was delivered by the Sheriff from the Council, viz:

"IN COUNCIL, Westminster, 16th March 1780.

"Whereas it appears to this Council that it will not be in the power of Joseph Bowker Esq$^{r.}$, commissary of purchases, fully to execute the

THURSDAY, In Council, 16 March 1780.

Met according to Adjournment.

Resolved that the Township or gore of Land granted to Doct. [Solomon] Harvey & his associates by the name of *Athens*, sixty seven in number, pay the Money for granting said Town on or before the first day of May next, at which time a Charter of Incorporation will be given, according to Resolve of Assembly.

Resolved that the Townships of *Philadelphia*[1] & *Chittenden*, granted this Sessions, [pay as follows:] that the Proprietors of Chittenden pay to the Treasurer of this State five hundred & forty pounds L. Money, made Good as in the year 1774. And that the Proprietors of Philadelphia pay him five hundred & eighty pounds, Money aforesaid, to be paid on or before the first day of June next, at which time Charters of Incorporation will be made out for said Towns—The conditions of settlement to be the Same as the other Townships Granted this Session to Colo. Roger Enos & others on or near Canada line, Except such settlement to be made within two years after the Circumstances of the War will admit to Settle in Safety.

---

business of his appointment to that important trust: They do therefore recommend to the honble Assembly to appoint an Assistant Commissary of purchases. By order of Govr. and Council,

"JOSEPH FAY, *Secy.*"

The aforesaid Recommendation of the Governor and Council being taken into consideration, Resolved that an Assistant Commissary of purchase be appointed this afternoon. [The foregoing message does not appear in the record of the Governor and Council. At the time fixed, Maj. Benjamin Wait was elected assistant; and on the same day Joseph Fay was elected to the same office for the lower part of Bennington county.]

On motion made, after long debate: Resolved that the following amendment be made to the Act entitled "An Act for the purpose of impowering the inhabitants of the respective towns in this State to tax themselves for certain occasions," viz:

"Always provided that no person be compelled by the major vote of said town to build, or repair a meeting house; or support a worship, or minister of the gospel, contrary to the dictates of his conscience; Provided said person or persons shall support some sort of religious worship as to them may seem most agreeable to the word of God, anything in this Act to the contrary notwitstanding."

The yeas and nays being required by Mr. [Matthew] Lyon whether the last clause of the amendment stand, viz.: "Provided said person or persons shall support some sort of religious worship as to him may seem most agreeable to the word of God"—they stand as follows, viz.:

Yeas—Mr. Speaker, Mr. Strong, Mr Brewster, Mr. E. Clark, [Ezekiel of Clarendon,] Mr. Ives, Mr. Roberts, Mr. Drury, Mr. Foot, Mr. Hamilton, Mr. Underwood, Mr. Williams, Mr. Barrett, Mr. Merrick, Mr. Knight, Mr. Webb, Mr. Jones, Mr. Upham, Mr. Curtiss, Mr. Howland, Mr. Whitcomb, Mr. Gilbert, Mr. Stephens, Mr. French.

Nays.—Mr. N. Clark, [Nathan of Bennington,] Mr. Lyon, Mr. Galusha, Mr. Comstock, Mr. Ormsby, Mr. M. Robinson, [Moses of Rupert,] Mr. Hibbard, Mr. Ward, Mr. Noyce, Mr. Harris, Mr. Hale, Mr. N. Robinson, [Nathaniel of Westminster,] Mr. Russell, Mr. Wild.

So it was Resolved in the affirmative.

For the act above referred to see Slade's *State Papers*, p. 396.

[1] Parts of Goshen and Chittenden.

Five pages are here left blank in the record, with this memorandum:

The following pages are left blank for the purpose of recording the remainder of the journals of Council at the Westminster Session which by some Mistake in the Transfer of the books from Mr. Tolman to me were not recd.

April 7th 1789. JOSEPH FAY, *Secy.*

The next entry on the record is of June 6, 1780, as of an adjourned meeting. It is probable, therefore, that there had been a meeting between March 16 and June 6, of which the record has been lost. There was a meeting of the Board of War, at which only two members of the Council seem to have been present. It is possible that a meeting of the Governor and Council had been called, and that the Councillors present, though not a quorum, adjourned to the 6th of June. The following are the proceedings of the Board of War:

RECORD OF THE BOARD OF WAR.

ARLINGTON, April 6th, 1780.

Board of War met. Present—Joseph Bradley, Ebenr. Allen, Jonathan Fassett, Ira Allen, Esquires.

April 7th, 1780.—Board of War met.—Saml Robinson Esqr. joined.

Resolved that Joseph Bradley Esqr. be Vice President.

Read a letter from the Inhabitants of the frontiers.

Adjourned to 2 o'clock.

Met at time and place, Col. Brownson in the Chair.

Resolved that this Board accept of the report of their Committee Respecting building a fourt at Pitsford, &c.

Resolved that said fourt be built near the north Line of Pitsford where Majr. Ebenr. Allen shall judge Proper; That said fourt be a Piquet with proper flankers, with Barracks sufficient for one Hundred and fifty men Inclosed; That such fourt be accomplished as soon as may be.

Resolved that a Picquet fourt with proper flankers be built at Hubbardton near Boardman's Place where Majr. Ebenr. Allen shall pitch; that there be Barracks sufficient for seventy-five men Inclosed, to be compleated as soon as may be.

Resolved that one Company of seventy-five men Exclusive of officers be immediately raised to joine Majr. Ebenr. Allen for the defence of the fronteers.

Resolved that said men be raised from the several Regt. in the following Proportion, viz.:

Colo. Herrick's Regt.	24
Colo. Allen's Regt.	18
Colo. Warren's Regt.	8
Colo. Fletcher's Regt.	13
Colo. Marsh's Regt.	12
Total	75

Resolved that Capt. Isaac Clark Take the command of said Company; That Lieut. Benj. Everst [Everest] be first Lieut.; that Rufus Branch be second Lieut.

Resolved that said officers and soldiers Continue in service untill the first day of January Next unless sooner discharged.

Resolved that the pay of said officers and soldiers be the [same as the] other Part of Majr. Ebenr. Allen's Command.

Resolved that Col°. Warren Raise said eight men out of the towns of Wells, Clarendon, Tinmouth, and Wallingford.

Resolved that the foregoing Resolutions be Recommended to His Excellency Thos. Chittenden Esqr. to carry into Execution.

Resolved that Capt. Jonathan Fassett be and he is Hereby appointed Commissary of Purchases with full power to appoint an assistant or assistants, and you or those you shall Hereafter appoint to assist you are fully impowered to purchase any kind of Provision or Camp materials for the use of this State's troops and pledge the faith of this State for the payment of the same, and to make up for any depretiation of money that may be from the time of Purchase to the time such money be paid, and you are further impowered to appoint such person or persons as you may from time to time find necessary to forward such Provision to the several necessary Posts in the frontiers, Taking the issuing Commissary's Receipts for the same. You will keep regular accounts of your time and Expenses and that of your assistants and all the purchases made as aforesaid in order to Exhibit to this Board for adjusting and Settlement when thereto required.

Whereas Capt. Jonathan Fassett is this day appointed Purchasing Commissary & to transport provision to this State's Troops, and whereas the Exigences of this State require that a quantity of Provisions be immediately Purchased and transported to the several Posts in the frontiers, and Whereas difficulties may from time to time arise in furnishing such supplies:

Resolved therefore that Capt. Fassett be directed when he shall judge the Exigences of the State require it to make application to the sivel authority who are desired to issue their warrant to seize any kind of Provision & to press a sufficient number of Carrages and Teams to forward such Provision to Camp, always provided that you leave with Each man a sufficient quantity of Provision for the use of such persons famaly & Dependance [dependents] untill the fifteenth day of September next.

Adjourned to 8 o'clock in the morning.

In Board of War, Arlington, April 8th 1780.

Whereas the General Assembly of this State did at their last session pass a Law impowering each Town in the State to lay Town Taxes to defray public expense, and Whereas the Exigences of this State often require the militia to turn out on the shortest notice, and for the due encouragement of that Patriotic Spirit they ought to be well rewarded for such services—and as the Assembly have not pointed out any way that such Extra Troops should be paid—it is therefore proposed that each Town by Taxes pay their own men for the time being, that each man have three shillings for each day (& officers in proportion to their Rank,) and Two pence for a Horse pr. mile as money went in 1774, Each person to furnish himself with provitions &c. and the depreciation made up when they receive their money, such roles to be examined by the select-men of such Town & charged to this State as money went in 1774, which will in future be allowed to such Town with the Interest. That all such expence since the rising of the last Assembly be paid as aforesaid.

Resolved that the foregoing be recommended to the several Towns in this State.

Extract from the minute. Ira Allen, *Sec'y.*

For the act of the Assembly referred to see Slade's *State Papers*, p. 396.

Procedures of the Board of War, April [8] 1780.

Whereas the present War with Great Britain is likely to be continued at least this Campaign and that the Continental Troops will be continued to the south of this, By which means there will be no movement to divert the Enemy in Canaday, it therefore becomes the indespensible duty of this State to make the best preparations in their power for the defence of the frontiers.

You are therefore directed without loss of time to repare to Col^o. Joel Marsh, Col^o. Peter Olcott, and such other persons as you shall judge necessary, and make Enquiry whether there is any Troops provided by New Hampshire or any other people for the defence of the frontiers of Cumberland County for this Campaign; Secondly whether any men has been raised within Col^o. Olcott's Reg^t. to join Capt^t. [probably Philip] Safford's Company, if so how many and whether the remainder are likely to be raised soon. 3^d to demand of Col^o. Olcott a Positive answer whether he will serve as Colonel of the fourth Regiment of Militia in this State or not. 4^thly to Enquire how the Militia of Cumberland County are supplied with powder, Lead, and flints, and make your return to this Board as soon as may be.

To Reuben Jones, Esqr.

Debenture of the Board of War, Arlington, April 8th 1780.

Hon. Tim^y Brownson, present,	£26 8 0
[Received] TIM^Y BROWNSON.	
Esq. Joseph Bradley,	38 8 0
Esq. Samuel Robinson,	36 0 0
Esq. Ira Allen,	36 12 0
Maj. Ebenezer Allen,	84 0 0
[Received] EBEN^R. ALLEN.	
Capt. Jonathan Fassett,	37 0 0

The above brought into Lawful money.

Esq. Joseph Bradley, £38 8 0	£1 4 0
The above paid by order from Pay-Table.	
Esq. Samuel Robinson, £36 0 0	1 2 6
Esq. Ira Allen, £36 12 0	1 2 10
Capt. Jonathan Fassett, £37 0 0	1 3 1

ARLINGTON, May 11th 1780.

Whereas the Board of War at their session February Last[1] Did Resolve that in case the Continent does not furnish provision for our Troops in the frontiers it be recommended to each town to furnish their Soldiers with provision, on such towns being acquainted by me that such provision will be wanted—and whereas the Continental provision is Stoped for the present, and provision of the meat kind is not now to be purchased, and as the Enemy are daily Expected on our frontiers and the soldiers now raised are almost intirely out of meat, and if they are obliged to quit the posts on our Frontiers for want of provision it will be attended with consequences that will be very distressing:

Therefore you are hereby directed to Collect thirty pounds of salt pork for Each man raised by your Town or ordered to be raised for the defence of said frontiers, and forward the same to the house of Col^o. Mead at Rutland Immediately, whose receipt you will take for said pork; and if the said pork cannot be collected without, you will take the same from the inhabitants in proportion to what they have & their families.

[1] There seems to be no record of the vote referred to.

You will use your utmost discretion in collecting said pork, and as it is of absolute necessity, you will not fail to carry this order into Execution, for which this shall be your sufficient warrant. You will keep accounts of the pork you furnish and the Expense of transportation, for which your town will be paid by this State. THOS. CHITTENDEN, *Gov'r.*
The Selectmen of the [*town of*] *Sandgate.*

This order was of course addressed to the selectmen of each town. Immediately following the order in a blank space on the page, these papers are recorded—apparently for the purpose of showing how the town accounts were presented and finally paid:

SANGATE, March 6th A. D. 1781.

We raised our Cate of Pork according to orders and sent it to head quarters being sixty weight of Pork.

this we atest TIMOTHY HURD, REUBEN THOMAS } *Select men.*

PAY-TABLE OFFICE, 2d of May, 1781, the Treasurer is directed to pay to the Select men of Sangate three pounds for the above pork and Eighteen shillings for Transportation.

pr. order, THOS. CHITTENDEN, JOHN FASSETT, } *Comittee.*

Received on the above Twenty six shillings and Eight pence. Received more Twelve shillings. REUBEN THOMAS.

5th of June, 1781, received Two pounds Twelve shillings the remainder of the above order pr. me REUBEN THOMAS.

Annexed to the above is the following list of towns with the number of men furnished by each:

	No. Men.		No. Men.		No. Men.
Sunderland,	4	Rockingham,	7	Pomfret,	3
Sandgate,	2	Whitingham,	2	Cavindish,	1
Dorset,	5	Townshend,	3	Wethersfield,	3
Shaftsbury,	18	Wilmington,	4	Woodstock,	5
Bennington,	24	New Fane,	3	Chester,	4
Rupert,	5	Londonderry,	2	Reading,	1
New Stamford,	2	Hinsdale,	4	Barnard,	2
Pownel,	13	Brattleborough,	10	Andover,	1
Arlington,	7	Dummerston,	6	Hertford,	5
Manchester,	10	Puttney,	9	Springfield,	4
Clarendon,	7	Hallifax,	7	Strafford,	3
Poultney,	4	Marlborough,	4	Ryegate,	1
Pittsford,	1	Guilford,	11	Newberry,	5
Rutland,	8	Athens,	1	Thetford,	3
Danby,	6	Westminster,	10	Fairlee,	1
Tinmouth,	7	Norwich,	7	Moortown,	3
Pawlett,	7	Royalton,	1	Barnet,	1
Wells,	2	Windsor,	8	Corinth,	2
Castleton,	2	Hartford,	6	Sharon,	2
Wallingford,	2				

RECORD OF THE GOVERNOR AND COUNCIL

AT AN

ADJOURNED SESSION AT ARLINGTON, JUNE 1780.

ARLINGTON, 7 June 1780.

In Council Wednesday 7th June 1780.

Met according to adjournment, & opened according to time & place and Adjourned to 9 oClock Tomorrow.

THURSDAY 8 June 1780.

Met according to Adjournment, and having taken into consideration the request of Silas Hamilton & Company, Resolved that the price of three thousand acres of Land Granted to them in Whitingham be one shilling pr. Acre money made good as in the year 1774, in lieu of two shillings, which price this Council set in March last.

Adjourned to 8 oClock Tomorrow morning.

FRIDAY 9 June 1780.

Met according to Adjournment.

Resolved, that whereas the Continental pay due to the troops who served the last season in this State, cannot be obtained of the Continent, that the Treasurer of this State be & he is hereby directed to advance the Money to Noah Smith Esqr. pay Master, to discharge the Same.

Adjourned to 8 oClock Tomorrow.

[SATURDAY, 10 June 1780.]

Met according to Adjournment.

Resolved that a Committee be appointed to receive the Charter of London Dary, [*Londonderry*,] And to dispose of the Same according to the Resolve of the General Assembly in March last. Members chosen, Colo. [Samuel] Fletcher, Deacon [Edward] Aikin & Major [Joseph] Tyler.

Adjourned until 8 oClock Monday next.[1]

MONDAY 12 June 1780.

Met according to Adjournment.

Resolved, that the payment of the Granting fees of the Township of Richford and Montgomery be suspended until the 15th day of August next.

---

[1] B. H. HALL states that on this day, June 10, 1780, Timothy Bartholomew was appointed commissioner for the sale of the confiscated estates of enemies in the towns of Norwich, Sharon, Thetford, Stratford, [Strafford,] Fairlee, and Mooretown [Bradford.] From the copy of an order and appointments of this kind in Slade's *State Papers*, p. 562, it seems that commissioners were appointed by the Governor and Council acting as a court of confiscation. For this reason, perhaps, the appointment of Mr. Bartholomew was not entered on the record of the Governor and Council.

Resolved that Joseph Fay Esq$^{r.}$ be and he is hereby appointed & requested to procure a printer in this State.

On petition of *John McNeil* to this Council in April 1779 requesting a pardon from the Sentence of the Court of Commissioners, destining him to banishment, the question being put it Passed in the Negative.

Whereas it has been represented to this Council that the Town of Norwich was under many inconveniences respecting the free exercise of Civil government for want of a Justice of the Peace in said Town, Therefore

Resolved, that this Council do recommend to such of the Inhabitants of Norwich as see fit to Assemble & recommend some suitable person to his Excellency Thomas Chittenden Esq$^{r.}$ to be Commissioned to act in the office of a Justice of the Peace until the rising of the General Assembly in October next.[1]

---

[1] From the Record of the *Board of War:*

In Board of War, Arlington, June 12^{th,} 1780.

Present—Timothy Brownson, Sam$^{l.}$ Fletcher, Joseph Bradley, Sam$^{l.}$ Robinson, Jonathan Fassett, & Ira Allen.

1$^{st.}$ Resolved that Paul Spooner Esq$^{r.}$ be & he is hereby requested to call on Doct$^{r.}$ [William] Page of Charles Town [N. H.] and purchase a State Store of medison for the use of this State's Troops that may be in service.

2$^{d.}$ Resolved to raise by inlistment without loss of time one Company of men to join Maj$^{r.}$ Eben$^{r.}$ Allen's Command for the deffence of the fronteers of this State. That said Company consist of one Capt$^{t.,}$ two L$^{t.,}$ four Serg$^{t.,}$ four Corporals and fifty two Privates; the Non-commissioned officers and Privates to have three pounds Bounty; their pay per month to be to a Captain Eight pounds, to a L$^{t.}$ five pounds Eight shillings, a sergeant two pounds eight shillings, a Corporal two pounds four shillings, a private two pounds in Hard money or specia equivalent; to continue in service untill the first day of December Next unless sooner discharged; their pay to commence six days before they march; that each man equip himself with every necessary accoutrement for War with half a pound of powder and lead answerable; and the members of this Board do hereby engage to use their influence that said Company have one Township of Land granted them (in Equal shares) towards their bounty and wages at the session of Assembly in October next as Cheap as any of such quantity shall be then granted.

3$^{d.}$ Resolved that this Board do recommend to his Excellency Tho$^{s.}$ Chittenden Esq$^{r.}$ to appoint and Commissionate officers for the aforesaid Company.

4$^{th.}$ Resolved that Sam$^{l.}$ Robinson Esq$^{r.}$ be requested to Call on Isaac Tichenor Esq$^{r.}$ and use his influence to obtain an order for fifty Barrels of salt Beef from the Continental Store at Charles Town for the use of this State's troops.

In Board of War, Arlington, June 12th 1780.

Sir,—I am directed to transmit to you the foregoing resolutions* and to Recommend to your Excellency to carry the same into Execution.

Ira Allen, *Sec'y.*

To His Excellency Tho$^{s.}$ Chittenden, Esq$^{r.}$

A Debenture of the Board of War.

Arlington, June 12th 1780.

Present—

Joseph Bradley Esq. one day's attendance 4 mile travel, £15 4 0

[Received] Joseph Bradley.

* Second and third resolves only.

RECORD OF THE GOVERNOR AND COUNCIL

AT A

SPECIAL SESSION AT ARLINGTON JULY 4-6 1780.

At a meeting of the Governor & Council by his Excellency[s] summons for that purpose holden at Arlington on the 4th day of July 1780—

Present His Excellency Thomas Chittenden Esqr. & the Honorable Members of his Council as follows—

Moses Robinson,	Jeremiah Clark, &
Jonas Fay,	John Fassett, Jur. Esqrs.
Timothy Brownson,	Joseph Fay, Esqr. *Sec'y.*

Adjourned to 8 °Clock Tomorrow.

WEDNESDAY 5th July 1780.

Met according to Adjournment & proceeded to business.

Whereas it is Represented to this Council that many of the soldiers which have inlisted in the service of this State who are [at] the Fortress of Pittsford & Castleton, are at this time destitute of Proper Clothing for a Campaign—And whereas it is also represented that the Inhabitants of the Frontiers, as also other towns in this State, are willing to Let them have such Clothing as they want provided it would be approved on by this Council and they could be paid—

It is therefore Recommended by this Council to the Inhabitants of the several Towns in this State to furnish their respective soldiers with such clothing as soon as they can Conveniently, & Take their orders on the Treasurer of this State for the pay to be deducted out of their Wages.

Adjourned to 8 °Clock Tomorrow.

THURSDAY, 6 July 1780.

Met according to adjournment and after finishing the business of the day adjourned Until the 17th Instant, then to meet at this place.

Attest, JOSEPH FAY, *Sec'y.*

Either there was no meeting on that day, or nothing transpired for record. Probably the special meeting of the 13th rendered another on the 17th unnecessary.

Samuel Robinson Esq. one day's attendance 14 mile travel, 23 4 0

[Received] SAMUEL ROBINSON.

Jonathan Fassett Esq. one day attendance, 12 0 0

The other members that composed this Board of War were members of the Council, and made up in the Debenture of the Council same time.

Jonathan Fassett Esq. one day attendance, £12 0 0 [as above,] paid in Hard six shillings.

RECORD OF THE GOVERNOR AND COUNCIL

AT A

SPECIAL SESSION AT ARLINGTON JULY 13 1780.

ARLINGTON, 13th July 1780.

In Council met according to his Excellency's summons for that purpose.

Present—His Excellency Governor Chittenden,

the Honble

Joseph Bowker,	Ira Allen,
Timo. Brownson,	John Fassett jr. Esqrs.
Jeremiah Clark,	Joseph Fay, Esqr. *Sec'y.*

Resolved that the Powder now to be dealt out to the Troops and Militia of this State be sold for Seven shillings Silver money or Seventy dollars in paper pr. pound & that the Lead be ——— pr. pound, & flints ——— pr. Doz.

Resolved the Honble Ira Allen Esqr. be & he is hereby appointed to proceed to Philadelphia to deliver a letter from Governor Chittenden of this day's date[1] to Samuel Huntington Esqr., President of Congress, containing an Answer to the President's Letter to Govr. Chittenden of the 10th of June last, containing several acts of Congress of the 2d and 9th of June last.

---

[1] See *Appendix G* for the action of Congress, the letter of Gov. Chittenden, and other papers on this subject. The letter as sent was dated July 25th instead of the 13th.

From the Record of the *Board of War*, July 14 1780:

IN BOARD OF WAR, Arlington, July 14th 1780.

Whereas it has been represented to this Board that Twenty thousand Brick are wanted to build chimneys in the Barracks in the fourt on the North Line of Pitsford: Therefore resolved that this Board do Hereby Recommend to Majr. Ebenr. Allen to furnish five fatigue men that are Experienced in that business if any there be to assist the Barrack master in making said brick, who shall be allowed one shilling Each in hard money or an Equivilant for Each day in addition to their pay.

Resolved that the Comedant of said fourt be allowed to keep one horse and one Cow in the State's pasture and the Barrack master see that there be no other cattle of any kind kept on the State's cost.

Resolved that there be no more barracks built in said fourt on the State's cost for the time being.

Whereas this Board did order three companies of Rangers be raised for the defence of the frontiers of this State and that Capt. Parmerly Allen* be first Capt. Wm. Hutchins be second and Capt. Jesse Safford be third Captain, & Whereas Capt. Jesse Sawyer has since been ap-

*Capt. PARMALEE ALLEN was connected by blood with the famous Ethan, Ira, and their relatives. Timothy Allen of Woodbury, Conn., was the father of Parmalee and cousin of Gen. Ethan Allen. Parmalee Allen came to Pawlet with his father in 1768, and was town clerk in 1770. He served with credit in Herrick's regiment of Rangers previous to the date of his appointment to command one of the three companies above mentioned.—See Hollister's *History of Pawlet.*

RECORD OF THE GOVERNOR AND COUNCIL

AT A

SPECIAL SESSION AT BENNINGTON JULY 24–5 1780.

BENNINGTON July 24th 1780.

At a meeting of the Governor & Council by his Excellency's order for that purpose in the Council Chamber Bennington date above—Present his Excellency Gov. Chittenden & the following members of the Honble Council vizt:

Hon. Moses Robinson,	Ira Allen, and
Jonas Fay,	John Fassett Jur. Esqrs.
Timo. Brownson,	Joseph Fay, Esqr. *Sec'y.*
Jeremiah Clark,	

Having opened the business to the Council and proceeded in debates relative to the Tories under Sentence of Banishment, agreed to Adjourn until Tomorrow Morning 7 oClock.

TUESDAY, 25th July 1780.

Met according to Adjournment & proceeded to the case of James Breakenridge who is under Sentence of Banishment. The question being put wheather the Sentence of Banishment be suspended for a Limited time it passed in the affirmative—That the Execution of said sentence be postponed during the pleasure of Council.

A Proclamation by his Excellency the Governor was read offering a free passport to all Tories who choose to join the Enemies of this & the United States of *America*, which was referred to a Committee to prepare and Lay before the Governor for his approbation. Members chosen Jonas Fay & Moses Robinson Esquires.

JOS. FAY, *Sec'y.*

---

pointed to command another Company in said detachment, who has heretofore ranked by Commission before Capt. Hutchins and Capt. Safford, Therefore resolved that Capt. Jesse Sawyer take rank according to his former commission.

Whereas the General Assembly did at their session in March last appoint Lieut. Enoch Hall to raise by enlistment Twelve men Every way Equiped for the Campaign to serve as Rangers for the defence of Guildhall and the ajoint towns, and Whereas it hath been represented that said number of men are not sufficient to answer that purpose, Therefore resolved That Lieut. Hall be and he is hereby directed to raise by inlistment six able bodied effective men every way Equiped for a Campaign in addition to those heretofore ordered to be raised and to continue in service untill the aforesaid men's Times are out or the whole discharged. Their pay to commence two days before they march, and to have the same pay as the other part of sd Company.

Sir,—I am directed to recommend to your Excellency to carry the foregoing Resolution into execution.

Extract from the minutes, IRA ALLEN, *Sec'y.*

To His Excellency Thomas Chittenden, Esqr.

Resolved that the sentence of Banishment passed on Benjamin Cole by the Court of Commissioners be & is hereby suspended during the pleasure of Council.

Adjourned without day. Jos. FAY, *Sec'y.*

On the record the above resolution follows the adjournment from July 6th to the 17th and immediately precedes the record of Aug. 15th which precedes that of July 24th and 25th. The resolution is presumed to belong to the record of the 25th.[1]

---

[1] From the Record of the *Board of War:*

SUNDERLAND, August 7th 1780.

The following members of the Board of War met, (viz.) Timothy Brownson, Joseph Bowker, Joseph Bradley, Ira Allen, Esquires.

Resolved to raise by a draft on the militia sixty able bodied Non-commissioned officers and soldiers, Every man Equiped, to join Majr. Ebenr. Allen's detachment of Rangers; that they be drafted from the several Regt. in the following Proportions, (viz.)

Colo. Samuel Herrick's Regiment,	24 men.
Colo. Ira Allen's Regt.	21 men.
Colo. Ebenr. Allen's Regt.	15 men.

Resolved that said men be commanded by one Capt., one Lt., & one Ensign. The Captain to be drafted from Colo. Saml. Herrick's Regt., that the Lieut. be drafted from Ira Allen's Regt. and the Ensign from Colo. Ebenr. Allen's Regt.

Resolved that the officers and soldiers in said company Receive for pay the same sum of money Per month in Hard money or an Equivalent as the Board of War have resolved to give the other part of said detachment, their pay to commence three days before they march. To Continue in Service two months from the time they march unless sooner discharged.

Resolved that the surgeon of said detachment be allowed pasturing for a Horse and Reasonable pay for the use of a Horse during the time he remains in this State's service.

Resolved to recommend to his Excellency Thos. Chittenden Esqr. to carry the foregoing Resolutions into Execution.

SUNDERLAND, Aug. 7th 1780.

A Debenture of the Board of War.

Timothy Brownson Esq. 1 day attendance,				£12	0	0
Joseph Bowker Esq. 1 day,	12	0	0	40	0	0
travil 35 miles,	28	0	0			
Ira Allen Esq. 1 day,				12	0	0
Joseph Bradley Esq. 1 day,				12	0	0
Samuel Robinson Esq. 1 day,	12	0	0	26	8	0
travil 18 miles,	14	8	0			

IN BOARD OF WAR, Arlington, August 21st 1780.

Whereas it has been represented to this board by Colo. Woods [probably Col. Ebenezer Wood] that the Enemy have taken several Prisoners from Barnard,* &c., In consequence of which a number of the militia officers & other principal gentlemen in the third and fourth Regiment of Militia assembled and agreed to raise fourty Volunteers to be Com-

* On the 9th of August 1780 a party of twenty-one Indians visted Barnard and captured Thomas M. Wright, Prince Haskell, and John Newton and carried them to Canada. Newton and Wright escaped in the spring of 1781, and Haskell was exchanged in the autumn of that year. They suffered many hardships, but on returning resumed their farms and lived upon them many years. —See article Barnard in Z. Thompson's *Vermont.*

RECORD OF THE GOVERNOR AND COUNCIL

AT A

SPECIAL SESSION AT BENNINGTON AUGUST 18 1780.

BENNINGTON, 18 August 1780.

Resolved that the agreement relative to a printer, between Stephen R. Bradley Esqr. in behalf of the State of Vermont & Mr. Timothy Green printer at New London, (Conn.,) be & hereby is Ratified on Condition that Mr. Green send his son to print for this State in Leu of Mr. Spooner.

Resolved that Mr. Ezra Stiles be and he is hereby appointed and impowered to repair as soon as may be to New London to inform Mr. Green of the Ratification [of the agreement] made between Stephen R.

---

manded by Capt. Cox & a Lieut. for the defence of the frontiers in that vicinity: Resolved therefore on said officers and soldiers joining Majr. Ebenr. Allen's detachment of Rangers that they are entitled to the same pay & rations as the other part of said detachment, such pay to commence Two days before they marched and to continue untill the first of December next unless sooner discharged.

Resolved that Colo. J. Marsh, Colo. J. Safford, Maj. B. Wait, Capt. Sever, Capt. J. [probably Jesse] Safford, & Capt. [Benjamin] Cox be a Committee to station Capt. Safford's & Capt. Cox's Companies of Rangers. That they stake out the ground for fourts and give directions how said fourts and covering shall be built. That said building be erected in the cheapest manner having refferance to the Present Campaign only, as the lands that the several surveyors are now surveying to the W. & North of you will be a settling next spring, which will make it necessary that a line of fourts should be erected further back.

Resolved that Maj. B. Wait furnish the necessary Implements for building fourts for Capt. Safford's and Capt. Coxes Companies and the necessary Camp Equipage for the same.

Resolved that the Commissary of Issues at Every Post where cattle are killed for the use of the army take the charge of the Hides and Tallow to see that the former are properly dried and that the latter is properly rendered and that both are disposed of as his Excellency the Governor shall direct from time to time.

ARLINGTON, Aug. 21st 1780.

A Debenture for the Board of War.

Col. Timo. Brownson 1 days attendance,				£12	0	0
Travil 4 miles,				3	4	0
				15	4	0
Joseph Bradley Esq. 1 day,	12	0	0	15	4	0
Travil 4 miles,	3	4	0			
Ira Allen Esq. 1 day,	12	0	0	15	4	0
Travil 4 miles,	3	4	0			
Maj. Benj. Wait 2 days,	24	0	0	84	16	0
Travil 76 miles,	60	16	0			
Samuel Robinson 1 day,	12	0	0	23	1	0
Travil 14 miles,	11	1	0			

Bradley Esqr. & Mr. Green aforesaid, & Facilitate as much as possible the moving of the Types and other apparatus for the purpose of Printing agreeable to said agreement.

Resolved that Stephen R. Bradley Esqr. be & he is hereby requested as agent to this State to repair to Philadelphia in Company with Colo. Ira Allen to Transact the Political affairs of this State & Report to this Council.

Letter of Gov. Chittenden on the Proclamation authorized July 25 1780.

ARLINGTON, 23d Sept. 1780.

Gentlemen—Your petition supposed to be yesterday's date has been this day recd by the hand of William Lincham & I have laid the same before the members of Council, which at present are not sufficient in number for a quorum. They are of opinion with me to inform you, that it would be an advantage to the Common Cause of Liberty, as well as for the Interest of this State, to permit such persons as choose to show themselves to be on the Enemys side to repair to them from amongst us agreeable to the proclamation, so that the mouths of all such as might in future appear and exhibit a disposition unfriendly to the Common cause might be stoped. Nine adult persons only have as yet made application for such permit and it is probable that no other will apply as the time is so far Expired that there is not sufficient time Left for them to make suitable preparation for their journey.

I must consider the Proclamation as a Legal act of the authority of this State, and that it would be an Illegal act of the authority to Engage by such proclamation safe conduct within the Enemies Lines & thereby afford an opportunity, or rather Lay a Trap or Snare for those disposed to go to Canada to discover their disposition and then take advantage of the discovery of such disposition, which was made on the faith and full confidence of the authority of the State, to punish them therefor.

I cannot conceive that any number of persons who have made themselves *duly* acquainted with the Nature of the act and the obligation the State is under to fulfil it, (Even admitting some may be of opinion that the act is Impolitic,) can reconcile it to their consciences for us thus to trifle with the Honor of the State. I should be happy in this to satisfy every individual Signer to the Petition in every particular of this affair, but it would be too Lengthy. I hope therefore that Colo. Robinson & others will fully make you Easy on this Subject.

I am Gentlemen your most Obedient
Humble Servant,
THOMAS CHITTENDEN.

True [copy] delivered in answer to the petition of a number of disaffected persons who wished to remove within the Enemies Lines on the aforesaid Proclamation. Attest, JOS. FAY, *Secy.* [1]

---

[1] The proclamation to which this letter refers and which was authorized by the Council on the 25th of July, has not been preserved. Its purport seems to have been to give a limited time within which tories might leave the state and join the enemy; their room probably being deemed better than their company.

THE FOURTH COUNCIL.

OCTOBER 1780 TO OCTOBER 1781.

THOMAS CHITTENDEN, Williston, *Governor.*
BENJAMIN CARPENTER, Guilford, *Lieutenant Governor.*

Councillors:

JOSEPH BOWKER, Rutland,	BENJAMIN EMMONS, Woodstock,
MOSES ROBINSON, Bennington,	IRA ALLEN, Colchester,
JONAS FAY, Bennington,	JOHN FASSETT, jr., Arlington,
TIMOTHY BROWNSON, Sunderland,	JOHN THROOP, Pomfret,
PAUL SPOONER, Hartland,	SAMUEL FLETCHER, Townshend,
JEREMIAH CLARK, Shaftsbury,	THOMAS CHANDLER, jr., Chester.

JOSEPH FAY, *Secretary.*
THOMAS TOLMAN, *Deputy Secretary* from Feb. 8 1781.

RECORD OF THE GOVERNOR AND COUNCIL

AT THE

SESSION OF THE GENERAL ASSEMBLY AT BENNINGTON,

OCTOBER AND NOVEMBER 1780.

At a General Election of the Governor and Council for the State of Vermont, Holden at Bennington the 12th day of October 1780,
Present—His Excellency Thomas Chittenden Esqr. Govr.
His Honor Benjamin Carpenter Esqr. Lt. Govr.
And the following Members of the Honble Council vizt.

Honble Moses Robinson Esqr.,	Paul Spooner,
Jonas Fay,	Ira Allen,
Joseph Bowker,	John Fassett, [jr.]
Timothy Brownson,	Samuel Fletcher,
Jeremiah Clark,	John Throop Esqrs.

Resolved that Jeremiah Clark, Jonas Fay, John Fassett, Joseph Bowker, Paul Spooner, & Moses Robinson Esqrs. be & they are hereby appointed a Committee to join a Committee from the House to receive, sort & count the Votes of the Freemen, and to declare those who are appointed to the several offices of Governor, Dep$^{y.}$ Governor, Councillors, and Treasurer for the year ensuing.

The aforesaid Committee having attended on the business of their appointment & made their report, it appears that the following Gentlemen were duly Elected viz$^{t.}$

His Excellency Thomas Chittenden Esq$^{r.}$ *Governor;* His Honor Benjamin Carpenter Esq$^{r.}$ *L$^{t.}$ Governor;* Honble Ira Allen, Benjamin Emmons, Samuel Fletcher, John Throop, John Fassett Jun$^{r.}$, Thomas Chandler, [jr.,] Joseph Bowker, Jonas Fay, Timothy Brownson, Paul Spooner, Moses Robinson, Jeremiah Clark Esq$^{r.}$, *Councillors.*

Adjourned until Tomorrow 8 °Clock.[1]

FRIDAY, 13th October 1780.

Met according to Adjournment.

Resolved that Captain Giles Wolcott be & he is hereby appointed a Commissary to purchase or procure & forward on provision to the Militia who are Collected & Collecting in this present Alarm.

Adjourned to 2 °Clock P. M.

Met according to adjournment.

Resolved that the Honble Jonas Fay Esq$^{r.}$ be & he is hereby appointed Sec'^{y} P. Tem, in the Absence of Joseph Fay Esq$^{r.}$

To Capt. Giles Wolcott:

You are hereby appointed purchasing Commissary for the time being to purchase provisions of every kind, & to Transport the Same to such place or places as may be Necessary to supply the Militia in the present Alarm.

And you are hereby impowered to pledge the faith of this State for the payment of all such Contracts & in case of Necessity you are further hereby impowered to seize such provision as may [be] Necessary & to Empress Teames, Horses & Carriages to forward such provisitions [provisions] to the Support of the Militia that may be in Service. You will keep regular accounts in your proceedings in order for settlement.

By order of Council,

THOMAS CHITTENDEN, *Gov$^{r.}$*

A similar appointment to the Above Issued to Capt. Samuel Billing [Billings, of Bennington,] as Assistant to Captain Wolcott.

Adjourned until 8 °Clock Tomorrow.[2]

---

[1] From the *Assembly Journal,* Oct. 12 1780:

The Governor and Council joined the Assembly in attending Divine worship, which was performed by the Rev'd M$^{r.}$ David Avery.

[2] From the *Assembly Journal,* Oct. 13 1780:

His Excellency the Governor requested the house verbally to accept his resignation of the office of Governor; but after repeated requests of a number of the members of Council and Assembly that he would withdraw his motion for resigning, he agreed to take upon him that office and accordingly took the necessary oaths to qualify him for the office of Governor the ensuing year.

The hon^{ble} Benj$^{a.}$ Carpenter Esq$^{r.}$ took the necessary oaths to qualify him for the office of Deputy Governor.

BENNINGTON 14 Oct. 1780.

Council met according to Adjournment.

Whereas it has been represented to this Couneil that there is a writing office [printing-office] in the Town of Westminster within this State the former property of ——— *Pale*[1] formerly an Inhabitant of that place, who has gone over to and Joined the Enemies of this and the United States of America,

Whereupon Resolved that Ezra Stiles Esqr. be & he is hereby authorized and empowered to Seize the same & Take it into possession for the use of this State & to retain the same until cause can be shown (by such as lay claim thereto) why it should not be adjudged forfeit & Confiscated to the use of this State.

By order of the Governor & Council,

JONAS FAY, *Secy. P. Tem.*

At the request of the General Assembly, choose Mr. Bowker & Mr. Troop, a Committee to join a Committee from the house to take into consideration the petition of Honah Bradley & *report.*[2]

Adjourned to 10 °Clock Monday next.[3]

---

[1] Possibly this is Gale. SAMUEL GALE was a loyalist and a prominent man in Cumberland county till the occurrence of the Westminster massacre. Though probably he was not a printer, he aspired to authorship and may have purchased printing materials. At the above date he was in the civil service of the Province of Quebec. No printer named Pale is mentioned in Thomas's *History of Printing.*

[2] Hannah Beardsley, as appears from the *Assembly Journal.*

[3] From the *Assembly Journal*, Oct. 14 1780:

The Governor laid before the house a Letter signed Saml. Huntington, President of Congress, enclosing Acts of Congress of the 9th and 11th [2d and 9th] of June last—and a letter under his signature to the President of Congress dated 25th July 1780—And desired Colo. Ira Allen to relate to the House his appointment, instructions and proceedings to Congress, &c., which he did in the following manner, viz.:

First.—A Commission appointing himself and Stephen R. Bradley Commissioners to wait on the Congress of the United States, &c., signed by Thomas Chittenden Esqr. &c., and attested by Joseph Fay, Esqr. Secretary &c.

2dly.—A letter signed Ira Allen and Stephen R. Bradley, directed to the President of Congress, acquainting him of their Commission, &c., dated at Philadelphia Septr. 12th 1780.

3dly.—A paper signed by Ira Allen and Stephen R. Bradley Esqrs. requesting to be admited personally in Congress when they should take the disputes &c. respecting Vermont into consideration—dated Philadelphia Septr. 13th 1780.

4th.—A paper signed Charles Thompson Secy. notifying that Congress would take the aforesaid dispute into consideration and that the said Commissioners attend &c.

5th.—A Remonstrance signed by Ira Allen and Stephen R. Bradley Esquires, directed to Congress, dated Septr. 22d 1780.

6th —A letter signed by Ira Allen and Stephen R. Bradley Esquires, directed to the President of Congress—dated Octr. 2d 1780.

The aforesaid papers were read; and an explanation and verbal account of the proceedings of said Commissioners was made by Colo. Allen.—See *Appendix G., post.*

BENNINGTON, In Council, Monday 16 October 1780.

Met according to Adjournment.

Resolved that a Committee of Two be appointed to join a Committee from the House to make out an Estimate of the Necessary Expense probable to be Incured the year ensuing. Members chose, Mr. Bowker & Mr. Allen.

Adjourned to 8 oClock Tomorrow Morning.

BENNINGTON 17 October 1780.
IN COUNCIL date above.

Met according to adjournment.

A bill from the House was read requesting a Committee from the Council to join a Committee of nine from the House to take into consideration the Lands ungranted & the several petitions therefor and Report their opinion what Lands ought to be Granted and what persons will be most conducive to the welfare of the State to have such Grants.

Resolved that a Committee of Four be chosen to join the above Committee. Members chosen Mr. Allen, Mr. Fassett, Mr. Fay & Mr. Spooner.

A bill from the House requesting a Committee from the Council to join a Committee of 7 to prepare for quieting the Ancient Settlers.

Resolved that a Committee of two to join the above Committee be appointed. Members chosen Mr. Brownson & Mr. Bowker.

Thomas Chandler [jr.] Esqr. who had heretofore presided as Speaker of the House of Assembly appeared before His Excellency & took the Necessary oaths to entitle him to a seat in Council.

The following message from the Governor and Council was read, viz.:

IN COUNCIL, Octr. 14th 1780.

This Council have had so much business in forwarding assistance to the frontiers that they have not had time sufficient to arrange the whole of the business that will likely be laid before you this session; shall therefore at this time lay before you the following for your present consideration, viz:

1st. The ways and means of supplying the treasury and securing the frontiers. [This was met by the House on the same day by the appointment of committees on petitions for land grants, and on the situation of the frontiers;* and on the 16th by a committee on finances.]

2d.—The procuring provisions and ammunition for the year ensuing.

3d.—The taking some effectual measures for securing such lands as heretofore have been and hereafter may be confiscated to the use of this State. [Oct. 16 the House appointed a committee on this subject.]

4th. The making such resolves concerning the unsettled rights of lands which have been heretofore granted as will appear just and reasonable and be a means of bringing forward the settlement of the unsettled towns within the lines;

And any other matters as they shall occur shall from time to time be laid before you for your consideration.

By order of Council, THOS. CHITTENDEN, *Govr.*

Resolved that the Members constituting the Board of War as appointed the last Session be and they are hereby impowered to do the business of said board until another board of War be chosen.

* Oct. 16th the committee on the frontiers reported about one hundred and fifty men in the garrisons at Pittsford and Castleton, and about eighty east of the mountains; and that four hundred men ought to be raised immediately, of whom three hundred and fifty should be assigned to the garrisons at Pittsford and Castleton.

The Governor & Council joined the House in a Committee of both houses for the purpose of appointing a Board of War.[1]

Adjourned to 8 °Clock Tomorrow Morning.

WEDNESDAY 18th October 1780.

Met according to adjournment & proceeded to the necessary business of the day.

The Honorable Moses Robinson Esqr. appeared before his Excellency & took the Necessary Oaths to qualify him to take his seat in Council.

Adjourned to 8 °Clock Tomorrow.[2]

THURSDAY, 19th October 1780.

Met according to adjournment.

Resolved that Josph Fay Esqr. be & he is hereby appointed Secretary to the Governor and Council for this State for the year ensuing, also took his seat & the necessary oath of office for Secretary of State.

Resolved that Jeremiah Clark Esqr. be a Committee to join a Committee from the House to prepare a bill for building a Bridge in Pittsford over a Certain river in sd Town.

Adjourned to 8 °Clock Tomorrow.

BENNINGTON 20 October 1780.
Friday In Council date above.

Resolved that Captain *Joseph Farnsworth* be & he is hereby appointed Commissary of Purchases to act in Conjunction with Majr. Samuel Billing as specified in a Warrant given him for that purpose.

Resolved that Edward Harriss Esqr., who was empowered to Sell a Farm in Wilmington as by a Resolve of Council of the 27.Oct. 1779, be directed to Sell the same to Captain Josiah Lock, for one hundred and Twenty seven pounds to be made Good as in the month of April 1777; & to receive Rects. for the Settlement with the Creditors for such Debts as are found to be justly due from Phinehas Fairbank Late of sd Wil-

---

[1] The persons elected were Timo. Brownson, Ira Allen, Samuel Robinson, Joseph Bowker, Stephen Pearl, John Fassett jr., Benja. Wait, Samuel Fletcher and Thomas Murdock—six of the nine being members of the Council. Col. STEPHEN PEARL was at this time a resident of Pawlet. He had been major previous to coming to Vermont, and was thus prepared for the duties of the office to which he was elected as above. In Nov. 1786 he commanded the Rutland county militia who put down the insurrection at that time. Shortly afterward he removed to South Hero, and from thence to Burlington, of which town he was a very popular citizen, being employed in various town and county offices. —See Hollister's *History of Pawlet; Vt. Hist. Magazine*, Vols. I and II; and Deming's *Catalogue*.

[2] From the *Assembly Journal*, Oct. 18 1780:

Resolved that a Committee of five to join a Committee from the Council be appointed to prepare instructions for the board of War. Members chosen, Mr. [Matthew] Lyon, Mr. [William] Williams, Mr. [Abner] Seelye, Mr. [Roswell] Post, and Mr. [William] Fitch. Mr A. [Amos] Robinson is appointed in the room of Mr. Lyon.

mington (who has joined the Enemies of this & the united states of America) in payment, & the surplus Paye to be paid to the Treasurer of this State.

Adjourned to 8 °Clock Tomorrow.[1]

SATURDAY, IN COUNCIL, 21[t] October 1780.

Met according to Adjournment.

The Governor and Council to whom was referred the Stating the fees for the Grant of Land made this day by the General Assembly of this State, having had the same under their consideration have stated the fees aforesaid at Four hundred and Eighty pounds for the said Land being one Township by the Name of *Montpelier*, in hard money or an equivalent in Continental Currency, to be paid by Col°. Timothy Bigelow[2] or his attorney, on the Execution of the Charter of Incorporation, on or before the 20 day of January next.

£480. Attest, JOSEPH FAY, *Secy.*[3]

---

[1] From the *Assembly Journal*, Oct. 20 1780:

Sundry letters from Genl. [Ethan] Allen to Govr. Chittenden, dated at Head Quarters Castleton, Octr. 18th and 19th were read.

[2] It is a remarkable fact, that the first, in a long series of land grants made for the special purpose of raising funds to be expended for the defense of the State at the most critical period of its history, should be of the township which afterward became its capital. Col. TIMOTHY BIGELOW was born in Worcester, Mass., Aug. 12 1739, and died there March 13 1790. He was a blacksmith, a leading patriot, and member of the Provincial Congress in 1774–5; marched at the head of a company of minute-men to Cambridge on hearing of the battle of Lexington; and was a major in Ward's Worcester regiment May 23 1775. In that capacity he went with Arnold on the celebrated march to Quebec, and ascended that mountain in Maine (to gain sight of the desired land,) which from the perilous adventure was named Mount Bigelow. He was captured in the attack on Quebec, and remained a prisoner until the summer of 1776. Feb. 8 1777, he was made colonel of the 15th Massachusetts regiment, at the head of which he assisted in the capture of Burgoyne. He served also in Rhode Island, at Valley Forge, and at West Point. After the war he had charge of the arsenal at Springfield, Mass. His son Timothy, a graduate of Harvard University in 1786, was one of the most eminent of the lawyers and legislators of Massachusetts in his day, whose daughter Katharine married the late Hon. Abbott Lawrence, M. C. for Massachusetts 1835–7 and 1839–41, commissioner to settle the north-eastern boundary question with Great Britain in 1842, and minister to England in 1849–1852.—See observations on the land grants of 1780, *post*.

[3] From the *Assembly Journal :*

Oct. 21 1780.—Resolved that this Assembly do approve and confirm the Resolution of Council desiring General Fellows [John, of Sheffield, Mass.,] to raise two Companies of Volunteers from his Brigade in Berk-

Blank pages are left in the record between Oct. 21 and 28, and the following explanation is entered:

These pages Left Blank for the purpose of Recording some of the journals which appear to be Missing, which I have not rec^d^ in the Transfer of the Books from Mr. [Thomas] Tolman, late Sec^y.^ or otherwise. The recess from the 21st to the 28th was during the Adjournment of Council & Assembly on acc^t^ of the Alarm of the aproach of the Enemy from Canada, which is not here specified.

Ap^l^ 9 1789. JOSEPH FAY, *Sec^y.^*

The recess of the Assembly was not from the 21st to the 28th, but from the 26th to the 30th. The Council was in session on the 28th, when the Assembly was not, and the Council records lost seem to be from Monday Oct. 23 to Saturday the 28th.

BENNINGTON, 28th October 1780.
Saturday, IN COUNCIL, date above.

Met according to Adjournment.

Resolved that those Gentlemen who have heretofore Attended Con-

---

shire County for the defence of the northern frontiers of this State. [This resolution does not appear in the record of the Governor and Council.]

Oct. 23.—Sundry letters from Genl. [Ethan] Allen to Govr. Chittenden, dated Head Quarters Castleton 22^d^ Octr. 1780, were read.

Oct. 24.—The Committee appointed to take into consideration the ungranted lands and the several petitions filed in the Secretary's office sent the following request to the House, viz:

"Your Committee having made considerable advancement in the business of their appointment have found it necessary to take the sense of the Committee [of the whole perhaps, including Governor and Council,] in what manner the several locations made by virtue of the Authority of New York since the King's prohibition shall be considered, who are unanimously of the opinion that they ought not to be considered as a sufficient bar against granting the same to other respectable worthy petitioners; they therefore wish to know the sense of the Assembly on this subject that they may govern their future conduct in the premises accordingly.

"by order of Com^ttee.^ PAUL SPOONER, *Ch^man.^*"

Which Request was read and thereupon

Resolved Unanimously that the several locations made by virtue of the authority of New York since the King's prohibition be and is hereby considered not a sufficient bar against granting the same to respectable and worthy petitioners.

Oct. 26.—Sundry letters from Genl. Allen, Col^o.^ Herrick and Capt. Sawyer were read, giving an account of the Enemy's approaching toward our frontiers, Therefore

Resolved, as the present alarm requires the assistance of a large number of the members for the purpose of joining the army or taking care of their families which are in immediate danger, that this Assembly be adjourned until Monday next—and that the several members who stay at this place are hereby appointed a Committee to join a Committee from the Council when necessary to prepare business to lay before the House at their opening, and all matters that are referred for a hearing this week are referred until the opening of the Assembly.

gress on behalf of this State be Allowed five shillings hard money for Each day Expended in Service exclusive of horse and Expenses.

The remaining part of the day being spent in preparing bills,

Adjourned to 10 °Clock Monday next.

Monday, IN COUNCIL, 30th October 1780.

Met according to Adjournment.

The members of Council sufficient for a quorum not being present, spent the day in preparing bills to Lay before the General Assembly to be passed into Laws.

Adjourned to 8 °Clock Tomorrow.

TUESDAY 31t October 1780.

Met according to Adjournt. & recd the following request from the General Assembly vizt:

IN GENERAL ASSEMBLY, Oct. 31st 1780.

Resolved that the Capt. General be & he is hereby requested to discharge the Volunteers raised for the defence of the frontiers.[1]

Extract from the journals, R. HOPKINS, *Clerk*.

The following Resolve received from the House vizt:

Resolved that this Assembly do approve of the Capt. Genl. and Commander in chief's making proposals to his Excellency Govr. Haldimand for settling a Cartel for exchange of Prisoners, and further advise and recommend to him to appoint and impower some suituable person or persons to further negociate the settlement of a Cartel with Majr. Carleton agreeable to Genl. Haldimand's proposals for that purpose.

Extract from the Minutes, ROSL. HOPKINS, *Clerk*.

True copy Recorded, JOSEPH FAY, *Secy.*

These resolutions were preceded on the *Assembly Journal* by the following entries of the date of Oct. 31 1780:

Several Letters were laid before the Assembly by the Governor, particularly one from Genl. Haldimand of Canada, dated at Quebec Octr. 22d 1780, directed to Govr. Chittenden: one from Majr. Chs. Carleton commanding a party of the British, &c., dated at Crown Point Octr. 26th 1780, directed to Genl. Allen, both of which contained proposals to settle a Cartel for exchanging prisoners; likewise a copy of a letter from Genl. Allen, directed to Colo. Webster [of New York,] dated Castleton, 29th Octr. 1780; a copy of a letter from Genl. Allen to Majr [Ebenezer] Allen, and a copy of a letter from Genl. Allen to Majr. Carleton, were read.

Likewise the Governor informed the House that he had wrote to Genl. Haldimand by advice of his Council making proposals to exchange prisoners, which occasioned the letters from Genl. Haldimand & Majr.

---

[1] This should have followed the next entry on the record of the Council, as the discharge of the volunteers was made in consequence of the agreement between Gen. Ethan Allen for Vermont and Maj. Carleton for Gen. Haldimand, in pursuance of which the British force was withdrawn to Canada.

Carleton, &c.—Whereupon Resolved, &c. [then followed the resolutions entered on the Council record of Oct. 31.] [1]

---

[1] The letters referred to, with these proceedings of the General Assembly, were the official initiation of what is known as "The Haldimand correspondence," between the commissioners of Vermont on the one hand and the Governor General of Canada and his agents on the other. The letters read to the Assembly, as entered above, that to Maj. Ebenezer Allen excepted, were as follows:

General Haldimand to Governor Chittenden.—Abstract.

QUEBEC, October 22 1780.

"If you will send a proper person with full power to Major Carleton at Crown Point, or St. Johns, to confer upon this business, I shall authorize the major to receive him;" but expressed an unwillingness to comply with the request [of Governor Chittenden for an exchange of prisoners] under the circumstances.

This abstract is probably inaccurate. Gen. Haldimand was not then ready for an exchange of prisoners, but desired a discussion of the subject.

Major Carleton to General Ethan Allen.

CROWN POINT, October 26 1780.

Sir:—By the bearer, Capt. Sherwood, I received General Haldimand's letter to Governor Chittenden, on the subject of an exchange of prisoners. I have authorized Captain Sherwood to treat with the Governor and you on the subject; though could I meet with you, or him, or both, perhaps the business would be sooner concluded, as, should any difficulty arise between Captain Sherwood and you, my instructions are so ample that I flatter myself that I could remove them.

During the continuation of this negotiation, no attacks or insults shall be offered to any post or scout belonging to your state or in your boundaries. I expect you will observe the same, and recall, as far as lies in your power, your scouts, to prevent through inadvertency on either part the appearance even of not adhering to the above.

I am, sir, your most obt. servt., CHAS. CARLETON.

Brigadier Gen. Allen.

General Ethan Allen to Colonel Webster.

HEAD QUARTERS, Castleton, 29 October, 1780.

Sir:—Last evening I received a flag from Major Carleton, commanding the British troops at Crown Point, with proposals from General Haldimand, commander-in-chief in Canada, for settling a cartel for the exchange of prisoners. Major Carleton has pledged his faith that no hostilities shall be committed on any posts or scouts within the limits of this state during the negotiation. Lest your state [New York] should suffer an incursion in the interim of time, I have *this day* dispatched a flag to Major Carleton, requesting that he extend cessation of hostilities on the northern posts and frontiers of New York. You will, therefore, conduct your affairs as to scouts, &c., only on the defensive until you hear further from me. I am, &c.,

ETHAN ALLEN.

To Col. Webster. To be communicated to Col. Williams and the posts on your frontiers.

WEDNESDAY 1t November 1780.

Met according to Adjournment.
Nothing passed this day to be recorded.[1]
Adjourned until tomorrow morning.

General Ethan Allen to Major Carleton.

HEAD QUARTERS, Castleton, 27th [29th] October 1780.*

Sir:—I received your letter to me, with General Haldimand's to Gov. Chittenden, last evening, by Capt. Sherwood.

Every respect will be shown your flag, and no hostilities will be permitted on my part; and it is expected you will extend your cessation of hostilities against any of the northern posts of the frontiers of the state of New York during this negotiation.

Special orders are given to prevent all hostilities until I receive your answer to this.

Major Clark is appointed to deliver this to you by a flag, and wait your answer. Your most obedient servant, ETHAN ALLEN.

P. S. Your letter, with Gennral Haldimand's, I have forwarded express to Governor Chittenden, and make no doubt some proper person will be appointed to settle the cartel as soon as possible. E. A.

To Chas. Carleton.

See *Vt. Hist. Soc. Coll.*, Vol. II, pp. 70, 71.

[1] From the *Assembly Journal* Nov. 1 1780:

Several letters from Colo. Udney Hay D. C. G. Purchases, [Northern Department of the continental army,] directed to Govr. Chittenden was read and refered to a Committee of three to make report. The Members chosen Mr. [Reuben] Jones, Mr. Lyon, and Mr. Williams.

A letter from Govr. Clinton, one from Colo. Webster, and one from Colo. Fletcher directed to Govr. Chittenden, were read.†

Nov. 2.—The Committee to whom was referred the papers &c. of Colo. Hay D. C. G. Purchases, brought in the following report, viz.

"That they have examined said papers and also conferred with Colo. Hay thereon and find that he is appointed by the Continental Commissary General to purchase provisions *in the New Hampshire Grants:*

"And that it is the opinion of your Committee that Colo. Hay by coming to this State and making application to the Legislature thereof has missed his instructions:

"And that it is further the opinion of your said Committee that (considering the imbarrasment this State lies under with regard to the claims of other States and the jurisdiction assumed over it; considering also the large supply of provisions already granted for the troops to be in the service of this State the year ensuing; should we suppose this State could be called the New-Hampshire Grants, which is by no means admissable,) the Legislature of this State ought not to undertake to supply Colo. Hay with the beef required.

"Your Committee would remind the House that there is no law that prevents Colo. Hay from purchasing what provisions he pleases in this State for the use of the Continent, and transporting the same where he thinks proper for that purpose. Signed M. LYON, *Chmn.*"

The aforesaid Report was read and accepted.

While the Legislature thus jealously guarded the independent position of the State and refused to recognize officially the officer of a government

* The date of this letter was the same as of the preceding one to Col. Webster.

† Col. Webster requested aid from Vermont, on Gov. Clinton's authority. Gov. Clinton wrote to Gov. Chittenden an indignant denial of such authority to Webster.—See *Vermont Historical Society Collections*, Vol. II, pp. 51, 67.

THURSDAY 2d November 1780.

Met according to Adjournment.

Resolved that Col. Brownson join a Committee [of the House] to take into consideration the petition from Colo. Warners Regiment.

His Excellency the Governor requested the opinion of the Council with respect to appointing some proper persons & authorising them to Treat with Maj. *Carleton* for the purpose of settling a Carteel for the exchange of Prisoners. Whereupon,

Resolved, to appoint two persons with full Powers to settle a Carteel with Major Carleton for the purpose aforesaid.

Resolved, that the Honble Ira Allen and Joseph Fay Esquires be & they are hereby appointed & empowered to repair forthwith to Crown-point or St. Johns & Enter upon the Establishment of a Carteel for the exchange of Prisoners.

Adjourned to 8 oClock Tomorrow.

FRIDAY 3d November 1780.

Met according to Adjournment.

Resolved that the Proprietors of the Township of *Lyndon* pay for each right in said Township, the number of Twenty four officers of the Rhode Island Line pay seven pounds for Each right, and the remainder to the Number of Forty pay Eight pounds Ten shillings Lawful Money in Silver, Gold, or other Curant money equivalent, to the Treasurer of this State, or a Committee appointed for that purpose, one half to be paid by the 20th day of February next, and the other half to be paid by the 15th day of May next—And that the Condition of settlement of said Township be as follows (vizt.) That each Proprietor of the Township of *Lyndon* his heirs or assigns shall plant and Cultivate five acres of Land in said Township, and build a house at Least Eighteen feet square on the floor on each respective right or share, within the Term of Four years next after the Circumstances of the war will admit of Settlement with safety, on penalty of his right or share of Land in said Township, & the same to revert to the freemen of this State to be by their representatives regranted to such persons as shall appear to Settle & Cultivate the same.—And said Committee so to be hereafter appointed is hereby authorised to Erase the Names of such proprietors as neglect or refuse to pay the Money aforesaid, and Enter others in their Room, and also that five equal Shares be reserved for public uses as shall hereafter

---

which would not recognize *Vermont*, it is worth observing that no harm was done to the national cause. Col. Hay was not prevented from buying beef if he could find any body who would sell it to him. Col. UDNEY HAY was a descendant from an eminent family of that name in Scotland, and the colonel himself is said to have been highly educated and distinguished for his talents—"a gentleman, an imposing man, rather of the Matthew Lyon cast." "He was opposed to the Constitution, and to the administrations of Washington and [John] Adams, and continued to the end a politician." Soon after the close of the revolution he settled in Underhill, and there lived and died. He represented that town in the General Assembly from Oct. 1798 to Oct. 1804.—See *Vermont Historical Magazine*, Vol. II, p. 942; and Deming's *Catalogue*.

be mentioned in the Charter of Incorporation of said Township, also all Pine Timber suitable for Mast & spars are reserved for the use of a Navy.

Adjourned until 8 °Clock Tomorrow, And continued from day to day by Adjournments until the sixth Instant.

BENNINGTON 6 Novr. 1780.
IN COUNCIL date above.

Met according to Adjournment and proceeded to business as follows—

Resolved that the Proprietors of *Randolph* in number sixty Eight pay for Each right Eleven Pounds L. Money in Silver or Gold coin or other Currant Money equivilent, to be paid to a Committee hereafter to be appointed to receive the same, on or before the first day of January next, & that the Conditions of settlement be as follows vizt. that Each Proprietor of the Township of *Randolph* aforesaid his heirs or assigns shall plant & cultivate five acres of Land on each respective right in said Town within the Term of three years on penalty of the forfeiture of his right or share of Land in said Township, & the same to revert to the Freemen of this State, to be by their Representatives regranted to such persons as shall appear to Settle & Cultivate the same. And the Neglect of payment & reservations to be the same as the Townships Granted to the Honble Jonathan Arnold[2] & Company by the name of *Lyndon*.

---

[2] Dr. JONATHAN ARNOLD was born in Providence, R. I., Dec. 14 1741. He was a member of the Assembly of Rhode Island in 1776 and author of the act of that year repealing the law requiring an oath of allegiance to the mother country to be taken. He was also a member of the Continental Congress 1782–4, and surgeon in the revolutionary army. After the war he removed to St. Johnsbury, Vt., and was its first town clerk in 1790. He was one of the Governor's Council in 1790, '91 and '92, and one of the judges of Orange county from 1792 until his death, Feb. 2 1798.—JOSIAH LYNDON ARNOLD, son of the doctor, was born in Providence, R. I., April 22 1768; graduated at Dartmouth in 1788; was tutor of Brown University until his father's death, when he removed to St. Johnsbury, which town he represented 1793–95. He died there June 7 1796. A volume of his poems was published the next year after his decease.—LEMUEL HASTINGS ARNOLD, another son of the Doctor, was born at St. Johnsbury, Jan. 29 1792; graduated at Dartmouth college in 1811; was a member of the Council of Rhode Island during the "Dorr rebellion" in 1842–3, governor of R. I. 1831–33, and member of Congress 1845–7. He died at Kingston, R. I., June 27, 1852.—Gen. RICHARD ARNOLD, son of governor L. H. Arnold, was born in Providence, R. I., April 12, 1828, graduated at West Point in 1850, and served with so much credit in the army as to be brevetted major general in August 1866.—SAMUEL GREENE ARNOLD was born in the same city on the 12th of April 1821, and the editor supposes was another son of the Governor. He was twice lieutenant governor of the State, U. S. Senator in 1863, and served with credit as aid to Gov. Sprague during the rebellion.—See Drake's *Dictionary of American Biography*.

Granted to Aaron Stores Esqr. & Company No. 4 on the plan.

Resolved that the Proprietors of the Township of *Washington*, Granted to Mr. Daniel Spooner, Steel Smith[1] & Elisha Burton & Co. and marked on the plan exhibitted by the Surveyor General No. 12, pay for each right nine pounds L. Money in silver or Gold coin or other currant money equivilent, to be paid on or before the first day of Jan. next, the Conditions of settlement to be the same as the Township of Randolph, which will be specified in the Charter of Incorporation.

JOSEPH FAY, *Sec'y*.

Resolved that the Proprietors of the Township of *Gilead*, Granted Elihu Marwin & Company Marked on the Plan No. 31, pay for each right £4. 10 Lawfull Money in Silver or Gold coin, to be paid on or before the 15th day of February next. The Conditions of settlement to be the same as the Township of Randolph, which will be specified in the Charter of Incorporation.

Resolved that the Proprietors of the Township of *Turnersburgh*, [Chelsea,] Granted to Bela Turner Esqr., Marked on the plan No. 8, pay for Each right Nine pounds Lawful Money in Silver or Gold Coin or other Currant Money equivolent, to be paid the first day of Feby. next. The Conditions of settlement to be the Same as the Township of Randolph, which will be specified in the Charter of Incorporation.

Resolved that the Proprietors of the Township of ———, Granted to Rosettee Griffin & Company being sixty four in Number, Marked on the plan No. 22, pay for Each right nine Pounds Lawful Money to be paid the First day of January next. The Conditions of Settlement to be the same as the Township of Randolph, which will be specified in the Charter of Incorporation.

Resolved that the Proprietors of the Township of *Cabbot*, Granted to Captain Jesse Levingworth & Company being sixty five in Number Marked on the plan No. 21, pay for Each right Nine Pounds Lawful Money, to be paid by the 1t. day of January next. The Conditions of Settlement to be the same as the Township of Randolph, which will be Specified in the Charter of Incorporation.

Resolved that the Proprietors of the Township of *Hydepark*, Granted to Captain Jedediah Hyde & Company Marked on the plan No. 45, pay for Each Right Eight pounds Ten shillings Lawful Money to be paid one half in silver money and the remainder in other current money equivolent, to be paid by the first day of January next, the terms of settlement to be the same as in the Township of Randolph, which will be specified in the Charter of Incorporation.

Resolved that the Proprietors of the township of *Greensborough*, Granted to Captain Timothy Green & Company, Marked on the Plan No. 24, pay for Each right Eight Pounds Ten shillings Lawful money in Silver or other Current money equivolent, to be paid by the 20 day of January next, the Conditions of settlement to be the same as the Township of *Randolph*, which will be specified in the Charter of Incorporation.

Resolved that the Proprietors of the Township of *Navy* [Charleston,] Granted to Comidore [Abraham] Whipple[2] & Company, Marked

---

[1] Capt. STEEL SMITH removed from Farmington, Conn., to Windsor, Vt., in August 1764, and was the first permanent settler in that town.—See Thompson's *Vermont*.

[2] Commodore ABRAHAM WHIPPLE, born at Providence, R. I., Sept. 26 1773. He was captain of a privateer in the French war, and in a

on the plan No. 32, pay for Each right in said [township] Eight pounds L. Money to be paid by the 10 day of January next in Silver, or other money equivolent, the Conditions to be the same as the Township of Randolph, which will be specified in the Charter of Incorporation.

Resolved that the proprietors of the Township of *Victory*, Granted to Captain Ebenezer Fisk & Comy. Marked on the plan No. 28, pay for Each right in sd. Township nine pounds Lawful Money in Silver, or other Current money Equivalent, to be paid by the 15 day of Feby. next, the Conditions of Settlement to be the same as in the Township of Randolph, which will be Specified in the Charter of Incorporation.[1]

Adjourned to 8 oClock Tomorrow.

---

single cruise captured twenty-three French vessels. In June 1772 he captured and burnt the British revenue cutter Gaspe in Narraganset Bay. He was appointed commodore in the Revolutionary war, and was very successful from 1775 until 1780, the prize money for his captures amounting on one occasion to a million of dollars. In 1780, while trying to save Charleston, he lost his squadron and was himself captured and held a prisoner during the remainder of the war. He dwelt in Cranston, R. I., until the formation of the Ohio Company in 1788, when he removed to Marietta, Ohio. He died there, May 26 1819 —*Drake's Dictionary of American Biography.*

[1] From the *Assembly Journal*, Nov. 6 1780:

The Committee appointed to prepare instructions for the board of War brought in their Report, which was read, and

Resolved that the members of the Board of War be and they are hereby directed to meet at some suitable time and place to choose their President and Secretary, which President shall have full power to call together the members of said board with the advice of one or more of the members and as often as may be found necessary—their Secretary to keep fair records of all their proceeding—and the duty of said Board shall be to examine into every necessary measure to be prosecuted for the defense of the frontiers of this State, and recommend to the Captain General of said State the raising any number of men and for such term of time as they may judge proper (not exceeding nine months,) and further shall have full power to appoint proper officers to command such men so raised, and to call out the Militia in such numbers and proportions from time to time as may be found necessary for the security of the frontiers. They will receive and examine the monthly returns of the Commissaries of purchases and issues, and likewise from the commanding officers of the troops in the service of this State, and order all kind of stores prepared for the use of said State to be transported in such quantities, at such times, and to such post or garrisons as they find necessary by said returns.

On the same day Ira Allen submitted a memorial, addressed "to his Excellency the Governor, the honorable Council, and Representatives of the State of Vermont," in which he urgently pressed for a settlement of his accounts as Treasurer, involving also the settlement of all accounts of Commissioners of sales of confiscated estates and Commissioners of Sequestration, and asked that whatever sum might be due him should be reduced to hard money value and payment be made to him and his associates in land, to be thereafter located under the same regulations,

TUESDAY 7th Novr. 1780.

Met according to Adjournment.

Resolved that Mr. John Burnham, Commissioner of Sales, be & he is hereby directed to repay the money paid to him by Timothy Green for a Certain Piece of Land in Pownal & make the money Good according to the rules prescribed by Congress.

By order of Council, JOS. FAY, *Secy.*

Resolved that the Proprietors of the Township of *Gatesborough*, Marked on the plan No. 43, Granted to Josiah Gates & Amos Jones & Company to the number of 120, pay for Each Right £4.10 L. Money in silver or other Current money Equivolent, to be paid by the fifth day of February next, the Conditions of Settlement to be specified in the charter of Incorporation.

Resolved that the proprietors of the Township of *Orange*, Granted to Amos Robinson, Ebenezer Green & Company, marked on the plan No. 15, pay for Each Right Eight pounds L. Money in Silver or other money equivolent, to be paid one half by the first day of Feby. next, the other half the first day of March next, conditions three years for Settlement & reservations to be Specified in the Charter of Incorporation.

Resolved that the Proprietors for the Township of *Pittsfield*, granted to Lt. Saml. Wilcox, Deacon Daniel Kinney, Deacon Josiah Wright, & Company being 65 in Number, Marked on the plan No. 1, pay nine pounds L. Money in silver or other money equivolent for Each right, to be paid by the 10th day of February next, to be settled in a term of three years next after the circumstances of the War will admit with Safety.

Resolved that the Proprietors of *Hancock*, Granted to Lt. Samuel Wilcox, Deacon Daniel Kinney, Deacon Josiah Wright & Company being sixty five in Number, Marked on the plan No. 2, pay seven pounds L. Money in Silver or an equivolent, to be paid First day of February next, to be settled in three years after the War will admit with safety, the reservation to be Specified in the Charter of Incorporation.

Resolved that the proprietors of the Township of *Morriston* [Morristown,] Granted to Mr. Moses Morse & Company being sixty four in Number, Marked on the plan No. 44, pay £7 L. Money in Silver or an equivolent in other Current money, to be paid by the first day of March next, the terms of Settlement is three years after the *War*, the reservations are to be Specified in the Charter of Incorporation.

Resolved that the Proprietors of the township of *Minden* [Craftsbury,]

---

restrictions and price as other lands of the same quality granted at that session: which was read, and it was

Ordered that the aforesaid Request or Memorial be granted in full.

On the same day also, detailed rules and regulations for the Commissary of Purchase Department, including Assistant Commissaries, were adopted; the latter, however, being reconsidered and postponed to the next session.

On the same day also the Assembly proceeded to try Brigadier General Ethan Allen (against his indignant remonstrance,) on complaints submitted by Capt. William Hutchins and Simeon Hathaway, the result being (on the 7th,) that the complainants were permitted to withdraw, and the thanks of the House were voted to Allen for his good service to the State.—See *Early History* pp. 323–325; and *Vt. Hist. Soc. Coll.*, Vol. II, pp. 78–80.

Granted to Col^o. Timothy Newel, Ebenezer Crafts Esqr.[1] & Company being 63 in Number, Marked on the plan N°. 37, pay Nine pounds L. Money in Silver or other Current Money equivolent, to be paid by the 16 day of January Next, to be settled in three years Next after the War will admit with Safety, the reservations to be Specified in the Charter of Incorporation.

Resolved that the proprietors of the Township of *Coventry*, Granted to Major Elijah Buel [of Coventry, Conn.,] & Company, being a Gore as is mentioned & described in the Grant of Assembly, pay for Each right Ten pounds L. Money in Silver, or other current money equivolent, to be paid by the last day of December next. And whereas the quantity of land cannot be ascertained, Whereupon

Resolved that Major Buel pay one hundred and fifty pounds money aforesaid at the time above mentioned & if on examination the full quantity of Land shall not be found as is Specified in said Buels petition as to make up 15 Rights Allowing 320 acres to Each proprietor agreeable to the Grant of said Land, then the money to be repaid without Interest, & if on Examination a Larger quantity shall be found, to be paid for when ascertained.

Resolved that the Proprietors of *Caldersburgh* [Morgan,] being 64 in Number, Marked on the plan N°. 33, pay for Each right Nine pounds L. Money, in Silver or an equivolent in other money, to be paid by the 26 day of December next, to be settled in the term of 3 years next after the war will admit with safety, the reservations will be Specified in the Charter of Incorporation.

Resolved that the proprietors of the Township of *Jamaca*, Granted to Col^o. Samuel Fletcher & Company being 54 in Number, described & Marked on the plan N°. 36, pay for each right in said Town nine pounds L. Money in Silver or other Curent money equivolent, to be paid by the Eighteenth of Feby. next, to be settled in three years—the reservations to be Specified in the Charter of Incorporation.

Resolved that the proprietors of the Township of *Brookfield*, Granted unto M^r. Phinehas Lyman and Company to the Number of 64, Marked on the Plan N°. 9, pay for each right Seven Pounds L. Money in Silver or other Current money equivolent, to be paid by the 19 Feby. next, to be settled within three years, the reservations to be specified in the Charter of Incorporation.

Resolved that the proprietors of the Township of *Wardsborough*, Granted to William Ward & Company being 53 in Number & Marked on the plan N°. 39, pay Eight pounds Ten shillings L. Money in Silver or other money equivolent for Each right, to be paid the 18th February next & to be settled within the term of three years after the War will admit with Safety, the reservations will be Specified in the Charter of Incorporation.

Resolved that the proprietors of the Township of *Fletcher*, Granted to Major [Joseph] Tyler & Company to the Number of 64, Marked on the plan N°. 46, pay for each right £8.10.0 L. Money in Silver or other Curent money equivolent, to be p^d. by the 17th of February next, the Conditions of settlement to be three years after the War will admit with Safety, the reservation to be Specified in the Charter of Incorporation.

Adjourned until 8 ^o Clock Tomorrow.

---

[1] Col. EBENEZER CRAFTS, of Sturbridge, Mass., founder of Leicester, Mass., Academy. He was a graduate of Yale college in 1759, and father of Gov. SAMUEL C. CRAFTS. Col. Crafts removed to Vermont in 1791, and died in 1810.

WEDNESDAY November 8th 1780.

Met according to Adjournment.

Resolved that the proprietors of the Township of *East Haven*, Granted to Mr. Timothy Andrews [Andrus,] Beach Tomlinson & Company, being sixty three in number, described and Marked on the Plan No. 29, pay for Each right in said Town Nine pounds L. Money in Silver or other Curent Money equivolent, to be paid the 15th day of February next, to be settled in three years after the present War will admit with Safety,—the reservations will be Specified in the Charter of Incorporation.

Resolved that the proprietors of the Township of *Westford*, Granted to Major Abraham Sedgick [Sedgwick,] Capt. Uriah Seymour & Company, being 63 in Number, described & Marked in the plan No. 42, pay for each right in said Town Eight pounds Lawful Money in Silver or an equivolent in other current money, to be paid by the seventh day of February next—to be settled in three years after the present War will admit with safety, the reservations will be specified in the Charter of Incorporation.

Resolved that the proprietors of the Township of *Sheffield*, Granted to Colo. Andrew Adams,[1] Mr. Stephen Kingsbury & Company sixty three in number, discribed & Marked in the plan No. 34, pay for Each Right in said Town Eight pounds L. Money, to be paid by the 25 of Decr. next, to be settled three years after the War—the reservations will be Specified in the Charter of Incorporation.

Resolved that the proprietors of the Township of *Newark*, Granted to Capt. Samuel Hulbert, Mr. Isaac Andrews & Company sixty three in Number, discribed & Marked on the plan No. 30, pay nine pounds L. Money on Each right on the sixteenth day of February next, to be settled in three years after the present War will admit with safety, the reservations to be specified in the Charter of Incorporation.

Resolved that the proprietors of the Township of *Kingston*, Granted to Messrs. Reuben King. Shelden Graham & Company sixty three in Number as discribed & Marked on the Plan No. 6, pay Seven pounds L. Money on Each right on the first day of March Next, to be settled in three years after the war will admit of a settlement with Safety, the reservations to be specified in the Charter of Incorporation.

Resolved that the Proprietors of the Township of *Braintree*, Granted to Messrs. Jonathan Temple, Jacob Spear, Nathan Putnam, Levi Davis & Comy. sixty one in number, as described and Marked on the plan No. 5, pay for each right Nine pounds L. Money on the first day of March next, to be settled in three years from the time of payment; the reservations will be specified in the Charter of Incorporation.

Resolved that the proprietors of the Township of *Hardwick*, Granted to Colo. Danforth Keyes and Mr. Eliakim Spooner & Company sixty three in Number, as discribed on the plan No. 23, pay Nine pounds L. Money on Each right on the first day of May next, to be settled after the War will admit with Safety—The reservations will be Specified in the Charter of Incorporation.

Resolved that the Proprietors of the Township of *Woodbury*, Granted to Colo. Ebenezer Wood, Mr. [William] Lyman & Company sixty three in Number, as discribed on the plan No. 20, pay Nine pounds Like Money on each right on the first day of April next, to be Settled three years after the war will admit with Safety—The reservations will be specified in the Charter of Incorporation.

---

[1] Possibly Hon. ANDREW ADAMS of Litchfield, Conn., member of the Continental Congress 1777–80 and 1781–2.

Resolved that the Resolution of yesterdays date relative to the fees, terms of settlement &c. of the Township of *Brookfield* Granted to Mr. Phinehas Lyman & Company be & is hereby reconsidered.

By order of Council, JONAS FAY, *Secy. P. T.*

Resolved that the proprietors of the Township of *Brookfield*, Granted unto Mr. Phinehas Lyman & Company to the No. [of] 64, Marked on the Plan No. 9, pay for Each right or share five pounds L. Money in Silver or other Curent money equivolent, to be paid one half on the first day of May next, the other half on the first day of October next, to be settled in three years. The reservations will be specified in the Charter of Incorporation.

Resolved that the proprietors of the Township of *Concord*, granted to Reuben Jones Esqr. & Company to the number of 65, marked on the plan No. 27, pay for Each right or share Eight pounds L. Money in Silver or other Currant money equivolent, to be paid on the 10 day of February next, to be Settled within three years.—The reservation will be specified in the Charter of Incorporation.

Resolved that the proprietors of *Williamstown*, Granted to Samuel Clark & Mr. Absalom Baker and Company 73 in Number, as described on the plan No. 13, pay for Each right in said Township Eight pounds L. Money in Silver or an equivolent in other Curent money, to be paid the fifteenth day of May next and to be Settled within three years after the war will admit with Safety—The reservations will be specified in the Charter of Incorporation.

Adjourned to 9 oClock Tomorrow.[1]

THURSDAY 9 November 1780.

Met according to Adjournnent.

Resolved that the proprietors of the Gore of Land [now *Landgrove*] bounded vizt. between the towns of Bromley [Peru,] Andover & Londonderry so as to Allow to Each proprietor three hundred and twenty acres or thereabouts, Granted to Captain William Utley, pay Each for such right in said Gore Eleven pounds L. Money in Silver or other Curent money Equivolent, to be paid on the first day of January next, & that the same be Settled within three years—the reservations will be specified in the Charter of Incorporation.

---

[1] Nov. 8 1780, the Assembly appointed the Governor, John Fassett, jr. and Timothy Brownson commissioners for examining accounts against the State, and authorized them to draw orders on the treasurer.

Col. John Strong, Col. Ebenezer Walbridge, Thomas Porter, Esq., Reuben Jones, Amos Robinson, and Stephen R. Bradley, Esqrs., were appointed auditors of public accounts, to look into the expenditure of the State's money, call all public officers to account and enforce collections of all sums due; and the Governor and Council and Court of Confiscation were requested to furnish them with all necessary papers.

On the same day Articles, Rules, and Regulations for the government of the militia and other military forces were adopted.

The following was also adopted:

Resolved that there be and hereby is granted unto his Excellency the Governor for his services the year ensuing one hundred and fifty pounds.

Adjourned until the first Wednesday of Feby. next, then to meet at Windsor.

Resolved that the proprietors of *Grotton*, Granted to Lt. Thomas Butterfield & Comy. in Number 66, as discribed on the plan No. 17, pay for Each Right Eight pounds L. Money in Silver money, or other Curent money equivolent, to be paid on the first day of March Next, to be settled three years after the present War will admit—the reservation will be set forth in the Charter of Incorporation.

Resolved that the Proprietors of the Township of *Cambridge*, Granted to Samuel Robinson Esqr. as discribed on the plan Marked No. 47, pay for Each right Eight pounds Lawful Money in Silver or other Curent money equivolent, to be paid on the 20th day of May next, to be settled within three years after the present war will admit with Safety. The reservations will be Specified in the Charter of Incorporation.

Resolved that the Proprietors of the Township of *Starksborough*, Granted to David Brydia and Company sixty four in Number, as described in the plan No. 41, pay Nine pounds L. Money in Silver or other Curent Money equivolent, to be paid on the 13th day of January next, and to be settled 3 years after the war permit with Safety. The reservations will be Specified in the Charter of Incorporation.

Resolved that the proprietors of *Warren*, Granted to John Throop Esqr. Capt. Steel Smith & Company 63 in Number, as discribed in the plan No. 11, pay on Each Right six pounds L. Money in Silver or other Curant money equivolent, on the 20 day of March next, & to be settled in four years after the present War will admit with Safety. The reservations will be specified in the Charter of Incorporation.

Resolved that the proprietors of the Township of *Roxbury*, Granted to Captain William Chaplin, Benjamin Emmons Esqr. & associates 63 in number, discribed on the plan No. 10, pay Eight pounds Ten shillings on Each right in Silver or other Current money equivolent, on the 25 day of March next, & settle the Same in three years after the present War will admit of Settlement with Safety. The reservations as usual.

Resolved that the Proprietors of the Township of *Northfield*, Granted Major Joel Matthews, Captain William Gallup & Company 63 in Number, as discribed on the plan No. 14, pay six pounds Ten shillings (on each right on the 18th day of January next) L. Money in Silver or other Curent money equivolent, & settle the Same after the present war will admit with Safety. The reservations to be Specified in the Charter of Incorporation.

Resolved that the Proprietors of the Township of *Littleton* [Waterford,] Granted to Gideon Horton & Company 64 in number, discribed on the plan No. 26, pay on Each Right Eight pound Ten shillings Lawful money in Silver or an equivolent in other Curent money, on the Seventh day of April next, and Settle the Same in three years. The reservations to be Specified in the Charter of Incorporation.

Resolved that the Honble Paul Spooner and John Throop Esqrs. be & they are hereby choosen a Committee to return the Names of the present settlers in the Township of *Brookfield*, Granted to Mr. Phinehas Lyman, &c.

Resolved that the proprietors of the Township of *Lincoln*, Granted to Colonel Benjamin Simonds [Simmons] & Company to the number of 64, discribed on the plan No. 40, pay for Each right six pounds L. Money in Silver, or an equivolent in other curent money, on the 19 day of February next, and Settle the Same in four years after the present War will admit with Safety. Reservations as usual.

Resolved that the proprietors of the Township of *Eden*, Granted to Colonel Seth Warner, Lt. Colo. Samuel Safford, the officers, soldiers, and the Heirs of the Deceased persons of His Regt. that did belong to this State when they Entered Service, discribed on the plan No. 48, pay on

Each right nine pounds. To Settle the Same after the present war will admit of a Settlement with Safety. The reservations to be Specified in the Charter of Incorporation.

Resolved that the Proprietors of the Township of *Rochester*, Granted to Asa Whitcomb Esq[r.] & Company 64 in Number, as discribed on the plan N[o.] 3, pay for each Right in said Town Nine pounds L. Money on the fifteenth day of March next, & settle the Same within three years after the present war will admit of Settlement with Safety. The reservations to be specified in the Charter of Incorporation.

Resolved that the Proprietors of the Township of *Wildersburgh* [Barre,] Granted to Colonel William Williams & Company 64 in Number, as discribed on the plan N[o.] 16, pay for Each right Eight pounds Ten shillings L. Money on the first Wednesday in May next, & settle the Same in three years after the war will admit with Safety. The reservations as usual.

Resolved that the Proprietors of the Township of *Vershire*, Granted to Capt. Abner Nealy and Company 64 in Number, discribed on the plan N[o.] 7, pay for Each [right] Ten pounds L. Money on the 10th day of January next, & Settle the Same in three years after the war will admit with Safety. The Reservations as usual.

Resolved that his Excellency the Governor, Hon[ble] John Fassett Ju[r.] Esq[r.] & the Hon[ble] Timothy Brownson Esq[r.] be a Committee to *receive* the Granting fees on the Several tracts Granted at the *present Session.*

Resolved that Jonas Fay & Moses Robinson Esquires be & are hereby appointed a Committee to revise the Laws for the press.

Resolved that Moses Robinson Esq[r.] make the draft of a Proclamation for a public Thanksgiving.

Resolved that the Proprietors of the district of *Ira*, Granted to Nathan Clark Esq[r.] & Company, pay Fifteen pounds on Each Right, Allowing to each proprietor 300 acres, to be paid in Silver or other money equivolent on the first day of June next. The reservations to be as usual.

The following Resolution Rec[d.] from the House & ordered to be recorded, viz[t.]

"IN GENERAL ASSEMBLY, Nov[r.] 8 1780.

Resolved that the Governor & Council be & they are hereby requested & authorised to appoint proper persons to Negociate for this State at Congress, & the other States, for the purpose of procuring assistants towards the defense of the Frontiers & any other Matters that shall be necessary for the benefit of this State.

Extract from the journals, ROS[L] HOPKINS, *Clerk.*"[1]

End of the Session held at Bennington in October and November 1780.

JOSEPH FAY, *Sec[y.]*

---

[1] By authority of this resolution Gov. Chittenden made "a positive demand" upon New York, Massachusetts, and New Hampshire to relinquish their claims to jurisdiction over Vermont, and proposed to those states, as well as to Connecticut and Rhode Island, "an alliance and permanent confederation with Vermont against the hostile attempts of British power."—See *Appendix G, post.*

RECORD OF THE BOARD OF WAR—NOVEMBER 1780.

Resolutions of Board of War Nov[r.] 29th 1780.

IN BOARD OF WAR, Arlington, Nov[r.] 29th 1780.

Members Present—Timothy Brownson Esq[r.], *President.*
Joseph Bowker Esq[r.]
Stephen Pearl Esq[r.]
John Fassett [jr.] Esq[r.]

Resolved to raise Eighty able bodied Effective men including Non commissioned officers for the defence of the fronteers of this State to be under the command of Capt. Jesse Sawyer. One Capt. one Lieut. and forty of the above Number of men to be raised forthwith out of Col[o.] Ira Allen's Regt. and march to fort Warren without Loss of time: and one Capt. one Lieut. and the other forty men to be raised forthwith out of Col[o.] Ebenezer Allen's Regt. and march to fort Vengeance and join Capt. Sawyer, and to continue in service fourteen days from the time they march unless sooner discharged, the pay of the Capt[ts.] to be eight pounds Hard money each p[r.] month or other money Equivalent and the other officers and soldiers Pay in proportion.

Resolved further to recommend to the Cap[t.] Gen[l.] to Issue his order to the Colonels of the within mentioned [above] Reg[t.] to put the within [above] resolve into Execution.

Resolved further to raise two Lieutenants and forty eight non-Commissioned officers and private men for the defence of the fronteers of this State for the ensuing winter, one of the above Lieutenants two sargeants two Corporals and twenty privates to be raised out of Col[o.] Fletcher's Reg[t.] and march to fort Vengeance at Pitsford by the first day of January and to Continue in service three months unless sooner discharged: and the other Lieutenant, two Sergeents two Corporals and twenty privates to be raised out of Col[o.] Sam[l.] Herricks Reg[t.] to march to fort Warren at Castleton by the first day of January and to continue in service three months unless sooner discharged—their pay to be as follows, viz: the Lieutenant's pay p[r.] month to be five pounds Eight shillings Hard money Each or other money Equivalent: the Sergeant's pay p[r.] month to be two pounds eight shillings Hard money Each or other money Equivalent: The Corporal's pay to be two pounds four shillings Hard money Each or other money Equivalent: the private's pay to be two pounds Hard money p[r.] month Each or other money Equivalent—their pay to commence six days before they march.

Resolved further that for the rations the officers and soldiers find on their march too and from camp they shall be allowed ten pence each Hard money.

Resolved further to recommend to the Cap[t.] General to issue his orders to the Colonels of the within [above] mentioned Regiments to put the within [above] Resolves into Execution.

Debenture for the Board of War, Arlington 29 [Nov.] 1780.

Timothy Brownson Esq[r.]	£0	15	4
Joseph Bowker Esq[r.]	1	9	0
Stephen Pearl Esq[r.]	1	1	2
John Fassett [jr.] Esq[r.]	1	12	4

The Honorable Col^{o.} Timothy Brownson
President of the Honorable the Board of War, Sunderland.

ARLINGTON, Dec[r.] 1st 1780.

Dear Sir:—I am directed by his Excellency to Copy the resolutions of the Hon[ble] Board of War and transmit the same to you, which have done & herewith enclose them. I have the honor to be

Sir, your most ob[t.] Servant,
THO[S] TOLMAN.

Hon. Col[o.] Brownson.

THE LAND GRANTS OF 1780—STATE FINANCES.

The numerous grants of townships made in the autumn of 1780 were designed to play so important a part in sustaining the State that a statement of the principal circumstances is desirable. Congress on the 2d of June preceding had declared that the acts of Vermont in asserting its independence and continuing its grants of lands, in violation of the resolutions of Congress of September and October 1779, "are highly unwarrantable and subversive of the peace and welfare of the United States;" and "strictly required" the people thereof "to forbear and abstain from all acts of authority, civil or military," over those residents in Vermont who preferred to accept the jurisdiction of another state. This had been accepted by the Governor and Council as a quasi declaration of war by Congress, and on the 25th of July Gov. CHITTENDEN had protested against this action, and notified the President of that body that "Vermont have, therefore, no alternative; they must either submit to the unwarrantable decree of Congress, or continue their appeal to heaven and to arms;" and announced that the State would appeal from Congress to the legislatures of the several states "and take such other measures as self-preservation may justify." In that critical condition of affairs, the General Assembly of Oct. 1780 deliberately determined to put Vermont on a war footing, by adopting elaborate rules and regulations for the militia, and framing others for the supply of provisions, &c. to its military forces in the field; by giving the Board of War full power to raise an army, or call out the militia, or both, for nine months, the term being increased to eleven months; and finally by numerous land grants to furnish the "sinews of war." Indeed the disposable land of the State,—the improved land of the tories that had been confiscated, and the ungranted lands that were to be sold—were the main features in the financial policy of the State.

When government was organized in March 1778, all the other states were groaning under the burden of taxes; and therefore, in Vermont, said IRA ALLEN:

It was thought good policy not to lay any taxes on the people, but to raise a sufficient revenue out of the property confiscated, and the ungranted lands. Hence it was found that those who joined the British were benefactors of the State, as they left their property to support a government they were striving to destroy. It is further to be observed, that not only the civil list was paid by the sale of the enemy's property, but new and firm friends were added to the government. While the States in New England were severely taxed to carry on the war, Vermont had no taxes to pay. This circumstance greatly promoted migration into Vermont, and those who came with that view were staunch friends to the new government, and added to its strength and consequence both at home and abroad.[1]

Such being the settled policy of the State, it is of course found that it was systematically pursued.

In 1779, further said ALLEN, a form of charter and rules for granting lands were adopted; and it appears, from the petitions in the Ms. State Papers in the Secretary of State's office, that a printed form of petition to the General Assembly for a land grant, was prepared. It is hardly necessary to add that these blank petitions were widely circulated, not only throughout New England, but in the middle States and in the army. In October 1779, IRA ALLEN was appointed to attend the legislatures of the middle and other states; and his account shows that his special business was in reference to the lands both of Vermont and of the continent. Several of the states visited owned no land outside of their own bounds, and ALLEN made a point of claiming that the immense public domain of wild land, wrested from Great Britain by the revolution, should not be the property of particular states, as Virginia, Pennsylvania, New York, &c., but the common property of all the states. In this view he proposed that the confiscated and ungranted lands of Vermont should be counted as part of the common property of all the states, and engaged that Vermont would account for all it received out of lands within her limits. This was a direct and powerful appeal to those states to make common cause with Vermont, as indeed on some occasions every one of them did.[2] Of course ALLEN did not neglect this opportunity to scatter broadcast the blank petitions to the General Assembly of Vermont for land grants. Land companies were formed in New Hampshire, Massachusetts, Connecticut, and Rhode Island; also by officers in the continental army; and members of the continental Congress were not excluded. In allusion to these companies, WASHINGTON said, in 1783:

Two things I am sure of, namely, that they [the Vermonters] have a powerful interest in those States, [New England,] and pursued very politic measures to strengthen and increase it, long before I had any knowledge of the matter, and before the tendency of it was seen into or suspected, by granting upon very advantageous terms large tracts of land; in which, I am sorry to find, the army in some degree have participated.[3]

Hence when the General Assembly met in October 1780, it found a large number of these petitions filed in the office of the Secretary of

[1] Ira Allen's *History*, in *Vt. Hist. Soc. Collections*, Vol. I, p. 393.

[2] See Observations relating to the influence of Vermont and the territorial claims on the politics of Congress, by JAMES MADISON, in *Vt. Hist. Soc. Coll.*, Vol. II, pp. 268, 269; and *Appendix F, post.*

[3] *Vt. Hist. Soc. Coll.*, Vol II, p. 325.

State, and the way apparently open to add materially to the funds in the treasury. This, said ALLEN, "furnished money to defray the expenses in part of the war, helped to alleviate, in a considerable degree, the burthens of the people, and to strengthen the frontiers against the common enemy."[1] At this particular juncture, however, it is obvious that the fund was raised in anticipation of a possible contest with New York, and even with Congress.

Oct. 14 1780 it was

Resolved that a Committee of five to join a Committee from the Council be appointed to take into consideration the situation of ungranted lands within this State which can be settled, and the several petitions filed in the Secretary's office praying for grants of such unlocated lands: and report their opinion what lands can be granted, and what persons will most conduce to the welfare of this State to have such grants. The Members chosen by ballot are Mr. Saml. Robinson, Mr. [Edward] Harris, Col°. [John] Strong, Mr. [Ebenezer] Curtiss, and Mr. [Joshua] Webb.

This phraseology shows that not money only was wanted, but influence to be used for the benefit of Vermont elsewhere.

Oct. 16, the limitation of grants to "land which can be settled" was stricken out, and the committee was enlarged, as follows:

Resolved that the words "which can be settled" be erased in the resolve appointing a Committee of five to take into consideration ungranted lands, &c. and that four persons be added to said Committee. The Members chosen Mr. [Matthew] Lyon, Mr. [Benjamin] Whipple, Mr. [Thomas] Porter, and Mr. [Thomas] Murdock.

Oct. 17, the Governor and Council appointed Messrs. Ira Allen, John Fassett, jr., Jonas Fay, and Paul Spooner, to join the committee of the House.

The first grant recommended by the committee was that of *Montpelier*, Oct. 21, when the House resolved that the grant be made to Col. Timothy Bigelow and Company, and that "the Governor and Council are hereby requested to issue a grant or charter of incorporation of said township of *Montpelier* under such restrictions, reservations and for such considerations as they shall judge best for the benefit of the State."

On the same day the Governor and Council "stated the fees" and conditions as follows:

At Four hundred & Eighty pounds for the said Land, being one Township by the Name of *Montpelier, in hard money or an equivalent in Continental currency*,[2] to be paid by Col°. Timothy Bigelow or his attorney, on the Execution of the Charter of Incorporation, on or before the 20th day of January next.

The House at the same session recommended grants of more than fifty townships, and in nearly all the cases the Governor and Council so far executed them as to name the grantees and the conditions of the charter. Thus the State designed to realize a very large sum of cash or its equivalent, in time to meet any probable emergency. Sufficient

[1] *Vt. Hist. Soc. Coll.*, Vol. I, p. 406.

[2] In later cases *lead* and *flints* were accepted instead of "hard money."

payments being expected in the winter of 1781, when no considerable military movement could be made against the State, there was supposed to be ample time to prepare for an active spring campaign, and it was improved by the Board of War for that purpose. As we know, however, this apprehended emergency was happily escaped by the diplomacy of ALLEN and FAY with the Governor General of Canada.[1]

In this connection a summary statement of the financial policy of the State may best be made. From July 1777 to October 1780, the main source of revenue was found in the sale of the confiscated property of tories. This, with funds derived from occasional land grants, sufficed for all purposes without levying any state tax. In October 1780, as has been seen, a large revenue was expected from the sale of ungranted lands, but in fact it soon became necessary to adopt another measure. Accordingly in April 1781 an act was passed "for the purpose of emitting a sum of Money, and directing the redemption of the same." It provided for the issue of bills of credit to the amount of £25,155, which were made "a lawful tender for payment on all contracts, executions, &c., as lawful money according to the face of the bill." These bills were to be redeemed by the first day of June 1782 in silver at the rate of six shillings for one Spanish milled dollar, or gold equivalent. For the act see Slade's *State Papers*, p. 424. For the redemption of these bills a tax of one shilling and three pence, lawful money, on the pound on the list of polls and ratable estate of the inhabitants of the state, was imposed—being the first state tax; and, in addition, a tax of ten shillings on each hundred acres of land in the state which would admit of settlement, public rights and college lands excepted. These three sources served the purpose for several years, the taxes proving in fact less than one seventh of the revenue raised. This is shown by the auditing of the state treasurer's [IRA ALLEN'S] accounts in February 1787, in which the sources and gross amount of revenue from March 1777 to October 1786 are specified, as follows:

	£	s.	d.
Continental money received of Commissioners [for confiscated property,]	£190,433	6	4
Lawful money received from Land Committee [for land granted,]	66,815	13	8
State notes [bills of credit] issued,	24,750	8	7
Cash received in lawful money from taxes,	38,536	17	11
Cash received on hard money taxes,	7,411	2	7
Total revenue March 1777 to October 1786, both years included,	£327,947	9	1

This covered ten financial years, and the average therefore was £3279 per annum. Five years later, in 1791, ALLEN stated the expenses of the State at £3219 9 9, and the average state tax *per capita* to be six pence three farthings to each inhabitant.

[1] See *Vt. Hist. Soc. Coll.*, Vol. II.

RECORD OF THE GOVERNOR AND COUNCIL

AT A

SPECIAL SESSION AT BENNINGTON DEC^R. 1780.

BENNINGTON 16 Decr. 1780.
IN COUNCIL, date above.

RULES AND REGULATIONS *directing in what manner the Troops employed in the Service of this State shall be paid.*

Resolved, that for the payment of the Troops that shall be in Service hereafter for the defence of this State, for any stipulated term of Time, there shall be one pay Master appointed whose duty it shall be, to pay the Troops agreeable to *pay Rools* which the Captains of Each Company shall make out, & which shall be examined & approved by the Committee of pay Table & the same certified on the back of said Roll before the paymaster shall pay any Money^s thereon, upon which a Warrant shall Issue on the Treasurer for the Pay Master to receive the Same & pay out the Several sums due to Each officer and soldier respectively.

There shall be duplicate Pay Rolls thus authenticated for each payment, on one of which shall be the Warrant to the Treasurer who shall take the pay master's Rec^t. thereupon keeping the Same as his Voucher, and the other shall be Lodged with the pay Master.

The pay Master shall be under a bond of one thousand pounds to the Treasurer of this State for the due and faithful performance of his duty. He shall keep regular Books of all monies rec^d. by him & paid out, & settle his acc^ts. with the Auditors of acc^ts. as often as they shall call upon him for that purpose. He shall take all his Rec^ts. for money Specifying the sums in words at Length & and not in figures, & no other Rec^ts. shall pass as a Voucher to his acc^ts. in Settlement.

All orders which officers or soldiers have drawn or may draw on their respective Captains while in Service for their Wages or any part of them shall be paid by the pay Master when Exhibitted to him to the ammount of such officers or Soldiers Wages, & such order with a Rec^t. thereon indorsed shall be a Sufficient Voucher to the pay master in a Settlement of his Accompts. Provided always that such be Exhibitted before such officer or Soldier may otherwise have received his pay.

And all like orders which the Captains or other Commanding officers have drawn or may draw upon the Treasurer & which are not paid before the pay *Roles* are made up and authenticated shall in Like Manner be paid by the pay Master who is hereby directed not to receive any other orders for pay until such orders and Receipts as the Treasurer may have are deducted and the Treasurer accounted to for the Same.

And Whereas there is now a number of Troops in Service & others that have been discharged which are not yet paid for their Services, it is further

Resolved that all Such Troops shall be paid by the pay Master in the Same manner as is prescribed by the foregoing Resolutions.

Resolved that the pay Master who shall be appointed be Allowed an Adequate Compensation for his Services, he keeping accounts of his Time and necessary expence in such Service.

The preceeding Rules & Regulations read & approved, Whereupon

Resolved that Thomas Tolman be & he is hereby appointed Pay Master to the Troops, heretofore and in future to be raised for the defense of this State for the year Ensuing.

By order of the Governor & Council,

JONAS FAY, *Secy. P. Tem.*

True Copy Recorded,

JOSEPH FAY, *Secy.*

RECORD OF THE BOARD OF WAR, JANUARY 1781.

Minutes of the proceedings of the BOARD OF WAR, *met at Arlington Jan. 2d and held by adjournment until the 10th inclusive* (1781.)

TUESDAY, Jan. 2d 1781.

Agreeable to an appointment of the Honble the President of this Board of War for the Honble Board to meet at this place on the 1st Tuesday in January, the same met—Present

Honble John Fassett Jun. Esqr.
Samuel Robinson Esqr.
Benjamin Wait Esqr. } *Members,*

and not being a full Board, adjourned 'till Tomorrow.

THOS. TOLMAN, *Secy. Pro Tem.*

WEDNESDAY, Jan. 3d.—Met according to adjournment, when the Honble Timo. Brownson Esqr. President appeared and took the chair.

But there being not yet a full board, adjourned till Tomorrow.

THOS. TOLMAN, *Secy. Pro Tem.*

THURSDAY, Jan. 4th.—Met according to adjournment, when Stephen Pearl Esqr. appeared and took his seat at the Board.

The Board proceeded to business by order of the President.

Resolved that Thos. Tolman be appointed *Secy. Pro Tem* to this Board during ye present sitting of this Board.

And upon motion made

Resolved, that the pay for Jonathan Fassett Esqr. late Comisy of Purchases be £13 10 0 pr. month, he to find his own Horse, and be allowed reasonable expences for himself and Horse, exclusive of his pay.

Resolved, that Elisha Clark Esqr. late Commissary of Issues be allowed £8 per month, and 3 rations pr. day—and that Messrs. Eli Cogsell, Lyman Chase & Amos Bicknel, late Assistant Commissaries of Issues, be allowed, each, £5 8 0 pr. month and two rations pr. day.

Resolved, that Capt. Joseph Safford late Barrack master be allowed while in actual service £7 pr. month, & 2 rations pr. day.

Resolved, that Mr. Gershom Beach, armourer, be allowed while in actual service £7 pr. month and 2 rations pr. day.

Adjourned 'till 12 othe Clock on Wednesday [Monday] next.

THOS. TOLMAN, *Secy. Pro Tem.*

MONDAY, Jan. 8th.—Met according to adjournment, when the Honble Joseph Bowker and Samuel Fletcher Esqrs. appeared and took their seats at the Board,—Stephen Pearl Esqr. not present,—and after deliberating upon sundry matters of Importance without entering into any Resolves, adjourned till Tomorrow morning 9 oclock.

THOS. TOLMAN, *Secy. Pro Tem.*

TUESDAY, Jan. 9th.—Met according to adjournment, when Stephen Pearl Esqr. appeared and took his seat at the Board.

The Board proceeded to consider the state of the frontiers, Whereupon

Resolved, that for the defence of the frontiers of this State for the ensuing Campaign there shall be one Regiment of INFANTRY raised, (to continue in service until the 15th day of Decmr. next, unless sooner discharged,) which shall consist of one Lt. Colo. Commdt, 2 majors, 9 captains, 18 subalterns, 1 Surgeon, 1 Surgs. mate, 1 Sergt. Majr, 1 Quarter Mast. Sergt, 36 Serjeants, 1 Drum Maj., 1 Fife Majr, 8 Drummers, 8 Fifers & 612 Rank and File.

Resolved, that 1 Adjt. and 1 Qr. Mastr. be appointed by the Lt. Col. Commandant out of the 18 Subalterns, To be allowed each £2 pr. month, in addition to their pay in the Line.

Resolved, that each company shall consist of 1 Capt. 1 first Lieut. 1 second Lieut. 4 Sergeants, 1 Drummer, 1 fifer, and 68 Rank and File, and that the Drums and fifes Major be annexed to the 1st Company in the Regiment.

Resolved, That the Field, Staff and Commissioned Officers appointed, with their rank, Pay & Rations, shall be as follows, namely:

	Names.	*Rank.*	*Pay pr. month.*	*Rations pr. Day.*
Field.	Samuel Fletcher,	Lt. Colo. Commdt,	£15	No. 6
	Benjamin Wait,	1st Major,	12	5
	Ebnr. Allen,	2d Major,	10	4
Commissioned.	Jesse Sawyer,	1st Captain,	8	3
	William Hutchins,	2d do.	do.	do.
	Jesse Safford,	3d do.	do.	do.
	Jonas Galusha,	4th do.	do.	do.
	John Powell,	5th do.	do.	do.
	Nathaniel [Nehemiah] Lovell,	6th do.	do.	do.
	[James] Blakesley,	7th do.	do.	do.
	James Brookins,	8th do.	do.	do.
	Josiah Fish,	9th do.	do.	do.
	Zebulon Lyon,	1st first Lieut.	£5 8 0	2
	Gideon Spencer,	2d first do.	do.	do.
	Bariah Green,	3d first do.	do.	do.
	Nathl. Holmes,	4th first do.	do.	do.
	Josiah Wright,	5th first do.	do.	do.
		6th first do.	do.	do.
	Benjamin Everist,	7th first do.	do.	do.
	Moses Evans,	8th first do.	do.	do.
	Elias Hall,	9th first do.	do.	do.
		1st second Lieut.	do.	do.
	Ebenezer Hoisington,	2d second Lieut.	do.	do.
		3d second Lieut.	do.	do.
	Benjamin Stevens,	4th second Lieut.	do.	do.
		5th second Lieut.	do.	do.
	Noah Chittenden,	6th second Lieut.	do.	do.
	David Powers,	7th second Lieut.	do.	do.
	John Boardman,	8th second Lieut.	do.	do.
	William Post.	9th second Lieut.	do.	do.
Staff.	Nathl. Dickinson,	Surgeon	£10	3
	John Hazleton,	Surgeon's Mate	8	2

Resolved, that the Lt. Colo. Commandant and Majr. Benjamin Wait be directed to nominate such Gentlemen as they shall judge worthy to fill the several places of a 6th first Lieut., a 1st second Lieut., a third second Lt. and a fifth second Lieut. agreeable to the above vacancies, and make returns of the Gentlemen thus chosen, with their several Ranks, to the Captain General, in order that they may be Commissioned accordingly.

Resolved, that the pay and Rations of the officers commence 14 days before the day of their entering into actual service, and that each Officer be allowed pr. month, for each retained Ration not drawn in Provisions, £1.

Adjourned 'till Tomorrow morning 8 o the clock.

THOS. TOLMAN, *Secy. Pro Tem.*

WEDNESDAY, Jan. 10th.—Met according to adjournment, and proceeded to business by order of the President—and upon motion made that the Board proceed to the method of raising the Troops to fill the Regiment of Infantry, resolved to be raised yesterday,

Resolved, that the several Militia Regiments within this State raise the following quotas of able bodied and effective men (viz.) Colo. Samuel Fletcher's Regt. 152 men, Col. Samuel Herrick's 112, Colo. Ebenezer Woods 99, The 4th Regiment as it stood before the last session of Assembly 111, Colo. Ebenezer Allen's 83, and Colo. Ira Allen's 111—Total 668.

Resolved, that each town furnish their proportion of men (agreeable to the foregoing Resolve) equipt, and ready for the field by the 10th day of February next, who shall march to the several places of Rendezvous of their respective officers, and be allowed, each, Pay 14 days, next before the day of marching from their respective towns.

Resolved that the pay of the Non Commissioned officers and Privates pr. month shall be as follows, (viz.)

Sergt. Majr.	£3		Drummers, each,	£2	4
Qr. Mr. Sergt.	3		Fifers, each,	2	4
Serjeants each,	2	8	Corporals, each,	2	4
Drum Maj'r	2	8	Privates, each,	2	
Fife Maj'r	2	8			

Resolved, that the Equipment of a non Commissioned officer and Soldier (exclusive of his Blankets & Cloathing) shall be as follows, (viz.)

1 Good Musquet,	1 Powder [flask or horn,]
1 Good Bayonet or Tomahawk,	1 Bullet Pouch, and a sufficient
1 Good Knapsack,	Tump Line[1] (or Sling for Packs.)

And whereas the Board consider it impracticable to appoint officers within the Bounds of the several militia Regiments in Exact proportion to the several Quotas of men raised by the same,

Resolved, That Colo. Fletcher's and Colo. Herrick's Regiment of militia compleat as many full companies as their Quotas will admit, and the Remainder, if more than half another full Company to be joined by, or if less than half another full Compauy to join themselves to the Quota of the next adjoining Regiment, who shall form Companies, and dispose of their Remainders in like manner, until the nine Companies be equally Compleated.

Resolved, that this formation of Companies, together with the arrangement of the officers to Each Company be under the direction of the Lt. Colo. Commandant, with the advice and consent of the other Gentlemen officers appointed.

And whereas it will be necessary, as well to avoid the needless cost of marching ineffective men into the Camp, as to prevent the after Trouble to the Towns who shall in this respect appear deficient,

. Resolved, that previous to the marching of the men from the several towns, there shall be a review made by such officers of the Regiment as reside in the said Towns respectively, whose duty it shall be to accept

---

[1]Tump line—a strap placed across the forehead to assist a man in carrying a pack on his back.—*Bartlett's Dictionary of Americanisms.*

none but able bodied, effective and well equipt men, and such as in their judgment are equal to, and capable for the service of a Campaign, and who shall pass in a General Muster of the Reg$^{t.}$ after their arrival in Camp by the muster master—and in case where towns have no officer appointed within the same to review the s ime previous to marching as above directed,

Resolved that the L$^{t.}$ Col$^{o.}$ Commandant and Major Benjamin Wait be directed to appoint such officer or officers as they shall judge best, to do said duty in such Towns.

And whereas it will be necessary that the Regiment of Infantry ordered to be raised be regularly mustered in Camp and enrolled in a muster master's office,

Resolved, that Thomas Tolman be, and he is hereby appointed Muster Master, whose duty it shall be to muster said Regiment as often, and in such manner, as the Captain General shall direct, and that he be allowed while in such service Six Shillings (6|) per day and 3 Rations; and that all Returns from the said Reg$^{t.}$ shall be made to the Cap$^{t.}$ General, as often, and in such manner & form as he shall from time to time direct.

And Whereas it will be necessary for equally securing the Frontiers of the two Counties that a part of this Regiment be detached,

Resolved, that a detachment of three full companies under the Command of Major Benjamin Wait be Stationed in the frontiers of the County of Cumberland until further orders from this Board or the Cap$^{t.}$ General, and that the Lieu$^{t.}$ Colonel Commandant, with the advice of Major Wait, shall direct those companies in the Regiment who shall be thus detached.

Resolved, that the surgeon's mate, Serj$^{t.}$ Major & Q. M$^{r.}$ Serjeant shall be annexed to do duty in Maj$^{r.}$ Wait's detachment, until further orders.

Resolved, that the Captain General be requested to issue his necessary orders, to put into effectual execution the foregoing Resolutions of this Board.

Resolved, that the preceding Resolutions of this Board for the defence of the frontiers of this State the ensuing Campaign, be published three weeks successively in the *Vermont Gazette.*

Resolved, in case either of the Majors who now Stand appointed shall not choose to accept, that Maj$^{r.}$ Isaac Clark be appointed to supply such vacancy, and the Captain General is requested to Commission him accordingly. By order of the Board, THO$^{S.}$ TOLMAN, *Sec$^{y.}$ Pro Tem.*

BENNINGTON, 9th Jan. 1781.

Sir,—Cap$^{t.}$ Putnam was yesterday with me (supposing that I was yet a member of the Board of War,) and has mentioned at the same time the services he has rendered this State in the capacity of Q. M. altho his appointment to that place was by the authority of the Continent. His services while acting in such Capacity, as far as come to my knowledge, were uniform, and such as merited him applause. It has been since suggested that in some degree he has been opposed to the establishment of this State—which has not sufficiently been proved to me.

It is well known that he has suffered in the present War by being drove from his possessions, and reduced to the necessity of obtaining a support of Himself and family by serving this or some other State in a Public capacity. As he has heretofore served with good acceptance, unless you can be fully satisfied that he has by his conduct forfeited the confidence of the State, I wish in his suffering condition he may have an appointment adequate to his merits.

I am, Gentlemen, your most ob$^{t.}$ humble servant,

JONAS FAY.

Honble Timothy Brownson.

Debenture of the Board of War met at Arlington Jan. 2d 1781 and continued by adjournment until the 10th inclusive.

To the Hon. Timothy Brownson Esq. President, 5 days at 7|	£1	15	0
8 miles travel at 4d.		2	8
Recd. pr TIMO. BROWNSON,	1	17	8
Hon. Joseph Bowker Esq. 3 days 21| 45 miles travel 15|	1	16	0
Recd. pr JOSEPH BOWKER.			
Stephen Pearl Esq. 3 days 21| double travel Amt. 40 miles, at 4d Recd. pr.	1	14	4
Hon. Samuel Fletcher Esq. 3 days 21| 42 miles travel 14| Recd. pr.	1	15	0
John Fassett Esq. Junr. 6 days 42| 2 miles travel at 4d. Recd. pr.	2	2	8
Benj. Wait Esq. 6 days 42| 80 miles travel, 26|8 Recd. pr.	3	8	8
Samuel Robinson 6 days 42| 28 miles [double] travel 9|4 Recd. pr me.	2	11	4
Total	£15	5	8

The above is a true Debenture.
Attest, TIMOTHY BROWNSON, *President.*

JOURNALS OF COUNCIL

AT THEIR

SESSION HOLDEN AT WINDSOR FEB. 8TH. 1781.

[WITH THE ADJOURNED SESSION OF THE GENERAL ASSEMBLY.]

STATE OF VERMONT. IN COUNCIL, Windsor 8 Feby. 1781.

At a meeting of His Excellency the Governor and the Honorable Council, the Legislature being Convened according to Adjournment—Present His Excellency Thomas Chittenden Esqr., His Honor Benjamin Carpenter Esqr. Lt. Govr. and the following Members of the Honble Council, vizt. Honble Joseph Bowker, Timothy Brownson, Paul Spooner, Benjamin Emmons, Ira Allen, John Throop, John Fassett, [jr.,] & Thos. Chandler [jr.] Esqrs.

Resolved that Thomas Tolman be & he is hereby appointed Secy. Pro Tempore.

A memorial from Doctor Thomas Clark was read, whereupon the Honble Ira Allen Esqr. [was] appointed a Committee from the Council to join a Committee from the house to take under Consideration the memorial.

A Letter Inclosing sundry papers to be Laid before the General Assembly signed Elisha Payne Chairman in behalf of a Committee appointed by a Convention held at Charleston [Charlestown, N. H.,] on the

16 of January Last was read, and upon a request from the house the Council joined them in a Committee of both houses to Confer on the Subject of said Letters.[1]

Adjourned to 9 °Clock Tomorrow.

FEB. 9th 1781.

Met according to Adjournment.

The Honble Samuel Fletcher Esqr. attended and took his seat in Council.

The Council having Attend[ed] on a Committee of both Houses until 10 °Clock—

Adjourned until 2 °Clock P. M.

Met according to Adjournment & again joined the House in a Committee of the whole until 6 °Clock and then Adjourned until 9 °Clock Tomorrow.

WINDSOR 10 Feb. 1781.

Met according to Adjournment and after Attending in a Committee of the whole until 11 °Clock the Committee adjourned & the Council proceeded to business.

A bill Entitled an Act for quieting the disorders prevailing in this State was laid before the Council, whereupon a Committee was appointed to join a Committee from the House for the purpose of Making such Alterations & amendments as they shall judge Necessary in said bill and make their Report. Members chose the Honble Samuel Fletcher & John Fassett, [jr.,] Esquires.

Adjourned until 9 °Clock Monday next.[1]

FEB. 12th 1781.

Met according to Adjournment.

A petition Signed David Haynes, Elisha Downs & sixteen others, inhabitants of Bennington [was read.]

A petition signed Nathan Roberts was read.

An act passed the General Assembly entitled an act to prevent a Multiplicity of Law Suits was read.

Adjourned to 2 °Clock P. M.

---

[1] Both Houses met in Committee of the Whole from time to time, until the unions of the forty-three New Hampshire towns and sundry districts of New York were effected. For the action of the Committee of the Whole, and of the General Assembly, with other documents on this subject, see *Appendix H.*

[1] From the Record of the *Board of War:*

IN BOARD of WAR, Arlington, Feby. 10th 1781.

On the Representation of Mr. Joseph Foster of Barnet and others Respecting that frontier,

Resolved, that Lieut. Beriah Green raise by Voluntary Inlistment thirty able bodied effective men Every way Equiped for war with Snowshoes to march Immediately, to continue in service one month unless sooner discharged, their pay to be the same as other Troops in this State's service. Their Pay to commence Ten days before they march.

Resolved, That Capt. John Strong asst. C. P. Procure Sixty Tin Kittles or other Pots & Kittles Equivilent for Camp Equipage.

Met according to Adjournment.

A petition of John Barret & others to the number of 31 was read requesting the General Assembly to Grant Liberty for making a Lottery for the purpose of Erecting two Bridges the one in Springfield over black river, & the other in Rockingham over a river by the name of Williams river, upon which a Committee of one was appointed to join a Committee of five from the House to Consider said petition and make report. Choose the Honble John Throop Esquire.

A Resolve of the General Assembly appointing a Committee to receive and inquire into the petition from the Several Towns respecting an over taxation was read whereupon a Committee of one was appointed to join said Committee of the House. The Gentleman choosen Honble Timo. Brownson Esquire.

Resolved that the Honble Benjamin Emmons Esqr. be appointed to join a Committee from the House for the purpose of prepairing a bill to be Laid before the General Assembly directing the Committee of Pay Table what sums shall be paid for the several Militia [services] done in this State in Alarms.

Deacon Dudly Chase prefered a Verbal petition to his Excellency & Council in behalf of the Proprietors of *Bethel*—That when the Charter of Royalton is given out it may not infringe on the sd. *Bethel*, he having causes of fear that might be the case unless due care be taken in discribing said lines.

Council Adjourned to 8 oClock Tomorrow.

FEBRUARY 13 1781.

Met according to Adjournment.

An Act to prevent a Multiplicity of Law Suits was again read & Concurred.[1]

A Resolve of the General Assembly appointing a Committee of Elevin to join a Committee from the Council to report their opinion to the House where the Frontier lines shall be established the Ensuing Campaign, was read—whereupon the Honble Timothy Brownson & Paul Spooner Esquires were appointed a Committee to join said Committee from the House.[2]

A resolve of the General Assembly appointing a Committee of three to arange the business that is Likely to be done this Session & report to

---

[1] This act permitted offsets on the most liberal scale. If one person commenced an action on contract against another, all matters of like character between the parties could be settled by the suit. For act, see Slade's *State Papers*, p. 423.

[2] From the *Assembly Journal*, Feb. 13 1781:

Resolved that a Committee of eleven to join a Committee from the Council be appointed to report their opinion where the frontier lines shall be established the ensuing Campaign. The member chosen Mr. [Benjamin] Whipple, Mr. [Abner] Seelye, Mr. [Ebenezer] Drury, Mr. [Elisha] Burton. Mr. E. [Elihu] Smith, Mr. J. [John] Powell, Colo. [Thomas] Lee, Maj. [Benjamin] Wait,* Mr. [Roswell] Post, Mr. C. [Calvin] Parkhurst, and Mr. A. [Amos] Robinson.

Resolved that a Committee of three be appointed to make such necessary alterations in the instruction of the Board of War as they shall judge best and Report to this House. The members chosen Mr. Ward 2d. [William, of Newfane,] Mr. [Samuel] Bartlet, and Mr. [John] Powell.

* Col. Lee and Maj. Wait were not members of the Assembly.

the House was read, whereupon the Hon[ble] John Throop & Ira Allen Esquires were chosen a Committee [to join the Committee] from the house.

Council Adjourned until 2 °Clock P. M.

A Report of a Committee upon John Chandler's selling Lands in Tomblinson, [Tomlinson, now Grafton,] was read & Concurred.[1]

Adjourned to 8 °Clock Tomorrow.

FEB. 14th 1781.

Met according to Adjournment.

A remonstrance Signed Thadeus Wait, William Hall, & Silas Wait was read.

A Resolve of the General Assembly equitting & releasing the Charter fee of Joseph Kneeland in the Township of Randolph was read whereupon the following was indorsed on said bill and Transmitted back to the House viz[t.]

IN COUNCIL Feb[y.] 14th 1781.

The Council having taken into their due consideration the within Resolve & altho they have a tender feeling for and are sincearely willing & desirous as in them lies consistent with Justice to the State in General to release the distressed yet as the Similar Sufferings of the Inhabitants of this State are so numerous they cannot see sufficient reason for the Grant made in this bill (at this Time) unless the General Assembly have it in their power and have a desire to Grant immeadiate relief to all those whose Misfortunes have been to Suffer loss of property in any degree more or less in the Present War.

THOMAS TOLMAN, *Sec[y.] P. Tem.*

An act entitled an Act in alteration of an Act entitled an Act concerning Delinquents was read & Concurred.

Council Adjourned until half after 1 °Clock P. M.

Met according to Adjournment.

A petition Signed Philip Smith was read. A Report of a Committee on Capt. Lees Petition was read.

Resolved that a Committee of three be appointed to join a Committee from the House for the purpose of Waiting upon the Committee appointed by a Convention held at Charleston [Charlestown, N. H.,] with a Report of a Committee of boath Houses of this State, upon the sub-

---

[1] Chandler had been attorney for Thomas Apthorp, who was owner of nine thousand acres of land in Tomlinson [Grafton.] After Apthorp had joined the enemy, Chandler conveyed this land by deed. The report and resolution of the House declared the fee of this land to be in the State, and required copies of Chandler's deed, and the power of attorney given to him by Apthorp, to be filed in the office of the clerk of the Assembly. JOHN CHANDLER was the oldest son of Thomas Chandler senior, of Chester, and came to Vermont with his father in 1763, and held several offices under New York until Feb. 25, 1772, when he was removed from the office of clerk of Cumberland county for misconduct. The transaction noted on the journal of the General Assembly indicates that his bad habit in business matters was strongly fixed. B. H. Hall said, little is known of his future career,—See *Eastern Vermont*, p. 638.

ject of Jurisdictional Claims, this day Brought in—members chosen Mr. Allen, Mr. Emmons, & Mr. Fassett.

Attest, THOMAS TOLMAN *Secy. P. Tem.*

Adjourned to 9 °Clock Tomorrow.[1]

IN COUNCIL Feb. 15th 1781.

Met according to Adjournment.

Resolved that it be recommended to the General Assembly, that the further Consideration of the Jurisdictional Claims laid & passed in boath Houses yesterday be postponed until the next Session of this Assembly, & that an Agent be appointed and fully authorised, Immeadiately to Wait upon the Legislature of the State of N. York now Convened in Albany to agree upon and establish the line between this State & the State of N. York.

Attest, THOMAS TOLMAN, *Secy. P. Tem.*

Resolved that this Council do recommend to the House that they do as Little business at this Session as may be, aranging & doing that which may be absolutely necessary at present & that they agree on some place to Adjourn to and Leave it with his Excellency with the advice of Council to call the Assembly when Necessary by Advertisement or otherwise when he may have returns from the Several States to which Letters are gone,[2] & further knowledge may be had respecting the War.

Attest, THOS. TOLMAN, *Secy. P. Tem.*

Adjourned to 2 °Clock P. M.

Met according to Adjournment.

A Resolve of the House appointing a Committee of two to join a Committee of Council for the purpose of Waiting upon the Committee of the

---

[1] From the *Assembly Journal*, Feb. 14 1781:

The Committee appointed to report their opinion to this House where the frontier lines shall be established the ensuing Campaign brought in the following Report, viz.

"That the line of defence on the west side of the Green Mountain be established at the forts of Pittsford and Castleton, by no means to be drawn further to the south unless by urgent necessity by the opposition of a superior force of the Enemy &c. and that a Committee be appointed on the west side the mountains by this Assembly with full power to remove the line from Castleton to the narrows on the lake or elsewhere if it shall be found proper to act in conjunction with the troops from N. York if any such should arrive at said narrows &c.

"That the troops destined to guard the frontiers on the east side of the Green Mountains be from time to time under the direction of a Committee elected on the east side the said mountains, and that the said Committee take to their assistance in either of the aforesaid instances the officers commanding the several detachments.

BENJA. WHIPPLE, *Chairman.*"

The aforesaid Report was read and accepted and

Resolved, That Colo. Gideon Warren, Colo. Thos. Lee and Mr. Ithamer Hibbard in the West side of the Mountains, and Capt. Abner Seelye, Benja. Emmons Esqr. and Capt. Elisha Burton on the east side of the mountains be and they are hereby appointed the Committees for the purposes mentioned in said Report.

[2] Referring to the letters of Governor Chittenden to the Governors of New York, New Hampshire, Massachusetts, Connecticut, and Rhode Island,—See *Appendix G.*

Cornish Convention[1] with a Letter Signed Beza [Bezaleel] Woodward, this [day] rec$^{d.}$ whereupon a Committee of two was appointed. Members chosen M$^{r.}$ Brownson and M$^{r.}$ Allen.

A petition Signed Sarah Simonds requesting Liberty to go to Canada, was read [as] passed the House. Granted & Concurred.

Adjourned to 9 °Clock Tomorrow.

WINDSOR 16 Feb$^{y.}$ 1781.
IN COUNCIL, date above.

Met according to Adjournment.

A resolve of the General Assembly appointing a Committee of Two to join a Committee from the Council to wait on the Convention Now Sitting at Cornish with the report of the Committee to propose an answer to the request of said Convention was read, whereupon M$^{r.}$ Allen was chosen as a Committee from the Council for the said purpose.

Attest, THOMAS TOLMAN, *Secy* [*P. Tem.*]

A Resolved of the General [Assembly] of the following purport was read, viz$^{t.}$

STATE OF VERMONT. IN GENERAL ASSEMBLY,
Windsor, Feb. 16 1781.

Resolved that two persons be appointed & added to the Board of War, the Members chosen by ballot are the Honble Benjamin Emmons Esq$^{r.}$ and Major Joseph Tyler.[2]

Extract from the Journals, ROS$^{L.}$ HOPKINS, *Clerk.*

Read & approved in Council,
THOMAS TOLMAN, *Sec$^{y.}$ P. Tem.*

The following Resolution was also read viz$^{t.}$

STATE OF VERMONT. IN GENERAL ASSEMBLY,
Windsor, Feb$^{y.}$ 16 1781.

Resolved that Instead of Instructions Given to the Board of War in the last Session of this Assembly, empowering them to raise Troops for

---

[1] The Charlestown Convention had adjourned to Cornish, N. H.

[2] JOSEPH TYLER came from Upton, Mass., and commenced the first settlement in Townshend in 1761. He was a patriot from the opening of the revolutionary war. In Nov. 1775 he was nominated by representatives of the towns in Cumberland county as first major of a regiment of minute-men, and was confirmed by the New York Committee of Safety in January 1776. He was a delegate for Townshend in Cumberland county Committee of Safety from June 1776 to June 1777, when the people of his town instructed him not to act in that capacity "agreeable to the new constitution of the State of New York, because it is our opinion that we do not belong to the jurisdiction of that state," &c. It seems that he had been friendly to the Vermont movement for some months, as in October previous he had been appointed by the Westminster Convention one of a committee of eleven to complete the work of obtaining signatures in Cumberland and Gloucester counties to the Vermont "Association," which pledged the signers to opposition to Great Britain. In Feb. 1781 he was made a member of the Vermont Board of War, as above. He represented Townshend in the General Assembly in 1783 and 1784.—See Vol. I; B. H. Hall's *Eastern Vermont;* and Deming's *Catalogue.*

the defence of this State, for a Term not Exceeding Nine Months, they be Impowered to raise such Troops for *Eleven Months*, & that the said board be authorized to Appoint a Commissary or Commissaries of Issues as they shall Judge necessary, and that they be authorised to direct the Commissaries of Purchase to provide such Camp utensils as they shall find necessary.

Extract from the Journals. Attest, R. HOPKINS, *Clerk.*

Read & Concurred in Council.

Attest, THOMAS TOLMAN, *Sec^y. P. Tem.*

Resolved that the Treasurer be directed to receive of Captain William Gallup Loan Office Certificates or Notes and his own Receipts to the amount of £1,118 13 6 for Confiscated Lands he has sold and pay to said Gallup £29 19 6, the Ballance due to him as by his account which was in Continental money the 26th of March 1778.

N. B.—The above mentioned ammount to the above sum without Interest, which Interest ammounts to £10 10 in like money.

The following is taken from a Manuscript Exhibitted by Captain [William] Gallup & Recorded in the journals by his particular request, vizt.

We the Subscribers being appointed by M^r. William Gallup of Hertford [Hartland] in the State of Vermont to appraise certain Lotts or parcels of Land belonging to Whitehead Hicks (& gone over to the Enemy,) agreeable to a Vote of the Honble House of Representatives of said State in March Last, have viewed and appraised sundry Lotts as follows being sworn to the faithful discharge of the Trust &c., vizt. one Lot the property of Stiversant[1] N°. 6, second Range, containing 300 acres Price 6| Per acre, Purchased by John Sumner & Nehemiah Liscomb.

One lot the property of Stiverstant 3 range N°. 7 288 acres price 7| p^r. acre, Purchased by Elias Wild & John Grove.

one Lot, the Property of the said Stiverstant N°. 5 3^d Range 300 acres price 7| purchased by James Dinnen.

one Lot, the property of White Head Hicks N°. 3 4 Range 300 acres price 7| Purchased by Samuel Grove.

one Lot the property of said White Head Hicks N°. 4 3^d Range 300 acres—Purchased by Daniel Buggbe the 2^d—Price 7| p^r. acre.

one Lot the property of the aforesaid Stiverstant N°. 4 R 4, 300 acres 7| p^r. acre—Purchaser William Cot'er.

one of White H. Hicks aforesaid N°. 4, 2^d Range 300 acres price 6| 6 —Purchased by D. Short.

one of Stiverstante N°. 2—3^d Range 300 acres price 6| 6 p^r. acre, Purchased by Benjamin Hayward.

one of White Head Hicks aforesaid N°. 2, 5th Range 329 acres Price 7| p^r. acre, Purchased by William Gallup.

Elnathan Walker 1 Lot 2^d range White H. Hicks containing 193 acres 6| 6 p^r. acre.

The above & foregoing is a true return of our doings as appears lits [lists] pr. us.

MATTHIAS RUST,
CHARLES SPAULDING, } *Appraisers.*

Recorded by order of Council.

Attest, THO^S. TOLMAN, *Sec^y. P. Tem.*

Council Adjourned until 2 ^oClock P. M.

---

[1] Perhaps Stuyvesant.

Met according to Adjournment.

A resolve of the General Assembly appointing a Committee of nine to join a Committee from the Council to Confer with the Committee appointed by the Convention now sitting at Cornish upon the Terms of a Union between the State of Vermont and the Inhabitants of the Hampshire Grants East of Connecticut river to the Mason Line, was read, whereupon a Committee of four was appointed. Members chosen Mr. Allen, Mr. Fassett, Mr. Spooner and Mr. Emmons.

Attest, THOS. TOLMAN, *Secy. P. Tem.*

Council Adjourned until 9 Tomorrow morning.

FEBRUARY 17th 1781.

Met according to Adjournment—not a quorum by reason of being detached into Committees.

Adjourned Until 9 oClock Monday Next.

WINDSOR 19 Feby 1781.

Council met according to Adjournment, And after [having] deliberated upon sundry Matters of Importance which are not required to be Entered on the journals, the Council adjourned to 2 oClock P. M.

Met according to Adjournment.

Resolved that the Committee for receiving the Granting fees for the Lands Granted Last October are directed to receive from the Proprietors of the Township of Rochester Two Hundred Bushels Wheat into Some proper Stores at Norwich, Hartford & Windsor at 6| pr. Bushel Towards said Granting fees.

A Resolve of the General Assembly appointing a Committee of three to join a Committee from the Council to report their opinion upon a Petition Signed Samuel Avery was read whereupon a Committee of two was appointed to join sd. Committee, Members chosen Mr. Brownson & Mr. Fletcher.

Adjourned to 9 oClock Tomorrow.[1]

---

[1] From the record of the *Board of War:*

IN THE BOARD OF WAR, Windsor, Feby 19th 1781.

Resolved that Capt. [Joseph] Farnsworth Commasary of Purchases be & he is hereby Requested to furnish all the Troops that are or may be in service at the fourt in Bethel or that Vicinity in the service of this State.

Resolved that Lieut. [Beriah] Green be and he is hereby Directed to take a Scout of fifteen men with Ten days provision and proseed in the most Likely Place to make Discovery of the Enemy to the Lake by the way of Onion River unless the Enemy Prevent his Proceeding so far & make Return of his Discovery to Major Wait.

Resolved that Capt. Farnsworth C. P. be & he is Hereby requested to furnish Eighty Iron pots or kettles sutible for Camp Equipage & Forward the same to Camp as soon as may be.

Resolved That Capt. Farnsworth C. P. Store provisions in the following places & Proportion (viz.) The Largest Store in Tinmouth, a small Store in Pollet, another in Reuport, another in Dorset, and one months provisions for the Troops that may be at Pitsford and Castleton.

Resolved That Capt. Farnsworth C. P. Pay be stated at Thirteen Pounds pr. month he to furnish his own horse & his Expence to be paid when from home he keeping regular accounts of the same.

WINDSOR February 20th 1781.
IN COUNCIL date above.

Met according to adjt.
A Resolve of the General Assembly appointing a Committee of Five to join a Committee from the Council to prepare a bill for a Land Tax

---

Resolved that the C. P. be allowed one Clerk, that his pay be five pounds Eight shillings pr. month and two Rations pr. day.
Resolved That Capt. John Strong asst. C. P. Pay be Stated at Nine pounds pr. month he to furnish his own horse & his Expences to be paid when from home he keeping regular accounts of the same.

Copy of Directions to Mr. Farnsworth for Mr. Strong in Issuing Provisions.

If Capt. Strong for ye time being Issues Provisions as an Issuing Commissary (in order for a proper settlement of accounts in the two Departments of the purchasing and Issuing Commissaries) he must take receipts on the back of provision returns, specifying the Quantity of the Provisions issued, and not specify Comsys name from whom the provisions are Received (but leave a Blank for ye purpose) in order that when an Issuing Commissary shall relieve him, the said Issuing Commissary shall rect. to him for the Quantity of such provision Returns, and the said Issuing Commissary's Rect. shall be a proper voucher to Capt. Strong in a Settlement of his accts. with Jos. Farnsworth Esqr. Comsy Genl. of Purchases in a proper Channel of a Purchasing Comsy's accounts. By order of ye Board.
Windsor 19th Feby. 1781. In Board of War.
To Jos. Farnsworth Esqr. C. Genl. of P.

IN THE BOARD OF WAR, Windsor, Feby. 22d 1781.

Resolved that fourt fortitude be the place for Issuing Provisions to the Troops for the Winter Campaign in that quarter.
Resolved that Windsor, Norwich, Woodstock and Newbury be the place for Repositing Provisions; that in several other Towns in the fronteers the provisions collecting in such Towns be stored there untill wanted.
Resolved That the Purchasing Commissary Purchase one Hundred wooden Boles and thirty Pales suitable for Camp Equipage.
Resolved that the Purchasing Commissary be directed to Purchase thirty Camp axes or the metirials to make them with.
Resolved that in case Capt. [James] Brookings shall when requested refuse to serve the Insuing Campaign in a Regt. raising for the defence of this State, that Capt. Abrm. Salisbury be appointed in his Stead. On the refusal of Capt. [Jesse] Sawyer, Capt. John Stark be appointed. That Capt. Daniel Comstock be appointed in the place of Capt. [Jonas] Galusha. That Lieut. [Charles] Dyer be appointed in the place of in Case Lieut. [Nathl.] Holmes Refuses. That Lieut. Coffin stand in nomination in Case [of] a vacancy of a first Lieut., & insign [Timothy] Mills in Case of a vacancy of 2d Lieut. That Capt. Abner Seely and Capt. [John] Benjamin be appointed. Lieutenant [Shubal] Cross, Lieut. [Joshua] Church, Lieut. [Samuel] Phipperen [in another entry, Phippen.]* That Benjamin Burton be 3d 2 Lieut. That Mr. Walk of Rockingham be armerer to Major Waits detachment. That Major [Joel] Matthews be Issuing Commasary.
Resolved that the Commasary of Purchases be requested to furnish fifty pair of snow shoes for Majr. Waits detachment without loss of time.

* These were appointments to fill vacancies in the new regiment of infantry.

and make report, was read, whereupon Mr. Bowker was chosen as a Committee from this Council.

Attest, THOMAS TOLMAN, *Secy. P. Tem.*

Adjourned until 2 oClock P. M.

Met according to Adjournment.

A Resolve of the General Assembly appointing a Committee to join a Committee from the Council to ascertain [in] what Manner this State shall make up the depreciation to Captain Lee and his Independent Company, being read,

Resolved that this Council do recommend to the General Assembly (as their opinion) that there needs no further order be taken on the Subject of Making Good the depreciation of the Wages of those that have been in Service but to resolve who shall be entitled to receive such priviledge from this State & direct Attested Roles of such persons thus entitled, to be exhibitted to the Committee of Pay Table who (unless some other Scale is designed by the House) will think it their duty to Liquidate such accts. agreeable to Such Roles and according to the Established Scale of Depreciation and Issue their Warrants to the Treasurer accordingly. Attest, THOS. TOLMAN, *Secy. P. Tem.*

Council Adjourned until 9 oClock Tomorrow.

IN COUNCIL Windsor 21t Feby 1781.

Met according to Adjournment.

A Resolve of the General Assembly appointing a Committee of three to join a Committee from the Council to assertain in what manner this State shall Make up the depreciation in Wages to Captain [then Col. Thomas] Lee's Independent Company, &c. was read, whereupon a Committee of two was appointed, Members chosen Mr. Fletcher and Mr. Brownson. THOS. TOLMAN, *Sec'y. P. Tem.*

A bill upon Highways was read and concurred with, with this alteration that in Lieu of 5 years for Rodes to be Surveyed by the Compas only two years be Allowed.

A bill postponing the payment of the Charter fees of the rights of the following persons in the Township of Randolph vizt. *Experience Davis, Timothy Miles, Zadock Steel & William Evans* for the Term of five years was read & Concurred provided that the Granting fees for said rights be secured to the State upon the Charter of said Town being Issued.

Attest, THOS. TOLMAN, *Sec'y. pro Tem.*

An Act repealing an Act for dividing the 4th Regt. & forming a 7th Regt. of Militia was read & Concurred.

An Act for dividing the first Regiment and Establishing a seventh Regt. was read & Concurred.

An Act directing County Elections was read & Concurred.

An Act for Establishing County Towns in the Several Counties in this State, & the time for holding Supreme & County Courts therein was proposed to the House in Lieu of one Sent from the Assembly.

Resolved That each man that furnish himself with a good pare of snow Shoes be paid for the same on their returning them into the States Store.

Resolved that his Excellency be requested to Call on Colo. Fletcher and Majr. Wait to enter service.

Resolved that the Commissary of Purchases be requested to procure one Hundred Wooden Boles and fifty Pails for Camp Equipage. [Repeated in the record.]

An Act in addition to & in Alteration of a Certain clause in an Act entitled an Act regulating Proprietors Meetings was read & Concurred.

An Act Continuing Sundry Civil officers as therein Specified Read & Concurred.

A Resolve of the General Assembly appointing a Committee of three to join a Committee of Council to Take into consideration the Expediency of Emitting a Sum of Money was read whereupon a Committee of two was appointed, Members chosen Mr. Bowker and Mr. Chandler.

Council Adjourned to 2 oClock P. M.

Met according to Adjournment.

An Act in addition to the Militia Act was read & Concurred.

An Act directing the payment of the Militia when Called into Service read & Concurred.

Resolved that an order be Drawn by his Excellency upon the Selectmen of the Town of Westminster for Forty Bushels of Wheat or an equivalent in flour to be Dilvd to Messrs. Spooner & Green they to be accountable.

Resolved that the Treasurer be directed to Call upon such persons as have recd. Guns being the property of this State to return them to him at a Limited time (which he may affix by advertisement) or the Value of said Guns in Money.

A Survey Bill signed Hazahel Shephard County Surveyor describing the Bounds of a tract of Land Granted to Captain Silas Hammilton was read, whereupon,

Resolved that a Charter be Given out accordingly.

A petition Signed David Haynes, Jonathan Griswould, John Kinsley, Caleb Harmon, Joshua Harmon, Medad Persons, Elisha Downs, Elisha Nichols, Phinehas Wright, David Powers, Eleazer Hawks, John Lawrence, Roswell Mossley, John Smith, Joseph Wickum, Elnathan Hubbell, Rufus Branch & Jedediah Merrill, Praying that the Several Fines laid on them by a Judgment of the Supreme Court holden at Bennington in the Month of January Last be remitted them & Each of them, was read, & the question being put wheather they be remitted it passed in the affirmative.

TOM TOLMAN, *Secy. P. Tem.*

Adjourned to 9 oClock Tomorrow.[1]

WINDSOR 22d: Feb. 1781.
IN COUNCIL, date above.

Met according to Adjournment.

A Resolve of the General Assembly appointing a Committee of five to join a Committee of Council to prepare Instructions for the Agents

---

[1] From the *Assembly Journal*, Feb. 21 1781:

Colo. Stephen Pearl desired to be dismissed as a member of the Board of War—Granted.

From the Record of the *Board of War:*

State of Vermont to Col. Stephen Pearl, Dr.			
To attending board of War in Nov. 1780 3 days at 7|	£1	1	0
" twenty miles travil at 4d.	0	6	8
" attending a Court of inquiry at Bennington 3 days in Aug. 1781 at 8| pr. day,	1	4	0
" 34 miles travil at 4d.	0	11	4

[Received] STEPHEN PEARL.

appointed to Wait on the Legislature of the State of New York was read, whereupon a Committee of two was appointed, members choosen Mr. Throop & Mr. Emmons.

A Resolve of the General Assembly appointing the Honble Ira Allen Esqr. & Major Joseph Fay Agents with full powers and Authority to Agree upon & establish the Line between this State and the State of N. York was read & Concurred.

A Resolve of the General Assembly Acquitting Aaron Rising, Tehan Noble, Levi Dones, [perhaps Doane,] & Ephraim Noble of Reupert of the Several quotors [quotas] of the provision Tax as prayed for by a petition signed by the said persons setting forth their Several Losses by Fire, was read and Concurred.

A Resolve of the General Assembly that the articles of Union agreed to and proposed by the Committee of this Legislature to a Committee of the Convention [at Cornish, N. H.,] be & is hereby confirmed, And assembly do pledge the Faith of this State that said articles be held sacred, was read, and the Question being put whether it be Concurred it passed in the affirmative.

A Resolve of the General Assembly confirming Reuben Harmon of Rutland[1] in some certain Rights of Land was read & Concurred.

Resolved that the term for the payment of the Granting fees of the Township of Wardsborough be postponed til the first Wednesday in April next.

A Resolve of the General Assembly granting the Prayer of a Petition signed Daniel West was read and Concurred.

A Resolve of the General Assembly postponing the payment of the Granting fees of the several proprietors under Named of the Proprietors of Royalton for the Term of five years, was read and Concurred—Also further Resolved that the time of the payment of the Granting fees for the remaining Proprietors of the said Township of Royalton be postponed until the first Wednesday of April next.

Attest, THOMAS TOLMAN, *Secy. P. Tem.*

Schedule of those persons or proprietors allowed 5 *years of payment*, vizt. Timothy Durkee Heman Durkee Aden Durkee Timo. Durkee Jur. David Fisk Joseph Fisk David Brewster Zebulon Lyon Elias Stevens Robert Hendey Calvin Parkhurst James Cooper Joseph Parkhurst Joseph Havens Elisha Kent Daniel Rix Gardner Rix Joseph John Rix, Medad Benton Nathan Morgan John Billings Benjamin Day Israel Wallow [Waldo] Peleg Parkhurst Phinehas Parkhurst, Jabez Parkhurst Ebenezer Parkhurst Daniel Gilbert Simeon Sheppard Jeremiah Trescott Nathaniel Moss [Morse] Wido. Sarah Rude [Rood] Isaac Morgan Elias Curtis Robert Havens Daniel Havens John Evans Martin Fuller John Hibbert & Jonathan Benton.[2]

An Act for quieting disputes concerning Landed property was read & Concurred.[3]

---

[1] Perhaps an error: Mr. Harmon resided in Rupert.

[2] This relief was of course granted on account of the burning of Royalton and the capture of sundry of its citizens in the preceding October.

[3] This act constituted the Governor, Council, and House of Representatives a court for the trial of cases where two or more charters had been made of the same tract of land to different proprietors. For the act, see Slade's *State Papers*, p. 424.

STATE OF VERMONT. WINDSOR 22d February 1781.

To the Honble General Assembly now sitting.—Your Committee appointed by the General Assembly impowering them to prepare Instructions for the Agents appointed to Settle the Line between the State of N. York & this State, beg Leave to report as follows, vizt. that it is our opinion that it be refered to the Governor & Council to give said Agents Instructions & full Power to Settle & Establish the boundary Line between the State of New York & this State.

BENJA. WHIPPLE, *Chairn.*

IN GENERAL ASSEMBLY 22d Feby.

The above report was read & accepted.

Attest, ROSL. HOPKINS, *Clerk.*

An Act for the Division of Counties within this State was read & Concurred.

An Act for the Division of Probate districts in the Several Counties was read and Concurred.

Adjourned until 9 oClock Tomorrow.

WINDSOR, 23d Feby. 1781.
IN COUNCIL date above.

Met according to Adjournment.

A Resolve of the General Assembly appointing a Committee to join a Committee from the Council to Consider the Matter of Making up the depreciation of Colo. Warner's Regiment, and Captain Lee's Company was read, whereupon Mr. Brownson was chosen as a Committee for the purpose from the Council.

Upon Motion Made that Bryant Brown of Windsor be appointed Sheriff in the Room of Major Benja. Wait for the County of Cumberland for the time being,

Resolved that the said Bryant Brown be & he is hereby appointed for the Time being.[1]

Attest, THOMAS TOLMAN, *Secy. P. Tem.*

The question being put who will be bound for the said Bryant Brown, John Throop Esqr. & Capt. Joel Ely appeared & in the Presence of His Excellency the Govr. Lt. Govr. & Council acknowledge themselves bound unto the Treasurer of this State in the just sum of £1000 Pounds to the Treasurer of this State.

The Condition of this obligation (or recognisance) is such that if the above said Bryant Brown doth well & truly discharge the duty of Sheriff in the County of Cumberland during the time he shall serve, then the above Obligation be void & none effect otherwise in full force and Virtue.

Attest, THOMAS TOLMAN, *Secy. P. Tem.*

A Resolve of the General Assembly appointing a Committee to join a Committee of Council to Take into Consideration a petition Signed William Williams was read, whereupon Mr. Brownson was appointed a Committee to join sd. Committee from the House.

A Resolve of the General Assembly appointing a Committee to join a Committee from the Council for Giving Instructions to the Committee appointed to direct & Inspect the printing of a Bank of Money was read, whereupon a Committee was appointed. Member chosen Mr. Fassett.

A Resolve of the Assembly upon a matter Relating to the Widow Sarah Chaffee was read and Concurred.

---

[1] Maj. Wait resigned this office to enter upon military service.

IN GENERAL ASSEMBLY, 23d. Feby. 1781.

Resolved that a Certain tract or Gore of Land Lying & being situate on the East side of Wallingford containing by Estimation Nine thousand seven hundred acres be Granted to Abraham Jackson Esqr. & associates to the number of thirty to be annexed to & Incorporated with the town of Wallingford and that the Governor & Council be requested to make out a Charter of Incorporation of the Same to the said Abraham Jackson Esquire & his associates on such Conditions and with such reservations as they shall [deem] Necessary.

Extract from the journals, R. HOPKINS, *Clerk.*

Resolved that the Granting fees for the Gore of Land Granted to Abr. Jackson Esqr. & associates to the Number of thirty be nine pounds pr. Right & be paid the first day of June Next & to be Settled in three years from the sd first day of June next which will be in the year 1784.

Attest, THOS. TOLMAN, *Secy. P. Tem.*

STATE OF VERMONT, IN GENERAL ASSEMBLY Feby. 23d 1781.

Resolved that there be & hereby is Granted unto Joseph Bowker Esqr., James Claghorn, Jehiel Andrus, & Thadeus Curtis Esqrs. & Company to the Number of thirty four, the following Tract of Land situate and Lying in this State bounded as follows vizt. beginning at the South east Corner of Rutland thence North 4 Do. East on Rutland East line five Miles & 80 Rods to the Southwest Corner of the Township of Chittenden, then East 20 Do. North two miles & 100 Rods in the South line of Chittenden to Killington West Line to the South west Corner thereof—thence East 28 degs. south five & half miles to Shrewsbury south east Corner, thence West four degrees North six miles to the first mentioned bounds containing about 8890 acres. The Governor and Council are hereby requested to Issue a Charter of Incorporation of said Tract unto Joseph Bowker Esqr. & Comy. by the name of *Medway* [afterward Parkerstown, now Mendon,] under such instructions & upon Such Conditions as they shall Judge best.

Extract from the Journals, ROSL. HOPKINS, *Clerk.*

Resolved that the Granting fees for the Tract of Land Granted to Joseph Bowker Esqr. & Comy. by the Name of *Medway* in number thirty four, be Seven pounds Ten shillings, the time of payment the first day of June Next & the time for the Settlement of said Land to Be within three years from the said first day of June Next.

Adjourned until 2 oClock P. M.

Met according to Adjournment.

A Resolution of the General Assembly directing the Method of appointing representatives read & Concurred.

A Resolve of the General Assembly Granting Certain Lands to the Widow Elizabeth Baldwin was read & Concurred.

An Act directing County Elections was read & Concurred.

An Act for the purpose of Emitting a Sum of Money was read & Concurred.

STATE OF VERMONT, IN GENERAL ASSEMBLY Windsor 23d Feb. 1781.

Resolved that a Grant of Land be made to Colo. William Williams & associates 26 in Number bounded as follows vizt. East on Willmington, Northerly upon Somerset, westerly upon Woodford, and Southerly upon a Tract of Land petitioned for by Benjamin Hinshaw [Henshaw] & others, Comprising a tract of Four Miles square & that His Excellency & Council be requested to Make out a Charter of said Township to Colo.

Williams & associates under such restrictions & reservations as they may think proper.[1]

Extract from the Journals.

Attest, ROSL. HOPKINS, *Clerk.*

Resolved that the Granting fees of the Tract of Land discribed in the above Bill in form Granted to Colonel William Williams & associates be £10 0 0 pr. Right, Time of payment to be June 1st 1781 and Settlement to be made on said Land within three years.

Attest, THOMAS TOLMAN, *Secy. P. Tem.*

STATE OF VERMONT, IN GENERAL ASSEMBLY 23d Feby 1781.

Resolved that a Grant of Land be made to Robert Bratten & associates 7 in Number in the North east Corner of Whitingham, Including the quantity of Two Thousand acres, and the Governor and Council are requested to Issue a Charter of said Land under such restrictions and reservations as they may think proper.

Extract from the Journals, ROSL. HOPKINS, *Clerk.*

Resolved that the Granting Fees to be paid on the Tract of Land Granted to Robert Bratten & associates in quantity 2000 acres as above be one shilling pr. acre, the Time for the payment to be on the 1t day of June next, & to be settled within three years.

Attest, THOMAS TOLMAN, *Secy. Pro Tem.*

END OF WINDSOR FEBRUARY SESSION.

RECORD OF THE GOVERNOR AND COUNCIL

AT A

SPECIAL SESSION AT ARLINGTON MARCH 1781.

ARLINGTON 6 April [March] 1781.[2]

IN COUNCIL Arlington date above.

Resolved that applicatiou to Majr. William Goodrich be made to furnish the State of Vermont with six Tons of Lead four Tons of which he is hereby Earnestly requested to Diliver to Major Fay at Bennington with 12,000 Good Gun Flints with all convenient dispatch and the other Two Tons and 6,000 Flints to be forwarded to Windsor in said State to be Consigned to Major Benjamin Wait.

Copy deld. to Majr. Goodrich. JOS. FAY, *Secy.*

ARLINGTON 6 March 1781.

In consequence of your being appointed to Procure some Lead for the use of this State which will be attended with Expense,

You are therefore hereby authorized to Call upon Gentlemen who may have money to pay into the Treasury of this State for Lands for

---

[1] Searsburgh.

[2] The Council was in session at Windsor from the 4th to the 18th of April, and this entry should have been March.

any sum you may have occasion for And your Rec$^{t.}$ shall answer on Settlement with the Treasurer for Granting fees.

THO$^{S.}$ CHITTENDEN.

Maj$^{r.}$ Goodrich.

On Motion made for sending the Commissioners appointed to Settle the boundary line between the States of N. York & Vermont to Albany with Instructions for that purpose, the question being put it passed in the Negative, as also not to write any further to General Assembly of N. York at present.

Adjourned to 9 °Clock Tomorrow.

MARCH 7$^{th.}$ April 1781.[1]

Council met according to Adjournment.

On application made to this Council by Captain Rayment [Raymond,] Resolved to authorize the Town Clerk of the Town of Stamford as follows viz$^{t.}$

To Israel Mead Town Clerk for the Town of Stamford, This is to authorize & fully to empower you in your Capacity of Town Clerk to administer the Oath of Alegiance to any Gentleman inhabitant of said Town of Stamford that may [apply] during your continuance in ^{sd} Clerk's office, as Also the oath prescribed in the Constitution of this State to Each respective officer Legally chosen in a Lawful Public Town Meeting, as Also the Oath of Alligeance & the freemans Oath to any Inhabitant of said Town who is or may in future be entitled to it by the Constitution, until some other proper Authority be appointed & Empowered in said Town. By order of Govr & Council,

Copy Delivered. JOSEPH FAY, *Sec$^{y.}$* [2]

Resolved that two Agents be appointed to proceed to Albany and make Enquiry with regard to the Measures pursued by the State of N. York for the defence of the Northern Frontiers & Report to this Council. Col$^{o.}$ Ira Allen & Major Joseph Fay is hereby appointed for the above purpose.[3]

RECORD OF THE BOARD OF WAR.

IN BOARD OF WAR, Arlington, 8th March 1781.

Sir:—I am directed to request you to give your answer whether you accept of your appointment as Capt$^{n.}$ in the Reg$^{t.}$ of Rangers or$^{d.}$ to be raised. Your answer is Expected in half an Hour or it will be taken in the negative.

To Cap$^{t.}$ J. Sawyer.[4]

Whereas a number of the officers appointed by this Board on the 9th day of Jan. last have declined serving agreeable to their appointment,

---

[1] So on the record. See foregoing note.

[2] This became necessary to prepare for an election of the first justice of the peace in Stamford, which had been fixed by the General Assembly for the last Tuesday in March 1781.

[3] The same gentlemen had been selected as agents to settle the boundary line, and it is not unreasonable to suppose that while inquiring as to the defence of the frontier, they would have eyes and ears for whatever might be done or said in reference to other Vermont affairs.

[4] Jesse Sawyer was appointed the first captain in the new regiment of *infantry* on the 9th of January preceding.

Resolved, that the following persons be appointed in their Room, (viz.)
Capts.—Daniel Comstock, John Stark.
1st Lieut.—George Saxton.
2d do.—Thomas Rowley, Junr.
And that the towns of Pownal and Shaftsbury be requested to nominate for each town one first and one second Lieut. and make returns of such nomination as soon as may be to the Capt. General.

Resolved that this Board do hereby Recommend That the Captn General ord. Capt. Hutchings & Lieut. Gideon Spencer & the men they have raised into service, and such others as he may think proper.

Memorandum, &c., Dates.

March 15 1781 Saml Phippen 1st Lieut.
Benja Wait Majr. Feby 10th.
Beriah Green 1st Lieut. Feby 10th.
Willis Hall 1st Lieut. Feby 10th.
Abner Seely Capt. do. do.
James Smally 1st Lieut. do. do.
Shubal Cross 2d Lieut. do. do.
John Benjamin Capt. do. do.
Nehemiah Lovel Capt. do. do.
Joshua Church 2d Lieut. do. do.
[In] Board of War.[1]

Debenture of the Board of War, Arlington, March 8th 1781.

Present—Hon. Timothy Brownson Esqr. 1 day 4 miles travil,	£0 8 4	
1781 Aug. 6th. Recd. the contents of the above. TIMOTHY BROWNSON.		
Ira Allen Esq. 1 day 4 miles travil,	£0 8 4	
Gideon Warren Esq. 1 day 35 miles travil,	0 18 8	
Samuel Robinson Esq. 1 day 14 miles travil,	0 11 8	
[Received,] SAMUEL ROBINSON.		
John Fassett [jr.] Esq. 1 day 1 mile travil	0 7 4	

[1] All of the above seem to have been officers in the new regiment of infantry. Capt. JOHN STARK, who was a cousin of Gen. John Stark, came to Pawlet from New Hampshire previous to 1770. He was a prominent citizen of the town, and commanded a company in the battle of Bennington. He was judge of Bennington county court, Rutland shire, from March 1778 to December 1779. He was one of the grantees of the "Two Heroes," which included Grand Isle, and about 1800 he removed to the last named town and was soon after killed by the kick of a horse. He left one son, Samuel, (who removed to Oswego county, N. Y.,) and twelve daughters. Samuel had ten daughters and four sons before he left Vermont.—See Hollister's *History of Pawlet.*

RECORD OF THE GOVERNOR AND COUNCIL

AT THE

SESSION WITH THE GENERAL ASSEMBLY AT WINDSOR,

APRIL 1781.

STATE OF VERMONT. IN COUNCIL, Windsor, 4th April 1781.

This day his Excellency the Governor & the following Members of the Honble Council met according to Adjournment, vizt. the Honble Jeremiah Clark, John Fassett, [jr.,] & Ira Allen. There not being a quorum present,

Adjourned to 9 oClock Tomorrow Morning.

Thursday, IN COUNCIL, 5 April 1781.

Met According to Adjournment—at which time the Honble Paul Spooner, Benjamin Emmons & Samuel Fletcher Esquires joined in Council, also Honble John Throop Esqr.

Adjd to 8 oClock Tomorrow.

WINDSOR 6 April 1781.
IN COUNCIL, Friday, date above.

Met according to Adjournment, at which Time his honor [Lieut.] Governor Carpenter took his Seat in the Council.

Resolved that the Honble Ira Allen & Paul Spooner Esquires be a Committee to join a Committee from the Assembly to arange the Necessary business of the present Session.

Resolved that Jeremiah Clark Esqr. join a Committee from the Assembly to Consider a petition from the Inhabitants of Sunderland in the State of Vermont.

Resolved that Ira Allen, Samuel Fletcher & John Fassett, [jr.] Esquires be a Committee to join a Committee from the Assembly to Consider & Provide for the defence of the Frontiers of this State.

Adjourned to 8 oClock Tomorrow.[1]

SATURDAY, IN COUNCIL, Windsor 7th April 1781.

Met according to Adjournment.

Abraham Ives Esqr. being Elected Sheriff for the County of Rutland And a Warrant Given for a Commission by which he is authorised to Execute that office & for the faithful discharge of duty Acknowledges

---

[1] From the *Assembly Journal:*

To the Honorable General Assembly of the State of Vermont:

Your Committee appointed to take into consideration the measures to be taken for defending this State against the common Enemy beg leave to Report—

That they conceive it necessary that one thousand five hundred men including officers be employed in the defence of the northern frontiers

himself bound & Recognised to the Treasurer of this State in the Sum of Two Thousand Pounds L. Money, Elihu Smith Esq[r.] & Lieut. Roswell Post Stand as Security.

Attest, JOSEPH FAY, *Sec[y.]*

Adjourned to 8 °Clock Monday Next.

---

of this State against the common enemy the ensuing season. That they find seven hundred men including officers are already ordered to be raised in the territory west of Connecticut·River, and reccommend that three hundred and ten men including a suitable proportion of officers be raised in the territory east of Connecticut River to be apportioned to the several Regiments and parts of Regt[s.] as follows, viz.

	Capt.	Lieut.	Non's & Priv.
1st Regt. in the 2[d] Brigade,	1	3	90
4th do. do. do.	1	2	68
1st Regt. in the 3[d] Brigade east of the River,	0	2	43
2[d] do. do.	1	0	47
3[d] do. do.	1	1	47
Total,	4 Capts.	8 Lts.	295 Non's & priv.

That there be an addition of a suitable number of persons to the Board of War from the east side of Connecticut River. That those members of the Board of War on the west side of the mountain have direction in Respect to the particular station of the men ordered by a quorum of the whole Board to be stationed west side of the mountains – and the members of the Board east of the mountains have direction of the particular station of the men ordered by a quorum of the whole Board to be stationed on the frontiers contiguous to Connecticut River. That matters in which a majority of either part of the Board of War cannot agree shall be determined by a quorum of the whole Board to be convened by the President on application of a majority of either part, or when he shall judge necessary. That the Board of War be directed and empowered at discretion to raise such number of volunteers by bounty from the State as shall amount to 1500 (including such men as have been or shall be raised by other measures already adopted by the State)—and that the whole be divided into two regiments to be properly officered and stationed in such proportion on the East and West side of the mountains as a quorum of the whole [Board] shall from time to time direct. That in apportionment of the men to be raised on the east side of the River particular regard be had by the officers who shall make the proportion to the several towns and that they make reasonable abatement to the towns for such men as they now have in Continental service. And That in order to defray the expence of defending the frontiers in the manner before mentioned, they conceive it necessary that the Assembly at their present Session devise ways and means to supply the Treasury with a sum not less than [£]30,000 lawful money.

IRA ALLEN, *for the Committee.*

The aforesaid report was read and passed and sent [to the Governor and Council] for concurrence April 12, 1781.

April 11 1781.—Resolved That this House will proceed to choose Brigadier Generals for each Brigade tomorrow morning.

April 12 1781.—Agreeable to the order of the day proceeded to choose by ballot Brigad[r.] Generals for each Brigade. The ballots being taken,

General Ethan Allen for the first,
Gen[l.] Benj[a.] Bellows for the second, and
Col[o.] Peter Olcott for the third Brigades

MONDAY, IN COUNCIL, 9 April 1781.

Met according to Adjournment.

Having proceeded to appoint Committees & Transact the necessary business of the day,

Adjourned to 8 °Clock Tomorrow.

TUESDAY, IN COUNCIL, Windsor 10th April 1781.

Met according to Adjournment,

And Having joined the General Assembly in a Committee of both Houses & Transacted the other necessary business of the day [by] sundry Sub Committees,

Adjourned to 8 °Clock Tomorrow.

WEDNESDAY, IN COUNCIL at Windsor 11 Apl. 1781.

Met according to Adjournment, and having met the Grand Committee according to the order of the day, & Transacted the other business by sundry Committees, &c.

Adjourned to 8 °Clock Tomorrow.

---

were chosen and are hereby appointed Brigadier Genls. for the Brigades aforesaid.

Resolved to add two members to the Board of War, and that this House will proceed to choose them tomorrow morning.

April 13 1781.—Agreeable to the order of the day proceeded to choose two members in addition to the Board of War. The ballots being taken, Colo. Timo. Bedle and Capt. Ebenr. Brewster were unanimously chosen.

To meet the recommendation of the committee for the supply of the treasury, the act was passed authorizing the emission of £25,155 lawful money, before noticed. An act was also passed authorizing the Commissary General of Purchases to draw funds from the treasury on orders from the Board of War.—See Slade's *State Papers*, pp. 424, 429.

ETHAN ALLEN had resigned the office of Brigadier General when the inquiry was instituted on the charges made against him in the Assembly by Hutchins and Hathaway. He now declined to accept the office to which he was again elected as above, but with the promise that he would render any service desired of him at any time, although not formally commissioned; and that promise was faithfully observed.

BENJAMIN BELLOWS, of Walpole, N. H., was a leading citizen of that portion of the country, and was chairman of the committee of the Walpole Convention, Nov. 15, 1780, which recommended a union of the western towns of New Hampshire with Vermont, and called the Charlestown [N. H.] Convention of January 1781. When, however, it became evident, at the close of that year and the opening of 1782, that very serious difficulties were certain to grow out of that union, he seems to have changed his opinion. In anticipation perhaps of this result, he declined to accept the office of Brigadier General tendered to him by the Vermont Assembly. On the 20th of June following Col. SAMUEL SAFFORD of Bennington was elected Brigadier General *vice* Allen resigned; and Col. SAMUEL FLETCHER of Townshend *vice* Bellows resigned.—For references to Col. Bellows, see *Vt. Hist. Soc. Coll.*, Vol. II, pp. 95–'6, 106, 112, 143, 226; and *Eastern Vermont*, pp. 224–'5, 739–742, 764–'5.

THURSDAY, IN COUNCIL, April 12 1781.[1]

Council met according to Adjour[t.]

A petition of Daniel Tilliston [Tillison,] Esq[r.] & others concerning the Township of Brookfield was read whereupon Resolved that the time

---

[1] From the *Assembly Journal*, April 12 1781:

Copies of two letters dated at "New York March 30th 1780," and "Feb[y.] 2[d] 1781," signed "Bev. Robinson Col[o.] Loy[l.] American Reg[t.]" and directed to "Col[o.] Ethan Allen," which were attested as true copies by "Ira Allen and M. Lyon," also a copy of a letter from General [Ethan] Allen to "Sam[l.] Huntington Esq[r.] President of Congress," which enclosed the original Letters from Bev. Robinson, were laid before this House and Read—whereupon his Excellency the Governor requested that the minds of the House might be taken whether the proceedings of Governor, Council, and Gen[l.] Allen were agreeable or approved by them —which question being put passed in the Affirmative.

After soliciting proposals from Allen to the British commander-in-chief, Sir Henry Clinton, Robinson wrote to Allen as follows:

I can make no proposals to you until I know your sentiments, but I think upon your taking an active part and embodying the inhabitants of Vermont in favor of the crown of England, to act as the commander-in-chief shall direct, that you may obtain a separate government under the king and constitution of England, and the men formed into regiments under such officers as you shall recommend, and be on the same footing as all the provincial camps are here. [In New York city, then in possession of the British.]

Allen "in thirteen minutes" exhibited this letter to Gov. Chittenden and other friends, and it was determined that no answer should be returned to Robinson, but that the governor should address Gen. Haldimand on the subject of an exchange of prisoners. The second letter of Robinson repeated the suggestions of the first, by authority of Sir Henry Clinton. This letter also was not answered. It was received on the 23d of February 1781, and on the 9th of March Allen sent both letters to the President of Congress. In doing this he declared that they were the only letters he ever received from Robinson, that he returned no answer, and never had the least acquaintance with the writer of them. He at the same time declared his opinion

That Vermont has an indubitable right to agree on terms of cessation of hostilities with Great Britain, provided the United States persist in rejecting her application for a union with them, for Vermont of all people would be the most miserable, were she obliged to defend the independence of United claiming States, and they at the same time at full liberty to overturn and ruin the independence of Vermont.

See *See Vt. Hist. Soc. Collections*, Vol. II, pp. 59–105.

It has already been stated that the resolution of the Assembly of Oct. 31 1780, (*ante*, p. 48,) was "the *official* initiation of what is known as 'The Haldimand Correspondence.'" Not till April 12 1781, however —as above—was the *actual* origin of that correspondence revealed to the General Assembly and the people of the State. Its revelation in that mode and at that time was undoubtedly made to relieve the Vermonters

for Making out the Charter of said Brookfield be postponed until the Session of Assembly in October Next.

Attest, JOSEPH FAY, *Sec'y*

---

engaged in it, and particularly ETHAN ALLEN, from a suspicion of infidelity to the cause of national independence. The letter of Governor General Haldimand to Gov. Chittenden, the correspondence between the British Major Carleton and the Vermont Brigadier General Allen, and the consequent armistice, had been made public in October 1780. Oct. 31 1780, Maj. General Schuyler informed Washington of it, and intimated unfavorable suspicions of a certain "*person.*" Nov. 6 following, Washington wrote to Schuyler "that matters in a certain quarter *carry a very suspicious face.*" Nov. 12 Gen. Schuyler communicated other facts to Washington, implicating, though not by name, "three members from the Vermont Assembly." On the 7th of November, however, Stephen Lush removed all mystery, in a letter to Gov. Clinton of New York, by openly charging Ethan Allen with "defection," and asserting that the Vermont Council were "trying Allen upon an impeachment containing eleven articles." It is true that Allen was on that very day "impeached" before the General Assembly on charges made by Lieut. William Hutchins and Simeon Hathaway. The charges are not stated in the record of the Assembly, but Lush's account shows that they were impeachable offences, and the armistice suggests with sufficient certainty that Allen was charged with infidelity to the country in that matter. The record does show that Allen was very indignant, declaring that the paper contained "such false and ignominious aspersions against him" that he would hear no more of it, "and went out of the house." He moreover resigned the office of Brigadier General, though prudently and patriotically promising "to serve the State according to his abilities," if the Assembly should think best to give him the command. The Assembly went on nevertheless with the investigation, and, on the testimony of Joseph Fay and Stephen R. Bradley, dismissed Hathaway's remonstrance, allowed Hutchins to withdraw, and by resolution appointed a committee to thank Allen for his good services, and informed him that his resignation was accepted "according to his offer," which has been stated above—that is, an offer of his best services when desired. See *Vt. Historical Society Collections*, Vol. II, pp. 68 to 82. It is obvious, from the various papers cited, that Allen was under a cloud in the minds of good and true men—of Washington and Schuyler in the continental army, of Lieut. Gov. Marsh, Gen. Jacob Bayley, and doubtless many others in Vermont. It was therefore both necessary and desirable to give the real origin of the armistice and the Haldimand correspondence, in the two letters of Beverly Robinson to Allen, and to make public the fact that Allen had communicated both of these letters to the President of Congress. This was done, as has been just shown, with explanations ample enough to vindicate his character

A Remonstrance signed Leonard Spaulding and a Number of Inhabitants against the County Elections for the County of Windham, requesting the Commissions of a Number who was appointed into office might be suspended [was read]—Whereupon

Resolved that the Commission for Samuel Knights [Knight][1] who Stands appointed to the office of Justice of the Peace—And Also Noah

---

and at the same time offer a powerful motive to Congress for doing justice to Vermont.

The avowals of Allen to the President of Congress were a good defense for him so far as the letters of Robinson were concerned. For the truce of 1780 he had still another good defense in the fact that it was made with the knowledge and approval of the Governor and Council and General Assembly of the State. Arnold betrayed his country's cause and joined the enemy. Allen betrayed nobody, but served his State. Strictly speaking, he owed nothing to the continental cause, as he was not in the service of Congress, nor was he or his State recognized by it. Allen retained his position as a friend of his country, and all his rights as a belligerent so far as the British were concerned; he conceded nothing to the British that was not conceded in return by them, for the benefit both of Vermont and of the confederacy. He was party to a truce which protected Vermont and New York alike, by dismissing a British force for a winter's residence in Canada. These facts show no stain upon his character as an officer or a patriot. But Allen's letter to the President of Congress reached far beyond the truce of 1780, and justified the policy which Vermont pursued until all danger from the British had ceased. It is true Congress had not conceded the independence of Vermont; but neither had it assented to or asserted the claims of New York, New Hampshire, or Massachusetts. Congress left Vermont standing alone, to defend herself as she could, and as she did, while from 1775 she had also contributed freely to the continental cause. Vermont declared herself to be, and in fact was, AN INDEPENDENT STATE; and as such she clearly had the *right* to protect herself by every means allowable to a sovereign—by any terms she chose to make with her enemies. That was Allen's ground, and it was also the ground assumed and asserted by Gov. Chittenden. As the result proved, it was the *true* ground. Vermont maintained her independence as a State, and at last that independence was acknowledged by all the other states in her admission to the Union.

[1] SAMUEL KNIGHT, of Brattleboro first, and afterward of Guilford, was commissioned as an attorney in "his Majesty's courts of record" in Cumberland County June 23 1772. In Feb. 1774 he was appointed a commissioner to administer oaths of office, the only office he ever held under New York. He was counted, however, among the unpopular Yorkers, and his profession brought him to Westminster, March 13 1775. It does not appear from any of the accounts of the tragic events of that day that Judge Knight was personally engaged in the assault upon the

Sabins [Sabin][1] who stands appointed as Judge of Probate, be suspended for the present.

Adjourned to 8 °Clock Tomorrow.

---

whigs, nevertheless the coroner's jury upon their oaths named him among the murderers of William French. Judge Knight escaped arrest, and did not return to Brattleborough until March 1776. He took no active part in the revolutionary struggle, but strenuously favored New York in the controversy with Vermont as late as Nov. 1778. Satisfied at length that New York could not maintain her claim, he submitted to the authority of Vermont, and was appointed a justice of the peace. The remonstrance of Spaulding and others was of course based on these above stated antecedents, and it served for a short time to postpone the employment of Judge Knight in official service. He was judge of Windham county court four years; judge of the supreme court 1789 and '90, and chief judge 1791, '2 and '3. He represented Brattleborough in the General Assembly in 1781, '83, '84 and '85. Dr. JOHN A. GRAHAM said: "He was bred to the law; is a gentlemen of great abilities; and has rendered many essential services to his fellow citizens, but, I am sorry to add, they have by no means been recompensed as they ought to be. To Mr. Knight that celebrated line of Pope may be truly applied,—

"'An honest man's the noblest work of God.'"

See *Eastern Vermont;* Graham's *Descriptive Sketch of Vermont;* Deming's *Catalogue; Legislative Directory,* 1870.

[1] NOAH SABIN was born in Rehoboth, Mass., Nov. 10 1714, a descendant of the Sabins [Saben, Sabin, Sabine,] whose names appear in the records of Plymouth Colony. He came to Putney in 1768, and was the first town clerk, 8th May 1770. In April 1772 he was appointed by New York judge of the inferior court of common pleas and justice of the peace for Cumberland County. He was one of the judges of the court at the time of the "Westminster massacre," and "was very earnest to have the law [the court] go on," discountenancing all opposition of the people to the court and the royal authority in the county. A conscientious man, he was a firm and avowed loyalist so long as there was a prospect that the royal authority could be maintained. For this he was extremely unpopular with the whigs, and for three years his life was in imminent danger because of his unpopular opinions. Not only was he denounced as a murderer because of his official connection with the court at Westminster, but in 1776 he was arrested by the Committee of Safety and confined to his farm on penalty of death at the hand of any man who should find him outside of its limits. As late as Dec. 7 1778, the church of Putney refused to receive him to "occasional communion" on account of his political opinions. He was admitted, however, in April 1781, (after he had submitted to the authority of Vermont,) and appointed judge of probate. As in judge Knight's case, the remonstrance of Spaulding and others postponed the issuing of the commission of judge

FRIDAY IN COUNCIL Windsor 13 April 1781.

Met according to Adjournment.

A petition signed by Mr. Abel Thomson in behalf of himself & associates pray [praying] for a Grant of a Township of Land [was read,] Whereupon the Council do Recommend to the General Assembly to Grant the Prayer of said Petition.

IN GENERAL ASSEMBLY 13th April 1781.

Resolved that there be & hereby is Granted unto Abel Thomson & Company being sixty in Number whose names are annexed to a Schedule anexed to the petition Exhibitted to this Assembly a Grant of a Township of Land situate and Lying in said State to Contain Twenty four thousand acres, bounding on the Towns of Middlebury, Salisbury & Leicester & to Cover part of Land *Governor Dunmore*[1] is said to have Given himself—that the Surveyor General be directed to Locate said Grant to said Thomson & Company accordingly—And that the Governor & Council be requested to Make out a Charter of Incorporation to the said Thomson & Company by the Name of *Ripton* under such Conditions reservations & restrictions as they shall Judge Best.

Copy Given pr. JOSEPH FAY, *Secy.*

Resolved that the Proprietors of the Township of *Ripton* Granted this day to Mr. Abel Thomson & Company pay six hundred & sixty Pounds L. Money in Silver or Gold, that one hundred Pounds be paid Down & one hundred Pounds by the 15th Day of June Next—if not paid by that time

---

Sabin. He was judge of probate for the district of Westminster in October 1781, and certainly again from Oct. 1786 to Oct. 1801—*probably* from 1781 to 1801. He died March 10 1811, in his ninety-sixth year. His son, NOAH SABIN, jr., represented Putney 1782 to 1785-6, and again in 1787; was register of probate for the district of Westminster from 1791 to 1801, and succeeded his father as judge from 1801 to 1808-9. He died Dec. 5 1827. See *Eastern Vermont;* Sabine's *Loyalists of the American Revolution;* and Deming's *Catalogue.*

[1] JOHN MURRAY, 4th Earl of Dunmore, was born in 1732, descended in the female line from the house of Stuart, and succeeded to the peerage in 1756. He was made governor of New York in Jan. 1770, and of Virginia in July 1771. From March 1773 he was in collision with the whigs of Virginia until June 1774, when he fled with his family and found refuge on board a British ship of war. Raising a band of tories, runaway negroes and British soldiers, he carried on petty and predatory warfare upon Virginia until July 1776, when he was dislodged and wounded, and shortly afterward he returned to England. He was made governor of Bermuda in 1786. While governor of New York, in a period of less than five months between Feb. 28 and July 8 1771, he granted land in Vermont to the amount of 511,900 acres, all of which had been previously granted by Gov. Benning Wentworth of New Hampshire. Of this quantity, 51,000 acres were granted, in the names of other persons, *for himself*, being the land referred to in the resolution of the Governor and Council. His fees for these grants amounted to $14,248.44. —See *Drake's Dictionary of American Biography; Early History of Vermont; Vt. Hist. Soc. Collections*, Vol. I.

so much of the Land to be sold as ammounts to the hundred pounds Last Mentioned—The remainder to be paid by the first Thursday in October Next, at which Time a Charter of Incorporation shall be given in which the Conditions & Reservations will be more fully Specified.

£660. Copy Given p^r. Jos. Fay, *Sec^y.*

State of Vermont, In General [Assembly,] 13 April 1781.

Resolved to Recommend & it is hereby Recommended to his Excellency the Governor to Issue his Proclamation appointing such day as he may Judge [best] to be Observed as a day of Public Fasting & Prayer Throughout this State. Attest, Roswell Hopkins, *Clerk.*

A Committee from the General Assembly being appointed vizt. M^r [Elisha] Payne, M^r. [Gideon] Ormsby, M^r. [Nathaniel S.] Prentice, M^r. [Bezaleel] Woodward, M^r. [Stephen] Pearl, M^r. [William] Page & M^r. [Benjamin] Giles to Confer with the Governor & Council relative to appointing officers boath Civil & Military on the East side of the [Connecticut] River[1]—

Adjourned to 8 °Clock Tomorrow.

Saturday 14 [April] 1781.

Met according to Adjournment.

Adjourned to 8 °Clock Monday next.

---

[1]The record here is imperfect. The resolution of the House of April 13 1781 was as follows:

Resolved that a Committee of Seven be appointed to confer with the Governor and Council respecting the appointing of county officers east of Connecticut River and Field officers in the Regiments now vacant, and make report to this House. The members chosen M^r. Payne, M^r. Ormsby, M^r. Prentice, M^r. Woodward, M^r. Pearl, M^r. Page and M^r. Giles.

Of these, all but Messrs. Ormsby of Manchester, and Pearl [Stephen, of Rupert,] were from New Hampshire towns, to wit: Col. Elisha Payne of Lebanon, Nathaniel Sartel Prentice of Alstead, Bezaleel Woodward of Dresden [part of Hanover,] Doct. William Page of Charlestown, and Benjamin Giles of Newport. The report of this committee was not entered on the journal of the House, but the substance of it was—as the above entry on the Council journal should be—that the Governor and Council be empowered to make all necessary appointments. This is indicated by the following resolution of the House, which was adopted on the same day:

Resolved that the Governor and Council be and they are hereby requested to appoint and Commissionate, for the time being, all officers civil and military which are necessary to supply vacancies in any counties, probate districts and Regiments within this State until they can be elected by the people agreeable to the 27th Section in the frame of government.

By the 18th section the Governor and Council had ample power "to supply every vacancy in any office;" and of course this resolution was unnecessary for the filling of vacancies in office within the meaning of the constitution. The intent of it therefore was to treat *the lack* of necessary Vermont officers east of Connecticut river as "vacancies." It will be seen that the Governor and Council acted promptly.

IN COUNCIL MONDAY Windsor 16 April 1781.

Met according to Adjournment.

Resolved that John Fassett [jr.] Esq.r join a Committee from the House to Make a Depreciation Scale.

Thomas Russel Esqr. [of Piermont, N. H.] is hereby appointed for the time being, an assistant Judge in and for the *County* of *Orange* in Lieu of Colo. Robert Johnson.

The following Gentlemen were Nominated and are hereby appointed for the time being Justices of the Peace & Judges of the County Court for the County of Windsor vizt.

Elisha Payne Esqr., [of Lebanon, N. H.,] *Chief Judge.*

Joseph Marsh Esqr., Benjamin Emmons Esqr., Beza Woodward Esqr., [of Dresden, now Hanover, N. H.,] & John Weld Esqr., *Side Judges.*

Samuel Chase, William Ripley, [of Cornish, N. H.,] Moses Whipple, [of Croydon, N. H.,] John Stevens, [of Plainfield, N. H.,] Abel Stevens, [of N. Grantham, N. H.,] John Wheatley, [of Lebanon, N. H.,] Elihu Hyde, [of Lebanon, N. H.,] Aaron Barney, Bazaleel Woodward, [of Dresden, now Hanover, N. H.,] & Jonathan Freeman, [of Hanover, N. H.,] Esquires, *Justices of the Peace for said County.*

Resolved that Bazaleel Woodward Esqr. be & he is hereby appointed Judge of Probate for the district of Dresden for the time being.

WINDSOR 16th April.

A Remonstrance signed by a Number of the Inhabitants of Rockingham against the Gentlemen who were appointed by County Election to the several offices of said County, Praying the Council to suspend Granting their Commissions, was read whereupon the question being put whether the Commissions be Suspended agreeable to sd. Remonstrance which passed in the Negative.

Adjourned to 8 oClock Tomorrow.[1]

TUESDAY, IN COUNCIL, Windsor 17th April, 1781.

Council met according to Adjournment.

The following Gentlemen were Nominated and are hereby appointed for the time being Justices of the Peace for the County of *Orange*, vizt. Joseph Paverly, Samuel Rise [Rice,] Elisha Cleaveland, [Bath, N. H.,] Timothy Bedle, [Bedel,] Thomas Russell, [Piermont, N. H.,] Israel Morey, [Orford, N. H.,] Jonathan Child, [Lyme, N. H.,] Joshua Copp, Enoch Page, Nathl. Rogers of Moristown [Franconia, N. H.,] & Nathl. Hodges, [Lyman, N. H.,] Esquires.[2]

---

[1] From the *Assembly Journal*, April 16 1781:

Resolved that the Governor and Council be and they are hereby requested to appoint Commissioners to lease out and take care of the estates of Absentees in such places as they shall judge best.

The House adjourned until the second Wednesday of June, then next, leaving the Governor and Council still in session.

[2] It seems there were two Timothy Bedels in the Assembly in 1781: Col. Timothy Bedel representing Lyman, Morristown, and Bath, N. H.; and Timothy Bedel, Esq., one of the representatives for Haverhill, N. H. It is presumed that all the above justices were for New Hampshire towns.

Resolved that Bazaleel Woodward Esq$^{r.}$ be and he is hereby appointed Secretary Pro tempore.

The following was agreed on by the Council as a form of a Commission for the Justices of the Several Counties in this State, viz$^{t.}$

His Excellency Thomas Chittenden Esq$^{r.}$ Gov$^{r.}$ Captain General and commander in Chief in and over the State of Vermont, To ——— Greeting:

You and Each of you being Elected and appointed Justices of the Peace within and for the County of ———, Know ye that I the said Governor in the name and by the Authority of the freemen of the State of Vermont, Do hereby Authorize and Empower you & every one of you Justices to keep the Peace in the said County of ——— And to keep & cause to be kept all ordinances & statutes Enacted for the preservation of the Peace & for the quiet rule & Government of the People within said County, according to the form force & effect of a Law of this State—And to chastise and punish according to Law all persons that offend against the same—And you are further to hear & determine all & singular the causes & suits (at any time) brought before you, according to the Laws and Statutes of this State, as in the Like cases it ought to be done.—And you and Each of you are to make & Cause to be kept true records of all and singular your doings in the premises as well of Writs precepts processes Indictments judgments and Executions as of all other matters or things which respect the Execution of your said office—And all persons are to take Notice hereof and Govern themselves accordingly.—Given under my hand and the seal of the State of Vermont this —— day of ———, A. D. ——.

Commissions were Issued for the Judges of the County Courts for the County of Rutland, Windham, Windsor, and Orange, & for the Justices of the county^{s} of Windsor and Orange, also a Warrant for the Judges of Probate for the district of Drisden in Windsor County, and Towns Adjoining.[1]

His honor the Deputy Governor & his Honor Paul Spooner Esquires left the Council Board.

Adjourned to 8 ^{o}Clock tomorrow.

Attest, BEZA. WOODWARD, *Sec$^{y.}$ P. Tem.*

WEDNESDAY, IN COUNCIL, Windsor 18th April 1781.

Bryant Brown who was Elected Sheriff for the County of Windsor resigned his said office of Sheriff which resignation was accepted by the Council and the office was accordingly Declared Vacant. The Governor & Council then took into their consideration the appointment of a Sheriff for the said County for the Time being, whereupon Resolved that Capt. Ebenezer Brewster of Dresden be & hereby is appointed Sheriff for the said County of Windsor for the time being in the Room of Bryant Brown resigned.

And the question being put who will be bound for the said Sheriff, the said Ebenezer Brewster as principal & Col$^{o.}$ Elisha Payne & Maj. Thomas Murdock as sureties, jointly & severally acknowledged them-

---

[1] In Feb. 1781, the eastern part of Vermont was divided into three counties—Windham, Windsor, and Orange. In April following the New Hampshire towns north of Claremont, Newport, Unity, and Wendell, were annexed to the counties opposite in Vermont, and the other New Hampshire towns embraced in the union were constituted a county named Washington.—See Slade's *State Papers*, p. 427.

selves indebted to the Treasurer of the State of Vermont in the sum of two thousand Pounds Lawful Money—Conditioned that if the above named Ebenezer Brewster shall well & faithfully discharge & execute the office of Sheriff for the County of Windsor for the time being then this recognisance to be void otherwise to be and remain in full force and Virtue—and a Warrant was Issued to the said Sheriff accordingly. Also Warrants to the Judges of Probate for the district of Windsor & Havrill [Haverhill.]

Attest, BEZA. WOODWARD, *Secy. P. Tem.*

Resolved that the fourth Wednesday in May next be and hereby is appointed for a day of public Fasting and prayer throughout this State.

The Governor, Council & General Assembly having Completed the business of the present Session Agreed to

Adjourn without day.

Attest, BEZA. WOODWARD, *Secy. P. Tem.*

The foregoing is a true Copy of the original Journals of Council.

Attest, JOSEPH FAY, *Secy.*

END OF WINDSOR APRIL SESSION.

RECORD OF THE BOARD OF WAR.

WINDSOR, April 17th 1781.

The Board of War met: Present, Joseph Bowker, John Fassett, [jr.,] Thos. Murdock, Benjamin Emonds, Timothy Bedel, Ebenr. Brewster,[1] & Ira Allen.

Timothy Bedel & Ebenr. Brewster being Elected were sworn to the faithful discharge of their Trust.

Joseph Bowker Esqr. was chosen President Protemporary.

Resolved that there be four Companies of Light Infantry Raised in this State East of Connecticut River for the defence of this State. That they consist of Sixty Eight Rank and file Each Company, to be commanded by one Capt., Two Lieuts. and four Sergeants, with a drum and fife.

Resolved that the several persons Hereafter named be and they are hereby appointed to the offices as hereafter specified:

Capt. John Prat of Chesterfield, [N. H.]; Lieut. ———— of Keen, [N. H.]; Lieut. ———— okes of Winchester, [N. H.]; Capt. Jonathan White, Charlestown, [N. H.]; Lieut. Edmond Waldo, Alstead, [N. H.]; Lieut. Jonathan Hall Jr., Walpole, [N. H.]; Capt. Daniel Clapp, Dresden, [N. H.]; Lieut. ——— ——— ———; Lieut. ——— ——— ———; Capt. Samuel Young, Haveril, [N. H.]; Lieut. James Butterfield, Westmoreland, [N. H.]; Lieut. Isaac Patterson, Piermont, [N. H.]

Resolved that Majr. B. Wait be and he is hereby requested to call on the officers in the Two South Compys ord to be raised on the East Side of Connecticut River to see whether they accept of their appointment or not and if either of them refuse serving That then in that case Majr. Wait consult the principle Gentlemen in that vicinity and make such

---

[1] Col. EBENEZER BREWSTER was a prominent citizen of Hanover, N. H., and represented that part of the town called Dresden in the Vermont Assembly of Oct. 1781.

nominations as may be then necessary & return such nominations with the names & Ranks of all that do accept to some of the members of this Board.

Resolved that Lieut. Dyre [and] Lieut. Joseph Andros of Shaftsbury be appointed Lieut. for Col^o. Fletcher's Reg^t. of Infantry.

Adjourned untill Nine o'clock to morrow.

Wednesday 9 o'clock, Mett.

Resolved that the Selectmen in the several towns (Through which it will be necessary to transport provision for the Troops for the defence of the frontiers) be requested to call on such Towns to do their work on the Roads agreeable to the Laws of this State as soon as may be so as to accommodate the transportation of provision as aforesaid.

Resolved that Maj. B. Wait be and he is hereby directed to call the officers and Soldiers of his detachment into service in such proportion & at such time as he may judge proper, & in case Maj^r. Wait on Confering with the Commissary of Purchase shall judge it necessary that some of the main Roades from the Country to some of the Garrisons to be hereafter specified ought to be mended or Cut in some new place, That then in such Case Maj^r. Wait Call out such numbers and proportion of his detachment to work on the road as he may think proper.

Resolved that the three southerly Companies now or^d to be raised on the east side of Connecticut River March as soon as may be into the frontiers on the West side of the Mountains and join Col^o. Fletcher, That the north Company join Maj^r. Waits Detachment.

Resolved that a Majority of the members of the Board of War that are on the West side of the Mountains be and hereby are Impowered (on confering with Col^o. Fletcher and such other officers as they may think necessary,) to determine for the time being the Stationing of the Troops for the defence of the frontiers, as also fourts, Barracks, &c. That a Majority of the members of this Board that are on the East side of the mountain be & hereby are Impowered (on confering with Maj^r. Wait & such other officers [as] they may think necessary,) to determine for the time being the stationing of the Troops for the defence of the frontiers, as also fourts, Barracks, &c.

Resolved that Capt. John Strong As^t. Comm^y. of Purchase be directed to purchase four Iron Kettles and fourty eight of a less size suitable for Camp Equipage and forward the same to the several Garrisons on the East side of the mountain as they may be wanted, and Eighty good axes.

Resolved that Mr. Elisha Clark be and he is hereby appointed Commissary of Issues for the West department the Insuing Campaign.

Resolved that Moses Johnson be 1 [first] Lieut., Isaac Lymond 2d Lieut. and Jonas Pierce 2[^d] Lieut. in Col^o. Fletchers Regiment of Infantry.

Resolved that the several Brigadier Gen^ls. in this State be and they are hereby directed to call on the officers Commanding Reg^ts. in his Brigade to make returns to him agreeable to an act of the Legislature of this State passed at their session in instant April. That the return be in the following form, (viz.)

(To be here inserted.)[1]

That the several B. Gen^ls. Compile such Reg^t. returns into a Brigade [return] & transmit one [copy] to the Capt. Genl. & one to the President of this Board, and where there shall appear to be any deficiency in accoutrements that B. G. direct that the Laws of this State in such Case made and provided be put in Execution without loss of time.

---

[1] This form was not inserted on the record.

A Debenture of the Board of War holden at Windsor, April 18th 1781.

Present—Joseph Bowker Esq. President P. T. one day,	£0 7 0
[Received] JOSEPH BOWKER.	
Ira Allen one day,	0 7 0
Benj. Emmons Esq. one day,	0 7 0
John Fassett, [jr.,] Esq. one day,	0 7 0
[Received] JOHN FASSETT, JR.	
Timothy Bedle two days,	0 14 0
[Received] TIMOTHY BEDEL.	
Thomas Murdock Esq. two days,	0 14 0
Ebenezer Brewster Esq. three days, twenty miles travil,	1 7 8
[Received] EBENEZER BREWSTER.	

IN BOARD OF WAR, Arlington, Apl. 25th 1781.

Whereas the Legislature of this State did at their session in instant April recommend that fifteen hundred men be raised for the defence of this State & Impowering this Board to proportionate and Station such men in such places as the Exigences of the State might Require which cannot be determined at this Time, & whereas a store house & some kind of Barracks are necessary to be built for the use of the Troops for the time being—Therefore

Resolved, that this Board do recommend that Commissary of Purchase with the assistance of the Troops on the Ground build in the cheapest manner a store house and some Barracks that may answer for the time being in fourt Warren.

Resolved, that Lieut. Jacob Fairman be appointed first Lieut. in the Regiment of infantry commanded by Colo. S. Fletcher. That in case said Fairman should decline serving, That then Lieut. Harris is appointed in his stead.

Resolved, that Mr. Garshom Buck be appointed Armorer for Colo. Fletcher's Regt. of infantry.

Resolved, that this Board do hereby recommend to his Excellency Thos. Chittenden Esqr. That he order all the officers and soldiers in Colo. Fletcher's Regiment of Infantry that are to join Colo. Fletcher's command on the West side of the Mountain & the three Companies East of Connecticut [river] that are to march to join Colo. Fletcher, that they march as soon as may be.

Resolved to & do Hereby Recommend to the Capt. Genl. that he give directions to the Troops in this State's service that their scouts cover the Inhabitants of Skeensborough, Grandvil [N. Y.] &c.

Debenture of the Board of War, Arlington, April 26th 1781.

Present—Honl Timothy Brownson, Esq. President one day 4 miles travil [Recd.] TIMOTHY BROWNSON.	£0 8 4
Joseph Bowker Esq. 1 day 45 miles travil	1 1 10
Ira Allen Esq. one day 4 miles travil	0 8 4
Gideon Warren Esq. one day 35 miles travil	0 18 8
[Recd.] GIDEON WARREN.	
Samuel Robinson Esq. one day 15 miles travil	0 12 0
[Recd.] SAMUEL ROBINSON.	
John Fasset Esq. one day 1 mile travil	0 7 4

From the following debenture account a meeting seems to have been called at Dresden, N. H., but no proceedings are recorded:

A Debenture of the Board of War at Dresden, May 7th 1781.

Timothy Bedel one day	£0 7 0
40 miles travil	0 13 4
	1 0 4
Thomas Moordock [Murdock] two days	0 14 0
3 miles travil	1
[Recd.] THOMAS MOORDOCK.	0 15 0
Ebenezer Brewster two days	0 14 0
Recd pr EBENEZER BREWSTER.	

Still another meeting, of which no record has been preserved, is indicated by the following debenture account:

A Debenture of the Board of War, Manchester, May 25, 1781.

Present—Hon. Timothy Brownson Esq. three days	
5 miles travil	£1 2 8
[Recd.] TIMOTHY BROWNSON.	
Joseph Bowker Esq. two days thirty-six miles travil	£1 6 0
[Recd.] in full JOSEPH BOWKER.	
Thos. Moordock Esq. three days 78 miles travil	£2 7 0
[Recd.] THOS. MOORDOCK.	
Samuel Robinson Esq. two days 22 miles travil	£1 1 4
Gideon Warren Esq. three days 38 miles travil	£1 13 8
[Recd.] GIDEON WARREN.	
Ebenr. Brewster Esq. three days 76 miles travil	£2 6 4
Recd pr EBENR BREWSTER.	
Joseph Tyler Esq. three days[1]	£1 12 0
Recd. pr JOSEPH TYLER.	
John Fassett Esq. three days 7 miles travil	£1 3 4
[Recd.] JOHN FASSETT.	
Benj. Emmons Esq. three days 83 miles travil	£2 8 8
[Recd.] BENJ. EMMONS.	

RECORD OF THE GOVERNOR AND COUNCIL

AT THE

SESSION OF THE GENERAL ASSEMBLY AT BENNINGTON,

JUNE 13 1781.

STATE OF VERMONT. IN COUNCIL, Bennington, 13 June 1781.

Present His Excellency Thomas Chittenden Esquire, His Honor Benjamin Carpenter Esqr. Lt. Govr. and the following Members of the Honble Council vizt.—Hon. Jonas Fay, Moses Robinson, Timothy Brownson, Ira Allen, John Fassett [jr.,] Paul Spooner, John Throop, Benjamin Emmons, Jeremiah Clark Esqr. Thomas Chandler Junr. Joseph Fay, *Secy.*

Whereas complaint has this day been Exhibited to this Council by Thomas Porter Esqr. & Colonel Ebenezer Walbridge, against Judah Padock Spooner, Timothy Green, Samuel Avery, and Ezra Stiles

---

[1] The travel is omitted, doubtless in copying into the record.

Esquire, Suspecting them to be confederate in Counterfeiting the bills of Credit of this State,

Therefore Resolved that a Warrant Issue from this Council to apprehend said persons to be Brought before this Council for Examination.

Resolved that this Council be & hereby is Adjourned to 8 °Clock Tomorrow Morning.

THURSDAY 14 June 1781.

To His Excellency Thomas Chittenden Esquire and the Honorable Council of the State of Vermont comes Ebenezer Walbridge and Thomas Porter Esquires, Committee for signing the Bills of Credit Emitted by this State, and on Oath Complain, inform & give said Governor and Council to Understand that this Instant 13th June Your Complainants have recd a forty shilling bill of Mr. Martin[1] of this State Currency No. 36 which your Complainants is very confident is not of their Signing, & Counterfeit, that your Complainants have just reason to suspect & do Suspect Judah Paddock Spooner, Timothy Green, Samuel Avery & Ezra Stiles Esqr. of Westminster in the County of Windham are concerned in the Wicked plan of Counterfeiting said Money, all which wicked conduct is contrary to the force and effect of a certain Statute Law of this State in such case made and provided, and against the peace and dignity of the Freemen of this State. Your Complainants therefore prays a writ may go forth to apprehend said persons that they may be examined and dealt with as the law directs.

EBENEZER WALBRIDGE,
THOMAS PORTER.

Bennington, June 13th 1781.
Sworn before me date above, MOSES ROBINSON, *Assistant.*[2]

STATE OF VERMONT, Bennington June 13th 1781.

To the Sheriff of the County of Windham, his Deputy, or Either of the Constables of Westminster, and for want of a proper officer to be had,

To Benjamin Fay Esqr. Greeting—

You are hereby authorised & commanded, in the name and by the authority of the freemen of the State of Vermont, to apprehend the bodies of the above named Judah P. Spooner, Timothy Green, Samuel Avery, Ezra Stiles Esqrs. all of Westminster in the County of Windham, & them forthwith bring before the Governor and Council in the Council Chamber in Bennington—And make diligent Search in all Suspected places & Break Locks and Doors for Counterfeit Money. Hereof fail not, & of this Writ & your doings make returns according to law.

pr order, JOSEPH FAY, *Secy.*

Westminster 15th June 1781.[3]

Then personally served the within Warrant by attaching the bodies of the within named Defendants and have them now in Court.

BENJAMIN FAY, *Sheriff.*

---

[1] Probably Daniel Martin, at that time a representative for Putney who was a speculator in money, as the journal of the House discloses.

[2] This was the title of members of the Executive Council when acting in their capacity as justices of the peace.

[3] This may have been the true date of the return, but it appears by the date of the return of the next warrant that two of the arrested parties were in Bennington on the 14th.

STATE OF VERMONT. IN COUNCIL, Bennington 13 June 1781.
To the Sheriff of the County of Bennington, or his Deputy, or either of the Constables of said Town, Greeting,—

You are hereby Commanded, in the name and by the Authority of the freemen of the State of Vermont, to apprehend the bodies of Samuel Avery and Ezra Stiles Esq$^{r.}$ & cause them to be brought forthwith before this Council to answer a Complaint this day Exhibited by Thomas Porter Esq$^{r.}$ & Col$^{o.}$ Ebenezer Walbridge against the said Avery and Stiles suspecting them to be confederate in Counterfeiting the bills of credit of this State. Hereof you may not fail, and return this Writ with your doings thereon.

Given under my hand date above.

By order of Council, JOSEPH FAY, *Sec$^{y.}$*

Bennington, June 14, 1781.

Then served the within Warrant by apprehending the bodies of the within named *Samuel Avery* and *Ezra Stiles*, and have them now before this Council. JONAS GALUSHA, *Sheriff.*

STATE OF VERMONT. { County & Town of Bennington, in Council Chamber, 14 June 1781.

To Sergeant Rufus Branch or M$^{r.}$ Stephen Hopkins.

You are hereby required and Commanded to take to your assistance three faithful men, with Arms and Ammunition, as soon as this shall come to your hand, and proceed to some narrow passing on the road on the east Mountain that leads to Woodford, and place your Guard at a proper distance from the Road so as to discover all persons who may pass and to Stop and to take into Custody all who you shall find passing to the Eastward, so as not to be discovered, till this Evening, then to return them to Bennington. You will take Special care not to discover yourselves to any who may be passing to the Westward. Hereof you may not fail.

By order of the Governor and Council, JOSEPH FAY, *Sec$^{y.}$*

According to the directions of the within Warrant, I proceeded to the East Mountain and fulfilled the directions of the within Warrant but found no person passing to the Eastward.

Pr STEPHEN HOPKINS.

Bennington, June 15th 1781.[1]

M$^{r.}$ Samuel Avery and Ezra Stiles Esquires, who were made prisoners on Suspicion of being confederate in Counterfeiting the bills of Credit of this State, were Examined and Liberated for the present.[2]

Adjourned until 7 o'Clock Tomorrow Morning.

---

[1] The probable purpose was to prevent the escape of any body then implicated, or who might be implicated, in the supposed crime of counterfeiting.

[2] On the 18th a like entry was made as to Mr. Spooner, and also as to *John Gould*, who was not named in either of the foregoing warrants. At the session of the General Assembly in the preceding April, the issuing of bills of credit by the State to the amount of £25,155 was authorized, and counterfeiting those bills was a capital crime. The bills were to be printed under the inspection of "Matthew Lyon, Edward Harris,

FRIDAY 15 June 1781.

Council met according to adjournment and proceeded to business.

Date above personally appeared Jonathan Hunt Esquire who is Elected Sheriff in and for the County of Windham within this State as principal, Luke Knowlton and Arad Hunt Esquires as Sureties, & acknowledge themselves jointly and Severally Recognized and bound

---

and Ezra Styles Esquires," and were to be delivered to "Honorable John Fassett, Ebenezer Walbridge, and Thomas Porter, Esquires, a committee for signing and numbering said bills."—See Slade's *State Papers*, p. 424. Mr. Styles, therefore, was one of the committee to inspect the printing. Spooner and Green were the printers employed. What connection Avery and Gould had with the work does not appear. They were both residents of Westminster probably, and it is possible Martin received the counterfeit bill from one of them. However this may be, the examination resulted finally in establishing the innocence of all the parties implicated, as appears from the following entry on the Assembly Journal under date June 21 1781:

The Committee appointed to inspect the press for printing the Bills of Credit &c. made a verbal Report—and one Chaffee and the printer-Boy were examined before this House by John Fassett and Paul Spooner Esq[rs.] Assis[ts.] relating to Counterfeiting the Bills of Credit of this State and both owned the fact.

EZRA STYLES, Esq., according to the Assembly Journal, represented Keene, N. H., in the Vermont Assembly in Oct. 1781; and according to Slade, EZRA STILES, Esquire, was one of the nine commissioners appointed at that time to settle boundary lines between Vermont and New York and New Hampshire. EZRA STILES, said to be a son of Rev. Dr. Ezra Stiles of New Haven, Conn., came to Westminster at an early day, settled there as an attorney, and "died long before his learned and venerated father," who died in 1795. He was more than once employed by the State in respect to printing, and probably he was the representative for Keene in 1781. See Thompson's *Gazetteer*, 1824. According to Drake's *Biographical Dictionary*, Dr. Ezra Stiles, jr., son of Rev. Dr. Stiles, died in North Carolina in 1784.

TIMOTHY GREEN, of New London, Conn., (a descendant of Samuel Green of Cambridge, Mass., the second printer in New England,) established a press at Norwich, Conn., in 1773, and afterward continued the business in New London. JUDAH-PADOCK SPOONER (he thus printed his name) was a brother in law of Green and served his apprenticeship with him. The two were partners in business at Westminster in 1781. See note *ante* p. 12; Isaiah Thomas's *History of Printing;* and Thompson's *Vermont*, Part II, p. 171.

SAMUEL AVERY of Westminster was deputy sheriff in Windham county in Oct. 1782, and in that capacity executed the sentence of banishment upon sundry violent "Yorkers." A person of the same name—probably another man—was sent to the legislature of New York

unto the Treasurer of this State in the Sum of two thousand pounds lawful money for the faithful performance of the said Jonathan in his said office of Sheriff in and for said County in discharging the duty and for the answering of all such Damages as any person or persons shall sustain for any unfaithfulness or neglect in the Execution of said office.[1]

Attest, JOSEPH FAY, *Secy.*

BENNINGTON 15 June 1781.

Personally appeared Col^o. Robert Johnson who is Elected Sheriff in & for the County of Orange within this State as principal, Capt. Luther Richardson & Col^o. John Taplin as sureties, and acknowledge themselves jointly and severally recognized and bound unto the Treasurer of this State in the Sum of two thousand pounds lawful money for the faithful performance of the said Colonel Robert Johnson in the said office of Sheriff in and for said county, in discharging the duty & for the answering of such damages as any person or persons shall sustain by any unfaithfulness or Neglect in the Execution of said Office.

Attest, JOSEPH FAY, *Secy.*

Council Adjourned until 8 °Clock Tomorrow Morning.

SATURDAY 16 June 1781.

Council met according to Adjournment.

Having passed the day & Nothing matter of record, Agreed to adjourn until Monday next one °Clock afternoon.

MONDAY 18 June 1781.

Council met according to Adjournment and proceeded to business.

Mr. Spooner *Printer* & John Gould having been made prisoners on suspicion of being confederate in Counterfeiting the bills of Credit of this State were Examined and Liberated for the present.[2]

Adjourned to 8 °Clock Tomorrow Morning.

TUESDAY 19 June 1781.

Council met according to Adjournment.

His Excellency the Governor and Council joined in a Committee of the whole. [On the union with the Western District.]

Voted Timothy Brownson Esqr. to join a Committee from the Assembly to receive the Militia Act & Report.

Voted that his Honor General Carpenter and John Throop Esquires join a Committee from the Assembly to make a bill of Depreciation for the payment of Col. Warner's Regiment.[3]

---

in March of the same year, as agent of Brattleborough, Halifax, and Guilford, to urge the enforcement in Vermont of the authority of New York.—See B. H. Hall's *Eastern Vermont.* The latter probably was the claimant to Vermont land under New York grants, subsequently noticed.

[1] A notice of Mr. HUNT is reserved for use when he appears as Councillor.

[2] See extract from the Assembly journal on the preceding page.

[3] For act see Slade's *State Papers*, p. 437. By the first section of the militia act of Feb. 1779, the Lieut. Gov. was made Major General. Gov. Chittenden gave that title to Lieut. Gov. Marsh in 1778.—See Vol. I, p. 257.

Voted that Colonel Robinson be added to the above Committee.

Voted that his honor Doctr. Spooner wait on the General Assembly to request them to appoint a Trustee of Loan Office.

The following is a Copy of a Resolution of the General Assembly vizt.

STATE OF VERMONT. IN GENERAL ASSEMBLY June 19 1781.

Resolved that Colo. Ira Allen be & he is hereby appointed Trustee of Loan Office for this State.

Extract from the Journals, ROSWELL HOPKINS, *Clerk*.

Resolved that Mr. Samuel Sherman be employed to ride post from his Excellency's in Arlington to Camp Head Quarters [at Castleton] once a week three months from the date hereof, to go up one road by the way of Tinmouth and return by the way of Pawlet; that for his Encouragement he be allowed fourteen shillings per week out of this State's Treasury, he to convey all public letters & dispatches free of all other expence.

Adjourned to 8 oClock Tomorrow Morning.

WEDNESDAY 20 June 1781.

Council met according to Adjournment.

No Matters of Record having passed this day Adjourned until 8 oClock Tomorrow Morning.[1]

THURSDAY 21t June 1781.

Council met according to Adjournment.

A remonstrance signed Benjamin Sutton, and others inhabitants of Stamford to the amount of two, against Benjamin Tupper being Commissioned as Justice of the Peace, was read. Said Tupper having been notified to appear at this time in Vindication if he see cause, Edward Higby and two others the remonstrants appeared. The said Tupper not having appeared to make defence, several Evidences were taken in Support of said Remonstrance. This Council having taken the same under

---

[1] From the *Assembly Journal:*

His Excellency Govr. Chittenden desired to be dismissed as one of the Committee of Pay Table. Granted.

On the same day Col. John Strong was elected to fill the vacancy.

Gen. JOHN STRONG was born in Salisbury, Conn., in 1738; married Agnes McCure, (a native of Edinburgh, Scotland,) in 1759; and settled in Addison in 1766. In 1777 he was captured by a party of British and Indians, but was paroled by Gen. Frazer; when, travelling through Vermont in search of his family, he found them at Dorset, where he remained until 1783, and then returned to Addison. He represented Dorset from 1779 to 1783, and Addison from 1784 until 1787—in all seven years. He was assistant judge for Bennington county in 1781 and '82, and chief judge for Addison county from 1785 until 1801—in all eighteen years. He was also judge of probate for Addison county from 1786 until 1802—sixteen years; member of the Council from 1786 until 1803—seventeen years; and a delegate in the Convention of 1791. He was a member of the Congregational church, and a consistent Christian. His death occurred in June, 1816. For other details see *Vt. Historical Magazine*, Vol. I, pp. 7-10; and see also Deming's *Catalogue*.

consideration are of opinion that his Appointment is Illegal and order that his Commission be suspended.

Attest, JOSEPH FAY, *Secy.*

Thomas Chandler [jr.] Esqr. moved for a dismission from Council for the present session which was granted.

Adjourned to 8 oClock Tomorrow Morning.[1]

FRIDAY, June 22, 1781.

Council met according to Adjournment.

Voted that Jeremiah Clark & Paul Spooner Esqrs. join a Committee from the General Assembly to take under Consideration the Bills of Credit of this State.

Voted that Colonel Moses Robinson be a Committee to join a Committee from the General Assembly upon a petition signed Jonathan Grant in behalf of the Inhabitants of Lunenburgh.

Voted that the Treasurer be & he is hereby directed to pay unto Joseph Farnsworth Esqr. Commissary General of purchases, the sum of Sixty pounds L. Money in specie for the purpose of disbursing the sum upon a particular Contract, made between him the said Commissary and Captain Arad Hunt of Hinesdil [Vernon] for Cattle purchased for the use of the State. He the said Commissary General to be accountable.

Attest, THOMAS TOLMAN, *D. Secy.*

STATE OF VERMONT. IN GENERAL ASSEMBLY June 20th 1781.

The votes being called for a Brigadier General of the first Brigade, Colo. Samuel Safford was Elected.

The votes being called for a Brigadier Genl. for the Second Brigade, Colonel Samuel Fletcher was Elected.[2]

Extract from the Minutes, B. WOODWARD, *Clerk P. T.*

---

[1] From the *Assembly Journal:*

THURSDAY, June 21st. [A. M.]

The Council sent back the Report of the Committee passed this House on the petition of Captains Frye Bayley [*Trye* Bayley in *Vt. Historical Magazine*, Vol. II, p. 939,] and Nehemiah Lovell [Lovewell] "not concurred with"—Therefore

Resolved that a Committee of three be appointed to confer with the Council (or a Committee appointed by them for that purpose) on the subject of said Report, and Report their reasons for not concurring with the same.—The members chosen Mr. Prentice, Mr. Whipple and Mr. [Gideon] Olin.

P. M.

Resolved to reconsider the Resolution accepting the Report of the Committee on the petition of Capt. Frye Bayley and Capt. Nehemiah Lovell and said petition is hereby dismissed.

[2] These elections were made to fill vacancies occasioned by the refusal of ETHAN ALLEN and BENJAMIN BELLOWS to accept this office, to which they had been elected on the 11th of the preceding April. Hon. HILAND HALL has a copy of a letter written by Ethan Allen, on the 14th of April 1781, and addressed to Gov. CLINTON, in which Allen tendered his own services, and the services of two other Vermont officers, *to New York*, to defend that State "against their cruel invaders." This letter is explained by Mr. Hall as an attempt to show Gov. Clinton that his distrust of Allen's patriotism was unfounded. Allen had

Voted that Nathan [Nathaniel Bartell] Prentice Esq[r.] of Alstead [N. H.] be and he is hereby appointed an Assistant Judge for the County Court in and for the County of Washington until another may be chosen by regular Election & qualified to succeed him Agreeable to the Constitution of this State.

By order of His Excellency & Council, THO[S.] TOLMAN, *D. Secy.*

Council Adjourned until Tomorrow Morning 8 oClock.

SATURDAY June 23[d] 1781.

Resolved that the Charter for the Township of Jamaca be drawn so as to Extend to the East line of Stratton, thereby Including a Gore of Land

---

been distrusted from the truce with Carleton in October 1780; he felt bound to defend himself; and he did so by his letter to Congress March 9 1781, accompanied by Beverly Robinson's letters, and by communicating the same documents to the Vermont Assembly on the 12th of April. Two days thereafter he made the third movement for the same purpose by this letter to Clinton. Remembering only the hostile relations of Allen and Clinton, this letter will be deemed extraordinary; but remembering further, that Allen compelled Carleton to include New York as well as Vermont in the truce, his act and his letter are seen to be in perfect harmony. About this time the command of all the Vermont troops in service was given to ROGER ENOS, but precisely how does not appear from any record. As the governor could not serve in the field as commander-in-chief without the assent of the Council, the editor presumes that Governor Chittenden, with the approval of the Council, designated Gen. Enos to take his place. "Gen. Enos commands this State's troops in service," wrote Ira Allen to Gen. Haldimand, July 10 1781. Maj. Gen. ROGER ENOS entered the continental army at the opening of the revolutionary war, and in the expedition of Arnold through the forest of Maine to Quebec in the autumn of 1775, he commanded the rear division, consisting of eleven hundred men. When the difficulties were so great as to make the enterprise questionable, a council of war was held, and under the spur of Arnold's zeal it was determined to go on, and Enos was ordered to bring up his strongest men and leave the sick and feeble to return; but he took the responsibility of returning with his whole command. For this he was at first harshly censured, but ultimately his conduct was excused by the circumstances of the case. Gen. Enos first appeared in Vermont history in March 1780, when the town of Enosburgh was granted to him and his associates. He appears next as above, commander of all Vermont troops in service, when he was among the few cognizant of the Haldimand correspondence, and governed his military movements accordingly. His residence was in Hartland until after 1791, as the record shows that he represented that town on several occasions from October 1782 to October 1792. The closing years of his life were spent with his daughter, Mrs. Ira Allen, in Colchester, where he died, Oct. 6 1808, in the seventy-third year of his age. He was a major general in the Vermont militia.

Lying East of said Stratton, and that the number of 10 persons be added as proprietors in said Township of Jamaca, and the Surveyor General is hereby directed to draw the bounds of said Charter accordingly.

Resolved that Judge Jones[1] be and is hereby directed to insert the name of Nathan [Nathaniel] S. Prentice Esquire in the Commission for the Judges of the County Court for the County of Washington as an Assistant Judge.

Council adjourned to 2 °Clock Afternoon.

Met according to Adjournment. Nothing passed as Matter of Record and Adjourned until Monday Morning Next 9 °Clock.

MONDAY June 25th 1781.

Council met according to Adjournment.

His Excellency Thomas Chittenden Esquire being absent by Illness his Honor the Lt. Governor in the Chair.

Having joined sundry Committees from the General Assembly,

Adjourned to 8 °Clock Tomorrow Morning.

---

[1] Daniel Jones of Hinsdale, N. H.

From the Record of the *Board of War:*

BENNINGTON, 23 June 1781.

We the subscribers being desiared by the Honble Bord of War to viset the frontiers of the State of Vermont and report where in our opine the garisons ought to be built for the best defence of the above said State

Begg leave to report first that the garisons at Pitsford ought to be removed back from the place where it now stands nigh Sutherland's mills or such particular spot as Colo. Fletcher shall direct. 2d. That the garison at Castleton ought to be removed West from where it now stands nigh to Blanchards mills, that the fort to be built at Skeensborough [Whitehall, N. Y.] ought to be built on a small hill where one Willson lives or Norwest about 5 or 6 hundred yards as Colo. Walbridge shall direct Taking into Consideration the conve'cy of Water. That Each of the above said forts ought to be built to Consist of a small picket and a strong block house. That the fortification at Castleton as it is most likely will be Considered Hed Quarters ought to be much the Largest. All which is submitted to your Hons.

Your very humble servants,

ROGER ENOS,
SAMUEL FLETCHER,
SAMUEL HERRICK,
GIDEON ARMSBURY [ORMSBY.]

STATE OF VERMONT. IN GENERAL ASSEMBLY June 23d 1781.

The within was read and ordered that a Committee of three be appointed to hold a conference with the within named persons respecting removing the Garison at Pittsford &c. and make report.—The members chosen Mr. E. Smith, Mr. B. Whipple and Mr. Post.

Attest, ROS. HOPKINS, *Clerk.*

IN GENERAL ASSEMBLY June 26 1781.

The above named Committee made a verbal report whereupon resolved that it be recommended to the board of War to order about one hundred men to be stationed at the said garrison as Pittsford for the support of it. Attest, B. WOODWARD, *Clerk P. T.*

TUESDAY 26 June 1781.

Council met According to Adjournment.

Resolved that Colonel Israel Morey be & hereby is appointed Judge of Probate for the time being in and for the district of Haveral [Haverhill, N. H.] in the County of Orange.[1]

Attest, JOSEPH FAY, *Secy.*

Adjourned to 8 °Clock Tomorrow morning.

WEDNESDAY 27 June 1781.

Met according to Adjournment.

Agreable to the request of the General Assembly of yesterday, Resolved that Colonel Henry Amanuel Lutterloh & Major Thomas Coggsel be and they are hereby Authorised & [empowered] to Locate a tract of Land Six Miles Square in some unappropriated part of this State in such form as to join in form to some Town or Towns Granted by this State & make returns of such Location to Ira Allen Esq. Surveyor General of this State in order to obtain a Charter of Incorporation.[2]

Per order of his Excellency the Governor and Council,

JOSEPH FAY, *Secy.*

Adjourned to 8 °Clock Tomorrow Morning.

---

[1] The territory on the east side of Connecticut river was divided into four probate districts, named Keene, Claremont, Dresden, and Haverhill.

Two incidents occurred in the Assembly on this day which illustrate peculiarities in the relations of the two houses under the first constitution. One was the presence of Councillor Fay in the House to make an important motion; and the other was the passage of an act by the House against the opinion of the Council.

IN GENERAL ASSEMBLY, June 26 1781.

On motion of Doct[r.] Fay,

Ordered that the doors be shut.

Resolved that a Committee of five to join a Committee from the Council be appointed to take into consideration the petitions from the Massachusetts line [officers] and Col[o.] H. E. Lutterloh and associates, and Report—The members chosen M[r.] Strong [John of Dorset,] M[r.] [William] Page, M[r.] [Edward] Harris, M[r.] [Isaac] Wyman, and M[r.] [Ebenezer] Curtiss.

On the 27th the Assembly voted grants in accordance with the petitions, and they were executed by the Governor and Council.—See observations on land grants, *ante* pp. 61-64.

The Governor and Council having proposed that the "Act" passed this day "to prevent turning streams of water out of their natural course" be referred to the next session—the question was put whether the said Act be referred; and it passed in the negative. The said Act was then read the 3[d] time and Enacted into a Law of this State.

[2] HENRY EMANUEL LUTTERLOTH of New York was appointed Deputy Quarter Master General by Washington, June 30 1777. The town of Albany was chartered by this resolution by the name of *Lutterloh.* Maj. THOMAS COGSWELL was from Haverhill, Mass., and ultimately a citizen of Gilmanton, N. H.

Resolved that Brigadier Generals John Glover and John Patterson be & they are hereby Empowered and fully Authorised to Locate a tract of Lands six miles Square in some unappropriated part of this State in such form as to join some town or towns Granted by this State & make returns to Ira Allen Esquire Surveyor General of this State in order to the Obtainining a Charter of Incorporation.[1]

By order of the Governor and Council, JOSEPH FAY, *Secy.*

Adjourned to 8 °Clock Tomorrow Morning.[2]

THURSDAY 28th June 1781.

Council met according to Adjournment and having passed a number of Acts and Transacted some other business of the day Resolved to Adjourn to 8 °Clock Tomorrow Morning.

FRIDAY 29th June 1781.

Resolved that Warrants be issued and directed [to] the respective Sheriffs in this State to Collect the British prisoners which may be found within the limits of this State and Cause them to be Safely conveyed to Head Quarters at Castleton by the 10 day of July next.

Resolved that Joseph Fay Esquire be and he is hereby appointed Commissary General of Prisoners for this State and that his Excellency the Governor be requested to make out a Commission for that purpose.[3]

Whereas Colonel William Williams[4] has made application for taking off part of the Granting fees for the lands Granted him formerly known

---

[1] Gen. JOHN GLOVER of Marblehead, Mass., raised one thousand men at the opening of the revolutionary war, which constituted what was popularly known as "the amphibious regiment," sailors and landsmen, and took rank among the best in the army. Glover's men manned the boats on the retreat from Long Island. He was appointed Brigadier General Feb. 21, 1777; was in active service until 1780; took part in the capture of Burgoyne, and conducted the captured to Cambridge. Col. JOHN PATTERSON of Massachusetts, afterward of New York, was promoted to a Brigadier Generalship at the same time as was Glover. The town of *Glover* was chartered to them and their associates.

[2] From the *Assembly Journal:*

Resolved that it be recommended to the board of war to order about one hundred men to be Stationed at the garrison at Pittsford for the support of it.

[3] It appears from *The Haldimand Correspondence* that as early as May 22 1781, Ira Allen had engaged that Haldimand should hear from Vermont about the middle of July, adding: "he thinks the commissioners will by that time be sent to exchange some prisoners, (provided he has a certainty of their being exchanged,) and will have power finally to determine whether Vermont is to be admitted as a province or not." Both Allen and Fay were commissioned in July; and Fay met Haldimand's agents about the first of August, but he was *not* authorised to close with the offer of the British general.

[4] Col. WILLIAM WILLIAMS moved from Northborough, Mass., to Marlborough, Vt., in 1769; and to Wilmington previous to 1777, as in that year he represented the last named town in the convention at Windsor

by the name of Reedsborough, whereupon Resolved that the Granting fees for Each right be Eight pounds in Silver or the value.

Whereas it has been represented to this Council that there is not a supply of provisions in Store for the use of the Troops of this State, and Whereas it is found Impracticable to prepare the Same

Therefore Resolved that the Secretary be and he is hereby directed to Issue his Warrants in behalf of the Governor and Council to the Commissary General to seize such quantities of provisions as necessity may require for the Support of the Troops of this State, and from such persons only as have more than for their families use, for which a reasonable price must be given.

Resolved that the price of the Township Granted to Col^o. Ira Allen & Company in February last lying north of Cambridge be nine pounds L. Money for Each Right, & that there be sixty five in number Exclusive of five public Rights.

Resolved that the Township of Land Granted to Col^o. Ira Allen in Feby last which is to be laid out between Misisque Bay and the main Lake to Include Windmill point, to have an equal number of proprietors to the quantity of Land as is Allowed in other Townships Granted by this State, that Each proprietor pay Twelve pounds for Each right.

Attest, JOSEPH FAY, *Sec^y.*

THE END OF JUNE SESSION HOLDEN AT BENNINGTON, 1781.

JOSEPH FAY, *Sec^y.*

---

which adopted the constitution. By that convention he was appointed one of a committee of three to procure arms for the State. He served in what is called "the French war," which ended in the treaty of peace signed at Paris Feb. 10 1763. In June 1775 Col. Williams offered his services to New York, in conjunction with Benjamin Wait and Joab Hoisington, to raise a regiment to serve as minute-men for the defence of Cumberland county against "regulars, Roman Catholics, and the savages at the northward." July 4 1775, Ethan Allen and Seth Warner commended him very highly for an appointment as major by Congress in Warner's regiment, should opportunity occur; and in August 1777 he distinguished himself as commander ot a regiment at the battle of Bennington. "As an officer," said B. H. HALL, "he was brave, energetic, skillful, and humane: as a citizen, enterprising, active, and progressive: as a neighbor, kind, polite, and attentive. The elegance and symmetry of his form were as perfect as his manners were agreeable. He was held in high estimation by the inhabitants of the various towns in which he dwelt at different times, and though of a wandering disposition, could easily accommódate himself to any circumstances in which he might be placed." Col. Williams was a deputy from Cumberland county in the provincial Congress of New York for the sessions commencing in May and November 1775, and May 1776; and representative of Wilmington in the General Assembly of Vermont from October 1779 to October 1781. In 1782 he seems to have been a resident of Marlborough again; but after the revolutionary war had been closed, he removed to Lower Canada, where he died in 1823.—See Vol. I; also *Vt. Hist. Soc.*

The following shows that the Board of War was in session on the 28th and 29th, though no proceedings are recorded. Doubtless the hundred men were ordered to Pittsford :

The Debenture of the Board of War, June 29th 1781.

Major Moordock 2 days		£0 14 0
[Recd.]	THOMAS MOORDOCK.	
Samuel Robinson 2 days		0 14 0
[Recd.]	SAMUEL ROBINSON.	

The rest of the Members made up in the Council.

The following entries are from the Record of the *Board of War:*

STATE OF VERMONT Dr. To JOSEPH BRADLEY,

To Sitting in the Board of War—

To three days at 7 shillings—4 miles travel	£1 2 4
" two " at 7 shillings—4 miles travel	0 15 4
" one " at 7 shillings—4 " "	0 8 4
" three " at 7 shillings—4 " "	1 2 4
" 1½ " at 7 shillings—4 " "	0 11 10
	£4 0 2

PAY TABLE OFFICE Sept. 5th 1781.

The within account examined and approved and the Treasurer is directed to pay the same to Joseph Bradley Esq. or bearer being 4 Pounds two pence Lawful money.

TIMOTHY BROWNSON, } *Committee of*
JOHN STRONG, } *Pay Table.*

TREASURER'S OFFICE, Sept. 6th 1781.

Received of Ira Allen Esq. Treasurer the contents of the above being four Pounds two pence Lawful money.

£4 0 2. JOSEPH BRADLEY.

[*Return of the "Training Band" in Rockingham.*]

Captains 1, Subalterns 1, Ensigns 1, Clerk 1, Sergeants 3, Drummers and fifers 0, Rank and file 53, Total Training Band 60, Arms in repair 20, Arms not in Repair 8, Arms wanting 35, Powder in Store 6 lbs., Powder wanting 54 lbs., Lead wanting 108 lbs., Flints in store 20, Flints wanting 340.

The above is a true List of the Training Band containing what Arms is Wanting, what in repair and out of repair, what powder in store and What is wanting and flints to complete said Company, attested

By us, WM. SIMONDS, *Capt.*
EBR. FULLER, *Lieut.*
EZRA WHITNEY, *Ensign.*

Rockingham, Oct. 6th 1781.

Collections, Vol. I; *Eastern Vermont;* Rev. E. H. Newton's Ms. *History of Marlborough*, in the library of the Vt. Historical Society; and Deming's *Catalogue.*

THE FIFTH COUNCIL.

OCTOBER 1781 TO OCTOBER 1782.

THOMAS CHITTENDEN, Williston, *Governor.*

ELISHA PAYNE, Lebanon, N. H., *Lieutenant Governor.*[1]

Councillors:

JOSEPH BOWKER, Rutland,
TIMOTHY BROWNSON, Sunderland,
PAUL SPOONER, Hartland,
MOSES ROBINSON, Bennington,
JONAS FAY, Bennington,
PETER OLCOTT, Norwich,
IRA ALLEN, Colchester,
BENJAMIN EMMONS, Woodstock,
JOHN FASSETT, jr., Arlington,
SAMUEL FLETCHER, Townshend,
JOHN THROOP, Pomfret,
BEZALEEL WOODWARD, Dresden, N. H.[1]

JOSEPH FAY, *Secretary.*

THOMAS TOLMAN, *Deputy Secretary.*

BIOGRAPHICAL NOTICE.[2]

BEZALEEL WOODWARD was a native of Lebanon, Conn., and a graduate of Yale college in 1764. He was professor of mathematics and natural philosophy in Dartmouth college, married a daughter of its first President Wheelock, and continued in that institution, of which he was a trustee, until his death, Aug. 25, 1804. He seems to have been active from the first in promoting the union of the western New Hampshire towns with Vermont. He represented Dresden, [the college lands in Hanover,] on the first union in 1778, and again on the second in 1781, officiating as Clerk of the House at one time, and at another as Secretary *pro tempore* of the Governor and Council. During the second union he was appointed judge of probate for the district of Dresden, one of a committee to revise the laws of the State, and one of the agents to

[1] Until February 1782.

[2] For notices of Messrs. FASSETT, FLETCHER, and THROOP, see *ante*, pp. 1–3; and of all other members of the Board except Mr. WOODWARD, see Vol. I.

Congress. He was also elected one of the judges of the Superior Court in 1781, but declined the office. His official service in Vermont of course terminated on the dissolution of the eastern and western unions in 1782. —See Blake's *Biographical Dictionary.*

RECORD OF THE GOVERNOR AND COUNCIL

AT THEIR

SESSION WITH THE GENERAL ASSEMBLY AT CHARLESTOWN, N. H., OCTOBER 1781.[1]

STATE OF VERMONT. IN COUNCIL Charlestown 11 Oct. 1781.

Present His Excellency Thos. Chittenden Esq. and the following members of the Honorable Council, vizt.

Moses Robinson,	Ira Allen &
Timothy Brownson,	Thomas Chandler Jr. Esqr.
Paul Spooner,	Joseph Fay, *Secy.*

Resolved that a Committee of five be appointed to join a Committee of the House to receive, sort & count the Votes of the Freemen and Declare the Several persons chosen into office for the year Ensuing.—Members chosen Mr. Robinson, Mr. Brownson, Mr. Chandler, Mr. Spooner and Mr. Allen.

Adjourned to 8 oClock Tomorrow.

FRIDAY 12th October 1781.

Council met according to Adjournment.

The Committee to receive, sort & count the Votes of the Freemen, Reported the persons hereafter named to be chosen into office respectively as follows vizt.—

His Excellency Thomas Chittenden Esqr. Govr.

Deputy Governor not chosen by the Votes of the Freemen.

Honble Ira Allen Esquire Treasurer and the

---

[1] From Ira Allen's *History of Vermont,* in *Vt. Hist. Soc. Collections,* Vol. I, p. 436:

In October 1781 the Legislature met at Charlestown, in the East Unions, when the Government of New Hampshire sent a Major Reynolds, with two hundred men, as was supposed, to stop the election and session of the Legislature; the friends of Vermont advised the Major, if he had any instructions from New Hampshire which were hostile to Vermont and the East Union, that it would be for the sake of humanity advisable for him to keep them to himself, as his force would not avail; this he prudently did, and the Assembly convened and proceeded to business without opposition.

Hon[ble] Jonas Fay,	Samuel Fletcher,	*[Councillors.]*
Paul Spooner,	Bezaleel Woodward,	
Moses Robinson,	John Throop,	
John Fassett Jun[r.]	Benjamin Emmons,	
Ira Allen,	Peter Olcott,	
Joseph Bowker,	Timothy Brownson[1] Esquires,	

The several Officers being present, Having taken the several qualifications required by Law, proceeded in conjunction with the General Assembly to the choice of a Deputy Governor. The Ballots being taken his honor Elisha Payne Esquire was declared chosen for the year ensuing.

Adjourned to 2 °Clock P. M.

Council met according to Adjournment.

Voted that Beza. Woodward Esquire join a Committee of the House to arrange the necessary business of the present Session and make Report.

The Governor and Council proceeded to the choice of a Secretary. The Ballots being taken Joseph Fay Esq[r.] was declared chosen.[2]

A petition Signed Hugh McCarty was read and referred to the General Assembly.

A number of papers signed Joseph Dyer relative to Fane Charter, or New Patmos, was read and referred to the Gen[l] Assembly.[3]

Council Adjourned to 8 °Clock Tomorrow.

SATURDAY 13 October 1781.

Council met according to Adjournment,

And in Conjunction with the General Assembly proceeded to the Choice of Judges of the Superior Court for the year ensuing. The Ballots being taken the following were duly elected and declared chosen viz[t.]

His Honor Elisha Payne Esq[r.] chief Judge.

Moses Robinson,	*Side Judges.*[4]
John Fassett, Jr.	
Beza. Woodward &	
Joseph Caldwell Esq[r.]	

---

[1] Mr. Brownson's name is not in this list, but is in another list in the record of the 13th.

[2] Until this day the Secretary of Council had been Secretary of State. On this day MICAH TOWNSHEND was elected to the last named office.

[3] Newfane, sometimes called Fane, and Patmos.

[4] Two of the judges elect were from the New Hampshire district, one from the western district, and two from Vermont proper—a distribution that was not satisfactory probably. Oct. 19 judge Robinson informed the House "that he should not accept his appointment as second judge of the Superior Court." He had been chief judge from the beginning. Paul Spooner was elected in his place. Oct. 23, Col. Caldwell, of Cambridge, N. Y., declined, and Jonas Fay was elected. Oct. 26, Bezaleel Woodward, of Dresden, N. H., declined, and Simeon Olcott was elected. Hon. SIMEON OLCOTT was born in Connecticut in 1737, and a graduate of Yale college in 1761. He settled in Charlestown, N. H., as an

Ira Allen Esq[r.] required the directions of Council relative to paying out the hard money in the Treasury. Whereupon

Resolved that the Treasurer suspend paying out any for the present as it is Wanted for Expences in voyages.[1]

Adjourned to 2 °Clock P. M. to meet at the house of Doct[r.] Page.

Council met according to Adjournment.

Voted M[r.] Robinson and M[r.] Brownson to join a Committee appointed by the House to nominate a member [number, or list of candidates] for the Board of War and make report.

Voted M[r.] Woodward and M[r.] Olcott to join a Committee from the House to Consider Col[o.] Waits Complaint for Want of Money to March a Company of Men to Camp.

Voted that the Members of Council shall Rank according to their former appointment which is as follows viz[t.]

Joseph Bowker,	Ira Allen,
Timothy Brownson,	Benjamin Emmons,
Paul Spooner,	John Fassett Jun[r.]
Moses Robinson,	Samuel Fletcher,
Jonas Fay,	John Throop &
Peter Olcott,	Beza. Woodward Esqr[s.]

Adjourned to 10 °Clock Monday next then to meet at the Council Chamber.

---

attorney, was judge of the superior court of Vermont from Oct. 1781 until Feb. 13, 1782, chief judge of the court of common pleas in New Hampshire in 1784, judge of the N. H. supreme court in 1790, and chief justice in 1795. He was United States senator for New Hampshire from 1801 to 1805.—See Drake's *Dictionary of American Biography.* The list of judges of the superior court of Vermont for 1781-2 in Slade's *State Papers*, and every subsequent printed list, is inaccurate. On the resignation of judge Simeon Olcott, Feb. 13, 1782, Samuel Fletcher was elected and declined to accept, when John Throop was elected. The judges from October 1781 until the dissolution of the eastern and western unions in February 1782, were Elisha Payne, Paul Spooner, John Fassett jr., Simeon Olcott, and Jonas Fay. Subsequent to the dissolution of the unions the list was as follows: Moses Robinson, Paul Spooner, John Fassett jr., John Throop, and Jonas Fay. In Slade's *State Papers*, pp. 553-5, it will be seen that Jonas Fay, Ira Allen, and Jeremiah Clark sat as assistant judges of the superior court when they had not been elected as such. This was done under the act of 1779 establishing the court, which provided that in case of necessity through the absence or inability of judges to form a quorum, any member of the Executive Council might sit as judge. See Slade's *State Papers* p. 299.

[1] Thus in the copy of the record in the office of the Secretary of State. The fact was that the money was wanted for the expenses of the agents of the State at Congress and elsewhere, as Vermont bills of credit would hardly serve their purpose. These were the "voyages" in view. This use of the word Ira Allen was apt to adopt, though *journeys* or *missions* would have been better.

[MONDAY, Oct. 15, 1781.]

Council met according to Adjournment.

Voted that Mr. Olcott & Mr. Robinson join a Committee of the House to provide ways and means for supplying the Treasury and consider the state of paper money.

Voted that Mr. Brownson & Mr. Spooner join a Committee of the House to Concert measures for Supplying the Army.

Voted that Mr. Allen Wait on the House with two letters recd from Brigadier General Stark and the orders given to the several Brigades of this State &c.[1]

Adjourned to 2 oClock P. M.

Council met according to Adjournment

And proceeded in conjunction with the House [to an election] of the Members of the Board of War, and a Committee of Pay Table. The ballots being taken the persons hereafter named were duly Elected and declared chosen vizt—

Honble Timothy Brownson Esqr.
Benjamin Emmons Esqr.
Ira Allen Esqr.
Roger Enos Esqr.
Joseph Caldwell Esqr.
Isaac Wyman Esqr.
Thomas Murdock Esqr.
John Fassett [jr.] Esqr.
Joseph Bowker Esqr., *Members of the Board of War.*

Honble Timothy Brownson Esqr.
Isaac Tichenor Esqr. and
Nathaniel Brush Esqr. } *Committee Pay Table.*[2]

Adjourned to 9 oClock Tomorrow Morning.

TUESDAY 16 October 1781.

Council met according to Adjournment

And agreeably to the order of the day His Excellency the Governor, The Honorable Council and General Assembly resolved themselves into a Committee of the whole to hear the report of the Agents to Congress, His Excellency Thomas Chittenden Esqr. in the Chair, Honble Beza. Woodward Esqr. Clerk.

Having heard the report of said Agents the Committee Adjourned to 2 oClock Afternoon.

Council met according to Adjournment.

The Honble Benjamin Emmons took his Seat in Council having taken the Necessary Oaths required by Law.

Agreeable to Adjournment the Govr. & Council met in Committee of the whole & his Excellency again resumed the Chair. Having debated largely on the Subject and taken sundry Votes, agreed to adjourn the Committee to 9 oClock A. M. Tomorrow.

---

[1] Gen. Stark was then stationed at Saratoga, within the district over which Vermont claimed jurisdiction. On a report that the enemy had passed lake George, he applied to Gov. Chittenden for aid, by letters of the 8th and 11th Oct. 1781, in response to which the Governor issued orders to Generals Safford and Enos and Col. Pearl.—See *Assembly Journal* of Oct. 15, 1781.

[2] The joint committee nominated eighteen candidates for the Board of War, and six for the Pay-Table, and the above named gentlemen were elected from the lists.

IN COUNCIL, &c.

Voted that Mr. Allen and Mr. Fay join a Committee of nine from the House to Take into Consideration the opening the Law for the Trial of the Title of Lands and quieting ancient settlers, &c. and make report.

Adjourned to 9 oClock A. M. Tomorrow.

WEDNESDAY 17th October 1781.

Council met according to Adjournment

And agreeable to the order of the day the Governor & Council again met [the House] in Committee of the Whole and proceeded as by their records may be seen. The Committee having adjourned to 9 oClock Tomorrow Morning the Council returned & proceeded to business.

Voted that Mr. Bowker and Mr. Allen join a Committee of five appointed by the House to adopt proper measures for the defence of the State for the year ensuing.

Adjourned to 9 oClock tomorrow.

THURSDAY 18 October 1781.

Council met according to Adjournment

And agreeable to the order of the day joined the General Assembly in a Committee of the Whole, & having Debated Largely on the Subject of making proposals to Congress relative to our being recd into the Federal Union, and several resolves being passed thereon, a Sub Committee appointed &c. as may be seen by the records of said Committee, Resolved to Adjourn to 9 oClock A. M. tomorrow, whereupon His Excellency & Council returned to the Council Chamber and proceeded to business as follows vizt—

Upon application made to this Council by Mr. Eliakim Spooner for some consideration for his giving up the Grant of the Township of Royalton to the State and for extraordinary expence & damages sustained thereby, Therefore

Resolved that Mr. Spooner be allowed Twenty pound L. Money in consideration of his Expences and damages aforesaid.

Adjourned to 2 oClock P. M.

Council met according to Adjournment.

The following resolution being read was ordered to be recorded vizt—

IN GENERAL ASSEMBLY October 18 1781.

Resolved that the first Thursday of December next be and is hereby appointed to be observed as a day of public *Thanksgiving* and *prayer* throughout this State, and the Governor is hereby requested to Issue his Proclamation accordingly.

Extract from the Journals, ROSL HOPKINS, Clerk.

Council Adjourned to meet in one hour at Doctr Pages.

Met according to adjournment and Adjourned to 9 oClock Tomorrow Morning.

FRIDAY 19th October 1781.

Agreable to the order of the day the Governor & Council joined the General Assembly in Committee of the whole, the sub Committee having made their report which was Accordingly Accepted. [1]

Adjourned for one quarter of an hour.

---

[1] This closed the sittings of the committee of the whole on the then recent action of Congress. For the result, see *Appendix H.*

IN COUNCIL.

His Honor Moses Robinson Esq. made application to be released during the present session, which was accordingly Granted.

Joseph Fay Sec^y. made a like application to be released during the present Session, which was accordingly Granted.

Adjourned to 2 °Clock P. M.

Met According to Adjournment.

A certificate of the choice of Joshua Tucker to the office of Justice of the Peace in the Town of Strafford Signed David Chamberlain Town Clerk being read and Considered—

Resolved that Joshua Tucker be and he is hereby appointed one of the Justices of the Peace within and for the County of Orange for the time being in the room of *William Brisco* resigned, and that the Clerk of the County Court of the said County of Orange be directed to insert the name of the said J. Tucker in the Commission of the Justices of said County.

The Honble John Throop Esqr. attended Council & took his seat after taking the necessary qualifications required by Law.

The Honble Timothy Brownson and Ira Allen Esquires were appointed a Committee to join a Committee from the House to point out the duty of Secretary of State.

Adjourned.

SATURDAY October 20, 1781.

Met According to Adjournment.

The Honble Jonas Fay Esquire was appointed to join a Committee from the house to prepare a bill on the report of the Grand Committee.

Leave of Absence was Granted unto the Honble Benjamin Emmons & Paul Spooner Esquires until Tuesday next.

Whereas the Warrants ordered by the Council held at Arlington on the 27 day of September last[1] to be issued to the Sheriff of the Counties of Windsor and Orange to collect from the several Towns the provitions assessed to them in consequence of an Act of Assembly in October last which still remains unpaid, have not yet been delivered to the said Sheriffs and there being Absolute Necessity that the provitions be forthwith Collected and delivered to the Commissary General or his deputy for supplying the Troops now on the Frontiers, therefore

Resolved that Warrants Issue to the said Sheriffs forthwith to collect the Taxes before mentioned and deliver them to the Commissary General or his Deputy for supplying the Troops now on the Frontiers, And that the Warrants to the said Sheriffs for that purpose Issued pursuant to the Resolve of Council before mentioned which are now in the hands of the Commissary General, be and hereby are declared to be void and of none effect.

The Honble John Fassett [jr.] Esqr. Attended.

Adjourned to Monday 9 °Clock.

MONDAY October 22^d 1781.

Met according to Adjournment.

The Honble John Fassett and John Throop Esquires were appointed to join a Committee from the House on a petition signed Timothy Andrus and Elijah Hinman upon the subject of assertaining the boundaries of Townships up Connecticut river.

The Honble John Fassett [jr.] Esqr. was duly qualified as Councillor.

---

[1]No record is found of a session of the Council between the 29th of June and the 11th of October 1781. See statement of Secretary Fay, following the record of Jan. 11, 1782.

An Act to remit to the Town of Danby the payment of a certain Tax therein mentioned was rec[d]. Read and returned to the House.

Adjourned until 9 oClock Tomorrow morning.

TUESDAY 23[d] October 1781.

Met according to Adjournment.

STATE OF VERMONT. IN GENERAL ASSEMBLY 22[d] Oct. 1781.

Resolved that the Governor and Council be requested to serve this Assembly at the opening of their next adjourned Session with Exact Copies of all their proceedings respecting the Fees, Limitations and Restrictions they have put on the Several Grants of Land made by this or a past Legislature in order for adjusting the same, and that the Committee for receiving fees on the Several Grants as aforesaid be directed to prepare their Accounts at the same time and Lay them before the Assembly that the same may be settled and fully closed.

Extract from the Journals, Attest, ROS. HOPKINS, *Clerk.*

Copy, THOM. TOLMAN, *D. Secy.*

The Hon[ble] Ira Allen Esquire was appointed to join a committee from the House upon a petition signed *John Barron* Praying for a Grant of Moortown, &c.[1]

A Commission was made out for the justices of the County of Rutland.

A request from the House to the Governor and Council to join in Committee [of the whole] to Elect a Judge of the Superior Court in the room of Col[o.] Caldwell who declines serving: the Ballots being taken Jonas Fay Esquire was Elected.

Adjourned to 9 oClock Tomorrow Morning.

WEDNESDAY 24 October 1781.

The Hon[ble] Peter Olcott & Joseph Bowker Esquires were appointed to join a Committee from the Assembly to take into Consideration the fees of the Superiour Court.

Adjourned to 2 oClock afternoon.

Met according to adjournment.

The Hon[ble] Jonas Fay Esq[r.] was appointed to join a Committee from the Assembly to take into Consideration the petition of Col[o.] Samuel Fairbanks.[2]

---

[1] Mooretown, now Bradford. This town was originally "laid out to himself and some others associated with him," by Sir Henry Moore, Governor of New York. May 3, 1770, says HILAND HALL, it was patented to Hon. William Smith of New York, judge and historian. A committee appointed on this subject by the General Assembly, reported in 1781, "That in the year 1770 said township was pattented by the then Gov[r.] of New York *to Sir Henry Moore's heirs*, whose agent, William Smith Esq[r.] of New York, in said Heirs behalf, conveyed to Samuel Sleeper Esq[r.] agent from [for] the Inhabitants of said town, three thousand acres," &c. Evidently the town was originally named for Gov. Moore. See *Vt. Hist. Soc. Collections*, Vol. I, p. 154; H. Hall's *Early History*, pp. 93–95; and Manuscript *Assembly Journal*, 1781–1785, p. 28.

[2] SAMUEL FAIRBANKS seems to have been a resident of that part of New York called the Western District of Vermont at that time. He

The Honorable Timothy Brownson, Esqr. was appointed to attend the House to propose a bill in amendment to one passed the Assembly yesterday for Laying a Tax of sixpence on the pound.[1]

Adjourned to 9 oClock Tomorrow Morning.

THURSDAY October 25th 1781.

Met according to Adjournment.

A bill was drawn to enable the Several towns within the State to Levy a Land Tax for the purpose of building meeting houses, School houses, and Bridges, which was laid before the General Assembly for their Consideration.[2]

Resolved that Noah Sabin Esqr. be and he is hereby appointed Judge of Probate in the district of Westminster,

And that Samuel Knights be and he is hereby appointed a justice of the peace within and for the County of Windham.

Attest, THOMAS TOLMAN, *Dep. Secy.*

The following is a Copy of a Resolution & Grant made by the General Assembly to Colo. Wm. Barton vizt—

STATE OF VERMONT. IN GENERAL ASSEMBLY, October 23, 1781.

Resolved that there be and hereby is Granted unto Colonel William Barton and Company, being sixty-five in number, a Township of Land by the name of *Providence*, and that the Surveyor General be and he is hereby directed to Survey to the said Colo. Barton and Company as soon as may be said Township to contain the quantity of six miles square, upon the unappropriated Lands Lying near to Lake Memphremagog, and the Governor and Council be and are hereby requested, as soon as the return of the Surveyor General be made as aforesaid, to make out a Charter of Incorporation to the said Colonel Barton and Company of said Township under such restrictions and reservations and for such fees as they shall judge proper.

Resolved that this Assembly having the highest sense of the Merit of Colonel William Barton as an active, Brave and Intrepped officer in the

---

was a private in Col. Van Rensselaer's New York regiment, but had been commissioned by Vermont as lieutenant colonel. He was arrested with others at Lansingburgh, early in October 1781, by Col. Van Rensselear, but made his escape, collected a body of men (or rather of Col. V. R.'s prisoners who escaped with Fairbanks,) and successfully resisted an attempt at their re-arrest, wounding two of the New York soldiers. —See *Vt. Hist. Soc. Collections*, Vol. II, pp. 184, 188. The petition referred to above was for a grant of confiscated land, which was for the time being refused.

[1] The bill was entitled "An act for raising sixpence on the poles and rateable estate," &c., and the Council preposed to substitute the words "An act for raising sixpence on the pound," &c. The Assembly record is that the amended act "was read and after some debate the act as it was passed yesterday was again read and passed into a Law." This was an effective way, if not a courteous one, of rejecting the amendment proposed by the Council. However, on the next day the bill was amended at the suggestion of Ira Allen, and then committed for further amendment.

[2] For this act see Slade's *State Papers*, p. 440.

Army of the United States, do Grant him two of said Rights in s[d] Township free of all expence.

Extract from the Journals, ROS[L] HOPKINS, *Clerk.*

STATE OF VERMONT. IN GENERAL ASSEMBLY, October 25 1781.

Colonel William Barton [1] made a verbal request to this house that they would reconsider the resolution granting him two rights free from fees in the Township of Providence as Granted to him and Company the 23d instant, which was accordingly reconsidered.

Extract from the Journals, ROSWELL HOPKINS, *Clerk.*

Copy Examined, THOMAS TOLMAN, *Dep. Sec[y].*

The Hon[ble] Ira Allen & Benjamin Emmons were appointed from the Council to join a Committee from the House to examine whether any lands are in a Situation to be Granted at the present Session of Assembly and to whom.

An Act of Assembly for Repealing all Laws prohibiting the trial of the Title of Lands &c. was laid before the Council. [2]

FRIDAY 26 October 1781.

Met according to Adjournment.

STATE OF VERMONT. IN GENERAL ASSEMBLY October 26 1781.

Resolved that this house will proceed to choose by Ballot a Committee of three to burn the bills of Credit of this State agreable to an Act

---

[1] Gen. WILLIAM BARTON was born in Providence, R. I., in 1747, and died there Oct. 22, 1831. July 10, 1777, as Lieut. Col. in the Rhode Island militia, he with a small party crossed Narragansett Bay, passing three British frigates, landed between Newport and Bristol ferry, and captured the British Brigadier, afterwards Lieut. General, Richard Prescott. For this service Congress honored Barton with the presentation of a sword and a commission as Colonel. His biographer, Mrs. C. M. WILLIAMS, adds that a grant of land to him in Vermont was made *by Cougress*, which is an error. In dealing with this land Gen. Barton became entangled in the law, was imprisoned many years in Vermont for debt, and until his release in 1825 by the generosity of the Marquis de LAFAYETTE on his visit to the state. Col. Barton was wounded in action in Aug. 1778 and disabled from further service. The name of the town was originally given from the Colonel's birth-place, but was changed to *Barton* in his honor. The title of General was probably conferred upon him in the militia service.—See *Life of*, by Mrs. C. M. Williams, 1839; and Drake's *Dictionary of American Biography.*

[2] The trial of land-titles was forbidden in February 1779, and the act was repeated in October 1780. In October 1781 the first "Betterment Act" was passed and at the same time the previous prohibitory acts were repealed. Again in 1783 and 1784 the trial of land-titles was prohibited, and this prohibition continued until the enactment of the second "Betterment Act" in October 1785.—See Slade's *State Papers*, pp. 388, 405, 442, 488, 494, 500.

passed this day. The Ballot being taken, the Hon[ble] Timothy Brownson, John Fassett [jr.] Esq[rs.] and Captain Mathew Lyon were elected.[1]

Extract from the journals, ROSWELL HOPKINS, *Clerk.*

True Copy, Examined, Attest, THOMAS TOLMAN, *D. Sec[y.]*

Adjourned until 2 oClock Afternoon.

Met according to Adjournment.

Resolved that the paymaster deliver £200 to Captain Luther Richardson taking his receipt for the same, he the said Richardson being accountable to deliver the Same to Captain Ward Bayley and the Officers and Soldiers of his Company at *Upper Cohos*, (being three months wages for said Company nearly,) and return proper accounts thereof to the said pay Master within two months from the date hereof.[2]

Attest, THOMAS TOLMAN, *D. Sec[y.]*

Hon[ble] Joseph Bowker Esquire moved for a dismission from Council during the present Session, which [was] accordingly Granted.

The Governor and Council was requested to attend the House for the Election of a Judge of the Supreme Court in the room of the Hon[ble] Beza. Woodward Esq[r.] who declines serving. Attendance was accordingly Given and the Ballots being taken the Hon[ble] Simeon Olcott Esquire was elected.

A Resolution of the General Assembly was read reconsidering the Grant of *Brookfield* and ordered to lie on the table.

An Act of the General Assembly assertaining the fees of the Superiour Court was read and Concurred.

Recognizence of £10.000.

The Hon[ble] Timothy Brownson & John Fasset [jr.] and Captain Matthew Lyon appeared and acknowledged themselves jointly and severally Recognized to the Treasurer of this State in the penal Sum of Ten thousand pounds Lawful Money for the faithful performance of their duty as a Committee appointed by the Legislature of this State this day for burning and effectually destroying the bills of Credit of this State emitted or bearing date February 1781,[3] & took the Oath of Office required by Law.

£10.000. Attest, THOMAS TOLMAN, *D. Sec[y.]*

Adjourned to 9 oClock Tomorrow Morning.

---

[1] The bills destroyed were those redeemed by reception in payment for taxes.

[2] *Coos* signified *the pines*. Upper Coos was the region of pines on both sides of the Connecticut river near Lunenburgh, and Lower Coos was the region below the fifteen miles falls in the vicinity of Newbury. The Indian inhabitants were called *Coossucks.*—Rev. Dr. SILAS MCKEEN, in *Vt. Hist. Mag.*, Vol. II, p. 802. Captain, afterward Colonel, WARD BAYLEY commanded three posts in the upper Coos and was a very efficient officer. He resided first at Maidstone and then at Guildhall. Capt. LUTHER RICHARDSON was one of a committee to run the lines of Guildhall in 1783.—See *Vt. Hist. Mag.* Vol. I.

[3] The only act authorizing the emission of state bills of credit was passed in April 1781; hence it appears from the above entry, and also from a copy of one of the bills, that they were antedated, "February, 1781"—no particular day stated. For fac simile of a Vermont bill of credit, see Thompson's *Vermont*, Part II, p. 134.

SATURDAY 27 October 1781.

Met according to Adjournment.

A Commission was made out and Executed to the Honble Israel Smith Esqr. Judge of Probate for the district of Thetford County of Orange.[1]

A Committee from the House Waited on the Governor and Council to know if any further business was to be laid before the House before the rising of the Session.

The Honble Peter Olcott Esqr. moved for leave of Absence, which was Granted.

STATE OF VERMONT. IN GENERAL ASSEMBLY October 25 1781.

Resolved that there be and hereby is Granted unto Samuel Benton and Company twenty three in number Including the said Benton, a Gore or Tract of Land in the County of Rutland containing about 5000 Acres, bounded on the north on a Tract Granted to Abraham Jackson Esqr. & Company, East on Andover, South on a tract Granted to William Uttley & Company, West on Harwich [now Mount Tabor,] and that the Governor and Council be requested to make out a Charter to the said Samuel Benton and Company of said Tract under such regulations and reservations and for such fees as they shall think fit.[2]

Extract from the Journals, ROSWELL HOPKINS, *Clerk.*

IN COUNCIL Oct. 26, 1781.

Read & Concurred. Attest, THOMAS TOLMAN, *D. S.*

Resolved that the fees on each right of Land in the Township of *Providence*, Granted to Colonel William Barton and Company, be nine pounds hard money to be paid the first day of March next, Subject to such reservations and restrictions as has been heretofore usually made on lands granted on like circumstances, and that the fees on each right granted to Nathan Fisk Esqr. be nine pounds for each Right.

His Honor Elisha Payne Esquire Attended as Lieutenant Governor being duly qualified to that Office According to Law.

A Commission was made out for Noah Sabin Esqr. Judge of Probate for the district of Westminster.

Resolved that the Treasurer be and he is hereby directed to pay unto Edward Harriss Esqr. the Sum of five pounds in hard money, it being part of the Sum which he has expended in the Service of this State.

Attest, THOMAS TOLMAN, *D. Secy.*

STATE OF VERMONT. IN GENERAL ASSEMBLY, Oct. 27 1781.

On motion made to choose a Surveyor General the Ballots being taken the Honble Ira Allen was Elected.

---

[1] Judge ISRAEL SMITH settled in Thetford in 1766, and was an active man in town and county affairs and for national independence. He represented the town for many years in the Assembly, and held the offices of judge of probate, and county judge, having been first assistant judge from 1786 to 1793, and chief judge from 1793 to 1797. He held offices under New York from 1770 to 1777.—See *Eastern Vermont*, and *Vt. Hist. Mag.* Vol. II. Governor Israel Smith was another person.

[2] This grant seems to cover that part of Weston which lies north of Landgrove. Weston was formed from a part of the original Andover, with the addition, it seems, of this gore. SAMUEL BENTON was among the first settlers of Cornwall, and represented that town from 1787 to 1790 and in 1791.—See Deming's *Catalogue*.

On motion made to choose a Commissary General the Ballots being taken Joseph Farnsworth[1] was declared Elected.

Extract from the Journals, ROSL HOPKINS, *Clerk.*

Copy Examined. THOMAS TOLMAN, *D. Secy.*

An Act Reviving the Laws of this State was read and Concurred.

An Act empowering David Pulsifer to sell Lands belonging to David Pulsifer Decd. was read and Concurred.

An Act empowering Mary Whipple to sell part of the Real Estate of Daniel Whipple Esqr. Decd. was read & Concurred.

An Act to empower the Sale of the Real Estate of Jorden Blaklee Decd. was read and Concurred.

An Act for Abating to the Town of Guilford part of a Tax therein mentioned was read and Concurred.

An Act repealing an Act passed at the last Session of Assembly, Entitled an Act for forming the Eleventh Regiment, was read and Concurred.

CHARLESTON [Charlestown,] October 27, 1781.

At a meeting of the Members of Council and Assembly for the County of Winsor, they agree to Nominate Major Thomas Chandler [jr.] and General Peter Olcott Judges of that County Court to fill up the Vacancies therein—And Major Francis Smith, Mr. Daniel Heald, John Simons, George Harris of Canaan [N. H.] & Simon Stevens Justices of the peace for said County to be Commissioned by His Excellency the Governor in Council for that purpose for the time being.

Attest, A. CURTIS, *Clerk.*

Copy. Attest, Pr. THOMAS TOLMAN, *D. Secy.*

STATE OF VERMONT. IN GENERAL ASSEMBLY October 26 1781.

Resolved that there be and hereby is Granted unto Nathan Fisk Esqr. and Company being Sixty five in number a Township of Land containing Six Miles square in some of the unappropriated Lands in this State, And that the Surveyor General be and he is hereby [directed] to Survey said Township to the said Nathan Fisk, George Duncan and Company, as soon as may be, on some of the unappropriated lands aforesaid ; And the Governor & Council be and they are hereby requested as soon as the return of the Surveyor General be made as aforesaid to Make out a Charter of *Incorporation* of said Township to the said Nathan Fisk, George Duncan & Company equally under such Restrictions, Reservations and on such conditions as they shall judge best, Provided they pay the fees in Lead, Flints or hard money by the first of Feby. next.

Extract from the Journals, ROSL HOPKINS, *Clerk.*

Copy, Attest, THOMAS TOLMAN, *D. Secy.*

STATE OF VERMONT. IN GENERAL ASSEMBLY 26 Octr. 1781.

Resolved that there be & hereby is Granted unto Major Theodore

---

[1] Capt. JOSEPH FARNSWORTH resided in Middletown, Conn., in 1771, in which year his son, Hon. Joseph D. Farnsworth of Fairfax, was born. At the opening of the revolutionary war Capt. Farnsworth was appointed assistant commissary in the continental army, and in that capacity he was in Bennington in 1777, to which town he removed his family. His appointment above, as commissary for Vermont, indicates that he had retired from continental service.

Woodbridge[1] and Company, and unto Mr. Joseph Jones[2] and Company to the number of sixty five a Township of Land Containing Six Miles Square, in some of the unappropriated lands within this State—And the Surveyor General is hereby directed to Survey said Township to the said Major Woodbridge, Jones & Companies as soon as may be on some part of the unappropriated Lands aforesaid—And the Governor and Council are hereby requested as soon as the returns of the Surveyor General be made as aforesaid, to Make out a Charter of *Incorporation* of said Township to the said Woodbridge, Jones & Companies equally ; provided they pay the fees in *Lead*, *Flints* or *hard money*, under such restrictions, Reservations & upon such Conditions as they shall judge best.[3]

Extract from the Journals, ROSL HOPKINS, *Clerk*.
Attest, THOMAS TOLMAN, *D. Secy*

IN COUNCIL Feby 8 1782.[4]

Resolved that the Proprietors of the Township Granted to Major Woodbridge, Mr. Joseph Jones & Companies pay nine pounds Lawful Money for Each Right.

Attest, JOSEPH FAY, *Secy*.

STATE OF VERMONT. IN GENERAL ASSEMBLY October 26 1781.

Resolved that there be and hereby is Granted to the Moheakunnuck Tribe of Indians a Tract of Land adjoining to and bordering around Lake Shalloon[5] Six Miles Square & the Governor & Council are hereby

---

[1] THEODORE WOODBRIDGE of Rhode Island, Major in the continental service. He was in the list of officers entitled to half pay, &c., under the acts of Congress.—*Records of the Revolutionary War*, by W. T. R. Saffell, 1858.

[2] This could hardly be JOSEPH JONES, member of the Continental Congress from Virginia, though under certain conditions he was not unfriendly to the independence of Vermont. He however censured the course of Vermont in securing influence in the army and in Congress by her land grants.—See Letter of *Joseph Jones to Washington*, Feb. 27, 1783, in *Vt. Hist. Soc. Collections*, Vol. II, p. 326.

[3] A charter of a town named *Woodbridge* was subsequently executed, but the grantees failed to comply with the prescribed conditions, and the charter was given by Gov. Chittenden to Ira Allen, as security for the indebtedness of the State to Allen at the time. The full history of this affair belongs to the date of 1788–9, and here therefore it is sufficient to say, that Gov. Chittenden was at first condemned and failed of a re-election in September 1789, but when the facts were fully understood the confidence of the people was again restored to him.—See *Vt. Hist. Soc. Collections*, Vol. II, pp. 479–'80.

[4] This entry of subsequent action seems to have been made here to complete the record as to this grant. Another case like it occurred on the same day.

[5] This vote covered land in that part of New York which had been annexed to Vermont. The Indians were Mohegans, who formerly resided in Stockbridge, Mass., and afterward in New Stockbridge, N. Y. After

Empowered and required to make out a Charter of *Incorporation* of said Tract as soon as the Limmits can be assertained, upon this *Condition* that said Tribe shall never have Authority to Aliene or Convey the whole or any part thereof to any person Whatever but those of their own Tribe, & such other restrictions & Limitations as they shall Judge proper. Extract from the Journals, R. HOPKINS, *Clerk.*

[Copy. Attest,] THOS. TOLMAN, *D. Secy.*

The following is a resolution of the General Assembly—

Whereas it appears to this Assembly that there was some irregularity with regard to the last choice of Field officers in the 3d Regiment, Wherefore

Resolved that it be and it is hereby recommended to the Captain General to order the Brigadier General of third Brigade to call on & Lead the 3d Regiment to a choice of such Field officers as were wanting to compleat the said third Regiment before the last choice, and make returns to the Capt. Genl of the officers chosen in order to their being Commissioned.

STATE OF VERMONT. IN GENERAL ASSEMBLY October 27 1781.

The above was read and passed into a resolution of this House.

Attest, ROSWELL HOPKINS, *Clerk.*

Copy, Attest, THOMAS TOLMAN, *D. Secy.*

Resolved that the Honble Paul Spooner and John Throop Esquires be and hereby are directed on application and at the expence of Messrs. Daniel Tilleston and John Payne, to Examine into the Circumstances of the settlers of the town of Brookfield, to determine whether any Mistakes are made in the return of settlers of said Town, to correct such Mistake if any there be. The persons whose rights shall be in dispute being first notified by said Tilleston & Payne to appear at the time of such examination in support of their respective Claims.

FEBY 9 1782.

Voted that Honble Joseph Bowker Esqr. to be one of the above Committee in Lieu of John Throop Esqr.

Adjourned until 9 oClock Tomorrow.[1]

---

the dissolution of the Western Union in 1782, another grant of land was voted to them, to be contiguous to the small lakes or ponds southward of Lake Memphremagog. In fact the grant covered the town of Marshfield.

The following account of the Indians above named is in Hoyt's *Indian Wars*, the author referring to *Massachusetts Hist. Collections*, Vol. IX, p. 99—old series:

To the west of Connecticut river, extending a short distance west of the Hudson, and into the present state of Vermont, was a nation called Mohicans, or Muhheakunnucks; their chief seat was at Albany, [N. Y.,] called by them Pempotawuthut, or the place of fire; the Stockbridge tribe belonged to this nation. Muhhaakunnuck in their language is said to signify a great water, or sea, that is constantly in motion, either flowing or ebbing; and these Indians state that they came from a country far to the west, where they lived in towns, by the side of a great water or sea; and were very numerous until compelled to scatter by reason of a great famine.

[1] From the *Assembly Journal*, Oct. 27, 1781:

Resolved that His Excellency the Governor's Sallary for the present year be two hundred pounds.

According to the minute of adjournment last entered on the journal, the following proceedings should be dated Sunday, Oct. 28 1781, but no date is recorded:

Resolved that the Granting fees of the Township of Land granted to Major Theodore Woodbridge, Joseph Jones and Companies be the sum of nine pounds each right to be paid on the 20th day of March next. The reservation will be the same as in Grants of Land heretofore made under similar Circumstances, and will be entered in the Charter of Incorporation of said Township. Attest, THOMAS TOLMAN, *D. Secy.*

Resolved that there be 1000 Copies [printed] of the Report of the Grand Committee at the Session held in Charleston this present Instant October, and that the same be promulgated for the Information of the Inhabitants of this and the United States in General.[1]

Resolved that *Henry Silsby* be and he is hereby appointed a Justice of the Peace in the County of Washington [in New Hampshire] for the time being & the register of said County is hereby directed to enter his name in the Commission of the Justices of said County.

This Council is adjourned to the last Wednesday in January next then to meet at Bennington.

THE END OF CHARLESTON SESSION.

The General Assembly closed its session on Saturday the 27th, but many of the members were in Charlestown on the 28th, when very exciting intelligence was received. Ira Allen thus described the scene :

In October, 1781, the Legislature met at Charlestown, in the East Unions, when the Government of New Hampshire sent a Major Reynolds, with two hundred men, as was supposed, to stop the election and session of the Legislature ; the friends of Vermont advised the Major, if he had any instructions from New Hampshire, which were hostile to Vermont and the East Union, that it would be for the sake of humanity adviseable for him to keep them to himself, as his force would not avail : this he prudently did, and the Assembly convened and proceeded to business without opposition. In the mean time, General St. Leger, at the head of the British army from Canada, ascended the Lake Champlain, and rested at Ticondaroga ; while General Enos had the command of the troops of Vermont on the frontiers, and his headquarters at Cas-

---

Resolved that Colo. Payne be and is hereby requested to inform this House whether he will accept of his Election to the office of Deputy Govr. of this State.

Colo. Payne informed the House that he would accept that office.

Resolved that his honor the Deputy Govr. have fifty pounds for his Sallary for the present year.

The Committee appointed to prepare Instructions for the Board of War for the year ensuing Made a verbal Report—Whereupon,

Resolved that the powers and Instructions heretofore given the Board of War be and they are hereby considered as their powers and instructions till the next Session of Assembly.

Resolved that the additional Sum of fifty pounds be granted unto his Excellency the Governor for his extraordinary services the year past.

[1]This was the official account of the action of Vermont on the resolutions of Congress adopted in August 1781. It is copied from the journal of Congress in *Appendix H, post.*

10

tleton; the General, and a number of officers under him, were fully acquainted with the negociations with the British in Canada, in particular Colonels Fletcher and Walbridge. Notwithstanding, it became necessary to keep up appearances, by sending frequently small scouts to Champlain to observe the movements of the enemy. One of these scouts fell in with a party of General St. Leger's; some shots were exchanged; Serjeant Tupper, who commanded the scout from Vermont, was killed on the spot, and his men retreated: the body was decently buried, and General St. Leger sent all his cloaths, with an open letter, to General Enos, informing him of his regret for the fate of the sergeant, and made an apology for his death. Perhaps this was done to try the spirit and disposition of the inhabitants, previous to the publication of the proclamation as conceded to at Skeensborough the September before. The dispatch and apparel were publicly delivered to General Enos, which made considerable noise among the troops: many of them were not acquainted with the subject of the negociation and armistice; and some that were, had no objection to raise difficulties, in hopes of gaining popularity.

Generals Enos, Colonels Fletcher and Walbridge, wrote letters, and sent immediately an express to Governor Chittenden at Charlestown, announcing the arrival at Ticondaroga of the British army; wherein they blended public matters and private negociation; Mr. Hathaway, the messenger, not being in the secret, failed not to proclaim the extraordinary message of General St. Leger through the streets of Charlestown, till he came to the Governor, which happened in the recess of the Legislature, and occasioned crowds of people to follow, to hear the news; the Governor and others were sitting in a large room; amongst whom were some persons that were eager to learn the negociations that were generally supposed to be carried on between the British in Canada and Vermont, to make an ill use thereof. The Governor opened one of the letters; he thought it prudent to peruse it himself before he allowed it to be publicly read. These letters were found to contain both public and private information, which occasioned some change of letters between the Governor, Messrs. Brownson and Fassett, who were in the secret, and next to the Governor. In this confused moment, Major Runnals came in, and enquired of Colonel Ira Allen what was the reason that General St. Leger was sorry that Sergeant Tupper was killed? Mr. Allen said that he could not tell. Mr. Runnals repeated the question; and Mr. Allen observed, that good men were sorry when good men were killed, or met with misfortune, which might be the case with General St. Leger. This answer enraged Mr. Runnals; and he again loudly enquired what reasons could possibly induce a British General to be sorry when his enemies were killed, and to send his cloaths to the widow? Colonel Allen then requested Major Runnals to go at the head of his regiment, and demand the reasons of his sorrow, and not stay there asking impertinent questions, eating up the country's provisions, doing nothing when the frontiers were invaded. Very high words passed between the Major and Colonel Allen, till Mr. Runnals left the room. This manœuvre drew all the attention from said letters; it was then proposed that the Board of War should be convened; and the Governor then summoned the members of the Board of War to appear as soon as possible in his chamber, leaving Mr. Hathaway to detail the news to the populace, the Board of War being all in the secret. New letters were made out from General Enos, Colonels Fletcher and Walbridge's letters, and, for the information and satisfaction of the public, read in council and assembly for the originals, and then returned to the Governor. Those letters contained every thing but the existing negociations which prudence and policy dictated to be separated from the other part of said letters.

In the mean time, Colonel Allen and Major Fay wrote to the British Commissioners, who were with General St. Leger, on the subject of their former negociations, in which they gave a list of the names of the members of the Legislature, with marks, denoting the new members, from which the change appeared great. They suggested the capture of Lord Cornwallis and his army, and added that, whether true or not, it had the same effect upon the people, who soon hoped for better news. In this critical situation, they thought it improper to publish the proposed proclamation, as several changes and circumstances seemed to presage more happy events, that should soon make all right. The packet containing Colonel Allen and Major Fay's letter was delivered at Ticondaroga about ten o'clock in the morning. About an hour after, an express arrived from the southward, which was supposed to contain the news of the capture of Lord Cornwallis and his army; for before evening, the troops, stores, &c. were embarked, and with a fair wind returned to Canada. Thus ended the campaign of 1781, with the accidental loss of only one man, on the extensive frontiers of Vermont, exposed to an army of ten thousand men; yet she did not incur any considerable debt. Such were the happy effects of these negociations.—Ira Allen's *History*, in *Vt. Hist. Soc.* Collections, Vol. II, pp. 436–438.

The negotiations referred to were with Gen. Haldimand; and the purpose of the proclamation was to declare Vermont to be a British province.—See *Vt. Hist. Soc. Collections*, Vol. II. Daniel Chipman stated that the expurgated copies of the letters above referred to, were prepared by Nathaniel Chipman.—See *Life of Chipman*, p. 38.

RECORD OF THE GOVERNOR AND COUNCIL

IN

NOVEMBER AND DECEMBER 1781 AND JANUARY 1782

STATE OF VERMONT. IN COUNCIL Arlington 14 November 1781.[1]

Resolved that Doctor John Page be & he is hereby remitted one fourth part of the Debt due from him to Colonel William Marsh on account of his debts being contracted in Continental Money.

STATE OF VERMONT. IN COUNCIL Arlington 21 Novr. 1781.

An order was Issued to the Treasurer to pay M^r. Samuel Sherman Postrider the sum of £10. 10. 0 for his services to the State agreable to resolve of Council of June last.

---

[1] On this day, doubtless on the approval of the Council, Gov. Chittenden wrote to Gen. Washington on the condition of the State and the correspondence with Gen. Haldimand.—See *Appendix H.*

STATE OF VERMONT. IN COUNCIL Bennington 19 December 1781.

Whereas Col^o. Nathaniel Brush[1] who was appointed by the Legislature of this State one of the Committee of pay table, declines serving in that capacity, and Whereas Colonel Timothy Brownson who was likewise appointed for that purpose is at this time Absent,[2] And Whereas it is absolutely Necessary that other persons should be appointed in their Stead—

I do therefore by & with the advice of a number of my Council appoint Amos Fassett and Noah Chittenden to Act in that Office until Col^o. Brownson shall return and Attend said business or until this order shall be revoked in due form.[3]

Signed THOMAS CHITTENDEN, *Governor.*

Copy Examined, THOMAS TOLMAN, *D. Sec^y.*

STATE OF VERMONT. IN COUNCIL Arlington 10 January 1782.

Resolved that the Honble Elisha Payne, Jonas Fay and Ira Allen Esquires & Abel Curtis[4] Esqr. be and they are hereby appointed Agents to repair to the Honble the Congress of the United States and in behalf of this State to Solicit Congress to Recognize the Independence thereof. And further to use their best endeavours with that honorable body that some equitable mode be prescribed for an Amicable Settlement of the boundary lines between this and the Claiming States. That either two or more of said Agents are empowered to proceed to business.

By order of the Governor and Council,

THOMAS TOLMAN, *D. Sec^y.*

Whereas Colonel Ira Allen had a Township of Land Granted to himself and associates by the General Assembly at their Session in February 1781 and it appears by said Grant that said Allen had leave to Lay said Township in any Vacant Lands in Good Form which he proposed to lay on a point of Land situate between Missisque Bay and the Main

---

[1] Col. NATHANIEL BRUSH came to Bennington about 1775; he commanded the militia of that town in the battle of Bennington; served as judge of probate in 1781 and from 1787 to 1794, and as clerk of the courts from 1787 to 1803.—See *Vt. Hist. Mag.*, Vol. I; *Memorials of a Century, Bennington;* and Deming's *Catalogue.*

[2] Col. Brownson was absent, bearing the letter of Gov. Chittenden of Nov. 14 1781 to Gen. Washington.

[3] AMOS FASSETT was a son of Deacon John Fassett of Bennington, and brother of Hon. John Fassett jr. He removed to Cambridge in 1784 (with Noah Chittenden,) and was assistant judge for several years. NOAH CHITTENDEN was the oldest son of the Governor, a resident of Cambridge and afterward of Jericho, and a prominent and valuable man, holding several important offices. He married a daughter of John Fassett, and a daughter by this marriage became the wife of Governor Galusha.—See *Memorials of a Century, Bennington; Vt. Hist. Mag.*, Vol. I, and II; and Deming's *Catalogue.*

[4] ABEL CURTIS resided in Norwich, was member of the Assembly in Oct. 1778 and in 1781 and 1782; and judge of Windsor county court in 1782 and 1783.—See Deming's *Catalogue.*

Lake Champlain, and Whereas it appears by his representation there is some reason to Apprehend that said Land has been before Granted, which induces him to make a new pitch for said Township, and as no Charter has yet been given him,

Resolved that in case the said Colonel Ira Allen make a Repitch of said Township in some of the Vacant Lands south of the Province of Quebec (Lat. 45° north,) East of Land heretofore Granted North of Onion River and West of Connecticut river, the Granting fees be nine pounds on Each right there being sixty-five rights in said Township.

Attest, THOMAS TOLMAN, *D. Secy.*

Adjourned to 8 oClock Tomorrow.

JANUARY 11th 1782.

Met according to Adjournment.

Resolved that the Charter or rather the Granting fees for the Gore of Land Granted to Samuel Benton and others be £5. 0. 0. pr right and that the time of payment be the first day of March next.

Resolved that his honor Elisha Payne Esquire Lt. Governor, Bezaleel Woodward Esqr., General Ethan Allen, John Fassett [jr.] Esquire and Colo. Matthew Lyon be and they are hereby appointed to make a Draught of the Political affairs of this State to be published.[1]

Attest, THOMAS TOLMAN, *Dep. Secy.*

Resolved that Captain Samuel Bartlett be and he is hereby appointed a member of the Committee of Pay Table to Act in that office until the rising of the next Session of the General Assembly of this State.

Attest, THOMAS TOLMAN, *D. Secy.*

[ENTRY ON THE JOURNAL BY SECRETARY FAY.]

Sundry proceedings of Council of which (Mr. Tolman's) Minutes were taken on loose papers the book not being present, are not to be found, which ought to be recorded in this place.

Attest, JOS. FAY.

WAR WITH VERMONT PROPOSED BY NEW HAMPSHIRE AND ATTEMPTED BY NEW YORK.

The missing records alluded to above contained proceedings of the Governor and Council at one of the most critical and important periods in the history of the State, when, at the same time, war was contemplated and prepared for by New Hampshire, on the one side, but was avoided by the adroitness of Ira Allen and the firmness of Gov. Chittenden and Lieut. Gov. Payne; and actually attempted by New York, on the other side, but was defeated by an overpowering force of the militia of the "Western District," so called, and from Vermont proper.—See *Appendix H.*

---

[1] A pamphlet entitled "*The Present State of the Controversy,*" &c., was the result, for which see *Appendix H.*

PROCEEDINGS OF THE GOVERNOR AND COUNCIL

AT AN

ADJOURNED SESSION WITH THE GENERAL ASSEMBLY,

JANUARY AND FEBRUARY 1782.

STATE OF VERMONT. IN COUNCIL, Bennington 31[t] January 1782.

Agreeable to Adjournment of His Excellency the Governor and his honorable Council to this day, His Excellency and Sundry Members of Council met at this place, and as a quorum of the Council were not present His Excellency and those of his Council present continued by adjournments until the 4th day of February 1782 at which time a quorum appeared consisting of the following Members viz[t]—

Hon[l] Joseph Bowker,	John Fassett,
Timothy Brownson,	Sam[l] Fletcher &
Moses Robinson,	Benj[a.] Emmons.

Adjourned to 8 oClock Tomorrow.

TUESDAY 5 February 1782.

Council Met According to Adjournment and Adjourned to 9 oClock Tomorrow Morning.

WEDNESDAY 6 February 1782.

Council Met According to Adjournment & Adjourned to 2 oClock Afternoon to meet at Major Jos. Fay's.

Council Met According to Adjournment and Adjourned to 9 oClock Tomorrow.

THURSDAY 7 February 1782.

Council Met According to Adjournment.

His Excellency the Governor moved the Council for an order on the Treasurer for two years salary which is yet behind—Whereupon

Resolved to make out an order as follows—

BENNINGTON 7th February 1782.

Sir—You are hereby directed to pay to His Excellency Thomas Chittenden Esq[r.] four hundred pounds L. Money in silver for his Salary Granted him by the Vermont Assembly for the years 1780 and 1781.

P[r] Order of Council, JOS. FAY, *Sec[y.]*

Ira Allen Esq[r.] Treasurer.

Adjourned to 2 oClock P. M. then to meet at this place.

Met According to Adjournment and Adjourned to 9 oClock Tomorrow.

FRIDAY 8 February 1782.

Council Met According to Adjournment, at which time the papers relative to the dispute Subsisting Between the Grantees of Brookfield and Wickham proprietors was read [and] ordered to be lodged on the files.

Adjourned to 2 oClock P. M. then to meet at Major Joseph Fay's.

Met According to Adjournment.

Having made a determination relative to the dispute between the proprietors of Brookfield and Wickham,[1] Resolved as follows, viz[t]

Whereas M[r.] Phinehas Lyman and his associates in October 1779 [Nov. 6, 1780,] Obtained a Grant of a Township of Land in this State by the name of Brookfield,

And Whereas a Matter of dispute arose between Colonel Israel Williams, Israel Williams Jun[r.] & M[r.] Pattridge [2] who Claim to be Associated with M[r.] Lyman in the aforesaid Grant, and have paid money therefor,

And Whereas the Governor recommended to them and Each of them to settle the matter in dispute by submitting it to Arbitrators Mutually chosen, and as it appears that they have not agreed upon a submission as aforesaid but each party chusing to submit the matter in dispute to the Governor and Council of this State—M[r.] Lyman appearing and Mess[rs.] Williams & Pattridge not appearing altho notified, this Council having heard the evidence and agreements that were exhibited on both Parties—

It is the opinion of this Council, that as Colonel Israel Williams, Israel Williams Jun[r.] and M[r.] Patridge did not choose to be Adventurers with M[r.] Lyman in Soliciting said Grant until almost one year after the Grant was made, they therefore cannot be considered as Grantees without the permission of Lyman, And as said Money was rec[d] through mistake it ought to be returned.

Attest, JOSEPH FAY, *Sec[y.]*

Resolved that the Proprietors of Moortown [Bradford,] sixty five in number pay for each acre [right ?] nine pounds L. Money in silver.

Adjourned to 9 oClock Tomorrow & Adjourned to 2 oClock P. M. and Continued the Adjournment to one oClock Monday next.

MONDAY 11th February 1782.

Council Met According to Adjournment, and being informed that the General Assembly had formed a house His Excellency and Council laid before the house a Letter from His Excellency General Washington, one from General Wolcott, and sundry other letters of a public nature which was publicly read after which the Governor and Council returned to Mr. Robinson's.[3]

---

[1] "Wickham" is a mystery the editor cannot solve. All the parties in this contest seem to have been claimants to Brookfield.

[2] Probably Col. Israel Williams and Samuel Patridge of Hatfield, Mass.—See B. H. Hall's *Eastern Vermont.*

[3] Undoubtedly the most important letters were those named above.—For letter of Gen. Washington see *Appendix H.* Gen. Wolcott's letter must have been of like tenor, and written with a knowledge of Washington's views. Both letters were written in Philadelphia, Washington's on the 1st and Wolcott's on the 18th of January 1782. OLIVER WOLCOTT, son of Gov. Roger Wolcott, was born at Windsor, Conn., Nov. 26, 1726, and graduated at Yale in 1746; served as a captain in the French war, and commissioner of Indian affairs in 1775; was member of the continental Congress and signer of the Declaration of Independence in 1776, colonel in active service under Gates, participating in the capture of Burgoyne, and for his services on that occasion was made

A bill from the House being rec[d] and read appointing a Committee to arrange the present business of this Session, Resolved that the Hon[ble] Moses Robinson Esq[r.] join said Committee and make report.[1]

---

brigadier general on the field. He was lieutenant governor of Connecticut from 1786 to 1796, and governor in 1796-7. He died in Litchfield Dec. 1, 1797.—See *Blake's* and *Drake's Biographical Dictionaries.* For the purity of his character, the value of his services, and his friendship for Vermont, Oliver Wolcott probably ranked next to Washington in the esteem of the leading Vermonters in his day. Chief Justice SAMUEL CHURCH, of Litchfield, Conn., in his address at the Centennial Jubilee at Salisbury Conn., in 1841, declared that the policy of Vermont, in the Haldimand Correspondence and the Eastern and Western Unions, was shaped at a council of the friends of Vermont in Litchfield county, held at the house of Oliver Wolcott. The statement, as quoted in John M. Weeks's *History of Salisbury, Vt.*, p. 216, was as follows:

The spirit of emigration, that same Anglo-Saxon temperament which brought our ancestors into the country, and which constantly pushes forward to the trial of unknown fortune, began its manifestations before the revolution, and sought its gratification first in Vermont. Vermont is the child of Litchfield county. We gave to her her first governor, and three governors [Thomas and Martin Chittenden, and Skinner;] beside as many as three senators in Congress, [Chipman, Seymour, and Phelps,] and also many of her most efficient founders and early distinguished citizens, Chittendens, Allens, Galushas, Chipmans, Skinner and others. The attitude assumed by Vermont in the early stages of the revolutionary war, in respect to Canada on the north, and the threatening states of New York and New Hampshire on either side, was peculiar and delicate, and demanded the most adroit policy to secure her purpose of independence. In her dilemma, her most sagacious men resorted to the councils of her old friends of Litchfield county, and it is said that her final course was shaped, and her designs accomplished, by the advice of a confidential council, assembled at the house of Governor Wolcott, in the village of Litchfield.

Accompanying the letters of Washington and Wolcott were several relating to the collisions in New Hampshire and New York, together with copies of Gov. Chittenden's letters and orders in reply. The most important of these, so far as preserved, are given in the appropriate places.—See *Appendix H.*

[1] This custom in the early history of Vermont legislatures, substantially supplied the place of the modern executive message. On this occasion the budget so fully showed the gravity and dignity of state legislation at that time as to deserve notice. The report of the committee was as follows:

The Committee appointed to arrange the most necessary business brought in the following Report, viz—

1[st.] To call upon his Excellency the Gov[r.] and his Council to lay before the House all official papers relating to the Interest of this State received since the Session in Oct. last.

2[d.] To call upon the Commiss[rs] appointed by the Legislature to treat

The Committee to whom was referred the petition of John Payne and Joseph Fisk, relating to a right of land in Brookfield [made a report] which is as follows vizt—

BENNINGTON 11 February 1782.

To His Excellency the Governor and the Council of the State of Vermont —Your Committee appointed to rectify any Mistakes that might heretofore have been made in the return of the Actual settlers in the Township of Brookfield within this State Beg Leave to report further that the Names of Jedediah Hyde, Amasa Hide and Ichabod Hide, remain as formerly, their Agent obliging himself in behalf of himself and constituents to Exchange their Obligations for Lands in said Brookfield which they hold against M$^{r.}$ Nubal Cross,[1] for the Obligations said Cross has Against said Hyde and his constituents for said Lands, at the request of M$^{r.}$ Cross.

Your Committee further report that Paul Spooner Esq$^{r.}$ have his name inserted in the Grant of the Township of Brookfield in the room of Noah or John Payne 3^{d} he engaging to convey a deed to John Payne 3^{d} if it shall appear on trial that the whole of said right properly belongs to him, or said Payne 3^{d} and said Noah Payne in partnership if on tryal it shall appear just that the aforesaid right should be so given, the Tryal to be had before John Throop & Paul Spooner Esquires on the application of either John Payne 3^{d} or Noah Payne and that the opposite party be duly cited to appear at time and place Agreed on, to be held at the expence of the party applying.

---

with Commiss^{rs} to be appointed by New-York and New-Hampshire relative to the boundary lines of this State to make their Report.

3$^{d.}$ To call upon the Committee for Revising the Laws.

4$^{th.}$ To call upon the Auditors of accounts for their Report.

5$^{th.}$ To adopt proper measures for the defence of this State against the common Enemy, &c.

6$^{th.}$ That the Surveyor Gen$^{l.}$ be called upon to lay before the House a survey of the State, as far as he has obtained it, as also a plan of all the townships granted and the vacant lands ungranted.

7$^{th.}$ To call upon the Treasurer to give an account of what paper money has been received into the Treasury since Oct$^{r.}$ last and how it has been disposed of.

8$^{th.}$ To lay before the Honble the Cont$^{l.}$ Congress in a decent and spirited manner our determination to Support our just Rights, and repeat our desire to be admitted into the federal Union.

9$^{th.}$ That a proper Check be put upon the Treasurer to enable the Auditors to adjust his accounts.

10$^{th.}$ To make provision for the payment of the Soldiers in the State's service in the last Campaign.

11$^{th.}$ To take under consideration the paper currency.

12$^{th.}$ To take proper measures to regulate the press.

MOSES ROBINSON, *Chairman.*

The last item was not legislation on the liberty of the newspaper press, there being no newspaper at that date, but to revive the then suspended newspaper at Westminster, or provide for the removal of the printing materials and the establishment of a newspaper at Bennington. This project resulted in the establishment, in the next year, of two newspapers, one at Bennington and the other at Windsor.—See *ante* pp. 12-13, note; and *post*, under date of March 1 1782.

[1] Shubael Cross in Brookfield charter.

Your Committee further report that the name of Ebenezer Brewster be inserted in s[d] Charter of Brookfield in the room of Joseph Fisk, he [Brewster] obliging himself to convey a deed of said right to Joseph Fisk or John Payne, or both in Partnership, as shall be determined on a fair hearing of said Fisk and Payne before Paul Spooner and John Throop Esquires and Transmitted to Ebenezer Brewster by said Throop and Spooner.

PAUL SPOONER, } *Committee.*
JOSEPH BOWKER, }

Copy Examined. Attest, JOSEPH FAY, *Sec[y.]*

Adjourned to 9 oClock Tomorrow Morning.

TUESDAY 12th February 1782.

Council Met According to Adjournment

And Adjourned to 2 oClock P. M.

Council Met according to Adjournment at which time His Honor Elisha Payne Esquire L[t.] Governor & the Hon. Peter Olcott Esq[r.] joined the Council and took their Seats.

Adjourned to 9 oClock Tomorrow Morning.

WEDNESDAY, 13 February 1782.

Council met According to Adjournment and Agreable to the Order of Yesterday joined the General Assembly and proceeded to the choice of a Judge of the Superior Court.[1] The ballots being taken the Hon[ble] Samuel Fletcher Esq[r.] was elected who declined serving in that office, whereupon the House [joint assembly] agreed to postpone the further Election for the present. Col[o.] Nathaniel Brush being appointed in October last one of the Committee of Pay table & having made his resignation was requested by the Governor, Council, and Assembly to attend and inform the house of the reasons why he did not serve in that Office, who appeared and upon the request of the House Agreed to Accept and Serve in that Office.

Adjourned to 2 oClock P. M.

Met according to Adjournment, His honor Governor Payne in the Chair.

Two petitions of the Inhabitants of Pownal was read, one praying for some mode to be pointed out to oblige the Town of Pownal to maintain and keep in repair the dug way in said Pownal, and one for building a Bridge over Hoosack River. A Committee from the Assembly being appointed to join a Committee from the Council and make report; Members chosen the Hon[ble] Joseph Bowker and Samuel Fletcher Esquires [to join from the Council.]

An Act of Assembly confirming to the Heirs of [James] Watkings late of Townsend Deceased certain Lands therein contained was read, whereupon Moses Robinson Esquire was requested to return with said

---

[1] No such order appears on the journal of either house. One of the letters presented to the Assembly on the 11th was from Hon. Simeon Olcott, dated Jan. 28 1782. and doubtless it was his resignation of the office of judge. The Assembly record of the 13th is that both houses met to elect a judge "in the room of Simeon Olcott Esq[r.] resigned."

Act to the Assembly to Gain some Explanation, which [act he] delivered to the Clerk [of the Assembly.][1]

Adjourned to 9 oClock Tomorrow.

THURSDAY 14 February 1782.

Council Met According to Adjournment.

A bill from the House appointing a Committee to Look into the situation of the vacant Lands and to report what Lands can be granted and to whom being read, Voted the Honb[ls] P. Spooner and Samuel Fletcher to join said Committee.

Adjourned to 2 oClock P. M.

Met According to Adjournment.

An Act granting a new tryal in a Case depending between John Alger & Enoch and Eliphalet Bean &c. having passed the General Assembly was read and Concurred.[2]

An Act passed the General Assembly Granting a quantity of Land to be sold in Londonderry for the purpose of building two Bridges over West river in said town was read and passed the Council.

An Act for Creditting the Town of Hinsdil [Vernon,] being Over Rated, &c. having passed the General Assembly, was read & Concurred.

Adjourned to 9 oClock Tomorrow.

FRIDAY 15 Feb[y] 1782.

An Act to convey to Taylor Brooks the title of fifty Acres of Land in Brattleborough having passed the House was read & Concurred.

Having rec[d] & read a number of bills which was sent back to the house for Explanation,[3]

Adjourned to 2 oClock P. M. to meet at Maj[r] Joseph Fays.

Met According to Adjournment.

Voted the Hon[ble] Moses Robinson Esquire to join a Committee from the House to consider the petition of M[r.] Timothy Andrews [Andrus] & Elijah Hineman [Hinman] Agents for the Townships of Guildhall, Maidstone, &c.[4]

---

[1] From the *Assembly Journal* of the same date :

The Hon[ble] Moses Robinson Esq[r.] brought back the Act confirming a piece of Land unto Sarah Watkins and gave some Verbal reasons why the Council would not concur in passing said Act. After some debate—

The question was put—Whether they would reconsider said Act? It passed in the Negative.

[2] For act see Slade's *State Papers*, p. 444. The parties were among the early settlers of Strafford.

[3] There were two bills returned, both of which were reconsidered by the Assembly. One was the act pointing out the office and duty of the Secretary of State, for which see Slade's *State Papers*, p. 444.

[4] Items of an account of Timothy Andrus against "the townships of Guildhall granby and Eight townships to the Northward":

"Timothy Andrus, Elijah Hinman appointed agents to settel the dispute with Col[o.] [Jonathan] groute relative to gilhall and granby at the assembly of Vermont holden at benington Expence 5 weeks myself and hors 18—0—0 Joseph Wooster Expence at bennington while in Capt Elijah Hinman absents agread uppon by him self and audrus for him to serve in his rome. Expence at that time 9—5—0."—See *Vt. Hist. Mag.*, Vol. I, p. 999.

A Committee on the petition of Samuel Avery being appointed [by the Assembly] to join a Committee of Council on Captain Lovels Pay roll, The Honble Joseph Bowker Esqr. was voted to join said Committee from the House.[1]

Adjourned to 9 oClock Tomorrow morning.

SATURDAY 16 February 1782.

Council met according to Adjournment

And joined the Assembly to appoint a Judge of the Superiour Court. The Ballots being taken the Honble John Throop Esquire was Elected.[2]

A Bill from the House was read, Referring the consideration of the petition of William Cockburn and Archibald Campbell to the Committee appointed to Consider the petition of Samuel Avery, whereupon the Honble John Fassett was appointed in addition to the Committee of yesterday.[3]

An Act Granting to Major Gideon Brownson six hundred and sixty Dollars and $\frac{90}{100}$ as depreciation was read and Concurred, Also

An Act or Resolution of Assembly requesting the Committee of Pay table to Adjust Captain Brownson, Ebenezer Allen & [Benjamin] Hickock's[4] Pay rolls.

Attest, JOSEPH FAY, *Sec^y.^*

Adjourned to 2 °Clock P. M. Monday Next.

---

[1] Capt. NEHEMIAH LOVEWELL, a famous fighter, as were others in New Hampshire of his name before him—Capt. John, the hero of Pigwacket, and John's son Col. Zaccheus, who served under Amherst in the reduction of Ticonderoga and Crown Point in 1759. Capt. Nehemiah served in Vermont as captain in 1780, '81 and '82, his first Vermont company having been raised in February, 1780, "on the west side of Connecticut river." Lovewell was one of the grantees of Goshen, and a representative for Corinth in 1783. The pay-roll of Lovewell's company, and a large number of others, can be seen in the office of the Secretary of State. He married Betsey Hazelton, the first white person born in Newbury. Samuel Avery had no connection with Lovewell's pay-roll, the Assembly journal showing that the two papers were referred to distinct committees.

[2] "In the room of Saml Fletcher Esqr. who did not accept the appointment," in the Assembly journal. Mr. Fletcher had been elected in place of Simeon Olcott, of Charlestown, N. H., resigned.

[3] Avery, Cockburne, and Campbell were all proprietors of land in Vermont under New York—the two first named of a large quantity; and each of them received a portion of the $30,000 paid to New York by Vermont.

[4] BENJAMIN HICKOK was a delegate for Hubbardton in the Convention at Dorset July 24 1776. His name is given as *Hitchcock* in the list of delegates, Vol. I, p. 15; *Hickok* in the signatures to the Association, *ibid* p. 23; and the editor suggested *Benjamin Hitchcock* as the true name. But in Z. Thompson's *Vermont Gazetteer*, first edition, in the

MONDAY 18th Feby 1782.

Council Met According to Adjournment.

A Pay roll signed Fry [Frye, commonly—the true name said to be Trye] Bayley Capt. dated at Newbury 8th May 1781 for service done by a number of men under his Command in Scoutting on the frontiers of this State, being read, whereupon

Resolved that it be and hereby is Recommended to the Committee of Pay table to adjust and draw an order on the Treasurer for the payment of said Pay roll. Attest, JOSEPH FAY, Secy.

A resolve of the House for the payment of Captain Nehemiah Lovells [Lovewell's] pay Rolls for the officers and Soldiers of his Company on the West Side of Connecticut River raised in February 1780; was read and passed the Council. Attest, JOSEPH FAY, Secy.

A petition Signed Samuel Herrick and Benjamin Wait was read praying the General Assembly to make Good the Depreciation of their Wages for Service done in the year 1777. The House having appointed a Committee to join a Committee of Council, Voted the Honble Benjamin Emmons Esqr. to join said Committee.

Adjourned to 9 oClock Tomorrow Morning.

TUESDAY, 19th February 1782.

Council Met according to Adjournment

And Agreable to the order of the day, His Excellency the Governor, the Honble Council & General Assembly resolved themselves into a Committee of the whole to take into Consideration the several Letters recd from abroad vizt.—one from his Excellency General Washington & one from General Wolcott and sundry others, together with other papers which relate to the Independence of Vermont and the relinquishment of the Unions with this State.[1]

---

article on Hubbardton, p. 156, the name *Hickok* is given. In the Ms. *Assembly Journal*, Vol. 2, p. 69, the record is as follows:

Resolved that the Committee of Pay-Table be and they are hereby directed to adjust the accounts of Capt. Gideon Brownson, Capt. Ebenezer Allen and Capt. *Benjamin Hecock* for the Companies that were raised by them in 1776 *by order of the Convention of the New Hampshire Grants*, and to give orders on the Treasury for what shall be found due to the officers and soldiers of said Companies—Provided they give sufficient evidence to the Committee of Pay-Table that they have never been paid for their services from the United States.

It appears from the record of the Convention at Dorset, Sept. 25, 1776, that there were "several colonels on the west side of the Green Mountains," with companies organized and armed for service, who were subject first to the Committee of War, and ultimately to the Convention. See Vol. I, pp. 33–35. It is stated in the *Gazetteer* we have referred to, that Benjamin Hickok, with others, was taken prisoner at Hubbardton, July 6, 1777, by a "party of Indians and tories under a Captain [Justice] Sherwood." The inference from that account is that he was released, while other prisoners were taken to Ticonderoga.

[1] The Committee of the Whole sat from day to day until the business was concluded.—For full record from the *Assembly Journal* see *Appendix H.*

A letter from Colonel Hinman [Heman] Swift[1] Commanding a Continental Regiment, directed to Brigadier General Samuel Safford, dated February 12th 1782, requesting the Generals assistance in taking up a number of Deserters from the Continental Army, in Supplying a Corporal Baker and three men with provisions, and was by the General laid before the Council, Whereupon

Resolved that the Commisary General of this State be & he is hereby directed to furnish said Corporal Baker and three men with necessary provisions for the Execution of the business above mentioned.

Attest, JOSEPH FAY, *Secy.*

Adjourned to 9 oClock Tomorrow.

WEDNESDAY 20 February 1782.

Council Met and Adjourned until tomorrow to meet in Grand Committee.

THURSDAY 21st February 1782.

The Grand Committee, composed of His Excellency the Governor, the Honble Council and General Assembly having dissolved, their report is as follows vizt. See the journals of the House in which they are recorded at large.

The Council being convened, the report of the Grand Committee was received from the House, with a Committee thereon to join a Committee of Council to draw a bill in form, whereupon voted that his honor Paul Spooner Esqr. join said Committee.[2]

Adjourned to 9 oClock Tomorrow Morning.

IN COUNCIL Friday 22d February 1782.

A bill from the house was read appointing a Committee to join a Committee of Council to point out some method to redress the injuries the Inhabitants of the unions have recd on account of their Alliance with this State. The Honble Joseph Bowker and Moses Robinson Esqr. was appointed to join said Committee.

An Act Granting the Prayer of Major Gideon Brownson, and Allowing him six hundred and sixteen dollars and sixty nine tenth parts[3] of a

[1] Col. HEMAN SWIFT (a brother of the Rev. Job Swift, who was for many years a distinguished clergyman in Vermont, and uncle of Hon. Samuel Swift of Middlebury and the late Hon. Benjamin Swift of St. Albans,) was born at Sandwich, Mass., in 1733, and died in Cornwall, Conn., Nov. 14, 1814. He was lieutenant in the French war, colonel through the revolutionary war, a member of the Council of Connecticut for twelve years in succession, and judge of Litchfield county court.—See Drake's and Blake's *Biographical Dictionaries*, and *Memorials of a Century, Bennington.*

[2] The "bill in form" was the official adoption of the report of the committee of the whole for the dissolution of the East and West Unions.—See *Appendix H.*

[3] "Sixty ninetyeth parts" in the act. In this case Vermont made good the depreciation of Major Brownson's continental pay from July 16 1779 to Aug. 1 1780. In the certificate of "Joseph Nourse, Register of

dollar was read having passed the General Assembly, Was agreed to by the Council and an order drawn on the back of said Act on the Treasurer for the payment of the same Signed by order of Council

JOSEPH FAY, *Secy.*

The Council joined the Assembly and proceeded to the choice of three Agents to the Congress of the United States to Agree on Articles of Union between this and the United States. The ballots being taken the Honble Moses Robinson, Paul Spooner Esquires and Isaac Tichenor Esqr. was Elected.

An Act of Assembly was read appointing certain persons therein named to repair to the Authority of New York, to request them to suspend the Execution of their Law in prosecuting those persons who have been active in joining Vermont, until they can have opportunity to petition for an Act of the Legislature of New York Granting Pardon &c. having passed the [House] was read and passed the Council.

Adjourned to 9 oClock tomorrow Morning.

SATURDAY 23d February 1782.

Council Met According to Adjournment.

An Act discharging the Town of Pownal from the payment of certain provision Taxes therein mentioned was read and Concurred by Council and returned to the House.

On motion made by General Olcott to be released from a Committee on the petition of Cockburn & Campbell, Voted that Honble Benjamin Emmons join said Committee in Lieu of General Olcott.

A Bill from the House was read as follows vizt—

STATE OF VERMONT. IN GENERAL ASSEMBLY February 23d 1782.

Resolved that the Governor & Council be & they are hereby requested to take the case of Asa Baldwin into their consideration, and if they judge best that Baldwin should have a tryal to give orders accordingly; if not that his papers and property be delivered up to him the sd Baldwin. Extract from the Minutes, ROSL HOPKINS, *Clerk.*

Agreable to the foregoing resolution of the General Assembly, This Council having taken into their consideration the case of said Bawldwin,

Resolved that he have Leave to dispose of his Farm in Dorset after the first day of May next, on Condition that said Bawldwin relinquish all pretensions of Claim or Demand on this State for the use of said Farm during the time it has been improved for the use of said State. Also that all the papers belonging to said Bawldwin be returned to him.[1]

Attest, JOSEPH FAY, *Secy.*

On application made by Mr. Brakenridge relating to John McNiel returning to this State,

Resolved that Mr. John McNiel be permitted to return to this State for the time being or until the Inhabitants [express] their uneasiness on that account.[2]

Attest, JOSEPH FAY, *Secy.*

---

the Treasury of Congress," to the Major, the space for the state of his residence was left unfilled, and the act required the word *Vermont* to be inserted; though by whom this was to be done was not prescribed. Probably it was done by the Secretary of State.

[1] See Vol. I, p. 146.

[2] See Vol. I, p. 193.

The following Bill rec[d] from the House & ordered by the Council to be recorded viz[t]—

STATE OF VERMONT. IN GENERAL ASSEMBLY February 22 1782.

Resolved that the Governor and Council be requested to write to his Excellency General Washington and desire him to furnish two thousand stand of Arms & a sufficient quantity of Ammunition for the use of this State.

Extract from the journals, ROS[L] HOPKINS, *Clerk.*

Copy Examined, JOSEPH FAY, *Sec[y.]*

Adjourned to Monday Next one oClock P. M. [1]

---

[1] From the *Assembly Journal*, Feb. 23 1782 :

The following Resolution of the Board of War was read—viz.—

"IN BOARD OF WAR Feb[y.] 22 1782.

"Resolved that it be and it is hereby recommended to the hon[ble] the "Gen[l.] Assembly now sitting in Bennington that this State raise one "Battallion consisting of 514 men officers included for the defence of "this State the ensuing Campaign, to be commanded by one Lieut. Col[o.] "Com[dt.] one Maj[r.] 8 Captains and 16 Subalterns, that they continue in "service till the 15[t] day of Dec[r.] unless sooner discharged, that each town "in this State raise, equip and pay their equal proportion of the afores'd "Battalion according to their lists given in to the Assembly in Oct[r.] 1781 "—that the Gen[l.] Assembly appoint some suitable person to repair im- "mediately to Maj[r.] Gen[l.] Heath, or to the Comand[g.] officer of the North- "ern department, and request him to furnish this State with 2000 Conti- "nental arms with a sufficient quantity of ammunition—And that the "Fort at Pittsford be removed to Capt. Jon[th.] Fassets house in said "Pittsford. Extract from the Minutes,

JOHN FASSETT, *Sec[y.] P. T.*"

The House took under consideration the Resolution of the Board of War and after some time spent in debating thereon,

Resolved there be raised for the ensuing Campaign 300 men officers included for the defence of this State. And that non Commissioned officers and privates be raised and paid by the different towns agreeable to their list returned last October—and that the Commissioned officers receive their pay out of this State's Treasury—and that the Gov[r.] and Council be and they are hereby requested to write to Gen[l.] Washington and desire him to furnish 2000 arms and a sufficient quantity of ammunition for the use of this State.

Resolved that a Committee of ten to join a Committee from the Council be appointed to Report their opinion what number of Commiss'[d] officers ought to be appointed to command the troops to be raised as aforesaid—and bring in a nomination of such officers to be appointed—except the Field officers which are to be appointed by ballot. The members chosen M[r.] [Matthew] Lyon, M[r.] [Gideon] Olin, M[r.] [Benjamin] Whipple, M[r.] [Samuel] Mattocks, M[r.] [John] Sargent, M[r.] [Zadock] Granger, M[r.] [Elisha] Burton, M[r.] [Thomas] Chandler, [jr.] M[r.] [Gideon] Ormsbee & M[r.] [Timothy] Bartholomew.

Messrs. Bowker, Fletcher and Emmons were joined from the Council.

Feb. 25 1782.—The Committee appointed to bring in a nomination of officers to command the troops to [be] raised the ensuing campaign brought in the following report—viz—

That in their opinion that the said troops be commanded by one Major, five Captains, ten Subalterns—That there be one Serjeant Maj[r.], one quarter Master Serg[t.], twenty Serjeants and twenty Corporals—and that the Adjutant and Quarter Master be appointed out of the Subalterns by

STATE OF VERMONT. IN COUNCIL Monday 25 February 1782.

Council Met according to Adjournment.

A bill from the House was read appointing a Committee of Ten members to Join a Committee of Council, for the purpose of nominating officers to command the Troops next Campaign, Whereupon

Voted that the Honble Joseph Bowker, Samuel Fletcher & Benjamin Emmons Esquires join said Committee.

Resolved that the Honble John Fassett and Timothy Brownson join the Committee appointed by the Assembly and Council to take into consideration the Petition of Samuel Avery Esquire.

A Bill from the House was Read appointing a Committee to prepare Instructions for the Agents appointed to setle Preliminaries with Congress &c. whereupon the Honble Moses Robinson & Samuel Fletcher Esquires [were appointed] to join said Committee.

An Act for enabling Communities to recover their rights, &c. having passed the House was read and Concurred.[1]

Resolved that the Proprietors of the Gore of Land Granted to General Samuel Safford and Company Eighteen in number pay for Each right nine pounds Lawful Money in Silver to be paid by the first day of May next, to be settled three years after the War. Reservations to be set forth in the Charter of Incorporation.

Resolved that the Proprietors of *Goshen* Granted to Captain *John Powel*, *Nehemiah Lovell*, *William Douglass*, Lt. *Samuel Beach* & Comp^y^ to the number of 65 pay for Each right Eight pounds Lawful Money in Silver to be paid on or before the first day of May next, the time of Settlement to be three years next after the War will admit of a Settlement with Safety, the reservations to be specified in the Charter of Incorporation.

---

the Major. That the following Gentlemen be appointed Captains and Subalterns—viz—

Capt. Jesse Sawyer,
Lieut. Jacob Fairman,
Lieut. David Dimmick.
Capt. Ithamir Brookings,
Lieut. Samuel Beach,
Lieut. David Powers.
Capt. Josiah Boyden,
Lieut. Jonas Royce,
Lieut. Amos Kellogg.
Capt. Beriah Green,
Lieut. [Joshua] Church,
Lieut. Elijah Knight.
Capt. Nehemiah Lovewell,
Lieut. James Smalley,
Lieut. Nathl. White.

Your Committee would further report that they have not attempted to rank the Companies. JOSEPH BOWKER *for the Com^tee^.*

The above report was read and accepted and

Resolved that his Excellency the Governor be and is hereby requested to Commissionate the persons to the several offices as mentioned in said Report.

Resolved that Benjamin Whipple Esqr. [of Rutland] be and is hereby appointed Muster-Master of the troops to be raised on the West side of the Green Mountains—and that Capt. John Benjamin [of Windsor] be and hereby is appointed Muster-Master of the troops to be raised on the East side of the Mountains.

Feb. 26 1782.—Agreeable to the order of the day, proceeded to choose a Major to command the troops to be raised the ensuing campaign. The ballots being taken, Major Gideon Brownson was Elected.

[1] This act prescribed the mode of discharging judgments in suits against towns.

Resolved that the Proprietors of a Small Gore of Land Granted to Edward Harris Esq[r.] and Associates to the number of seventeen pay for Each right Eight pounds Lawful Money in Silver to be paid by the first day of May next. Terms of Settlement to be three years after the War. Reservations to be as in the other Towns.

Resolved that the Proprietors of the Township of *Sterling* 65 in number Granted to General Samuel Fletcher and Company pay for Each right Eight pounds Lawful Money in Silver to be paid by the first day of May next. The terms of Settlement to be the same as other Towns within the lines.[1] Reservations to be Specified in the Charter of Incorporation.

Resolved that the Proprietors of a Gore of Land Granted to Lieutenant Moses Johnson & Company thirty three in number containing about five thousand & 45 acres pay for each right Seven pounds Lawful Money in Silver, to be paid by the first day of May Next, to be settled in three years from this date.

Resolved that the Proprietors of a Gore of Land Granted General Peter Olcott and Company pay for each Right Eleven pounds L. Money in Silver, Each right to contain three hundred and thirty acres, to be paid by the first day of June next. To be settled in three years from this date. Reservations to be specified hereafter.

Resolved that the Proprietors of a Gore of Land Granted to M[r.] John Wheeler & Com[y.] cantaining about two thirds of a Township pay for Each right in said *Gore* nine pounds L. Money in Silver each right to contain three hundred and thirty acres, to be paid by the first day of May next. Terms of Settlement to be three years after the War will admit. The reservations to be Specified in the Charter of said Grant.

Resolved that the Proprietors of the Township of *Waitsfield* Granted Gen[l] Roger Enos, Colonel Benjamin Wait and Company to the number of sixty-five pay for Each right Eight pounds L. Money in silver to be paid by the first day of May next. To be settled in three years after the war will admit with safety.

Resolved that the proprietors of the Gore of Land Granted unto Amos Green, Samuel Moulton and Company to the number of sixteen pay for each right nine pounds L. Money in silver to be paid by the first day of May next. To be settled in three years from this day. Reservation to be Specified in the Charter of said Grant.

Adjourned to 9 °Clock to morrow Morning.

[TUESDAY, February 26, 1782.]

An Act from the House was read empowering a Committee to sell Colonel Peters Estate in More Town [Mooretown, now Bradford,] in which the Council Concurred.[2]

Resolved that the Proprietors of the Township of *Burk* Granted to M[r.] Justice Rose, Captain Uriah Seymour & Company to the number of sixty five pay for Each right nine pounds L. Money in silver to be paid by the first day of May next, to be Settled in three years after the War

---

[1] Beyond the lines of military defence, and in the territory which was common ground for the scouts of both parties in the war.

[2] The confiscated land of the tory Lieut. Col. John Peters of Hebron, Conn.—See Vol. I, pp. 267–8. The resolution of the Assembly authorized a sale to Capt. Nehemiah Lovewell.

will admit with Safety. The reservations to be Specified in the Charter of Incorporation of said Town.

Resolved that the Proprietors of the Township of *Browington* Granted to Timothy and Daniel Brown Esquires, sixty five in number, pay for Each right Eight Pounds L. Money in silver fifty pounds of which is to be paid down, sixty pounds the first day of August next, the Termes of Settlement to be three years after the circumstances of the War will admit with Safety. The reservations to be Specified in the Charter of Incorporation of said Township.

An Act of Assembly for the Annual Settlement of the Treasurers Accompts at Each October Session was read and Concurred.

A petition signed Timothy Andrews [Andrus] and Elijah Hinman was read, praying to be discharged from certain Land Tax therein mentioned, having been read in Assembly and a Committee of Council appointed [asked] to join a Committee from the House—Member Chosen the Honble Benj^a.^ Emmons Esqr.

A petition signed Seth Smith, praying to be discharged from a certain Indictment, was read and the prayer thereof Granted, on condition of his taking the Oath of Allegiance to this State, [and] returned to the house.[1]

A Petition signed Joseph Burt, praying to be discharged from certain bonds therein mentioned, was read and approved, said Burt taking the Oath of Allegiance to this State. Returned to the House.[2]

An Act relinquishing to the Settlers of Royalton certain Taxes therein mentioned was read and approved.—[on account of "the ravages of the enemy" in the burning of the town.]

Adjourned to 2 oClock P. M.

Council Met According to Adjournment.

An Act empowering the Surveyor General to perambulate the lines of the several Towns therein mentioned was read & the Council proposed as an Amendment *that the Surveyor General report to this Assembly* in *lieu* of his *line* being conclusive.

An Act discharging a number of persons & Inhabitants of Bennington from their four folds was read and Concurred.[3]

Resolved that Joseph Fay Esqr. Commissary of Prisoners be & he is hereby directed to Give Terrence Smith Son of Doctor George Smith his Parole as a prisoner of War.[4]

---

[1] SETH SMITH of Brattleborough was an agent of the adherents to New York in Windham county, and in that capacity visited Gov. Clinton, who sent him to represent Vermont matters to Congress; which he did so unfavorably that the grand jury of the county indicted him for attempting to betray the state "into the hands of a foreign power."—See B. H. Hall's *Eastern Vermont;* and *Vt. Hist. Soc. Collections*, Vol. II.

[2] JOSEPH BURT of Brattleborough, who gave a bond for the appearance of the above named Seth Smith for trial.

[3] By the act of Feb. 1779, directing listers in their office and duty, any person owning real estate in any town, other than that in which he resided, was required to return a true list without warning, "or be liable to be fourfolded."—See *Slade's State Papers*, p. 295.

[4] DR. GEORGE SMYTHE, or SMITH, was one of Gen. Haldimand's Commissioners to treat with Vermont. He was a physician of Albany, N. Y., and a tory. Lorenzo Sabine supposes he was a brother of judge William Smith of New York, afterward chief justice of Canada.—See *post* p. 152.

On application made by Col^o. W^m. Barton, Resolved that the payment of the Granting fees of the Township of *Providence* [Barton] Granted to Colonel William Barton & Company be postponed until the first day of June next, then one half to be paid, the time of Payment of the other half to be determined upon at that time.

An Act repealing an Act forming a Sixteenth Regiment having passed the General Assembly was read and Concurred.[1]

An Act directing the Selectmen of Pownall to repair certain Diged Highways [dugway in the Assembly journal] having passed the General Assembly was read & Concurred.

Resolved that the Proprietors of the Township of *Billy Mead* [Sutton] Granted to the Honble Jonathan Arnold Esquire and Company to the number of sixty-five pay for each right Eight pounds L. Money in silver to be paid (including what is already paid) by the first day of June next, except Twelve rights which is to be paid by the first day of August next, the Terms of Settlement to be three years after the circumstances of the War will admit with Safety. The reservations to be specified in the Charter of Incorporation of said Township.

Adjourned to 9 oClock Tomorrow.

WEDNESDAY 27 Feby 1782.

Council Met according to Adjournment.

An Act for abating the Town of Wells from Certain Tax therein specified was read and approved.

On the request of Colonel William Barton to have the Granting fees of his Township Suspended,

Resolved that on the punctual payment of the Granting fees of said Town by the time agreed on that Ten shillings on each right be relinquished.

Resolved that the Proprietors of the Township of Fayston Granted to Colonel Ebenezer Walbridge, Major Gideon Ormsby & Company to the number of sixty five pay for each right Eight pounds Lawful Money to be paid on the first day of May next, to be settled three years after the War, other Conditions & reservations to be set forth in the Charter of Incorporation.

Resolved that the Proprietors of the Gore of Land Granted to Beza. Woodward Esqr. and Company Twelve in number, pay for Each right four pounds L. Money to be paid by the first day of May next.

A Bill recommending the Draught of a bill giving Instructions to the Committee for receiving the Granting fees, was read and the Honble John Fassett Esqr. & Moses Robinson Esqr. were appointed to join said Committee.[2]

An Act to compel the more punctual Attendance of the Members of Assembly was read and approved.[3]

An Act relinquishing a part of a Tax of the district of *Ira* was read and approved.

A Bill from the house for raising three hundred men was read, appointing a Committee to devise ways and means for that purpose,

---

[1] This regiment consisted mainly of militia in the "West District."

[2] The committee "to take the granting fees for Lands, &c." consisted of Gen. Samuel Safford, Col. John Strong, and Hon. Thomas Porter.

[3] This act imposed a fine of one pound ten shillings for each day of absence without excuse, the daily roll or register of the clerk being conclusive evidence.—See Slade's *State Papers*, p. 446.

whereupon the Hon[ble] Joseph Bowker [was] appointed to join said Committee.

An Act Granting Arms and Ammunition to certain persons who were taken prisoners &c. was read and Concurred.[1]

A petition signed by the Inhabitants of Shrewsbury was read, a Committee being appointed by the house to join a Committee of Council, Whereupon Voted the Hon[ble] Samuel Fletcher to join said Committee.

An Act directing the Treasurer to distroy the bills of Credit of this State &c. was read and approved.

Adjourned to 9 oClock Tomorrow.[2]

THURSDAY, 28 February 1782.

Council Met According to Adjournment.

Resolved that the proprietors of the Gore of Land Granted to Captain Daniel Smith & Co. Ten in number, pay for each right Eight pounds Ten shillings L. Money to be paid by the first day of May next, Each right to contain three hundred and thirty Acres. Terms of Settlement to be three years after the War will Admit with Safety. Reservations to be set forth in the Charter of Incorporation.

Resolved that the Proprietors of the Township of *Johnson* Granted to the Rev[d.] Jonathan Edwards, M[r.] [William] Samuel Johnson, Charles Chauncey Esquires & Company[3] being sixty five in number, pay for

---

[1] Vermonters recaptured from the British.

[2] From the *Assembly Journal*, Feb. 27 1782:

Resolved that M[r.] Ward Bayley be and is hereby appointed a Lieutenant to command the troops to be raised in the upper Cohoss and his Excellency the Gov[r.] is hereby requested to Commissionate him accordingly.

The act for raising three hundred men did not apply to the towns north of Barnet. These towns, by another act, were required to raise a guard of twenty-one men for their own protection. Col. Bayley served, of course, on this occasion, with the rank and pay of Lieutenant only.

Resolved that the Board of War be and are hereby empowered to take such measures to provide ammunition for the use of this State as they shall judge will be necessary to put the same in a state of Defence.

Resolved that the Captain General be and is hereby empowered and directed on advice of the Board of War, to order into service such number of militia as they shall judge necessary, and for such time not exceeding thirty days from their arrival in Camp.

Resolved that the Governor and Council be and they are hereby requested and empowered to give the officers &c. of the Connecticut line a reasonable time to pay the Charter fees of a township granted by this State to them—And if they should neglect or refuse to pay the fees aforesaid then they are hereby requested and empowered to grant said township to such persons as shall most conduce to the benefit of this State.

Resolved that Capt. [Daniel] Cumstock be and is hereby appointed a Captain to command a Company of men in the service of this State the ensuing campaign in the room of Capt. Jesse Sawyer who will not accept of his appointment—And the Governor is hereby requested to commissionate the said Capt. Cumstock accordingly.

[3] Rev. JONATHAN EDWARDS, D. D., then of New Haven, Conn., and afterward President of Union College, N. Y. WILLIAM SAMUEL

Each right Eight pounds Ten Shillings L. Money to be paid immediately, the Terms of Settlement and reservations to be specified in the Charter of Incorporation.

An Act for the purpose of raising a Certain Number of Troops for the defence of the Inhabitants of the upper Cohoos [Coos] was read and approved.[1]

On recommendation of the representatives of the County of Winsor, Resolved that Major Benjamin Wait Esqr. be and he is hereby appointed Sheriff in and for said County for the time being.

A petition Signed Asa Bawldwin was read praying for leave to return to this State, whereupon Resolved that His Excellency the Governor be requested to Grant said Bawldwin a pass for that purpose.

A petition Signed Lewis Walker, Daniel Briggs, Francis Matison & Joshua [thus on the record] Praying for certain fines therein mentioned to be remitted, was read, whereupon Resolved that said fines be and they are hereby remitted & the aforesaid persons are hereby fully discharged therefrom. Attest, JOSEPH FAY, *Secy.*

An Act for taking off the Tender of paper Money was read and Concurred.[2]

IN GENERAL ASSEMBLY 28 Feby 1782.

On motion made, Resolved that this Assembly will Appoint one person in addition to the Agents already appointed to transact the business of this State in Congress. The Ballots being taken the Honorable JONAS FAY Esquire was Elected.

Attest, ROSWELL HOPKINS, *Clerk.*

Resolved that the Proprietors of the Gore of Land Granted to Captain Elijah Dewey & Comy fifteen in number pay for each Right in said Gore Eight pounds Ten Shillings L. Money, the one half to be paid Down, the other half to be paid the first day of May next—the Terms of Settlement and reservations to be Specified in the Charter of said Gore.

Adjourned to 9 oClock Tomorrow.[3]

JOHNSON, LL.D., of Stratford, Conn., was agent for Connecticut in England from 1766 to 1771, and a firm friend to Vermonters then and during his life; a member of the Continental Congress and of the Convention which adopted the federal constitution, U. S. Senator for Connecticut from 1789 to 1791, and President of Columbia College, N. Y. city. The town of Johnson seems to have been named in his honor. CHARLES CHAUNCEY, LL.D., then residing at New Haven, Conn., was a distinguished jurist, and President of the first agricultural society organized in Connecticut.

[1] See note, *ante* p. 124.

[2] This applied to the bills of credit issued by the State. These bills were a legal tender from the issue under the act of April 1781 until June 1 1782, when they were redeemable in specie.—See Slade's *State Papers*, pp. 424–426, 446.

[3] From the *Assembly Journal*, Feb. 28 1782:

Resolved that the Secretary to the Governor and Council be and is hereby allowed nine shillings pr. day while attending on Council.

The Committee appointed to see what hard money there is now going into the Treasury and how the same should be paid out, brought in the following report, viz—

FRIDAY 1[t] March 1782.

Council met according to Adjournment and Adjourned until Thursday next then to meet at Captain David Galushas, Shaftsbury.

END OF FEBRUARY SESSION 1782.

Copy of Instructions to Committee for procuring a Printer.

BENNINGTON, IN COUNCIL 1[t] March 1782.

To Colonel John Barret, Benjamin Burt, and *John Sessions Esquires*—You having been appointed by the General Assembly to Superintend and provide for the printing office in this State—

These are therefore to Instruct and direct you to Examine into the Cause why the printing office [at Westminster] has not answered the purposes Expected, and to Engage some Suitable person or persons in the vicinity of Westminster to Supply every Material for the said press on as reasonable conditions as can be obtained, and to Engage some suitable post rider or riders to Circulate & distribute the public acts & news papers through the several Towns in this State. And if you cannot Engage a person or persons that answer that purpose you are hereby authorized & directed with the Consent of the proprietors to remove said Office with the Materials to Bennington on this States Cost if any person will Engage to Supply the Materials at that place for the purpose aforesaid. And if the proprietors refuse to accede to these terms & will not Engage to carry on said business punctually and with dispatch, you are hereby directed to dismiss him & procure an other printer, that will answer the purposes expected, and make returns to the Governor & Council of your doings as soon as may be. By order of the Governor & Council,

JOSEPH FAY, *Sec[y].*

That they find there is £369 in hard money now to go in to the Treasury; and that they find it will take £226–17–10 to pay one third of the Debenture of Council and Assembly not reckoning this days pay, and that when £100 is laid by for the Agents to Congress there will be left £42–18–2 out of which it is the opinion of your Com[tee] that [Lieut.] Governor Paine [Payne] have £8 on account of the order he has on the Treasury—Gen[l.] Enos £6 on his like order—M[r.] Spooner £8 on his like order, M[r.] Townshend [Secretary of State,] £6 on his like order.

M. LYON, *for the Com[tee].*

The aforesaid report was read and accepted and the Treasurer is hereby directed to govern himself accordingly.

Resolved that the Land Office Committee be and they are hereby directed to pay unto the Commissary General of Purchases from time to time, such monies as they shall judge necessary, considering the exigencies of the State—as soon as the orders specially directed by this House are paid, and said Commissary to give his receipt to be accountable to the Treasurer for the said monies.

Resolved that Col[o.] John Barrêt, Benjamin Burt, and John Sessions Esq[rs.] be and they are hereby appointed to Super Intend the press and Supply the same—And the Governor and Council are hereby requested to give said Committee their instructions.

Resolved that the Board of War be and they are hereby empowered and directed to proportion the men to the several towns that are ordered to be raised for the ensuing Campaign.

PROCEEDINGS OF THE GOVERNOR AND COUNCIL AT THEIR SESSIONS IN MARCH AND MAY 1782.

STATE OF VERMONT. IN COUNCIL,
Shaftsbury, Thursday 7th March 1782.

The Council met according to Adjournment at which time intelligence was recd of the arrival of the Honble Jonas Fay & Ira Allen Esqrs. Agents to Congress.

Adjourned to 9 oClock Tomorrow.

FRIDAY 8 March 1782.

Council Met According to Adjournment at which the Agents to Congress arrived and proceeded to make their Report &c.[1]

Adjourned to 8 oClock Tomorrow Morning.

SATURDAY 9 March 1782.

Met According to Adjournment.

Resolved that General Samuel Safford and Abel Curtis Esquires be & they are hereby appointed Members of the Board of War in [place] of Colonel *Wyman* and *Caldwell*, and was duly qualified to that office.

On motion made, Resolved that Nathan Canfield[2] be and he is hereby discharged from the bond that he is under to appear before this Council to answer his Conduct &c.

Resolved that Alexander Brush [of New Haven] be and he is hereby appointed Captain to Command a Company of Men in the Service of this State the Ensuing Campaign.

Resolved that the Proprietors of the Township of *Lutterloh* [Albany,] *Glover*, *Wyllys* [Jay,] and the Township Granted to Major Woodbridge and Company pay the Granting fees of said Townships by the first day of August next.

Resolved that Joseph Fay Esqr. Commissary General of prisoners, be & he is hereby directed to Parole Terence Smith son of Doct. [George] Smith & permit him to go to Canada on Condition of his returning or sending out Lt. Michael Duning in Exchange.[3]

WARRANT FOR THE COLLECTION OF A PROVISION TAX OF DELINQUENT SELECTMEN.

The following is a Copy of a Warrant Given the several Sheriffs to Collect Provision Tax vizt—

To the Sheriff of the County of ——— or his deputy, Greeting:

Whereas by an act of the Legislature of this State passed in October 1780 entitled "An Act for the purpose of procuring provisions for the

---

[1] *See Appendix H.* [2] See Vol. I.

[3] MICHAEL DUNNING of Pownal was one of the Commissioners of Sequestration in 1778-9.—See Vol. I.

Troops to be employed in the Service of this State for the Ensuing year" among other things therein enacted, the then Select men of the Several towns within this State were authorized, empowered and directed to Levy a Tax on their respective Towns for the procuring such quotas of Provisions as they are respectively assessed by the said Act with the necessary cost of package &c.

And Whereas it is represented by Joseph Farnsworth Esq[r.] Com[sy] General of Purchases, that the Select men of several Towns within the said County of——have neglected their duty herein and have not returned to him or his deputy their respective quotoes of Provisions as directed in said Act.

And furthermore Whereas no due information hath been made whereby the Select men of any Town in said County can be availed by the provision made in said Act for them in case of the opposition of the Inhabitants of a Town or one third part thereof, and as the time for the payment of those quotoes is now Long elapsed and special need requires that such arrears be forthwith made Good to the public in order that the State may be better enabled to provide for the Troops who shall go forth in our defence the ensuing Campaign as well as to discharge those Necessary Debts contracted by the public the last season in Consequence of the delinquency aforesaid—

These are therefore in the name & by the Authority of the Freemen of the State of Vermont to command you, that of the Goods or Chattels of the Select men (whose right or duty it hath been to procure such quotoes) of such Towns in the said County of—— as shall be certified to you by the said Commissary General delinquent of such quoto, or any part thereof, or sum or sums of Money in Lieu thereof, of which quotoes or Coplements, Sum or Sums of Money, you will be certified and receive the particular directions of the said Commissary General, and which after being availed of in your own possession by virtue of this Warrant, you will deliver over to him the said Commissary General or his Deputy taking his receipt therefor hereon Indorsed. And also of the said Goods or Chattels to satisfy yourself for your own fees as by Law you are intitled.

Hereof fail not, but make due returnes of this writ with your doings thereon within ninety days from the date hereof.

Dated at Arlington this Eighteenth day of March A. D. 1782.

By order of His Excellency the Governor with the advice of Council.

THOMAS TOLMAN, *D. Sec*[y.]

STATE OF VERMONT. IN COUNCIL, Arlington 7th May 1782.

This Council having taken into consideration the manner in which the prisoners Lately taken should be disposed of, whereupon

Resolved that Joseph Fay Esquire Com[y] General of Prisoners be and he is hereby directed to take a list of said Prisoners and such as have been actually in the British Service to cause to be immediately Sent to Canada to be exchanged & the remainder[1] to remain in close Confinement until further orders from this Council.

Attest, THOMAS TOLMAN, *D. Sec*[y.]

---

[1]Tories and disaffected persons, probably. When Mr. Fay proceeded to execute this resolution by returning seventeen prisoners, strong opposition to the release of any of the prisoners of war was made by citizens of Bennington and vicinity, and Gov. Chittenden ordered a military force to take the prisoners to the frontier to be exchanged

Whereas it appears to this Council that there is not a sufficiency of provision collected for the present support of the Troops in service and that unless immediate exertions be made the Troops cannot be supported, Therefore

Resolved that it be and hereby is recommended to the Inhabitants of the Several Towns within this State to take some immediate & effectual measure to raise a Sufficiency of Provision at Cost to Support the number of Soldiers sent from such Town, until they can be other ways supplied by the present Crops on the Ground.

Attest, JOSEPH FAY, *Secy.*

END OF THE FIRST VOLUME.

The second commencing with the proceedings of Council at Windsor June 13th 1782. Attest, JOSEPH FAY, *Secy.*

NOTE BY THE EDITOR.—The first manuscript volume in the Secretary of State's office in fact ends with April 18, 1781, and Secretary Fay's copy of the original minutes preceding June 13 1782 was attached to the second manuscript volume; doubtless by a blunder of the binder of the books. The second manuscript volume commences as above indicated by Secretary Fay.

JOURNALS OF COUNCIL

AT THE

SESSION WITH THE ASSEMBLY AT WINDSOR, JUNE 1782.

WINDSOR June 13th 1782 (Thursday.)

Agreable to an Adjournment in February last, The Council met at this Place—(at Mr. Hawley's.)

Present—His Excelly Thos. Chittenden Esqr. Governor. Members—The Honble Ira Allen & Saml. Fletcher Esqrs. Thos. Tolman *Dep. Sec'y.* Benja. Wait Esqr. *Sheriff.*

Col. Seth Warner, with a committee from Bennington, remonstrated with the Governor and threatened to bring them back. The Governor replied that he had acted by the authority of the Council, (the above resolution;) that Col. Allen's regiment would be sufficient to execute his orders; and he advised the committee to return to Bennington and quiet the people. The seventeen prisoners were sent to Canada and exchanged for forty citizens of Vermont and neighboring states who had been captured by the British. Upon this, all opposition ceased and the course of the Governor was approved by all parties.—See Ira Allen's ***History***, in ***Vt. Hist. Soc. Collections***, Vol. I, pp. 459, 460.

But not being a Quorum, adjourned 'till Tomorrow Morning 10 o th Clock—Then to meet at this Place.

FRIDAY, June 14th 1782.

Council met according to Adjournment. Present His Excelly the Governor.—Members present—The Hon. Ira Allen, Saml. Fletcher, John Throop, Benja. Emmons, Esqrs.

The Hon. Paul Spooner Esqr. attended the Board. Not being a Quorum to transact Business, adjourned 'till Tomorrow Morning at 8 o'thClock —Then to meet at this Place.

SATURDAY, June 15th 1782.

Council met according to adjournment.—Present His Excellency the Governor. Members—The Hon. Jonas Fay, Ira Allen, John Fasset Junr., Saml. Fletcher, John Throop, & Benja. Emmons Esqrs.

His Excellency and Council then waited on the House, when his Excellency the Governor laid before the Assembly the following Letters and Copies which were read in order by the Secretary, viz.

Copy of a Letter from Thos. Tolman D. Secy by order of His Excellency to Governor Clinton Dated Aprl. 15th 1782. Copy of a Letter from His Excelly to General Washington Dated Mar. 16th 1782. Copy of a Letter from His Excelly to Oliver Wolcott Esqr. do. Letter from Barzilla Rice to Jona. Hunt Esqr dated May 14th 1782.[1] Letter of May 15th from Jona. Hunt Esqr. to His Excelly the Governor. Letter of May 16th from Jno. Shepardson Esqr to His Excelly. Letter of May 23d from Wm. Biggelow[2] to His Excelly the Governor. Copy of a Letter from His Excelly the Govr. to Majr. Shepardson Dated May 23d 1782. Copy of a Letter from His Excelly to Jona Hunt Esqr Sheriff Dated May 22d 1782. Copy of a Letter from His Excelly to Stephen R. Bradley Esqr Dated do. Copy of a Letter from His Excelly. to Genl. Fletcher, Dated do. Copy of a Letter to Jotham Biggelow, Danl. Lynde, Josiah Biggelow, and others—from His Excelly. Dated the same as above.[3]

His Excellency then laid before the Assembly the necessary Business of the Session—after which His Excellency and Council returned to the Council Room.[4]

The Honble Paul Spooner Esqr attended the Board.

---

[1] Hunt was sheriff of Windham county, and Rice was one of his deputies. These letters related doubtless to the resistance of the Yorkers in Guilford.

[2] An adherent to New York, residing in Guilford.

[3] These were all residents of Guilford, who were indicted by the grand jury in September 1782 for resisting the authority of Vermont.

[4] From the *Assembly Journal:*

After reading the aforesaid letters [noted in the Council journal above] his Excellency requested that there might be some alterations made in the following Acts viz—the Act directing the laying and serving executions—the Act respecting the making up the depreciation to Colo. Warners Regiment—and the provision Act.

The Agents appointed to wait on Congress requested that Monday next might be assigned to hear their report—therefore Ordered that Monday next at the opening of the House in the afternoon be assigned for that purpose.

A Resolution of Assembly appointing a Committee of five to arrange the Business of the Session, was rec'd and read, whereupon a Committee of Council was appointed to join said Committee. Members chosen, General Fletcher and John Fasset, Jun$^{r.}$ Esq$^{r.}$

Upon an application to this Council by M$^{r.}$ Benj$^{a.}$ Jacobs of Salem in the Common Wealth of Massachusetts, producing a Letter directed from the Com^{sy} of Prisoners at Boston to the Commiss^{y} Genl of Prisoners at Quebec, and desiring a Permit for the Purpose of passing into Canada to negociate the Exchange of a number of Prisoners agreeable to the Request of said Letter—

And Colonel Chase appearing and informing the Council that from an acquaintance with the said Jacobs he could recommend him as a gentleman of good Character, Therefore

Resolved that it be and hereby is recommended to his Excellency the Governor to grant a Permit agreable to the said Request—and also to include in said Permit one Jos. Taylor to attend the said Jacobs—

N. B. (A Copy of the Permit granted is on the Files of Council.)

☞ The Permit was altered as will appear by the Copy on File.

Adjourned to 2 o^{the}Clock afternoon, to meet at this place.

Met according to adjournment.

Jonas Fay Esq$^{r.}$ was appointed to join a Committee from the House to draw a Bill for the Appointment of a Special Superior Court in the County of Windham. [On account of the disturbances at that time.]

The Honble Moses Robinson Esq$^{r.}$ attended the Board.

An Act altering the name of Hertford (the Name of a Town in this State) to Waterford was read, and concurred. [See journal of the 17th.]

An Act pardoning John Arms was read and concurred.[1]

A Resolution of Assembly appointing a Committee of three to take under Consideration the 1st Article in the Report arranging the Business of the Session, which is "that an Amendment be made in the Act directing the levying Executions" was received and read, Whereupon a Committee of Council was appointed to join s^{d} Committee. Members chosen, Moses Robinson & Samuel Fletcher Esq$^{rs.}$

A Resolution of Assembly appointing a Comm^{tee} of five to take under Consideration the 4th Article in the Report of Arrangement which is "To take under Consideration the Act for levying a Tax on the lands in this State," was received and read, whereupon a Committee of Council was appointed to join said Committee. Members chosen John Fasset Jun$^{r.}$ & Ira Allen Esq$^{rs.}$

Council adjourned till Monday next at 9 o^{the}Clock in the Morning. Then to meet at this place.

MONDAY, June 17th 1782.

Council met according to Adjournment—Present His Excell^{y}. Members—The Honble Ira Allen, Jonas Fay, Moses Robinson, & John Fasset Jun$^{r.}$ Esq^{rs}.

The Honble Paul Spooner and General Fletcher attended the Council Board.

---

[1] JOHN ARMS was one of the first settlers of Brattleborough, and held several offices under New York from 1766 until 1770. He joined the enemy, but repented and returned to Vermont, and was pardoned on taking the oath of allegiance to Vermont. He wrote a poetical account of the Westminster massacre, which is one of the most truthful of the tory accounts.—See B. H. Hall's *Eastern Vermont*.

The Governor and Council joined the House in a Committee of the whole to hear the Report of the Proceedings of our Agents at Congress, in Consequence of their two last Missions—In hearing which Reports, the greater part of the Afternoon was taken up.[1]

The Act mentioned in yesterday's Journal, "altering the name of Hertford to Waterford" as concurred by Council, was this Day reconsidered, and proposed to the Assembly by Paul Spooner Esqr. from the Council, to be altered from "Waterford" to *Hartland.*

A Resolution of Assembly appointing a Committee to prepare a Bill in addition to an Act intituled "an Act directing and regulating the levying and serving Executions" and make report—was received and read; whereupon

Resolved that a Committee of Council be appointed to join said Committee. Member chosen—Paul Spooner Esq.

Council adjourned to Tomorrow Morning at 8 o^th Clock—Then to meet

---

[1] From the *Assembly Journal :*

The following are the proceedings of the Grand Committee viz—

"WINDSOR, June 17th 1782.

"His Excellency the Governor and Council having joined the Assembly in a Committee of the whole to hear the report of the hon^ble Jonas Fay and Ira Allen Esq^rs. and Abel Curtiss Esqr. and of the hon^ble Moses Robinson, Jonas Fay and Paul Spooner Esq^rs. and Isaac Tichenor Esqr. late agents to Congress—His Excellency in the Chair—Micah Townshend Esqr. Clerk—

1st. A Resolution of the Governor and Council appointing the Honble Elisha Payne, Jonas Fay and Ira Allen Esq^rs. and Abel Curtiss Esqr. Agents to Congress dated Jany. 10th 1782 was read.

2^d. A Letter from Messrs. Fay and Allen to the President of Congress dated 30th Jany. 1782—read.

3^d. A Letter from the hon^ble Saml. Livermore Chairman of a Committee of Congress to Messrs. Allen & Fay dated Feby. 1st.—read.

4th. A Letter from Messrs. Fay & Allen to M^r. Livermore Chairman &c. dated 5th. Feby. 1782,—read.

5th. A paper delivered by Messrs. Fay & Allen to a Com^tee of Congress on the 6th. Feb^y.—read.

6th. A Memorial delivered by Messrs. Fay, Allen & Curtis to the Committee of Congress dated 7th. Feby. 1782—read.

7th. Written observations delivered by Messrs. Fay, Allen and Curtis to the Committee of Congress dated 12th. Feby. 1782--read.

8th. A letter to the President of Congress from Messrs. Fay, Allen and Curtis dated 13th. Feby. 1782—read.

9th. A letter from the same persons to the President of Congress dated 16th. Feby. 1782—read.

10th. Another Letter from the same persons to the President dated 21st. Feby. 1782—read.

In the Report of the hon^ble Moses Robinson, Jonas Fay and Paul Spooner Esq^rs. and Isaac Tichenor Esqr. the following papers were read viz—

1st. A commission under the signature of his Excellency the Governor appointing the persons above mentioned Agents and Delegates to Congress, dated 13th. March 1782.

2^d. A written Report of the said Agents of their proceedings and the proceedings of Congress respecting this State."

See *Appendix H.*

at the Meeting House in order to join the General Assembly in the Committee of the whole, which still stands adjourned.

TUESDAY, June 18th 1782.

Met according to adjournment.

Present His Excellency the Governor. Members—Ira Allen, Saml. Fletcher, Jonas Fay, John Fasset Junr. John Throop, Benj:a Emmons, Paul Spooner, Moses Robinson Esqrs.

Then attended the House in a Committee of the whole, after which returned to the Council Room. [This was in reference to the report of the Auditors' accounts, but nothing was done.]

Resolved that a Committee be appointed to join a Committee from the House to form an Act for suppressing the Disturbances in the County of Windham.—Members chosen Mr. Fletcher and Mr. Emmons.[1]

Resolved that Mr. Fletcher be and he is hereby appointed to join a Committee from the Assembly on the within Petition, agreeable to a Bill from said Assembly. The Petition mentioned is that of Lt. David Hitchcock praying for the Grant of a Gore of Land adjoining Athens.

A Letter of June 10th 1782 from Capt. Robert Pattison requesting to resign—was rec'd and read.

A Letter of the same Date was rec'd from Lt. Thos. Taggart and read, purporting the same request.

Adjourned 'till Tomorrow Morning 8 o thClock, then to meet at this place.

WEDNESDAY June 19th 1782.

Council met according to Adjournment.

Present His Excellency the Governor.—Members—Ira Allen, Saml. Fletcher, Benj:a Emmons, & Moses Robinson Esqrs.

Resolved that Mr. Robinson be and he is hereby appointed to join a Committee from the House "to prepare a Bill to adjust and settle the Estates of Absentees."

Resolved that Mr. Emmons be and he is hereby appointed to join a Committee from the House "to prepare a Bill directing the Committee of P. Table not to answer the Militia P. Rolls of the late East and West Unions" &c.—

Resolved that Mr. Allen be and he is appointed to join a Committee from the House "to take under Consideration the Situation of the Proceedings of the Legislature of this State respecting Moretown" [Mooretown *alias* Bradford.]

Adjourned 'till tomorrow Morning 8 o thClock—then to meet at this place.

THURSDAY June 20th 1782.

Council met according to Adjournment.

Present His Excellency the Governor. Members—Jonas Fay, Ira Allen, Saml Fletcher, John Fasset Junr., John Throop, Benja. Emmons, Moses Robinson Esqrs.

---

[1] For act see Council record of Aug. 29 1782, *post*. June 19th, Jonas Fay and Paul Spooner were requested to call upon the disaffected inhabitants of Orange county and the northern towns of Windsor county, explain the action of Congress, and "use their utmost endeavors to unite the disaffected people to this Government." Isaac Tichenor was sent for the same purpose to the towns of Brattleborough, Halifax, and Guilford.—Ms. *Assembly Journal*, Vol. 2, p. 134.

An Act confirming a Right of Land unto Reuben Bloomer in the Township of Dorset was read and concurred.

The following is a Bill received from the House,—

"STATE OF VERMONT, *In General Assembly* June 20th 1782.

Resolved that there be and is hereby granted unto Lieut. David Hitchcock and his Associates seven in Number herein after named a Gore or Tract of Land containing by Estimation *One Thousand Acres*, bounded Northerly upon Athens, Easterly upon Putney, Southerly upon Dummerston, and Westerly upon New Fane and Townshend, viz: To Jonas Moore two Hundred and Thirty five Acres, David Hitchcock 235 Acres, Benjamin Butterfield Junr. one Hundred and Fifty Acres, Oliver Cheney Ninety Acres, Ebenezer Ober Ninety Acres, Moses Benson Fifty Acres, Daniel Benson Fifty Acres, and Joseph Enos one Hundred Acres.—And the Governor and Council are requested to issue a Grant for the same to the said Persons under such Restrictions and Reservations as to them shall appear proper—annexing the sd Gore to the Town of Putney upon this Condition—That if any other Inhabitants than are above named are included in the Bounds of said Gore, the said Grantees shall relinquish to the actual Settlers what they have severally heretofore purchased or improved."

IN COUNCIL (date above.)

Resolved that the Granting Fees upon each Acre of Land in the above Gore be Two Shillings and the Time for the Payment of the same be on or before the first Day of August next.

Attest, THO. TOLMAN, *D. Secy.*

Resolved that the Treasurer be, and he is hereby directed to pay unto Captain William Gallup the sum of Twenty three pounds Sixteen Shillings and two pence Lawl Money, it being in full of a Ballance due the sd Gallup as a Commissioner for the Sale of confiscated Lands which will appear drawn in Continental Money—viz £40 9 6 March 1778 on the Journals of Council of February 1781—reference thereto being had.

By Order of the Governor and Council, THO. TOLMAN, *D. Secy.*

£23 16 2.

Adjourned till tomorrow Morning 8o thClock then to meet at this Place.[1]

FRIDAY June 21st 1782.

Met according to adjournment. Present His Excellency the Governor. Members—Ira Allen, Saml Fletcher, Jonas Fay, John Fasset junr., John Throop, Benja. Emmons, Paul Spooner & Moses Robinson Esqrs.

Upon a Reconsideration of the Time for the Payment of the Granting Fees of the Gore of Land granted to Lt. David Hitchcock and Associates on the 20th Instant,

Resolved that the Time for the Payment of said Fees be on or before the Day of the rising of the General Assembly in October next.

The Honble Paul Spooner Esqr. requested Liberty to resign his Office of Judge of Probate for the District of Hartford, whereupon

Resolved that Elias Wild Esqr. be and he is hereby appointed Judge of Probate within and for the District of Hartford, in the Room of the Honble Paul Spooner Esqr. resigned.

---

[1] From the *Assembly Journal:*

The Governor and Council joined this House to choose a Chief Judge of the Superior Court. The ballots being taken The Honble Moses Robinson was Elected. [In place of Elisha Payne, who by the dissolution of the union with the "Eastern District" had become a citizen of New Hampshire.]

The following Acts which had previously passed the House of Assembly, were this day passed in Council with the several Proposals of Amendment added to each viz—

An Act establishing the Constitution of Vermont and securing the Privileges of the People.

An Act adopting the Common Statute Law of England.

An Act defining and limiting the Powers of the several Courts within this State.[1]

An Act regulating all Processes in Civil Causes.

An Act directing County Election in the County of Windsor.

An Act in Addition to an Act directing and regulating the levying Executions.[2]

---

[1] See Slade's *State Papers*, p. 450.

[2] For this act see Slade's *State Papers*, p. 455. Another act which was passed by the Assembly on the same day, entitled "An act for the punishment of conspiracies against the peace, liberty, and independence of this State," is not noticed on the Council journal. This act provided that the assembling of six or more persons, "with weapons of terror," to hinder the execution of the laws; or if any person or persons shall conspire, or attempt, any invasion, insurrection, or rebellion against the State—the punishment should be banishment, or imprisonment, and forfeiture of property. The third section provided that if any person banished under this act should refuse to depart, or after departure should return without leave, and be convicted thereof, "he or they shall suffer death."—See Slade's *State Papers*, p. 454. Attested copies of this act were sent immediately to the towns of Brattleborough, Halifax, Guilford, and Marlborough.

The acts establishing the constitution of Vermont, &c., have occasionally been criticised, and to the discredit of the critics. The fact that at that day the General Assembly was intended to be omnipotent, and was made so by the constitution, except as to altering, or infringing upon, that instrument, is a sufficient answer to these criticisms.—See *Vt. Historical Soc. Collections*, Vol. II, pp. 277, 429, 448; and D. Chipman's *Memoir of Chittenden*, pp. 100–113. The act of June 1782 was for "establishing the Constitution of Vermont, and securing the Privileges of the People,"—not to infringe upon either. It originated in the 5th clause of the items of business agreed upon for the session, which was in these words: "That a Statute be made in explanation of the 25th Section of the Constitution." That section related to the personal liberty of debtors, and the admission of prisoners to bail. The act was drawn probably by MICAH TOWNSHEND, a lawyer of good reputation, who was then Secretary of State. The first section, establishing the constitution, was enacted "to prevent disputes respecting the legal force of the Constitution of this state;" and the remaining section gave the general privileges of the constitution and laws of the state to "all the people of the American States, within this State, whether they be inhabitants or not." See Slade's *State Papers*, p. 449.

Council adjourned with the General Assembly to the Second Thursday in Oct[r.] next agreeable to Constitution, to meet at Manchester—Unless necessary Business shall require some intermediate Meetings of this Board, to be called by His Excellency the Governor.

END OF JUNE SESSION AT WINDSOR, 1782.

Attest, THOMAS TOLMAN, *D. Sec[y.]*

PROCEEDINGS OF THE GOVERNOR AND COUNCIL

AT A

SPECIAL SESSION AT MANCHESTER, AUGUST 29[th.] 1782.

STATE OF VERMONT. IN COUNCIL Manchester Aug[t.] 29th 1782.

AN ACT *empowering the Governor to raise men to assist the Sheriffs.*

Be it enacted and it is hereby enacted by the Representatives of the Freemen of the State of Vermont in General Assembly met and by the authority of the same, that His Excellency the Captain General of this State be, and hereby is empowered to order & direct any Officer or Officers in this State to raise any number of Men in the same, and to march them to any part thereof, to assist the Sheriffs in their respective Counties in the due Execution of their Office—And that His Excellency be empowered to appoint and commissionate any Person or Persons with full power for all the Intents & Purposes aforesaid—And that His Excellency call on the Commissary General to furnish the Men when so raised with Provisions as need may require; and for that purpose that he grant a Warrant to said Commissary to levy by Distress and take Provisions wherever it may be found, a sufficiency to supply said Troops while in actual Service for the Purposes aforesaid.

WINDSOR June 22[d] 1782.

The preceeding is a true Copy of an Act of the Legislature of the State of Vermont passed yesterday.

Attest, MICAH TOWNSEND, *Secr[y.]*[1]

IN COUNCIL at the House of M[r.] Elias Gilberts in Manchester, August 29th 1782.

The Council having met at this place, agreable to Request of His Excellency the Governor, & a Quorum being present, the Board proceeded to Business.

The present situation of the County of Windham being taken under the due Consideration of this Board,

---

[1] This act and a resolution requiring a special session of the superior court in Windham county, were, by a resolution of the Assembly of June 21, to be kept secret until the session of the court.

Resolved, that His Excellency the Governor be advised to raise 150 Men as Vollunteers within Col°. Ebenr Walbridge's Regiment, and 100 within Col°. Ira Allen's Regiment, for the purpose of assisting the Civil Authority of this State in carrying into Execution the Laws thereof in the said County of Windham.

Resolved, that His Excellency the Governor be also advised to appoint and commissionate B. Genl Ethan Allen, to take the command of the said Vollunteers.

Resolved, that the Honble Jonas Fay Esqr. be, and he is hereby appointed Judge of Probate for the District of Bennington, in the Room of Col°. Nathl. Brush resigned—This appointment to remain in full Force & Virtue, until some other Person shall be regularly elected & commissionated to that Office, according to Constitution.

The Hon. Jonas Fay being duly sworn to that office was accordingly commissionated.

Upon the Application of Benjamin Bennet to this Council by his Attorney Stephen R. Bradley Esqr requesting that the Sentence given by the Hon. Superior Court of this State, at their Session in Tinmouth the last week, against the said Bennet, be mitigated by this Board,

Resolved, that as it is the Desire of this Council when consistent with Constitution, & in Case of Penitency, to mitigate the Rigours of the Law upon Offenders, the said Benjamin Bennet is hereby discharged from Three Months & an half of the Imprisonment ordered by said Sentence, upon Condition that he pay to the Sheriff of the County of Bennington, the Fine ordered by said Court, with Costs of Prosecution, Committment, &c ; or procure good and sufficient Security to the Acceptance of the said Sheriff, that the same shall be paid within Three Months after liberation,

And the Sheriff of the said County of Bennington, upon such Payment or Security being made, at the Expiration of Fourteen Days next after the rising of said Court, is hereby directed to liberate & discharge the said Benjamin Bennet from his Confinement in the Goal in Bennington.

By Order of the Governor and Council, THO. TOLMAN *Dep. Secry.*

Resolved that the Secretary of Council, or Deputy, be directed to redraught in a plain and legible Manner the former minutes of this Council, and compile the same into one Book in Folio.

Attest, THOMAS TOLMAN, *Depy Secry.*

A COMMISSION, WITH INSTRUCTIONS, TO BRIGADIER GENERAL ETHAN ALLEN.

To the Honorable Brigr General Ethan Allen.—In pursuance of an Act of the General Assembly of this State at their Session in the month of June last, entitled "An Act empowering the Governor to raise Men to assist the Sheriffs" by & with the advice of the Council Board of this State met at Manchester on the 29th day of August last, which is as follows, vizt. "Resolved, that His Excellency the Governor be also advised to appoint & commissionate B. General Ethan Allen to take the command of the said Vollunteers" and reposing Special Trust & confidence in your Fidelity & good Conduct, I do by these Presents, In the name, and by the authority of the Freemen of the State of Vermont, fully authorize and empower you, the said Ethan Allen, to act and transact the following matters, for the purpose of assisting the Civil Authority in the due Execution of the Laws of this State, for the suppression of the late, and present tumultuous Insurrections in the County of Windham.

Firstly. You will proceed to raise as Volunteers, Two Hundred and Fifty men (One Hundred & Fifty of which in Colonel Walbridge's, and One Hundred in Colonel Allen's Regiment of Militia) & see them equipt with Horses, Arms and Accoutrements. Provisions and Ammunition will be furnished by the Commissary General.

Secondly. The Men when raised & thus equipt you will march into the County of Windham as a Posse Comitatus for the Assistance of the Civil Authority in the said County of Windham as aforesaid, In pursuance of the Trust reposed. Given under my Hand at Arlington this Second Day of September Annoque Domini 1782.

(Signed) THOMAS CHITTENDEN, *Capt. General.*

By His Excellency's Command,
THOS. TOLMAN, *D. Secry.*

Attest, THOMAS TOLMAN, *D. Secry.*

In the spring and summer of 1782, the adherents to New York in the southern part of Windham county were very active in their opposition to the authority of Vermont, being encouraged therein by Governor Clinton, by whom civil and military officers, residing in that county, were commissioned. The opposition culminated on the 22d of August, in successful resistance to an attempt of Jonathan Hunt, the Vermont sheriff, to arrest Timothy Church of Brattleborough, on an execution. Thereupon the special session of the Council of August 29 was called, and the above commission was given to General Allen. On the 8th of September the General gathered his *posse;* on the 9th the party of mounted men reached the scene of disturbance; on the 10th the principal offenders were arrested; and by the 19th they were convicted and sentenced by the superior court, some to banishment and confiscation, and others to fines.—See *Vt. Hist. Soc. Collections*, Vol. II, pp. 272–'3, 286–'7, 295–303; *East. Vermont*, pp. 424–455; *Early History*, pp. 394–397.

JOURNALS OF COUNCIL BELONGING TO THE FIRST VOLUMN.

COMMENCING WITH THE

PROCEEDINGS AT ARLINGTON APRIL 25th 1781.[1]

ARLINGTON April 25, 1781.

This day the following Members of Council Met by His Excellency's Summons vizt. Jonas Fay, Moses Robinson, Ira Allen, and John Fassett Esquires—There not being a quorum,

Adjourned to 8 oClock Tomorrow.

---

[1] Owing to an erroneous memorandum at the close of Vol. 1 of Secretary FAY's records, the following minutes of special sessions of the Council were omitted in copying for the press, and are now necessarily inserted here, instead of preceding the minutes of June 13 1781 on p. 101. In fact these and other minutes are misplaced in the official record.

APRIL 26, 1781.

Met according to adjournment.

The Honble Timothy Brownson & Jeremiah Clark Esquires joined the Council.

Resolved that the Honble Ira Allen Esquire and Major Isaac Clark, be and they are hereby appointed Agents, to proceed to the Province of Canada, & to Treat with Commissioners to be appointed on the part of the British in Canada, to agree on and settle a Carteel for the Exchange of prisoners and make returns to this Council.[1]

Resolved that the Captain General Notify the officers of the Militia in the Counties of Bennington and Rutland to make returns of the deficiency of ammunition in their respective Regiments &c. and receive orders for their Supply which will be delivered on Account of Money due to the Militia for services done.

Resolved that Joseph Farnsworth Esquire Commissary of Purchases, be and hereby is directed to receive and receipt the Ammunition belonging to this State and be accountable.

Resolved that Moses Robinson Esqr. be and hereby is appointed in lieu of Ira Allen Esqr. to attend the Convention to be holden at Cambridge [N. Y.] on the second Wednesday in May Next.

Resolved that there be and hereby is appointed four persons to Take a Tour into the new Teritory Lately Claimed by the State of Vermont adjoining to and lying East of Hudson River, to Learn the sense of the people relative to joining this State. Persons chosen, Mathew Lyon, Jonathan Fassett, Joseph Fay, and Thomas Butterfield. Either two of the above persons are directed to proceed as above specified.

Resolved that whereas it has been Represented that Colonel Gideon Warren has Removed with his effects out of the Ancient jurisdiction of this State, and Whereas it is viewed by this Council to be necessary that a quorum of the Board of War Convene on business at this Time, therefore Resolved that Jonathan Fassett Esquire be and hereby is appointed for the time being to Supply the place in the Board of War of Colo. Warren.

JOSEPH FAY, *Secy.*

Adjourned without day.

BENNINGTON 30th April 1781.

Personally appeared Jonas Galusha who is Elected sheriff in and for the County of Bennington, Captain David Galusha, and Captain Abiather Waldo as his Sureties, and acknowledge themselves jointly and severally recognized and bound unto the Treasurer of this State in the sum of two thousand pounds Lawful Money for the faithful performance of the said Jonas in his said office of Sheriff in & for the county aforesaid in discharging of the duty and for the answering all such damages as any person or persons shall Sustain by any unfaithfulness or Neglect in the Execution of the said office.

Attest, JOSEPH FAY, *Secy.*

ARLINGTON May 26, 1781.

In Council Resolved that an *Embargo* be and hereby is laid on the Exportation of all kinds of provision out of this State that is Necessary and Suitable for the Army for thirty days next coming.

---

[1] Allen alone went on this service.—See Allen's *History*, in *Vt. Hist. Soc. Collections*, Vol. I, pp. 420–421.

COUNCIL-CHAMBER.

CATAMOUNT-TAVERN.

APPENDIX A.

THE FIRST VERMONT COUNCIL CHAMBER,

IN

THE OLD CATAMOUNT TAVERN AT BENNINGTON.[1]

BY HILAND HALL.

[From *The American Historical Record*, number for Jan. 1872.]

ON the 30th of March 1871 the old "Catamount Tavern" House which had long been the most notable relic of early times in the Center Village of Bennington, Vermont, was burnt to the ground. It had been unoccupied for a short time and the origin of the fire is unknown. The house, which was in a tolerable state of preservation, had been built over a hundred years, having been erected by Captain Stephen Fay, a year or two prior to 1770. It was a wooden building about 44 feet by 34, two stories high, having two high chimneys with high fire places in each story, besides which there was a very large fireplace in the cellar or basement, part of which was used as a wash room, and a cook room as occasion required. The two chimneys are now standing (Autumn of 1871) exhibiting their spacious fire places, with heavy iron cranes in those of the lower story and basement. On the marble mantle of one of the fire places the words "Council room" appear, cut there in early times.[2] On the top of the high sign post was placed the stuffed skin of a Catamount, from which came the name of the house, though in its early days it was, in accordance with the custom of the time, more generally spoken of as "Landlord Fay's."

During the period of the early settlement of the state, the house was a great resort for travellers and emigrants, and it was also widely known

---

[1] The Illustrations for this paper, are from Photographs furnished by the author, ex-Governor Hiland Hall, of North Bennington, Vermont, and a pen-and-ink sketch by his grand-daughter.—EDITOR OF THE RECORD.

[2] The carver of the words on the fire-place left out the *n* in the word Council.

as the Head Quarters of the settlers in their contest with the New York land claimants. It was the home of Ethan Allen for several years from 1770, when he first came to the "New Hampshire Grants," as Vermont was then called. The settlers held their lands under grants from New Hampshire, to which the territory was supposed to belong, but in 1764 the king, by an order in council, placed them under the jurisdiction of New York. Whereupon the governor of that province declared their titles to be void, and re-granted their lands to speculators, who recovered judgments in the New York courts against the settlers, and sent their sheriffs and posses to execute them, who were resisted by the occupants and forcibly prevented from obtaining possession. This controversy raged for years, and the settlers appointed committees of safety before whom offenders against the integrity of their titles, styled "Yorkers," were brought for trial. On conviction they were variously punished, sometimes by banishment from the territory, and sometimes by whipping on the naked back, a mode of punishment for crime then in common use throughout the country. The latter punishment, in allusion to the Great Seal of the Governor of New Hampshire affixed to their charter titles, and to the instrument with which it was commonly inflicted, the settlers humorously called "the application of the *beech seal*."[1]

Another mode of punishment was devised for one offender residing within their own limits. One Doctor Samuel Adams of Arlington who had held his lands under a New Hampshire charter, suddenly became an open advocate of the New York title, advising his neighbors to purchase it. This tended to weaken the opposition to New York by producing division among the settlers, and he was repeatedly warned to desist from such discourse. But he persisted in his offensive language, and arming himself with pistols and other weapons, threatened death to any one who should molest him. What followed is related in the language of a contemporary: "The Doctor was soon taken by surprise, and carried [15 miles] to the Green Mountain [Landlord Fay's] tavern, at Bennington, where the committee heard his defence, and then ordered him to be tied in an armed chair and hoisted up to the sign (*a catamount's skin stuffed, sitting upon the sign post, 25 feet from the ground, with large teeth, looking and grinning towards New York*) and there to hang two hours, in sight of the people, as a punishment merited by his enmity to the rights and liberty of the inhabitants of the New Hampshire Grants. The judgment was executed, to the no small merriment of a large concourse of people. The Doctor was let down and dismissed by the committee, with an admonition to go and sin no more. This mild and exemplary disgrace had a salutary effect on the Doctor and many others."[2] Dr. Adams, on Burgoyne's invasion, became a violent tory, and fled to Canada, from which he never returned.

When Sir Wm. Tryon, governor of New York in 1771, issued a proclamation offering a reward of 20 pounds each for the apprehension of Ethan Allen, Remember Baker and Robert Cochran for their riotous opposition to the New York government, they retaliated by publishing over their names a counter proclamation offering a reward of 15 pounds for James Duane and 10 pounds for John Kempe, their two leading land-claiming antagonists, styling them "those common disturbers of the public peace," the rewards so payable on their being brought to "Land-

---

[1] Slade's Vermont *State Papers*, page 36.

[2] Ira Allen's *Natural and Political History of Vermont* p. 47. The same in *Vermont Historical Collections*, Volume I, page 357.

lord Fay's at Bennington."[1] Colonel Ethan Allen was sojourning at the "Catamount Tavern" in the spring of 1775 and from the "Council Room" of that house went forth his order of May 3rd, for mustering the Green Mountain Boys for the capture of Ticonderoga which was effected seven days afterwards in the name of "the great Jehovah and the Continental Congress."

In this noted tavern house sat the Vermont Council of Safety during the trying campaign of 1777 guiding and directing the patriotic exertions of the Green Mountain Boys to stem the torrent of Burgoyne's invasion; and here also Stark and Warner, with the aid of the Council, planned the famous attack on Baum's entrenchments, where was won the brilliant victory of Bennington, which turned the current of success from the British to the American arms, and was followed in a few weeks, by the capture of Burgoyne and his army at Saratoga. Captain Fay, the proprietor of the house, had five sons in the Battle of Bennington one of whom was killed. On being told that one of his sons had fallen in the fight, the venerable patriot, through his deep grief "thanked God that he had a son who was willing to die for his country."[2]

Here, in 1778, was tried and condemned, one David Redding, a traitor and spy; and in a field in front of the house a gallows had been erected, and a great crowd had assembled to see him executed. But on the morning fixed for the execution, the Governor and Council granted him a reprieve for one week, for the reason that he had been tried by a jury of six, while by the common law there ought to have been twelve. The multitude, who as well as the six jurors, had condemned the traitor, were clamorous at their disappointment, and violence was seriously apprehended, whereupon Col. Ethan Allen, who had just returned from his long English captivity,[3] mounted a stump and waving his hat and exclaiming *attention the whole!* proceeded to announce the reasons which produced the reprieve, advised the multitude to depart peaceably to their habitations, and to return on the day fixed by the Governor and Council, adding, with an oath, "you shall see somebody hung at all events, for if

---

[1] See Hiland Hall's *History of Vermont*, page 134.

The following is a copy of the Proclamation:

£25 REWARD.

Whereas James Duane and John Kempe of New York, have by their menaces and threats greatly disturbed the public peace and repose of the honest peasants of Bennington, and the settlements to the northward, which peasants are now and ever have been in the peace of God and the King, and are patriotic and liege subjects of George III. Any person that will apprehend those common disturbers, viz. James Duane and John Kempe, and bring them to Landlord Fay's at Bennington, shall have £15 reward for James Duane and £10 for John Kemp, paid by

ETHAN ALLEN,
REMEMBER BAKER,
ROBERT COCHRAN.

Dated Poultney, Feb 5, 1772.

[2] *Memorials of a Century*, by Rev. I. Jennings, pages 253, 254.

[3] In September, 1775, Colonel Allen was in command of a body of Canadian Volunteers, on the borders of the St. Lawrence River. He was captured near Montreal and sent a prisoner in chains to England. He was exchanged, in New York, in May, 1778, when he returned to his home in Vermont.

Redding is not then hung I will be hung myself." Upon this the uproar ceased and the crowd dispersed. Redding having been afterwards tried and condemned by a jury of twelve, was hung on the day to which his reprieve had been granted, in accordance with Allen's prediction.[1]

The children of Captain Stephen Fay were numerous and respectable, and several of them have been prominent in the affairs of the state of Vermont. He died in 1781, and the house, not many years afterwards, became a private dwelling for two of his sons, in succession ; then for a grandson and finally for a great grandson, John Fay, Esq., who died Feb. 25, 1866.

---

[1] Slade's *State Papers*, page 269.

APPENDIX B.

RESOLUTIONS OF CONGRESS IN SEPTEMBER AND OCTOBER 1779, AND ACTION OF VERMONT THEREON.

THE AGENTS OF VERMONT TO CONGRESS.

PHILADELPHIA, July 1st 1779.

Gentlemen,—We ever have been and still are willing that every part of the conduct of the people we represent, (so far as relates to the measures which have been come into for establishing the State of Vermont,) should at any convenient time be fully laid before the Grand Council of America, together with the solicitation of our constituents for a union with the other free and independent States of America; as agreeable to the declaration of said constituents (in full Convention) made at Westminster on the fifteenth day of January A. D. 1777, and exhibited to Congress soon after.[1] They always stand ready, in conjunction with their fellow brethren in the United States, to pay their equal proportion of the expenses of the present just war with Great Britain.

But being sensible of the inconvenience which might attend your honors in the deliberation and final determination of a matter of such importance while the War with Great Britain and the circulating medium remain in the present condition, we would be far from urging a decision in the premises until you can have leisure to take it up deliberately, confidently relying (in the mean time) that when ever such opportunity shall present, we shall have seasonable notice to prepare and lay in our defence. Therefore (at this time) we enclose you only a copy of our appointment and instructions, with a printed hand-bill containing viz. Governor Chittenden's orders to Col. Allen dated the 6th day of May last, an extract of the proceedings of an adjourned Superior Court held at Westminster on the 26th day of the same month, and his Excellency's Proclamation of the 3d of June;[2] and transmit you a book containing a code of Laws as established in the State of Vermont; and have the satisfaction to be, with real sentiments of esteem,

Gentlemen, Your honors' most
Obdt. Hble Servts.

ETHAN ALLEN,
JONAS FAY.

The Hon. the Congress.[3]

---

[1] See Vol. I, p. 48. [2] See Vol. I, pp. 305, 442.

[3] *Ethan Allen Ms. Papers*, p. 283.

MEMORIAL OF A CONVENTION HELD AT LEBANON, N. H., JULY 27 1779, BY A COMMITTEE OF THE CONVENTION.[1]

To the honorable Committee appointed by Congress to repair to the New Hampshire Grants and inquire into the reasons why the inhabitants refuse to continue citizens of the respective states which heretofore exercised jurisdiction over them &c.

A Committee appointed by a convention of delegates from nineteen towns on said grants on both sides of Connecticut river beg leave to exhibit the following sentiments of the people and peculiar circumstances of the grants from which they form apprehensions that they ought not to be holden to the States of New York and New Hampshire.

The people in these parts conceive that in the formation of Republican States no class or body of men ought to be holden or considered as part of any community without their consent and that such consent must be given in one of the following ways. 1st By their express and direct act for that purpose. 2nd By their acquiescence in the measures taken by the State for an establishment of such government. 3d By their being duly represented in a State after it is formed. Or 4, By their holding some charter of privilege by which they are necessarily connected with the State in order to an enjoyment of ye privileges contained in the charter.

To have them holden to a State without such consent they apprehend is inconsistent with republican government; which (as they imagine) supposes the subjects to be governed by their free consent, by a legislature in which they are duly represented, by officers in whose appointment they have a voice (at least) by their representatives, and in a manner which the majority of those who unite for the purpose of government agree upon—which they conceive to be clearly stated in *an address to the people of New Hampshire—a public defence of the rights of the grants*, and in a pamphlet entitled, *a Republican;* which accompany this.[2]

---

[1] *New Hampshire Grants*, *Vol.* I, No. 40, p. 277, in the Archives of the State Department, Washington. This memorial was addressed to the committee of Congress which had been appointed in June 1779 to visit Vermont; as was also the letter of JOSEPH MARSH, which is appended to it. As this committee had returned to Philadelphia before the convention met at Lebanon, these papers were of course addressed to the committee at Philadelphia, and were thus brought to the knowledge of Congress. At the same session of Congress, in August 1779, a memorial of a Convention of the towns of Hartford, Norwich, Sharon, Royalton, Fairlee, Newbury and Barnet was presented, dated March 1779. It was again presented by Peter Olcott in Feb. 1780, and will be found in *Appendix G.* These documents, so far as the editor can ascertain, have never been printed.

[2] The document first named is a pamphlet of sixteen small pages, entitled as follows: "An ADDRESS of the INHABITANTS of the TOWNS of Plainfield, Lebanon, Enfield, (alias Relhan,) Canaan, Cardigan, Hanover, Lime, Orford, Haverhill, Bath, and Landaff, to the Inhabitants of the several Towns in the Colony of New Hampshire. Norwich: (Conn.) Printed by JOHN TRUMBULL, M,DCC,LXXVI." It was signed by NEHEMIAH ESTERBROOK, Chairman, and BEZALEEL WOODWARD, Clerk; and

Those pamphlets, the people apprehend, clearly evince that the only band which held the grants connected with New York & New Hampshire was dissolved by the declaration of Independence of the United States. In order to a more full understanding whereof it will be necessary to attend to various and peculiar circumstances the Grants have been under in the different stages since they were first granted. And 1st. No one will deny that the fee of the tract of land now called the *New Hampshire grants*, before it was chartered appertained to the crown of Great Britain as the law of the land then stood and that it never had been vested in any subject whatever. That in the course of the last war and soon after the close of it, without an express annexation of it to the jurisdiction of any particular government, the governor of New-Hampshire by express direction or (at least) concurrance of the crown, alloted the said grants on both sides of Connecticut river into townships and granted charters of them in the name of the King to such persons as were willing to undertake the settlement of them, by which charters the grantees not only became entitled to the lands as granted but were also erected into bodies corporate, with certain immunities and privileges.

The grantees by receiving a title to their lands and such ample incorporations from the governor of New Hampshire, conceived they had good reason to expect to be subject to that government, & no other, as they viewed that act of the King to be of the nature and complexion of an engagement on his part that he would not remove them to another government & in confidence and expectation thereof large numbers of the grantees removed their families and substance on to those lands and underwent infinite hardships, toils and fatigues to put them under cultivation.

---

was dated Hanover, July 31, A. D. 1776. To it was appended a notice for an adjourned meeting at College Hall, Hanover, on the second Thursday of October following; at which meeting possibly the next document referred to in the text was adopted. The pamphlet, of which the title is given above, complains that the former government of the colony was absolute; that the desire of the people in 1776 was to adopt a republican government; but that the convention which formed the council and assembly then in existence had defeated this purpose, by apportioning representation according to population, thus depriving many towns of representation at all, and many others so in effect—and, further, by "confining the electors in their choice of a representative to persons of £200 estate and so on, in that manner, as they of their sovereign pleasure thought fit to dictate." The case is forcibly presented and ably argued. The three documents referred to were doubtless of the same character and for the same purpose; and, though unsuccessful in New Hampshire, it is apparent they were influential in Vermont.—See first Constitution of Vermont, chap. II, section sixteen. JEREMY BELKNAP stated that the N. H. Convention of Nov. 14 1775 required every elector to possess real estate of *twenty* pounds value; every candidate for election of *three hundred pounds;* and fixed the number of representatives at 89, of which Cheshire and Grafton counties (western New Hampshire,) had only 21.—See Belknap's *History of New Hampshire*, Vol. II, p. 305–309.

2. Through the influence of vigorous exertions on the part of New York and default on the part of New Hampshire a decree was obtained in 1764 from the King in council (without the grantees of the lands ever being notified in the matter) whereby the grants were divided by a line at the western bank of Connecticut river and those west of the river subjected to the government of New York, while those east of the river were continued under the government of New Hampshire. The people on the grants were surprised and confounded at being thus divided and especially those west of the river who found themselves thereby annexed to a government very disagreeable to them—the settlement of the lands thereby retarded and the whole thrown under the greatest possible disadvantage as to taking measures for a redress of those grievances. Some part of them however combined for the purpose of obtaining redress and were at the expense to send agents to Great Britain to endeavor it; which joined with the exertions of the governor of New Hampshire and humble petitions of the people from other parts of the grants had brought the matter again under consideration; and the inhabitants with reason solaced themselves in the prospect of being again re-annexed to New Hampshire, & thereby have the whole of the grants united: But the attention of the King at that time being more closely engaged in absolute dominion over his American subjects than in a redress of their grievances the matter was delayed till the commencement of the present war.

The governor of New York in the mean time had threatened the inhabitants who had been thus unjustly subjected, that unless they would resign up the grants which they had obtained from the governor of New-Hampshire and receive patents of their lands from him, he would grant them to other persons, which he actually did in sundry instances - by means of which and other artifices many of the grantees were prevailed on to suffer their charter to be deposited in the hands of the council of New York. This being the case those who were able and willing to pay the exorbitant demand of two thousand three hundred dollars & suffer an enhancement of their quitrents, obtained grants or promises of charter from that governor—while others opposed the New York measures *by force of arms*, for which their leaders suffered an outlawry. The governor of New York being at length prohibited making re-grants—those who had been so submissive as to trust him with their New Hampshire charters (except the few above mentioned) could neither recover them nor obtain new grants.

The most of the inhabitants west of the river did notwithstanding submit to the government of New York and those east of the river continued under the government of New Hampshire until the declaration of independence of the United States.

By that declaration the people conceived themselves freed from that unrighteous act in 1764 which they have ever viewed as being of the same nature as those measures of Great Britain, on account of which the United States disowned subjection thereto, with this difference only that the former had respect to a certain district of the American colonies only, while some of the latter had respect to the whole. They have conceived that a division of them by a line at the river which was viewed by disinterested judges as cruel, arbitrary and unjust and which has ever been complained of as such by those who were immediately affected, ceased on the declaration of independence, as the immediate ground and object of that independence was to free y[e] inhabitants of the United States from the inquisitous and tyrannical measures Great Britain had for a number of years been concerting against us, of which this was one —hence the inhabitants on the two sides of the river conceive it to be manifest that they had good right to connect themselves together when independence took place.

For the foregoing and other important reasons suggested at the proceedings of a late convention at Dresden and which accompany this,[1] the people on the grants west of the river have ever been very uneasy at being subjected to the jurisdiction of New York, and since the commencement of the war by far the greatest part of them have constantly determined no longer to submit to that jurisdiction.

The foregoing representation of the circumstances of the grants we apprehend also clearly shows the injury done to the inhabitants east of the river in their being separated from those west of the river, as they were by that separation exposed to such measures as New Hampshire saw fit to impose on them. And the wide difference in sentiments in respect to representation between the inhabitants within the Mason-claim, and those on the grants, occasioned a number of towns on the grants as early as Decem. 1775 to remonstrate against the measures taken by the convention of that state—a copy of which is herewith exhibited—and no satisfactory answer being obtained thereto they in the next place published an address to the people of New Hampshire on the subject.[2]

By the declaration of independence the people [who] were aggrieved, supposed themselves freed from further obligations to New Hampshire but were notwithstanding willing to connect with them in case they could agree on terms—in consequence whereof proposals were made to unite with them, which are also inclosed with their answer which last was esteemed so vague and indeterminate that it gave no satisfaction of relief in the point of representation which had primarily occasioned their controversy with New Hampshire.

The inhabitants on the grants west of the river had in the mean time declared independence from New York and taken measures to procure government among themselves, and also invited those east of the river (who were unwilling to connect with New Hampshire under present circumstances) to unite with them therein, which on consideration of the dissolution of their connection with New Hampshire by the declaration of independence, and the reunion of the grants on the the two sides of the river by the extinction of the decree in 1764 they agreed to accept.

About half of the inhabitants on the grants east of the river have notwithstanding continued to act with New Hampshire and exerted themselves to have the whole of the grants re-united to that State, to which opposition has been all along made by the other part of the inhabitants and which they are still averse to, as New Hampshire by their late plan of government still give evidence that their intention is to establish their representation according to numbers, which the people in this quarter of the grants are unwilling to unite upon.

On the whole the body of the people in the northern half of the grants east of the river, for the reasons before mentioned conceive they are under no obligations to connect with New Hampshire. And the whole

---

[1]Probably the Convention alluded to by Ira Allen as having published a pamphlet in 1778 for the first Union.—See Vol. I, p. 405. The pamphlet is not in the Archives at Washington.

[2]The New Hampshire scheme of representation complained of was adopted Nov. 14 1775; the protest was made in Dec. 1775; and the address was dated July 31 1776.—See *ante*, p. 170, note[2].

are unwilling to be separated from the inhabitants west of the river, whom they view as brethren and of the same family, which endearing connection they think ought not to be dissolved.

Lebanon on the New Hampshire Grants July 27th, 1779.

JOSEPH MARSH
ELISHA PAYNE
PETER OLCOTT
JONA CHASE
BEZA WOODWARD
Committee.

Joseph Marsh to the Committee of Congress.

LEBANON ON THE NEW HAMPSR. GRANTS
July 27th 1779.

Gentlemen,—When the people on the New Hampshire grants were informed of your appointment by Congress to repair to these parts to enquire into the reasons of the difficulties subsisting among them relative to their not continuing citizens of the respective States to which they had belonged &c. it gave universal satisfaction in expectation that they should in that way have an opportunity of laying before Congress those matters of difficulty which have long subsisted between those states and the people on these grants ; but when they were informed that the committee had been on some part of the grants and were returned, they were much disappointed. Notwithstanding, being anxious of having those matters brought to a speedy issue they have met in convention and ordered a brief representation of their political circumstances, together with their reasons for not submitting to the government of said states, to be transmitted to your Honors, which is now done by Col. Olcott, hoping the committee will receive them so far at least as to inform themselves that those difficulties are still subsisting in these parts of the grants and will probably continue until the interposition of Congress shall bring them to an issue.

We would beg leave earnestly to request that in case the committee shall not think themselves authorized to make their report on the information which we have exhibited & what they have otherwise obtained, that they will devise some way whereby ye people may be heard so that Congress may be fully availed of the true situation and circumstances of the people on the grants before any decisive decree shall be made thereon. We would beg leave further to inform that the people on the grants are so divided that unless the whole of the grants can be made an entire state we apprehend the only alternative left which will bring the dispute to a happy close will be by connecting the whole of the grants with New Hampshire as they were before the decree in 1764.

And as the state of anarchy and confusion which we have for a number of years been and still continue under, lays us under the greatest difficulty in performing our part as members and citizens of the American States—We therefore earnestly request that those matters may be in some proper way and manner brought to a speedy issue, whereby we may both do & pay our part of the continental cause & dispute with Great Britain—At the same time humbly expecting will never suffer any tryal or decision of the matters of controversy whereby the people on the grants will be affected without providing for them an opportunity of being heard and defending themselves.

I write this in behalf of the general committee in ye northern district of the New Hampshire grants, in compliance with directions from their constituents, and am with much respect gentlemen

your honors most obedient and most humble servant,

JOSEPH MARSH, *Chairman.*

Honble Committee of Congress.

IN CONGRESS Friday, July 2, 1779.[1]

A letter of the 1st, from Ethan Allen and Jonas Fay, was read, enclosing a paper endorsed col. Allen and Dr. Fays' appointment and instructions, and accompanied with a book entitled "Acts and laws of the State of Vermont in America."

Ordered to lie on the table.

July 31 1779, Jonas Fay and Paul Spooner, two of the Committee appointed by the General Assembly on the 16th of the previous February, were instructed to wait upon Congress and request copies of such letters and resolutions as they might deem necessary, and to transact any other business concerning this State.[2] They promptly discharged this duty, and also delivered the following letter.

GOVERNOR CHITTENDEN TO CONGRESS.[3]

BENNINGTON August 5th 1779.

Gentlemen,—After reading a resolution of your Honorable Body of June last, purporting that any further consideration on the dispute subsisting between the States of New York & Vermont should be postponed until your Committee (appointed to examine the said dispute) should have made their report specially in the premisses: I cannot but take notice with some concern of your resolution of the 16th of the same month which was sent to your Committee by Express while they were in this Vicinity, resolving unanimously, that "the officers acting under the State of N. York who were lately restrained of their liberty by certain persons of a district called the N. Hampshire Grants. ought to be liberated."

This last resolve I find creates some jealousies in the minds of many of the inhabitants of this State on several accounts, viz.

1st. Because it appears to be counter to the resolution of the first of June aforesaid.

2d. Because it enters into the merits of the controversy subsisting previous to the report of said Committee, And

3d. Because it appears that the resolve was made Ex parte, and that the real facts on which it was founded with the many circumstances attending that matter, would not (at that time) have been particularly known to Congress: and that under such circumstances it appears to those inhabitants that the authority of this State ought not to be impeached or Censured by any resolve.

What the said officers (alias delinquents) had suffered, was for a high-handed breach of the peace, in rescuing several Cattle taken by legal authority for the payment of fines imposed on certain persons who refused to do any proportion in guarding the frontiers of this State from the invasions of the British, Savages, &c. and the said officers were liberated before the date of said resolution.[4] But as this matter necessarily terminates with the grand controversy subsisting between the two contending Governments, I shall omit making any particular remarks (by

---

[1] *Journal of Congress*, Folwell's edition, 1779–80, Vol. v, p. 209.

[2] See Vol. I, p. 307–'9.

[3] *New Hampshire Grants*, Vol. I, No. 40, p. 246, in Archives of the State Department, Washington. Now first printed in full.

[4] See Vol. I, pp. 298–300, 518–525.

way of defense) in the premises, until Congress shall appoint a future time when N. York and Vermont may be heard on the subject at large; at which time I shall respectfully present to you, a vindication of the conduct of this State, from its early conflict with N. York down to the present Æra; and a representation of the many good consequences which have already accrued to these independent States, by their assuming Government. In the mean time I renew the application of Mess^r. Allen & Fay (Agents for this State) to your hon^ble Body, of the first of July ultimo, for a union with the free, Sovereign and independant States of America, and in behalf of the people over whom I preside, [offer] to pay a just proportion of the expence of the present War with G. Britain when thereto legally requested.

It is evident the inhabitants of this State are in alliance with the States of America already; that they have fought, bled, and a great number of them suffered by being driven, by the enemy, from their possessions, with the loss of their most valuable effects, while many of their patriotic fellow citizens have nobly fallen in the Glorious Conflict: Witness the memorable Battle fought at this place on the 16th day of August 1777, the taking a number of British and delivering about one hundred American prisoners at the landing near Ticonderoga (soon after the Battle aforesaid) by a detachment composed principally of Col. Herrick's Regiment of Rangers raised within this State, with other Green Mountain Boys, (commanded by Col^o. John Brown,) and the many other important services rendered in the common cause by your friends in this State; for which nothing can make an adequate compensation but their being admitted to a union with the other independant States of America.

Congress will doubtless bear in mind that this important controversy subsisted many years before the late revolution took place, that it was not occasioned in consequence of it, and consequently that it does not equally affect Congress to settle it as tho' their own measures had given rise and existence to it; so that Governor Clinton's extraordinary and repeated importunities to you, to come to any determination of the matter exparte, and his hints of co-ercive measures in case of procrastination in the affair, are the more reprehensible. I find by a Copy of his letter of the 29th of May last to Congress, that he should defer taking any decisive measures, except issuing the necessary order to the Militia of this State,[1] and notwithstanding I am far from countenancing a measure so disagreeable in its nature, while I am sensible that the assistence of every power (which has and continues to operate for the happiness of these independent States) ought to be exerted wholly for their defense and security—Yet the free-born Citizens of this State can never so far degrade the dignity of humane nature, or relinquish any part of that glorious Spirit of patriotism which has hitherto distinguished them in every conflict with the unrelentiug and long-continued Tyranny of Designing men, as tamely to submit to his Mandates or even to be intimidated by a challenge from him. There is a large number of able bodied effective men in the lower halfshire of the County of Cumberland, some of whom are persons of very considerable property, that have been averse to taking up arms in defense of these States, who take the advantage of the dispute between N. York & Vermont to screen themselves from service, and by their living in the more interior part of the State are necessarily protected by the exertions of their neighbors; the Militia officers who pretend to act under N. York have been repeatedly applied to to furnish a quota to assist in defending the frontier in any way themselves might

[1] See Vol. I, pp. 519, 520.

choose, and have as often refused; I heartily wish that some method may be adopted, by Congress, to rouse them to their duty.

I wish you every happiness and am gentlemen with the highest sentiments of esteem, Your Honors most obedient and very Humble servant,

THO^S. CHITTENDEN.

The Honble Congress etc.

JONAS FAY AND PAUL SPOONER TO CONGRESS.[1]

PHILADELPHIA Aug. 20th 1779.

Most Honour'd Gentlemen,—We inclose herein to you a Copy of our instructions (which alludes to our appointment) to wait on you for the purposes therein named ; and as complaints have from time to time been exhibited to Congress against the conduct of our constituents, who, have not the favour of a seat in the grand council of America ; We humbly conceive ourselves (in our Capacity) justly entitled to copies of all such complaints and therefore beg that we may be furnished with those named in the list herewith exhibited, with any other papers we may have omitted naming (that concerns the people we represent) together with any resolutions that have been had thereon by Congress, since the commencement of the present war with G. Briton.

And as we are here, at the expense of a State who furnish men, to defend not only their own, but the frontiers of Several other States, we pray that we may be indulged in the request with all convenient speed, and are in the mean time, with the highest esteem and confidence in your Wisdom and integrity

Gentlemen your Honors most Obedient & very Humble Servants,

JONAS FAY,
PAUL SPOONER.

The Honble the Congress &c.

IN CONGRESS, Tuesday, August 24, 1779.[2]

A letter, of August the 5th, from Thomas Chittenden, and one of the 20th, from Jonas Fay and Paul Spooner, with two papers enclosed, were read :

On motion of Mr. M'Kean, seconded by Mr. Holten,

Resolved, That copies of the following papers be delivered to Jonas Fay and Paul Spooner, as private persons, viz.

1. Proceedings of Congress on the petition from the representatives of the New Hampshire Grants dated January the 17th, 1776, and read the 8th of May following :[3]
2. Report on Joseph Woodward's letter, dated the 17th of January, 1776, and read the 30th of May following :[4]

---

[1] *New Hampshire Grants,* Vol. I, No. 40, p. 253, in the Archives of the State Department, Washington.

[2] *Journals of Congress,* Folwell's edition, 1779–80 Vol. V, p. 245.

[3] See Vol. I, pp. 16–21.

[4] Joseph Woodward was chairman of the Convention of Jan. 1776 at Dorset. For resolutions reported by the committee of Congress, see Vol. I, p. 20 note [2].

13

3. Proceedings of Congress on the extracts of the proceedings of the convention of New Hampshire Grants, 24th of July and 25th of September 1776 :[1]

4. · A letter from Pierre Van Cortlandt, President of New-York, to Congress, dated May the 27th, 1777, and proceedings of Congress thereon :[2]

5. Governor Clinton's letter of May [July] the 8th, 1778, and read the 18th of September following, and the resolution thereon :[3]

6. Gov. Clinton's letters of the 27th [18th] and 28th [29th] of May, with three papers enclosed, and of the 7th of June, 1779, and resolves of Congress :[4]

7. The several papers relating to the trial of Hilkiah Trout, [Grout,] dated February the 18th, 1779.[5]

---

[1] The Convention at Westminster of Jan. 15 1777 seems to have been omitted. This convention adopted "the Declaration and Petition to Congress ;" and the proceedings of Congress above referred to are the resolutions of June 30 1777, *dismissing* the petition of Vermont.—See Vol. I, pp. 48, 396.

[2] See Slade's *State Papers*, p. 77. This letter hastened the resolutions of Congress of June 30, 1777, referred to in the preceding note. This letter and the Vermont petition were referred to a committee of the whole, June 23 1777, and both were disposed of by the resolutions adopted a week later.

[3] In this letter, Gov. Clinton complained, among other things, of the draft of every fourth man in Vermont to recruit Warner's regiment.—See *Eastern Vermont*, p. 324.

[4] See Vol. I, pp. 518–522.

[5] Major HILKIAH GROUT, of Weathersfield, was born in Lunenburgh, Mass., July 23 1728. He came to Vermont previous to June 27 1755, as on that day he, with several others, was captured by Indians at Bridgman's Fort in Vernon. In 1758 or 9, being released, he returned to Cumberland County. He adhered to New York, and was employed in various offices under that state, having been appointed captain of the Weathersfield company, in the upper regiment for Cumberland county, in 1775, and first major of the regiment in 1776 ; delegate for Weathersfield in the County Congress, or Committee of Safety, in 1777 ; assistant of inferior court of common pleas in 1778 ; and justice of the peace, commissioner to administer oaths of office, and justice of the court of oyer and terminer in 1782. On the 17th of Feb. 1779, he went to Shrewsbury, in the exercise of his office as a New York magistrate, and took sundry affidavits, for which he was seized and tried by a court-martial, Feb. 18, consisting of several officers of Warner's regiment, the decision being that the charge was not supported. To this trial the above vote of Congress doubtless referred. Grout was afterward tried, convicted, and fined by a Vermont civil court. He represented Weathersfield in the Vermont Legislature of 1785.—See *Eastern Vermont;* Deming's *Catalogue* ; and Slade's *State Papers*, p. 552.

IN CONGRESS, Wednesday, September 8, 1779.[1]

The delegates for the state of New-York laid before Congress certain instructions which they have received from their constituents, accompanied with sundry papers, which were read; also a petition of the committees of Cumberland county to Congress was read, praying their speedy interposition in settling the disturbances upon the New-Hampshire Grants, accompanied with sundry papers:[2]

Ordered, That the same be referred to a committee of five:

The members chosen, Mr. McKean, Mr. Paca, Mr. Holten, Mr. Huntington and Mr. Smith.

INSTRUCTIONS *of the New York Legislature to its delegates in Congress relative to the disorders prevailing in the north eastern parts of the state of New York.*[3]

KINGSTON, August 27, 1779.

Gents.—We anxiously expected that, by an effectual Interposition of Congress, our deluded Fellow Citizens in the North Eastern Parts of the State would before our present meeting have peaceably returned to their duty, and prevented the necessity of coercive Measures to compel a submission to the authority of Legal Government. This we were the more readily induced to hope as we conceive the Terms we have offered to them to be not only perfectly just and equitable but even generous; these pacific Overtures have been disregarded, Violence and Outrage are daily committed upon, and the Severest punishment threatened against (the latter of which will appear from the inclosed Copy of an Act of the Legislature of the pretended State of Vermont[4]) our good subjects in Brattleborough and other well affected Towns, who now claim from us that Protection which we have Solemnly promised to them and which consistent with justice we can no longer withhold.

While on the one hand we view with a degree of Horror the dreadful consequences of having Recourse to Force, not only to this State, and especially to the unhappy People who will be its immediate Object, but also to the common cause of America—yet on the other we are persuaded our Successful efforts, to expel a foreign Tyranny will avail us little while we remain Subject to the domestic Usurpation; earnestly wishing however by every attempt to Peace, to prevent the evils of a Civil War, we must direct you to entreat once more the mediation of Congress.

A Quorum of the Committee, appointed by the Resolution of the first of June last, having never met,[5] and as we have not been informed that

---

[1] *Journals of Congress*, Folwell's edition, 1779–80, Vol. v, p. 257.

[2] Petition dated July 23 1779. See *Doc. Hist. of New York*, Vol. 4, pp. 590–593.

[3] From the *Documentary History of New York*, Vol. 4, pp. 594–596.

[4] The act here referred to was that of June 1779, entitled "An act to prevent persons from exercising authority, unless lawfully authorized by this State;" which, of course, prohibited all exercise of authority under New York in Vermont.—See Slade's *State Papers*, p. 389.

[5] Messrs. Root and Ellsworth, of the committee of Congress, reached Bennington on the 26th of June, a few hours after Messrs. Atlee and Witherspoon had left. John Sessions, and an associate from Cumberland county, followed Messrs. A. and W. to Albany and endeavored, but

Congress have since proceeded in the business, we presume it is remaining before them in the same State it was prior to that day. Upon this suposition we shall take the Liberty of suggesting several matters for their consideration and proposing certain measures, not only just and satisfactory in themselves, but such as we believe will be effectual in restoring the Peace of the State.

It is to be observed that all the Lands in that District of Country, which has attempted a Separation from this State under the name of Vermont, is 1st either unpatented and unoccupied or 2dly unpatented and actually occupied or 3dly Patented by New Hampshire or Massachusetts Bay and not afterward patented by New York or 4thly Patented by New York prior to any patent under New Hampshire or Massachusetts Bay or 5 Patented by New Hampshire or Massachusetts Bay and afterwards patented by New York.

With respect to the first Case the Lands must remain for the future Disposition of Government. With respect to the second we have engaged to confirm to the Occupants their respective Possessions together with as much vacant adjoining Land as to form convenient Farms not exceeding three hundred acres each.

With respect to the third we have engaged to confirm the Patents under New Hampshire or Massachusetts Bay as fully as if they had been made under New York without taking any advantage of a non performance of Condition.

With respect to the fourth and fifth Cases we have engaged besides confirming such Possessions as were made under New Hampshire or Massachusetts Bay prior to any Patent for the same Lands under New York to submit the Determination of the Right of Soil to Commisrs. to be appointed by Congress who are to determine agreeable to Equity and Justice without adhering to the strict Rules of Law Provided nevertheless that the actual Occupants under New York shall be confirmed in their respective Possessions.

It is further to be observed that every part of the above District was indisputably included within the Jurisdiction either of New York or New Hampshire or Massachusetts' Bay and that the Right of Jurisdiction as Congress themselves have declared was not altered by these Communities respectively becoming Independent States.

Having made these observations we would premise further that in order to remove every objection, fully to evince the Uprightness of our Intentions and our earnest desire for an accommodation, We are willing that if Congress should deem the above mode of determining the Right of Soil between interfering Claimants under New Hampshire or Massachusetts Bay on the one and under New York on the other part ineligible, we will consent that it shall be determined either immediately by Congress themselves or in such other manner as they shall think proper. We will also concede that on all Questions relative to such Right of Soil this State shall not vote in Congress, that Congress shall guaranty to the Inhabitants on the Grants the Performance of these Terms and that no Proceeding of Congress requiring or recommending it to the Inhabitants to submit to the Authority of this State shall be construed to injure any Right of Jurisdiction which the States of New Hampshire or Massachusetts Bay may respectively have to the above Territory or any part thereof.

---

in vain, to persuade them to return to Bennington.—Micah Townshend to Gov. Clinton, July 5, 1779, in Ms. *Clinton Papers*, N. Y. State Library, No. 2428.

This last Proposal does not arise from an apprehension that probably these States will claim the jurisdiction of any of the Grants lying West of Connecticut River but is mentioned solely with a view that nothing would remain which can possibly have even the appearance of a Difficulty. We will at all Times chearfully submit the Right of Jurisdiction to the desision of Congress agreeable to the 9th Article of Confederation.

These Terms and Proposals We conceive must satisfy every Claim either upon our Justice or Generosity and we trust they will appear to Congress, to whom we instruct and authorize you immediately to communicate them, to pledge the public Faith of this State for the Performance of them, and thereupon to sollicit the immediate Interferance of Congress recommending to such of the Inhabitants of the Grants who at the Commencement of the present War were within the Jurisdiction of New York again to submit to the Government & Authority of this State, with a Proviso (should the same be deemed necessary) that such Interference shall not be construed to injure a Right of Jurisdiction existing in any other of the United States.[1]

We presume it will be needless at this time particularly to recapitulate all the Reasons which induced this State to apply to Congress for a Declaration of their Sence of the Conduct of our revolted fellow subjects, as they are fully contained in the numberless Papers which we have from time to time transmitted to Congress. Respecting this matter let it suffice to mention as a principal Inducemt that the Revolters asserted and their adherents believed that their attempts to a separation from this State were agreeable to and favored by Congress or some Members of Weight and Influence.

Every Delay on the Part of Congress explicitly to disavow and disapprove of is construed by these People as countenancing and has a manifest tho' we do not say a designed Tendency to establish and confirm the secession. Their Pretended Legislature has already confiscated and are now disposing of the Estates of Persons who have joined the Enemy and probably will soon proceed to grant the unappropriated Lands. By these means they raise moneys for the Support of their Government and obtain a great and dayly accession of Strength not only by an additional number of Settlers but every other Purchaser will be interested to maintain an authority upon which their Title depends.[2] These Proceedings

[1] For the formal propositions of Gov. Clinton to the inhabitants of Vermont, in his Proclamations of February and October 1778, and the Vermont view of the same, see Ethan Allen's *Vindication*, in Vol. I, Appendix I.

[2] It is obvious that Vermont might have retorted, that the most active enemies to the independence of the State were the men to whom New York had granted Vermont lands. In seeking to strengthen her cause by enlisting the interest and influence of citizens of other states, as landholders in her own, Vermont opposed them to New Yorkers who had been interested in like manner against Vermont. In March 1781, Gen. Alexander McDougall, a delegate of New York in Congress, advised Gov. Clinton to adopt the same course, using "*vacant lands in the Grants*" as the material in part to be used in purchasing the influence of New England officers for New York, and tempering "the leveling principles" of the yeomanry of New England. At that time Gov. Clinton was hopeful of an early decision of Congress favorable to New York, but recon-

also will increase the Confusion and render the Restoration of Peace at a future day more difficult. As they bear no Share in the present public Burthen, that part of the Country is become an Asylum for all Persons who wish to avoid Military Duty or the Payments of Taxes, and Numbers are daily emigrating thither influenced merely by this Motive. They will also attempt to enforce their cruel Edict and oblige the Inhabitants of Brattleborough and the other Towns who have remained in Allegiance to this State to submit to their usurpation. These Inhabitants will resist and the Justice, Peace and Safety of the State demand that we should and we are resolved to assist and protect them. In short, for we cannot enter into particulars. Matters are bro't to a Crisis, and we must in this session determine with Decision upon the important Question of protecting our faithful Subjects and supporting the rightful Jurisdiction of the State. What the Consequences will be, we forbear to mention. They may easily be imagined and Congress can prevent them.

One principal Design of our Present Meeting was to deliberate upon this momentous Subject. We shall notwithstanding suspend all further proceedures and continue sitting till we are favored with the Sentiments of Congress which you will transmit to us by the messenger who conveys this and whom you will detain for that purpose.

Should we however be disappointed and Congress decline to interpose by an express Recommendation as above proposed, we do in such Case direct Mr. Jay, to whom we have in a special manner committed this Business, immediately to withdraw and attend us at this Place.[1]

Gents,—With this you will receive a Letter in the nature of Instructions which you will observe is wrote upon a Presumption that no Proceedings relative to the Vermont Business have been had in Congress since the appointment of the Committee on the 1st of June last. Should subsequent measures however have been adopted by Congress which you may conceive equally effectual and beneficial to the State with those we have instructed you to propose, you are in such Case at Liberty to suspend the Communication of these Instructions till our further Direction and immediately inform us of the measures by a special messenger.

We are with due Respect, Gentlemen,

your most obedient Servants.

By order of the Senate. }
By order of the Assembly. } [Signatures omitted in the copy.]

IN CONGRESS, Friday, September 17, 1779.

The committee to whom was referred the petition of the committees of Cumberland county, together with instructions from the senate and

---

ciled to almost any decision—even to the extension of Vermont to the Mason line in New Hampshire—rather than have the controversy prolonged; else, even at that late day, he might not have declined the advice given by his friend. In his reply to the general, the governor did not allude to the subject.—*Clinton Papers*, in N. Y. State Library, Nos. 3575 and 3616. For an extract from Gen. McDougall's letter, and Gov. Clinton's in full, see *Appendix G.*, *post.*

[1] Mr. JAY was chief justice of New York, and could not serve that state in Congress except on a special emergency. The controversy with Vermont was treated as such an emergency, and he was sent to Congress "in a special manner" on that subject.

assembly of the state of New-York to their delegates in Congress, and other papers accompanying the same, brought in a report.[1]

IN CONGRESS, Friday, September 24, 1779.

Congress took into consideration resolutions reported from the committee of the whole, which were agreed to as follows:[2]

1. Whereas, on the first day of June last, Congress, by a certain resolution reciting "that whereas divers applications had been made to Congress on the part of the state of New-York, and of the state of New-Hampshire, relative to disturbances and animosities among inhabitants of a certain district known by the name of the New Hampshire Grants," praying their interference for quieting thereof, did resolve, "that a committee be appointed to repair to the New-Hampshire Grants, and enquire into the reasons why they refuse to continue citizens of the respective states which heretofore exercised jurisdiction over the said district; for that, as Congress are in duty bound, on the one hand, to preserve inviolate the rights of the several states, so, on the other, they will always be careful to provide that the justice due to the states does not interfere with the justice which may be due to individuals; that the said committee confer with the said inhabitants, and that they take every prudent measure to promote an amicable settlement of all differences, and prevent divisions and animosities so prejudicial to the United States:" and did further resolve, "that the farther consideration of this subject be postponed until the said committee shall have made report."

2. And whereas it so happened that a majority of the committee appointed in pursuance of the aforementioned resolution, did not meet in the said district, and therefore have never executed the business committed to them or made a regular report thereupon to Congress:

Ordered, That the said committee be discharged.

3. And whereas the animosities aforesaid have lately proceeded so far, and risen so high as to endanger the internal peace of the United States, which renders it indispensably necessary for Congress, to interpose for the restoration of quiet and good order:

4. And whereas one of the great objects of the union of the United States of America is the mutual protection and security of their respective rights:

5. And whereas it is of the last importance to the said union, that all causes of jealousy and discontent between the said states should be removed; and therefore that their several boundaries and jurisdictions be ascertained and settled:

6. And whereas disputes at present subsist between the states of N. Hampshire, Massachusetts-Bay and N. York, on the one part, and the people of a district of country called N. Hampshire Grants, on the other, which people deny the jurisdiction of each of the said states over the said district, and each of the said states claim the said district against each other as well as against the said people, as appertaining in the whole or in part to them respectively:

---

[1] *Journals of Congress*, Folwell's edition, 1779–1780, Vol. v, p. 273.

[2] The resolutions are copied from the journals of Congress, but the preambles and resolutions are divided and numbered from the copy in the *Documentary History of New York*, to correspond with Mr. Jay's explanatory letter to Gov. Clinton, which follows the resolutions as amended Oct. 2 1779.

7. *Resolved unanimously*, That it be, and hereby is most earnestly recommended to the states of New-Hampshire, Massachusetts-Bay and New-York, forthwith to pass laws, expressly authorizing Congress to hear and determine all differences between them relative to their respective boundaries, in the mode prescribed by the articles of confederation, so that Congress may proceed thereon by the first day of February next at the farthest:

8. And further, that the said states of New-Hampshire, Massachusetts-Bay and New York, do, by express laws for the purpose, refer to the decision of Congress, all differences or disputes relative to jurisdiction, which they may respectively have with the people of the district aforesaid, so that Congress may proceed thereon on the first day of February next.

9. [And also to authorize Congress to proceed to hear and determine all disputes subsisting between the grantees of the several states aforesaid, with one another or with either of the said states, respecting title to lands lying in the said district, to be heard and determined in the mode prescribed for such cases by the articles of confederation aforesaid :][1] and further, to provide that no advantage be taken of the non-performance of the conditions of any of the grants of the said lands, but that further reasonable time be allowed for fulfilling such conditions:

10. *Resolved unanimously*, That Congress will, and hereby do, pledge their faith to carry into execution and support their decisions and determinations in the premises, in favour of whichsoever of the parties the same may be, to the end, that permanent concord and harmony may be established between them, and all cause of uneasiness removed.

11. *Resolved unanimously*, That Congress will, on the said first day of February next, proceed, without delay, to hear and examine into the disputes and differences relative to jurisdiction aforesaid, between the said three states respectively, or such of them as shall pass the laws before-mentioned on the one part, and the people of the district aforesaid who claim to be a separate jurisdiction on the other; and, after a full and fair hearing, will decide and determine the same according to equity; and that neither of the said states shall vote on any question relative to the decision thereof. And Congress do hereby pledge their faith to execute and support their decisions and determinations in the premises.

And whereas it is essential to the interest of the whole confederacy, that all intestine dissentions be carefully avoided, and domestic peace and good order maintained :

12. *Resolved unanimously*, That it is the duty of the people of the district aforesaid, who deny the jurisdiction of all the aforenamed states, to abstain in the mean time from exercising any power over any of the inhabitants of the said district who profess themselves to be citizens of, or to owe allegiance to, any or either of the said states: but that none of the towns, either on the east or west side of Connecticut river, be considered as included within the said district, but such as have heretofore actually joined in denying the jurisdiction of either of the said states, and have assumed a separate jurisdiction which they call the state of Vermont. And further, that in the opinion of Congress, the said states afore-named ought, in the mean time, to suspend executing their laws over any of the inhabitants of the said district, except such of them as shall profess allegiance to, and confess the jurisdiction of, the same respectively. And further, that Congress will consider any violences committed against the tenor, true intent and meaning of this resolution as a breach of the peace of the confederacy, which they are determined to keep and main-

---

[1] Repealed Oct. 2 1779 and another clause substituted.—See next page.

tain. And to the end, that all such violences and breaches of the public peace may be the better avoided in the said district, it is hereby recommended to all the inhabitants thereof, to cultivate harmony and concord among themselves, to forbear vexing each other at law or otherwise, and to give as little occasion as possible to the interposition of magistrates.

13. *Resolved unanimously*, That in the opinion of Congress, no unappropriated lands or estates which are or may be adjudged forfeited or confiscated, lying in the said district, ought, until the final decision of Congress in the premises, to be granted or sold.

Ordered, That copies of the aforegoing resolutions be sent by express to the states of New-York, New-Hampshire and Massachusetts-Bay, and to the people of the district aforesaid, and that they be respectively desired to lose no time in appointing their agent or agents and otherwise preparing for the hearings aforesaid.

The aforesaid resolutions being read over, and a question taken to agree to the whole,

Resolved, unanimously in the affirmative.[1]

IN CONGRESS, Saturday, October 2, 1779.[2]

On motion of Mr. Gerry, seconded by Mr. Peabody, Congress came to the following resolution:

Whereas in the first resolution of Congress of the 24th of September last, relative to a district of country called "New Hampshire Grants," is the following clause, viz. [Here follows that part of clause 9 on page preceding which is enclosed in brackets:] and whereas no provision is made in the said articles of confederation for hearing and determining disputes between any State and the grantees of any other State:

Resolved unanimously, That the clause above recited be repealed.

Resolved unanimously, That it be, and hereby is recommended to the states of N. Hampshire, Massachusetts-Bay and N. York, to authorize Congress to proceed to hear and determine all disputes subsisting between the grantees of the several states aforesaid, with one another, or with either of the said states, respecting title to lands lying in the said district, to be heard and determined by "commissioners or judges," to be appointed in the mode prescribed by the 9th article of the confederation aforesaid.

Ordered, That a copy of the preceding resolves be transmitted to the states of N. Hampshire, Massachusetts Bay and N. York, and also to the inhabitants of the New-Hampshire Grants.

LETTER OF JOHN JAY, *President of Congress and Delegate for New York, to Gov. Clinton of New York—explanatory of the foregoing resolutions of Congress.*[3]

Dear Sir,—Whether the resolutions of Congress of the 24th inst., providing for the settlement of all disputes between New-York and her neighbours, as well as revolted citizens, will please my constituents as much as they do me is uncertain. Nor am I convinced of the prudence of committing to paper all the reasons which induce me to think them (all

---

[1] *Journals of Congress*, Folwell's edition, 1779–80, Vol. v, pp. 276–278; *Documentary History of New York*, Vol. 4, pp. 596–598.

[2] *Journals of Congress*, Folwell's edition, 1779–80, Vol. v, p. 283.

[3] *The Life and Writings of John Jay*, Vol. I, pp. 88–94.

circumstances considered) perfectly right. Some of them, however, I shall communicate. My first object on coming here was to prevail upon Congress to interpose though in the smallest degree ; well knowing, that if they once interfered ever so little, they might with more ease be led to a further and more effectual interposition.

Soon after my arrival, I found the following objections to an interference with Vermont generally prevailing.

1st. That Congress, being instituted for the sole purpose of opposing the tyranny of Britain, and afterward of establishing our independence, had no authority to interfere in the particular quarrels of any State. Hence all their former resolutions on the subject were merely negative. 2d. That the confederation had not yet taken place, and that the business should be postponed till all the States had acceded ; an event then daily expected. 3d. That it was an improper season to interfere, and that the attention of Congress ought not to be diverted from the general objects of the war. 4th. That harsh measures against Vermont might induce them to join the enemy and increase their force. 5th. That they possessed a strong country, were numerous, warlike, and determined ; and that more force would be required to reduce them, than could be spared from the general defence.

These were some of the ostensible objections. Besides which I had reason to suspect the following private ones. 1st. That divers persons of some consequence in Congress and New-England expected to advance their fortunes by lands in Vermont. 2d. That Vermont, acquiring strength by time, would become actually independent, and afterward acknowledged to be so. 3d. That being settled by New-England people, and raised into consequence by New-England politics, it would be a fifth New-England State, and become a valuable accession of strength both in and out of Congress. 4th. That ancient animosities between New-York and New-England naturally inclining the former to side with the Middle and Southern States, the less formidable she was the better, and therefore the loss or separation of that territory was rather to be wished for than opposed. These and many other considerations of the like nature induced me to postpone bringing on the matter till I could have an opportunity of preparing the way for it by acquiring a knowledge of the characters then in Congress, &c.

It is also proper to observe that the House was for the greater part of the winter so heated by divisions on points of great general importance, that it would have been improper and improvident to have called upon them to decide on this delicate business till more temperate calmness had taken place. When these began to appear the subject was introduced, and you have had a copy of the resolutions proposed by New York on that occasion.[1] Against them, all objections before mentioned operated, with this additional one, that it would be highly unjust and

[1] The reference here doubtless is to several resolutions proposed by the New York delegation May 22 1779, which were not adopted. They declared that the several states in the confederacy are entitled to the territory they held while colonies of Great Britain; that no state should be divested, unless by judgment of Congress in favor of some other state in the union, as prescribed by the articles of confederation; and that no part or district shall be permitted to separate from a state except by consent of that state. Other resolutions were similar to what had been adopted previously, or were adopted afterward. See *Journals of Congress*, Folwell's edition, 1779–80, Vol. v, p. 164.

impolitic to determine against Vermont without previous inquiry into the merits of their claims, and giving them an opportunity of being heard. This objection, so far as it respected their claim to independence, was absurd though plausible; but it was not to be overcome, and though we might have carried a resolution against it by a slender majority, that majority would have consisted of southern members against a violent opposition from New-England and their adherents. A resolution carried under such circumstances would rather have encouraged than disheartened Vermont, and was, therefore, ineligible.

Hence I conceived it to be expedient to promote the measure of appointing a committee of inquiry; knowing that if Congress proceeded to inquire, it would be a ground for pressing them to go further and determine; especially as I was apprized that the result of these inquiries would be in our favour.

The committee, you know, never had a formal meeting;[1] it nevertheless had its use. The individual reports of the members who composed it advanced our cause; and even Mr. Witherspoon, who was and is suspected by New-York, made representations in our favour.

Your last resolutions[2] were of infinite service, by evincing the moderation, justice, and liberality, and at the same time the spirit of the State. On the other hand, the law of Vermont for whipping, cropping, and branding your magistrates made an impression greatly to their disadvantage.[3] Before these emotions should have time to subside, as well in observance of our instructions, I pressed Congress from day to day to adopt such measures as the public exigencies called for, and thereby prevent the flames of civil war from raging. It would not, I believe, have been difficult to have obtained what some among you would call very spirited and pointed resolutions, but which, in my opinion, would have been very imprudent ones; because, among other reasons, they would not have been unanimous. You will find the recitals and particular resolutions numbered in the margin of the copy herewith enclosed, from 1 to 13. I shall trouble you with a few explanatory remarks on each of them, under heads numbered in like manner.

1st and 2d. These recitals were inserted to show the reason why Congress now proceed without the report of the committee, after having resolved to postpone the further consideration of the subject till their report should be made.[4]

3d. This recital justifies the facts set forth in your representations, and in case an appeal to the public should become necessary, may be used with advantage to New-York.

4th. This recital destroys the doctrine that the Union (independent of the articles of confederation) had no other object than security against foreign invasions.

5th. This recital is calculated to impress the people with an opinion of the reasonableness and policy of the requisition or recommendation which follows, and therefore will the more readily induce those States to adopt the measures recommended to them.

6th. You may inquire for what reason I consented to this recital, as it puts Massachusetts and New-Hampshire on a footing with New-York; whereas I well knew that New-York alone had a right to claim jurisdiction over Vermont. My reasons were these: Vermont extends over

---

[1] The committee appointed to visit Vermont in June 1779.

[2] The resolutions of instruction of Aug. 27 1779, *ante*, pp. 179–182.

[3] The temporary act of June 1779.—See Slade's *State Papers*, p. 389.

[4] Such was the resolution of June 1 1779.—See Vol. I, p. 521.

Connecticut River into the acknowledged jurisdiction of New-Hampshire:[1] as to Massachusetts, the recital admits only her *claims*, not her *title;* and it is as impossible to deny the existence of claims when made, as it is to prevent them. Their delegates pointedly asserted and insisted on the claim of Massachusetts; and it appeared to me expedient to provide for a speedy determination of all claims against us, however ill founded. You may further ask, Why Vermont is made a party? the reason is this: that by being allowed a hearing, the candour and moderation of Congress may be rescued from aspersions; and that those people, after having been fully heard, may have nothing to say or complain of, in case the decision of Congress be against them; of which I have no doubt.

7th. It is true, that by this resolution the merits of former settlements with these States will be again the subject of inquiry, discussion, and decision; and therefore it may at first sight appear improper; but these settlements will still remain strong evidence of our rights, however objectionable they may be represented to be by those States. Nor will Congress be easily prevailed upon to annul them, because in that case all their boundaries would be afloat. Besides, in my opinion, it is much better for New-York to gain a permanent peace with their neighbours by submitting to these inconveniences, than by an impolitic adherence to strict rights, and a rigid observance of the dictates of dignity and pride, remain exposed to perpetual dissensions and encroachment. Peace and established boundaries, under our circumstances, are, I think, almost inestimable.

8th. The reason of this is assigned in the last sentence under the 6th head.

9th. For the same purpose of preserving the appearance of equality in claims, whatever difference there may be in titles, the three States are mentioned in this recommendation. The object of it is a settlement of all disputes respecting interfering grants, in case Vermont should be abolished, and that district in part, or in the whole, adjudged to either of the three States.

10th. I am sure you will admit my prudence in giving your voice for this resolution.

11th. As it was not absolutely certain that New-Hampshire and Massachusetts would pass the laws in question, and as I was sure that New-York would, it appeared to me highly expedient to provide, by this resolution, that the dispute between New-York and Vermont should be determined, whether the other two States came in or no: and, lest the former guarantee contained in the 10th resolution might be construed to be contingent, and to depend on the event of all the three States adopting the measures recommended to them, it is here repeated. You will observe that neither of the three States are to vote on the decision.

12th. On the plan of hearing Vermont, this resolution, however inconvenient, became indispensable. Care, however, has been taken in it to exempt all persons from their jurisdiction who profess allegiance to

---

[1] An error, the first union with the New Hampshire towns having been dissolved in the previous February, and the second union having been effected subsequently. It was true, however, that some towns in New Hampshire were claiming the right to unite with Vermont, which purpose was favored by a few towns in Eastern Vermont. This was a distinct party at that time, represented at Congress by its own Agent, Gen. PETER OLCOTT; while "Vermont" was represented by Agents officially appointed by it—JONAS FAY and PAUL SPOONER.

either of the three States. But you will say, Why to the *three* States? Why not to New-York only; from whom they revolted, and under whose actual jurisdiction they last were? Because it would have clashed with the equality of claims before mentioned, and the least opposition to which would have prevented these resolutions from being unanimous; a circumstance, in my opinion, infinitely more valuable than the preservation of useless etiquette. And, further, because the district is here so described as to extend over the river and affect New-Hampshire.[1] In a word, the necessity of the resolution was so obvious that there was no avoiding it. These inconveniences will be temporary, and, if the principles laid down in it are observed, will not be very great; especially as Congress have determined a violation of it to be a breach of the peace of the confederacy, and have declared their resolution to maintain it.

13th. This resolution needs no comment, the policy and justice of it being extremely evident. Anxious to avoid a moment's delay in sending you these resolutions, I have not time by this opportunity of adding any thing further than that upon this occasion I have acted according to the best of my judgment, after having maturely considered and well weighed the force and tendency of every consideration and circumstance affecting the business in question. When I first received my special commission, I did not apprehend that this matter was in a more particular manner confided to me than to my colleagues, though some of them considered it in that light. The commission vested me with no further power than what any other of your delegates possessed; nor was any matter given more particularly in charge to me than to the others by the Legislature. Their late instructions, however, speak a different language. I am satisfied to be viewed in that light, that is, to be the responsible man; and, provided the measures I adopt are not thwarted, I am confident that I shall be able to bring all these matters to a happy conclusion. I hope, however, that this will not be considered as a hint for my being continued in the delegation; I assure you, nothing but an adherence to the resolutions and principles of action I adopted and professed at the commencement of the war would induce me to remain here at the expense of health as well as property; for though I shall always be ready to serve my country when called upon, I shall always be happy to find it consistent with my duty to remain a private citizen.

I am, sir, your most obedient servant, JOHN JAY.

ACTION OF VERMONT ON THE RESOLUTIONS OF CONGRESS OF SEPT. 24 1779.

As Mr. JAY was satisfied to stand as "the responsible man" for the resolutions of Congress of the 24th of September 1779, it is reasonable to infer that he shaped them. Certain it is, that they were skillfully adapted to bind Congress to a decision in favor of New York, and that result was confidently expected by Mr. JAY. The States of Massachusetts and New Hampshire were nominally admitted as parties with New York, adverse to Vermont; but Vermont, *as a State*, was studiously ignored, and so far, the question of her independence was decided against her in advance. "The people of a district of country called New Hampshire Grants" were cited to appear by their agents, but not as guests to

---

[1] See preceding note to the sixth clause.

a feast, but rather as a sacrificial offering for the occasion, the only question being whether New York should have the whole of Vermont, or whether it should be divided between New York, New Hampshire, and Massachusetts. It is very clear that Mr. JAY relied upon the adjudications of the questions of jurisdiction by Great Britain as they stood at the declaration of American Independence—that is, adverse to both New Hampshire and Massachusetts, and in favor of New York; and that he counted upon the states in Congress to affirm the jurisdiction of New York, because, otherwise, "all their boundaries would be afloat." It is to be noted, that in case of a decision adverse to Vermont, Congress was bound to execute and support it with all the power of the confederacy. Were Vermont to consent to a trial *on the issue as made up for her*, she would have to submit to New York, or rebel against the confederacy. Were she to refuse to appear at all, Congress would be bound to decide the question in the succeeding February, if New York alone insisted, although Massachusetts and New Hampshire should not appear. So the danger of collision between Vermont and the confederacy was imminent, and the patriotism of the Vermonters tempted them to submission. "The influence of Congress at that time," [October 1779,] said IRA ALLEN, "was great, being considered as the pillar of liberty; and their advice was deemed a law; the friends of New York exulted, and doubled their exertions against Vermont. When the Assembly convened, nine tenths were for suspending the sale of confiscated property, and the granting of lands till after the 1st of February, the time assigned by Congress to examine into the disputes and differences;" and Allen went on to say, that after spending fourteen days in deliberation, the Governor and Council and General Assembly unanimously resolved "to grant the whole of their unlocated lands, and sell their confiscated estates."[1] But they did more; and first of all, they resolved to put the State before Congress on Vermont's chosen issue, and not on New York's—"TO SUPPORT THEIR RIGHT TO INDEPENDENCE, at Congress, and to the world, in the character of a free and independent State." Gov. CHITTENDEN, in his speech at the opening of the October session of the General Assembly in 1779, recommended the suspension of the laws intended to have been executed on offenders against Vermont in Cumberland county, "in consequence of a letter received from his Excellency John Jay, Esquire, President of Congress, inclosing certain acts passed by that honorable board, [the resolutions of Sept. 24 1779,] relating to a final settlement of all difference subsisting between this and the adjacent States, which I now submit to you for your consideration; a subject of the greatest importance, and demands your most serious attention."[2] The record in the journal of the General Assembly is as follows:

---

[1] Allen's *History of Vermont*, in *Vt. Hist. Soc. Collections*, Vol. I, p. 405.

[2] See speech, *ante*, p. 5.

SATURDAY, October 16th 1779.

Resolved that a Committee of four be appointed to join a Committee from the Council to form the outlines of the plan to be persued by this State for defence against the neighbouring States in consequence of the late acts of Congress for that purpose. Committee chosen Genl. E. Allen, Mr. [Reuben] Jones, Mr. N. [Nathan] Clark, and Mr. Fassett, [John, jr., of Arlington.[1]]

TUESDAY October 19th 1779.

Resolved that this Assembly join with the Governor and Council in a Committee of the whole to-morrow morning to take into consideration several acts of the honorable the Congress of the 24th Septr. last relating to a settlement of all disputes between the States of New Hampshire, Massachusetts Bay and New York on the one part and the State of Vermont on the other.

WEDNESDAY October 20th 1779.

The Assembly with the Council according to their Resolution of yesterday resolved into a Committee of the whole to take into consideration several acts of the honble the Congress of the 24th Septr. last relating to a settlement of all disputes between the States of New Hampshire, Massachusetts Bay and New York on the one part and the State of Vermont on the other, &c.

The Committee of the whole being dissolved the Speaker resumed the chair and the House proceeded to business.

THURSDAY October 21 1779.

The Committee of the whole brought in the following report vizt.

"Agreeable to the order of the day his excellency the Governor, the "Council and House of Representatives were resolved into a Committee "of the whole, to take into consideration the letter of the 25 ult. from "his excellency John Jay Esqr. late president of the Congress of the "United States of America,[2] enclosing certain acts of Congress, for an "equitable settlement of all differances subsisting between the States of "New Hampshire, Massachusetts Bay and New York on one part, and "this State on the other, and after some time spent thereon the Governor "resumed the chair, and the following Resolutions being read several "times were agreed to vizt.

"Resolved unanimously, that it is the opinion of this Committee that "this State ought to support their right to independance, at Congress, "and to the World, in the character of a free and independant State.

"Resolved that this Committee recommend it to the General Assembly, "to make Grants of all, or any part of the unappropriated lands within "their Jurisdiction, that does not interfere with any former Grants, as "their wisdom may direct. Extract from the Minutes,

"JOSEPH FAY, *Clerk.*"

---

[1]The Governor and Council passed a similar resolution on the 15th, appointing Jonas Fay, Ira Allen, and Paul Spooner as committee on the part of the Council.

[2]Sept. 27 1779, Mr. JAY was appointed minister plenipotentiary to Spain, and he then resigned the chair and his seat in Congress.

On motion made, Resolved unanimously by this Assembly that they agree to the aforesaid Report.

Resolved that this Assembly in granting lands will have reference to the convenience, quality and situation of the lands, and that they will not take into consideration any petition for lands until a plan thereof be laid before this House by the Surveyor General, or such plan or plans as have been previous to their being laid before the Assembly been properly approved by the Surveyor General and duly certified.

On the same day ETHAN ALLEN was chosen an agent of the state to wait on the Council and General Court of Massachusetts;[1] and IRA ALLEN was chosen an agent to visit the states of New Jersey, Pennsylvania, Delaware, and Maryland, and instructed to furnish the assemblies of those states with copies of Ethan Allen's "*Vindication.*"[2]

FRIDAY October 22d. 1779.

Resolved, that five persons be chosen by ballot, Agents in behalf of the freemen of this State, to appear at the Congress of the United States of America, on the first day of February next; and that they, or any three of them, are hereby fully authorised and empowered by the Representatives of the Freemen aforesaid, to vindicate their right to independance at that honourable Board.

And, furthermore, our said Agents, or any three of them, are hereby amply empowered to agree upon, and fully to settle Articles of Union and Confederation in behalf of this State, with the United States, which shall be binding on us, on our constituents and our successors. And our said Agents are hereby further empowered, to transact all other political affairs of this State at Congress, as a free and independant State, and report their proceedings herein to this Assembly as soon as may be.

Agents chosen, General Ethan Allen, the honorable Jonas Fay and Paul Spooner Esquires, Stephen R. Bradley Esqr. and the honorable Moses Robinson Esqr.

SATURDAY October 23d. 1779.

Resolved, that the Surveyor General be and he is hereby directed to advertise in the public papers for all Charters of lands that have been granted by either of the States of the Massachusetts-Bay, New-Hampshire or New-York to be recorded in his office at the expence of this State.

---

[1] See *Appendix C.* [2] See *Appendix F.*

APPENDIX C.

THE CLAIM OF MASSACHUSETTS TO PART OF THE TERRITORY OF VERMONT.

THE first knowledge the Vermont authorities had, that Massachusetts had entered in Congress a claim to part of her territory, was in October 1779, about a month later than the resolutions of Congress of Sept. 24 1779, wherein it was "most earnestly recommended to the states of New Hampshire, Massachusetts-Bay, and New-York, forthwith to pass laws, expressly authorizing Congress to hear and determine all differences between them relative to their respective boundaries," &c. This claim was at the time a surprise to Vermont, and it was promptly met by a direct appeal to Massachusetts from Gov. Chittenden, which was borne by Ethan Allen, who had been appointed by the General Assembly to negotiate on the subject. It was also met and argued in Bradley's "*Appeal*,"[1] and Ethan Allen and Jonas Fay's "*Concise Refutation*,"[2] to which the reader is referred.[1] That the intervention of Massachusetts was friendly to Vermont in its design is now well understood, and is in fact shown by the record.

Appointment of ETHAN ALLEN *as Agent to the Council and General Court of Massachusetts.*

IN GENERAL ASSEMBLY, Oct. 21, 1779.

Resolved, that an Agent be chosen to wait on the honorable the Council, and General Court, of the State of Massachusetts-Bay, to negotiate the public business of this State.

Chose for the above purpose, by ballot, Brigadier General Ethan Allen. Extract from the Journals,

Attest, ROSWELL HOPKINS, *Clerk.*

Sent up for Concurrence.

IN COUNCIL, Manchester, October 22, 1779.

Read and Concurred. JOSEPH FAY, *Secretary.*[3]

---

[1] See *Appendix D.* [2] See *Appendix E.*

[3] *Ethan Allen Manuscript Papers*, p. 286. These were Allen's credentials. The resolution is in the Assembly journal, but the concurrence was not noted in the Council journal.

Gov. Chittenden to Samuel Adams, President of the Council of Massachusetts.

MANCHESTER, October 28th, 1779.

Sir,—I am directed by my Council and the General Assembly of this state, now sitting, to signify to your honor, that his Excellency John Jay, Esq. the late President of the Congress of the United States, has, by express, communicated a letter to me, bearing date the 25th ult. enclosing certain acts of Congress, for an equitable settlement of all differences subsisting between the state of Massachusetts-Bay, New-Hampshire and New-York, on the one part, and this state, on the other; by which I obtained the first intelligence of a claim being set up and continued, by Massachusetts state, over any part of this.

The General Assembly have been pleased to appoint the bearer, Brig. Gen. Allen, to wait on your honorable Council and General Court, to learn over what part of this state you mean to extend your claim, and how far you mean to carry such pretensions into execution, in the trial at Congress, on the first day of February next, agreeable to the acts of Congress, with which, I am informed, you are served with a copy. Every necessary step shall be invariably pursued, on my part, to bring about an equitable accommodation of all differences aforesaid, agreeable to the strict rules of justice and equity; which cannot be attended to, in my opinion, without an explicit acknowledgment of the independence of this state; for

First. Can any, even the least, reason be given for this state's being put under the jurisdiction of New-York, contrary to their will? Have not the inhabitants of Vermont suffered an infinity of evils, by New York's pretending to exercise jurisdiction over them, when neglected by every friendly power on the continent, even the authority which gave them being not excepted?

Second. Have not Vermont, for many years before the late revolution took place between Great-Britain and America, been forced to the last alternative, the absolute necessity of having recourse to arms, to defend their interest, purchased at the dearest rate; and of exhibiting that same spirit of patriotism, which has, so far, brought America out of a state of threatened slavery, into the fruition of freedom and liberty?

Third. Does not that same spirit of freedom now exist among the free citizens of Vermont, which is absolutely necessary to be continued, by the United States of America, in order to carry into execution the declaration of Congress, on the 4th of July, 1776? Surely it does.

Fourth. Can such a people be draged, or flattered, into a subjection to any one of the United States, or be divided to two or more of them, merely to allow them a stretch of jurisdiction, and thereby augment their power? Surely they cannot.

If you will please to lay this before your honorable Council and General Court, and write me your answer, by the bearer, the favor shall be ever gratefully acknowledged by,

Sir, your honor's most obedient humble servant,

THOMAS CHITTENDEN.

The honorable the President of the Council of Massachusetts State.[1]

---

[1] This letter was not entered in the record of the Governor and Council. It is inserted here literally as it was printed in Slade's *State Papers*, pp. 114–115.

Samuel Adams to Thomas Chittenden.[1]

Sir,—Your letter dated Manchester, the 28th of October, [1779,] and directed to the President of the Council of this State, has been laid before the General Assembly, according to your request, and duly considered. Two questions of importance are therein proposed, viz.

---

[1] *Life and Public Services of Samuel Adams*, by WILLIAM V. WELLS, Vol. III, pp. 144–147. The author introduced the letter as follows:

The correspondence of Mr. Adams makes occasional reference to the claims of New York, Massachusetts and New Hampshire to the territory of Vermont, which in 1777 had declared itself an independent State, and in the following year elected Thomas Chittenden Governor. As the Green Mountain Boys were determined to support their right, and the growing importance of the dispute had given the common enemy encouragement to open negotiations with Vermont, Congress, in well-grounded alarm, had essayed to effect an arrangement between the several claimants to the lands in question. A civil war seemed at one time to be impending. Mr. Adams, it was thought, had, from the first, been favorable to the independence of Vermont, and in 1776 was reported to have advised Colonel Warner to that effect.* Massachusetts was now anxious that the new State should be formed, but refused to come into the proposed Congressional conference on the subject, fearing some ulterior designs of New York and New Hampshire on the disputed territory.

Governor Chittenden, a man of great ability, and universally respected in Vermont, addressed a letter to Samuel Adams, desiring to have the position of Massachusetts defined on the subject of her particular claim to any portion of Vermont. The following draft of a reply is in the handwriting of Mr. Adams. [Here follows the letter given above.] The letter, continued Mr. Wells, is without date, but was written not long after that of Chittenden, of which the original is missing. It is a plain exponent of the position of Massachusetts in this interesting question, and a fair instance of the direct, comprehensive, and yet perfectly simple style of Samuel Adams's writings on all subjects. The letter of Chittenden was evidently penned with a careful observance of state formality; addressing Mr. Adams as President of the Senate, with the expectation that, in returning the courtesy, he would unguardedly acknowledge him as Governor of the State of Vermont. The habitual caution of Adams is shown in the reply, which recognizes Mr. Chittenden only as a private citizen. * * * * The matter was repeatedly before Congress, and in August of this year [1781] that body offered to recognize the independence of Vermont, and admit her into the Union upon the indispensable condition that she would relinquish her encroachment upon the lands of New Hampshire and New York, several townships from both of which States had been absorbed. New York

* I had lately some free conversation with an eminent gentleman [Dr. Franklin] whom you well know, and whom your 'Portia, in one of her letters. admired for his expressive silence about a confederation; a matter which our much valued friend, Colonel W——, [Col. Seth Warner.] is very solicitous to have completed. We agreed that it must soon be brought on, and that if all the Colonies could not come into it, it had better be done by those of them that inclined to it. I told him that I would endeavor to unite the New England Colonies in confederating, if none of the rest would join in it. He approved of it, and said if I succeeded, he would cast his lot among us.—*Samuel Adams to John Adams*, Jan. 1776, quoted in Wells's *Life and Services of Samuel Adams*, Vol. II, p. 358.

The friendship of Samuel Adams to Vermont is evident, also, from the following:

'Tis reported Colonel Warner has said he was advised to petition Congress to have the Hampshire grants set off in a new State, by Mr. Adams, one of the delegates [in Congress.] The people are much divided,- some for a new State, some for joining Hampshire, others Massachusetts, many for remaining under New York. I endeavored to dissuade them from persisting in such idle and delusive schemes.—*John Taylor to Pierre Van Cortlandt*, dated Albany, Nov. 3, 1776, in Force's *American Archives*, Fifth Series, Vol. III, pp. 503-4.

"Over what part of this State (by which we suppose is to be understood Vermont) we mean to extend our claim?" and "How far we mean to carry such pretensions into execution, in the trial at Congress on the first day of February next."

This State hath an ancient and just claim to all the territory referred to in your letter lying between the rivers Connecticut and Hudson, bounded as follows: viz. easterly by Connecticut River; westerly by the eastern line of New York; northerly by the northern boundary of Massachusetts Bay; and southerly by the northern limits of the Massachusetts jurisdiction as it was settled by the King of Great Britain in the year 1739.

This we take to be a full answer to your first question, according to its true intent, because we suppose a part of the district of Country which has been commonly called the New Hampshire grants, and is contained within the bounds above described, is a part of that territory which you call the State of Vermont. Over this tract of country we mean to extend our claim, notwithstanding the decision of the King of Great Britain aforesaid in favor of the Province of New Hampshire, in 1739, which we have ever considered to be unjust.[1] And as the General Assembly hath no authority to divest the State of any of its constitutional rights, we mean to continue, assert, and maintain the said claim, before any body competent to try and determine the same, against the protestations of any people whomsoever.

However necessary you, Sir, may judge it that an explicit acknowledgment of the independence of the State of Vermont should be made, in order to bring about an equitable accommodation of the difficulties subsisting between the States mentioned in your letter, this State cannot come into such an acknowledgment consistently with its connection with the United States of America and the engagements it has solemnly entered into with them. We have, therefore, reason to expect that such formality of state in this address to you as would be correspondent with

---

protested against this, but the Massachusetts delegation in Congress, doubtless by instruction, voted in the affirmative. The desire of Massachusetts, in asserting its claim, probably was to secure the independence of Vermont, and prevent its partition between New York and New Hampshire. After the resolution of Congress, New York determined to prosecute her claim, proposed to assert it by force, and marched troops for the purpose, and New Hampshire threatened a similar course. A timely letter from Washington to Chittenden induced the Legislature of Vermont to establish the western bank of the Connecticut River on the one part, and a line drawn from the northwest corner of Massachusetts northward to Lake Champlain on the other, as the eastern and western boundaries of the State, relinquishing all claim of jurisdiction without those limits; and the impending danger of a civil war was thus averted.

[1] By this rejection of the king's decision in 1739, the claim of Massachusetts was extended far west of the limits of Vermont, to wit, in the words of HILAND HALL: "from the well known southern boundary of that state to a line of latitude running through a point three miles north of the source of the Merrimac river, and reached for that width west to the Pacific ocean, thus including southern Vermont and central and western New York, as well as a vast territory across the continent to the west."—*Early History*, p. 301.

that which is adopted in your letter will be candidly dispensed with at this time.

In the name and by the order of the General Assembly,

I am with due respect, Sir,

Your most obedient and very humble servant,

SAMUEL ADAMS.

Thomas Chittenden, Esq., at Manchester.

Oct. 27 1777, Charles Phelps, of Marlborough, Vt., presented a memorial to the Council of Massachusetts "in behalf of the sacred rights" of that state to fifty townships in the southern part of Vermont, asserting title by virtue of a purchase, by the state, of the lands from the Indians, and that the territory so purchased had been divided into townships in the days of Gov. Belcher, but that the papers had been destroyed in the burning of the provincial court-house in Boston, in December 1747. Mr. Phelps proposed to support this claim by the then only surviving witness, Col. Israel Williams of Hatfield. The Council resolved to take the deposition of Col. W., and in 1779 the General Court declared that the State of Massachusetts had "a clear and indisputable right" to the southern part of Vermont; but when, in the year 1780, the subject was brought before Congress, the General Court decided that the claim was an "infringement on the rights of Vermont," and refused to prosecute it further.[1] The records of the General Court of Massachusetts for 1779 show, that Mr. Phelps was still urging the claim of that state, and that a committee, consisting of James Bowdoin, Samuel Adams, and John Lowell, was appointed to examine into the matter.[2] The declaration of 1779, referred to by B. H. HALL, was probably the result of this examination. Gov. Chittenden asserted, however, in his letter to the President of Congress, dated July 25th 1780, that Massachusetts had "not, *as a legislative body*, laid any claim to the territory of Vermont; nor have they enacted laws judicially authorizing Congress to take cognizance thereof." The last statement was certainly true; but it is evident, from the resolutions of Congress of Sept. 24 1779, that *in some form*—HILAND HALL says "officially"[3]—the claim of Massachusetts had been presented.

In September 1780 Congress proceeded to hear the claims of New Hampshire and New York, and on the 27th of that month postponed further consideration. Contemporaneously with this action of Congress, the legislature of Massachusetts instructed the delegates of that state in Congress to move and use their influence for a postponement of the question "till time and circumstances will admit of a full and ample discussion, and that Congress in the mean time take proper steps to pre-

---

[1] B. H. Hall's *Eastern Vermont*, pp. 306, 307.

[2] Resolution of the General Court of Massachusetts, Dec. 28 1779.

[3] *Early History*, p. 301.

vent any grants of the aforesaid lands [in Vermont] being made by any person or persons."[1]

Gov. Chittenden to Gov. John Hancock of Massachusetts.

STATE OF VERMONT.
IN COUNCIL, Arlington, 12th December, 1780.

Sir,—Enclosed I transmit your Excellency a copy of my letter to Congress of 25th of July last, which, together with this, I request may be laid before the Legislature of the State over whom you preside, for their perusal and consideration.

The arguments and representations therein exhibited are equally applicab le for the consideration of the several Legislatures of the United States separately.

Many and great are the evils which Vermont labors under: Congress claiming a jurisdiction over them; three of the United States claiming their territory in whole or in part, and Vermont at the same time a frontier in part to those very States, and exposed to British invasion from Canada, who being possessed of the Lake can suddenly bring their whole force into this State, which, beyond hesitation, will be their object next campaign, unless some immediate measures be adopted to prevent it, as they have already destroyed the frontier settlements of the state of New York.[2] In a word, their force will undoubtedly be so great that it will be out of the power of the State to form magazines and to support a body of troops sufficient to withstand them, and the consequence must inevitably be, either that the people of this State be sacrificed; or, 2dly, be obliged to retire into the interior parts of the United States for safety; or 3dly, be under the disagreeable necessity of making the best terms with the British that may be in their power. Nearly the same would be the condition of either of the United States separately considered from their Union (as they would be unable to withstand the British power,) which may abundantly serve to evince that it is out of the power of Vermont to be further serviceable to them, unless they are admitted into Union.[3]

---

[1] Resolution of Sept. 29 1780. [2] In October 1780.

[3] Agents were appointed by the Governor and Council, Nov. 1 1780, "to treat with Major Carleton," of the British force in Canada under General Haldimand, "for the purpose of settling a cartel for the exchange of prisoners." This was done pursuant to a resolution of the General Assembly of the previous day. Out of this grew the so called Haldimand Correspondence; but at the date of the above letter to Gov. Hancock, nothing had been done, the truce with Maj. Carleton for the time then being excepted. The letter of Chittenden to Congress, July 25 1780, to Gen. Washington of Jan. 5 1781, and his letters in December 1780 to the Governors of Massachusetts, Connecticut, and Rhode Island, all gave timely notice that Vermont might be forced, for the protection of her people, to make terms of some sort with the British; and the preservation of Vermont in that emergency was due to the diplomacy alone of Gov. Chittenden, Ira Allen, and their associates. No aid was given in that crisis to Vermont by either Congress or any of the neighboring states, while her own continental regiment of Green Mountain Boys, under Warner, was serving in New York.

This State are of opinion that it is high time she had better assurances from the several States now in Union, whether, at the conclusion of the present War, she may without molestation enjoy her Independence, or whether she is only struggling in a Bloody War to establish neighboring States in their Independence to overthrow or swallow up her own and deprive her citizens of their landed estates. I do, therefore, in behalf of this State, demand your Legislature that they relinquish their pretensions of a claim to jurisdiction over any and every part of this State, and request them to join in a solid Union with Vermont against the British forces which invade the American States. Such a Union for the mutual advantage of both States, I am ready to ratify and confirm on the part of this State. I have the honor to be, Sir, your Excellency's

most obedient and most humble servant,

THOS. CHITTENDEN.

A true copy. Attest, THOS. TOLMAN, *P. T. Sec^y.*

His Excellency Governor Hancock.[1]

Resolution of the General Court of Massachusetts, March 8 1781, *in response to the letter of Gov. Chittenden.*

This Court having maturely and deliberately considered the same, feel themselves disposed to comply with the request of said Inhabitants, and to concede that the said territory and the Inhabitants within the same should be a sovereign independent State, in such way and manner and upon such terms as shall be agreed upon and established by the Congress of the United States of America:

Therefore *Resolved* that in case the territory called Vermont be recognized by Congress as a sovereign independent State and enter into the Confederation with the other American States, this Commonwealth will and do hereby relinquish their claim of jurisdiction in and over the said territory and every part and parcel thereof from the North side of the town of Northfield on the West bank of Connecticut river in the County of Hampshire to the North West corner of the town of Williamstown in the county of Berkshire, in such manner and by such other bounds as shall be established by the delegates of the United States in Congress assembled, reserving nevertheless to each and every individual within and without said territory of Vermont, their full right and title to such lands within the same as are held and enjoyed by virtue of any right or grant derived from the Province, State, or Commonwealth of Massachusetts.

Approved by the Governor.

---

[1] From the *Haldimand Papers;* a copy of this letter, and also one of like tenor to Gov. Trumbull of Connecticut, having been transmitted to Gen. Haldimand by Ira Allen. See *Vt. Historical Soc. Collections*, Vol. II, pp. 84–86.

APPENDIX D.

VERMONT'S APPEAL TO THE CANDID AND IMPARTIAL WORLD. CONTAINING A FAIR STATING OF THE CLAIMS OF MASSACHUSETTS-BAY, NEW-HAMPSHIRE, AND NEW-YORK. THE RIGHT THE STATE OF VERMONT HAS TO INDEPENDENCE. WITH AN ADDRESS TO THE HONORABLE AMERICAN CONGRESS, AND THE INHABITANTS OF THE THIRTEEN UNITED STATES. BY STEPHEN R. BRADLEY, A. M.[1]

The LORD hath called me from the Womb, from the Bowels of my Mother hath he made mention of my Name.
And said unto me, Thou art my Servant, O V------! in whom I will be glorified.
And I will feed them that oppress thee with their own Flesh, and they shall be drunken with their own Blood as with sweet wine, and all Flesh shall know that I the LORD am thy Saviour and thy Redeemer, the Mighty One of Jacob. ISAIAH XLIX.

HARTFORD: Printed by HUDSON & GOODWIN.

STATE OF VERMONT,

IN COUNCIL, Arlington, 10th Dec. 1779.

THE following Treatise, intitled, Vermont's Appeal to the Candid and Impartial World, containing, &c. being read and carefully perused, is approved of; and Resolved, that the same be published to the World.

By order of the Governor and Council, JOSEPH FAY, *Sec'ry.*

---

[1] STEPHEN ROW BRADLEY, LL.D., was born in what is now Cheshire, [until 1780 part of Wallingford,] Conn., Feb. 20 1754. He was son of Moses Bradley and Mary Row, and grandson of Stephen Bradley of New Haven, Conn., one of several brothers who served under Oliver Cromwell, but came to America about the year 1650, a short time previous to Oliver's "crowning victory" over King Charles at Worcester. The grandson inherited the military spirit of his English progenitor. Having graduated at Yale College in July 1775, he became captain of a company of "Cheshire Volunteers" in the continental service in January 1776. In December of that year he undertook other military service with the rank of adjutant; and soon after was aide-de-camp to Gen. David Wooster, and was present when that general was slain at Danbury in April 1777. In 1778 he served as commissary, and in the summer of 1779 as major at New Haven, Conn.* In the mean time he had pursued

* So stated in B. H. HALL'S biographical chapter in *Eastern Vermont.* Mr. Bradley's service as major could not have exacted much of his time, since it is evident his investigation of the Vermont question must have been made in the summer of 1779.

INTRODUCTION.

THE reader doubtless will wish to see a fair stating of the claims, of *Massachusetts-Bay*, *New-Hampshire*, and *New-York;* before he enters on the important subject of the independence of *Vermont.* On the eighth day of October last past, his Excellency Governor Chittenden,

---

the study of the law under Tapping Reeve, the distinguished instructor at Litchfield, Conn. His first appearance in Vermont was at Westminster, May 26 1779, when he was admitted to the bar of the superior court of this State, and was appointed its clerk. His attention must have been turned at once to the controversy of Vermont with the three adjoining states, since he was appointed on the 22d of Oct. as one of the agents to present the case to Congress, and his "Appeal" was written previous to the 10th of December of the same year. In February 1780 he attended upon Congress in his capacity as Agent, but the case was deferred. In June 1780 he was appointed State's attorney for Cumberland county; and in September he again attended Congress in behalf of Vermont and united with Ira Allen in making a vigorous remonstrance at that time against the course taken with Vermont.—See *Appendix G.* From his first settlement in the state in 1779 until he retired from the United States Senate in 1813—a period of thirty-four years—Mr. Bradley was almost constantly employed in public service, and for about half of that time in offices that interfered with his professional business. He represented Westminster in the General Assembly in 1780, 1781, 1784, 1785, 1788, 1790 and 1800. He was Clerk of the House in 1779, and in 1785 its Speaker. From Dec. 1781 to March 1791 he was register of probate for Windham county; in 1783 a judge of the county court; and in 1788 a judge of the supreme court. He was one of the commissioners appointed in Oct. 1789 to settle the controversy with New York, and a delegate in the state convention of 1791 which adopted the constitution of the United States. On the admission of Vermont to the Union in 1791, Mr. Bradley was elected the first U. S. Senator for the eastern side of the state, holding that office until March 1795. He was again and still again elected to the same office, holding it from March 1801 to March 1813. His early services to the state, in the controversy for its independence, were eminently useful and entitle him to lasting and grateful remembrance, but he most highly honored it by his ability and reputation as a Senator. He received five elections as President of the Senate; the third office in the government highest in rank. He was President of the convention of Republican members of Congress, and as such, Jan. 19, 1808, he summoned the convention of members which met and nominated Mr. Madison as President. He did this apparently on his own responsibility, and hence offence was taken by many members—notably by the New York delegation, only one of whom attended. Nevertheless the nomination thus made was confirmed by the country. Mr. Bradley was at that time the leading Republican Senator from New

received by express from John Jay Esq; late President of Congress; a copy of an act of Congress of the 24th of September last, informing, that each of said states, claimed the state of *Vermont* against each other, as well as against the inhabitants, as appertaining in the whole or in

---

England, but he was opposed to a war with Great Britain and "earnestly counselled Madison against it." "So dissatisfied," said B. H. HALL,—doubtless on the authority of the late Hon. WM. C. BRADLEY—"did Mr. Bradley become with the national policy of this period, that, on the 4th of March, 1813, at the close of his congressional labors, he withdrew altogether from public life, determined, since he was unable to prevent a needless war, not to continue in any position where he would be subjected to the calumnies and odium of a majority from whom he dissented." In two biographical notices which the writer has read, Mr. Bradley is described as "an erratic man." That phrase is often the penalty affixed for originality and independence, and in this case, knowing many of the admirable peculiarities of WILLIAM C. BRADLEY the son, it is deemed most just to count it as a compliment to the father. Certain it is that Senator Bradley has been described by those who knew him well, as "a lawyer of distinguished abilities, and a good orator." "Few men have more companionable talents, a greater share of social cheerfulness, a more inexhaustible flow of wit, or a larger portion of unaffected urbanity."* A much later writer, a son-in-law of Mr. Bradley, said: "he was distinguished for political sagacity, a ready wit, boundless stores of anecdote, a large acquaintance with mankind, and an extensive range of historical knowledge."†

It is evident, not only from the honors conferred upon Mr. Bradley by the Senate, but also from the part he took in the business and debates of that body, that he ranked among its active and influential members. The journals of the Senate show that he was placed on committees to which the most important and delicate questions were referred: for examples,—on the special message of President Jefferson, Jan. 13 1806, transmitting the claim of Hamet Caramelli, ex-bashaw of Tripoli, which involved the then late war with the ruling bashaw, and Mr. Bradley made the report, including a bill for Hamet's relief, and a resolution of thanks to Gen. William Eaton ‡ and his American associates, for their

* *A Descriptive Sketch of the present State of Vermont*, 1797, by JOHN A. GRAHAM, LL.D., p. 41.

† *Recollections of a Lifetime*, by Hon. S. G. GOODRICH, widely known as "Peter Parley."

‡ Gen. WILLIAM EATON, as a citizen of Vermont for some years, deserves more than this reference. He was born in Woodstock, Conn., Feb. 23 1764, entered the continental army at sixteen, and came out in 1783 with the rank of sergeant. Entering Dartmouth college, he graduated in 1790, having spent his vacations in Vermont as a school-teacher from 1788 to 1790, and also the subsequent year. From 1791 till 1793 he was clerk of the Vermont house of representatives, but in 1792 he obtained a commission as captain in the U. S. army, which he held until July 11 1797, when he was appointed consul to Tunis, where he arrived in March 1799. He concerted with Hamet Caramelli, the lawful chief of Tripoli, then in exile, an expedition against the usurping chief, which was done on the authority of the United States, whose fleet was to co-operate. In fifty days he crossed the Lybian desert with an army of five hundred men, and encamped before Derne, the capital of the richest province of Tripoli, April 26, 1805. This town contained a population of 15,000, and was defended by a port, batteries, and a strong garrison. Eaton increased his force to

part to them respectively; together with a resolution of Congress, to

---

eminently brave and successful services in Hamet's behalf; on the confidential message of President Jefferson, Dec. 18 1807, proposing an embargo; and on the confidential message of President Madison, Jan. 3 1811, suggesting that the United States take possession for the time then being of East Florida, and publish "a declaration that the United States could not see, without serious inquietude, any part of a neighboring territory, in which they have, in different respects, so deep and so just a concern, pass from the hands of Spain into those of any other foreign power." This was aimed against Great Britain, though the terms were general, and thus in fact contained the germ of the famous "Monroe doctrine" of 1823. The committee, by Henry Clay, its chairman, reported a bill and declaration accordingly. A still more important service was rendered by Mr. Bradley in 1803, as a member of the committee on a proposal of amendment to the constitution as to the mode of electing President and Vice President, he having been the author of that part of the existing constitution which requires that the Vice President, like the President, shall be chosen by a majority of the electoral votes.

Mr. Bradley resided in Westminster until 1818, when he removed to the neighboring village of Walpole, N. H., "where he lived in ease, independence and honour, until he took his willing and not painful departure, with the cheerful expression of a mind at peace with itself, with the world, and with heaven." He died on the 9th of December, 1830. The dates of his birth and death—stated otherwise in different sketches—are taken, with nearly all other facts, from the biographical chapter by B. H. HALL in *Eastern Vermont*, pp. 593–601, to which, and to the portrait there given, the reader is referred. Mr. HALL's account is undoubtedly more complete and accurate than any previously published, he having had the assistance of the late Hon. WILLIAM C. BRADLEY.

2,500, by the addition of Arabs, and, with the co-operation of three U. S. frigates, captured the place in two hours. Twice he was attacked by a superior force, and twice he repulsed the assailants and so completely on the 10th of June that his way was open to the gates of Tripoli, with a fair prospect of re-instating the rightful ruler and accomplishing the original design of the U. S. government. At this crisis he learned that a peace had been made by Tobias Lear, the American consul, which put an end to further proceedings. On his return to the United States, he was complimented by the President, and special thanks were proposed in both houses of Congress, which seem to have failed on disagreements as to form—as by a sword, or medal, or a simple resolution of thanks. The Secretary of State, however, was empowered to settle his accounts upon just and equitable principles. The king of Denmark, more generous if not more just, presented General Eaton with an elegant acknowledgment in a gold box, for rescuing captured Danes; and the State of Massachusetts, for like relief to her citizens in captivity, gave him a thousand acres of land. This grant was located in the north-eastern corner of Maine, and probably the General never derived any benefit from it personally. He was greatly disappointed that the national government did not better repay his services, and as a consequence fell into the habit of intemperance. Aaron Burr endeavored, ineffectually, to enlist him in his conspiracy, and on the trial of the conspirator, Eaton was a witness against him. The General died at Brimfield, Mass., June 1, 1811.—See *The Life of General Eaton*, by Charles Prentiss, published in 1813, with a portrait; Memoir by C. C. Felton in Sparks's *American Biography;* Blake's *Biographical Dictionary;* and Drake's *Dictionary of American Biography.*

judge and determine the cause on the first day of February next. But as the inhabitants of this state, view themselves intitled with the rest of the world, to that liberty which heaven bequeathed to Adam, and equally to all his posterity: we cannot think it worth our while, to show the absurdities, and clashing inconsistencies, of various grants made by the British crown, from the time of King *James* the first, A. D. 1606, down to the present Æra. We do not expect to stand upon any derived power from an arbitrary king; we cannot conceive human nature fallen so low, as to be dependant on a crowned head for liberty to exist; we expect to stand justified to the world, upon that great principle of reason, that we were created with equal privileges in the scale of human beings, among which is that essential right of making our own laws, and chusing our own form of government; and that we, nor our fathers, have never given up that right to any kingdom, colony, province, or state, but retain it now among ourselves as sacred as our natural existence.

AND here the reader is desired to observe, that the claims are not for property only, but they claim a right to jurisdiction, a power of governing us as a people, and pretend to derive that right from the British crown: when the crown of *Great Britain*, never had any right, but the mere consent of the people, and of course that right died when the people assumed government.

'TIS very curious to see how many shapes, *Massachusetts-Bay*, *New-Hampshire*, and *New-York*, are able to make his most sacred Majesty appear in; he certainly according to the vulgar notion, much exceeds the devil.

WHILE his adjudications were in their favour he had the immutibility of a God, but when against them, the design of a villain.

THE claims of *Massachusetts-Bay* and *New-Hampshire*, especially at this period of time are very extraordinary in their nature, and unaccountable upon any other principle, unless they think by putting in so many frightful claims, they scare us to surrender to some one, rather than to run our chance of being devoured by the whole. It is now upwards of forty years, since *Massachusetts-Bay* and *New-Hampshire* came to a full settlement of boundaries; there had for a long time before, disputes and controversies subsisted, between them: And for settleing the same his Majesty was pleased, by his order in Council, dated the 22d of January 1735, to direct, that Commissioners should be appointed to mark out the dividing line, between the said provinces, and on the 9th day of February 1736, a commission was accordingly issued out; with liberty to either party who should think themselves aggrieved by the determination of the said Commissioners, to appeal therefrom to his Majesty in Council, which said Commissioners did make their report, too tedious to insert here. The cause was appealed to his Majesty in Council, for a final determination, and the following is an authentic copy of what then [March 1740] passed.

" AND whereas appeals from the determination of the said Commis- " sioners, have been laid before his Majesty by the agents for the respec- " tive provinces, of the *Massachusetts-Bay*, and *New-Hampshire*, which " said appeals have been heard before the Committee of Council for hear- " ing appeals from the plantations, who after having considered the " whole matter, and heard all parties concerned therein, did report unto " his Majesty as their opinion, that the northern boundary of the said " province of the *Massachusetts-Bay*, are and be a similar curve line, " pursuing the course of *Merrimack* river, at three miles distance on the " north side thereof, beginning at the atlantic ocean, and ending at a " point due north of a place (in a plan returned by the said commission-

"ers) called *Pantucket* [Patucket] falls: and a straight line drawn from "thence due west cross the said river, till it meets with his Majesty's "other governments; and that the rest of the commissioners said report, "or determination, be affirmed by his Majesty. Which said report of "the committee of council, his Majesty hath been pleased with the ad- "vice of his privy council to approve, and to declare, adjudge, and order, "that the northern boundary of the said province of the *Massachusetts-* "*Bay*, are, and be a similar curve line, pursuing the course of *Merrimack* "river, at three miles distance on the north side thereof, beginning at "the atlantic, and ending at a point due north of a place in the plan re- "turned by the said Commissioners, called *Pantucket* falls, and a straight "line, drawn from thence due west cross the said river, till it meets with "his Majesty's other governments; and to affirm the rest of the Com- "missioners report or determination Whereof the governor or comman- "der in chief of his Majesty's said provinces for the time being, as also "his Majesty's respective councils and assemblies thereof, and all others "whom it may concern are to take notice."

THIS boundary line as then established by his Majesty in Council, *Massachusetts-Bay* did fully acquiesce in, and hath now for above forty years observed it as sacred, and acted accordingly. We find in the year 1744, *William Shirley*, Esq; then Governor of the province of *Massachusetts-Bay*, complained of *New-Hampshire* to the Duke of *New-Castle*, one of his Majesty's principal Secretaries of State, for neglecting to take possession of, and to provide for a fort, called *Fort Dummer;* which had been built by the *Massachusetts* government, about twenty years before, but by the above recited line, fell within the limits of *New-Hampshire*, in which complaint are these words: "Not thinking ourselves obliged to "provide for a fort which no longer belongs to us."

WHICH complaint, being laid before the king and council on the 6th day of Sept. 1744; his Majesty was pleased to order, that as said fort was within the province of *New-Hampshire*, they must support and maintain the same; "or his Majesty will find himself under the necessity of re- "storing that *fort*, with a proper district contiguous thereto, to the prov- "ince of the *Massachusetts-Bay*, who cannot with justice be required, to "maintain a *fort* no longer within their boundaries."

THIS *Fort Dummer* was several miles north of *Massachusetts* line, as then established, and west of *Connecticut* river. All which shews that *Massachusetts-Bay* ever since, conceived that line to be their northern boundary, and fully agreed to it. So late as the 3d of October 1767, the commissaries [commissioners] on the part of the *Massachusetts-Bay*, among which was *Thomas Hutchinson*, their great historian; dont doubt to treat that line as sacred; they say in their proposals to *New-York*, to establish a boundary line between the two governments, in the following words, viz.

"THAT a line being extended due north from the north corner of the "colony of *Conecticut*, until it comes to the distance of twelve miles "from *Hudson's River*, and another line being extended due west, *upon* "*the north boundary of the Massachusetts province, according to the settle-* "*ment thereof with New-Hampshire*, until such line comes to the like "distance, &c."

WHICH evidently proves, that there was a fair tryal before the king and council, and a boundary line established between *Massachusetts Bay* and *New Hampshive;* which has ever since been agreed too, and deemed as sacred on all sides above forty years, and is now the fixed line between the *Massachusetts-Bay* and *Vermont.* And for *Massachusetts Bay* to claim over that line a part of this state, by virtue of a right derived from the crown of *Great-Britain*, when by that, they are expressly bounded to that line; is very surprising, after their own tacit consent so long. They and all the world must acknowledge, that had we not bravely defended our rights against the state of *New-York;* but had tamely submited to that government, *Massachusetts-Bay*, would not at this time of day have laid in a claim.

We shall trouble the reader no further with the *Massachusetts* claim, being persuaded he must see the principle on which it stands, and how frivolous it is in itself.

The states of *America*, cannot now judge of the propriety and fitness, by which the crown of *Great-Britain* established the various lines on the continent. This undoubtedly should be observed as an invariable rule; that wherever the parties have mutually agreed for a succession of years, and acted accordingly down to the late revolution, those lines, and adjudications, ought to be held as unalterable and sacred.

The claim of *New-Hampshire*, stands on nearly the same principles as the former. Every unprejudiced mind will acknowledge, that after the beforementioned line was established, down to the year 1764, *New-Hampshire* had an exclusive right to all this territory. This appears from the before recited adjudication, and especially in the instance of *Fort Dummer;* as well as from the various Commissions, sent the Governors of *New-Hampshire*, impowering them to sell and dispose of all this territory; in which period of time the inhabitants of *Vermont*, purchased all the territory they are now in actual possession of; excepting some small remnants; of the Governor of *New-Hampshire*, and gave a valuable consideration to the benefit of the crown. After this there arising a dispute respecting boundaries; the government of *New-York*, by very unfair means, obtained an adjudication in the following words *to wit.*

"*At the Court at St. James's, the 20th day of July* 1764.

"PRESENT,

"THE KING'S MOST EXCELLENT MAJESTY,

"*Lord Steward.*	*Earl of Hillsborough.*
"*Earl of Sandwich.*	*Mr. Vice Chamberlain.*
"*Earl of Halifax.*	*Gilbert Elliot, Esq.*
"*Earl of Powis.*	*James Oswald, Esq.*
"*Earl of Harcourt.*	

"Whereas there was, this day, read at the board, a report made by "the Right Honorable the Lords of the Committee of Council for "plantation affairs, dated the 17th of this instant, upon considering a "representation from the Lords Commissioners for trade and planta-"tions, relative to the disputes that have, some years, subsisted between "the Provinces of New-Hampshire and New-York, concerning the "boundary line between those Provinces:—His Majesty, taking the "same into consideration, was pleased, with the advice of his privy "council, to approve of what is therein proposed, and doth accordingly, "hereby order and declare the western banks of the river Connecticut, "from where it enters the Province of the Massachusetts-Bay, as far "north as the forty fifth degree of northern latitude, *to be* the boundary "line between the said two Provinces of New-Hampshire and New-"York. Wherefore, the respective Governors and Commanders in Chief "of his Majesty's said Provinces of New-Hampshire and New-York, for "the time being, and all others whom it may concern, are to take notice "of his Majesty's pleasure, hereby signified, and govern themselves "accordingly.

W. BLAIR."

WHICH royal mandate, was most fully agreed too by the province of *New-Hampshire*, and they governed themselves accordingly down to the late revolution; and cast the people of the Grants, now the inhabitants of *Vermont*, out of their government, and refused any connection with them, published a proclamation, ordering the said people to conduct accordingly, which they have done, and by their own valour, under God, have maintained their liberties; and now *New-Hampshire* in their fit of frenzy, are claiming us back again; like a peevish child, flings away its play-thing, and then roars for it.

THE governor of *New-Hampshire* wrote to governor *Tryon*, on the 19th day of October 1771 in these words: "That he had invariably rec-"ommended implicit obedience to the laws of *New-York*, and upon all "occasions positively disavowed any connection with those people." By the same reason that *New-Hampshire* disavowed any connection with us when in distress, we now positively disavow any connection with that government, and mean to govern ourselves accordingly. We could mention many public acts of their legislature; one so late as the 8th day of January 1772, viz.

"At a Council held at *Portsmouth* by his Excellency's summons on "Thursday the 8th day of January, 1772.

"PRESENT,

"His Excellency *John Wentworth*, Esq; Governor, and

"Theodore Atkinson,	"Daniel Pierce,
"Daniel Warner,	"George Jeffrey, [Jaffrey,]
"Peter Levius, [Livius,]	"Daniel Rogers,
"Jonathan Warner,	"Peter Gilman,
"Daniel Rindge,	"Thomas W. Waldron.

"The premises being read, it is considered, that by his Majesty's or-"der in Council 20th July 1764, the western banks of *Connecticut* river "was then commanded to be the west bounds of this province, and that "this government has been and is entirely obedient thereto." Which shews that *New-Hampshire* did fully agree to, and acquiesce in that royal mandate. We might further observe that the State of *New-Hampshire*, by the writings of their supreme legislature, since the revolution, have implicitly acknowledged the State of *Vermont*,* and given encouragement to our agents, sent there from time to time, that we think it very ungenerous for *New-Hampshire* to claim us now, after they have publickly disavowed any connection with us more than fifteen years; and ordered us to govern ourselves accordingly. That we shall forever dismiss the claim of *Massachusetts-Bay* and *New-Hampshire*, after reminding them, that 'tis very similar to the claim the Pretender has to the Crown of *Great-Britain*. And it is more probable he will govern the British nation, than either of those States will *Vermont*.

*The reader will here observe how implicitly they acknowledged Vermont by the following letter, viz.

"EXETER, July 19, 1777.

"SIR,—I was favoured with yours of the 15th instant yesterday by Express, and laid the same before our General Court, who are sitting. We had previous thereto determined to send assistance to your State: They have now determined that a quarter part of the militia of twelve regiments shall be immediately drafted, formed into three battalions, under the command of Brigadier General John Stark, and forthwith sent into your State, to oppose the ravages and coming forward of the enemy; and orders are now issuing and will go out in a few hours to the several Colonels for that purpose. Dependence is made that they will be supplied with provisions in your State, and I am to desire your Convention will send some proper person or persons to No. 4, by Thursday next, to meet General Stark there, and advise with him relative to the rout and disposition of our troops, and to give him such information as you may then have, relative to the manœvres of the enemy.

In behalf of the Council and Assembly, I am, Sir, your most obedient humble Servant,

MESHECH WEARE, *President.*

Ira Allen, Esq; Secretary of the State of Vermont."

WE now pass on to the old dispute, *New-York* against *Vermont.* In the first place we absolutely deny, and we believe the candid world will join with us, that *New-York* ever had the least pretended right to this territory, before the adjudication of the King and Council A. D. 1764; though they pretend the Dutch first discovered the continent, and took up all the land west of *Connecticut* river, to *Delaware* bay. No person of sense will ever believe that, for they were ever considered by the English as intruders, and no historian that ever wrote, has been able to give any charter of the government of *New-York*, or bounds to its territory.*

THEY have likewise made much noise about a grant to *James Duke of York*, afterward King of *England*, but after all they prove too much, for if that proves any thing, it will give them a right to all the lands west of *Connecticut* river, which will take a great part of *Connecticut* and *Massachusetts-Bay*, and a large tract from the province of *Quebec*. And further it is very evident from what passed by the King and Council 1744, that the territory of *Vermont* was then considered and adjudged to be within the province of *New-Hampshire*, for the adjudication was expressly, "That *Fort Dummer* was within the province of *New-Hampshire.*" And *Fort Dummer* was west of *Connecticut* river, and most clearly within the territory of *Vermont*, now claimed by *New-York*. Hence we say that the territory of *Vermont*, never did belong to the *Dutch*, and was never considered as appertaining to *New-York* government before the royal mandate passed in 1764; on the other hand they could not claim by any authority but a few miles east of *Hudson's* river.

AND thus stood the case on the 20th day of July 1764: *New-Hampshire* relinquished all their claim to this territory, and *New-York* obtained a royal command affixing it to their government, over which before they could not have the least pretended right.

AND upon this point turns the whole dispute, between *New-York* and *Vermont*, without going one step back from the year 1764; either that royal mandate is absolutely unavoidable in its nature, and binds all beings within its limits equal to the moral law, or if it is voidable unquestionably *Vermont* is entitled to freedom and independence. For never, no never, did a people take more pains to avoid the operation of an oppressive act, than the people of *Vermont* have done. Our greatest enemies cannot say we ever associated with the government of *New-York*, or ever admitted their jurisdiction further than compelled by force. But on the contrary, we have ever since 1764, opposed them with all our might and strength even to blood.

*Says Mr. Trumbull [Rev. Benjamin,] an able historian, in a treatise upon the ancient charters:

But is it not very strange indeed if there ever were any grants made to the Dutch of this country, that they never were obtained, and exhibited in the controversy between the Dutch and English, which subsisted for more than twenty years? Equally strange is it also, that all the historians who have written concerning them have given no account of the country which they described, or of any limits or boundaries whatsoever expressed in them. The authorities and vouchers which have been now recited give abundant evidence, that the Dutch claim to New England, or to any part of North America, was without any legal foundation: and that their title to any part of the country, was never, at any period, allowed in England. The court of England ever disowned it, and treated them as usurpers. They were not the first discoverers of the country and therefore could not claim it on that footing. They had no grant of it, specifying any particular boundaries, first or last, which any historians have ever been able to certify. A grant for an exclusive trade on Hudson's river in 1614, and a grant to the West-India Company in 1621, without any description of the country granted, without the least mention of boundaries, is all that their ablest historians pretend. A grant to the West-India company, observe, not to any corporation, or body of men, in New-Netherlands, or in New-England. Nay, this grant was so far from warranting the Dutch to settle on the lands at New-Netherlands, now New-York, and exercise jurisdiction there, distinct from the government of England, that even the States General, who, it is pretended, made the grant, disowned their ever having given orders for any thing of this nature.

FURTHER, it appears that the English, of the united colonies, ever considered the right of the Dutch, as confined entirely to the lands which they had purchased and settled, AND NO MORE. In a word, governor Hutchinson has said, on the best ground, that the suffering the Dutch to extend so far as Greenwich, 20 miles east of Hudsons river, was mere favor and indulgence to these intruders. The New-England patents and the derivative grants, had a western extension to the south sea, included the whole province of New-York, and made an ample conveyance of all that part of it, which had not been settled prior to them.

THE cause must then stand upon these two points, in view of every unprejudiced mind, first had *King George the III* on the 20th of July 1764, any right to grant the fee of the land, now called the State of *Vermont*, to the government of *New-York?* and secondly had the King of *Great-Britain*, ever a right by his royal mandate to abridge the *Americans* of that great privilege, of making their own laws, and chusing their own form of government?

To the first we answer, that 'twas always a maxim in the English nation, that "the King is not above the law" and that "The law cannot do wrong." Now, as we had before purchased this territory, and given a valuable consideration to the Governor of *New-Hampshire*, who was authorized by the King of *Great-Britain* to sell it, and acted as an agent under him when he gave grants of this very territory, 'twas the same, and as binding on his Majesty, in the eye of all law and reason, as if the king had sold it himself. If then the king had once sold this territory, and taken a valuable consideration, had he any right the second time to convey it away? and if he could the second time, might he not as well twenty or a hundred, and so on *ad infinitum?* and consequently there could be no security from a king. The voice of reason and common sense tell us, that he could not convey it away but once, and as we had before purchased it, 'twas out of the king's power to convey it to *New-York*, therefore that royal mandate which *New-York* obtained A. D. 1764, was null and void in itself, as conveying any fee of the land.

To the second question we answer as every true American whig ought to do, that 'tis not a king, nor any other beings, under God, that have a right to abridge mankind of their natural liberties without their consent. What right ever had king *George* delegated to him to frame government for us, and to bind us in all cases whatsoever? None; he had in the nature of things as good a right on the 20th of July 1764, to have subjected the Angels of God, to the government of *New-York*, as he had the people of *Vermont*. For if he could abridge twenty thousand, he could one hundred thousand, and equally three millions of their liberties. And if *Vermont* had not a right to resist that act of oppression, *America* has now no right to resist, but ought to submit to all the usurpations of the British crown.

So that, view that royal command in what light soever, as either granting the fee of the land, or the right of jurisdiction; it can be of no validity longer than *George* stands with an iron rod of tyranny to support it; but is now as dead, as all other of his arbitrary acts, committed heretofore in *America*, against the peace and dignity of human nature. Will any one pretend to say that his royal mandate respecting the Quebec bill is now to be observed as sacred? Certainly not. And yet the Quebec bill much exceeds in point of authority. The truth is, those sovereign acts of oppression and tyranny, went out, and died, when the king in the declaration of independence, was removed to his Britannic regions of despair; and they who now seek to revive them, are as great enemies to the civil liberties of mankind as George III.

HENCE then we are imbolden[ed] to say that *Vermont* must live over the claims of all her enemies. *Massachusetts-Bay*, and *New-Hampshire*, by their dereliction, or utter forsaking, have lost all their pretended right; or in the words of the *Mosaic Law* they have given *Vermont* a bill of divorce, and have sent her away, and now she may not in any wise return to them again.

AND let *New-York* ground their claim upon what principle they please, when reduced to a scale of reason, it must like self-righteousness fail, and leave *New-York* without hope.

THUS we have briefly stated the controversy to the world, [and] we now proceed to treat of the independence of *Vermont*.

VERMONT'S APPEAL, &c.

WERE it possible for rational men to entertain so mean an idea of the Great Author of our existence, as to believe he intended a part of the human race should hold an absolute unbounded power over others, destined by his Sovereign will and pleasure to wear out a servile life, as vassals and tenants, to cruel lords and masters; in that case *Vermont* might demand of *New-York*, and all others who pretend to that power, some evidence of their having such a dreadful commission from Heaven; for condemned criminals are not obliged to submit to the awful sentence till the executioner has shewn his warrant.

BUT reason and common sense must convince all those who reflect upon the subject one moment, that all the claims made to this State, are founded on principles of the greatest injustice, cruelty and oppression, subversive of the rights of mankind, tending to destroy those great revolution principles upon which the United States are built up, and do in the end point an insult to the divine author of our existence. They need only a candid stating to receive a compleat refutation, for with as great propriety in the fitness of things might *Vermont* claim the territory of *New-York*, and demand their right to independence, as *New-York* can *Vermont's*. In which case we make bold to say, *Vermont* would get no other answer than *Britain* has frequently got from the mouths of cannon in asking the same question. "Yet knowing to what "violent resentment, and incurable animosities, civil discords are apt to "exasperate and influence the contending parties; we think ourselves "required by indispensable obligations to Almighty God, to our fellow "countrymen, and to ourselves, immediately to use all the means in our "power" not incompatible with our independence, for stoping the effusion of human blood, and to make known to the impartial world the justice of our cause.

BUT before we enter thereupon, must beg leave to inform the world, of the unfair means that have been used to deprive *Vermont* of her unalienable and inestimable rights. For the truth of which, we can appeal to many worthy characters, and to the august council of Congress, whether *New-York* has not in the darkest hours of the present conflict with *Great-Britain*, when our united wisdom and strength were requisite to oppose the common enemy, made the greatest struggles at Congress, and even by threats, has attempted to obtain a decree exparte against the State of *Vermont*, from no other view but because she thought her own political importance in the scale of *America* was vastly superior to that of *Vermont's;* and that Congress would rather crush *Vermont* than loose the friendship of *New-York;* when not only *New-York*, but every person, who has taken the least pains to inform himself, knows that they never had any other right of jurisdiction over the territory of *Vermont*, but what they obtained by their own wicked craft and *British* tyranny; and that the inhabitants of *Vermont*, as a people, have never submitted to the jurisdiction of *New-York*, no not from the very earliest period. For the proof of which we can now appeal to the marks on the backs of their then civil Magistrates (if any there be who have not joined the common enemy) who came from time to time, to execute cruel laws, such that the Satarp [satrap] of an eastern Despot would blush at; made on purpose to ruin the inhabitants of *Vermont*, which will be an eternal disgrace to the records of *New-York* so long as it has a political existence; for particulars of which the reader is referred to *General Allen's* "*brief narrative of the proceedings of the government of New-York.*"—[Published in 1774.]

BUT finding Congress possessed of too much wisdom and integrity to carry their vile purposes into execution, they have left no stone unturned, whereby they might ruin *Vermont.* And to gain their point, to the great detriment of the United States, have imbraced, and nourished in the bowels of this State, sworn enemies to the liberties of *America*, and endeavoured to screen them from contributing their might, toward the salvation of their country in times of the greatest danger; and that too, when called upon by officers under commissions from the *American* Congress; for no other reason, but because those persons were avowed enemies to *Vermont.*

THEY have secretly confered commissions on the sculking neutrals, who leaving to others the heat and burden of the day, have used all their diabolical schemes, to dishearten and divide the freeborn sons of *Vermont.*

THEY have received private persons, stealing away from this State, into their legislature, under pretence of their being representatives from certain towns, contrary to the very letter and spirit of their own constitution.

IN a word, they have tryed all means in their power, to extirpate and distroy the State of *Vermont;* altho' we have in all our public writings assured *New-York* of our readiness to settle all controversies, respecting lands in dispute, in some equitable way, when the great cause of *America* would permit.

AND now diffident of our own opinion, we leave the candid world to determine, how far *New-York* might have their own influence in view, by strenuously urging, and insisting, that Congress should determine such an important cause, at a period of time, when they think their State from many circumstances, is become the great key of the continent and to affront them must be very detrimental to the confederacy; but let *New-York* remember, that we have a northern as well as they a southern key,[1] and are determined to maintain and support our independence and freedom, or take refuge in that blessed State; *where the small and great are, and the servant is free from his master.*[2]

THE independence of *Vermont*, will be argued under the following heads, viz.

I. The right the State of *Vermont* has to independence.

II. Her interest and advantage in being independant.

III. The necessity she is under of supporting her independence.

IIII. The advantage that has and will accrue to the other States of *America* from the independency of *Vermont.*

---

[1] This was written several months before the Haldimand correspondence was commenced, but clearly foreshadowed it. Six months later, July 25 1780, Gov. Chittenden stated to Congress the thought expressed above in more emphatic language—that, to their protection, if necessary, the people were "at liberty to offer, or accept, terms of cessation of hostilities with Great Britain." In May 1781, Dr. George Smith, who was one of the British commissioners to treat with Vermont, wrote to Gen. Haldimand that he heard Col. Allen declare "*that there was a north pole and a south pole*, and should a thunder-gust come from the south, [Congress,] they would shut the door opposite that point and open the door facing the north," [Canada.]—See *Vt. Hist. Soc. Coll.*, Vol. II, p. 132.

[2] Job III, 19.

UNDER the first of these heads, we can support the right the State of *Vermont* has to independence, upon the same scale of reason, that all kingdoms and States maintain theirs. In a state of nature man knows no ruler, every one (under God) is his own legislator, judge, and avenger, and absolute lord of his property. Had man continued, pure and holy through time, as he came from his Creator at first, there would doubtless have been no need of government; his wants would have naturally created society, but wickedness would never have produced government. Obeying the dictates of a pure conscience, man would have needed no other law-giver; and *jurisdiction*, that necessary evil at best, would never had its name. But conscience, nature's great foundation of legislation, being corrupted by the introduction of sin, necessity absolutely required man to be under some further regulation, than the mere impulse of a depraved conscience; which we find soon after the fall, excited the perpetration of most horrid crimes in the children of disobedience, and would fill the world, with the greatest horror and misery unless restrained. From hence government took its rise, to prevent and punish wickedness, or in other words, negatively, to promote the happiness of society by restraining vice.

FROM whence it most evidently follows, that the very end and design of government, is security of life, liberty, and property, to every member of society; and the form that best answers that end, is of all others the most preferable.

THE human race being in the order of creation, all equal, that there is neither high or low, rich or poor, bond or free, for they are all one; until that equality be destroyed by some subsequent circumstance, they are all intitled to equal privileges of society; and have each one a sacred indefesible right, to choose that form of government, that shall best secure life, liberty, and property.

OR to give a more clear representation of the case, let us suppose a number of persons to move and settle within the polar circle, unconnected with any other part of the world. At their first arrival, they would form into society; and while each one remained strictly honest and just, they would need no further regulations; their views would be the reciprocal good of each other. But so soon as vice, that pest of society, began to creep in among them, they would then find the necessity of establishing some form of government to make each other honest: In framing of which, every person ought to have an equal share, in the legislative, judicial, and vindictive powers; and would have an indisputable right, to adopt such a mode of government, as to them shall seem best, and ought to enjoy the benefits thereof, unmolested, equal with any other kingdom, or State under Heaven; and for any foreign power to exercise jurisdiction, and enforce laws upon that people, would be the essence of tyranny.

WE'LL suppose still further, that as soon as our new emigrants are formed into a state of society, before they have established any form of government, an eastern monarch should pass that way with a large host of the dogs of war and sons of tyranny the disgrace of human nature, and discover this little honest feeble band, whereupon he should make a formal declaration, "that he had full power and authority, to make laws "and statutes, of sufficient validity, to bind this society in all cases "whatsoever." And should order and decree that these new settlers in the wilderness, should be abridged of all their natural rights, and be bound to *New-York*, and subjected to the laws, ordinances and jurisdiction of the same, upon pain of having his dogs of war let loose to destroy them. And notwithstanding frequent petitions, remonstrances, and asserting their just rights, were nevertheless compelled to remain in this condition, for ten long years, at which period of time, they arrive to that degree of strength, with the assistance of some honest neighbors, that they rise and cut in two that power, *which was of sufficient validity, to bind themselves in all cases whatsoever*, and thereby git loose from the cords of bondage. We ask in the name of reason, whether the world ought to assist in spliceing that power, to bind them again to *New-York;* or whether they ought not in equity, and the eternal rules of right, immediately to be put in full possession of that inestimable privilege, which they have so long been unjustly deprived of, *that of making their own laws, and choosing their own form of government.*

SIMILAR is the State of *Vermont;* whose inhabitants, at the expence of their fortunes, and hazard of their lives, without the least charge to any Colony, Province, or State, from which they removed, by hard labour and unconquerable spirit, they have procured settlements, in the wilderness of *Vermont;* have faced death and danger; undergone unspeakable hardships, in perils by savages, in perils by wild beasts of prey, in cold, in nakedness, in hunger, and in want. That above all have they suffered, from the cruelty of *Great Britain* and her emissaries. Nevertheless, from the first day of their entering into said wilderness, they never adopted, or choose any kind of government, any further than compelled by the murdering sword, nor did they ever form into a State of society, with any other Colony, Province, or State, but kept a well regulated association among themselves, for the protection of life, and property, until the 15th of January 1777, when by the united voice of the people, they declared themselves a free and independant State. For the truth of these things we can appeal to many undeniable facts; so late as March 1774, [1775,] previous to the battle of *Lexington*, the judges of *New-York*, were led in fetters of iron, within the gates of their own city, for shedding innocent blood at *Westminster*, in murderously attempting to enforce the laws of that province, upon the people of *Vermont.* And as the territory of *Vermont* did not originally appertain to *New-York*, and seeing the inhabitants never did associate with that province, it is manifest they have as good a natural right to independence, to make and execute their own laws, as any body of people on this continent.

AGAIN, the State of *Vermont* has an undoubted right to independence, from the situation and extent of it's territory.

As we have before shewn, the government that best answers the ends of society, is of all others the most preferable, being instituted to promote happiness, and not increase misery: Now whenever government fails in answering the ends of it's institution; or in other words creates more evils than it prevents, it becomes a burden, and ought in the course of things to be dismissed; hence it is, when the reason of parental government ceases, the government of course ceases. And by the same reason that the other *American States* have assumed government, *Vermont* is of age to act for herself. And to suppose the territory of *Vermont*, which is 160 miles in length, and 60 miles in breadth, with near thirty thousand souls, at this time of day, after 3 years independence, under as good regulation, and code of laws as any State on the continent, ought to be affixed to the government of *New-York*, whose morals, manners, and interests are diametrically opposite, is as absurd, as to suppose the *American States* ought to be reaffixed to *Great Britain.* Add further, that if *Vermont* was affixed to the jurisdiction of *New-York*, many individuals must travel 400 miles to the seat of government; which would render it an intolerable burden, and pervert the very ends for which government was instituted.

AGAIN, we might observe, that *Great-Britain*, previous to the declaration of independence, had made a distinct government of this territory, and had granted a commission accordingly. But as matters are now situate, *Vermont* cannot obtain a copy of those writings. And that may be one great reason why *New-York* has wearied Congress to obtain an immediate decisive adjudication, before that evidence can possibly be obtained, least otherwise they should be self-condemned upon their own stating.[1]

AGAIN, the State of *Vermont* has merited an indisputable right to independence, in the esteem of every true whig; by her brave and noble conduct, in the gloomy struggle of *America* with *Great-Britain.* First in *America* were the Green Mountain Boys, (to their immortal honor be it written) that commenced an offensive war against British tyranny. Under every disadvantage in being a frontier, they nevertheless with their lives in their hands, took *Ticonderoga*, and other important garrisons in the north; so early that *New-York*, as a government, was considered as a dead weight in the continental scale. And like men determined to obtain liberty or death, they pursued the war into *Canada;* there they fought, blead, and died, not counting their lives dear, that they might obtain the prize at the race end. Many heroes can *Vermont* boast in the territory of *Canada*, who fell fighting in the glorious cause of American liberty and freedom. Let the brave immortal *Gates*, and deathless *Stark*, tell posterity, that in the year 1777, assisted by the militia of the State of *Vermont*, they humbled the long boasted pride of *Great-Britain*, and brought the towering General *Burgoyne*, with his chosen legions, to ask mercy at their feet. In a word, *Vermont*, by her blood and treasure, at the point of the sword, has fairly merited liberty; and by the eternal rule of reason, has a right to independence, from every consideration; she has received it from God, as being created with equal liberties in the scale of human beings; from nature in the formation of her territory; and from her own victorious struggles with *Great-Britain.*

II. THE interest and advantage of the State of *Vermont* in being independant is very certain. This territory has been one continued scene of legislative confusion, and contention, since the royal mandate passed A. D. 1764, till the late revolution, which gave *Vermont* an opportunity to take the staff of government into her own hands. And this contention, being unavoidably founded in the natural opposition of interests, between the State of *New-York*, and that of *Vermont;* that were they to be under one and the same jurisdiction, 'twould render the whole State an eternal theatre of contention, bloodshed and misery. That taking every circumstance into consideration, the greatness and situation of its territory; the strength to which it has already arisen, with the rapid progress of its future settlement; the difference of the morals, and manners of its inhabitants from those of *New-York*, the clashing interests, together with that bitter jealousy, not to say hatred that would forever exist, were they to be affixt to *New-York*, must oblige every impartial man to say that it would be greatly for the interest of *Vermont* to be independent.

III. VERMONT is under a necessity of supporting her independence. Freedom is the gift of the beneficent Creator, to all his subjects: Slavery only appertains to the devil and his followers. All rational beings have a right to expect that from their natural parents which God bequeathed to them, and left in trust to be handed down unimpaired, to the last child to be born of the human race.

THE State of *Vermont*, we have now clearly shewn, has a natural right to independence; honor, justice and humanity forbid us tamely to sur-

---

[1] See *post*, *Appendix G*, note to the letter of the Agents of Vermont to the President of Congress, under date of Feb. 1 1780.

render that freedom which our innocent posterity have a right to demand and receive from their ancestors. Full well may they hereafter rise up in judgment against us, if, like profane Esau, we mortgage away their birth rights, and leave them at the expence of their lives, to obtain freedom. The righteous blood, already spilt in *Westminster* court-house, calls louder than thunder for an everlasting separation from *New-York.*

FURTHER, the State of *Vermont*, is under an absolute necessity of supporting her independence, or incurring, as a people, the greatest guilt in the eye of heaven. They have declared to the world that they are, and of right ought to be, a free independent State; have appointed officers civil and military, who have discharged their various betrustments, punished offenders, ratified and dissolved the most solemn contracts in nature, joined man and wife, have in some instances granted bills of divorce, strictly forbidding the parties ever to cohabit together, have pronounced sentence of death, when twelve men of the vicinage, under the oath of God have declared life was forfeited by the law of the land, and have issued a warrant to take away the same; that should they now give up independence, and thereby confess that they had no right to found government: they would acknowledge themselves guilty of the crying sins of murder, adultery, fornication, robbery, &c. and deserving of that curse pronounced by God on those who part man and wife.

AGAIN, we are under a necessity of supporting our independence, arising from our plighted faith to individuals: Upon the declaration of independence of the State of *Vermont*, many persons of fortune, admiring its constitution, sold all that they had in neighbouring states, moved in and purchased large interests of the government, laid out all their effects, taking the plighted faith of the freemen of the State of *Vermont* for their security; and now to give up our independence, would be destroying all their security, and reducing them by our perfidy, from a state of affluence, to a wretched condition of beggary and want; that could it be possible, every virtuous person would stigmatize the inhabitants of *Vermont*, to the latest posterity.

IIII. WE are now to point out the advantage that has and will accrue to the other States of *America* from the independence of *Vermont.*

OMITTING a few ******, whom *New-York*, by their bribery and corruption, have prevented from doing much in the common cause; we venture to assert that no one of the fourteen states[1] now at war with *Great-Britain*, according to their numbers, have done more for the interest of the whole, than *Vermont.* During the first stages of the war, not one State, excepting *Connecticut*, (a free government,) excelled the Green Mountain Boys for vigor, spirit and resolution. We will appeal to those Generals who have had the northern command, whether by applying to the Governor and Council of *Vermont*, in times of the most pressing danger, they did not receive much speedier, and as effectual help as by applying to *New-York.* That all the world must confess who have had the least knowledge of the war in the northern district, that the State of *Vermont* has been of great advantage to *America*, and much more so than if that territory had belonged to any other State.

AGAIN, many advantages must hereafter accrue to the other States of *America*, from the independency of *Vermont;* for we cannot expect those States who are ambitiously grasping at territories to which they have not the least shadow of right, will use the wealth arising therefrom to any better purpose than to oppress their less wealthy and less powerful neighbors. It never will be for the interest of the United States, to have some great, overgrown, unwieldy States. *New-York* is now large

[1] This includes Vermont as the fourteenth state.

enough; and 'tis very probable that if *New-York* should obtain this territory, and the Green Mountain Boys submit to their aristocratical form of government; she would in time, by the same spirit, overrun and ruin many of the United States.[1]

VERMONT'S APPEAL

To the General CONGRESS of the *United States.*

CALLED upon as we are to address your honorable board, on matters of the last importance to the State of *Vermont;* and probably to the thirteen United States, over which you preside: we wish most earnestly to perform this office with the utmost decency, reverance, and respect; trusting, that should necessity, which knows no law on so uncommon an occasion, oblige us to deviate from that delicate line of honor observed by courts, your candour will impute it to a just attention, due to our own preservation, against those artful and designing States, who abuse your confidence and authority, for the purpose of effecting our destruction; rather than disrespect to your august body.

WE glory in being allied to your government, in being connected by the strongest ties of nature, gratitude, and friendship, to those illustrious personages, who by their valour and wisdom, have extricated *America* from ruin, and by securing happiness to others, have erected the most noble and durable monuments to their own fame. We solemnly assure you, that we most ardently wish a permanent union and confederation might be established between this and the United States, upon so firm a basis, as to transmit its blessings to posterity uninterrupted by any future dissensions. Under a full expectation, of reaping equal blessings at the end of the conflict with Great-Britain; the inhabitants of this State have ever stood forth with their lives, and fortunes, to assert and maintain the rights and interests of *America.*

BUT to our unspeakable grief, we find neighboring States, usurping a more tyrannic power, if it were possible, than ever Great-Britain grasped after, wallowing in luxury, and wanting provinces to drain of wealth, like the debauched Romans, to defray their extravigancies, are using the wisdom of serpents, and the intrigue of courtiers, to make the inhabitants of *Vermont* dupes, and slaves, to their unbounded lust of domination and prey.

AND to our great astonishment, we find some so base, as to be willing their countrymen should be made tributary to such birds of prey; if they might have a small pittance for gathering the tax, even on condition it were demanded at the point of the bayonet.

THE petty tyrants of every country always wish to have the people dependant on such a power, for under colour of authority from that power, they can carry on their oppressions, vexations, and depredations, and sin without controul.

---

[1] This appeal to the small states was effective. In 1782 Mr. Madison named New Jersey, Delaware, and Rhode Island as favoring Vermont in Congress with a view "of strengthening the interests of the little states." Connecticut and Maryland, of the comparatively small states, were also for Vermont at that time, and Massachusetts and Pennsylvania of the large states.—See *Vt. Hist. Soc. Coll.*, Vol. II, pp. 268, 312.

THAT could any thing add to our grief and surprise, it must be to find your act of the 24th of September last, containing the following Resolutions, *viz.* [For these resolutions, see *ante*, *Appendix B*, pp. 183-185.]

As *Americans*, as freemen, or as men of common sense, we cannot view ourselves holden, in the sight of God or man, to submit to the execution of a plan, which we have reason to believe, was commenced by neighbouring States without policy; and must be prosecuted by means incompatible with the fundamental principles of liberty; which appears, not only big with injustice and impiety, but carries immediate ruin to ourselves and posterity, as soon as they become human beings. We have examined it minutely, we have viewed it in every point of light in which we were able to place it; and with pain and grief, we sincerely declare we cannot close with the terms of those resolutions, for these reasons.

1. BECAUSE, all the liberties and privileges of the State of *Vermont*, by said resolutions, are to be suspended, upon the arbitrament and final determination of Congress; when in our opinion, they are things too sacred ever to be arbitrated upon: and that we cannot stand acquitted to our own conscience, to the world, or posterity, to give them up, by reason of the adjudication of any man or body of men, but must hold ourselves under the most sacred obligations to posterity, to defend them at every risk.

2. BECAUSE, the Congress of the United States has no right to meddle with the internal police, and support of civil government in this State; for us, not for Congress, has government been instituted here, and we cannot conceive that any other legislature has a right to prescribe modes to determine our fate, or abolish our own internal institutions. We most chearfully at the same time will accede to any propositions made by Congress for the equitable settlement of all disputes relative to property, when admitted to union with the other States.

3. BECAUSE, we conceive this State to exist independant of any of the thirteen United States, and not accountable to them, or their representatives, for liberty, the gift of the beneficent Creator; having existed as an intire corporation, or body politic, before the union or confederation of the other States: the first association, and oldest body politic on the continent, upon the late revolution establishment; and therefore cannot belong to the confederacy.

4. BECAUSE, the State of *Vermont* is not represented in Congress, we cannot submit to resolutions passed without our consent, or even knowledge, which put every thing near and dear at stake. We esteem it an essential unalterable principle of liberty, the source and security of all constitutional rights, that no State or people can be bound by the acts of any legislature without being represented. "It is with the deepest "concern that we have seen the sacred security of representation, that "great bulwark of liberty, silently passed over," and acts, rendering the liberty, and lives of the inhabitants of *Vermont* precarious, passed unanimously. We have carefully weighed the matter, and can see no material difference, in being dragged to *Philadelphia* or *Great-Britain;* and there, untried and unheard, obliged to deliver ourselves up as victims to court pleasure. Let the prejudiced amuse the world, and confound the ignorant with their jargon; freedom and dependence on a power, over which we have no influence nor controul, is slavery, or we are yet ignorant of the word.

5. BECAUSE, there appears a manifest inequality, not to say predetermination by said resolutions, in that Congress should request of their own constituents, power to judge and determine in the cause, and never

ask the consent of thousands whose all are at stake, which evidently purports one of these two things: either that the rest of the world are not intitled to equal privileges with their constituents, and that Congress have a right *to make laws to bind them in all cases whatsoever*, without their consent or even knowledge: or, that Congress already have predetermined us to belong to the thirteen United States and of course have a delegated right to judge in the cause; either of which, as freemen, it is our indispensible duty by all lawful means to oppose.

6. BECAUSE, said resolutions are either inconsistent in themselves, or incompatible with the liberties of free States; in that Congress implicitly acknowledge, that as Congress, they have no right to take up the matter, by requesting of *New-Hampshire*, *Massachusetts-Bay*, and *New-York* special laws to authorize them to judge of the cause; and then go on to pledge the faith of Congress, to execute and support their decisions, and determinations, in the premises, if only one State, *to wit*, *New-York* should pass the law, which amounts to this: that *New-York* can give Congress power to pledge the faith of the United States; and even of those States who refuse to submit the cause to Congress.

THESE are our sentiments upon this important subject, and least they should be misconstrued, or misunderstood, we again declare to you, sirs, and to the world, that we are not contending for lucre or filthy gain, we are willing to agree with any equitable proposals, made for the settlement of all differences relative to the fee of lands in dispute; and are not anxious of being judges in our own cause. We further most solemnly assure you, that we are, and ever have been willing, to bear our proportion of the burden and expense of the present war with *Great-Britain*, from its first commencement, whenever admitted to union with the other States: Esteeming it just, that those who equally participate of the blessings of liberty, should bare equally the burdens of the war in obtaining it. At the same time, we cannot be so lost to all sense, and honor, or do that violence to our feelings, as freemen, and as *Americans*, that after four years war with *Great-Britain*, in which we have expended so much blood and treasure, we should now give up every thing worth fighting for, *the right of making our own laws and choosing our own form of government*, to the arbitrament, and determination of any man or body of men under heaven.

"Who noble ends by noble means obtains;
"Or failing smiles, in excile, or in chains,
"*That man is great indeed.*" POPE.

VERMONT'S APPEAL

To the Inhabitants of the UNITED STATES of *AMERICA*.

COUNTRYMEN, FELLOW CITIZENS, & BRETHREN.

UNDER the strongest ties of friendship, as men who have equally suffered together, from the iron rod of tyranny, in the late cruel measures of *Great-Britain;* and have gone hand in hand, and stood by each other, in times when threatened with ruin, tyranny, and death; we beg your most serious attention by our address to this very important subject. And whilst like the Dove in the fable, you bend the branch, to save the poor Bee struggling for life; remember it may be in our power to sting the fowler so severely, when drawing the net to ensnare the Dove, as may hereafter procure your liberation. We can never believe that the present inhabitants of the United States are so lost to all feelings of humanity, benevolence, and religion, that while they extend their right hands to Heaven, and weary unbounded grace, in praying to be delivered from *British* tyranny and oppression; they should with their left hands, be forming shackles of slavery for their *American* brethren. It gives us pain and grief, to mention the intrigues, and artifices, used by wicked and designing men, to destroy the inestimable liberties, and priviledges of the State of *Vermont;* and that too by those ungrateful ones, who have been preserved from Indian cruelty, by our brave and strenuous exertions during the present war.

WE need not inform you, that all those despotic claims of jurisdiction, over this State, made by any powers of the neighbouring States, originate from the same seeds of corruption and tyranny, that raised the war between *Britain* and *America*, to wit the power of taking from us our property without our consent; or in other words, to reduce us to a state of abject tenantry, binding us down as tenants, and then domineering over us as Lords.

WE need not warn you of the dangers that threaten you in our destruction; those who have once feasted on the spoils of their countrymen, and tasted the sweet of living upon the labor and sweat of tenants, like the voracious wolf, will never leave till they have devoured the whole flock of *American* yeomanry. We have seen the liberties of *Poland*, and *Sweeden*, swept away in the course of one year, by treachery and usurpation; the free towns in *Germany*, like dying sparks are quenched one after another in the destructive greatness of their neighbours.

WE beg leave to recall your attention to the present most critical situation of the inhabitants of the State of *Vermont;* many of us were soldiers in the provincial army during the last war, between *France* and *Great-Britain*, and suffered inconceivable hardships, in successive campaigns, in striving to support the honor of the *British* nation, and to conquer and defend this territory of land from Indians, Canadians, and French, at which time 'twas that we discovered the excellency of the country, and determined if ever circumstances would permit to settle the same.

AT the close of the war, *Canada* being ceded to the British crown, and a general peace prevailing in *North-America*, gave us an opportunity to begin settlements on the Green Mountains, then a wilderness, filled with savages, scorpions and beasts of prey ; and notwithstanding all our fatigue in assisting to conquer said territory, that we might not give offence, we applied to the governor of *New-Hampshire*, at that time an agent or factor, to sell extra-provincial or crown lands in *America*, for the king of *Great Britain;* and purchased all the territory of *Vermont* at a very high price, excepting a small tract in the northern part of this state, and continued making settlements in the wilderness, [and] by an invincible fortitude, surmounted every obstacle. In this situation, in the midst of a howling wilderness, we had very little to do with any other colony, or province, never sending abroad to obtain legislation, but kept a very good regulation among ourselves; acknowledging *New-Hampshire* to be our parent State, because we had purchased our land there, and expected to have it warranted and defended by them, but never associated with them as a people in a state of society; for we never had a single voice in their house of representatives, and consequently were not contained within the jurisdiction of their laws. In this situation the king of *Great-Britain*, starting the idea of raising a revenue from the American colonies, and considering the *New-England* colonies too popular to begin with, and entertain any prospect of success, he therefore adds all the territory north of ***Massachusetts*** line, and west of ***Connecticut*** river, (which we had before purchased) by an arbitrary command, to the jurisdiction of *New-York;* thinking as part of that province was held by tenure, he could carry on his plans with greater ease, by adding greater power to the servants of the crown, decreasing the number of freemen, and consequently increasing the number of slaves: We think the greatest reason will justify this assertion, for no sooner had the governor of *New-York* obtained jurisdiction, but he patented out all the territory we were in possession of, to a few of his nobility and lords, who were favorites of administration, and ordered us to pay the annual rents usual for servile tenants, or quit our possessions immediately; and that "we should not tarry to reap the crops then growing." We replied in the most humble, but positive terms, "That we had purchased our lands "of the crown at a dear rate, and had suffered infinite hardships in gain- "ing settlements, and now to give them up, or acknowledge ourselves "tenants to any lord, was what we would not at the risk of our lives." And from thence sprung the long dispute; we, on our part, refusing to submit to their government, and they striving to dispossess us of our lands and tenements; in the course of which time, we frequently petitioned *New-Hampshire* most earnestly, that they would take us under their protection, and prevent our being devoured by those who sought our ruin; and had as often the misfortune to find them deaf to all our intreaties, and at last the bitter mortification to see a proclamation, issued by the Governor and Council of *New-Hampshire*, wherein they relinquished all right to the jurisdiction of said territory; put us out from under their protection, and directed us to govern ourselves accordingly. We then found ourselves reduced, to the melancholy necessity of quitting all, and from a state of affluence to commence beggars; to submit as servile tenants to haughty lords; or as freemen, to face death and danger and support our rights; we determined upon the latter, and choose rather to die with honor than live with shame. In this condition, detachments of their militia were frequently sent to dispossess us, whom we opposed even to blood. It ought to be observed, that as soon as *New-Hampshire* refused us any relief, and relinquished their claim, we sent immediately agents after agents to *Great-Britain*, with petitions in their hands, to lay at the foot of the throne, praying for relief, who at first were received very cooly, but after the plan of the stamp-act failed in *America*, the crown listened to our cries, and gave a decree, in part suspending that jurisdictional power in *New-York*, *until his Majesty's further will and pleasure should be known;* afterwards we obtained one or two reports of the Board of Trade in our favour, but remained very much in that situation, until the eve of the present war, when we understood that king *George*, to answer some other tyrannic views, had given Governor *Skeen* a commission to preside as governor over most of this territory, who came once to visit us, but finding the inhabitants no better disposed toward him, than toward *New-York*, soon made his exit and left us to govern ourselves.[1]

"WE shall decline the ungrateful task, of describing the irksome vari- "ety of artifices, the acts of oppression, the fruitless terrors, and una- "vailing severities," that for the course of twelve years were dealt out by the legislature of *New-York*, in their endeavours to execute their unreasonable and cruel measures. And not to wound humanity, leave untold those black acts of outlawry and death, passed against Englishmen, and

---

[1] This statement is not embraced in Ira Allen's later account, for which see note on the subject, *post*, *Appendix G.*

freemen, and that too by a legislature, wherein they could have no representation, placing them as common marks for the arrow, wherein they not only proffered absolution to any person that should kill them, but even offered rewards, to those who would imbrue their hands in their blood, for no other crime but defending their just rights and privileges. Driven as we were by fatal necessity, while we remained in that condition, to submit either to ruin, slavery and death; or declare ourselves a free and independent State; we determined upon the latter, being assured, that our struggle would be glorious, since in death we could obtain that freedom, which in life we were forbid to enjoy.

WE have now existed as a free independant State almost four years, have fought Britains, Canadians, Hessians, Waldeckers, Dutchmen, Indians, Tories and all, and have waded in blood to maintain and support our independence. We beg leave to appeal to your own memories, with what resolution we have fought by your sides, and what wounds we have received fighting in the grand *American* cause; and let your own recollection tell what *Vermont* has done and suffered in the cause of civil liberty and the rights of mankind. And must we now tamely give up all worth fighting for ? No, sirs, while we wear the name of *Americans*, we never will surrender those glorious privileges for which so many have fought, blead and died; we appeal to your own feelings as men of like sufferings, whether you would submit your freedom and independence, to the arbitrament of any court or referees under heaven ? if you would, after wasting so much blood and treasure, you are unworthy the name of *Americans;* if you would not, condemn not others in what you allow yourselves. To you we appeal as the dernier resort under God; your approbation, or disapprobation, must determine the fate of thousands. It is not the intrigueing courtier, the eloquent lawyer, or the learned judge that we fear; we tremble least posterity should read, that the arms of the glorious *Americans*, after working wonders in the cause of liberty, were tarnished and disgraced, and vilely used as instruments to deprive their brethren of their inestimable rights and privileges.

OUR enemies give us opprobrious names, they call us insurgents and rebels. We have stated the matter clearly before you in the course of this *pamphlet;* you see wherein our rebellion consists, and if that can be called rebellion, shew us a period in the history of the present war, in which you have not been equally rebellious. We conjure you by that friendship which has so long subsisted between us, by the blood and sufferings we have exhibited in your cause, by your own honor, and liberties which are at stake, to rise and crush that spirit of oppression, now exercised in seeking our destruction. Be assured that if you suffer us tamely to be devoured by those greedy powers who have laid plans for our ruin, that spirit will not sleep long, before you must fare the same fate; for we conceive the liberties of the whole, to be absolutely connected with every part of an empire, founded on the common rights of mankind. We have coveted no man's estate, we have at all times been ready to submit all differences relative to the fee of lands in dispute to impartial judges, and now solemnly declare to all the world that we are contending only for liberty, the gift of the Creator to all his subjects, the right of making our own laws, and choosing our own form of government, and will God be pleased to dispose the hearts of our countrymen to save the inhabitants of the State of *Vermont* from tyranny and oppression, to grant them their liberties in peace, and to see the things which belong to their political salvation, before they are hidden from their eyes.

To the Commonalty of *New-Hampshire, Massachusetts-Bay* and *New-York.*

WE conclude this address to you, in short, to remind you that your liberties are challenged as well as ours; you are now engaged in a bloody war in defence of the same; remember, the measure you meet out to others, heaven will measure back to you again. Can you stand before the throne of God and seek to be protected and defended in your cause, while you are striving to overthrow and destroy the liberties of the State of *Vermont*, which stands on as large a scale of reason for independence as any other State on the Continent.

AGAIN we request you seriously to consider, whether the object is worth the pursuit before you rush head-long like the horse into the battle. Force is seldom imployed with success to change the opinions, or convince the minds of freemen. But admitting that you should conquer us and affix us to any of your governments. Will that enrich you? Certainly not: Will it make us better neighbours? it cannot. Will our destruction secure your liberties? By no means. What then will you obtain finally, for all your trouble and expense, not to say bloodhshed. Nothing but a conquered depopulated territory, where every single inhabitant, will be so imbittered against you, that you will be necessitated to keep a standing army perpetually, to keep them in subjection, and support government. And that very army in time, being accustomed to trample upon the liberties of mankind, will, with the assistance of the disaffected, like the worm at the root of *Jonah's* gourd, eat up and devour the whole of your liberties, and thus the righteous Judge of the universe will give that people that deprive *Vermont* of her rights, slavery to drink for they will be worthy.

THE END.

APPENDIX E.

A CONCISE REFUTATION OF THE CLAIMS OF NEW-HAMPSHIRE AND MASSACHUSETTS-BAY TO THE TERRITORY OF VERMONT; WITH OCCASIONAL REMARKS ON THE LONG DISPUTED CLAIM OF NEW-YORK TO THE SAME. Written by ETHAN ALLEN and JONAS FAY Esqrs. Published by order of the Governor & Council of Vermont.

BENNINGTON the first day of January 1780.

JOSEPH FAY, *Sec'ry.*

HARTFORD: Printed by HUDSON & GOODWIN.[1]

THIS Government, astonished at the late extraordinary claims of New-Hampshire and Massachusetts-Bay to the territory of Vermont and the following remarks having been omitted in any piece heretofore published on the subject, laid themselves under the disagreaable necessity of publicly exposing the imbecility and depravity of those governments, whose candour on the very first attempts should have suggested to them that in prosecuting such claims they would unavoidably become accomplices with the government of New-York in their many aggravated and long continued oppressions of the people of this State. This Government, sensible of the devices of certain leading gentlemen of the government of New-York against them, and being apprised that they had some time since proposed to certain leading gentlemen in the States of New-Hampshire and Massachusetts-Bay to divide this State among the three States aforesaid which are now actually claiming it severally,[2] and

---

[1] *Ethan Allen Ms. Papers*, pp. 295–325.

[2] The allusion in this and other Vermont documents, to a design to divide Vermont between at least two of the contending states, was not without foundation. Oct. 7 1779—nearly three months preceding Allen and Fay's *Concise Refutation*—John Jay wrote to Gov. Clinton that one of the delegates in Congress from New Hampshire "seems much inclined to make the ridge of mountains instead of Connecticut river the boundary line between us;" and Mr. Jay favored the proposal.* Feb. 9 1780, after several unsuccessful attempts to induce Congress to proceed to a hearing of the controversy, the New York delegates in that body addressed a formal letter to Gov. Clinton, recommending *an accommodation of the dispute with New Hampshire.* Feb. 21, Gov. Clinton commu-

* *Clinton Papers*, No. 2549, an extract from which is in H. HALL'S *Early History*, p. 307.

sensible likewise of our danger from the frontier situation to the Province of Quebec, and of the influence which the government of New-York (especially if corroborated by those of New-Hampshire and Massachusetts-Bay) might have in the Congress of the United States in which we have [are] not represented—These apprehensions excited this Government to remonstrate at the General Courts of New-Hampshire and Massachusetts-Bay against their making and prosecuting such claims which in their nature and tendency are cruel, unjustifiable, and without any reasonable foundation for their support:—And having received several acts of Congress of the 24th of September last, among which is contained a recommendation to the several States of New-Hampshire, Massachusetts-Bay and New-York, to pass laws expressly authorizing the Grand Council of America to hear and determine the differences which have subsisted between them on one part and the inhabitants of a district of country called the New-Hampshire Grants (as they are pleased to term them) on the other, on the first day of February next; and a citation (only) to the inhabitants of the latter to choose Agents and otherwise prepare for the hearing aforesaid, [this Government] have therefore thought it expedient to exhibit to the world, and to the honorable Congress as a very respectable part of it, the apparent impropriety of those claims.

---

nicated this letter by message to the Assembly. Feb. 22, the message and letter were referred to a joint committee of both houses, of which Micah Townshend of Brattleboro' was chairman on the part of the House. March 8, Mr. Townshend reported an answer to their delegates in Congress, which declared it "ineligible at present to attempt an accommodation with New Hampshire in the mode you have proposed;" but declared that "at a future day possibly the measure may appear not only expedient but necessary."* April 10 1780, Mr. Townshend wrote from Brattleboro' to Gov. Clinton as follows: "By what I can learn the legislature of New Hampshire or at least some of their members, and their partizans west of Connecticut river, entertain an opinion that the western boundary of that state will be fixed at the *Green Mountains*."† Under date of Jan. 16, 1783, at Philadelphia, John Taylor Gilman, delegate to Congress from New Hampshire, wrote to President Weare for instructions, saying: "The Legislature of New York are now in session, and from some information which I have had this Day think it is probable they will Repeal their Act by which the Desision of this matter was Submitted to Congress, if it should be proposed in the present state of this matter and without Deciding on the Question of their Independence, that it be Recommended to New York and New Hampshire to adjust this matter between themselves Reserving to Massachusetts the Right of Claiming, and a trial upon the principles of Confederation, and that Congress pledge themselves for carrying into effect their agreement."‡ For other memoranda on the same subject see H. HALL's *Early History*, p. 415.

* *Assembly Journal of New York*, cited in H. HALL's *Early History*, pp. 307-309.

† *Clinton Papers*, No. 2791.

‡ From manuscript copy in possession of Hon. HILAND HALL.

And first we shall consider the pretensions of Massachusetts-Bay.[1] It is admitted that previous to the adjudication of the boundary line in 1739 between New-Hampshire and Massachusetts-Bay the latter had claimed a considerable part of the present jurisdiction of New-Hampshire, from the Atlantic Ocean on the east part (which claim did equally interfere with the territory now in dispute) and in longitude through the main land to the South Sea, on the west part, as described in the charter of the Colony of Massachusetts-Bay. This antiquated claim of Massachusetts-Bay was referred to the King and Council by an appeal from a Court of Commissioners previously authorized by the same authority to determine, and mark out the boundaries between the said two provinces, as may appear from the following extract of the settlement of that line viz.

"And whereas appeals from the determination of the said Commis-"sioners have been laid before his Majesty by the Agents for the re-"spective Provinces of the Massachusetts-Bay and New-Hampshire; "which said appeals have been before the Committee of Council for "hearing appeals from the plantations, who after having considered the "whole matter and heard all parties concerned therein did report unto "his Majesty as their opinion that the northern boundary of the said "Province of Massachusetts-Bay are and be a similar curve line, pursu-"ing the course of Merrimack river at three miles distance of [on] the "north side thereof beginning at the Atlantic Ocean and ending at a "point due north of a place on a plan returned by said Commissioners "called Pantucket [Patucket] Falls and a strait line drawn from thence "due west cross the said river till it meets with his Majesty's other gov-"ernments, which said report of the Committee of Council, his Majesty "hath been pleased with the advice of his Privy Council to approve, and "to declare, adjudge and order that the northern boundary of the said "Province of Massachusetts-Bay are and be a similar curve line, pursu-"ing the Course of the *Merrimack* River at three miles distance on the "north side thereof beginning at the Atlantic Ocean and ending at a "point due north of a place on the plan returned by the said Commis-"sioners called Pantucket Falls and a strait line drawn from thence due "west crost the said river till it meets his Majesty's other governments."

This adjudication was made in 1739[2] which was forty years ago and the government of the Massachusetts-Bay have regulated their jurisdiction accordingly ever since which is too notorious to be disputed and may be further illustrated by a variety of acts of their own as well as of the British government. One of them respects Fort Dummer which was built by the Massachusetts-Bay Province in 1724, and garrisoned at their expence a number of years, but upon its being excluded from their jurisdiction by the settlement of the boundary line aforesaid, the Bay Province represented to the government at home that the said district of land claimed as aforesaid and Fort Dummer having been determined to be the property of New-Hampshire they were no longer obliged to garrison and maintain it, and praying that as it was necessary for the defence of that part of the country that New-Hampshire might be directed to support it: In consequence of which an order passed the King and Council in 1744 as follows viz. "That the Governor and Comman-"der in Chief of New-Hampshire should forthwith move the Assembly "in his Majesty's name to make a provision for that service;" and at the

[1] See *ante, Appendix C;* and *Appendix D*, pp. 204–206.

[2] The date of the decision is March 5 1740, in Belknap's *History of New-Hampshire*, Vol. II, p. 132.

same time informing them "that in case they refused to comply with so "reasonable and necessary a proposal, his Majesty would find himself "under the necessity of restoring that fort with a proper district of land "contiguous to it, to the Province of Massachusetts-Bay, who cannot "with justice be required to maintain a fort no longer within their "boundary." In consequence of this requisition New-Hampshire did actually maintain Fort Dummer and paid a demand of arrears for its previous support to Massachusetts-Bay and the receipt thereof remains in the Secretary's office of New-Hampshire to this day.

After these solemn governmental transactions, and actual compliance of Massachusetts-Bay to the said royal adjudication, their pretensions to the jurisdiction of Vermont appear to be not only impertinent but arbitrary, and should such a precedent take place would make an end to all jurisdictional limitations through the United States as well as those of Vermont, as in this case no ancient settlement of boundary lines respecting them could be valid, and consequently the greatest confusions and disorders would necessarily ensue. Furthermore, if there be any thing in those pretensions of Massachusetts-Bay they equally effect [affect] the actual jurisdiction of New-Hampshire to the eastward of Connecticut River, over which eastern part when Massachusetts-Bay shall exercise their jurisdiction, it will be early enough for them to do the same over an equal width of the jurisdiction of Vermont. After all provided there be any reality in those pretensions there is a great deal in them as they are founded on a charter right, and consequently challenge the right of soil: This the principal gentlemen of their Court gave our Agent to understand that they demanded with jurisdiction, which opens another scene of expence to the inhabitants (provided their pretended claim takes place.) This will undoubtedly be displeasing to the present occupants, their lands having been (the greater part of them) already granted by New-Hampshire and New-York, but [as] there is no probability of satisfying the many unwarrantable and avaricious claims of the several contending governments, the citizens of Vermont therefore judge it reasonable to eject them.

This Government have such a sacred regard to the occupancy of land within their jurisdiction that they would not wish to have the possessors and *occupants* disturbed in their possessions, notwithstanding such lands may have been appropriated by either of the contending governments (New-York not excepted.)

We come now to the consideration of the pretensions of New-Hampshire to the jurisdiction of Vermont by introducing the settlement of the boundary line between them in [and] New-York as follows viz:

"At a Court of *St. James* the 20th day of July 1764.

"PRESENT

"The King's most Excellent Majesty,

"Lord Stewart,[1]	Earl of Hillsborough,
"Earl of Sandwick,[2]	Mr. Vice Chancellor,[3]
"Earl of Halifax,	Gilbert Elliot Esq.
"Earl of Powis,	James Oswald Esq.
"Earl of Harcourt,	

[1] Lord Howard in Slade's *State Papers*, and Lord Steward in Bradley's *Appeal*. [2] Earl of Sandwich in *Slade*. [3] Wm. Vice Chamberlain in Slade's *State Papers*, p. 19, and Mr. Vice Chamberlain in Bradley's *Appeal*. The Lord Chancellor and Lord Chamberlain both seem to have been members of the Council, and probably the Vice Chancellor and Vice Chamberlain sat in the absence of their principals.

"Whereas there was this day read at the Board, a report made by the "right honorable the Lords of Committee of Council for Plantation "affairs, dated the 17th of this instant, upon considering a representation "from the Lords Commissioners for trade and Plantations relative to the "disputes that have some years subsisted between the Provinces of "New-Hampshire and New-York concerning the boundary line between "those Provinces: His Majesty, taking the same into consideration, was "pleased, with the advice of his Privy Council, to approve of what is "herein [therein] proposed and doth accordingly hereby order and de-"clare the west bank [western banks] of the river Connecticut, from "where it enters the Province of Massachusetts-Bay, as far north as the "forty-fifth degree of northern latitude, to be the boundary line between "the said two Provinces of New-Hampshire and New-York, wherefore "the respective Governors and Commanders in Chief of his Majesty's "said Provinces of New-Hampshire and New-York, for the time being, "and all others whom it may concern, are to take notice of his Majesty's "pleasure hereby signified and govern themselves accordingly.

"WILLIAM BLAIR."

Probably the advocates for the pretensions of the claim of New-Hampshire to this territory, will advert to the 47th and 48th pages[1] of our Vindication of the right of the inhabitants of Vermont to form into an independent State, where we show the nullity of the said adjudicated line of 1764, in consequence of the declaration of independence of the United States and the annihilation of the British government in America, asserting, that in consequence of our arguments alluded to as aforesaid they open a door for the claim of New-Hampshire to take place by making void that line in order to defeat the claim of New-York. The attention of the reader is requested very particularly to the following observasions viz. The territory of Vermont, until the people's declaration of independence, was extra-provincial land and the governments of New-Hampshire and New-York claimed the jurisdiction of it by turns, merely from the sovereign will and pleasure of the King as neither of these governments were possessed of any charter-right as a body politic which they could call their own or challenge in their own right. Had New-Hampshire been possessed of such a charter-right their claim would have been more respectable and permanent and would have operated against the adjudication of 1764 aforesaid provided such boundaries had been previously ascertained. But this disputed territory being in those times crown lands and without the limits of any of the (then) colonies or plantations, the King's authority over it was therefore absolute and while this power remained in being, the last royal decree was valid and binding, which was that of 1764 aforesaid, which extended the jurisdiction of New-York over the said territory at which time the claim of New-Hampshire to the premises became extinct and finished, nor is it in their power to renew their claim to this government, being wholly destitute of any charter right thereto, and having lost it by the same arbitrary power by which they acquired it, and ought therefore to be finally silent about it, as well on account of their own relinquishing of such claim, and not affording the inhabitants any protection or jurisdictional support for a succession of years but since the declaration of the independence of this State have not only relinquished their said claim by their governmental transactions explicitly acknowledging the independence of this State. The proper credentials of this last fact will be exhibited in the following sheets with some further illustrations, being at present impatient to observe, that as the claim of New-

[1] See *Appendix I*, Vol. I, p. 464.

Hampshire to this territory was nullified, and became extinct in consequence of the royal decree of 1764 aforesaid, as before argued, and as the claim of New-York to this territory was as equally deficient as that of New-Hampshire to any charter right as a body politic or inherent constitutional jurisdiction; the claim of New-York therefore only survived that of New-Hampshire from the arbitrary decree of 1764 to the glorious æra of AMERICAN LIBERTY and INDEPENDENCE which was declared the fourth day of July 1776 and then expired also, to the inexpressible joy of the free citizens of Vermont, who in consequence thereof reverted to a state of nature, and have since formed government on the true principles of liberty.

This royal arbitrary line in the time of the kingly power was in the nature of it incompatible with the rights of a free people as they were thereby divested of the inestimable priviledge of choosing their own form of government, and of electing their chief magistrates, nor were they in such circumstances in any condition to know what form or alteration of government might next take place, as the King and his creatures were the sole arbitrators of it. In fine this people have suffered every indignity and oppression that prodigal and lucrative governors, and their swarm of hungry dependents could invent, and carry into execution, and it is surprising, that any persons that live in these days of liberty still entertain any idea that the said boundary line should operate in favour of the claim of New-York. From this short review of the claims of Massachusetts-Bay and New-Hampshire, they cannot affect the claim of Vermont to independence, which may be further illustrated by a two fold argument viz. provided those adjudicated boundary line of 1739 and 1764 aforesaid be deemed authentic and valid, their claims to Vermont must be considered as nugatory and abortive, but on the other hand if those adjudicated lines be considered as null and void, in this case the claim of Vermont, to the jurisdiction of this territory, would be much better grounded than those of Massachusetts-Bay or New-Hampshire, inasmuch as their government hath for a long time been formed by the authority of the people at large, or their legal representatives, who under God have a natural and indisputable right to form their own governments, so that the claims of Massachusetts-Bay and New-Hampshire to this territory are bar'd either by the aforesaid adjudication or in consequence of the legal establishment of the government of Vermont, nor is it possible for any one or both of those governments to set up a third principle whereby they can deduce a legal or just claim to any part of this government, for if their claims are not founded on the lines formerly ascertained by the British government [or] on the free consent and mutual association of the people of this territory, their pretensions are frivolous or tyrannical. This two fold argument is not viewed as being absolutely necessary in order to defeat the claims of those governments to the said premises but was introduced by way of supererogation. Sufficient it is in order to vindicate the claim of independence of the State of Vermont against those of Massachusetts-Bay and New-Hampshire, that these governments have for a series of years conformed to those settlements of 1739 and 1764 in their legislature [legislative] and executive capacities, and acted uniformly agreeable to those limitations until within a few months last past. Sundry years before the commencement of the present British war with the colonies, the people of this territory solicited both of those governments, at different times to extend their governmental protection to them, and prevent the ruin with which they were threatened by the oppressive iron rod of the government of New-York but could obtain none. But it appears by their late claim that they have since altered their minds although their motives herein (it is presumed) are far from being honourable—for it is a great fundamental and universal principle in all free governments, that government and protection are inseperably connected together, so that without protection or at least an attempt to extend it when earnestly solicited as aforesaid, government naturally and necessarily ceases to be, or in other words, such a refusal of protection implicitly disavows any right of jurisdiction or forfeits any supposed right either by neglecting such claims or refusing such protection. From whence we may infer that all pretenders to government which have not ultimately the good of the governed in view and do not afford, or endeavour to afford protection to those over whom they pretended such claims, should instead of the respects due to legislatures, courts and the like, be esteemed and treated as enemies to society and the rights of mankind. Thus it appears from the great and most universally received maxims in all free governments that the citizens of Vermont are and ought to be independent of the three governments which lay claim to them; and that every of their said pretensions are daring usurpations and insults on the liberty of an independent, brave and free people, who have never received any governmental protection or benefit from either of them, but instead thereof have every thing to apprehend from their venality and usurpation. Had New York succeeded in their various and insidious attempts to subjugate the people of Vermont, the recent claims of those other governments would never have been mentioned and the jurisdiction of New-York over this territory would at this day have been indisputable, so that Massachusetts-Bay and New-Hampshire have taken advantage of the controversy between New-York and Vermont, and even of the bravery of the latter in defending their natural rights and liberties, as the only possible ground of laying their frivolous claims. They have furthermore taken the advantage of the bravery of the United States in general and Vermont likewise, in bringing about the present revolution by which means they dare extend their pretended claims which it is presumed they would not have had the hardiness to endure [against] the British government over the head of those royal adjudications of 1739 and 1764 aforesaid, and it is worthy a remark that these claims have been started about three years since the declaration of the independence of the United States. Still the people of Vermont, legally speaking, remained under the British Government (over which Governor Philip Skeene was commissioned chief magistrate and next to this Government has the best claim to the jurisdiction of Vermont) from the 4th day of July 1776 to the 15th day of January next following and then in a solemn manner disavowed the British government and rejected the pretensions of Mr. Skeene, and all other pretenders to the jurisdiction of this territory, and declared themselves *a free and Independent State;* and have as they humbly conceive, in their various struggles for liberty, fairly merited the enjoyment of it.[1] This they consider as the ultimate reason of their many expences, labours, toils, battles, victories and hazards, and for the attainment of which they have chearfully suffered such an uncommon series of concomitant evils.

The following exhibits will set the pretensions of the claim of New-Hampshire in a true light. Not long after the settlement of the jurisdictional line in 1764 between New-York and New-Hampshire, Governor Benning Wentworth, who then presided over the latter, issued his proclamation, the principal import of which is, "That whereas it was the "King's pleasure that this territory should be under the jurisdiction of "New-York—That New-Hampshire paid a ready obedience—further-

[1] For note on the project of Skene, see *post*, p. 239.

"more advertising such persons as held either civil or military commis-"sions (in this district) under the authority of New-Hampshire to sur-"cease from any further administration." At the same time "directing "the inhabitants to conform to the government of New-York." We likewise find the following extract in a letter from the Governor of New-Hampshire to Governor Tryon, [of New York,] of the 19th of October 1771 viz. "That he had invariably recommended" to those inhabitants "implicit obedience to the law of the province of New-York and upon "all occasions positively disavowed any connections with those people."

We next exhibit the minutes of the Council of New-Hampshire, viz.

"PROVINCE OF NEW-HAMPSHIRE.

"At a Council held at *Portsmouth* by his Excellency's summons, on "Thursday the 8th day of January 1772.

PRESENT,

"His Excellency *John Wentworth* Esq; Governor, and

"Theodore Atkinson Esq.,	Daniel Pearce [Pierce] Esq.,
"Daniel Warner Esq.,	George Jaffery [Jaffrey] Esq.,
"Peter Levires [Livius] Esq.,	Daniel Rogers Esq.,
"Johnathan Warner Esq.,	Peter Gilman Esq.,
"Daniel Rindge Esq.,	Thomas W. Waldren [Waldron] Esq.

"His Excellency the Governor having laid before the Council for their "advice two letters from his Excellency Governor Tryon of New York "dated October [2d] 1771, and December 23, 1771, the latter enclosing a "proclamation, also a copy of his Excellency's answer to the first letter,[1]

---

[1] The record of the Council of New York embraces the substance of Tryon's letter and Wentworth's reply, as follows :

[From the *Documentary History of New York*, Vol. 4, p. 455.]

MINUTES OF COUNCIL

Relative to the Governor of New Hampshire's letter touching the riotous behaviour of the New Hampsnire grantees.

IN COUNCIL November 13th 1771.

His Excellency was pleased to communicate a Letter of the 19th day of October last, from Benning [John] Wentworth Esq[r]* Governor of the Province of New Hampshire, in Answer to a Letter from his Excellency the Governor of this province, complaining of an Exparte Survey of the River Connecticut lately made by the Government of New Hampshire, also informing Governor Wentworth of the Riotous Behaviour of Persons within this province claiming Lands under Grants of New Hampshire, and that the Riotous Spirit of those people seems to be greatly owing to the assurances they pretend to have received from Governor Wentworth that the Line will be altered so as to include the said claimants within the Jurisdiction of his Government—*in which Letter Governor Wentworth utterly disclaims any such or the like Assurances, and declares that he had invariably recommended implicit obedience to the Laws, and upon all occasions positively disavowed any connections with those people, and observes that he thought it unnecessary to consult this Government previous to the late Survey of Connecticut River, as that River is comprehended within the Limits of his own Government.*

The Board Taking into Consideration the dangerous Tendency of the Disturbances at present prevailing in that part of the Country, and that

* *Note by the Editor.*—This is a remarkable error. Benning Wentworth was allowed "opportunity to resign," to escape removal; and John, a nephew, was commissioned as his successor Aug. 11, 1766.—See Belknap's *New-Hampshire*, Vol. II, pp. 260, 261.

"—The premises being read, it is considered that by his Majesty's order "in Council of the 20th of July 1764, the western banks of Connecticut "River was then commanded to be the west bounds of this Province and "that this Government has been and is entirely obedient thereto. There-"fore the said proclamation relating wholly to matters and things with-"out the boundaries of this province, it is advised that the publication "thereof, by the authority of this province, is extra-provincial, and there-"fore in our opinion his Excellency is further advised not to issue any "proclamation relating to the premises. Secondly, that it is not expedi-"ent for the government in any wise to interfere with, or concern in "running the lines between his Majesty's province of New York and "Canada, which by his Excellency Governor Tryon's letter of the 23[d] "December 1771 is already begun, by Commissioners appointed for that "service agreeable to his Majesty's instructions, wherein it does not ap-"pear that this province is referred to or mentioned.

"A True Copy from the Minutes of the Council,

"Attest, GEORGE KING, *Deputy Secretary.*"

The following is a copy of a letter from the President of the Council of New Hampshire to the (then) Secretary of this State, viz.

[Here was inserted a copy of the letter of Meshech Weare of July 19 1777, addressed to "*Ira Allen Esq. Secretary of the State of Vermont*"—for which see *ante, Appendix D*, p. 207. Next followed the letter of President Weare of Aug. 22 1778, on the first union of New Hampshire towns, addressed to the honorable Thomas Chittenden—all but the first paragraph; for which letter see Vol. I, p. 414.]

The foregoing letter was laid before the General Assembly of this State at their session in October 1778 agreeable to President Weare's request, and a joint Committee was thereupon appointed from the Council and Assembly and the said Union was dissolved and President Weare's demands fully and amply adjusted and settled at the then next

---

Governor Wentworth had not thought proper by public act of his Government to disavow the assurances, the Rioters pretend to have received from him, humbly advise his Excellency, and it is accordingly ordered by his Excellency the Governor with the Advice of his Council, that a proclamation be prepared notifying the declaration of Governor Wentworth on this subject contained in his Letter above mentioned—Stating the claim of this Province to the Lands Westward of Connecticut River —Strictly injoining the Inhabitants of those Lands to yield Obedience to the Laws within this Government: And derecting the Magistrates and other Civil Officers to be vigilant in their Duty and attentive to the Preservation of the public Peace; and to transmit the Names of all offenders herein, that such measures may be taken for their punishment, as the Nature of their Crimes shall require—And that the Draft of such proclamation when prepared be laid before his Excellency for the approbation of this Board.

Gov. Tryon issued a proclamation accordingly, dated Dec. 11 1771, a copy of which was sent to Gov. Wentworth Jan. 8 1772. Wentworth acknowledged the receipt of the proclamation and renewedly disavowed any connection with the "violence & illegal opposition to Government" of the New Hampshire grantees.—For Tryon's letter to Wentworth, Oct. 2 1771, see *Doc. History of New York* Vol. 4, pp. 445–6; and for Tryon's proclamation see the same, pp. 456–459.

adjourned session of Assembly held at Bennington on the 12th day of February 1779 as will appear by the following extract of the report of said Committee and the Resolution of the Assembly thereon, viz.

[Here followed the report and resolution, certified by "M. LYON, *Clerk;*" for which, Lyon's certificate excepted, see Vol. I, pp. 430, 431.]

It is presumed that from the settlement of the boundary line between New York and New Hampshire in 1764, to the date of President *Weare's* letter of the 22d August aforesaid, which is more than fourteen years, that New Hampshire, (during this period) had given up in the most explicit and public manner, all pretensions to the jurisdiction of any and every part of the lands comprehended in this State. Governor *Benning Wentworth's* proclamation aforesaid sets this matter in a clear light, soon after the alteration of jurisdiction, directing the settlers under New-Hampshire to conform to the laws of New York.[1] The letter from the Governor of New Hampshire [John Wentworth] to Governor Tryon, of the 19th of October 1771, speaks the same language, viz. "That he had "invariably recommended implicit obedience to the laws" of New York, "and upon all occasions positively disavowed any connection with "those people." The Governor and Council of New Hampshire the 8th of January 1772 wholly renounced their claim to the premises: "It is "considered that by his Majesty's order in Council of the 20th July 1764 "the western banks of Connecticut river was then commanded to [be] "the west bounds of this province; and that this government has been "entirely obedient thereto." President *Weare's* letter to Ira Allen Esq. proceeds still further, and positively *concedes* to the independence of this State. It appears that the Court of the State of New Hampshire, by their President, address him in his official character, viz. as "Secretary of the State of Vermont;" and in the contents of the letter when writing to the Secretary of this State, not less than three times gives it the appellation or stile of "your State;" and observes in the finishing clause of the letter, "in behalf of the Council and Assembly I am," &c. From all which it appears that the said letter has the authority of the General Court of that State for its support, and which in the most express terms, acknowledgeth the independence of this State which is of itself a final bar to the claim of New Hampshire. For if Governments can relinquish their claim of jurisdiction when they please and assume it again at pleasure, the whole notion of governmental jurisdiction is reduced to a mere romance and nothing permanent, obligatory or binding in it, and therefore such a precedent is inadmissable, as it would, if admitted to become general, destroy all order and decorum in the universe.

It should be acknowledged that the Court of New-Hampshire, through the channel of their President's letter to Governor Chittenden, before inserted,[2] offered a number of reasons relative to the impropriety of this State's taking into union sixteen towns east of Connecticut river, which reasons are equally conclusive against the claim of New-Hampshire to the westward of the same river. Says Mr. *Weare*, their President: "Is

---

[1] The proclamation of Benning Wentworth, surrendering the jurisdiction of the territory of Vermont to New York, seems to have been issued immediately after the order of the king of July 1764 was received, and before the proclamation of the Governor of New York of April 10 1765.—See Ira Allen's *History of Vermont*, in *Vt. Hist. Soc. Collections*, Vol. I, p. 341; and Hiland Hall's *Early History*, p. 478.

[2] See Vol. I, p. 414.

"there any ascertaining the boundaries between any of the United States "of America but by the lines formerly established by the authority of "Great Britain? I am sure there is not." This being admitted, we are equally sure New-Hampshire has no right to any territorial jurisdiction to the westward of said river. Notwithstanding, it appears that the Court of New-Hampshire, in the first place, plead the settlement of the line in 1764, as the main ground of their title to those sixteen towns aforesaid, (west of the Mason line) by which means they are included in their jurisdiction, and in a few months afterward break over the said line of 1764 and lay claim to the State of Vermont, when at the same time nothing can be more apparent than that the same arguments by which they establish their claim to those said sixteen towns east of the river effectually bars their claim to the westward of the same river, and leaves the contested territory to be disputed between New-York and Vermont. "I am surprized," says the President, that "they," speaking of the inhabitants of this State, "should supply their enemies with arguments "against them, by their connecting themselves with people (having ref- "erence to those sixteen towns) whose circumstances are totally differ- "ent from their own, and who are actually members of the State of New- "Hampshire." This last clause, affirming that the inhabitants of those sixteen towns were actually members of the State of New-Hampshire, at the same time implicitly affirms that the inhabitants on the west side of the said river were not, which is fully explained in the preceding part of the same paragraph, viz. "whose circumstances are wholly different from their own," that is, the members of the State of Vermont, which is still further explained from another paragraph of the same letter, when, after stating the facts relative to the aforesaid union with those sixteen towns before frequently mentioned, says, "on which I am directed to "represent to you, and to desire it may be laid before the representatives "of your people." As this was addressed to the Governor of Vermont from the Court of New-Hampshire to be laid before the representative body or General Assembly in which the claim of New-Hampshire is clearly set up, and their right vindicated to a number of towns over which Vermont on a mistaken and wrong representation had encroached, upon the representation whereof, the General Court of the State of Vermont dissolved the Union as aforesaid and agreeable to the claim and request of the Court of the State of New-Hampshire relinquished every connection, as a political body, with those sixteen towns east of Connecticut river. And thus the respective governments of New-Hampshire and Vermont having mutually settled their boundary line on the west banks of Connecticut river agreeable to the adjudication thereof in 1764 between New-York and New-Hampshire cannot fail of opperating as a final bar against any subsequent claim of New-Hampshire to any part of the State of Vermont. For New-Hampshire made their claim and Vermont very readily closed with them and gave them their whole demands in which the minds of both governments met and the dispute naturally and necessarily ended, and it is but children's play for New-Hampshire to make a second demand on the State of Vermont; for if one settlement is not decisive and binding, neither would a second be, a third, and so on *ad infinitum.*

Previous to the Claims of Massachusetts-Bay and New-Hampshire to Vermont the simplicity of the inhabitants of this Government and their veneration for Congress was so great, that it is highly probable that they would have very frankly submitted the long controversy between them and New-York, to the final decision of the Congress of the United States, though at the same time they were far from an opinion that Congress had any legal inherent or constitutional right (exclusive of their own consent and approbation) so to do : But the recent claims of Massachusetts-Bay and New-Hampshire in concert with New-York, and it is suspected in confederacy with each other to divide this State among those three governments has excited their apprehensions for though it may not prove a triple league as is imagined, it is at least a strong combination of interests which will undoubtedly agree in the ruin of this State, whatever disputes may happen between themselves relative to the jurisdiction thereof. And as to the States of Virginia, N. Carolina, and S. Carolina, whose territory's are immensely large, and whose interest it is to maintain their respective sovereignties over their extensive claims, which may in natural probability influence their delegates in Congress to oppose the independence of Vermont as it may in future operate as a precedent to divide those large territories into different States, (not that it is apprehended by us that there is any similarity in the circumstances of this tract of country to any other part of America,) and thus from views of their own particular interests be very partial and biased judges of the right of Vermont to independence, and instead of judging on the principles of justice and equity which respects Vermont as opposed to the claims of Massachusetts-Bay, New-Hampshire and New-York, may rather determine the matters agreeable to their own ambition and interest, so that were Vermont to calmly submit their indubitable claim of independence to Congress, though they are as respectable a body as the world ever produced, it would be by no means certain that Vermont could have an impartial tryal ; as there may be many connections of interests very prejudicial to them which at present we cannot conceive of and which is out of our power to come at the knowledge of as this State is not represented in Congress.

These things being premised and as the freemen of this State have never had any voice in electing, forming or creating Congress, as a political body, or had any representation therein; but have rather been misrepresented: And whereas this State held their charter of liberty from Heaven and not " of man or the will of man," [they] have upon a full and candid examination and consideration determined not to submit HEAVEN BORN FREEDOM to the arbitrament of any tribunal below the stars, which through infirmity might deprive them of it: But as they have closely embraced it in the most critical and hazardous times, are determined to hold it fast, except it be torn from them by the hand of power; which resolution we trust will be justified by the Court of Heaven, and commended by all true friends to the liberty and happiness of mankind.

The following is an extract from the proceedings of the General Assembly of Vermont at their session in October last, viz.

Here followed the proceedings of the General Assembly of Vermont of Oct. 20 and 21 1779, on the resolutions of Congress of Sept. 24 1779, for which see *ante*, *Appendix B*, pp. 191, 192.

APPENDIX F.

MISSION OF IRA ALLEN TO NEW JERSEY, PENNSYLVANIA, DELAWARE, AND MARYLAND.

IN GENERAL ASSEMBLY OF VERMONT, Oct. 21, 1779.

Resolved that an Agent be chosen to wait on the General Assemblies of the States of New-Jersey, Pennsylvania, the lower Counties on the Delaware, [now Delaware,] and Maryland, and to transmit to them the pamphlets entitled "a vindication of the [opposition of the] inhabitants of Vermont to the Government of New-York, &c." and to transact any other business with either of the said Assemblies as may be found necessary (in behalf of this State) and report to this Assembly.

Chose for the above purpose the honorable Ira Allen Esq[r.]

The letter of Ira Allen to the Council of Pennsylvania undoubtedly embraces substantially the representations made to the other states named in his commission, but it is deemed best to prefix, by way of introduction and further explanation of that letter, Allen's account of his mission given in his history of Vermont, which was as follows:[1]

To discover the several interests and dispositions of each State south of New-York, respecting the interest and independence of Vermont, and to shew the consequence of that State heretofore in the common cause, as well as to demonstrate the natural and divine right the people have to form a government for themselves, the General Assembly appointed Ira Allen, Esq. to attend the Legislatures of New Jersey, Pennsylvania, Delaware, Maryland, and other states, if time permitted, before the first of February, 1780, and on that day to be at Philadelphia, and join Jonas Fay, Moses Robinson, and Stephen R. Bradley, as a committee, by the Assembly of Vermont appointed to wait on Congress, and shew the just claim the State had to be independent, and to hold the lands under New Hampshire Grants.

Mr. Allen, according to his appointment, attended the Legislatures of the fore-named States, and distributed sundry pamphlets written in vindication of the claims and doings of Vermont. Many questions arose respecting the local interest of Vermont, by a junction with the other States, and their views, touching the unlocated lands, and the confiscated property of the royalists. It is to be observed, that a question subsisted in Congress, respecting the unappropriated lands, and the property of the loyalists, who had joined the enemy against the independence of the United States. These four States were of opinion that all property wrested from the king of Great Britain and his adhe-

---

[1] See *Vt. Hist. Society Collections*, Vol. I, pp. 405–407.

rents, by the efforts of the people of the United States, ought to be disposed of for defraying the expences of the war, and not for the emolument of any one State in which it was situated or was claimed. These States (Pennsylvania excepted) had no claims of consequence in the west; neither had Vermont; therefore upon a similar interest, and on the assurance of Mr. Allen, that if Vermont was admitted to a seat in Congress, she would adhere to those principles, they seemed to wish to favour the interest of Vermont. Mr. Allen urged, that an account of the lands granted and confiscated in Vermont, should be accounted for as a small part of their unlocated lands and confiscated estates throughout the United States; that as partners in common and new beginners, it was necessary to make use of a part of their share for the common good, being very much exposed to the common enemy, from an extensive frontier contiguous to Champlain and Canada, and from whence eruptions might easily be made into the State of New York, and the New England States, in case of rendering Vermont of no importance in the union; further, that the disposal of such lands and property furnished money to defray the expences in part of the war, helped to alleviate, in a considerable degree, the burthens of the people, and to strengthen the frontiers against the common enemy. These reasons, with the political consequence of Vermont in the capture of Ticondaroga, Crown Point, &c. and the cutting off the first wing of General Burgoyne's army, operated in a two-fold degree, and had a salutary effect on Congress. On the first of February, 1780, the Commissioners from Vermont met at Philadelphia, but nothing conclusive was done, and the agents returned home, after having made official offers in behalf of the State, to bear full and just proportion of the expences of the war, on their being admitted to a seat in Congress.

From February 1780, when it was supposed the Vermont question was to be decided, until Oct. 29 1782, contemporaneously with the prosecution of her claim to Vermont, New York labored persistently, skillfully and successfully, to deprive Vermont of the favor which Allen had gained in several of the states by means of the land question. Though New York failed at last in the controversy with Vermont, she gained the honor of making the first cession of western lands to the United States, and of forcing Virginia to follow her example, which settled the question in the other five land-claiming states.—See *The Constitution*, by W. HICKEY, sixth edition, pp. 414–422; and HILAND HALL'S *Early History*, pp. 316, 403–414.

Ira Allen to the Council of Pennsylvania.[1]

PHILADELPHIA, Jany 20th, 1780.

Honored Sirs,—I doubt not but your Excellency, & most, if not all your Honors have heard more or less of the Controversy subsisting between the State of New York on the one, & the State of Vermont on the other Part; and as it is thought by some to endanger the Internal Peace of America, I beg leave to make a few observations thereon; and first, said Controversy was occationed by the undue influence of Governor Colden and his adhearance [adherents] at the Rotten Court of Britain, in 1764, by obtaining jurisdiction over that Part of the then Province of New Hampshire, situate to the west of Connecticut River, and by the undue Exercise of the same, in laying subsequent Pattens [pa-

---

[1] *Pennsylvania Archives*, Vol. VIII, 1779–1781, p. 88.

tents] on those antisedantly derived from New Hampshire, in Prejudice to the first Grantees & Settlers, and by the undue Exercise of law to bring aboute their vile and mercinary Purposes, by which means the Contending Parties were greatly Exasperated towards each other, and had appealed to armes before the Present Revolution.

At which time the Inhabitants of the now State of Vermont took an active Part with their Country, thinking to swallow up their old Quarrel with New York, in their General Conflict for Liberty.

Since which time said Inhabitants have assumed to themselves (amongst the Powers of the Earth) that inestamable Blessing of Heaven, sivil Government (on the same Grand, Original, Basis, or Great Rule, of Eternal Right, that the other free States of America did, and on which a number of the Present Powers of Europe revolted from the Kingdoms to which they paid allegiance), and have Governed their Internal and External Police by the same more than three years.

Yet the uneasy, and never-to-be-contented Citizens of New York, have Indeavoured to surprise Congress into a Determination of that Important Controversy in their favour, and as they would have it Exparta (Thereby to carry into Execution the reduction of Vermont, an Enterprise they attempted some years ago, and could not Effect, and which their own Militia seem not inclined to undertake,) which has Occationed the Governor and Council of Vermont to Publish a Vindication of the Opposition of said Inhabitants to the Government of New York, and their right to assume Government, and exhibit some of said Vindications [the pamphlet of that title] to Congress, and to the Legislature of each of those States, and to the Principal Officers of the Continental Army, for their Consideration.

The Citizens of Vermont view themselves virtually in Union with the other free States of America, ever since they took Ticondaroga, Crown Point, &c., in favour of the United States, and have from the beginning of this War, and are still willing, to furnish their Quota of men in the field, and have offered to Congress to Pay their full Proportion of the Expence of the War, when the Policy of America will admit them [to] a seat in Congress.

It is to be observed that this Controversy was not Occationed by the Present Revolution, But subsisted many years before, Consequently it doth not Equally Effect Congress to settle it, as tho. their own measures had given rise to it. The Citizens of Vermont will cheerfully submit to all the Disadvantages that doth, or may, attend them, by not having a seat in Congress, untill the Present troubles shall subside; Rather than to Crowde for it, while it might be thought Prejuditial to the Common weale of the American Empire; yet they consieve themselves justly intitled to a seat in Congress, and will not sell their Birth rite for a mess of Potage, as Profane Esau did.

I am with due Respect, Your Excellencies & Honors
most obedient Humb'le serv't, IRA ALLEN.

N. B. In the vindication I herewith Exhibit, there is no mention made of the clames of the States of the Massachusetts Bay, or New Hampshire, as they were not announsed to Vermont on the 23d of August last, when said Vindication was Published, But will be shortly done, and Published in a similar manner. I. A.

Directed,

To his Excellency Joseph Reed, Esqr., & Hon'ble Council.

Indorsement,

From Ira Allen, of the State of Vermont. Read in Council, January 25. T. M., [Col. Timothy Matlack,] Secretary.

APPENDIX G.

ACTION OF CONGRESS IN REFERENCE TO VERMONT, FEB. 7 TO OCT. 6 1780, AND LEGISLATIVE PROCEEDINGS AND DOCUMENTS CONNECTED THEREWITH.

Feb. 1 1780 was the day assigned by Congress, by the resolution of Sept. 24 1779, for action on the claims of New York, New Hampshire, and Massachusetts to the jurisdiction of Vermont. On that day no action was had upon the subject, (in fact there is no record of any proceedings on that day in the journal,) but the agents of Vermont transmitted the following letter to the President of that body.[1]

Agents of Vermont to the President of Congress.

PHILADELPHIA, Feb$^{y.}$ 1, 1780.

Sir:—Inclosed your Excellency will receive a copy of an act of the Legislature of the State of Vermont, appointing and empowering Agents to appear and transact their political affairs at the Congress of the United States as a free and independent State.[2] Herewith likewise will be communicated to you "A Vindication of the opposition of the inhabitants of Vermont to the government of New York,"[3] and "Vermont's Appeal to the candid and impartial World,"[4] published by order of the supreme executive authority thereof, the last of which contains some of the principal reasons upon which the inhabitants of Vermont acted, and their right in assuming government, with an address to the honorable American Congress in answer to their act of the 24th of September last, together with a book containing a constitution and code of laws as established by the freemen of said State, and have only to add that we

---

[1] In the *Clinton Papers*, No. 2714, covering this letter, it is stated that it was read in Congress Feb. 7 1780. The journal of Congress of that date, (Folwell's edition of 1800, Vol. VI, pp. 15, 16,) show that other papers on the subject were presented and read, but this letter is not mentioned. Probably the omission was an error of the transcriber or printer.

[2] See *ante, Appendix B*, p. 192. [3] See Vol. I, pp. 444–517. [4] See *ante, Appendix D.*

are now in this town, and are ready with full powers on the part of the State of Vermont to close an equitable union with the other independent States of America, and to pledge the faith of our constituents to pay a just proportion of the expence of the present war with Great Britain whenever a constitutional requisition therefor shall be made.

Nevertheless we are not authorized, neither does the State whom we have the honor to represent view themselves holden to close with the terms of the resolutions of the 24th of September aforesaid, for the reasons published in the Appeal referred to. But could the Honorable Congress pass over those reasons and determine that they have an uncontrolable right and power to compel Vermont to abide their determination in the premises, yet they cannot conceive it to be just and equitable that such an important cause, in which not only property, but even liberty for which we have been so long contending, [are involved,] ought to be tried, and a final decision so hastily had thereon, on a footing so unequal as it must inevitably be, on the part of Vermont, if done at this time.

All the evidence that can possibly be exhibited, as the case is now unfortunately placed, must be *exparte*, and that evidence which must finally prove the claim of New York and all others groundless upon their own stating, is at present out of our power, for if we are allowed proper time to prove that in consequence of our remonstrating and petitioning the court of Great Britain, that power had made a distinct government of the tract now comprehending the State of Vermont, and appointed Governor Skeene to preside over the same, previous to America's denying its supremacy, it would silence all our enemies, and oblige every man, even those interested, to acknowledge that the State of Vermont had an equal right with the other American states to assume an independent government.

And until we are allowed sufficient time to collect and publish our evidence, the freemen of Vermont can never voluntarily surrender those liberties which God and nature has vested them with, by reason of any partial adjudication, for if the claims of the one side are founded on arbitrary adjudications of the crown, of course a subsequent adjudication of the same power, respecting the premises, must render the former adjudication null and void.[1] If they are built on a right of purchase they

---

[1] See biographical note on Col. PHILIP SKENE, in Vol. I, p. 153. In Bradley's *Appeal*, Dec. 1779; Ethan Allen and Fay's *Concise Refutation*, Jan. 1780; Ethan and Ira Allen's *Defence of Vermont in uniting with portions of New York and New Hampshire*, Jan. 1782, and in Ira Allen's letter to Gen. Haldimand, July 1782, (for the last two documents see *Vt. Historical Society Collections*, Vol. II, pp. 238 and 283–4,) representations similar to the above were made concerning Skene's province or charter. It is evident that the representations of the Vermont Agents to Congress, and in Ira Allen's letter to Haldimand in July 1782, were made *as pleas for delay;* and it should be observed that in neither is it affirmed absolutely that a charter of the territory of Vermont was granted to Skene. The Agents said, " if we are allowed proper time to prove," &c.; and Ira Allen said, " it is reported and generally believed in the colonies, that Governor Philip Skene had a charter," and he suggested that Haldimand should " write to Governor Skene *for this charter so much wanted.*" It must be admitted, however, that in Bradley's *Appeal* this

must fail, for *we* possess that in exclusion of all others, being of a prior date and for a valuable consideration, which no other party can pretend to. If on a right of conquest, they fail. If on a right of settlement and occupancy, in this likewise, as well as on every principle of the law of nature and nations, they certainly fail.

We sincerely lament that neighboring states, from local prejudices, or otherwise, should raise internal animosities during the severe contest with Great Britain, and thereby give fresh reasons to our common enemy to procrastinate the war, and unnecessarily continue the effusion of human blood. And are, sir, your

Excellency's most ob[t.] humble serv[ts.]

JONAS FAY,
MOSES ROBINSON,
STEPHEN R. BRADLEY.

His Excellency Samuel Huntington Esq. Prest. of Congress.

---

matter was less cautiously stated, though there it was admitted that Vermont had no proof. The truth was probably given in Ira Allen's *History of Vermont.* This was written and printed in London in 1798, and it is not presuming too much to say, that Allen would have procured a copy of Skene's charter if one had ever been granted. He did say, that the approaching revolutionary war [in 1774–5,] "*put an end to the proposed negociation.*" His account was as follows:

Hence, in the year 1774, to get rid of the colony of New York, a plan was formed by Col. [Ethan] Allen, Mr. Amos Bird, and other principal characters among the people, in conjunction with Colonel Philip Skene, to have established a new royal colony, which was to contain the grants of New Hampshire, west of Connecticut River, and the country north of the Mohawk River, to latitude 45° north, and bounded west by Iroquois River and Lake Ontario.

Colonel Skene had been an officer in his Majesty's service, and had retired on a large patent of land lying at the south end of Lake Champlain, which was called Skenesboro', [Whitehall,] a proper scite for the capital of the new colony, of which he was proposed to be Governor.

The honor and lucrative prospects thus presented to Colonel Skene, stimulated him to go to London at his own expence, to solicit the accomplishment of an important object to individuals, and to the public: for had he succeeded, the people who had settled under the royal grants of New Hampshire would have been quiet, and relieved from the oppressive conduct of the Governor and Council of the colony of New York.

Colonel Skene's first object, after his arrival in London, was to get himself appointed Governor of the garrisons of Ticonderoga and Crown Point, which being effected, his friends advised him that, to obtain the grand object in view, he should bring forward a petition from the people on the premises to the King and Privy Council, stating, that in order to restore harmony in the said district, and for the convenience of administering justice in a department very remote and extensive, his Majesty would be pleased to establish the territory aforesaid, with colonial privileges, and appoint Colonel Philip Skene Governor thereof.

Information of these matters was transmitted from London to the people of the said district; but the calamity of an approaching war in America put an end to the proposed negociation for a royal colony, that was to surround that important water LAKE CHAMPLAIN.—See *Vt. Historical Society Collections*, Vol. I, pp. 360, 361.

PROCEEDINGS OF CONGRESS.

MONDAY, February 7, 1780.[1]

Mr. Samuel Livermore, a delegate from New Hampshire, attended and produced the credentials of his appointment, which were read.

The delegates of Massachusetts-Bay laid before Congress their Commission and instructions. which were read.

A representation from Peter Alcot [Olcott,] and Bezaleel Woodward, stiling themselves agents from the greater part of the towns in the northern district of the New Hampshire grants, on both sides of Connecticut river, and between the heights of land on the two sides, accompanied with a paper, signed "Joseph Marsh, Chairman of said Convention," purporting to be powers granted them by a convention of members from the towns aforesaid, were read.

An act of the legislature of the state of New Hampshire was laid before Congress, and read, as follows: [Here followed the act, which submitted the claim of New Hampshire to the territory of Vermont to the decision of Congress.]

The two documents referred to in the journal of Congress of Feb. 7 1780 are as follows. To these the editor has added other documents which were presented to Congress but are not named in the printed journal.

Credentials of Peter Olcott and Bezaleel Woodward.[2]

To Peter Olcott and Bezaleel Woodward, Esquires, Gentlemen:

Pursuant to a Vote of a Convention of Members from the towns in the northern parts of the New Hampshire Grants on both sides of Connecticut river, being part of the district known by the name of the State of Vermont, on the seventh day of december last,—You are authorized and empowered jointly or individually to appear as Agents for the people in this part of the Grants at the hearing proposed by certain resolutions of the honorable Continental Congress of the 24th of Sept. last to be had before them on the first day of Feby next respecting the disputes and differences relative to jurisdiction betwixt the States of New Hampshire, Massachusetts Bay and New York on the one part and the people of the said New Hampshire Grants who claim to be a separate jurisdiction on the other part. You are to act for the people in this part in all matters relative to said Grants which shall come under the consideration of Congress, or any court to be appointed agreeable to said resolves, and therein to pursue the objects which have heretofore been pointed out to Congress by said Convention and by the people in this part of the Grants so far as the state of matters at the trial shall in your opinion admit.[3]

P order, JOSEPH MARSH, *Chairman of said Committee.*

[Endorsed]
New-Hampshire Grants Jany 1st A. D. 1780.

---

[1] From the *Journals of Congress*, Folwell's edition, 1780-81, Vol. VI, p. 15.

[2] *N. H. Grants*, Vol. I, No. 40, p. 309, in Archives of the State Department, Washington.

[3] See *Appendix B;* and also the *Representation* presented to Congress Aug. 1779 by Peter Olcott, *post*, p. 244.

Representation of Peter Olcott and Beza. Woodward to Congress.[1]

To his Excellency the President and the honorable Members of the Congress of the United States of North America:

Peter Olcott and Bezaleel Woodward Agents for the greater part of the towns in the northern destrict of the New Hampshire Grants on both sides of Connecticut River, and between the heights of land on the two sides, Humbly beg leave to represent

That our Constituents by their Agent in the month of August last laid before a Committee of Congress sundry papers relative to the political situation, to which we beg leave to refer in the hearing relative to said Grants; the great object of which is to communicate the earnest desire of the Inhabitants in the northern destrict from Connecticut river to the highlands on each side that they may not be subjected to separate jurisdiction, and that in case Congress shall see fit to approve an establishment of a new State on the Grants, that the whole so far as the highlands east of the river may be included in it—otherwise that the whole of the Grants be annexed to New Hampshire—as they conceive a divisional line at the river will be injurious not only to the interest of the inhabitants but also to the public weal.

For the following reasons—

1. The inhabitants on both sides of the river received grants of their lands and charters of incorporation from New Hampshire, which they apprehended gave them good reason to expect to be continued subjects of one and the same State, as they were by their incorporations entitled to the same privileges, which could not (after being granted) be justly taken from them without their consent. The decree in the year one thousand seven hundred and sixty four by which the inhabitants on the two sides of the river were subjected to separate jurisdictions, viz: one part to New York while the other part was continued subject to New Hampshire, was passed without any previous notice to the inhabitants who were most immediately interested in the matter, to whom it was both grievous and injurious, and who never acquiesced therein—and as it was rendered efficacious only by that arbitrary power which has in vain attempted to enslave the United States, the inhabitants conceive that the operation of it cannot be fairly construed to continue since the declaration of independence.

2. The situation of the country in respect to means of communication is such as renders a division at the river greatly injurious to the inhabitants. The range of mountains on the west side and highlands on the east side, at the distance of about twenty miles, extend through the Grants from north to south near one hundred and fifty miles, the valley betwixt which heights is at the river, which will ever occasion the principal communication and traffic of that part of the country to center at the river—therefore a line at the river will bring the center of that business to the extreme parts of the two states; which must ever be inconvenient in a country situated as that is.

3. To have a line at the river will throw each part into a very incommodious situation in respect to government. In that case the State must be about one hundred and fifty miles in length from north to south and not more than from forty to fifty miles in width east and west through the longest extent of which from north to south is a range of mountains which will bring the body of inhabitants on the two extreme parts, render a management of their political affairs very inconvenient and ever have a tendency to create divisions and parties among them.

---

[1] *N. H. Grants*, Vol. 1, No. 40, p. 319, in Archives of the State Department, Washington.

Again if a State be formed west of the river only, county business in that and New Hampshire must center either at the extremities of the States, or on the heights of land remote from the principal part of inhabitants.

4. The coincident sentiments of the people on the Grants on both sides of the river in respect to government and their desires to be united point out the inexpediency of a division at the river.

We think ourselves warranted to assure Congress that for the foregoing and other reasons a large majority of inhabitants on either side of the river are desirous of an establishment of an union of the whole and that no division be made at the river.

Our Constituents rejoice at the interposition of Congress in the affair, and their assurance of a speedy issue of the contest, by the continuance of which they have been involved in innumerable difficulties; and mean to govern themselves according to the resolutions of Congress on the premises.

We entreat a decision on the subject as soon as Congress in their wisdom can judge expedient, as every delay is productive of new confusions and animosities among the people.

And as in duty bound shall ever pray.

PETER OLCOTT,
BEZA. WOODWARD.

Philadelphia Feb. 1st 1780.

[Endorsed]
Messrs. Olcott & Woodward Representation
Read Feby. 7 1780.

Letter of Messrs. Fay, Robinson, and Bradley, to the President of Congress.[1]

PHILADELPHIA, Feby. 5th 1780.

Sir,—In pursuance of our appointment from the State of Vermont, we have, in discharge of our betrustment, waited on the Grand Council of the United States of America; have delivered to them a Copy of our Credentials, empowering us to close a Union and Confederation with the other States &c. And are now about to take our leave of this city to meet the Assembly of the State we represent, which are shortly to convene to adopt measures for protecting our infant frontiers, and vigorously prosecuting the War against our common enemy.

We are assured that nothing on our part shall deter us, from spiritedly opposing the Savages of the Wilderness or the power of G. Britain. And have full confidence that neither States or individuals, that are attached to the American cause, can wish to divert us from our fixed purpose. And shall ever stand ready to acquiesce in any requisition made by Congress, not incompatible with our own internal police.

And are with the highest sentiments of esteem

Your Excellency's most humble Servants,

JONAS FAY,
MOSES ROBINSON,
STEPHEN R. BRADLEY.

His Excellency Samuel Huntington Esq. President Congress.

[Endorsed]
Read Feby 7 1780.

---

[1] *N. H. Grants*, Vol. 1, No. 40, p. 315, in Archives of State Department, Washington.

Representation of inhabitants of Hartford, Norwich, Sharon, Royalton, Fairlee, Newbury, and Barnet, presented by PETER OLCOTT *to Congress in August* 1779, *and again presented Feb.* 8 1780.[1]

To the honorable the Congress of the United American States:

The inhabitants of the under mentioned Towns on the New Hampshire Grants west of Connecticut River and east of the Green Mountains so called, Humbly beg leave to represent

That about the time of the declaration of independence of the united States, sundry persons from the western part of the said Grants made known to us that the inhabitants west of the Green Mountains were very desirous of having a new State formed on the said New Hampshire Grants—that many among us expressed our willingness for such an event in case the Grants east of Connecticut river might join us in pursuing that object, as we have ever thought their circumstances in almost every respect similar to ours—they having received the grant of their landed property in the same channel, their manners and habits the same, and the local situation of the country such as makes it very inconvenient for us to be divided from them &c.—That we were by an arbitrary decree of the King unjustly deprived of that union with the Grants east of the river, and that we are well assured the Grants in general have ever been desirous of having it restored and influenced principally by a prospect of such union a considerable number of towns from among us did unite with the inhabitants west of the green mountains in forming a constitution for a State.—That the towns on the Grants east of Connecticut River were about the same time invited to join in pursuing that object and in conformity to said invitation a number of towns east of the river were in the month of June last received into union with said new State (then known by the name of Vermont) by a resolve of the Assembly, the members thereof being previously instructed so to do. That said Assembly have since in violation of their faith and honor, deprived the towns east of the river of their protection and actually extinguished the union with them. In consequence whereof a large number of the members of the council and Assembly have withdrawn their connection with that Assembly, to the very general approbation of their constituents. That the said Assembly have ordered a confiscation of the estates of those persons called *tories*, and have actually disposed of lands in that way to a very great amount, and have sold many estates for but little more than half their real value, of which they have given deeds in the name and behalf of the freemen of said State and appropriated the avails to many frivolous and unnecessary purposes, instead of depositing them in continental loan offices agreeable to a resolve of Congress. Since the withdraw of those members they have resolved to dispose of more than one hundred thousand acres *gratis* to particular favorites without any advantage accruing thereby to the good people in general.[2] That from an apprehension of danger to the liberties of the people from designing and ambitious men and for other important reasons a considerable number of towns east of the said green mountains and west of the river have ever from the first refused to unite with said State or own allegiance thereto—So that for the reasons foregoing and others too numerous to mention, the towns which had united with said State having withdrawn their

---

[1] *N. H. Grants*, Vol. 1, No. 40, p. 311, in Archives of the State Department, Washington.

[2] The editor is aware of no evidence anywhere of such a disposal of land by the State.

connection with it, there now remain but very few towns east of said mountains which continue connected with said State or own any allegiance thereto.

Notwithstanding all which we are assured that the members who continue to act in assembly have last month appointed a Committee to apply to Congress for an establishment of a State on the said Grants west of Connecticut river, which in the present situation of affairs we beg leave to represent that we utterly refuse our compliance with.

We therefore humbly pray that Congress will be pleased to do nothing relative thereto which may in the least encourage the establishment of a State under those disagreeable circumstances, but on the contrary that they will in some way express their disapprobation of it, and grant such relief to their injured petitioners as in their wisdom may seem fit. And that previous to a determination relative to said State we may have proper notice and opportunity more fully to show our reasons why a new State under present circumstances ought not to be established.

And your petitioners as in duty bound shall ever pray.

New Hampshire Grants,
March A. D. 1779.

An original petition of which the foregoing is a copy, and which is regularly certified to have been voted by the inhabitants of the towns of Hartford, Norwich, Sharon, Royalton, Farlee, Newbury and Barnet on said Grants, was in the month of August last delivered by the subscriber to the Committee of Congress on the affairs of the New Hampshire Grants, to be by them communicated to Congress.

Peter Olcott, *Agent*
Feby 8, 1780. *of the Inhabitants on said Grants.*

Messrs. Olcott and Woodward to the President of Congress.[1]

Philadelphia, Feb. 17th A. D. 1780.

Sir,—May it please your Excellency.

As we are informed that the papers referred to in our petition to Congress of the first instant are not in the Secretary's office, we beg leave in this way to exhibit copies of those which we view as most material in the stating our case in the hearing relative to the New Hampshire Grants.

We have the honor to be, with highest sentiments of duty and respect,
Your Excellency's most obedient
and most humble servants,

Peter Olcott,
Beza. Woodward.

His Excellency Samuel Huntington Esq.
President of Congress.[2]

Feb. 9 1780, the delegates from New-York wrote to Gov. Clinton recommending "an accommodation of the dispute with New-Hampshire." Alarmed by this, the N. Y. Assembly on the 22d of Feb. required James

---

[1] *N. H. Grants*, Vol. 1, No. 40, p. 323, in Archives of the State Department, Washington.

[2] The documents referred to here, and also in the "Representation" dated Feb. 1 1780, were doubtless the papers presented to Congress by Gen. Olcott in 1779, for which see *Appendix B.*

Duane or John Morin Scott "to proceed to Congress with all possible dispatch." Mr. Scott took his seat in Congress March 6, and Philip Schuyler on the 7th; on which day also R. R. Livingston presented a resolution of New York extending his term until the first of October.

IN CONGRESS, THURSDAY, March 2, 1780.[1]

Resolved, That Tuesday next be assigned for taking into consideration the disputes and differences relative to the jurisdiction of the states of New-York, Massachusetts-Bay, and New-Hampshire, or such of them as have passed laws agreeable to a recommendation of Congress of the 24th of September last, on one part, and the people of a certain district of country called the New-Hampshire Grants, who claim to be a separate jurisdiction, on the other part.

Massachusetts had passed no act under the resolution of Sept. 24 1779. The question should have been taken up by Congress on the 7th of March, but it was not considered until the 21st, when it was postponed necessarily, as appears from the following:

IN CONGRESS, TUESDAY, March 21, 1780.[2]

On motion to proceed to the order of the day for taking into consideration the disputes and differences relative to the jurisdiction of the states of New-York, Massachusetts-Bay and New-Hampshire, or such of them as have passed laws, agreeably to a recommendation of Congress of the 24th of September last, on the one part, and the people of a certain tract of country called the New-Hampshire Grants, who claim to be a separate jurisdiction, on the other part:

Ordered, That the same be postponed, nine states, exclusive of those who are parties to the question, not being represented in Congress.

April 17 1780, Mr. Folsom, a delegate in Congress for New Hampshire, writing to Josiah Bartlett, said: "As to Vermont, there were several violent attempts by the delegates of New-York and New-Hampshire to bring the matter before Congress, but without the least appearance of success. I have no expectation of any settlement till after the war is over, if I can believe the present members."—H. HALL'S *Early History*, p. 305.

Resolutions of Congress adopted June 2, 1780.

FRIDAY, June 2, 1780.[3]

Congress resumed the consideration of the report of the committee on sundry papers respecting the New-Hampshire Grants, and thereupon came to the following resolutions:

Whereas it is represented to Congress, and by authentic evidence laid before them it appears, that the people inhabiting the district of country, commonly known by the name of the New-Hampshire Grants, and claiming to be an independent state, have, notwithstanding the resolutions of Congress of the 24th of September, and 2d of October, pro-

---

[1] *Journals of Congress*, Folwell's edition, 1780–81, Vol. VI, p. 26.

[2] Same, p. 34.

[3] Same, p. 56.

ceeded as a separate government to make grants of lands and sales of estates by them declared forfeited and confiscated; and have also in divers instances, exercised civil and military authority over the persons and effects of sundry inhabitants within the said district, who profess themselves to be citizens of and to owe allegiance to the state of New-York:

Resolved, That the acts and proceedings of the people inhabiting the said district, and claiming to be an independent state as aforesaid, in contravening the good intentions of said resolutions of the 24th of September and the 2d of October last, are highly unwarrantable, and subversive of the peace and welfare of the United States.

That the people inhabiting the said district, and claiming to be an independent state as aforesaid, be and they hereby are strictly required to forbear and abstain from all acts of authority, civil or military, over the inhabitants of any town or district who hold themselves to be subjects of and to owe allegiance to any of the states claiming jurisdiction of the said territory, in whole or in part, until the decisions and determinations in the resolution aforementioned shall be made.

And whereas the states of New-Hampshire and New-York have complied with the said resolutions of the 24th of September and the 2d of October last, and by their agents and delegates in Congress declared themselves ready to proceed in supporting their respective rights to the jurisdiction of the district aforesaid, in whole or in part, according to their several claims, and in the mode prescribed in the said resolutions: and whereas Congress, by their order of the 21st of March last, did postpone the consideration of the subject of the said resolutions, nine states exclusive of those who were parties to the question not being represented; and by their order of the 17th of May last[1] have directed that letters be written to the states not represented, requesting them immediately to send forward a representation:

Resolved, That Congress will, as soon as nine States exclusive of those who are parties to the controversy shall be represented, proceed to hear and examine into and finally determine the disputes and differences relative to jurisdiction between the three states of New-Hampshire, Massachusetts-Bay and New-York, respectively, or such of them as shall have passed such laws as are mentioned in the said resolutions of the 24th of September and the 2d of October last, on the one part, and the people of the district aforesaid, who claim to be a separate jurisdiction, on the other, in the mode prescribed in and by the said resolutions.

Joseph Marsh to the President of Congress on Vermont affairs, April 12 1780.[2]

NEW HAMPSHIRE GRANTS, DRESDEN, 12 Apr. 1780.

Sir,—May it please your Excellency:

A continuation of the unsettled and unhappy state of affairs in the New Hampshire Grants on Connecticut River induces us to trouble Congress with this on the subject.

The people on said Grants in consequence of the resolves of Congress of the 24th Sept. last flattered themselves with the prospect of being soon

---

[1] The record of Congress of that date, Folwell's edition, does not contain this order.

[2] *New Hamp. Grants*, Vol. 1, No. 40, p. 325, in the Archives of the State Department, Washington.

happy in the enjoyment of civil government;—the want of which at present so greatly threatens their prosperity and tranquility.

By the positive determination and assurance in said resolves of Congress the people were confident that a final settlement would soon take place and are not a little distressed that the affair is still postponed —as they with reason greatly fear the unhappy consequences of our broken situation.

There being such a variety of parties in the country in favor of the different claims of jurisdiction renders it impracticable to conduct the concerns of civil society with any tolerable regularity—but what is of still greater moment and concern is that should this quarter (which is principly a frontier) be attacked by ye enemy from Canada our disunion is such that devastation and ruin would in all probability be the consequence. whereas were these difficulties adjusted by Congress and we assured of what jurisdiction we ought to submit to we might contribute considerable force against the common enemy.

Perhaps Congress are not availed of the dangerous and alarming steps taken by the Assembly of that territory called Vermont—we say dangerous and alarming as we apprehend a foundation is laying not only for private but general disturbances. At their last session charters of several townships were granted—some to officers of the army & others to gentlemen of different States. These measures we apprehend are big with consequences which may be extensively detrimental. We take the liberty of repeating our earnest desire that the difficulties above hinted at may be under the wise direction of Congress settled as speedily as possible.

I write this in behalf of the general committee in the northern district of the New Hampshire Grants contiguous to Connecticut River—and have the honor to be with the highest sentiments of duty and esteem

Your Excellency's most obedient
and most humble servant,
JOSEPH MARSH, *Chairman.*

His Excellency Sam$^{l.}$ Huntington Esq. President of Congress.

[Endorsed]
Read June 5, 1780.

IN CONGRESS, FRIDAY, June 9, 1780.[1]

Nine states represented, exclusive of New-Hampshire, Massachusetts-Bay and New-York.

A motion was made by Mr. Livingston, seconded by Mr. Scott, [both of New York,] agreeably to the resolution of the 2d instant, to proceed to hear and examine into and finally determine the disputes and differences relative to jurisdiction between the three states of New-Hampshire, Massachusetts-Bay and New-York, respectively, or such of them as shall have passed such laws as are mentioned in the resolutions of the 24th of September and 2d of October last, on the one part, and the people of the district commonly known by the name of the New-Hampshire Grants, who claim to be a separate jurisdiction, on the other, in the mode prescribed in and by the said resolution.

But it being represented on the part of New-Hampshire, that the agent specially appointed for that business, is not now present, and, from the great distance, cannot soon attend Congress,

On motion of Mr. Walton [of Georgia,] seconded by Mr. Folsom [of New Hampshire,]

---

[1] *Journals of Congress*, Folwell's edition, 1780–81, Vol. VI, p. 58.

Ordered, That the second Tuesday in September next be assigned to proceed to hear and examine into and finally determine the disputes and differences relative to jurisdiction, between the three states of New-Hampshire, Massachusetts-Bay and New-York, respectively, or such of them as shall have passed such laws as are mentioned in the resolutions of the 24th of September and 2d of October last, on the one part, and the people of the district commonly known by the name of the New-Hampshire Grants, who claim to be a separate jurisdiction, on the other, in the mode prescribed in and by the said resolutions.

Ordered, That copies of the aforegoing order be sent to the States of New-York, New-Hampshire and Massachusetts-Bay, and to the people of the district aforesaid.

Proceedings in Congress on the Vermont question in September 1780, and Documents connected therewith.

Evidently the following document was presented to Congress in anticipation of the promised action of that body in September 1780—at what date, however, does not appear. It is here inserted in the order of its date.

Letter of Joseph Marsh, Peter Olcott, and Beza. Woodward to the President of Congress.[1]

Dresden on the New Hampshire Grants,
July 20, A. D. 1780.

Sir,—May it please your Excellency:

We are sensible Congress have reason to expect their resolves of the first of June last would have such influence that the people on these grants might wait patiently their decisions respecting them; but such is the disposition of those who have assumed an independent jurisdiction that not only their measures but professions are in direct opposition to those resolves. They have ever since their sessions in March been assiduous to obtain surveys of the ungranted lands and have now sundry parties of men out for that purpose, who instead of resting matters are hastened on account of the late resolves of Congress with a view to obtain surveys of the whole before the sessions of their assembly in October next, and we understand are determined at that time to make grants of the whole to such persons as they shall apprehend will be most useful to assist in an establishment of a new State, and thereby at one stroke prevent an occasion for any further prohibition of Congress, purchase advocates in adjacent States and procure supplies of money to accomplish their purposes. They are also taking like speedy measures in confiscating estates of persons whom they are pleased to call *tories;* in respect to which it ought to be noted that their virulence is most poignant against those friends to order who oppose their rash procedures.

Vast numbers are continually making application for lands, and become advocates for their establishment in order to obtain them. Agents are at the same time employed to impress the minds of the people with an apprehension that Congress are conscious they have no right to decide the question in respect to their being an independent state and mean to postpone it from time to time, that they may establish it themselves, and construe every delay in that light. And experience shows that such suggestions however ill-grounded have too much influence.

---

[1] *N. H. Grants*, Vol. 1, No. 40, p. 341, in Archives of the State Department, Washington.

In short no measures are omitted which may tend to weaken the authority of Congress in the minds of the people and destroy the salutary influence of their late resolves, which they say were passed only to quiet New York, till they can establish their state.

New Hampshire continüe to call on those towns east of the river (who have connected themselves with those west) for men money and provisions, but as there is no authority to which they can consistently own allegiance, till Congress decide the dispute, and as they know not any right which New Hampshire (rather than the Massachusetts or New York) have to call on them consistent with the resolves of Congress on the subject in Sep'r last, they do not comply with their orders in respect to paying taxes, and think it unreasonable that a proposition[1] be allotted to them, till they are put in a condition to perform it, which can be done only by the decision of Congress; they are [as] zealously affected in the contest with Great Britain as any part of America—have ever had their quota of men as full as any part, and are now exerting themselves to raise their quota of recruits, from a sense of the importance of the cause; but cannot act with that vigor as though the dispute respecting the grants was decided.

The people in these parts mean to abide the decision of Congress and abhor the sentiments of those who deny their right.—They will cheerfully acquiesce in any thing Congress may judge proper, but ardently wish a union of the two sides of the river. New Hampshire will be their choice, if a new state be not admitted, which they have generally done expecting.

We entreat a speedy decision in respect to a new state, and in case one is not admitted, that commissioners may come into the territory to decide the claim of the other States, as we apprehend the future happiness of the inhabitants who are most nearly interested ought to be consulted, inasmuch as they will be principally affected by that decision.

We add nothing in respect to the merits of the case, as we have already laid our own submission and representation of the matter before Congress last winter; which we trust will be considered in its place.

A decision to be published on the Grants before a new election of officers in Vermont (in the beginning of Sep'r) is greatly desired, and in our view absolutely necessary before a meeting of their Assembly (the beginning of Oct'r) in order to prevent their involving hundreds of people in inextricable difficulties, by purchasing their grants of land.

More than thirty thousand people on these grants must be involved in difficulties while the matter is delayed, and the eyes of the greater part are to Congress for relief; and unless it can be speedily obtained we are undone.

We write in behalf of the inhabitants in the northern part on both sides of Connecticut river; and have the honor to be with the highest sentiments of duty and esteem, Sir,

Your Excellency's most obedient and most humble Servants,

JOSEPH MARSH,
PETER OLCOTT, } *Committee.*
BEZA. WOODWARD,

His Excellency the President of Congress.

[1] *Proportion* perhaps was the word intended.

Bez. Woodward's petition in behalf of people above Charlestown, N. H. Grants.[1]

[By order of a Convention holden at Dresden Aug. 30 1780.]

To His Excellency the President and the Honorable Members of the Congress of the United States of North America—Humbly sheweth

The petition of the principle inhabitants on Connecticut river on both sides and northward of Charleston, met in a convention at Dresden on the New Hampshire Grants August 30th 1780—

That the union of Canada with the united States is in our opinion of the greatest importance to them for the following reasons viz: there is but one seaport in that country which we shall ever have need to defend, yet good water carriage for near two thousand miles, stretching itself in a circular manner round the thirteen united States, through an excellent country of land, great part of which is inhabited by savages, whose furr and skin trade produces to our enemies an annual profit which is immense.

The annual produce of wheat in that country for exportation is very great, by which the British armies in America receive essential advantage. The capture of that country will be a leading step towards securing to the united States the profit of the fish, oil &c. produced at and near the St. Lawrence, which would be a greatly beneficial acquisition. While they hold possession of Canada, our frontier must be very extensive, and the savages at their command, and we had almost said the enemy destroy and take yearly from the frontiers bordering on Canada as much in value as the cost of reducing and holding that country. We are sure the defence of our frontiers costs more.

The securing that country in our favor will be the only effectual means to enable us to secure those of Ohio and Missisipi both on account of obtaining in that way the interest of the savages in our favor and as the conveyance for the enemy (while they hold possession of Canada) of men, ammunition and provisions to those parts is not only as easy but more expeditious and safe by the waters St. Lawrence than by the Gulf of Mexico. And in our opinion those countries cannot otherwise be effectually secured. By obtaining Canada we add to our force thirty thousand fighting men and destroy the efficacy of the bill passed in the British parliament in the year 1774 for extending the province of Quebec which includes the province of Main and great part of New Hampshire, these Grants &c, the establishment of which is without doubt the main object of the enemy in taking & holding possession at Penobscot, and within the extent of which the united States have not a single fortress to cover their claim in opposition to that of the British. In short that bill is so extensive that should it be established the united States would have little or nothing left worth contending for, and we see not how it can be effectually destroyed but by a union of Canada with them.

The body of inabitants in that country are desirous of such union and unless it can be bro't about speedily by sending a force into Canada they will be under necessity to take an active part against us, which they have hitherto avoided.

The whole force of Britain now in arms in Canada at all their posts from Quebec to Detroit including one thousand five hundred tories and Indians (who are continually roving and destroying our frontiers) does not exceed five thousand men, one thousand are stationed in the district

[1] *N. H. Grants*, Vol. I, No. 40, p. 559, in the Archives of the State Department, Washington.

of Montreal, and six hundred of the rovers have that district for their head quarters.

The communication from the settlements on this river to St. Charles on Chamblee river is easy—the road already opened more than half the way, the rest may be opened at very little expence, and the whole will be very good—the distance about one hundred miles.

A good commander with few continental troops in addition to such voluntiers as may be raised for that purpose on these Grants and in the New England States, with a suitable quantity of arms and ammunition to furnish those Canadians who are now eager for such an expedition and will at once join us on arrival of an army there, will easily take possession of and keep the district of Montreal, and that being secured, the country above even to and beyond the Western lakes must soon submit to the united states.

Your petitioners are confident that fifteen hundred men from these Grants will turn out (if called for) to assist in taking possession of that country. They can and will chearfully furnish five hundred horses, one hundred teams and ten thousand bushels of wheat, and more if necessary, also such other grain as may be wanted on the credit of the continent, from the district of country between the heights on the two sides of Connecticut river and north of the Massachusetts Bay, the inhabitants of which (more than five thousand families) are now cheifly obliged to hold the sword in one hand and tools for husbandry in the other, and probably must continue so to do till that country is reduced, unless we have a large continental force continually supported here to defend us from their ravages, as our frontier is very extensive.

We therefore humbly pray that Congress will be pleased to order an expedition into Canada by the middle of September next, or as soon as possible and publish a recommendation to the people on the Grants and to the New England States for voluntiers to join such continental forces as shall be sent on the expedition and that we make ready necessary provisions which your petitioners will chearfully comply with to the utmost of their power.

And as in duty bound shall ever pray &c.

Per order of the Convention,

BEZA. WOODWARD, *Clerk.*

Beza. Woodward as to [Gen. Peter] Olcott being a delegate in Congress.[1]

DRESDEN ON THE NEW HAMPSHIRE GRANTS,
August 31st 1780.

May it please your Excellency.—Col. Olcott [is] again appointed agent in behalf of the people on both sides Connecticut river from Charleston upward in the dispute betwixt the claiming States and the N. Hampshire Grants.[2]—We entreat that a determination of the question "Whether a new State be allowed on the Grants" may be deferred no longer, as every confusion is taking place among the people and will continue while that point is unsettled, of which he can give particular information and to whom we beg leave to refer Congress.

We trust our petition by our agents last winter and the committees letter of the 20th ult. will be brought to the view of Congress when the

---

[1] *N. H. Grants*, Vol. 1, No. 40, p. 361, in the Archives of the State Department, Washington.

[2] Appointed by the Convention at Dresden, Aug. 30 1780.—See preceding document.

trial comes on. There is no one point in which the people can agree so well as in an union with N. Hampshire in case the whole on both sides of the river shall not be permitted to unite in a new State which the body of the people have now done expecting [two or three words erased.] We would however entreat that after the determination that a new State be not admitted the people may be called upon to show which of the States they wish to be united with, as the happiness and prosperity of the inhabitants will greatly depend on their being gratified in that respect; such a measure also will have the most effectual tendency to procure an universal acquiescence in the resolves of Congress respecting the matter, as it will evidence a tender concern in Congress for their well-fare.

Great numbers think they have an undoubted right to demand a union with New Hampshire, by virtue of the compact made with them by the King in the grants he made of the lands by the governor of New Hampshire.

It has been suggested that the people will take arms and claim protection of Canada under the Quebec bill in opposition to any resolve Congress may pass against a new State, which we can assure them is without foundation in respect to the body of the people who are waiting with earnest expectation the decision of Congress on the subject and mean to conform their conduct to it—there are very few but what will readily acquiesce—none of any consequence on this side the green mountains and few on the other, however some of their leaders may desire to raise a tumult in opposition to them.

Col. Olcott is vested with all the power which our people can confer while in our present distracted situation, and we hope his measures in the matter conformable to this and other papers from this quarter may be considered as the voice of the people.

I write this by order and in behalf of the general committee in the northern district of the grants and have the honor to be with highest sentiments of respect, Sir,

Your Excellency's most obedient and most humble servant,

BEZA. WOODWARD, *Clerk.*

His Excellency the President of Congress.

[Endorsed]

Read Sept. 18, 1780.

Ira Allen and S. R. Bradley as to their Commission.[1]

PHILADELPHIA, Sept. 12th 1780.

Sir,—We do the Honour to forward your Excellency a duplicate of the appointment of Commissaries [commissioners] from the State of Vermont to wait upon the Honorable Congress of the United States.

Herewith you will receive a letter from his Excellency the Governor of Vermont, with a pamphlet [Bradley's *Appeal*] refered to in said letter, which we have positive orders to lay before Congress, And are

Your Excellency's Most Obedient Humble Servants,

IRA ALLEN,

STEPHEN R. BRADLEY.

His Excellency Saml. Huntington, Esq. Pres. of Congress.

[Endorsed]

Letter from Ira Allen & Stephen R. Bradley
Sept. 12, 1780.
Read the same day.

---

[1] *New Hampshire Grants*, Vol. 1, No. 40, p. 555, in the Archives of the State Department, Washington.

The commission and letter referred to follow:

Commission of Ira Allen and Stephen R. Bradley.[1]

STATE OF VERMONT. BY THE GOVERNOR.

{ SEAL. } Whereas the Supreme Legislature of this State did at their Sessions in october last past, resolve "that five persons be chosen by ballot Agents in behalf of the freemen of this State, to appear at the Congress of the United States of America on the first day of February next and they or any three of them are hereby fully authorized and empowered by the freemen aforesaid to Vindicate their right to independence at the Honorable Board":

And whereas the said Agents appeared at Congress on the said first day of February officially and transmitted [transacted] the business of their appointment agreeable to their instructions and made report to Supreme Legislature of their doings, at the session in March last:

And Whereas by late advice received from Congress, it appears requisite that Commissaries [commissioners] should be appointed for the time being to attend and deliver officially to Congress such dispatches as shall be sent from the authority of this State, from time to time, and also to remonstrate against any acts of Congress which may infringe the rights and sovereignty of this State:

I have therefore tho't fit by and with advice of council to appoint and commissionate IRA ALLEN and STEPHEN R. BRADLEY, Esquires, and they are hereby appointed with full power to transact the business aforesaid. Given under my hand and the Common Seal of this State in the Council Chamber at Bennington this 16th August, 1780.

THOS. CHITTENDEN.

By his Excellency's Command,

JOSEPH FAY, *Sec. State.*

[Endorsed]

Commission of Ira Allen & Stephen R. Bradley,
August 16th 1780.
Read Feby. [September 19 1780.]

Governor Chittenden to the President of Congress, in reply to the resolutions of that body of June 2 and 9, 1780.[2]

BENNINGTON, *July 25th*, 1780.

SIR,

Your Excellency's letter of the 10th ult. enclosing several acts of Congress, of the 2d and 9th of the same month, I accidentally received, the 6th inst. have laid them before my Council, and taken their advice thereon, and now beg your Excellency's indulgence, while I treat on a subject of such moment in its nature, and which so nearly concerns the citizens of this state.

However Congress may view those resolutions, they are considered by the people of this state, as being, in their nature, subversive of the

---

[1] *New Hampshire Grants*, Vol. 1, No. 40, p. 357, in the Archives of the State Department, Washington.

[2] From a copy in Slade's *State Papers*, furnished by Hon. STEPHEN R. BRADLEY, who made thereon the following memorandum: "Delivered Congress Sept. 12, 1780, and read, *eodem die.*" In this, as in other intances, the journal of Congress contains no notice. The probable reason is that the Vermont papers, not noticed in the journal, were read in committee of the whole.

natural rights, which they have to liberty and independence, as well as incompatible with the principles on which Congress ground their own right to independence; and have a natural, and direct tendency to endanger the liberties of America, which have, hitherto, been defended at great expence, both of blood and treasure.

Vermont's right to independence has been sufficiently argued, and the good consequences resulting to the United States, from its first assuming government, clearly vindicated, in sundry pamphlets, which have been, officially, laid before Congress. I beg leave to refer your Excellency to "Vermont's appeal," &c. particularly from the thirty second to the forty second page;[1] in which, among other things, is contained a particular answer to the resolutions of the 24th of September, referred to in the resolves of the 2d of June last; and a denial of the authority of Congress over this state, so far as relates to their existence as a free and independent government.

I find, notwithstanding, by a resolution of the 9th ult. that Congress have assigned the second Tuesday of September next, to judge, absolutely, of the independence of Vermont, as a separate jurisdiction. Can Congress suppose this government are so void of reason, as not to discern that the resolves of the 2d and 9th of June aforesaid, so far as the authority of Congress may be supposed to extend to this state, are leveled directly against thier independence?

Vermont, as before mentioned, being a free and independent state, have denied the authority of Congress to judge of their jurisdiction. Over the head of all this, it appears that Congress, by their resolutions of the 9th ult. have determined that they have power to judge the cause; which has, already, determined the essence of the dispute; for, if Vermont does not belong to some one of the United States, Congress could have no such power, without their consent; so that, consequently, determining they have such a power, has determined that Vermont have no right to independence; for it is utterly incompatible with the rights and prerogatives of an independent state, to be under the control or arbitrament of any other power. Vermont have, therefore, no alternative; they must either submit to the unwarrantable decree of Congress, or continue their appeal to heaven and to arms.

There may, in future, be a trial at Congress, which of the United States shall possess this territory, or how it shall be divided among them; but this does not concern Vermont. And it is altogether probable that there have been proposals for dividing it between the state of New-Hampshire and New-York, the same as the King of Prussia, the Empress of Russia, and the Empress of Hungary divided Poland between those three powers; with this difference only, that the former are not in possession of Vermont.

The cloud that has hovered over Vermont, since the ungenerous claims of New-Hampshire and Massachusetts-Bay, has been seen, and its motions carefully observed by this government; who expected that Congress would have averted the storm: but, disappointed in this, and unjustly treated as the people, over whom I preside, on the most serious and candid deliberation, conceive themselves to be, in this affair, yet, blessed by heaven, with constancy of mind, and connexions abroad, as an honest, valiant and brave people, are necessitated to declare to your Excellency, to Congress, and to the world, that, as life, liberty and the rights of the people, intrusted them by God, are inseparable, so they do not expect to be justified in the eye of Heaven, or that posterity would call them blessed, if they should, tamely, surrender any part.

---

[1] See *ante*, pp. 216–218.

Without doubt, Congress have, previous to this, been acquainted, that this state has maintained several posts on its frontiers, at its own expence; which are well known to be the only security, to this quarter, of the frontier inhabitants of the states of the Massachusetts-Bay and New-Hampshire; and it is highly probable that Albany, and such parts of the state of New-York, as lie to the northward of that, would, before this time, have been ravaged by the common enemy, had it not been for the indefatigable exertions of this state, and the fears, which the enemy have been, and are still possessed of, that their retreat would be interrupted by the troops from those posts and the militia of this state.

Thus, by guarding the frontiers, has this state secured the friendship of part of the private gentlemen and yeomanry, even of those states, whose representatives, it seems, are seeking its destruction. And having the general approbation of disinterested states, this people are, undoubtedly, in a condition to maintain government; but should they be deceived in such connexions, yet as they are not included in the thirteen United States, but conceive themselves to be a separate body, they would still have in their power, other advantages; for they are, if necessitated to it, at liberty to offer, or accept, terms of cessation of hostilities with Great-Britain, without the approbation of any other man or body of men: for, on proviso that neither Congress, nor the Legislatures of those states, which they represent, will support Vermont in her independence, but devote her to the usurped government of any other power, she has not the most distant motive to continue hostilities with Great-Britain, and maintain an important frontier for the benefit of the United States, and for no other reward than the ungrateful one of being enslaved by them. True, Vermont have taken an active part in the war, subsisting between the United States and Great-Britain, under an expectation of securing her liberties; considering the claim of Great-Britain to make laws to bind the colonists, in all cases whatsoever, without their consent, to be an abridgment of the natural rights of mankind: and it appears that the said resolves of the 2d and 9th of June, are equally arbitrary, and that they furnish equal motives to the citizens of Vermont, to resist the one as the other; for, if the United States have departed from the virtuous principles upon which they first commenced the war with Great-Britain, and have assumed to themselves the power of usurping the rights of Vermont, it is time, high time, for her seriously to consider what she is fighting for, and to what purpose she has been, more than five years last part, spilling the blood of her bravest sons.

This government have dealt with severity, towards the tories, confiscated some of their estates, imprisoned some, banished some, and hanged some, &c. and kept the remainder in as good subjection, as any state belonging to the union. And they have, likewise, granted unto worthy whigs, in the neighboring states, some part of their unappropriated lands; the inconsiderable avails of which, have been faithfully appropriated for the defence of the northern frontiers; which, eventually, terminates in the support of the interest, and securing the independence and sovereignty of the United States: and, after having faithfully executed all this, have the mortification to meet with the resentment of Congress, circulated in hand-bills and the New-York publick papers, representing their conduct, "in contravening the good intention of Congress, as being highly unwarrantable, and subversive of the peace and welfare of the United States." Those resolves serve only to raise the expiring hopes and expectations, and to revive a languishing flame, of a few tories and scismaticks, in this state, who have never been instrumental in promoting the common cause of America.

With regard to the state of the Massachusetts-Bay, they have not, as a legislative body, laid any claim to the territory of Vermont; nor have they enacted laws, judicially authorizing Congress to take cognizance thereof, agreeable to the before mentioned resolves; a majority of their legislative body considering such pretensions to be an infringement on the rights of Vermont; and, therefore, the state of the Massachusetts-Bay cannot be considered as a party in this controversy.

As to the state of New-Hampshire, although they have judicially authorized Congress to make a final adjudication of their late started and very extraordinary claim to the territory of Vermont, yet, by recurring back to the original proceedings between the two states, it appears, the General Court of New-Hampshire had, previous to laying the said claims, settled their boundary line with the state of Vermont, and established Connecticut river as the boundary between the respective governments; and, as far as the approbation of the government of New-Hampshire can go, have, previously, conceded to the independence of Vermont; the particulars of which are too prolix to be given in this letter, but are exhibited, at large, in a pamphlet, entitled "A concise refutation of the claims of New-Hampshire and Massachusetts-Bay to the territory of Vermont," and which is herewith transmitted as a bar against the right of New-Hampshire to a trial for any part of Vermont.

The government of New-Hampshire, ever since the royal adjudication of the boundary line between them and the government of New-York, in 1764, have cast the inhabitants of the contested territory, out of their protection, and abandoned them to the tyranny of New-York: and have very lately, over the head of the settlement aforesaid, laid claim to the said territory, and enacted laws as aforesaid, to enable Congress to judicially determine the merit of said claim. How glaringly illegal, absurd and inconsistent, must their conduct as a legislative body, appear, in this respect. Such irregularity among individuals, arises from the ill government of the human passions; but when that takes place in publick bodies, it is unpardonable, as its influence is more extensive and injurious to society.

Hence it appears, legally speaking, neither the states of New-Hampshire or Massachusetts-Bay, can be, with propriety, considered as parties in the controversy; and, consequently, New-York is left alone, a competitor with Vermont, even admitting Congress are possessed of sufficient authority to determine those disputes, agreeable to their resolutions; which, by this government, is, by no means, admissible.

Notwithstanding the usurpation and injustice of neighboring governments towards Vermont, and the late resolutions of Congress, this government, from a principle of virtue and close attachment to the cause of liberty, as well as a thorough examination of their own policy, are induced, once more, to offer union with the United States of America, of which Congress are the legal representative body. Should that be denied, this state will propose the same to the Legislatures of the United States, separately, and take such other measures as self-preservation may justify. In behalf of the Council, I am, Sir,

Your Excellency's most obedient, humble servant,

THOMAS CHITTENDEN.

His Excellency SAMUEL HUNTINGTON, *Esq. President of Congress.*

Ira Allen & S. R. Bradley asking admission in person to proceedings of Congress.[1]

To His Excellency Samuel Huntington, Esq. President of the Congress of United States of America.

Sir,—We request your Excellency whenever debates come before Congress that may in any wise affect the rights, Sovereignty or independence of the State of Vermont, that you take the sense of Congress whether we be admitted a personal attendance the better to enable us to discharge the end of our appointment, And are

Your Excellency's Most Humble Servants,

IRA ALLEN,
STEPHEN R. BRADLEY.

Dated Philadelphia, Sept. 15th 1780.

[Endorsed] Read the same day.[2]

Luke Knoulton's Commission.[3]

STATE OF NEW YORK.

CUMBERLAND CO. SS:

At a Convention of the Committees of the said County held at Brattleboro' the 30th Day of August 1780,—

Resolved that LUKE KNOWLTON, Esq. be and he hereby is nominated and appointed an Agent on behalf of the Inhabitants of said County who are professed subjects of the State of New York, to attend the Trial proposed to be held before Congress, or a Committee thereof, at Philadelphia in the beginning of September next, relative to the jurisdiction over the Tract of Land commonly called the New Hampshire Grants, lying west of Connecticut River.

By order, JOHN SERGEANT, *Chairman P. T.*

[Endorsed] Read Sept. 19, 1780.

Letter of introduction [from Gov.] G. Clinton.

POKEEPSIE, 12th Sept'r 1780.

Gentlemen,—This will be handed to you by Mr. Knowlton a Gentleman from Cumberland County for whose Character and Business I beg leave to refer you to the enclosed Copy of a Letter and to his Credentials.—I should be happy if he may be enabled to return with such Intelligence as will prove satisfactory to his Constituents whose Patience in their present disagreeable Situation appears to be nearly exhausted.

The Legislature is now sitting and will soon adjourn, I would therefore wish if Congress have any Matters which may require their attention that they be forwarded without Delay.

I am, Gentlemen, with the highest Respect & Esteem Your most Obedient, GEO. CLINTON.

The Honorable the Delegates of the State of New York in Congress.

[Endorsed] Read Sept. 18, 1780.

---

[1] *N. H. Grants*, Vol. 1, No. 40, p. 557, in the Archives of the State Department, Washington. So entitled there.

[2] Probably read in committee, as no entry of the reading appears on the printed journal.

[3] *N. H. Grants*, Vol. 1, No. 40, p. 371, in Archives of the State Department, Washington.

[4] *Same* p. 365.

In the letter of introduction to Gov. Clinton, furnished by the Cumberland County committee, Mr. K. was described as a gentleman of "penetration and probity."[1] LUKE KNOULTON (so written by Mr. K., says Hon. JAMES H. PHELPS,) was born in Shrewsbury, Mass., in 1737, and died in Newfane, Dec. 12 1810, aged seventy-three years. He was a resident of Newfane in 1772, and with John Taylor proprietor of that town, under a New York grant, from May 12 1772, and he received $249.53 of the $30,000 paid to New York by Vermont to settle the controversy between those states. May 17 1774, on the organization of the town, he was chosen town clerk, and he held that office sixteen years. April 14 1772 he was appointed by New York one of the justices of the peace for Cumberland county. June 1776 to June 1777 he was a member of the Cumberland county Committee of Safety. He next appeared as above in September 1780, as agent for Cumberland county against Vermont in Congress, in which service he had a recommendation from Gov. Clinton. It is pretty certain that, from knowledge then gained, Mr. Knoulton changed his opinion on the Vermont question. Writing of the period when Knoulton and Ira Allen were at Philadelphia on this business, the latter said: "*A plan was then laid between two persons at Philadelphia*, to unite all parties in Vermont, in a way that would be honourable to those who had been in favour of New York,"[2] &c., stating that it was to call a convention of delegates of all parties interested, including those residing east of Connecticut river, to meet at Walpole, N. H., Nov. 15 1780. Mr. Knoulton is the first named of several Cumberland county gentlemen who, Oct. 31 1780, initiated measures to bring about this proposed convention at Walpole,[3] which met and called another to meet at Charlestown, N. H., Jan. 16 1781.[4] Of the last convention Mr. Knoulton was an active member, and doubtless he acted in concurrence with Allen, who was present and very influential, according to his own account, though he did not present his credentials as a delegate. This convention resulted, first, in the union with Vermont of thirty-five New Hampshire towns, and, consequent upon that, a like addition of that part of New York lying east of Hudson river and extending from north latitude 45° to the north line of Massachusetts. In 1782, Mr. Knoulton and Samuel Wells of Brattleboro' assisted in exchanging letters between the British commander in Canada, Gen. Haldimand, and British agents in New York city, of which a complaint was made to Gen. Washington, and through him to Congress, which resulted in resolutions directing the arrest of Knoulton and Wells, and information to the executives of New Hampshire, Massachusetts, Connecticut and New

---

[1] *Eastern Vermont*, p. 381.

[2] Ira Allen's *History of Vermont*, in *Vt. Historical Soc. Collections*, Vol. I, p. 412.

[3] *Eastern Vermont*, p. 401; *Vt. Historical Soc. Collections*, Vol. II, p. 96.

[4] See *Appendix H*, *post*.

York "of the treasonable practices with which some of their subjects are charged."[1] Jan. 27 1783, Gen. Washington transmitted to Congress Lieut. Israel Smith's report of Knoulton's and Wells's escape, which was charged to information given by Jonathan Arnold, a delegate in Congress from Rhode Island.[2] It is certain that Wells's escape was aided by Ethan and Ira Allen,[3] and it is not unreasonable to presume that Knoulton was favored by them or their associates. The fact is that Vermont was then carrying on a correspondence with Gen. Haldimand, who had to consult the British commander and his agents in New York city, and hence this exchange of letters through the agency of Knoulton and Wells was but an incident of the Vermont policy at that time. That Wells was so much of a loyalist as to be rewarded by Great Britain is true, but Knoulton received no such recognition, and there is no evidence impeaching his patriotism beyond the fact that on this occasion he aided the work in which Chittenden, the Allens, and other leading Vermonters were engaged for the purpose of preserving the independence of the state and protecting its people from the ravages of war. Nov. 16 1783, a party of a dozen adherents to New York, two of them of Newfane, arrested Mr. Knoulton, ostensibly on account of the order of Congress of the preceding year. They contented themselves, however, with taking him over the Vermont line into Massachusetts, leaving him there. Gen. Fletcher raised a force for a rescue; but Knoulton returned, and the Yorkers dispersed, so the military force was disbanded. Mr. Knoulton represented Newfane in the General Assembly in 1784-6, and 1788-9, five years; was a member of the Council from Oct. 1790 to Oct. 1801, eleven years; a member of the Convention of 1793; judge of Windham County Court from 1787 to Dec. 1794, and in 1802, fifteen years; and judge of the Supreme Court in 1786.—See Deming's *Catalogue*. In Graham's *Descriptive Sketch* Mr. Knoulton is represented as "a leading character, and a man of great ambition and enterprize, of few words, but possessed of the keenest perception, and an almost intuitive knowledge of human nature, of which he is a perfect judge. This gentleman, owing to the particular method in which he has transacted business, has obtained the appellation of Saint Luke."—See B. H. HALL's *Eastern Vermont*, pp. 503-4, 675-6, 720-723.

IN CONGRESS, MONDAY, September 11, 1780.[4]

Mr. J. Sullivan, a delegate for the State of New Hampshire, attended and produced his credentials, which were read.

---

[1] *Secret Journals of Congress*, 1775-81, Vol. I, pp. 244, 245.

[2] *Vt. Hist. Soc. Collections*, Vol. II, p. 323.

[3] Ira Allen's *History*, in *Vt. Hist. Soc. Collections*, Vol. I, p. 467.

[4] *Journals of Congress*, Folwell's edition, 1780-81, Vol. VI, p. 124.

TUESDAY, September 12, 1780.[1]

Nine states, exclusive of the states interested, not being represented:

Resolved, That the order of the day, to proceed to hear and examine into and finally determine the disputes and differences relative to jurisdiction, between the three states of New Hampshire, Massachusetts-Bay and New-York, respectively, or such of them as shall have passed such laws as are mentioned in the resolutions of the 24th of September and the 2d of October last, on the one part, and the people of the district commonly known by the name of the New Hampshire Grants, who claim to be a separate jurisdiction, on the other, in the mode prescribed in and by the said resolutions, be postponed till Thursday [Tuesday] next, and that the members in town be notified to attend the house at 10 o'clock in the morning of that day.

TUESDAY, September 19, 1780.[2]

Resolved, That the order of the day, to proceed to hear and examine into and finally determine the disputes and differences relative to jurisdiction between the three states of New Hampshire, Massachusetts-Bay and New York, respectively, or such of them as have passed such laws as are mentioned in the resolutions of the 24th of September and the 2d of October last, on the one part, and the people of the district commonly known by the name of New Hampshire Grants, who claim to be a separate jurisdiction, on the other, be postponed till six o'clock.

On motion of the delegates of New-York,

Ordered, That the Secretary notify Messrs. Ira Allen, Stephen R. Bradley, Luke Knoulton, and colonel Olcott, to attend this afternoon, on the hearing of the question respecting the jurisdiction of the tract of country commonly called the New Hampshire Grants.

Six o'clock P. M.

Congress met according to adjournment, and proceeded to hear, &c. the persons notified attending, when the following papers were read:

The act of the state of New-York, passed Oct. 21st, 1779, and the act of the state of New-Hampshire, of Nov. 1779, both passed pursuant to the resolutions of Congress of September 24th and October 2d:

A commission to Ira Allen and Stephen R. Bradley, Esq'rs. dated August 16th, 1780,[3] signed Thomas Chittenden, under a seal in the instrument, called the seal of the state of Vermont:

An appointment of Luke Knoulton, as agent on behalf of the inhabitants of Cumberland county, at a convention of the committees of the said county, Brattleborough, Aug. 30, 1780, and signed John Sergeant, chairman *pro tempore*.[4]

An appointment of Peter Olcott and Bezaleel Woodward, Esq'rs. agents from the towns in the northern parts of the New-Hampshire Grants, on both sides of Connecticut river, being part of a district known by the name of the State of Vermont, pursuant to a vote of a convention of members from the said towns, November 17, 1779, signed

---

[1] *Journals of Congress*, Folwell's edition, 1780–81, Vol. VI, p. 125.

[2] Same,, p. 127.

[3] See *ante*, p. 254. The resolution of the Governor and Council, requesting and authorizing Mr. Bradley to attend Congress as agent with Mr. Allen, is entered on the record as of August 18, 1780, but the commission is dated Aug. 16.

[4] See *ante*, p. 258.

Joseph Marsh, chairman of the said convention, and dated New-Hampshire Grants, January 1, 1780.[1]

The delegates of New-York, as agents for the state, delivered in sundry papers, which were read, with an intent to prove that the land known by the name of the New-Hampshire Grants, on the west side of Connecticut river, is within the limits of the state of New-York; that the state of New-Hampshire have acknowledged this, and that the people on the said tract have been represented in the legislature of New-York, since the year 1764.

WEDNESDAY, September 20, 1780.[2]

Congress proceeded to the order of the day, the parties being present as yesterday, except the delegate for the state of New-Hampshire, who was absent through sickness; when the state of New-York, by its delegates, proceeded in stating evidence to prove that the inhabitants of the tract of country known by the name of the New-Hampshire Grants, west of Connecticut river, as part of the state or colony of New-York, were duly represented in and submitted to the authority, jurisdiction and government of the Congress and Convention of the said state, till late in the year 1777; and that, therefore, the people inhabiting the said tract of country have no right to a separate and independent jurisdiction.

Sept. 22 1780, the Vermont Agents remonstrated against the proceedings of Congress; and this, probably, influenced to some extent the postponement, which was ordered as follows:

WEDNESDAY, September 27, 1780.[3]

Congress proceeded in the order of the day respecting the jurisdiction of the tract of country commonly called the New-Hampshire Grants, all the parties being present except Ira Allen and Stephen R. Bradley, who being duly notified, declined to attend, when the agent for the state of New-Hampshire proceeded to state evidence tending to prove, that the tract of country known by the name of the New-Hampshire Grants, was within the state of New-Hampshire, and that therefore the people inhabiting the said tract of country, have no right to a separate and independent jurisdiction. The gentlemen appearing in behalf of sundry inhabitants of the said Grants having nothing to add, and pressing Congress to come to a determination, withdrew.

Resolved, That the farther consideration of the subject be postponed.

FRIDAY, October 6, 1780.[4]

Congress proceeded to the consideration of the subject relative to the jurisdiction of the tract of country commonly called the New-Hampshire Grants, when a letter of the 2d, from Ira Allen and Stephen R. Bradley was read.

This letter was as follows:

Ira Allen and Stephen R. Bradley to Congress.[5]

PHILADELPHIA Oct. 2 1780.

Sir,—We have the honour to inform Congress that the time of our appointment to attend on Congress expired yesterday in consequence of which we set out this morning to meet the General Assembly of the State which are to convene the 12th instant to adopt measures for

---

[1] See *ante*, p. 241.

[2] *Journals of Congress*, Folwell's edition, Vol. VI, 1780–81, p. 129.

[3] Same, p. 135. [4] Same, p. 145.

[5] *N. H. Grants*, Vol. I, No. 40, p. 579, in Archives of State Department, Washington.

prosecuting the war in conjunction with the thirteen united States & for regulating their own internal police. We are assured the General Court of the State of Vermont will make every effort in their power to establish the sovereignty and independence of America and could wish that principle might be invariably observed by every man in authority throughout the American States.

The dispute concerning the State of Vermont is of such great concern it appears to us of the highest importance Congress should be rightly acquainted with the dispute before they interpose on either side, which at present they cannot while America is in her present Situation. We can further observe that we have many papers more authentic than those that have been exhibited to Congress that will shew our right to sovereignty over the claims of all our adversaries; which we have not here at present.

For these and for many other reasons we must request Congress to postpone a further inquiry into the premises til a future day.

And have the honor to be your Excellency's

Most Obedient Humble Servants,

IRA ALLEN,

STEPHEN R. BRADLEY.

His Excellency Saml Huntington, Esq. President of Congress.

IRA ALLEN'S ACCOUNT OF THE HEARING IN CONGRESS IN SEPTEMBER 1780.[2]

In August, 1780, Ira Allen and Stephen [R.] Bradley Esquires attended Congress, as agents from Vermont, in order to be prepared for the second Tuesday in September (to which time Congress had referred the determination of the cause of Vermont.) The people in the south-east part of the State who professed allegiance to the state of New York, sent their agent, Luke Knowlton, Esq; to attend Congress; and the people in the north-east part of the State, who were, in opinion and politics, with the revolting members of the Legislature of Vermont in 1778, also sent their agent, Peter Olcott, Esq; to Congress; thus, to that body, all parties appeared to be represented. The agents of Vermont had frequent interviews with the members of Congress, in particular those from New York, with whom they spent several evenings in the most sociable manner. Very different views and objects seemed to be pursued by all parties; indeed, all parties seemed determined to carry their point. Therefore, to gain as great an advantage as possible, the agents of Vermont requested in writing, that when any debates came before Congress which might affect the rights, the sovereignty, or independence of the State of Vermont, they might be present. On this request, the opponents to Vermont took courage, supposing that by getting the agents to attend in Congress, they would make some remarks on the evidence adduced against the independence of Vermont, or, in some way, put it in the power of that body to consider the cause to them submitted by the agents of Vermont.

On the 19th of September, 1780, they received a notification to attend Congress, to hear the question respecting the jurisdiction of the New Hampshire Grants. The claims of New Hampshire and New York were put in, and both of these States plead that Vermont had no

---

[2] See his *History of Vermont*, in *Vt. Historical Society Collections*, Vol. I, pp. 408–412.

pretensions to independence, but belonged to them. The agents of Vermont, though present, were not considered or treated by Congress as the agents or representatives of any State or people invested with legislative authority. Part of two days were spent in hearing the evidence exhibited by New York, to shew that the people on the New Hampshire Grants belonged to, and of right were under the authority and jurisdiction of New York, and therefore had no right to a separate independent jurisdiction, a day being assigned to hear the claim and evidence of New Hampshire. During this time the agents of Vermont retained minutes of the proceedings of Congress, and of the evidence exhibited by the Agents of New York, that they might the better be prepared to remonstrate against them, as they had no idea of submitting the independence of Vermont to the arbitrament of Congress, or even of speaking on the matter in Congress, or of objecting in any way to the evidence adduced against Vermont, however irregular or provoking. The principles upon which the Agents of Vermont went, were to remain quiet, let the business be conducted as it would: the worse, the more advantage they would have in remonstrating; they concluded it not advisable to attend and hear the claim and evidence of New Hampshire when it was taken up by Congress, therefore sent in their remonstrance to that body, and declined attending. Mr. Thompson, Secretary, (of Congress) called on and urged them to attend, which they refused; he then requested to know what report he should return to Congress; when he received for answer, *that while Congress sat as a Court of Judicatory, authorized by the claiming States ex parte, and Vermont was not put on an equal footing, they should not again darken the doors of Congress;* the remonstrance was as follows.

Remonstrance of the Vermont Agents against the proceedings of Congress, Sept. 22, 1780.

"To the Honourable CONGRESS of the UNITED STATES of NORTH AMERICA.

"The remonstrance of Ira Allen and Stephen R. Bradley, Commissioners from the free and independent State of Vermont, appointed for the time being to attend on Congress.

"With pleasure they embrace this first opportunity to testify their thanks for the personal honour done them by Congress, in giving them an attendance, though in a private capacity, with their honourable body: At the same time they lament the necessity which obliges them to say, they can no longer sit as idle spectators, without betraying the trust reposed in them, and doing violence to their feelings, to see partial modes pursued, plans adopted, ex parte evidence exhibited, which derives all its authority from the attestation of the party; passages of writings selected giving very false representations of facts, to answer no other end but to prejudice your honourable body against the *State of Vermont;* thereby to intrigue and baffle a brave and meritorious people out of their rights and liberties. We can easily conceive the Secretary's office of the State of New York may be converted into an inexhaustible source to furnish evidence to answer their purpose in the present dispute.

"Needless would it be for us to inform Congress, that by the mode of trial now adopted, the State of Vermont can have no hearing without denying itself: And to close with those resolutions, which we conceive our enemies have extorted from your honourable body, and on which the trial is now placed, would be, in fact, taking upon ourselves that humility and self abasement, as to lose our political life, in order to find it.

"We believe the wisdom of Congress sufficient to point out, that pursuing the present mode, is deviating from every principle of the laws of nature, or nations: For if the dispute is between the States claiming on the one part, and the State of Vermont on the other, whether the latter be a State *de jure*, or an independent jurisdiction *de facto*, they ought to be considered in the course of the dispute, until the powers interposing have determined whether the latter be an independent jurisdiction *de jure;* if not they of course ought to annihilate the jurisdiction *de facto;* but to annihilate the State *de facto*, in the first place, is summarily ending the dispute; to deny the latter any independent jurisdiction *de facto*, is to deny there is any longer parties in the dispute.

"Again, we conceive the means connected with the end, and upon no principle whatever can we justify, that either part should establish the modus, or rules to be pursued in determining disputes, without confounding every idea of right and wrong. In the present case, on the one part might the end as justly have been established as the way and means to effect the end.

"We are far from being willing those brave and strenuous efforts made by the State of Vermont, in the controversy with Great Britain, should be buried by our grasping adversaries (thirsting after domination and prey) in the specious pretext of riotously assuming Government; and we thereby lose all credit for the men and money we have expended.

"Thus, while we are necessitated to remonstrate against the proceedings of Congress on the present mode, we are willing, at the same time, any equitable enquiry should be made, the State of Vermont being allowed equal ptivileges with the other States in the dispute.

"And that the State of Vermont might stand justified to your honourable body, and to the world, both as to her present and future conduct, we are induced, as well from principles of attachment to the American cause, as a regard we have for peace and harmony among the states of America now at war with Great Britain, to make the following proposals, viz.

"1st. That the State of Vermont will, as soon as may be, forward to the Secretary of Congress, an attested return of all male persons, liable to do duty agreeable to a militia act heretofore exhibited to Congress in a code of laws, entitled "The Laws of Vermont;" and the State of Vermont shall, for and during the present war with Great Britain, from year to year, furnish an equal number of troops in the field, in proportion to their numbers, as Congress shall estimate the quotas of the several United States, in proportion to their numbers; which troops shall be clothed, quartered, and paid by the State of Vermont. And, at the close of the war, the dispute shall be equitably settled by the mediation of sovereign powers; and nothing herein contained, shall be construed to take away the right any of the United States claim to have in or over the State of Vermont: Or

"2dly, We are willing to agree upon some one or more of the Legislatures of the disinterested States to interpose as mediators, and settle the dispute: Or

"3dly, We are willing Congress, being possessed of sovereignty, should interpose to prevent the effusion of human blood; at the same time, we reprobate every idea of Congress sitting as a Court of Judicatrue, to determine the dispute, by virtue of authority given them by the act or acts of the State or States that make but one party.

"It gives us pungent grief that such an important cause at this juncture of affairs, on which our *all* depends, should be forced on by any gentlemen professing themselves friends to the cause of America, with such vehemence and spirit as appears on the part of the State of New York: And shall only add, that if the matter be thus pursued, we stand ready to appeal to God and the world, who must be accountable for the awful consequences that may ensue.

Done at Philadelphia, this 22d day of September, A. D. 1780.

"IRA ALLEN,
"STEPHEN R. BRADLEY."

Congress having heard the evidence on the part of New Hampshire, on the 27th of September, resolved that the further consideration of the subject should be postponed.

Proposals of Vermont for a permanent Alliance and Confederation with adjoining States.

Oct. 14 1780. Governor Chittenden communicated to the General Assembly the action of Congress in June preceding, his protest to the President of Congress of July 25, and a report of the hearing in Congress in September,—the latter being supplemented by a verbal account by Ira Allen. No legislative action was had, however, in *direct* response to Congress, but much was done to enable the state to maintain its independence,[1] and on the 8th of November a resolution was adopted,[2] under which Governor Chittenden proceeded according to his notice of the 25th of July, which was that, should Congress deny to Vermont an admission to the union, "*this state will propose the same* [*an union independent of Congress,*] *to the legislatures of the United States, separately, and take such other measures as self-preservation may justify.*"[3]

Gov. Chittenden to Gov. Clinton of New York.

State of Vermont,
In Council, Arlington, November 22d, 1780.

Sir:—Inclosed I transmit your excellency a copy of my letter to Congress of the 25th of July last, and on a full examination of the controversy between the State of New York and this State, and duly considering the present peculiar circumstances of both States, I am induced to make a positive demand on the Legislature of the State over whom you preside, to give up and fully relinquish their claim to jurisdiction over this State, and also propose to them to join in a solid union with this State for mutual defence against the British forces which invade the American States, particularly such part as make incursions on the frontiers of the two States from the Province of Quebec. Such a union for the reciprocal advantage of both governments, I am willing to ratify and confirm on the part of this State.

Col. Ira Allen, who delivers this, waits your answer to these proposals.

---

[1] See note on the Land Grants of 1780, &c., *ante*, p. 61.

[2] *Ante*, p. 59.

[3] The last clause covered other measures of Vermont at that period, and notably the Haldimand Correspondence. See Gov. Chittenden's letter to the President of Congress, *ante*, p. 256.

In behalf of the Council and General Assembly, I have the honor to be with great esteem your Excellency's very obedient humble servant,

THOMAS CHITTENDEN.

His Excellency George Clinton Esq. Governor, &c. of the State of New York.

To be communicated to the Legislature thereof.

The Legislature of New York had been summoned to meet on the 3d of January 1781, but a quorum did not attend until about the first of February.[1] On the 5th Gov. Clinton transmitted Gov. Chittenden's demand with the message following:

Gov. Clinton to the New York Assembly.

Gentlemen,—You will receive with this message a letter from Thomas Chittenden dated the 22d of Nov. last, making a positive demand on the legislature to give up and fully relinquish the jurisdiction of this state over the part thereof generally distinguished by the name of the New Hampshire Grants, with a copy of his letter to Congress of the 25th of July last.

Nothing but the desire of giving you the fullest information of every matter of public concern, could induce me to lay before you a demand, not only so insolent in its nature and derogatory to the honor of the State and the true interests of your constituents, but tending to subvert the authority of Congress (to whom the determination of the controversy is solemnly submitted) and establish a principle destructive in its consequences to the power and happiness of the United States.

GEORGE CLINTON.

Albany, Feb. 5, 1781.

This message, with the accompanying letters, was referred in the Senate to a committee of the whole, and in the House to a committee of nine. Feb. 21 the Senate considered the subject; chancellor Robert R. Livingston, who had been a special delegate for the state at the then recent hearing in Congress, was heard by the committee, which reported resolutions declaring it inexpedient for the state to insist further on its right to jurisdiction over Vermont, and providing for commissioners to meet commissioners of Vermont to settle the terms for a cessation of jurisdiction by New York. On the same day the Senate adopted the resolutions, with only one dissenting voice, and sent them to the House for concurrence. In that body, the resolutions were made the order of the day for February 27th. The result is stated by HILAND HALL as follows:

On that day the entry on the Assembly journal is as follows, viz:

"The order of the day being read, for taking into consideration the "resolutions of the honorable the Senate, relative to the tract of country "commonly called the New Hampshire Grants, Mr. Speaker put the "question, whether the House will now proceed to take the said resolu- "tions into consideration. Debate arose and it was carried in the affirm- "ative."

Upon the declaration of this vote, the governor's private secretary, who, it seems, had been waiting the result, announced a message from his Excellency which was immediately read. In his message the gover-

---

[1] Gov. Clinton to Gen. Alexander McDougall, *Clinton Papers*, No. 3616, *post*, p. 269.

nor stated that he had received information "in a manner that claimed his credit, that certain resolutions, originating in the Senate, had been sent to the Assembly for concurrence, proposing the relinquishment of jurisdiction to that part of the State commonly designated by the name of the New Hampshire Grants," and declaring that "if the House should agree to carry those resolutions into effect, the duties of his office would oblige him to exercise the authority vested in him by the constitution and *prorogue them.*"

This message, threatening to put an abrupt end to the session of the Assembly, in case they should proceed to concur with the Senate in the passage of the resolutions, had its intended effect of preventing their adoption. But for this extraordinary threat to exercise an odious power, which has since been expunged from the constitution, there is every reasonable probability that the controversy would have been brought to a speedy and happy close, and all the troubles and heart burnings which resulted from it, for several succeeding years, would have been thereby prevented.[1]

The time for this experiment upon New York was well chosen by Gov. CHITTENDEN and his advisers. The northeastern frontier of that state had been ravaged in the preceding October by a British force from Canada, and would be exposed to like ravages in the coming spring from both the British and their Indian allies, so the aid of Vermont had become exceedingly important to all the citizens of eastern New York between Lake Champlain and Albany. Hence Vermont had many friends in that section, and among them was Maj. Gen. PHILIP SCHUYLEY, who bore a leading part in the adoption of the Senate resolutions of the 21st of February. The postponement of the Vermont question by Congress in the preceding September had also been discouraging to New York, and from the fact that the Senate was all but unanimous for a settlement with Vermont on the day Chancellor LIVINGSTON had given his opinion, the inference is fair that he, too, favored the project. Another busy actor in the scene was IRA ALLEN. The following letter is interesting, not only for Gov. CLINTON's account of this matter, but for the fact it reveals that even he, within a few weeks after he had defeated the proposed settlement of the controversy, was almost prepared to concede the independence of Vermont, and to extend its jurisdiction over a large part of New Hampshire.

Gov. Clinton to Maj. Gen. Alexander McDougall.[2]

POKEEPSIE, 6 April 1781.

Dear Sir,—In my hasty scroll from Albany I promised you a more lengthy epistle the first leisure hour. It is not yet arrived and if I was to wait for it I am apprehensive I should be charged with inattention.

Our official letters and the copies of laws transmitted with them to Congress with the list of the acts enclosed to Mr. Duane will give you a general idea of the business of the last meeting, and the enclosed copies

---

[1] See *Early History of Vermont*, pp. 329–336.

[2] *Clinton Papers*, No. 3616; from a manuscript copy in the possession of HILAND HALL. Gen. MCDOUGALL was one of the New York delegates in Congress.

of Message and resolutions[1] will serve to explain the conduct of the legislature, or rather the Senate, respecting our controversy with the inhabitants of the Grants. I have therefore only to give you a detail of the management of a measure, which, had it succeeded, I am persuaded you will agree would have reflected lasting ignominy and disgrace upon the state, and this consideration alone ought to have forbid it.

By my proclamation the legislature was to have convened at Albany the 3d of January, but the unpunctual attendance of members prevented their forming a quorum until about the first of February. In this period Mr. Ira Allen arrived at Albany, the members who attended met daily to arrange and prepare the business, and on the idea of promoting dispatch, Mr. Allen was introduced and the letter[2] opened in my absence. The proposition it contained was immediately though informally agitated and every engine set to work to prepare the minds of the members as they arrived to accede to it: Our northern and western frontier could only be protected from the ravages of a treacherous and ruthless savage enemy by the numbers and military prowess of the state of Vermont; that we could not expect their assistance without relinquishing our jurisdiction over them and yielding to their claim of independency; that in this case we should conciliate their affections and be enabled to enter into a compact with them and be safe. The greater part of the citizens of Albany and Schenectady and the inhabitants of the northern frontier were easily gulled by the leaders for this measure into a belief of all they said in favor of it, and daily reports of the intention of the enemy to penetrate the country in force as soon as the lakes were froze, at times that they were actually on their way, circulated to promote the favorite object.[3] The discontents and commotion which at the time too generally prevailed in the state were also in some instances employed to answer the end, and among the grievances complained of by some districts not the best affected to the cause of the country, the opposition given to the independency of Vermont was a noted one. On more minute inquiry I discovered that measures as early as last fall had been taken to promote this hopeful business, and that a certain gentleman (an old friend of ours[4]) had then declared his sentiments on the subject and his

---

[1] Doubtless the Senate resolutions of Feb. 21 and the threatening message of Feb. 27.

[2] Chittenden's of Nov. 22 to Gov. Clinton.

[3] Less than a month previous to the date of this letter, Gov. Clinton himself had given a dismal account of the condition of New York to Gen. Washington, the letter being dated Feb. 14 1781. The enemy, he wrote, had commenced their barbarities in Tryon county and the best part of the remaining territory would be totally depopulated; "a want of ability to raise a competent body of troops for the defence of the frontiers" was confessed; artillerists and field artillery were wanted; they had exhausted all their stock of ammunition; the troops were destitute of provisions of the meat kind; all the money in the treasury had been advanced; and even from that little success was expected, as there were no beef cattle within the state. This account could not have been exceeded by anything Allen and "the leaders for this measure" could say.—See *Vt. Hist. Soc. Collections*, Vol. II, pp. 53, 54.

[4] Gen. SCHUYLER.

intention to agitate and support it at the next meeting of the legislature. This I have reason to suspect induced some of our monied gentlemen, to what on such occasions you may judge would be easily obtained, to speculate in lands and solicit grants under the government of Vermont, and by this means they became warmly interested.[1] Under these circumstances it is not strange that a majority of our honest and well meaning Senate, speaking of them as a body, should have been led into a measure from which they were inclined to believe so much good was to result, and not sufficiently apprized of the evils attending it, nor that my message to the Assembly on the subject declaring my intention to prorogue was an unpopular one in Albany. Your official letter informing that there was reason to hope for a speedy and just decision of the controversy by Congress arrived very opportunely and it changed the sentiments of some and for the present stopped the mouths of all, and occasioned the laying aside a long address moved in the Senate in consequence of my message to the Assembly, but not yet agreed to.[2]

---

[1] To this suggestion the following extract from the letter of Gen. McDougall, to which Gov. Clinton was replying, is amusingly pertinent:

Maj. Gen. Alexander McDougall to Gov. Clinton.—Extract.

PHILADELPHIA, March 12, 1781.

The influence of the officers of the New England line is considerable in their states, and the habits of thinking which they have acquired in the army are more conformable to the genius of our [New York] constitution than [are those of] the yeomanry of those states who will unavoidably come into ours, and it is necessary the leveling principles of the latter should be tempered by those of the former.* It will be a good stroke of policy *to grant those gentlemen land in our state*, and it might be expedient to extend it to those of New Jersey—*vacant lands in the Grants might make a part of it.* If this should be judged prudent, the grant should extend to the officers of those lines who have resigned with good reputations, and to all the soldiers who have served three years, and to all who shall serve during the war. Certain I am we shall derive great utility from such a measure, if it is soon done, and in my opinion no time is to be lost in doing it. I understand a bill of this nature was prepared in the fall of 1779 at Kingston, but was rejected from considerations of narrow and niggardly policy. If it had been done, the influence of the Vermont land-jobbers would ere this have been at an end. I would give you some conclusive intelligence on this subject if time permitted.—*Clinton Papers*, No. 3575.

*In 1756 Lieut. Gov. COLDEN of New York wrote to the British Lords of Trade thus: "The New England Governments are formed on republican principles, and these principles are zealously inculcated on their youth, in opposition to the principles of the Constitution of Great Britain. The Government of New York, on the contrary, is established, as nearly as may be, after the model of the English Constitution. Can it then be good Policy to diminish the extent of Jurisdiction in His Majesty's Province of New York, to extend the power and influence of the others."—For this extract, and a note thereon by Gov. HALL of Vermont, see *Vt. Hist. Society Collections*, Vol. II, p. 510.

[2] March 12 1781, the Senate appointed Mr. Schuyler and Mr. Platt to draft an address to the governor on this subject, but Gen. McDougall's letter of the same date, representing Congress to be favorable to New York, prevented further action. Gen. McDougall wrote as follows in reference to the controversy in Congress:

The question of the New Hampshire Grants will soon be settled as the state of that name urge its delegates to press for a decision, and there is great reason to expect it will be a just and honorable one for

While these matters were transacting in Albany and the revolters (who had their emissaries among us) had every reason to expect that their demand would be fully complied with, their Council and Assembly then sitting at Windsor came to the resolutions, a copy of which I enclose you, extending their claim to the deepest channel of Hudson's river, &c. These resolutions you will observe is [were] prior to those of our Senate four days, and you will easily perceive the use which was to be made of them if we had been mad enough to have relinquished our jurisdiction. These resolutions appear to me to have been a secret transaction. I obtained a copy by mere accident, and I am the more inclined to believe this to be the case, as by the proceedings of a convention composed of the friends of New York, Chittenden and all parties including two counties on the east side of Connecticut river, though it appears they have agreed to unite and form an independent government including the several townships on the east side of Connecticut river to Mason's line, not a word in the minutes is said of this western extension to Hudson's river, and I am persuaded the inhabitants on the east side of the Green Mountains (who now compose a large majority) would not readily accede to it, as it is a capital object with them to establish their seat of government on the bank of Connecticut river, against which this western extension would militate and in the end defeat.[1]

---

our state. The cession [of land] made by New York to the United States has removed the cause of opposition which Maryland gave, to have our dispute settled, and the other small states not near us will cease their opposition, as the cause of it is removed. Pennsylyania will urge a determination of their dispute with Connecticut as soon as the business of their legislature is over. This I had from the President [Samuel Huntington of Connecticut] in a confidential conversation with him on the subject of the New England encroachments.—*Extract from No.* 3575 *of the Clinton Papers.*

[1] The initiatory proceedings, commenced Oct. 31 1780 and continued until June 16 1781, were public, and the propositions for both the east and west unions resolved upon Feb. 14 1781 were referred to the towns concerned, and of course were public. Feb. 15 1781, the Governor and Council recommended to the Assembly a postponement of further consideration of the jurisdictional claims to the next session, and the appointment of an agent to wait immediately upon "the legislature of the State of New York, now [then] convened at Albany, to agree upon and establish the line between this State and the State of New York." Not until more than three months after Gov. Clinton had defeated the resolutions of the New York Senate, and more than two months after the date of the above letter to Gen. McDougal, was the west union effected. The consummation of the unions resolved upon Feb'y 14th was postponed to the April session, and Ira Allen and Joseph Fay were appointed agents to New York on the 17th of February, as proposed by the Council. Allen bore Chittenden's demand to Clinton probably in January 1781, and may have remained in Albany until the project was defeated on the 27th of February; but there was ample time to send to Albany notice of Allen and Fay's appointment as special agents previous to the action of the New York Senate on the 21st, and the strongest of reasons

I most devoutly wish this unhappy controversy was decided. I wish for a just and honorable decision, but I am persuaded almost any that Congress can have in contemplation is better than further delay. To their decision, made by the proper tribunal, we must and can with honor submit, and a decision by them will in a great measure destroy the bad effects which would result from these turbulent people establishing themselves in defiance of their and our authority. They daily gain strength at our expense, and the dissensions which this dispute excites among ourselves, I fear, will have an unhappy effect in our

---

existed for doing so, as it would show that Vermont had on its part appointed agents to meet with like agents or commissioners, as proposed in the Senate resolutions of New York. Thus it appears from the record that Vermont acted frankly and fairly. Gov. Clinton was not *officially* apprized of the action of the General Assembly, because the Vermont agents were not authorized to treat with him, but with "the legislature of the State of New York." Gov. Clinton's indignant message of Feb. 5 was a sufficient notice to Vermont against any further official or friendly appeals to him. It is not possible, however, that Gen. Schuyler and associates could have been ignorant of Vermont's action, or that they, as Gov. Clinton said he had been, were dependent upon "mere accident" for information on a project which they were zealously pressing. Indeed, the very terms of the resolution of the New York Senate show, and Gov. Clinton was thus in fact notified, that it was expected Vermont would appoint commissioners to settle the controversy. The readiness with which twelve districts of New York agreed, on the 9th of May following, to unite with Vermont, is another reason for believing that these things were not done secretly.—See *Appendix H.* There are still other facts pertinent, showing conclusively that Connecticut and Rhode Island were apprized of the purpose of Vermont to seek a settlement of the controversy with the co-operation of New York; and it is highly probable that the legislatures of those states had information from Gen. Schuyler and Gov. Chittenden which warranted at least a hope of a happy settlement of the then dangerous controversy. Jan. 21 1781, Gen. Schuyler wrote to Gen. Washington that he had moved in the New York Senate to request the Eastern States to join in a Convention for settling boundaries so as "*to create a new State in this quarter* on conditions to be stipulated by the Convention."—See Sparks's *Revolutionary Correspondence*, Vol. 3, p. 213. On the 4th of May following he again declared his desire on this subject to Washington, and added that Gov. Clinton had "*put a stop to the business.*"—See Sparks's *Washington*, Vol. 8, pp. 42, 43, note. Vermont *projected* the east and west unions by one act only, Feb. 14th, but *suspended* both for a settlement of the controversy by the states interested in it, which Gov. Clinton defeated. New Hampshire also persisted in its claim. Then Vermont resumed hostilities by effecting the threatened encroachments on New York and New Hampshire—the east union April 5, and the west June 16. For resolutions of Connecticut and Rhode Island, see *post*, p. 275.

public councils. If they are to be a state, which however I deprecate, it is essentially our interest that they should extend to Mason's line, as for the reasons above mentioned it will be our best security against future encroachments, besides in this case the weight and influence of government will be in the hands of sober, discreet people, and many of them warmly attached to us. I am &c. yours sincerely,

GEORGE CLINTON.

To Maj. Gen. McDougall.

On the 22d of February the Vermont Assembly authorized the Governor and Council to prepare instructions to their agents (styled "commissioners," in their commission,) appointed to settle the boundary line with New York, and they were commissioned by Gov. Chittenden, (according to the *Index to the Stevens Papers*, p. 27,) "*to settle boundary lines between Vermont, New Hampshire, and New York*"—thus showing that Vermont intended a fair settlement of the controversy by a mutual agreement between the three States. Gov. Clinton seems to have had no idea of the real purpose of Vermont, thus clearly indicated, when he wrote the letter to Gen. McDougall on the 5th of the succeeding April. On learning of the defeat of the project on account of the extraordinary conduct of Gov. Clinton, it was resolved by the Governor and Council, March 7 1781, not to send the agents to Albany, or to write any further to the General Assembly of New York at present.[1] Thus, a really hopeful scheme of conciliation was most unfortunately ended.

Gov. Chittenden to Gov. Hancock of Massachusetts and Pres't Weare of New Hampshire.

Dec. 12 1780, Gov. Chittenden sent demands, similar to that to Gov. Clinton of New York, to the governors of Massachusetts and New Hampshire. For his letter to Gov. Hancock of Massachusetts, see *Appendix C, ante* p. 198. It is presumed his letter to Pres't Weare was substantially the same, as both are described as the same in the *Index to the Stevens Papers*, in these words: "to join in the common defence or Vermont will be obliged to join the British," in one letter; and "to join in the common defence or Vermont will be obliged to join the Enemy" in the other.[2] Gov. Chittenden wrote to Gov. Trumbull on the same day, that he had made "a demand on the legislatures of the states of New York, New Hampshire, and Massachusetts Bay, to relinquish their claims of jurisdiction to Vermont, with proposals to unite with them in a like union." Massachusetts responded favorably by the action of the General Court, March 8 1781, relinquishing its claim and consenting to

---

[1] *Ante*, p. 85.

[2] *Index to the Stevens Papers*, pp. 66, 79. The original letter to President Weare was in the manuscript volume of *New Hampshire State Papers* on the Vermont controversy, p. 175, but it has been lost; and the copy of it contained in the *Stevens Papers* was burnt with the Vermont capitol in 1857.

the independence of Vermont.[1] No direct reply from New Hampshire can be found, but the following document shows the position of that state at the time.

Resolutions of New Hampshire, Jan. 13 1781, *instructing its Delegates in Congress.*[2]

STATE OF NEW HAMPSHIRE. IN HOUSE OF REPRESENTATIVES, January 12th 1781.

Whereas this State is Subjected to many hardships & Inconveniencies on Account of the unsettled Situation of the Inhabitants of the Tract of Land called the New Hampshire Grants, west of Connecticut-River —A respectable Number of whom, being desirous of having said Tract confirmed to this State, considering the same as part thereof—And it being highly necessary as well for the good of this State, as for the Interest of the Inhabitants of said Tract that a speedy Decision be had thereon—

Therefore Resolved, that the Agents & Delegates from this State to the Continental Congress be instructed, and they are hereby instructed to use every possible means to induce Congress to make a speedy and final Determination of the Disputes relating to the Tract of land aforesaid—And as soon as Congress shall proceed in this matter, it is the Opinion of this State, that the said Agents and Delegates ought to use their Endeavours to have the Question "Whether the said Tract of Land shall be a Separate and Independent State," first determined.—That, if the same shall be determined in the Negative, they and each of them urge all proper Motives & Arguments to have the same Tract confirmed to the State of New Hampshire—for which purpose they are directed to make use of the papers now in their possession respecting said Dispute —and to procure such others as may be of service.

It is further Resolved that the Honorable the President be desired to enclose an Attested Copy of this Resolve & transmit the same to the said Agents & Delegates as soon as may be.

Sent up for Concurrence.

JOHN LANGDON, *Speaker.*

IN COUNCIL, Jany 13th 1781. Read & concurred.

M. WEARE, *Prest.*

Gov. Chittenden to Gov. Trumbull of Connecticut.[3]

STATE OF VERMONT. IN COUNCIL, Arlington, 12th December, 1780.

Sir:—Enclosed I transmit your excellency a copy of my letter to Congress of the 25th of July last, which, together with this, I request may be laid before the legislature of the state over whom you preside for their perusal and consideration, as it is the only method that Vermont has at present in her power of soliciting a union with the United States to propose it to their several legislatures separately, and as I have not received any answer from congress to my proposal of union in my said letter to them, nor to sending other similar offers from this government with additional proffers to that honorable body to bear a just proportion

---

[1] See *Appendix C, ante*, p. 199.

[2] Manuscript volume of *New Hampshire State Papers, Vermont Controversy*, 1764–91, p. 206.

[3] *Haldimand Papers*, in *Vt. Hist. Soc. Collections*, Vol. II, p. 84.

of the expence of the present war with Great Britain, it does not appear that congress have determined to admit this state into union. The arguments and representations exhibited in my said letter to congress are equally applicable for the consideration of the several legislatures of the United States. This being premised, I proceed to propose an alliance and permanent confederation between the states of Connecticut and Vermont against the hostile attempt of British power, on such conditions as may be agreed upon for the mutual advantage and security of the liberty and independence of the two states respectively. Similar proposals are made to the legislature of Rhode Island and Providence Plantations by this government, and also a demand on the legislatures of the states of New York, New Hampshire, and Massachusetts Bay, to relinquish their claims of jurisdiction to Vermont, with proposals to unite with them in a like union.

The citizens of this state are of opinion that it is owing to the undue influence which those contiguous claiming states (to this territory,) have in congress that Vermont has hitherto been prevented from a union with the United States. This they consider the greatest injustice and ingratitude, as they have ever since the commencement of the present war been a frontier, in part, to every one of them, and in such circumstances have nothing better to expect from them at the conclusion of this war, than to be obliged to wage another war with them to protect their liberties against their exorbitant claims, or fall a prey to them, notwithstanding such a series of sufferings and beneficial service done to the United States in general, and to them in particular, in the course of this war. And although these considerations, abstracted from all others, are sufficiently discouraging, yet additional evils arise when we consider the force of the enemy in Canada; the probability of their being reinforced between this and the conclusion of the next campaign, together with their advantages of the navigation of the lakes, by which means they can suddenly bring their whole force into this state, which cannot fail to be their object next campaign, unless some measures be immediately adopted to prevent it, as the frontier settlements of the state of New York are already destroyed. In a word, their force will be so great that it will be out of the power of this state to form magazines and support a body of troops sufficient to withstand them, and the consequence must inevitably be either that the inhabitants of this state be sacrificed; or, 2dly, they must be obliged to retire into the interior parts of the United States for safety; or 3rdly, be under the disagreeable necessity of making the best terms with the British that may be in their power. Nearly the same would be the condition of either of the United States separately considered from their union, (as they would be unable to withstand the British power,) which may abundantly serve to evince that it is out of the power of Vermont to be further serviceable to them, unless they are admitted into the union.

I am, your excellency's most obedient,
and most humble servant, THOS. CHITTENDEN.

Copy attest, THOS. TOLMAN, *P. Sec'ty.*

His Excellency Governor Trumbull.

The foregoing shows that Gov. Chittenden addressed substantially the same letter to Rhode Island, a copy of which he transmitted to Gen. Washington Jan. 15 1781.[1] The responses of Connecticut and Rhode Island were as follows:

---

[1] *Vt. Hist. Soc. Collections*, Vol. II, p. 6.

Proceedings of the General Assembly of Connecticut, relative to the admission of Vermont, as a State, into the Union of the United States of America.[1]

At a General Assembly of the Governor and Company of the state of Connecticut, holden at Hartford (by special order of the Governor,) on the 21st day of February, Anno Domini 1781,—

Resolved by this Assembly, that the commissioners who are, or may be, appointed on the part of this state to meet the commissioners from the other three New England states, and the state of New York, in convention to be holden at Providence, at the call of his Excellency the Governor of Connecticut, be instructed, in addition to the commission already given them by this Assembly, to propose as a subject of consideration, in said convention, the request of the people calling themselves the State of Vermont, to be admitted into union and confederation with the thirteen United States of America, as a free and independent state, and report their doings, consultations and conclusions thereon, to this Assembly.

And it is further resolved, that His Excellency the Governor be, and he is hereby, desired, as soon as may be, to notify the several states expected to meet by their commissioners, in said convention, of the above resolution, in order that said states may, if they see proper, make similar enlargements of instructions to their commissioners; and His Excellency the Governor is further desired to make a call of said convention as early as possible. A true copy of record; examined by

George Wyllys, *Sec'ry.*

Resolution of the General Assembly for the State of Rhode Island and Providence Plantations, at a session holden on the third Monday in March 1781.[2]

It is voted and resolved, that the Honorable William West, Esq., William Bradford and Esek Hopkins, Esqs., be, and they are hereby, appointed a committee to meet the commissioners from the other New England states, and the state of New York, in convention, to be holden in Providence, on the 12th day of April next, for the purpose of consulting and devising ways and means that Congress may be invested with power to collect and raise a permanent fund for the paying, clothing and supporting the army, and for discharging the interest arising upon the debts which have been contracted; that the said committee be, and they are hereby fully empowered to consult, deliberate and advise with said convention, in all and every subject and matter which may be brought into contemplation, respecting the welfare of the United States or our allies; and in particular to take into consideration the subject-matter of the policy and justice of admitting into union and confederation with the thirteen United States of America, the people calling themselves the state of Vermont.

Provided, that nothing which shall be done in the said convention, in consequence of this appointment, be binding upon this state, until ratified by this Assembly.

---

[1] From the *Rhode Island Colonial Records*, 1780–1783, Vol. IX, p. 343.

[2] From the same, p. 365.

APPENDIX H.

THE SECOND UNION OF NEW-HAMPSHIRE TOWNS WITH VERMONT, AND UNION WITH PART OF NEW YORK, IN 1781.

THE action of Congress in June 1780, and the hearing and postponement in September, exasperated the Vermont government, and disheartened both the adherents to New York in Cumberland county, and the persons in eastern Vermont and western New Hampshire who favored an extension of the jurisdiction of New Hampshire over the whole of Vermont, or the establishment of a new state bounded by the Mason grant on the east and the main ridge of the Green Mountains on the west. The prime movers in a "plan," which resulted in annexing western New Hampshire and a large part of the north eastern section of New York to Vermont, were IRA ALLEN and LUKE KNOULTON. In Allen's *History*, immediately succeeding the last paragraph in his account in the preceding appendix,[1] he said:

A plan was then laid [September 1780,] between two persons at Philadelphia, to unite all parties in Vermont in a way that would be honourable to those who had been in favour of New York, and said sixteen towns, [which united with Vermont in 1778,] that would also justify the Legislature of Vermont, to effect which, measures were taken to induce some of the western members of the Council and Assembly of New Hampshire, who had exerted themselves to extend the jurisdictional claim of New Hampshire over the territory of Vermont, to write circular letters to convene a Convention at Walpole, which met in December 1780.[2]

Of the adherents to New York who made the earliest public movement, Oct. 31 1780, the first man named was LUKE KNOULTON, and he had for associates several of the leading supporters of New York in Cumberland county, as the following account, by B. H. HALL, of that convention, and of a second on the 8th of November, indicates:

---

[1] *Appendix G, ante*, p. 266.

[2] See *Vt. Hist. Soc. Collections*, Vol. I, p. 412. The Convention met on the 15th of November, instead of December.

On this occasion, Luke Knoulton, Hilkiah Grout, Oliver Lovell, Col. John Sergeants, Micah Townshend, Maj. Jonathan Hunt, Simon Stevens, Charles Phelps, Benjamin Henry, James Clay, Maj. Elkanah Day, Thomas Cutler, and Barzillai Rice, were appointed a committee to take into consideration the feasibility of a new government, and to meet such persons as should be authorized, to consult upon the same question by a convention or a committee of the people of Gloucester [Orange] county on the west, and Grafton county on the east side of Connecticut river. The design of Cumberland county in these proceedings was "to devise and carry into execution such measures as should be deemed best calculated to unite in one political body all the inhabitants from Mason's grant on the east to the height of land on the west side the said river."—The idea thus brought forward of establishing the western line of a new district at the ridge of the Green Mountains, manifested clearly the unwillingness of the New York adherents to acknowledge the jurisdiction of Vermont, provided they could ensure their own safety in any other way.[1]

Delegations from three counties having by previous agreement met on the 8th of November, at Charlestown, New Hampshire, measures were taken to learn the sentiments of the inhabitants residing in the towns included in the district which it was proposed to establish. Until the result of this inquiry should be declared, ultimate action was postponed. Desirous of engaging in the union, the towns in the county of Cheshire, New Hampshire, sent delegates to a meeting which was held at Walpole on the 15th of November.[2]

PROCEEDINGS OF THE CONVENTION AT WALPOLE, NOV. 15 and 16, 1780.[3]

At a CONVENTION of DELEGATES from the several towns in the County *of* Cheshire, *in the* State *of* New-Hampshire, *held at* Walpole, *in said county, on the* 15*th day of* November, *in the year of our Lord, one thousand seven hundred and eighty:*

VOTED, That *Dr. Page, Col. Hunt, Capt. Holmes, Daniel Jones, Esq.* and *Col. Bellows*, be a committee to confer with gentlemen from any parts of the territory, called the New-Hampshire grants, concerning the jurisdiction of the said grants, and to consider what is proper to be done by the inhabitants thereof, relative to their jurisdiction; that the same may be ascertained and established. Which committee, after due enquiry and consideration, report as follows, viz. The committee appointed by the convention, held at Walpole, November 15th, 1780, do report, that we have conferred with the several gentlemen present, who were committees from the different parts of the territory, called the New-Hampshire grants, viz. *Cumberland, Gloucester* and *Grafton* counties, and do find, that many matters lately agitated, with respect to the jurisdiction of the New-Hampshire grants, render a union of the inhabitants of that territory indispensably necessary. The said inhabitants

---

[1] True as this was, this and the three succeeding conventions were undoubtedly parts in "the plan" of Allen and Knoulton—parts assigned respectively to the adherents to New York, and the movers of the first union of New Hampshire towns with Vermont.

[2] *History of Eastern Vermont*, p. 401.

[3] Slade's *State Papers*, p. 126.

received the grants of their lands from the same jurisdiction, and settled them while a union was extant; which was an implicit engagement of authority, that it should be continued. But we were unjustly deprived of the advantages resulting from it, in the year 1764, by an arbitrary decree of Great Britain, to which we never acceded: which decree, however, cannot be esteemed efficacious, since the declaration of independence; it being one of those iniquitous measures, by which they were attempting to oppress the colonies; and for which we have since thrown off subjection. This being the case, the union re-exists. And shall we throw it off? God forbid. The situation of the territory aforesaid, by reason of their being a frontier, as well as many other matters, which are obvious, respecting commerce and transactions of a public nature, makes it expedient that they be united in all their interests, in order to make their efforts, in that quarter, against the common enemy, more vigorous and efficacious. In respect to government, great disadvantages may arise by a division. In that case, delinquents may easily evade the operations of justice, by passing from one state to another, and thereby be induced more readily to practice iniquity in that part where the body of inhabitants, and the principal traffick, center. And we imagine that a union of public interests is the only means by which the contentions and animosities, now subsisting among the inhabitants of the territory aforesaid, can be brought to a happy issue: for, so long as the course of justice is in different channels, where people are so nearly allied, disturbances will arise. From authentic information, we cannot but apprehend, that the state of New-Hampshire is greatly remiss, if not grossly negligent, (to call it by no harsher name) in trusting affairs of such great importance as the settlement of their western boundary, to a committee, some of whom, we conceive, would risk the loss of half the state, rather than New-Hampshire should extend their claim west of Connecticut river. And from the best authority that can be obtained, it appears that the agent of the state aforesaid is endeavouring to confirm a division of the grants, contrary to their true interests; which has given the people, on the grants, just occasion to rouse and exert themselves in support of an union of the whole. We, therefore, earnestly recommend, as the only means to obtain an union, preserve peace, harmony, and brotherly love, and the interest of the community in general, that a convention be called from every town from within the said grants, to be held at Charlestown, on the third Tuesday of January next, at one of the clock, in the afternoon; and that one or more members be appointed from each town, with proper instructions to unite in such measures as the majority shall judge most conducive to consolidate an union of the grants, and effect a final settlement of the line of jurisdiction.

B. Bellows,
S. Hunt,
D. Jones, } *Committee.*
L. Holmes,
W. Page,

In Convention, *at Walpole, November* 16*th*, 1780.

The above report being repeatedly read,—Voted,

That it be accepted; and a sufficient number of copies be printed and transmitted to the several towns on the New-Hampshire grants, on both sides of Connecticut river, for their notice, to appoint one or more members to attend the said general convention; which shall be deemed a sufficient notification. *By order of the Convention,*

Benjamin Bellows, *Chairman.*

A true Copy—Attest, Daniel Newcomb, *Clerk.*

Journal of the Convention of Delegates from Forty-Three Towns on the New Hampshire Grants, January 16, 1781.[1]

At a Convention of Members from forty-three Towns on the New Hampshire Grants begun and held at Charlestown, January 16th, 1781.

The Honorable Samuel Chase,[2] Esq; was chosen *Chairman* and Bezaleel Woodward,[2] Esq; *Clerk.*

Resolved, that General *Bellows,*[2] *Daniel Jones,*[2] Esq; Col. *Hunt,*[2] Mr. *Woodward,*[2] Col. *Bedel,*[2] Col. *Paine,*[2] Col. *Olcott,* Capt. *Curtiss,* Mr. *White,* Col. *Wells,* Mr. *Knoulton* and Mr. *Townsend* be a Committee to prepare matters necessary to be transacted by this Convention; and that they report the same with all conveuient speed.

January 18*th,* 10 *o'clock A. M.*

T H E Committee above named made report, which being read, is in the words following, Viz, Whereas the Governor of New Hampshire, before and after the close of the last war, did exercise jurisdiction over and grant the greatest part of the Lands within the territory commonly called the *New Hampshire Grants,* on both sides of Connecticut-River, to sundry companies of persons, principally inhabitants of New England; who offered to undertake, and carry into effect, settlements thereon, subject to the jurisdiction of the crown of Great-Britain, in connection with the colony of New Hampshire.

And whereas the said undertakers did undergo infinite hardships, toils and fatigues, in forming settlements in the several townships, on both sides of the river, agreeable to their engagements; induced by the happiness in prospect for themselves and posterity, resulting, in great measure, from an happy union of their settlements on the two sides of the river, under the same jurisdiction; the benefits of which had long been experienced in adjacent governments, and which were plighted to them by the circumstances and conditions under which they received and held their grants.

And whereas the King of Great-Britain did, in the year 1764, pass an arbitrary decree, that the said territory should be divided at Connecticut River, subjecting one part to the jurisdiction of his Governor of New-York, and continuing the other part under the jurisdiction of his Governor of New-Hampshire, whereby the said territory was divided without the consent or knowledge of the owners and proprietors, in violation of the royal engagements, and contrary to the true interest of the inhabitants; against which measure those most immediately affected, so soon as the matter came to their knowledge, did in the most humble, earnest and affecting manner remonstrate and petition; sent agents to Great-Britain to state before the King their grievances, and humbly interceded for redress; and at the same time took every prudent measure to obtain the interest of adjacent Colonies in their favor, especially that of New-Hampshire, from connection with which they had been separated.

And whereas the said connection rendered the government of New-Hampshire more extensive than the object of their first incorporation, viz. the Mason patent; which extension has ever been a source of uneasiness and discontent, to several persons of influence and importance in that government, and the Assembly of New-Hampshire therefore refused to use their influence in favor of a re-union of the grants, after the division of them by the decree in 1764, when applied to for that purpose, in behalf of the owners, proprietors and inhabitants of the said territory.

---

[1] From Henry B. Dawson's *Historical Magazine,* number for January, 1871—furnished by the late Capt. W. F. Goodwin, U. S. A.

[2] Of New Hampshire.

AND WHEREAS the obligations of the inhabitants of the said territory, as well as of all others in the United States, to allegiance and subordination to the crown of Great-Britain have ceased, on account of the series of unconstitutional and oppressive measures of that authority, towards the American plantations; and independence has therefore been declared by the inhabitants of the said grants, with the United States, whereby all those connections have ceased which resulted from, and were dependant on a subordination to Great-Britain. And as the said territory was never annexed by Charter to any one or more of the American colonies, nor otherwise connected, than by an order of the King to his Governors, to exercise authority there in behalf of the crown, and by a grant of the feoffees to claim a right to be continued in union with one another in matters of Government; the jurisdiction was of consequence, by the declaration of independence, transferred to the inhabitants; which they had good right to undertake and exercise, whenever they should see fit—Yet the said inhabitants, influenced by attachments to the different governments with which they had been connected (resulting from an habituated submission to despotic power) and not immediately attending to the singular circumstances, under which independence from the power of Great-Britain left them, did many of them passively submit to, and act with those governments, to which the King of Great-Britain had last annexed them; While on the other hand, a considerable part of the inhabitants of the said territory, influenced by uneasiness with the measures of those governments, and being early led to enquire into our peculiar situation (to which others were inattentive) did observe, and publish to the world, their views in respect to our independance; and in conformity thereto, broke off connection with the states of New-York and New-Hampshire,—And of those on the west side of the river, who had withdrawn connections from the state of New-York, viewing only the operation of independence from Great-Britain, in respect to themselves and not attending that the whole of the Grants were thereby placed in similar situation, did associate together, and set up a new and independent government.

AND WHEREAS as the states of New-York and New-Hampshire, influenced by the refusal of a respectable number of inhabitants of those parts of the Grants, which they severally claimed, to submitt to their respective jurisdictions, complained to the Congress of the United States, of measures taking by the said inhabitants in respect to their independency; and also, made known to Congress, that they had claims to the said territory: And as Congress, on the 24th of September, 1779, did resolve and publish, that they would take upon themselves a final settlement of the disputes respecting the said Grants, provided the states concerned should agree thereto; (and, among other things, recommended that no state should exercise jurisdiction over any of the inhabitants of the said district, except such as should profess allegiance to, and confess the jurisdiction of the same)—which was complied with by the states. And as sundry periods have elapsed, which Congress had appointed for a decision of the said matter, in controversy, without anything material being transacted on the subject; and as, notwithstanding the claim of New-Hampshire to the whole of the Grants, the evident object of both states, by their agents at Congress, has of late been to establish a division at the river, contrary to the true interest of the inhabitants; as they would thereby be deprived of those advantages, in respect to commerce, and transactions of a public nature, which would naturally result from that union of the two sides of the river, which they had warrant to expect, and have right to demand, from the nature, tenor, and circumstances of the grants which they hold.

AND WHEREAS a considerable part of the inhabitants on the said territory, having disavowed connection with any state already formed, have subsisted for some time without any regular form of government, and have been destitute of civil regulations, for want of which they are reduced to lamentable circumstances; and as they are thereby prevented, in a great degree, from performing that part in the present contest with Great-Britain, which might otherwise reasonably be expected, and which might be of essential service in the grand dispute:—And as the contiguity of the said Grants to the province of Canada, renders the inhabitants a frontier to the New-England states; and as the parliament of Great-Britain have done what in them lies, towards annexing the greater part of the said territory to the province of Canada, by the act commonly called the *Quebec Bill;* for the purpose of obtaining an establishment whereof, it is to be expected they will further employ their force, in attempting the reduction of the inhabitants, or destruction of them and their property. And as the British forces, in conjunction with their savage allies, have of late begun a new scene of devastation among us, by burning some of our towns, and carrying the peaceable inhabitants into captivity: and it is to be expected that great part of the said territory will be treated in the same manner, unless vigorous measures are taken to prevent them: — And as there is no military force employed by the continent, or any of the states, for our defence, which renders an union without delay absolutely necessary, or great numbers will immediately abandon their habitations, which will give such advantage to the cause of Britain, and so open and extend this frontier, that a much greater force will then be necessary for its defence:—And as nothing considerable can be done by the inhabitants of the said territory, tending to their own defence, until they are firmly united for that purpose, and in measures of government.

THIS CONVENTION THEREFORE, taking the aforesaid matters into their most serious consideration, and being duly authorized by their constituents, the inhabitants of the said territory, do hereby publish and declare, that notwithstanding all the unjust measures which have been, or may be, taken to divide us, the right of union still remains to the inhabitants of the said territory, which we are determined to maintain and support; and bind ourselves *by the ties of virtue and honor*, as we are already bound by the ties of interest, to unite in all such lawful measures as the majority of the representative body of the inhabitants of said territory, duly convened, or such as they may appoint under them, shall agree upon, to maintain and support a union of the inhabitants on the whole of the said Grants; *holding ourselves in duty bound to abide the decisions of Congress on the subject, when the matter shall be properly stated before them, and their resolutions thereon be obtained.*

As the primary object of this Convention is, that an union of the whole of the Grants be formed and consolidated, upon principles that the majority think proper; and as a considerable part of the said Grants are represented in the state of Vermont,

RESOLVED, That a Committee be chosen to confer with the said Assembly, at their next session, on the subject of said union; and invite them to join in measures which may be most conducive to obtain the object proposed.

RESOLVED, That the proceedings of this Convention be laid before the several towns on the Grants, for their approbation; recommending that those towns which concur in the measures, and have no representatives or delegates in this Convention, appoint members for that purpose; and that each and every town impower their members, to join with the representatives of other towns on the Grants, who shall agree to unite together, in all such measures as shall be necessary for our internal regulations and defence.

Which declaration and resolutions having been repeatedly read, and maturely considered, the question was put, whether this Convention do agree with their Committee in their said report?—which was carried in the affirmative.

Whereupon

RESOLVED, That Dr. William Page, Daniel Jones, Esq; and Mr. Elijah Frink, of the county of Cheshire; Luke Knoulton, Micah Townsend, and John Bridgman, Esqs. of the county of Cumberland; Col. Peter Olcott, Noah White, Esq; and Capt. John Strong, of the county of Gloucester; and Col. Paine, Bezaleel Woodward, Esq; and Mr. Davenport Phelps, of the county of Grafton, be a Committee to confer with the Assembly of Vermont, agreeable to the foregoing resolutions.

RESOLVED, That the proceedings of this Convention be printed, and one copy thereof transmitted to each town on the Grants; and that Maj. Day, Mr. Townsend, and Mr. Lovel, be a Committee for that purpose.

RESOLVED, That this Convention do adjourn, to meet at the meeting House in Cornish, on the first Wednesday in February next, at one of the clock in the afternoon.[1]

[PROTEST OF A MINORITY OF THE DELEGATES.]

" *In Convention at Charlestown, January* 18, 1781.

"WE the subscribers, delegates from the several towns to which our " names are affixed, wishing for, and endeavoring to form a union of the " New-Hampshire Grants on both sides of Connecticut River, and con- " tented that they be annexed to New Hampshire, or be a seperate state, " as Congress may judge proper; but thinking ourselves not authorized " by our constituents to unite with the said Grants, in the method re- " solved by the said Convention; and being of opinion that their pro- " ceedings have a tendency to weaken the reins of government—to re- " tard the exertions of those who are engaged to oppose the public " enemy—to introduce irregularity and disorder in the county of Chesh- " ire, and not conducive to the end proposed; think it our duty to protest " against the proceedings of said Convention.

" *Winchester*,	SAMUEL ASHLEY, REUBEN ALEXANDER.
" *Walpole*,[2]	BENJAMIN BELLOWS.
" *Charlestown*,[3]	SAMUEL HUNT.
" *Richmond*,	OLIVER CAPRON.
" *Keene*,	TIMOTHY ELLIS, DANIEL NEWCOMB.
" *Alstead*,	NATHANIEL S. PRENTICE.[4]
" *Claremont*,	OLIVER ASHLEY, MATTHIAS STONE.[4]
" *Newport*,	BENJAMIN GILES."[4]

Extract from the Minutes. BEZA. WOODWARD, *Clerk*.

---

[1] The proceedings of the adjourned session of the Convention, so far as known, appear in the record of the Vermont Assembly, *post.*

[2] There were two members attending from Walpole.—W. F. G.

[3] Three members attended from Charlestown, two of whom agreed to the Report of the Committee.—W. F. G.

[4] These gentlemen were all members of the Vermont Assembly after the union. The towns named in this protest were all in New Hampshire, and the signers of the protest were, at its date, members of the Assembly of that state.

Secret History of the Charlestown Convention, &c., by Ira Allen.[1]

The Governor and Council appointed Colonel Ira Allen to repair to Charlestown to meet that Convention, and to take such measures as his prudence should dictate, and which might be conducive to the interest of the State. Mr. Allen took credentials from Sunderland, as a member, to meet the Convention, from that town, agreeable to invitation; before he arrived, the Convention had been in session two days, and had appointed a Committee to state the business of their meeting. Forty-three towns were represented in the Convention; twelve of those representatives were members of the Council and Assembly of New Hampshire. Mr. Allen did not take a seat as a member of the Convention, nor produce his credentials. At length the Committee reported to unite all the New Hampshire grants to New Hampshire, which was adopted by a great majority, and went in fact to annihilate the State of Vermont. Mr. Allen informed some confidential persons, that the Governor, Council, and some other leading characters, on the west side of the Green Mountains, were for extending their claim of jurisdiction to the Mason line; and that if the Convention would take proper measures the Legislature of Vermont would extend their claim at their adjourned term in February, 1781; and that he was authorized to give such assurance.

A motion was made and carried, to consider the report, and re-commit it to the committee, to be corrected and fitted for the press, as it would be a matter of public notoriety, and to lay it again before the Convention next morning. The friends of New Hampshire were much pleased with their success, and well enjoyed the night; but the scene changed the next morning, and the committee reversed their report, and reported to unite all the territory of New Hampshire, west of Mason's east line, extending to Connecticut river, with the State of Vermont; and which report was accepted by a great majority of the Convention, it being principally opposed by twelve members of the Counucil and Assembly of New Hampshire, who, thereupon, withdrew to remonstrate against the proceeding.

This bare-faced conduct of the members of the Legislature disclosed their intention at once, and furnished Vermont with fair pretensions to extend her jurisdiction on grounds of similar policy and self-preservation.

The Convention then appointed a Committee to confer with the Legislature of Vermont at their next term, and adjourned to meet at Cornish (only three miles from Windsor, the place of session of the Legislature of Vermont, agreeable to adjournment) on the same day with them.

On February 10th, the Committee informed the Assembly, then sitting at Windsor, that "the Convention of the New Hampshire towns was desirous of being united with Vermont, in one separate independent Government, upon such principles as should be mutually thought the most equitable and beneficial to the whole." In consequence of this application, the Legislature resolved, on February 14th, that "in order to quiet the present disturbances on the two sides of the river (Connecticut) and the better to enable the inhabitants on the two sides of said river to defend their frontier, the Legislature of this State do lay a *jurisdictional claim* to all the lands whatever, east of Connecticut river, north of Massachusetts, west of the Mason line, and south of latitude 45°; and that they do not exercise jurisdiction for the time being."

---

[1] From Ira Allen's *History*, in *Vt. Historical Society Collections*, Vol. I, pp. 413, 414.

The Convention of the New Hampshire towns was then sitting at Cornish, on the opposite side of the river; and on February 22d, the articles of union were agreed upon, and confirmed; nevertheless, the right of dissolving the union of the district was retained by the State of Vermont.

THE JOINT ACTION OF THE CHARLESTOWN CONVENTION AND THE GENERAL ASSEMBLY OF VERMONT, ON THE UNIONS, FEBRUARY 1781.[1]

THURSDAY, Feby. 8th 1781.

A letter signed "Elisha Payne Chairman" of the Convention [the adjourned Charlestown Convention then sitting at Cornish,] directed to the "Honble Thomas Porter Esqr. Speaker of the Assembly of the State of Vermont," requesting to be heard on the business of their appointment—and likewise enclosing sundry resolutions of a Convention of members from forty-three towns in the New Hampshire Grants began and held at Charlestown Jany. 16th 1781," was read and [it was]

Resolved that the Governor & Council be requested to attend this House in a Committee of the whole to confer together before the said Committee be heard.

The Governor & Council attended accordingly and [both Houses] Resolved themselves into a Committee of the whole.

The Comtee of the whole having adjourned, the House formed and adjourned.

The committee of the whole met on the 9th, 10th and 12th. The proceedings of the day last named were recorded in the Assembly journal of the 14th as follows:

STATE OF VERMONT, Windsor Feby. 12th 1781.

Agreeable to the order of the day, the Governor, Council and House of Representatives met, and formed into a Committee of the whole, for the purpose of taking into consideration the matter of laying a jurisdictional claim east and west—His Excellency Thos. Chittenden Esqr. in the Chair. After some debate, a Committee of seven were appointed to prepare a Report, to be made to this Committee, which Report was made as follows, viz. [on the 14th:]

To the grand Committee consisting of his Excellency the Governor the honble Council and House of Representatives—

Your Committee to whom was refered the several papers from the Committee of the Convention at Cornish and also the requests of the inhabitants living north of a line being extended from the north line of the Massachusetts to Hudsons River and east of the same River and South of Latitude forty five beg leave to Report—viz.—

That whereas the district of country formerly known by the name of the New Hampshire Grants was peopled in consequence of grants of lands from New Hampshire and whereas the former government of New York did by cunning in the year 1764 obtain a Royal order to exercise jurisdiction to the west bank of Connecticut River which was against the consent of the people of said district. New York proceeded to grant subsequent pattents, erect courts, issue writs of ejectment, possession &c. in prejudice to the first grantees and occupants; the inhabitants necessitated to it declared a defensive war against the government of New York and that government made acts of outlawry against said inhabitants and warlike preparations was making on both

---

[1] Extracts from the Ms. *Assembly Journal*, Vol. I.

sides. In the interim the people governed themselves by conventions who at several times made application to New Hampshire to exert themselves to obtain jurisdiction who by a Proclamation &c. wholly rejected any such connections. Thus stood the case at the grand æra of American Independence when in Kingly governments all jurisdiction and jurisdictional lines ceased and all governmental powers devolved on the people, when they, continuing said Convention, emerged into independence, declaring themselves on the fifteenth day of Jan$^{y.}$ 1777 to be a sovereign, free and independent people—and

Whereas the general court of New Hampshire did on the 19th day of July 1777, by a letter signed "Meshech Weare President" directed to "Ira Allen Esq$^{r.}$ Secretary of the State of Vermont," acknowledge the independence of this State, and whereas on the representation of a Committee inhabiting several towns east of and contigious to Connecticut River made to the Assembly of this State at their Session in March 1778 that a number of towns east of and adjoining to said River were unconnected with any State with regard to their civil police, this State upon said Representation did admit sixteen towns east of said River to Union and extended jurisdiction over them--and

Whereas the General Court of New Hampshire did, by their letter dated Aug$^{t.}$ 22$^{d.}$ 1778 signed "Meshech Weare President of the Council of New Hampshire" directed "To the hon$^{ble.}$ Tho$^{s.}$ Chittenden Esq$^{r.}$" demand of the State of Vermont a surrendery of their jurisdiction east of said River which will appear in the following paragraph in said letter viz—"I beseech you Sir for the sake of the people over whom you "preside and the [said] people for the sake of their future peace and "tranquility to relinquish every connection as a political body with the "towns east of Connecticut river who are members of the State of New "Hampshire entitled to the same privileges as the other people of the "said State from which there never has been any attempt to restrain "them."—The Legislature of Vermont at their session in Feb$^{y.}$ 1779 on the reception of President Weares said letter, considering their territory to be larger and more fertile than that of New Hampshire allowing [including] the latter said sixteen towns east of said River and being unwilling to have a controversy with a neighbouring State, did close with the demand of New Hampshire and relinquished jurisdiction east of said Connecticut River. In this the minds of the two governments met and virtually settled upon the River as the boundary line between the respective States. An agent was then appointed to transact the dissolution of said Union to the General Court of New Hampshire who on his arrival there found, after delivering his message, that there was a plan on foot for laying a jurisdictional claim to the territory of Vermont under pretext of friendship and to baffle the claims of New York. Said agent made strenuous efforts against such claims being laid, arguing that it could not be of much service to Vermont as she had little to fear from New York, and the further consideration was postponed to their next Session. In the interim an agent was again sent to attend said General Court with a letter from the Governor of this State requesting the Legislature of New Hampshire in the most urgent manner not to lay claim to this State. After a hearing before both houses and the most pressing arguments used, the legislature did insist that they would do Vermont a favour, and accordingly laid their claim and directed their agents to lay said claims at Congress, which together with the claims of the neighbouring States has prevented this State from obtaining a seat in Congress.[1]

---

[1] Ira Allen was the agent of Vermont on both occasions. For his account, see Vol. I, pp. 407–409.

It is to be here observed that New Hampshire have from the time of laying her aforesaid claim endeavoured to support internal broils in the eastern part of this State contigious to Connecticut River. Some gentlemen inhabitants of the County of Cheshire, that are or have been members of the General Court of New Hampshire, not long since in Convention when fatal necessity obliged them to it, publickly declared that their intentions were to unite the whole of the grants (meaning Vermont) to N. Hampshire.—And whereas Sundry applications have been made by the people inhabiting west of the line known by the name of the Mason line, and east of Connecticut river, to unite with this State in one distinct government—Their last application is in the words following viz—

"*To the hon*ble *the Gen*l. *Assembly of the State of Vermont now sitting in* "*Windsor.*"

"The Committee appointed by the Convention holden at Charlestown "the 16th of Jany. last to confer with the Assembly of said State beg "leave to inform that the Convention are desirous of being united with "the State before mentioned in one seperate independent government "upon such principles as shall be mutually thought the most equitable "and beneficial for the whole, desiring an answer as soon as may be.

"By order of the Committee. ELISHA PAYNE.

"Windsor Feby. 10th 1781."

Therefore your Committee do recommend, in order to quiet the present disturbances on the two sides of the River and the better to enable the inhabitants on the two sides of said River to defend the frontiers, that the Legislature of this State do lay a jurisdictional claim to all the lands situate east of Connecticut River north of the Massachusetts and South of latitude 45—and that they do not exercise jurisdiction for the time being.

[ON THE WESTERN UNION.]

Whereas the government of New York have for more than sixteen years last past made use of every art and cunning in their power to usurp the rights and properties of the people of this State; while every measure hitherto adopted has proved abortive for settling a controversy of such magnitude, so necessary to be settled for the peace and welfare of the United States at this critical period, the unfortunate situation of this State being that of having an extensive frontier of more than one hundred miles in length to defend against the British invasion from the Province of Quebeck, by the avaricious and ambitious claims of the neighbouring governments and by the powers assumed over them by Congress, [this State has] have at several times been embarrassed in raising men and money for the defence of her frontiers; and by resolutions of Congress, obtained by the claiming governments, notwithstanding the brave exertions of this State in the Bennington Battle &c., every article belonging to the Continent has been called for and ordered out of the State even to pick-axes and spades at a time when the State was erecting a new line of forts on her frontiers, at which time the State of New York evacuated their fort at Skeensborough [now Whitehall,] which necessitated the people [1] to petition this State for protection, when this State reinforced her guards and directed her scouts to cover said people.

---

[1] The people of that part of New York, or the part covered by the supposed government of Skene, mentioned in the next section.

And whereas it appears by the best accounts hitherto obtained that there was a government established by the Court of Great Britain before the æra of American independence, including all the lands this State at present exercises jurisdiction over, as also a much greater western extent, over which Governor Philip Skene was to have presided, which overturns the claims of New York on their own stating [1]—

And whereas it appears that the government of New York is still determined to do everything in her power to embarrass and overturn the jurisdiction of this State, and have made no answer to Governor Chittenden's letter of the 22d Novr. last past which was sent to the Legislature of New York demanding of them to relinquish their claim of jurisdiction to this State and inviting them to join in the mutual defence of the frontiers of the two States against British invasion from the Province of Quebec—

Therefore your Committee do recommend that the Legislature of this State do lay a jurisdictional claim to all the land situate north of the north line of the State of Massachusetts and extending the same to Hudson's River the east of the center of the deepest channel of said River to the head thereof, from thence east of a north line being extended to latitude 45 and south of said line, including all the lands and waters to the place where this State now exercises jurisdiction—and not to exercise jurisdiction for the time being.

By order, JOSEPH BOWKER, *Chairman.*

Windsor Feby. 14th. 1781.

IN COMMITTEE OF THE WHOLE, Feby. 14th 1781.

The aforesaid Report was read and accepted.

Attest, ROS. HOPKINS, *Clerk.*

[IN GENERAL ASSEMBLY, Feb. 14, 1781.]

The aforesaid Report was read and accepted, and thereupon

Resolved that this state have and do hereby lay a jurisdictional claim to all the lands and waters described in the aforesaid Report.

Resolved that a Committee of five be appointed to join a Committee from the Council for the purpose of waiting upon the Committee appointed by a Convention held at Charlestown with the Report of the Committee of both houses upon the subject of jurisdictional claims and passed the house this day.

The members chosen Mr. Harris [Edward of Halifax,] Mr. Strong [Col. John of Dorset,] Mr. Pearl [Col. Stephen of Rupert,] Mr. Walbridge [Col. Ebenezer of Bennington,] and Mr. Murdock [Major Thomas of Norwich.] [2]

IN GENERAL ASSEMBLY, Feby. 15th. 1781.

A request from the Convention was delivered to this House by their Committee, and

Resolved that a Committee of three to join a Committee from the Council be appointed to prepare an answer to the aforesaid request of the Convention now sitting at Cornish—and report to this House as soon as may be. The members chosen Mr. Walbridge, Mr. A. Robinson [Amos of Hartford,] and Mr. Webb [Joshua of Rockingham.] [3]

---

[1] See *ante*, p. 239, note.

[2] Three Councillors were joined the same day—Messrs. Allen, Emmons, and Fassett.

[3] The Councillors joined were Messrs. Allen and Brownson.

Resolved that the Committee from the Convention be informed that it is not likely that an answer to their request can be given until tomorrow morning 9 °Clock.

Resolved that the Report of the Committee of the whole which passed this House yesterday respecting jurisdictional claims be referred until tomorrow morning for further consideration.

FRIDAY, Feby. 16th. 1781.

The Committee to whom was refered the request of the Convention now sitting at Cornish &c. brought in the following Report viz.

That this Assembly is willing to receive the inhabitants of the New Hampshire Grants east of Connecticut River and west of the Mason line into union with this State if we can agree on terms that shall be safe for this State and beneficial for the whole.

The reason why some public papers was not delivered to the Committee of said Convention as agreed upon are—that the bill was long and took longer to copy it than was expected, that the appointment of the Committee happened to be laid aside among other papers and could not be found till 12 oClock, that it was expected that Doct^r. Page would have waited at Windsor till the copies were ready, that about one oClock the copies were offered to him—and he did not take them.

P^r. order, TIM^O. BROWNSON, *Ch^m.*

The aforesaid Report was read and accepted and

Resolved that a Committee of two to join a Committee from the Council be appointed to wait on the Cornish Convention with the aforesaid Report. The members chosen M^r. Walbridge and M^r. E. Smith [Capt. Elihu of Clarendon.][1]

After the intervention of other business the journal proceeded as follows:

A Resolution from the Convention passed this day was delivered to this House by a Committee appointed by said Convention for the purpose mentioned in the said Resolve; and thereupon,

Resolved, that a Committee of nine to join a Committee from the Council be appointed to confer with the said Committee from the Convention according to said Resolve and make Report of their proceedings as soon as may be.—The members chosen Col^o. Strong, M^r. E. Smith, M^r. Walbridge, M^r. S. Robinson [Samuel of Bennington,] M^r. Murdock, M^r. Webb, M^r. M. Powell [Martin of Manchester,] M^r. Harris, and M^r. Whipple [Benjamin of Rutland.][2]

The following, from Slade's *State Papers*, embraces details of the negotiation between the committees of the Convention and the Legislature, and the remaining action of the latter as extracted from the journals of the Assembly and Council and certified by their recording officers for publication.

" *Articles of Union, agreed upon between the Committee of the Legislature of the State of* VERMONT, *and the Committee of the Convention of the New-Hampshire Grants, at Windsor, in Feb.* 1781.

ARTICLE 1. That the Constitution of said state be adopted as it now stands, subject to a revision, when the people, at large, shall judge proper.

---

[1] Councillor Allen was joined.

[2] Councillors Allen, Fassett, Spooner, and Emmons were joined.

ANSWER—We cannot agree to a revision of the Constitution, in any other way than is pointed out therein.

REPLY—The answer of the committee of the Legislature to our first article, not objected to.

ART. 2. That so soon as the circumstances of the state shall admit, the Legislature of the state shall apply to the Congress of the United States, to be admitted into confederation with them.

ANSWER—Agreed to.

ART. 3. That no farther grants of land shall be made by the Legislature of Vermont, until the towns included in the Union have opportunity to be represented in the Assembly.

ANSWER—Not admissible.

REPLY—Agreed to omit the third article, in confidence the Assembly will act on principles of honor, in respect to it.

ART. 4. That all expences of the several towns, non-represented in the Legislature of Vermont, and those which shall be admitted into the Union, which shall have accrued in respect to the war, be, at some future period, properly adjusted, and that the whole be at equitable charge therein.

ANSWER—Admitted, on condition the losses of the suffering inhabitants of this state, be included.

ART. 5. That a general and full act of oblivion be passed for the persons who, on the first day of October last, professed themselves subjects of the state of New-York: and that all judgments for fines, forfeitures, &c. against any, or either of the said persons, for opposing the authority of the state of Vermont, be annulled; and that no judgments be, hereafter, rendered against any of the said persons for offences heretofore committed against said state.

ANSWER—Agreed to.

ART. 6. That no civil suits shall hereafter be maintained against any, or either, of the said persons, for trespasses, heretofore committed by them, against any of the officers of the said state or their assistants.

ANSWER.—Agreed to.

ART. 7. That where unappropriated lands were granted by the late government of New-York, antecedent to 1st of September, 1775, the property of such grantees, now residing upon the New-Hampshire grants, shall be secured to them, free from expence; and where the same, or any part thereof, has already been granted by this state, compensation in value, shall be made in other unappropriated lands, free from expence.

ANSWER.—Not agreed to.—Whatever compensation of that kind is made, it must be done on application to the Legislature, according to equity, arising out of each particular case.

A Message from Committee of Convention to Committee of the Legislature.

In order that the committee of Convention may the better determine on articles necessary to be proposed, respecting the regulation of Militia, present defence, &c. we would request the committee of the Legislature of Vermont to suggest to us their ideas in respect to the time and manner, in which the Union shall be completed, in case other articles can be mutually agreed on; and wish for an answer, before we proceed further.
E. PAYNE, *for the Committee.*

To the honorable the Committee of the Legislature.
Saturday, 12 o'clock, February 17th, 1781.

The answer of the Committee of the Legislature to the foregoing Message.

The committee are of opinion that, if articles of Union are fully agreed on, it ought to be completed, at farthest, by the first Wednesday of April next; and that the manner be as follows, viz.

The Legislature shall call on all the towns, in the state of Vermont, and also on all the towns on the New-Hampshire grants, east of Connecticut river, to give their sentiments relative to the Union's taking place, as soon as may be; and that the votes of each town be returned to the assembly, at their adjourned session, on the first Wednesday of April next; and, on condition that two thirds of the towns in the state of Vermont, at a legal town meeting, vote for the union, and also, two thirds of the towns, on the New-Hampshire grants, east of Connecticut river; at the same time, those towns that vote for the Union (who are not represented) be directed by the Legislature, to choose members to sit in the assembly, who will be admitted, in case the Union is completed as aforesaid. By order. I. ALLEN, *Clerk.*

To the honorable the Committee of Convention.
Saturday, 2 o'clock, February 17th, 1781.

The Reply of the Committee of the Convention, to the above Answer of the Committee of the Legislature.

In order to facilitate the raising and subsisting men for the present defence, according to the act of the Legislature of Vermont, for that purpose, the committee of Convention concur with the proposals of the honorable committee of that Legislature, in respect to the time and manner of completing the Union, with the following explanations and alterations, viz.

1. That those towns only, who make returns, be reckoned in computing the proportion.

2. That an extent of only those towns, east of the river, which are within about twenty miles of it, be referred to.

3. That the towns, not represented in Assembly, shall be immediately called on to elect members to take their seats in Assembly, on the said first Wednesday of April next, in case the Union shall be concurred in by a major part of the towns who act on the matter; which will, doubtless, include two thirds of the inhabitants.

E. PAYNE, *for the Committee.*

To the honorable Committee of the Legislature.
Tuesday, 10 o'clock, A. M. February 20th, 1781.

The Assembly's committee give for answer to the committee of Convention, to their proposed explanation and alteration of the proposals of this committee, as to the manner and time of completing the Union:—

ART. 1. Agreed to.

ART. 2. Agreed to.

ART. 3. That the towns, proposed to be in Union, be immediately called on to choose members to sit in Assembly, on the first Wednesday in April next, in case the Union shall be concurred to, by a major part of the towns in this state, and two thirds of the towns, east of, and within about twenty miles of Connecticut river.

By order, J. FASSETT, *Chairman.*

To the honorable Committee of Convention.
Tuesday, 3 o'clock, February 20th, 1781.

ART. 8. Proposed by the Committee of Convention.

That wherever persons, who professed themselves subjects of New-York, have heretofore been fourfolded, for not giving in their list to the assessors, or if such cases shall happen before the approbation of the several articles of Union by the Assembly and Convention, respectively, the fourfold shall be relinquished, upon the party's giving in his list to the assessors.

ANSWER.—Agreed to.

ART. 9. That wherever property has been taken, under the authority of Vermont, or shall be taken, before the several articles of Union shall be ratified by the Assembly and Convention, respectively, from any of the persons in the county of Cumberland, who, at, or before, the time of such taking, professed themselves subjects of New-York, for fines, forfeitures, &c. credit shall be given to the persons aforesaid, for the full value of such property, in future military services.

ANSWER.—Not agreed to, in the extensive sense that it may be taken in; yet, it is expected that whatever personal service has been done, or fines, will be duly considered.

ART. 10. That all actions, pending in any court in the counties of Cheshire and Grafton, shall be transferred in the situation they shall be in, at the time of completing the Union, to Courts to be then, forthwith, erected, under the authority of Vermont, without cost to the parties, other than would have accrued, had they been terminated in Courts under the jurisdiction of New-Hampshire.

ANSWER.—Agreed to.

ART. 11. That those towns, east of the river, who have paid their proportion, or any part thereof, of the sixty million of dollars, apportioned to New-Hampshire, shall have credit for what they have severally paid to the treasury of said state, in case Vermont, at any future period, shall have to pay their proportion of the Continental assessment for the money emitted by Congress.

ANSWER.—Answered in the answer to the fourth article.

A Message from the Committee of the Convention, to the Committee of the Legislature.

The Committee of Convention beg leave to inform the Committee of the Legislature of Vermont, that they have, at present, no additional articles, and agree to wave any further objections to answers received to those already proposed, and wish to receive whatever the Legislature's Committee have to add, on the treaty. E. PAYNE, *for the Committee.*

The honorable Committee of Legislature.
Tuesday, 5 o'clock, P. M. February 20th, 1781.

A Message from the Committee of the Legislature to the Committee of Convention.

As no further proposals are to be made by the Convention's Committee, at present, the Assembly's Committee propose the following articles, as really necessary for the peace and well being of this state, and the United States.

ART. 1. That the independence of the state of Vermont be held sacred; and that no member of the Legislature shall give his vote or otherwise use endeavors to obtain any act or resolution of Assembly, which shall endanger the existence, independence or well being of the state, by referring its independence to the arbitrament of any power.

ART. 2. That whenever this state becomes united with the American States, and there shall then be any dispute between this and either of the United States, respecting boundary lines, the Legislature of this state will then (as they have ever proposed) submit to Congress, or such other tribunal as may be mutually agreed on, the settlement of any such disputes. By order, J. FASSETT, *Chairman.*

The honourable Committee of Convention.
Wednesday, 11 o'clock, A. M. February 21st, 1781.

A Message from the Committee of Convention, to the Committee of the Legislature.

The Committee of Convention agree to article first and second of the proposals of the Committee of the Legislature of Vermont.

E. PAYNE, *for the Committee.*

Wednesday, 12 o'clock, February 21st, 1781.

By order, JOHN FASSETT,
Chairman of the Committee of the Legislature.
ELISHA PAYNE,
for the Committee of Convention.

The Committees of Legislature and Convention agree to recommend that the assembly of Vermont adjourn to the first Wednesday in April next, then to meet, at Windsor: and that the people, in the several towns proposed to be united, on both sides of the river, be requested to express and make return, at that time, of the sense of the towns in respect to a completion of the Union; and that those towns who agree to the Union, on either side of the river, who are not duly represented in the assembly, be requested to appoint members to attend the assembly, at the proposed adjournment; and that the constable or selectmen be requested to warn meetings of the inhabitants of such towns, seasonably for that purpose. JOHN FASSETT,
Chairman of the Committee of the Legislature.
ELISHA PAYNE,
for the Committee of Convention.

WINDSOR, February 21st, 1781."

Proceedings of the Legislature of Vermont and the Convention on the foregoing articles.

STATE OF VERMONT, IN GENERAL ASSEMBLY, February 22d, 1781.

The aforesaid report was read and accepted; and

Resolved, That the articles of Union agreed to, and proposed, by the Committee of this Legislature, to the Committee of the Convention, be and are hereby confirmed; and this Assembly do pledge the faith of this state, that said articles be held sacred. Attest, ROS. HOPKINS, *Clerk.*

IN COUNCIL, February 22d, 1781.

Read and concurred. THOS. TOLMAN, *Sec'ry pro tem.*

IN CONVENTION at Cornish, February 22d, 1781.

The foregoing articles and recommendation were read and agreed to.

SAMUEL CHASE, *Chairman.*

IN GENERAL ASSEMBLY, Thursday Feb$^{y.}$ 22$^{d.}$ 1781.[1]

A Resolve of the Convention of this day's date appointing a Committee to deliver the articles of Union to this House for their approbation and ratification was read and

Resolved that a Committee of three be appointed to wait on the Convention with the Articles of Union that have passed this House and likewise the articles that have passed the Convention which are ratified by this Legislature; and bring back the original Articles that have passed this House when ratified by the Convention.—The members chosen M$^{r.}$ Bartlet [Capt. Samuel of Sunderland,] M$^{r.}$ Pearl and M$^{r.}$ Burton [Capt. Elisha of Norwich.][2]

---

[1] From the manuscript *Assembly Journal*, Vol. I.

[2] The purpose of this resolution seems to have been to preserve a copy of the ratified articles. This committee made no formal report, but its duty was performed, as the published articles indicate.

FRIDAY Feb$^{y.}$ 23$^{d.}$ 1781.

Resolved that Ezra Styles [Stiles] Esq$^{r.}$ be and he is hereby appointed and impowered to get the several Acts and Articles of Union that have passed this session printed and forward the same to Martin Powel Esq$^{r.}$ of Manchester in the County of Bennington, Sol$^{o.}$ Bingham Esq$^{r.}$ of Tinmouth in the County of Rutland, Briant Brown Esq$^{r.}$ of Windsor in the County of Windsor, Tim$^{o.}$ Bartholomew Esq$^{r.}$ of Thetford in the County of Orange and Nath$^{l.}$ Robinson Esq$^{r.}$ of Westminster in the County of Windham, who are hereby requested to forward them to the several towns in their several Counties as soon as may be.

Whereas there are several towns unrepresented in this Assembly through neglect of the proper officers for warning freemens meetings or some other reasons which does by no means interfere with their right of Representation; and

Whereas there is a Union formed or about to be formed between this State and the New-Hampshire grants east of Connecticut River and in case that Union proves to be agreeable to the people it will be necessary for them towns to be represented in this Assembly in their next Session —Therefore

Resolved that the respective Constables of such towns in the west and east side of Connecticut River, or the Selectmen where there are no Constables, be and they are hereby impowered and desired to warn the freemen in their respective towns to meet at some convenient place in such town at least four days before the next Session of this Assembly for the purpose of chosing a Representative or Representatives for such town, and it shall be the duty of the freemen then and there to attend and proceed to elect a Representative or Representatives according to law, and the Representatives on the Grants east of Connecticut River shall be fairly intitled to seats in this Assembly on the said Unions appearing to be agreeable to the people according as is proposed in the Articles of said Union.[1]

Resolved that this Assembly be and is hereby adjourned until the first Wednesday of April next then to meet at Bennington.

The General Assembly met at Windsor, (not at Bennington, as per entry in the Assembly journal of the adjournment of the February session,) on Wednesday the 4th of April, but a quorum did not attend until the afternoon of the 5th. The record of the 5th and 6th gives the completion of the eastern union as follows:

THURSDAY, 2 o'clock, P. M. April 5^{th,} 1781.

The following was delivered the Speaker by the Committee appointed for that purpose, viz.

"IN CONVENTION at Cornish, Thursday, April 5^{th,} 1781.

"*Voted*, That a committee of three be appointed to wait on the Assembly of Vermont, now sitting at Windsor, to inform them of the state of the returns from the towns on the east side of Connecticut River and that the way is clear on our part for the proposed union agreeable to the articles of the treaty, and to Request information whether the Assembly are ready to receive the members returned to sit in the Assembly, on the unions taking place. The Committee chosen, Col$^{o.}$ Payne, M$^{r.}$ Woodward and Doct. Page.—Extract from the Minutes.

"BEZA. WOODWARD, *Clerk*."

"List of those towns east of Connecticut River which have made returns acceding to an Union with the State of Vermont, viz:—Hinsdale,

---

[1] Concurred in by the Governor and Council on the same day.

Walpole, Surry, Gilsom, Alstead, Charlestown, Acworth, Lemster, Saville, Claremont, Newport, Cornish, Croydon, Plainfield, Grantham, Marlow, Lebanon, Grafton, Dresden, Hanover, Cardigan, Lyme, Dorchester, Haverill, Landaff, Gunthwait, Lancaster, Piermont, Richmond, Chesterfield, Westmoreland, Bath, Lyman, Morristown *alias* Franconia, and Lincoln. The Convention have received no returns of any town dissenting.

ELISHA PAYNE,
BEZA. WOODWARD, } *Committee.*"
WILLIAM PAGE,

The several Representatives were desired to give in the votes of the towns that they represent concerning the union; and the following towns were found to have voted to accept the same agreeable to the articles, viz.—Shaftsbury, Arlington, Sandgate, Sunderland, Dorset, Reuport, Pawlet, Poultney, Castleton, Danby, Tinmouth, Rutland, Pittsford, Bethel, Pomfret, Peacham, Fairlee, Guilford, Moortown, Whitingham, Marlborough, New-Fane, Wilmington, Putney, Westminster, Athens, Chester, Windsor, Reading, Thetford, Strafford, Barnard, Royalton, Sharon, Norwich and Hinsdale; and the following towns disapproved of the said Unions taking place, viz:—Bennington, Manchester, Clarendon, Dummerston, Londonderry, Woodstock and Hertford.

Note.—The following towns have not sent in their opinion, viz:—Wells, Wallingford, Townshend, Wethersfield, Cavendish and Hartford.

Resolved, That a Committee of three be appointed to wait on the Convention and inform them that the Union is agreed on by a major part of the towns in this State agreeable to the Articles of Union as proposed; and that this Assembly will wait to receive the members returned to sit in this Assembly, on the Unions takeing place to-morrow morning nine o'clock to take their seats. The members chosen, Mr. Walbridge, Mr. [Stephen R.] Bradley and Mr. Lyon.

FRIDAY April 6th 1781.[1]

Mr. Woodward [Bezaleel,] a Representative from the East side of Connecticut River, informed this House that the Representatives elected in the several towns east of said River were waiting to take their seats agreeable to the Articles of Union and the order of the day—whereupon

Resolved that a Committee of three be appointed to wait on the Representatives returned to sit in this Assembly from the towns east of Connecticut River and introduce them to this House—the members chosen Mr. Bradley, [Stephen R., who took his seat for Westminster at this session,] Mr. Walbridge and Mr. [Matthew] Lyon.

The following are the several members chosen to Represent the towns east of Connecticut River, who were introduced by the aforesaid Committee, and produced their Credentials and took the necessary oaths to quallify them to a seat in this House viz—

Deacon Silas Thompson and Capt. Saml. King, Chesterfield; Mr. Absalom Peters, Landaff; Lieut. Jno. Stevens, Plainfield; Capt. Josiah Russell, Plainfield; Mr. Moses Whipple, Croyden; Daniel Jones Esqr., Hinsdale; Willm. Ripley Esqr., Cornish; Mr. Silas Gaskill and Mr. Daniel Cass, Richmond; Doctr. Wm. Page, Capt. Saml. Wetherbee, Charlestown; Thos. Russell Esqr., Piermont; Mr. John Dunton, Acworth; Mr. Saml. Canfield, Marlow; Mr. Moses True, Saville; Nathl. S. Prentice Esqr., Alstead; Mr. Elijah Frink, Lempster; Mr. Wolston Brockway, Surry; Benja. Giles Esqr., Newport; Deacon Matthias Stone, Capt. Oliver Ashley, Claremont; Capt. Abel Stevens, N. [North] Grantham; Mr. Russel Mason, Grafton; Colo. Elisha Payne, Lieut. Elihu Hyde, Lebanon; Jonth. Freeman Esqr., Colo. John House, Hanover; Mr. Sawyer Bullock,

[1] From the Ms. *Assembly Journal*, Vol. I.

Cardigan; Maj[r.] Jon[th.] Child, M[r.] Walter Fairfield, Lime; M[r.] Davenport Phelps, Orford; Col[o.] Tim[o.] Bedle, Lyman, Morristown, and Bath; Tim[o.] Bedle Esq[r.] and Maj'[r.] Joshua Howard, Haverill; M[r.] John Young Jun[r.] Gunthwaite; Bezaleel Woodward Esq[r.], Dresden—except Deacon Silas Thompson and M[r.] Sawyer Bullock.[1]

On the preceding day twelve representatives from Windham, Windsor, and Orange counties—doubtless elected under the resolution of the preceding February—took their seats. On the 6th of April, after the admission of the representatives from New Hampshire towns, Stephen Tilden and Lieut. Gov. Joseph Marsh presented credentials as representatives for Hartford, in place of Elkanah Sprague and Amos Robinson, who were the sitting members, but were "recalled." Gov. Marsh had been very active against the Vermont government from the dissolution of the first union with New Hampshire towns, but at this period doubtless he was anxious to identify himself again with Vermont. These credentials were referred to a committee, which reported immediately that the town was "duly represented" by the sitting representatives, and the report was accepted.

SATURDAY April 7th 1781.

Resolved that the Clerk of this Assembly send a summons to the Constables of each town that is not Represented in this Assembly on the east side Connecticut River directing them forthwith to warn the freeholders &c. to meet at some suitable place and there to choose a Representative or Representatives to sit in this Assembly as soon as may be.[1]

SETTLLMENT OF BOUNDARY WITH NEW YORK PROPOSED.

IN COUNCIL, February 15[th.] 1781.

Resolved that it be recommended to the General Assembly, that the further Consideration of the Jurisdictional Claims read & passed in both Houses yesterday be postponed until the next Session of this Assembly & that an Agent be appointed and fully Authorised, Immediately to Wait upon the Legislature of the State of N. York now Convened in Albany to agree upon and Establish the line between this State & the State of N. York.

Attest, THOMAS TOLMAN, *Sec[y.] P.T.*

IN GENERAL ASSEMBLY, SATURDAY Feb[y.] 17[th.] 1781.

Resolved that there be two Agents appointed and fully authorized immediately to wait upon the Legislature of the State of New York now convened at Albany to agree upon and establish the line between this

---

[1] An additional representative, Jonathan Cole, of Westmoreland, was admitted on the same day; and subsequently, Israel Mead of New Stamford, Lieut. John Graves of Walpole, and Ebenezer Dewey of Gilsum—all from New Hampshire towns—were admitted.

[1] For the appointment of civil and military officers in the New Hampshire towns embraced in the union, see *ante*, pp. 88, 89, 96–99, 108, 116, 118.

State and the State of New York.—The Agents chosen (by ballot) are Col°. Ira Allen and Maj^r. Joseph Fay.[1]

Resolved that a Committee of five to join a Committee from the Council be appointed to prepare instructions for the aforesaid Agents and Report to this House.—The members chosen M^r. Whipple, M^r. Ward 1st,[2] M^r. Pearl, M^r. Murdock and M^r. Webb.[3]

IN GENERAL ASSEMBLY, Feb. 22, 1781.

The Committee appointed to prepare instructions for the Agents appointed to settle the line between this and the State of New York brought in their Report which was read, and

Resolved that the Governor and Council be and they are hereby requested to make out instructions to said Agents whenever it shall be judged necessary, under such restrictions as they shall judge proper for the benefit of this State.

March 7, doubtless having heard of the failure of the proposition of the New York Senate to settle the controversy, the Governor and Council declined to give instructions at that time.—See *ante*, pp. 266–273.

UNION WITH VERMONT OF A PART OF NEW YORK, APRIL AND JUNE, 1781.

IN GENERAL ASSEMBLY OF VERMONT, Tuesday, April 10, 1781.

The House formed themselves into a Committee of the whole with the Governor and Council to take into consideration the several petitions from the inhabitants of Cambridge, Campden, Granville, Skeensborough &c.[4]—[New York towns.]

---

[1] Concurred in by the Governor and Council, Feb. 22.

[2] William Ward of Shaftsbury is first on the list of representatives. Another William Ward represented Poultney, and still another Newfane.

[3] Councillors Throop and Emmons were joined.

[4] Three of these petitions are preserved in the Secretary of State's office. The following is the petition of inhabitants of Granville. It is more forcible than elegant.

To Thos. Chittenden Esqr. Capt. General Govr. and Commander in Chief in and over the State of Vermont.

this petition of the Subscribers Inhabitants of the town of Granvill in the County of Charlottee and State afore said humble Shueth that your Excellency['s] humble petitioners are fully Sensable that the Extent [of] Juridiction of Said State includes us and we Dearly feel the Sad Consequence of Not Being Enexed to Said State of Vermont for Reasons that ever since the year 1777 we have been Left without any provition for defence against the Merciless Indevations [invasions] of our unnatierl Enemy and we Being a frontier town to the Northward but Ever Called upon to Raise our Equl Dotto [quota] of men year by year and [who have been] ever Stationed fair [far] below us—

and whereas the Right and Lawfull Juridiction of the State of Vermont Extend to the west of us we your Excellency['s] humble petitioners Begeth that your Excellency would Except of us as true and faithfull Subjects to the afore Said State of Vermont and adopt some Mesher

The Committee of the whole having adjourned—The House formed and the Speaker resumed the Chair.

WEDNESDAY April 11th. 1781.[1]

Agreeable to the order of the day the House formed themselves into a Committee of the whole with the Governor and Council. Said Committee having dissolved, the speaker resumed the chair.

The Committee of the whole made the following report of a Sub-Committee, viz.

"To the Grand Committee consisting of his Excellency the Governor, the honble the Council and the General Assembly.

"Your Committee to whom was referred the consideration of the several petitions and letters from the inhabitants of Granville, Cambridge, &c. requesting this State to exercise jurisdiction over them for the reasons therein specified, beg leave to report

"That the Legislature of this State do recommend to the people inhabiting that part of the former government over which Govr. Philip Skeene was to preside, to which this Legislature at their session in Feby. last laid a jurisdictional claim, to appoint members to attend a Convention at Cambridge [N. Y.] the second Wednesday of May next; that the Legislature of this State appoint a Committee to meet said Convention at said time and place: that said Convention and Committee take into consideration the defence of the frontiers, and if they can mutually agree on articles of Union that then such Convention proceed to resolve to raise their quota of men for the defence of the frontiers, with a proper proportion of officers, which shall be returned to the Board of War and commissioned in the same manner that the troops heretofore ordered to be raised for the present defence of this State are and do duty in the same manner: that in case said Convention and Committee do agree on

---

whearby we may be Better Governed, Agreeable to the Ruels and Laws of the Constitution of the Aforesaid State of Vermont.

Your Excellency['s] Humble petitoners Intreat your Greacious attention to this our Humble petition As we in duty Bound will Ever pray

Granvill March 28th 1781

[Signed by Isaac Bennett and one hundred and seven other persons.]

The petitions of Lieut. John Patterson and thirty-seven other citizens of Camden, and of John Austin and seventy-nine others of Cambridge, set forth as reasons for annexation to Vermont that "the Goverment of New York have neglected guarding our Northern frontier;" that, aided by the militia of Vermont, a force sufficient for defence could be raised in case of emergency; and that the territory had been formerly embraced in "a government" "over which Govr. Skeen was to have presided."—See *Vermont State Papers*, (manuscript,) Vol. 17; being *Petitions*, Vol. 1, 1777-87, pp. 39, 40 and 44.

On the return of these towns to their allegiance to New York, in 1782, their conduct in joining Vermont was excused by allegations of the neglect or inability of New York to protect them, which were even more emphatic than the above.—See *Documentary History of New York*, Vol. 4, pp. 605, 606. For other evidence of the weakness of New York at this period, see *Early History of Vermont*, pp. 341-344; and *Vt. Hist. Soc. Collections*, Vol. II, pp. 49-55.

[1] From Slade's *State Papers*, p. 138.

articles of union, raising men, &c. then such articles of union shall be transmitted to the several districts in said claim, when the people of said districts are requested (provided they agree to such articles of union) to choose members to attend this Assembly, except such districts had instructed their member or members, in case articles of union were agreed on, that their members should be impowered to take seats in this Assembly: that in case two thirds of the districts, in district meeting, choose members as aforesaid, that then such members shall take their seats in this Assembly: that this Assembly adjourn to the second Wednesday of June next, at Bennington.

"JOHN FASSETT, *Chairman.*"

"WINDSOR, April 11th, 1781.

"IN THE GRAND COMMITTEE, April 11th, 1781.

"The above report was read and accepted,

"Attest, JOSEPH FAY, *Clerk.*"

The aforesaid Report was Read and after some debate the question was put and the Yeas & Nays were requested and they are as follows viz—

YEAS 48.—Mr. Walbridge Mr. Lyon Mr. Petibone Mr. Ormsby Colo. Strong Mr. Harmon Mr. Pearl Mr. Fitch Mr. Moss Mr. Ward Mr. Higley Mr. Rowley Mr. Jackson Mr. J. Smith Mr. E. Smith Mr. B. Whipple Mr. Post Mr. Drury Mr. Harris Mr. Underwood Mr. Bratten Mr. Burlinggame Mr. Weston Mr. Eli Mr. Weld Mr. Seelye Capt. Strong Mr. Cottle Mr. Sprague Mr. A. Robinson Mr. J. Powell Mr. Foster Mr. Murdock Mr. Spooner Mr. Aiken Mr. Bradley Mr. Putnam Mr. Taplin Mr. W. Baley Mr. McConnell Mr. Wells Mr. Giles Mr. J. Stevens Mr. Brockway Mr. Frink Mr. Whipple Mr. Young Mr. Gaskill.

NAYS 39.—Mr. Shepherd Mr. Knight Mr. N. Robinson Mr. Holton Mr. Curtiss Mr. C. Parkhurst Mr. Burton Mr. [Joel] Marsh Mr. J. Baley Mr. Dana Mr. Kent Mr. Payne Mr. Woodward Mr. Bedle Mr. Prentice Mr. Child Mr. Hyde Doctr. Page Mr. Phelps Mr. Ripley Mr. House Mr. J. Russell Mr. Fairfield Mr. Freeman Mr. Wetherbee Mr. Howard Mr. Stone Mr. Thos. Russell Mr. King Mr. Mason Mr. True Mr. Hunt Mr. Canfield Mr. Duncan Mr. A. Stevens Mr. Peters Mr. Cass Mr. Cole Mr. Ashley.[1]

So it passed in the affirmative.

Resolved that a Committee of two to join a Committee from the Council be appointed to prepare a Bill agreeable to the aforesaid Report and make Report to this House.—The members chosen Mr. Lyon and Mr. Wells, [Samuel of Brattleborough.]

Resolved that a Committee of six to join a Committee from the Council[2] be appointed to meet a Convention to be held on the second Wednesday of May next at Cambridge [N. Y.] for the purpose specified in a Report of a Committee of both Houses of this day's date; and that a majority of such Committee are hereby impowered to transact the business pointed out for the said Committee in said Report and make a Report of their doings to the [General Assembly at their] next session for their approbation.—The members chosen Mr. Walbridge, Mr. Porter

[1] Of the yeas, 7 were representatives of New Hampshire towns, leaving 41 Vermonters. Of the nays, 27 were from New Hampshire towns, leaving 12 Vermonters. This list is taken from the Assembly journal.

[2] The Council journal of this day gives no details; hence it does not appear from the record what Councillors were joined to these committees. It does appear, from the report of the committee last named above, that Moses Robinson was one of the committee from the Council.

[Thomas of Tinmouth,] Mr. Williams [Col. William of Wilmington,] Mr. Prentice [of Alstead, N. H.,] Mr. Curtiss [Capt. Ebenezer of Windsor,[1]] and Mr. Child [of Lyme, N. H.]

MONDAY April 16th. 1781.

Resolved that this Assembly be and is hereby adjourned until the second Wednesday of June next then to meet at Bennington.

The adjournment was to the 13th of June, but a quorum was not in attendance until the afternoon of the 15th, when the following occurred:

IN GENERAL ASSEMBLY OF VERMONT, June 15, 1781.

The representatives of the western District informed this House in writing that they were ready to take their seats according to the Articles of Union, &c.

The Committee, who was appointed to treat with the Convention holden at Cambridge in June [May] last reported the following articles, viz.

"Articles of Union proposed by the Convention composed of representatives from the several districts of Hoosack, Scorticook, Cambridge, Saratoga, Upper-White-Creek, Black-Creek, Granville, Skeensborough, Greenfield, Kingsbury, Fort Edward and Little Hoosack, convened at Cambridge aforesaid the 9th day of May 1781, and by several adjournments to the 15th of the same month inclusive.

"ARTICLE 1st. That the district or tract of land lying north of a line being extended from the north line of the Massachusetts to Hudson's River, and east of said river and south of latitude 45, as comprehended in the late jurisdictional claim by the Legislature of the State of Vermont, be considered as part of said state, and the inhabitants thereof as free citizens.

"ANSWER.—Agreed to by the Committee of the Legislature of the State of Vermont.

"ARTICLE 2d. That the whole military force of the State of Vermont (as occasion may require) shall be exerted in our defence, as free Citizens, against any insurrection, invasion or incursion whatsoever; but especially against the common Enemy.

"ANS.—Agreed to.

"ARTICLE 3d. That application be made by the Legislature of the state of Vermont to the Congress of the United States to be admitted with them as soon as circumstances will admit.

"ANS.—Agreed to.

"ART. 4th. That as the people within the aforesaid late claim have been called upon and have paid a considerable part of the Continental taxes into the treasury of the State of New-York, they shall have credit for the same in case the State of Vermont at some future period should be called upon to pay their proportion of money emitted by Congress.

"ANS.—Agreed to, provided the services done by the state of Vermont in the present war be included.

"REPLY OF CONVENTION.—Agreed to, provided the expence of said district in the present war be likewise included.

"ARTICLE 5th. That all actions depending within the late claim shall be transferred in the situation they shall be in at the time of completing the union to courts that may be then forthwith erected under the Authority of Vermont, without cost to the parties other than would have accrued had they been terminated in courts under the jurisdiction of the State of New-York.

---

[1] Mr. Curtis was excused and John W. Dana of Pomfret was appointed in his place.

" ANS.—Agreed to.

" ART. 6th. That the change of jurisdiction shall not be understood to effect, [affect,] or alienate, private property.

" ANS.—Agreed to.

" Articles of union proposed by the Legislature of the State of Vermont.

" ART. 1st. That the Independence of the State of Vermont be held sacred, and that no member of the Legislature shall give his vote or otherwise use his endeavours to obtain any act or resolution of Assembly that shall endanger the existence, independence, or well being of said State by referring its independency to the arbitrament of any power.

" ANSWER.—Agreed to by Convention.

" ARTICLE 2d. That whenever this State becomes united with the American states and there shall then be any disputes between this and any of the United States respecting boundary lines, the Legislature of the State of Vermont will then (as they have ever proposed) submit to Congress or such other tribunal as may be mutually agreed upon for the settlement of any such disputes.

" ANS.—Agreed to.

" The foregoing articles were severally mutually agreed to by the Convention and Committee at Cambridge the 15th May 1781.

" Attest, JOHN ROGERS, *Chairman of Convention.*
MOSES ROBINSON, *Chairman of Committee.*"

The aforesaid Articles were read and after some debate

Resolved that this House form themselves into a Committee of the whole with the Governor and Council to take the aforesaid Articles under consideration. The Committee of the whole having dissolved, the House formed themselves, and the Speaker resumed the Chair—

And after some time spent in debating on the said report it was referred until tomorrow morning, for further consideration.

A declaration of the Inhabitants of the western District, giving their reasons for disavowing allegiance to the State of New-York, with their disavowal, was read.

Adjourned until to-morrow morning, eight o'clock.

SATURDAY, June 16th 1781.

Met, according to adjournment.

The House again took up the consideration of the Articles of Union, agreed on between the Committee appointed to treat with the Cambridge Convention, and said Convention, and after some debate the question was put—whether this House would approve of said articles, as agreed between said Committee and Convention ? It passed in the affirmative.

The yeas and nays on the question being requested by Mr. Woodward, and the question being put whether the yeas and nays should be taken—passed in the affirmative, and they are as follows, viz.

YEAS 53.[1]—Mr. Barber Mr. Briggs Mr. S. Robinson Mr. Olin Mr. Ward 1st[2] Mr. Walbridge Mr. Lyon Mr. Ormsby, Mr. Powell Mr. Bartlet Col. Strong Mr. Underhill Mr. Harmon Mr. Pearl Mr. Everest Mr. Moss Mr. Ward 2d[2] Mr. Rowley Mr. Gage Mr. Speaker [Porter,] Mr. Bingham Mr. J. Smith Mr. B. Whipple Mr. Post Mr. Thurber Mr. Harris Mr. Underwood Mr. Ward 3d[2] Mr. Williams Mr. Martin Mr. Hayward Mr. N. Robinson Mr. Webb Mr. Burlinggame Mr. Curtiss Mr. Weld Mr. Bratten Mr. Cottle Mr. Sprague Mr. A. Robinson Mr. J. Powell Mr. Murdock Mr. Aiken Mr. Putnam Mr. Taplin Mr. Wells Mr. Giles Mr. J. Stevens Mr. Ripley Mr. Frink Mr. M. Whipple Mr. Wyman Mr. Sherman.

[Forty-eight Vermonters in the affirmative.]

---

[1] **Yeas and nays from the *Assembly Journal.*** [2] **See p. 297, note[2].**

NAYS 24.—Mr. Holton Mr. Bartholomew Mr. Foster Mr. Burton Mr. Dana Mr. Woodward Mr. Hyde Mr. Wm. Page Mr. Phelps Mr. House Mr. Stone Mr. Freeman Mr. Wetherbee Mr. T. Russell Mr. King Mr. Hunt Mr. Canfield Mr. Duncan Mr. Peters Mr. Cole Mr. Ashley Mr. Graves Mr. Jones Mr. B. Smith.

[Six Vermonters in the negative.]

Resolved that a Committee of three be appointed to wait on the members returned from the Western District to sit in this Assembly and inform them that this House are ready to receive them as members of this House upon their producing their several appointments &c.—The members chosen Mr. S. Robinson, Mr. Lyon and Mr. Harris.

The following are the several members chosen to Represent the Western District and were introduced by the aforesaid Committee and produced their Credentials which were read and approved, viz.—

Mr. Thos. Benedict & Mr. Benja. Hicks, Scorticook; Capt. John Abbot and Lieut. Jno. Johnson, Hoosack; Colo. Gidion Warren,[1] Greenfield; David Randall Esqr. & Doct. Abm. Burdick, Little Hoosack; Mr. John Shepherd, Black-Creek; Mr. Joseph Craw, South-Granville; Capt. Asaph Cook, Granville; Aaron Fuller, Esqr., Skeensborough; Mr. Thos. Smith & Mr. John Rogers, Saratoga; Mr. Phineas Whiteside, Colo. Joseph Caldwell, Cambridge; and they all took the necessary oaths to qualify them to a seat in this House, except Lieut. John Johnson and Mr. Benja. Hicks who did not attend.

MONDAY, June 18th. 1781.[2]

Resolved that a Committee of three to join a Committee from the Council be appointed to arrange the civil and military departments in the Western Territory lately united to this State and make Report.—The members chosen Mr. Warren [of Greenfield, N. Y.,] Mr. Whiteside of Cambridge, N. Y.,] and Mr. S. Robinson, [Samuel of Bennington.]

Resolved that the Governor and Council be and they are hereby requested to join this House in a Committee of the whole to morrow morning nine o'clock to take under consideration proper measures for informing the Congress of the United States of the political situation of Vermont &c.

Resolved that an inquiry be made into the grounds of the report of a treaty with Canada &c. to morrow morning when the Committee of the whole meet.[3]

The Committee of the Whole met on the 19th and after consultation adjourned to the 22d. On the 20th the committee appointed by the Assembly to arrange the civil and military affairs of the Western District made a report, annexing so much of the District as was in Albany county to the county of Bennington, and so much as was in Charlotte county to the county of Rutland; dividing the militia in four regiments and annexing them to the first brigade; providing for the election of magistrates and town officers, and also of militia officers—all for the time being; which report was accepted.

---

[1] Col. Warren had removed from Vermont a short time previous.

[2] From the *Assembly Journal.*

[3] The report of the committee indicates nothing on this subject; but an inquiry was made, and Ira Allen contrived a report so ingeniously as to satisfy all parties.—See *Vt. Hist. Soc. Collections*, Vol. II, pp. 133–135 and 142.

FRIDAY June 22d. 1781.

The House formed themselves into a Committee of the whole with the Governor and Council agreeable to their adjournment.

The Committee of the whole having dissolved, the House formed and the Speaker resumed the Chair.

The Committee of the whole made the following Report of a Sub Committee viz.—

"*To the Grand Committee consisting of Governor, Council and Assembly—*

"Your Committee appointed to prepare a draught to send to Congress to inform them of the political situation of this State &c. Beg leave to recommend,

"That an Annunciation of the late extention of the boundaries of this State with some of the capital reasons for such extention be transmitted to adjacent states.

"That three delegates be appointed to repair to Congress with full powers to propose to and receive from them terms for an union of this with the United States—and to transact any other matters at Congress which may be necessary for the welfare of this State—such terms of union or other treaty agreed on by them to be subject to the ratification of the Legislature of this State previous to their establishment—such delegates to give Congress whatever information they may desire of the political situation of this State—And that they be vested with full and ample powers to take seats in Congress as Delegates from this State when terms of union shall be agreed on and ratified as before mentioned. Two delegates to be nominated by the members within the ancient limits of the state, and two by the members from each newly added territory.

"Which is humbly submitted by JONAS FAY *Chm.*

"Bennington June 22d. 1781."

" IN GRAND COMMITTEE June 22d. 1 81.

"The aforesaid Report was read by paragraphs and approved.

"Attest JOSEPH FAY, *Clerk.*"

The aforesaid Report was read and accepted.

Resolved that this House will proceed agreeable to the aforesaid Report to choose Delegates to wait on Congress &c.

Ordered that the members of the Districts proceed immediately to bring in their nomination agreeable to said Report—And the following Nomination was returned by them viz.—

Middle District	JONAS FAY IRA ALLEN	Esquires.
Eastern District	BEZALEEL WOODWARD ELISHA PAYNE	Esquires.
Western District	JONAS FAY IRA ALLEN	Esquires.

The ballots being taken the Honble Jonas Fay and Ira Allen Esquires and Bezaleel Woodward Esqr. were Elected Delegates as aforesaid.

Resolved that a Committee of three to join a Committee from the Council be appointed to prepare the ANNUCIATION to send the adjacent States; and make Report.—The members chosen Mr. Woodward, Mr. Lyon and Mr. Whiteside.

Resolved that a committee of five to join a Committee from the Council be appointed to prepare instructions for the members appointed to wait on Congress &c.—The members chosen Mr. Jones [probably Daniel

Jones of Hinsdale, N. H.][1] Mr. Phelps [Davenport of Orford, N. H.] Mr. Giles [Benjamin of Newport, N. H.] Mr. Walbridge [of Bennington,][2] and Mr. Webb, [Joshua of Rockingham.]

Resolved that a Committee of three be appointed to run the South line of this State from the southwest corner of Pownal to Hudson's River.—The members chosen Mr. S. Robinson, Mr. Caldwell [of Cambridge, N. Y.,] and Mr. Barber, [Elisha of Pownal.]

On the 25th of June the committee appointed to draw up instructions to the delegates to Congress, reported in the language of the report of the committee of the whole on that subject; also a resolution desiring the Governor to commission them; and the instructions and resolutions were adopted. July 10, Gov. Chittenden delivered the commission in substantially the words of the report of the committee of the whole.—See commission in proceedings of Congress of Aug. 17 1781, *post.*

WEDNESDAY June 27th. 1781.

An Annunciation of the extention of the boundaries of this State was read and agreed to.[3]

Ordered, that his Excellency the Governor be desired to transmit copies of the annunciation to all the United States.

Resolved that the delegates appointed to repair to the American Congress be and they are hereby directed to set off on the business of their appointment by the first day of August next.

THURSDAY June 28th. 1781.

Resolved that Jonas Fay, Ira Allen, and Bezaleel Woodward Esquires, appointed Delegates to repair to Congress, be impowered to draw on the Treasurer of this State for such sum or sums of money as may be necessary to enable them to discharge their commission to Congress agreeable to the orders of this House—and that an order on the Treasurer issue accordingly signed by his Excellency the Governor, and that they be accountable for such sums as they shall receive.

ACTS OF THE GENERAL ASSEMBLY, JUNE 1781, FOR THE ORGANIZATION OF THE WESTERN DISTRICT.

AN ACT for the purpose of forming the Western Territory, lately taken into Union with this State, into Townships, and for annexing it to the Counties of Bennington and Rutland.

Whereas it is found necessary, for the purposes of representation, and for exercising civil government, that the inhabited part of the following

---

[1] Doct. Reuben Jones and Joshua Webb representated Rockingham in the Assembly in October 1780, but at the adjourned session in February Jonathan Holton presented credentials from that town and was a representative with Mr. Webb at the session of June 1781. It is presumed that Mr. Holton was elected in place of Doct. Reuben Jones resigned.

[2] Edward Harris of Halifax was appointed in place of Col. Walbridge excused.

[3] This document the editor has not been able to find.

described district, viz.—Beginning at the north-west corner of Williamstown,[1] and extending west, ten degrees north, to the centre of the deepest channel of the waters of Hudson's River; then up said river, and extending through the centre of the deepest channel thereof, to the head thereof; thence north, by the needle of the compass, to the latitude forty-five—(lately taken into union with this State) be divided into townships, with the usual incorporate privileges; and that the said district be annexed to said counties. Therefore,

Be it enacted, &c. that the districts of land, in said territory, commonly known by the names of Hosack, Cambridge, White-Creek, alias New-Perth, Black-Creek, Skeensborough, Kingsbury, Scotch-Patent, alias Argyle, and Fort Edward, be, and they are hereby incorporated, each of them, into a distinct township, and to be severally known and distinguished by the aforesaid names respectively; and are hereby vested with all the privileges and immunities, which other towns within this State do of right exercise and enjoy.

Be it further enacted, that the tract of land within the said territory, lying west of, and adjoining to, Pownal, and north of the south line of said territory, and west of a line extended from the east line of the tract of land known by the name of Scorticook district, and south of Hosack district, be and is hereby incorporated into a township, by the name of Little-Hosack; and that the tract of land, lying bounded west on the north river, south on the south line of said territory, north on the tract of land, commonly called Scorticook district, and east on Little-Hosack, together with the district of land, commonly known by the name of the district of Scorticook, be and is hereby incorporated into a township, by the name of Scorticook; and that such part of the tract of land, known by the name of the district of Saratoga, as is included in said territory, be and is hereby incorporated into a township, by the name of Saratoga-East; and that the tract of land, lying west of, and adjoining to, Pollet, and north of, and adjoining to, Black-Creek, and westerly on Kingsbury and Skeensborough, be and is hereby incorporated into a township, by the name of South-Granville; and that the tract of land, north of said South-Granville, as far north as the west-line of the township of Wells extends, be and is hereby incorporated into a township, by the name of North Granville; and that the tract of land, northward of said North-Granville, extending north to the East-Bay, bounded eastward on Fairhaven, and westward on Skeensborough, be and is hereby incorporated into a township, by the name ol Eastborough. And that each of said townships be and are hereby vested with the same privileges and immunities as other towns within this State do of right exercise and enjoy.

And be it enacted, that the townships of Little-Hosack, Hosack, Cambridge, Scorticook, and Saratoga-East, being that part of said territory which formerly belonged to Albany county, be and are hereby annexed to the county of Bennington; and that all the remaining part of the aforesaid townships, be and are hereby annexed to the county of Rutland.

AN ACT directing the holding Town Meetings in the Western Territory lately taken into Union with this State, and directing the Listers in said Territory in their Office and Duty.

Whereas, for the purpose of civil government, it is found necessary that the inhabitants of the towns lately formed in the western territory, lately taken into union with this State, be directed and impowered

[1] Williamstown, Mass.

to hold town meetings, and choose the town officers necessary for the present year.

Therefore,

Be it enacted, &c. that the inhabitants of each of the respective towns, formed and incorporated by this Assembly, in said territory, be, and they are hereby authorised and impowered to hold town meetings in their respective towns, at such time in the month of July next, and at such places as usual, or most convenient in their respective towns, as the persons hereafter impowered to warn such meetings shall direct; and to appoint such officers at their said meetings, as other towns, in this State, by law, are directed and impowered to choose, in their annual March meetings: which officers, when sworn to the faithful discharge of their office, shall be, and they are hereby impowered to execute such office as they are appointed to, as other officers of the like kind, in the other parts of this State are.

And it is hereby recommended to the inhabitants of each of the said towns, at their said meeting, to choose one or two meet persons for justices of the peace in and for the county to which they belong, and make return to the Governor and Council, of such choice, in order that such persons be appointed and commissioned, in case they are approved of by them.

Be it further enacted, that the persons hereafter named, be, and they are hereby impowered to warn town meetings in the towns to which they respectively belong; that is to say,—Capt. William Sheppard, for Scorticook; Mr. Thomas Smith, for Saratoga; Mr. Stutson Benson, for Hosack; Col. Joseph Caldwell, for Cambridge; Mr. Benjamin Randal, for Little-Hosack; Capt. Solomon Brown, for White-Creek, alias New-Perth; Capt. Aaron Osgood, for Black-Creek; Capt. David Blakesley, for South-Granville; Capt. John Grover, for North-Granville; Mr. James Burroughs, for Skeensborough; Mr. Lemuel Hide, for East-Borough; Mr. Gilbert Harris, for Kingsbury; Capt. Batty, for Scotch-Patent, alias Argyle; Mr. Daniel Paine, for Fort-Edward.

And whereas the time the law directs that the inhabitants of the respective towns in this State be warned to give in the list of their polls and rateable estate, is now elapsed, and there is a necessity of the said lists being regularly taken in the towns in the said territory:

Therefore,

Be it enacted, that the listers chosen in the respective towns in the territory aforesaid, be, and they are hereby authorised, for the present year, to warn all the inhabitants of their respective towns, some time in the month of July, to give in, to them, their respective lists, according to law, by the 15th day of August next, of all their rateable polls and estate they were possessed of on the twentieth day of June; which list shall be inspected by said listers, and returned to the General Assembly, agreeable to the law of this State.

And the said listers shall govern themselves in their said office, according to said law, in all respects, the times therein mentioned only excepted.

AN ACT to impower Heads of Classes in the Western District to tax the Members of said Class, &c.

Whereas sundry persons in the western district, have been appointed heads of classes, by the authority of the State of New-York; in consequence of which appointment, they have engaged, and are further to engage, sundry persons in the service of this and the United States; to some of whom they have given their obligations promissory, for their county; which heads of classes are, by a law of the State of New-York, vested with authority to levy a tax on the several members of each class, for the payment of such sum or sums of money as have been, or shall, from time to time, be found necessary by such heads of classes, to be paid or engaged to be paid, for such man or men, as shall, at any time, be called for from such class. Therefore,

Be it enacted, &c. that each and every such head of classes be, and they are hereby authorised with full power and authority, to call on the several members of their classes for their proportion of such sum or sums; and in case of neglect or refusal, to proceed against them as the law directs in case of debt; and such men so raised be directed forthwith to join a company in this State.

Proclamation of Gov. Chittenden, July 18, 1781.

BY HIS EXCELLENCY

THOMAS CHITTENDEN, ESQUIRE,

Captain-General, Governor and Commander in Chief, in and over the State of VERMONT.

A PROCLAMATION.[1]

WHEREAS the Legislature of this State, at their Session in June last, for the reasons hereafter exhibited, did extend their Claim of Jurisdiction from the North-West corner of the Commonwealth of Massachusetts Westerly in the same Direction with the North Line of said Commonwealth, until it reaches the deepest channel of Hudson's River; thence running Northerly in the deepest Channel of said River, to the Source thereof, and from thence a due North Direction to Latitude 45° North (or the southern Boundary of the Province of Quebec.)

AND whereas no Part of the Lands contained in said Claim, were ever included in any original Charter from the Crown of Great Britain to the Government of New-York, but were known to be extra-provincial Lands, without the Limits of any of the chartered Colonies, and annexed to the former Government of New-York, merely by the Decree of the Crown, manifested in its Commissions to the respective Governors of New-York: which Jurisdiction in its own nature became null and void in Consequence of the Declaration of Independence by the United States, and the Annihilation of Kingly Power in America. And in consequence of a subsequent Commission from the same royal Authority to Governor Philip Skeene, which vested him with Powers of Jurisdiction over the same Territory, and which on the Position of the Validity of royal Traditions and Boundaries, would fatally operate against the Claim of the State of New-York. And although there may have been what some People call a mutual Association and Connection between the Inhabitants included in said Claim, and the State of New-York since the Declaration of Independence, yet the Nature of such Allegiance must be founded on a reciprocal Protection; for Government and Protection are by Nature so connected together, that the one cannot exist indepen-

---

[1] *Clinton Papers*, No. 3831. The editor is indebted to HENRY L. LAMB, Esq., for this document. The Proclamation was not entered upon the record of the Governor and Council, and it is here given from a copy printed in 1781.

dent of the other; nor can any Allegiance be lawfully had or demanded by any Government, except at the same time it affords the salutary Influences of Support or Protection to its Citizens.

AND whereas the Government of New York, for a Number of Years, have been very deficient in succoring, defending or protecting the Citizens inhabiting the said claimed Territory, and of late have wholly abandoned them to the Ravages of the common enemy. And whereas this State have been their main Support and Protection for several years last past, and have lately entered into a governmental League and Combination with them, for the mutual Happiness and Security of each other, under the same Constitution and Code of Laws; being urged thereto by the Refusal of the Government of New-York to unite with this Government for their mutual Defense, and from the local Situation of both to the Waters of Lake Champlain, and the British Government of Canada, from whence a powerful Force can suddenly invade this State including its late Western Union.

AND whereas Commissions both civil and military have been lately issued from the supreme Authority of this State to Persons chosen, agreeable to the Laws and Customs thereof, in the several Districts and Corporations within the Limits of the said western Claim of Jurisdiction:

I HAVE therefore thought fit, by and with the Advice of my Council, to issue this Proclamation, and do hereby strictly require, charge and command all Persons of whatever Quality or Denomination residing within the said Western Claim of Jurisdiction, to take due Notice of the Laws and Orders of this State, and govern themselves accordingly, on Pain of incurring the Penalties therein contained.

AND I do hereby further strictly require and command all Magistrates, Justices of the Peace, Sheriffs, Constables, and all other civil, and all military Officers to be active and vigilant in executing the Laws aforesaid, without Partiality.

{ SEAL. } Given under my Hand, and the Seal of this State, at Arlington, this 18th Day of July, A. D. 1781, and in the 5th Year of the Independence of this State.

THOMAS CHITTENDEN.

By his Excellency's Command, THOMAS TOLMAN, *Dep. Sec'ry.*

GOD save the PEOPLE.

PROCEEDINGS IN CONGRESS RELATING TO VERMONT—JULY 19 TO AUG. 20, 1781.[1]

July 9 1781, the following letter was referred by Congress to a committee consisting of Mr. Sherman of Connecticut, Mr. McKean of Delaware, Mr. Carroll of Maryland, Mr. Varnum of Rhode Island, and Mr. Madison of Virginia:

---

[1] In the interim, between the proceedings in Congress in Sept. 1780 and July 1781,—to wit, March 1 1781—the Confederation was completed by the accession of Maryland; and on the same day New York, by its delegates in Congress, relinquished to the United States its claim to lands west of its present boundary. Of this claim Mr. MADISON said:—"The claim of New York is very extensive, but her title very flimsy. She urges it more with the hope of obtaining some advantage or credit by its cession, than ever of maintaining it. If the cession should be

President Weare of New Hampshire to the Delegates of that State in Congress.[1]

(COPY.) EXETER, June 20th, 1781.

Gentlemen,—Enclosed you have copies of three petitions from different towns in the county of Cheshire, by which you will see the embarrassed situation we are in, occasioned by the dispute relative to the New Hampshire Grants not being settled.

New Hampshire flattered herself that dispute would have been long since adjusted by Congress, and have been at great expense in sending agents to Philadelphia for that purpose. The amazing unexpected delay therein has been attended with the greatest mischief to the United States in general, and to the State of New Hampshire in particular. It has given an opportunity to many disaffected persons, who are the principal leaders in the disturbances, to do much injury, and who, it is said, and not without foundation, have entered into a negociation with the enemy. In short, New Hampshire is brought into such a dilemma, and the Government thrown into such confusion by this delay in Congress, that it is impossible for her to comply with the requisitions of Congress, to any great degree, while this dispute remains unsettled; and it is in vain for them to expect it of her, as no supplies of men, money or provision can be collected at present from more than ⅔rds even of that part of the state which lies east of Connecticut River, and unless Congress brings matters to an immediate issue, we cannot tell how far the contagion may run, but very much fear that the state will be very soon ruined, in a great measure, and not able to contribute farther towards the war. Therefore you are directed to lay this dispatch before Congress as soon as may be, and earnestly request that they would immediately take the matter under consideration, and make a final decision thereon without any further delay, as it is of much greater consequence than can be described. I am, gentlemen, your most humble servant,

(Signed) M. WEARE.

By order of the General Assembly.

Hon. Sam'l Livermore, and John Sullivan, Esquires.

Secretary's Office, August 21, 1781.

The foregoing is a true copy of the original, filed in this office.

GEO. BOND, *Dep'y Sec'y of Congress.*[2]

---

accepted, and the affair of Vermont terminated, as these are the only ties which unite her with the southern states, she will immediately connect her policy with that of the eastern states, as far at least as the remains of former prejudices will permit."—See *Madison Papers*, Vol. I, p. 121; and *Vt. Hist. Soc. Collections*, Vol. II, pp. 268–9.

[1] *Haldimand Papers, in Vt. Hist. Soc. Coll.*, Vol. I, p. 137.

[2] Aug. 13 1781, Prest. Weare wrote to Gen. Washington on the same subject as follows:

Had it not been for this unaccountable and altogether unexpected destruction of our currency, [by the people of Massachusetts refusing to take continental bills,] the only one we had, I doubt not we should have been able to carry the acts [for completing the quota of New Hampshire in the continental army] fully into effect, excepting in that part which, as I mentioned in my letter of the 23d of July, under pretence of joining what they call Vermont, have refused to raise men or furnish supplies of any kind, so that there will be a deficiency *on that account* of more than quarter part, both of men and supplies, until Congress, before whom the matter lies, shall determine upon it.—*Correspondence of the Revolution, Letters to Washington*, Vol. VIII, p. 385.

From a letter of Hon. John Sullivan, in Congress, to President Weare, (in the *N. H. Papers on the Vermont Controversy*,) July 10 1781, it seems that several documents were presented to Congress on the 9th. These were in the lost *Stevens Papers*, and are named in the *Index to the Stevens Papers*, in connection with Weare's and Sullivan's letters, as follows:

Instructions to delegates in Congress to prosecute their claims as to Vermont, March 31st 1781.

Walpole petition opposed to union with Vermont.

Westmoreland petition as to Vermont.

Swanzey petition do. do.

July 20, according to one memorandum, and July 31 according to another,[1] the committee above named submitted a report, which opened with an acknowledgment of the zealous exertions of New Hampshire and New York in the common cause, and a conviction that they would not ever suffer it to languish by their means; recited briefly the case of Vermont, describing its boundaries as they existed previous to the Unions, and the relinquishment by Massachusetts of her claim on condition that a like relinquishment be made by New Hampshire and New York, and concluded with the following resolutions:

Resolved that it be recommended to the states of New Hampshire and New York respectively to declare the inhabitants of the district called Vermont, bounded as aforesaid, unamenable to any jurisdiction under their authority and to renounce all territorial claims thereto, but to refer to Congress to determine on what terms this concession shall take effect, in case Congress shall recognize the independence of the said people of Vermont.

Resolved that Congress will consider all the lands of New Hampshire and New York respectively, lying without the limits of Vermont aforesaid, as coming within the actual guarantee of territory contained in the articles of confederation: and that the United States will accordingly guarantee such lands and the jurisdiction over the same against any claims or encroachments from the inhabitants of Vermont aforesaid.

Gov. HALL suggested that this report was prepared in the absence of the delegates of New York, and in the expectation that both New Hampshire and New York would assent to its recommendation, and so end the encroachments of Vermont upon their territory. But, as will be seen, the delegates of New York resumed their seats on the 31st of July, and on the 3d of August presented a memorial of that state persisting in its claims to Vermont; whereupon the above named report was recommitted.

[1] The appointment of the committee and its report are not noted in Folwell's edition of the *Journals of Congress*, and the statements made here are from notes taken by Gov. HALL from the Committee Books of the Continental Congress in the State Department at Washington.—See H. HALL's *Early History*, pp. 350, 351.

TUESDAY, July 31, 1781.[1]

Mr. Duane and Mr. L'Hommedieu, two delegates for the state of New York, attended.

WEDNESDAY, August 1, 1781.

A motion was made by Mr. Varnum, seconded by Mr. L'Hommedieu, that a committee be appointed to enquire into the facts mentioned in the intercepted letter of the 7th February last, from lord George Germain to sir Henry Clinton, and report the result of their enquiries to Congress.

Mr. Bland moved to postpone this motion, which failed for want of the vote of a majority of the States. *Yeas*—New-Hampshire, New Jersey, Delaware, Virginia, South Carolina; *nays*—Massachusetts, Rhode Island, Connecticut, New York; divided, Maryland; not counted one member *yea* for North Carolina, and one member *nay* for Georgia. The question to agree to the motion was also lost for the same reason: *yeas*, Rhode Island, Connecticut, New York, Maryland, and Virginia; *nays*—New Hampshire, Massachusetts, New Jersey, Delaware, and South Carolina; one vote on each side from North Carolina and Georgia not counted.[2]

This dispatch, and the encroachments of Vermont on New Hampshire and New York, thoroughly alarmed Congress and contributed essentially to the pledge in the resolutions of the 7th and 20th of August on which the final acknowledgment of the independence of the State was founded. This appears fpom the following:

Ezra L'Hommedieu (in Congress) to Gov. Clinton.—[Extract.]

July 31, 1781. Some intercepted letters from Lord George Germaine on this subject [Vermont] and the solicitations of New Hampshire, it is said, induced them [congress] to take up this business without a repre-

---

[1] From the *Journals of Congress*, 1781–2, Vol. VII, Folwell's edition.

[2] The intercepted dispatch was as follows:

Lord George Germaine to Sir Henry Clinton.—[Extract.]

WHITEHALL, [London,] February 7, 1781.

The return of the people of Vermont to their allegiance, is an event of the utmost importance to the king's affairs, and at this time, if the French and Washington really meditate an irruption into Canada, may be considered as opposing an insurmountable bar to the attempt.* General Haldimand, who has the same instructions with you to draw over these people, and give them support, will, I doubt not, push up a body of troops, to act in conjunction with them, to secure all the avenues through their country into Canada; and when the season admits, take possession of the upper parts of the Hudson and Connecticut Rivers, and cut off the communication between Albany and the Mohawk country. How far they may be able to extend themselves southward, or eastward, must depend on their numbers, and the disposition of the inhabitants; but, if Albany should take part with them, the inducement to attempt to open a communication with them by Hudson's river will appear irresistible to people here.—*Vt. Hist. Soc. Coll.*, Vol. II, p. 93.

* Washington *had* entertained such a design at times from September 1778 to December 1779.—*Life and Writings*, Vol. VI, pp. 56, 423. Vermont was to aid in this expedition.—See Vol. I, p. 217.

sentation from New York.[1] The plan is, which is a report of a committee, to recommend it to New York and New Hampshire to relinquish their jurisdiction, or to consult on the propriety of doing it, to the state of Vermont, according to her former claims—the Massachusetts having already passed a law for that purpose, provided the other states would do the same. This report being the order of the day was recommitted. This plan probably might in some degree exculpate congress from blame, and they might refer the sufferers to the state, who had voluntarily relinquished their jurisdiction, for compensation for their lands. 'Tis said a person from our state [New York] lately informed some members of congress that a majority of the assembly and a greater part of the senate were in favor of granting their independence. Probably this might have some effect.—*Clinton Papers*, No. 3862.

James Madison to Edmund Pendleton.

PHILADELPHIA, August 14, 1781.

Dear Sir:—The controversy relating to the district called Vermont, the inhabitants of which have for several years claimed and exercised the jurisdiction of an independent state, is at length put into a train of speedy decision. Notwithstanding the objections to such an event, there is no question but they will soon be established into a separate and federal state. A relinquishment made by Massachusetts of her claims; *a despair of finally obtaining theirs on the part of New York and New Hampshire, the other claimants on whom these enterprising adventurers were making fresh encroachments;* the latent support afforded them by the leading people of the New England states in general, from which they emigrated; *the just ground of apprehension that their rulers were engaging in clandestine negotiations with the enemy;* and lastly, perhaps, the jealous policy of some of the little states, which hope that such a precedent may engender a division of some of the large ones, are the circumstances which will determine the concurrence of congress in this affair."—See *Early History*, p. 346-353; *Madison Papers*, Vol. I, p. 96.

Referring to the intercepted dispatch, IRA ALLEN said:

This information had greater influence on the wisdom and virtue of Congress than all the exertions of Vermont in taking Ticonderoga, Crown Point, and the two divisions from General Buogoyne's army, or their petition to be admitted as a State in the general confederation, and offers to pay their proportion of the expenses of the war.—I. Allen's *History*, in *Vt. Hist. Soc. Collections*, Vol. I, p. 429.

IN CONGRESS, FRIDAY, August 3, 1781.

A memorial of the delegates, as agents for the state of New-York, respecting the controverted jurisdiction of the district called the New Hampshire Grants, was read.

The memorial was as follows:

Memorial of the Delegates of New York to Congress.[2]

To the United States of America in Congress assembled:

The underwritten delegates for the state of New York have the honor, in obedience to an express instruction from the Legislature of the state of New York, to represent, that on the 24th of September, 1779, it

---

[1] That is, previous to July 31 1781, referring, doubtless, to the action of the committee, created July 9, on the letter of President Weare of June 20.

[2] From the *Haldimand Papers*—furnished to Gen. H. by Ira Allen.

was unanimously resolved by Congress that it be most earnestly recommended to the states of New Hampshire, Massachusetts and New York (among other things) forthwith to pass laws to refer to the decision of Congress all differences and disputes relative to jurisdiction over the district called the New Hampshire Grants, which they respectively had with the people of that district, so that Congress might proceed thereon on the first day of February then next, and Congress did thereby pledge their faith to carry into execution and support their determination and decision in the premises.

That Congress having declared it to be essential to the interests of the whole Confederation that all intestine dissentions be carefully avoided, and domestic peace and good order be maintained, it was further unanimously resolved: that it was the duty of the people of the district aforesaid who denied the jurisdiction of all the aforesaid states, to abstain in the meantime from exercising any power over any of the inhabitants of the said district who profess themselves to be citizens of, or to owe allegiance to, any or either of the said states, but that none of the towns either on the east or west side of Connecticut River were to be considered as included within the said district, but such as had heretofore joined in denying the jurisdiction of either of the said states, and had assumed a separate jurisdiction which they called the state of Vermont; and further, that in the opinion of Congress the three states aforesaid ought in the mean time to suspend executing their laws over any of the inhabitants of the said district, except such of them as professed allegiance to and confessed the jurisdiction of the same respectively; and further, that Congress would consider any violence committed against the tenor, true intent and meaning of that resolution as a breach of the peace of the Confederacy, which they were determined to keep and maintain. And it is further resolved unanimouslv, that in the opinion of Congress no unappropriated lands or estates which were or might be adjudged forfeited or confiscated, lying in the said district, ought, until the final decision of Congress in the premises, to be granted or sold. That in pursuance of the said recommendation the Legislature of the state of New York passed a law fully authorizing Congress (among other things) to hear and determine all differences and disputes relative to the jurisdiction between the state of New York and such of the inhabitants of that part of the said district which lies on the west side of Counecticut River as denied the jurisdiction of that state; and that the said decision being duly made and published, should be and remain final and conclusive against that state forever. That in conformity to the said resolution, law and at great expense, the state of New York made the necessary preparations for supporting their territorial rights, and similar steps were taken on the part of the state of New Hampshire. That on the 19th of September, '80, all the parties concerned in the said controversy (Massachusetts Bay excepted) attended, namely: the delegates and agents from the states of New Hampshire and New York respectively, Ira Allen and Stephen R. Bradley in behalf of the people of the Grants claiming a separate and independent jurisdiction, Luke Knowlton, agent in behalf of a number of towns within that part of the said district known by the name of the county of Cumberland, and Peter Olcot and Bezaleel Woodward, agents for the towns in the northern parts of the said district on both sides of the Connecticut River, and the delegates as agents for the state of New York, laid before Congress evidence with an intent to prove that the district known by the name of the New Hampshire Grants on the west side of the Connecticut River is within the limits of the state of New York; that the state of New Hampshire had acknowledged this, and that the people of the said district had been represented in the Legislature of New York since the year 1764, and submitted to the authority, jurisdiction and government of the Congress and Convention of the said state till late in the year 1777, and therefore have no right to a separate and independent jurisdiction. That on the 27th of the same month, all the parties being present except Messrs. Allen and Bradley, agents for the people of the Grants claiming a separate and independent jurisdiction, who, although duly notified, declined any further attendance, the agents of the state of New Hampshire proceeded to offer evidence tending to prove that the tract of country known by the name of New Hampshire Grants was within the state of New Hampshire, and that therefore the people inhabiting the said tract of country can have no right to a separate and independent jurisdiction. That Luke Knowlton, agent in behalf of part of the county of Cumberland, within the said district, and Peter Olcott and Bezaleel Woodward, agents from the towns in the northern parts of the New Hampshire Grants on both sides of Connecticut river, being respectively called upon and having nothing to add, and pressing Congress to come to a determination, withdrew. That the delegates of the state of New York have repeatedly entreated Congress to decide the matters in question respecting the claim of an independent state, set up by some of the inhabitants of the district aforesaid, but a decision hath hitherto been deferred. The underwritten delegates are further instructed to represent that the state of New York, in compliance with the resolutions of Congress before recited, have hitherto suspended the execution of their laws over any inhabitants of the said district, except such as professed allegiance to, and confessed the jurisdiction of, the same, and have refrained from granting any lands within the said district. The inhabitants who deny our jurisdiction, on the contrary, have strengthened their party by disposing of those lands, and exercising force to compel their neighbors, within the said district, who profess themselves to be citizens and to own allegiance to the state of New York, to submit to their authority, and in violation of the express resolutions of Congress, have passed acts to include with their assumed jurisdiction several considerable districts extending westward from the claim they set up at the time of passing the said resolution, to the middle of Hudson's River. That their high-handed encroachments have greatly interrupted the raising of levies and supplies within the state of New York for the support of the war, and must be productive of further weakness and disorder, and render the said state, already greatly exhausted and desolated, altogether unable to contribute to the common cause. From these weighty considerations the underwritten are expressly instructed by the Legislature of the state of New York to urge Congress, agreeable to their said resolutions and engagements, to decide the controversy so long subsisting respecting the claim of independent jurisdiction set up under the pretended state of Vermont, and to take measures in the meantime for restraining the encroachments of the said inhabitants, at least within the bounds which they themselves, till the late extraordinary extention, considered, represented and claimed as comprehending the New Hampshire Grants. The underwritten do therefore, by this public act, (which they pray may be received amongst the records of the United States,) make known the just expectations and earnest request of the Legislature of the state of New York, declaring their readiness to lay before such of the members of Congress as may be uninformed, satisfactory evidence of the title of New York to all that part of the controverted district which lies on the west side of Connecticut River.

Done at Philadelphia, in obedience to the express instruction of the

Legislature of the State of New York, the 3d day of August, 1781, and in the sixth year of our Independence.

(Signed) JAMES DUANE,
EZRA LEHOMMEDIEU,
Delegates for the state of New York and agents in the controversy referred to.

SECRETARY'S OFFICE, CONGRESS, August 21, 1781.

The foregoing is a true copy of the original filed in this office.

(Signed) GEORGE BOND,
Deputy Secretary of Congress.

IN CONGRESS, TUESDAY, August 7, 1781.

Congress took into consideration the report of the committee, consisting of Mr. Sherman, Mr. McKean, Mr. Carroll, Mr. Varnum, Mr. Madison, to whom was recommitted their report on a letter of the 20th June from the President of New Hampshire, together with a motion relative to the subject; and thereupon came to the following resolutions:

Whereas the states of New-Hampshire and New-York, have submitted to Congress the decision of the disputes between them and the people inhabiting the New-Hampshire Grants, on the west side of Connecticut river, called the state of Vermont, concerning their respective claims of jurisdiction over the said territory, and have been heard thereon; and whereas, the people aforesaid claim and exercise the powers of a sovereign independent state, and have requested to be admitted into the federal union of the United States of America: in order thereto, and that they may have an opportunity to be heard in vindication of their said claim:

Resolved, That a committee of five be appointed to confer with such person or persons, as may be appointed by the people residing on the New-Hampshire Grants, on the west side of Connecticut river, or by their representative body, respecting their claim to be an independent state, and on what terms it may be proper to admit them into the federal union of these states, in case the United States in Congress assembled, shall determine to recognize their independence, and thereof make report:

And it is hereby recommended to the people of the territory aforesaid, or their representative body, to appoint an agent or agents to repair immediately to Philadelphia, with full powers and instructions to confer with the said committee on the matters aforesaid, and on behalf of the said people, to agree upon and ratify terms and articles of union and confederation with the United States of America, in case they shall be admitted into the union; and the said committee are hereby instructed to give notice to the agents of the states of New-Hampshire and New-York, to be present at the conference aforesaid.

Resolved, That in case Congress shall recognize the independence of the said people of Vermont, they will consider all the lands belonging to New-Hampshire and New-York respectively, without the limits of Vermont aforesaid, as coming within the mutual guarantee of territory contained in the articles of confederation; and that the United States will accordingly guarantee such lands and the jurisdiction over the same, against any claims or encroachments from the inhabitants of Vermont aforesaid.[1]

---

[1] These resolutions were sent to Gov. Chittenden by Gen. Washington, by a special messenger—Capt. Ezra Heacock,—who was also charged

WEDNESDAY, August 8, 1781.

Congress proceeded to the election of a committee of five, to confer with such person or persons as may be appointed by the people residing on the New-Hampshire Grants, on the west side of Connecticut river, or by their representative body, respecting their claim to be an independent state, and on what terms it may be proper to admit them into the federal union of these states, in case the United States in Congress assembled, shall determine to recognize their independence:

The members chosen, Mr. Boudinot [of New Jersey,] Mr. Vandyke [of Delaware,] Mr. Carroll [of Maryland,] Mr. Montgomery [of Pennsylvania,] Mr. Randolph [of Virginia.]

FRIDAY, August 17, 1781.

Congress took into consideration a report of the committee appointed in pursuance of the resolution of the 7th, to confer with agents to be appointed by the people of the New-Hampshire Grants, on the west side of Connecticut river; and to whom was referred a letter from Jonas Fay, Ira Allen, and Bezaleel Woodward, wherein they represent, that the said J. Fay, I. Allen and B. Woodward, have produced to them a commission, under the hand of Thomas Chittenden Esq; empowering them among other things, to repair to the American Congress, and to propose to and receive from them terms of an union with the United States; whereupon,

Resolved, That it be an instruction to the committee to confer with the said Jonas Fay, Ira Allen and Bezaleel Woodward, on the subject of their mission.[1]

---

with a verbal inquiry, whether the people of Vermont would be satisfied with the independence suggested by the resolutions, or really designed to join the enemy. Gov. Chittenden conversed freely on Vermont affairs with Capt. Heacock; assured him that the negotiation with Canada was to secure the state from invasion; that the people of Vermont were zealous supporters of national independence, and desired the admission of their state into the union; but that under no circumstances would they submit to the jurisdiction of New York: "that they would oppose this by force of arms, and would join with the British in Canada, rather than to submit to that government." Capt. Heacock was requested to report these declarations to Gen. Washington.—*Vt. Hist. Soc. Collections*, Vol. II, p. 158.

[1] The letter referred to was as follows:

PHILADELPHIA, 14th Aug. 1781.

Sir,—We have the honor to enclose a duplicate of our commission to attend on the Honorable the Congress, and have to add that we are ready to enter on the business of our appointment. We are, &c.

JONAS FAY,
IRA ALLEN,
BEZ'L WOODWARD.

His Excellency the President of Congress.

*Commission to the Vermont Delegates to Congress.**

By His Excellency Thomas Chittenden Esquire Captain-General, Governor and Commander-in-Chief in and over the State of Vermont.

To the Honorable Jonas Fay and Ira Allen Esq[rs.] and to Bazaleel Woodward, Esq[r.] Greeting.

* From the *Haldimand Papers*—copy furnished to Gen. H. by Ira Allen.

On the 18th the committee of Congress and the Agents for Vermont had an interview, the record of which does not appear on the journal of Congress. The two documents annexed are from the *Haldimand Papers*, having been furnished to Gen. Haldimand by Ira Allen:

Vermont Delegates to Committee of Congress.

To the Honorable Committee of Congress:

Whereas, the state of Vermont hath formed jurisdictional union with people inhabiting a district of land known by the name of New Hampshire Grants, east of Connecticut River, on apprehension that the said district does not of right belong to New Hampshire; also with a district 20 miles in breadth, lying west of the New Hampshire Grants, on apprehension that it does not of right belong to the state of New York, by means of which union it is impracticable for the people on the New Hampshire Grants, west of Connecticut River only, to perform any public act as a state, exclusive of the districts above mentioned, and that the claims of the people on the said districts to independence from the states of New Hampshire and New York respectively, may have a full and fair hearing, and that a final decision may be had thereon as soon as may be: Therefore, the subscribers, delegates from and in behalf of the state of Vermont, beg leave to propose the following as terms which appear to them necessary in order to a Federal union between that and the United States:

1st. That Vermont be recognized as an independent state, under the following description, viz: Beginning at the northwest corner of the state of Massachusetts, which is the northwest corner of the town of Williamstown, and from thence extending eastward in the north line of Massachusetts to the west bank of Connecticut River; thence up the river as it tends to the 45th degree of north latitude; thence west in said latitude line to the centre of Lake Champlain, (west of Missisquy Bay); thence southwardly in the deepest channel of the said Lake, as also the channels of the South and East Bays, to the head of the latter; thence up the deepest channel of Poulteney River, and the west line of the town of Poulteney; thence southward on the westward line of the seve-

---

Agreeable to a Resolution of the General Assembly of this State passed at their Session in June last, appointing You Delegates in behalf of this State to repair to the American Congress; with full powers to propose to and receive from them terms for an Union of this State with the United States, and to transact any other matters at Congress which may be necessary for the Wellfare of this State: such terms of Union or other Treaty agreed on to be subject to the ratification of the Legislature of this State previous to their establishment, and You are to take Seats in Congress as Delegates in behalf of this State when terms of Union shall be agreed on and Ratified as aforementioned.

These are therefore to authorize and impower You, the said Jonas Fay, Ira Allen and Bezaleel Woodward, Esq$^{rs.}$ or either two of you to attend on the Honorable the Congress of the United States of America as soon as may be, then and there to do and transact the business of your appointment.

Given under my hand and the seal of this State in the Council Chamber at Bennington this 10th day of July A. D. 1781, and in the fifth Year of the Independence of this State.

(Signed) THO$^{S.}$ CHITTENDEN.

By His Excellency's Command.

(Signed) JOSEPH FAY, *Sec$^{y.}$*

ral towns of Poulteney, Wells, Pawlet, Ruport, Sandgate, Arlington, Shaftsbury, Bennington and Pownall, to the place of beginning.

2nd. That delegates to represent the state of Vermont in Congress be elected by the representatives of the freemen of the state, as it is now extended, until the several claims of New Hampshire and New York to the said districts be heard and determined.

3rd. That the several claims of New Hampshire and New York be determined as soon as may be, and agreeable to the mode prescribed by the Articles of Confederation for the decision of disputes between two or more states concerning boundary, jurisdiction, &c.

4th. That Vermont have the same right as any other state, on application to Congress, to have an hearing on the said disputes, and to be admitted in like manner by their agents (to be appointed for that purpose) as a party in support of the claim of the people within the said districts to independence from the said states of New Hampshire and New York respectively. In case that on trial the districts aforesaid shall [not] be found to belong of right to the states of New Hampshire and New York respectively, they shall be thenceforth considered as belonging to the jurisdiction of the state of Vermont.

(Signed) { JONAS FAY, IRA ALLEN, BEZ'L WOODWARD.

Philadelphia, August 18th, 1781.

Indorsed: "Copy. (No. 27.) Proposals from the agents of Vermont to Congress, dated Philadelphia, August 18th, 1781."—From the *Haldimand Papers*, in *Vt. Hist. Soc. Collections*, Vol. II, p. 164.

Questions by Committee of Congress to Vermont Delegates, and their answers thereto.

PHILADELPHIA, 18th August, 1781.

Query 1*st.* Are the boundaries, set forth in the written propositions delivered in by the said agents, at this time, claimed by the State of Vermont, as the lines of jurisdiction, the same as contained in the resolution of Congress of the 7th of August instant?

Answer. They are the same, with the addition of part of the waters of Lake Champlain, for the benefit of trade &c.

Query 2*d.* What part do the people of Vermont mean to take, as to the past expences of the present war, and what aid do they propose to afford as to men and money, to the common defence?

Answer. Such proportion as shall be mutually judged equitable, after their admission to a seat in Congress, which has been several times officially proposed by agents on the part of Vermont.

Query 3*d.* What are the ideas of the people of Vermont relative to the claim of private property, under grants or patents from New-Hampshire, or New-York, previous to the present revolution?

Answer. Altho' the State of Vermont hath not, hitherto, authorized any court to take cognizance of such causes, as respect titles of lands, nevertheless, they have had, and still have it in contemplation to adopt such modes, as the circumstances, arising out of each case, may justify, without adhering to the strict rules of law.

Query 4*th.* What are the intentions of your constituents, in regard to the patents that were granted on conditions of settlement within a given time, and which have been prevented by the claims of the people of Vermont, and the present revolution?

Answer. No forfeitures have been taken by the state of Vermont, on any such grant, for non-performance of conditions of settlement, and we conceive it to be the intention of our constituents to grant a further reasonable time for fulfilling such conditions.

Query 5th. What are the number of inhabitants within the lines mentioned in their propositions above mentioned?

Answer. As the citizens of Vermont have not been lately numbered, we can therefore only estimate them at about thirty thousand, which we conceive to be nearly a true estimation.

Query 6th. What quantity of land is contained within the said bounds?

Answer. There has been no accurate survey of the state of Vermont, but we conceive it to contain about five million acres.

Query 7th. What applications have been made, either publicly or privately, by the enemies of the United States, or their adherents, to draw off the people of Vermont from their affection to the United States of America?

Answer. The honorable committee are possessed of copies of Bevy. Robinson's letters, enclosed in B. General Allen's letter of the 9th of March last, to the then President of Congress; and any private offers we cannot avouch for.

Query 8th. In case the enemy should attempt an invasion of the northern frontiers, what aid, as to men and provisions, could be raised in the State of Vermont, for the public defence, (you can suppose the invasion made in different quarters) and within what time?

Answer. The number of militia, within the lines herein limited, we suppose to consist of about seven thousand, in general well armed and accoutred, and have ever shown themselves spirited in case of alarms, &c. In regard to provisions, the country is fertile but new and considerable emigrations from other states to Vermont.—The Legislature, at their session, in October last, levied a tax on the inhabitants for provisions sufficient for victualling one thousand five hundred troops in the field for twelve months; and we are of opinion a larger store may be, in the same manner, collected, the ensuing autumn.

Indorsed: "Copy (No. 28) 1781. Queries from the Committee of Congress to the agents of Vermont and their answers, 18th August."—From the *Haldimand Papers*, in *Vt. Hist. Soc. Collections*, Vol. II, p. 165.

Of this interview IRA ALLEN gave other details in the following account:

A Committee of Congress was appointed to meet and agree with the Agents of Vermont, respecting lines and boundaries; they accordingly met. The eastern boundary line [Connecticut river] proposed by the [delegates of Vermont to the] Committee of Congress was not disputed, but the western boundary afforded a tedious dispute. Mr. James Duane, and Colonel Allen, managed the controversy, both being greatly interested in the lands liable to be affected by the boundary line. Different proposals had been made, without producing any effect, and the Committee often adjourned for deliberation, and went out of the Committee-room in Congress. At length Colonel Allen drew an abstruse line that would answer Vermont; gave it to the late Roger Shearman, Esq. member for Connecticut, just as Congress were impatient to adjourn, praying him to redraft it, and propose it as his own, which he complied with, and laid it before Congress, which was immediately received and passed into a resolve, and Congress adjourned, before Mr. Duane properly understood the motion, or rather, the operation of such proposed line, which added to Vermont beyond the original claim of New Hampshire, (which was a line from the north-west corner of the Massachusett's north, ten degrees east, in the west line of the towns of Pownal, Bennington, Shaftsbury,&c.) the towns of Fairhaven, Benson, South Hero, North Hero, and Isle of Mott, and several other Islands, and put out of dispute Alburg, and some other lands, as also the navigation of Lake Champlain. Had the Legislature of Vermont described Pawlet River, instead of Poultney River, in their act of relinquishment of jurisdiction, they would have held a much larger tract, and been equally consistent with the resolve of Congress, and if disputes arose respecting said line, they could not have been used against Vermont, as her Agents did not consent to them. —*I. Allen's History*, in *Vt. Hist. Soc. Collections*, Vol. I, p. 432.

IN CONGRESS, MONDAY, August 20, 1781.

The committee appointed to confer with J. Fay, I. Allen and B. Woodward, delivered in a report, which was taken into consideration; and, thereupon, Congress came to the following resolution:

It being the fixed purpose of Congress to adhere to the guarantee to the States of New-Hampshire and New-York, contained in the resolutions of the 7th instant:

Resolved, That it be an indispensable preliminary to the recognition of the independence of the people inhabiting the territory called Vermont, and their admission into the fœderal union, that they explicitly relinquish all demands of lands or jurisdiction on the east side of the west bank of Connecticut river, and on the west side of a line beginning at the north-west corner of the state of Massachusetts, thence running twenty miles east of Hudson's river, so far as the said river runs north-easterly in its general course; then by the west bounds of the townships granted by the late government of New-Hampshire to the river running from South-Bay to Lake-Champlain, thence along the said river to Lake-Champlain, thence along the waters of Lake-Cha.nplain to the latitude of forty-five degrees north excepting a neck of land between Missiskoy-Bay and the waters of Lake-Champlain.

On the question to agree to this, the yeas and nays being required by Mr. Sharpe,

New-Hampshire,	Mr. Livermore,	*ay*	*	*Delaware,*	Mr. M'Kean,	*ay*	*ay*
Massachusetts,	Mr. Patridge,	*ay*	*ay*		Mr. Vandyke,	*ay*	
	Mr. Osgood,	*ay*		*Maryland,*	Mr. Jenifer,	*ay*	*ay*
Rhode-Island,	Mr. Mowry,	*ay*	*		Mr. Carroll,	*ay*	
Connecticut,	Mr. Ellsworth,	*ay*	*ay*	*Virginia,*	Mr. Madison,	*ay*	*ay*
	Mr. Sherman,	*ay*			Mr. Bland,	*ay*	
New-York,	Mr. Duane,	*no*	*no*		Mr. M. Smith,	*ay*	
	Mr. L'Hommedieu,	*no*			Mr. Randolph,	*ay*	
New-Jersey,	Mr. Boudinot,	*ay*	*ay*	*North Carolina,*	Mr. Sharpe,	*ay*	*
	Mr. Elmer,	*ay*		*South Carolina,*	Mr. Matthews,	*no*	*ay*
Pennyslvania,	Mr. Atlee,	*ay*	*ay*		Mr. Bee,	*ay*	
	Mr. Clymer,	*ay*			Mr. Eveligh,	*ay*	
	Mr. T. Smith,	*ay*		*Georgia,*	Mr. Walton,	*ay*	*ay*
					Mr. Howley,	*ay*	

* Not counted, not being a majority of the delegates of the state.

So it was resolved in the affirmative.

It will be observed that New York only voted in the negative. From the affirmative vote of Mr. Livermore of N. H. the inference is that the instructions of New Hampshire of March 31 1781 were in harmony with those of the preceding January, on p. 274, *ante*.

PROCEEDINGS OF THE GENERAL ASSEMBLY OF VERMONT, OCTOBER 1781, ON THE RESOLUTIONS OF CONGRESS OF AUGUST 1781.

The deliberations and action of the legislature were mainly in a committee of both Houses, and for that reason the journals do not give an account in detail. Ira Allen stated in his history of Vermont that much difficulty was encountered on account of the conflicting interests growing out of the eastern and western unions; however, a result was reached on the 19th of October, when Jonas Fay of the Council, and Messrs. Ezra Stiles, Stephen R. Bradley, and John Barrett of the House, were appointed a committee to "prepare a Bill" agreeable to the report of the committee of the whole. A "bill," in the language of the record, meant an official statement of the action of the legislature. It was as follows:

[From Slade's *State Papers.*]

STATE OF VERMONT, CHARLESTOWN, October 16th, 1781.

The Governor and Council having joined the general assembly, in a committee of the whole, to take into consideration the report of the honorable Jonas Fay, Ira Allen and Bezaleel Woodward, Esquires, who were appointed by the Legislature of this State, in the month of June last, to repair to the American Congress, with powers to propose to, and receive from, them, terms for an union of this, with the United States, &c.

His Excellency THOMAS CHITTENDEN, *Esquire, in the chair:*

The said agents laid before the committee the following papers, which were read by the secretary in their order, viz.

1*st* and 2*d*. A copy of their letter to the President of Congress, of the 14th of August last, enclosing a duplicate of their commission.

3*d*. The resolutions of Congress, of the 7th and 8th of August last.

4*th*. Brigadier General Bellows, and associates, petition to New-Hampshire, 25th of May, 1781.

5*th*. Petition of the selectmen of Swanzy to New-Hampshire, June 9th, 1781.

6*th*. Honorable Mesheck Weare's letter, to be laid before Congress, dated 20th June, 1781.

7*th*. Messieurs Duane and Ezra L'Hommedieu's memorial and prayer to Congress, of the 3d day of August, 1781; together with Ira Allen and Stephen R. Bradley Esquire's remonstrance to Congress, dated September 22d, 1780.

8*th*. Resolve of Congress, dated 17th August, 1781.

9*th*. Written proposals to committee of Congress, dated August 18th, 1781.

10*th*. Questions proposed to the agents of Vermont by the committee of Congress, August 18th, 1781.

11*th*. The foregoing questions, with the answers annexed.

12*th*. Resolutions of Congress of the 20th August, 1781.

The further consideration of the report being referred, adjourned till to-morrow morning, nine o'clock.

October 17.

Met, according to adjournment.

The committee proceeded to the consideration of the resolutions of Congress, of the 20th day of August aforesaid, and other papers mentioned in the report of said agents; and, after some time spent thereon, resolved that, in the opinion of this committee, the Legislature cannot comply with the resolutions last referred to, without destroying the foundation of the present universal harmony and agreement that subsists in this state, and a violation of solemn compact entered into, by articles of union and confederation.

The further consideration of the report being postponed, adjourned to nine o'clock to-morrow morning.

October 18.

The committee having resumed the further consideration of the said report:

Resolved, That, inasmuch as the resolutions of Congress of the 7th and 20th of August last, did, by no means, comport with, but entirely preclude, any propositions made by our agents; it is, therefore, the opinion of this committee, that the propositions made by our agents to the committee of Congress, on the 18th of August last, ought not, in future, to be considered as binding on the part of Vermont.

Resolved, That it be and is hereby recommended to the Legislature of this state, that their thanks be returned to their honourable agents, for their good services in behalf of this state, on the business of their late mission to the Congress of the United States of America.

And this committee recommend to the Legislature of this state, to remain firm in the principles on which the state of Vermont first assumed government; and to hold the articles of union which connect each part of the state with the other, inviolate; and, for the further information and satisfaction of the honourable the Congress, and the world, do recommend to the Legislature to publish the following articles, which respect the admission of Vermont into the fœderal union, viz.

ART. 1st. That the independence of the state of Vermont be held sacred, and that no member of the Legislature shall give his vote, or otherwise use his endeavours, to obtain any act or resolution of Assembly, that shall endanger the existence, independence and well being of said state, by referring its independency to the arbitrament of any power.

ART. 2d. That whenever this state becomes united with the American States, and there shall then be any disputes between this and any of the United States, the Legislature of the state of Vermont will then (as they have ever proposed) submit to Congress, or such other tribunal as may be mutually agreed on, for the settlement of any such disputes.

And that the impartial world may be fully convinced of the good and laudable disposition of Vermont, and of her readiness to comply with any reasonable proposal, for the adjustment of the disputes, respecting boundary lines, between this and the neighbouring states of New-Hampshire and New-York, this committee further recommend to the Legislature to make the following proposals to the said states of New-Hampshire and New-York, respectively: that whereas, disputes have arisen between the states of New-Hampshire and Vermont, relative to jurisdictional boundary lines, &c. the Legislature of Vermont, being willing and desirous, as much as in them lies, to promote unity and good accord between the two states, do propose to the state of New-Hampshire, that all matters relating to the aforesaid dispute, shall be submitted to five, or more, judicious, unprejudiced persons, who shall be mutually agreed on, elected and chosen by a committee of Legislature, on the part of each state, respectively.

And that the states of New-Hampshire and Vermont do pledge their faith, each to the other, that the decision had, by the persons so elected, being made up in writing, signed by the President of such Commissioners, and delivered to the secretary of each state, respectively, shall be held sacredly binding on each of the said states of New-Hampshire and Vermont for ever.

And that proposals of the same tenor, be also made to the Legislature of New-York.

And this committee do further recommend, that nine persons be elected Commissioners, by the Legislature, on the part of Vermont, to treat with Commissioners to be elected on the part of New-Hampshire and New-York, respectively, for the adjusting the aforesaid jurisdictional boundary lines.

And that they be commissioned by his Excellency the Governor, and the faith of this state be by him pledged in behalf of the state, that the decision, thus had, shall, in future, be held as sacredly binding on the part of Vermont.

The committee further recommend to the Legislature, that the Proceedings of this committee, be officially transmitted to the Congress of the United States; and that they be enclosed in a letter, under the signature of his Excellency the Governor, and directed to the President of Congress.

And this committee do further advise the Legislature to recommend to the authority in every part of the state, to remain firm in the support of government, and the punctual execution of the laws, notwithstanding the various measures taken to create divisions and discord.

The commissioners chosen for the above purpose,--the honourable Elisha Paine, Jonas Fay, Ira Allen, and Peter Olcott, Esquires, Daniel Jones, Esquire, Colonel Gideon Warren, Phineas Whiteside, Esquire, Colonel Joseph Caldwell, and Ezra Stiles, Esquire.

Resolved, That it be an instruction to the said Commissioners, that they prepare, and make, the necessary defence in the premises, and that they introduce the said matters to New-Hampshire and New-York, in such way as to them shall appear best.

October 19, 1781.

Voted that this committee be dissolved.

(Signed) BEZA. WOODWARD, *Clerk of Committee.*

"STATE OF VERMONT, IN GENERAL ASSEMBLY,
CHARLESTOWN, October 19th, 1781.

The aforesaid report being read, and question being put, it was unanimously approved and accepted. (Signed) ROSWELL HOPKINS, *Clerk.*

IN COUNCIL, October 19th, 1781.

Read and concurred,
(Signed) JOSEPH FAY, *Secretary.*"

PROPOSALS OF VERMONT TO NEW HAMPSHIRE AND NEW YORK FOR THE SETTLEMENT OF BOUNDARIES—OCT. 1781.

Pursuant to the foregoing resolutions of the General Assembly, Gov. Chittenden issued a commission to the commissioners on the 27th of October; and on the same day copies of the resolutions and commission were forwarded to the President of New Hampshire, as appears from the following documents in the volume of New Hampshire *State Papers on the Vermont Controversy.*

Elisha Payne to President Weare.[1]

CHARLESTOWN, October 27th. 1781.

Sir,—The Commissioners appointed by the State of Vermont to negotiate and compleat the settlement of the boundary lines between that

---

[1] N. H. *State Papers on the Vermont Controversy*, p. 255; it is preceded by a copy of the proceedings of the Vermont Assembly of Oct. 16 1781.

State and the States of N. Hampshire and New York respectively agreeable to the resolutions of the Legislature of Vermont, beg leave herewith to transmit those resolutions together with a duplicate of their Commission for the consideration of the Legislature of New Hampshire.

The Commissioners are ready to attend [to] the business of their appointment whenever they shall receive an answer in the premises.

In behalf of the Commissioners, I am Sir

Your most Obedient Hum^ble^ Servant,

ELISHA PAYNE.

*The Honble Meshech Weare Esqr.*

President Council of New Hampshire.

Commission of the Vermont Commissioners.[1]

{ SEAL. } His Excellency THOMAS CHITTENDEN Esq; Captain-General, Governor and Commander in Chief in and over the State of Vermont.

To the Honorable *Elisha Payne, Jonas Fay, Ira Allen*, and *Peter Olcott*, Esq^rs.^: *Daniel Jones* Esq: Colonel *Gideon Warren, Phinehas Whiteside*, Esq; Colonel *Joseph Caldwell* and *Ezra Stiles* Esq:

GREETING.

Agreeable to a Resolution of the Governor, Council and House of Assembly at their Session held at Charlestown this Instant October, appointing you Commissioners for and in behalf of the STATE OF VERMONT to enter upon a Negociation for the Settlement and Adjustment of the Boundary Lines, as well between the State of NEW HAMPSHIRE and VERMONT as between the State of NEW YORK and VERMONT agreeable to your Directions contained in the Resolution aforesaid.

THESE ARE THEREFORE, in the Name and by the Authority of the Freemen of the State of VERMONT, to authorize and amply empower you the said Elisha Payne, Jonas Fay, Ira Allen, Peter Olcott, Daniel Jones, Gideon Warren, Phinehas Whiteside, Joseph Caldwell and Ezra Stiles, or any five of you the said Commissioners, to compleat and carry into Execution the Negociation and Settlement of the said Boundary Lines of Jurisdiction between the said States of NEW-HAMPSHIRE and NEW YORK with the said State of VERMONT respectively agreeable to said Resolutions.

AND I DO HEREBY PLEDGE THE FAITH of the said State of VERMONT, that the determinations had in the Premises shall be held sacredly binding on the part of VERMONT.

IN TESTIMONY whereof, I have hereunto set my Hand, and caused the Seal of this State to be affixed, In Council, this 27th Day of October Anno Domini, One Thousand Seven Hundred & Eighty one—And in the 5th year of the Independence of this State. THO^S.^ CHITTENDEN.

By His Excellency's Command,

THO: TOLMAN, *Dep. Sec^y.^*

(Duplicate.)

Ira Allen regarded the failure to send agents personally, in October, to New Hampshire and New York as a great mistake; first, because he believed New Hampshire could have been then persuaded to assent to Vermont's proposition; second, that New York would have been forced either to assent or refuse, probably the latter; and third, that with the assent of New Hampshire, and her aid with that of the states then

[1] *N. H. Papers on the Vermont Controversy*, p. 257.

friendly, "Vermont would have retained her west union to the present day, if not extended her claims further west."[1] In December, Gov. Chittenden sent Allen to urge the assent of New Hampshire, and an effort was made in conjunction with other agents appointed by Lieut. Gov. Payne; but at that date New Hampshire had resolved upon forcible measures, as will appear hereafter, and the attempt at conciliation was fruitless.

Gov. Chittenden to Ira Allen.[2]

ARLINGTON, December 15th 1781.

Sir,—I have Consulted a Number of the members of my Council on the Controversy between this & the State of New Hampshire Respecting the Boundary lines between the Two States Whereupon I do hereby appoint & authorise you to Repare to the Genl. Court of New Hampshire & there use your Influence that they Comply with the Proposals of the Legislature of this State for an amicable Settlement thereby if Possible to Prevent the Effution of Human Blood as the appearence of Civil War will but too much give Countenance to the Common Enemy of these States. THOS. CHITTENDEN.

To Colo. Ira Allen.
(Copy.)

Lieut. Gov. Payne to Gen. Enos and Sheriff Page.[3]

STATE OF VERMONT.

To Brigadier General Roger Enos and William Page Esq.

Gentlemen,—By advice of sundry members of the council of this State You are hereby appointed and empowered to repair forthwith to the Assembly of New Hampshire and in conjunction with Colo. Ira Allen (already there by appointment of the Governor) use your endeavours that said Assembly consider and concur in the proposals made to them for settlement of the dispute between the two States relative to jurisdiction, and agree on measures to prevent hostilities till an equitable and impartial determination of the said disputes can be obtained.

ELISHA PAYNE, *Lieut. Govr.*

Charlestown, Decr. 21 A. D. 1781.

Roger Enos and Ira Allen to Josiah Bartlett.[4]

EXETER, Decr. 29th 1781.

Sir,—You will herewith Receive a Duplicate of our Commission to attend the Genl. Court of New Hampshire and have to add that notwithstanding one of our Colleges [colleagues] Wm. Page Esqr. being Confined in Goal Contrary as we Conceive to the Laws of States or Nations We are so Desirous of an Accomodation we [are] Ready to Enter on the Business of our mission. We are with sentiments of Esteem your Humble Servts.

ROGER ENOS,
IRA ALLEN.

The Honble Elisha [Josiah] Bartlett Esqr.
President of Committee of Safety.

---

[1] IRA ALLEN'S *History, in Vt. Hist. Soc. Collections*, Vol. I, pp. 439–441.

[2] N. H. *State Papers on the Vermont Controversy*, p. 267.

[3] *Same*, p. 303. [4] *Same*, p. 315.

FORCE AGAINST VERMONT ATTEMPTED BY NEW YORK, AND CONTEMPLATED BY NEW HAMPSHIRE—1781-2.[1]

The actual exercise of jurisdiction by Vermont in the East and West Unions, after the failure of the attempts to induce New Hampshire and New York to settle the controversy, very naturally excited the hostility of those states, and the most extraordinary thing is, that both failed to maintain their authority. New York was manifestly unable to do it, mainly from the fact that the sympathies of a majority of the people north of Albany, (from whom her military force was at that time necessarily drawn,) were in favor of Vermont;[2] while New Hampshire seems to have been reluctant to push matters to the extreme of a civil war, in which eastern New Hampshire would have been confronted by a majority of her people in the west, and all the force that Vermont could bring into the field. Moreover it appears from the vote of Mr. LIVERMORE, (the only delegate from New Hampshire present,) for the resolution of Congress, Aug. 20·1781,[3] that the government of New Hampshire was friendly to the independence of Vermont on condition of the relinquishment of the Unions.

COLLISIONS IN THE WESTERN DISTRICT.

New York was the first to commence active measures. Oct. 15 1781, Gen. Peter Gansevoort jr. notified Gov. Clinton of the arrest, at Lansingburgh, by Col. John Van Rensselaer, of Samuel Fairbanks, who had been a private in the colonel's regiment, but had joined those who after the union considered themselves Vermonters, and had received a lieutenant colonel's commission.[4] This was sharply resented by the following letters of Vermont officers to Gen. John Stark, who then commanded the continental troops on the northern frontier.

---

[1] The spirited "*Song of the Vermonters*," which has been assigned to 1779, was undoubtedly written on this occasion. This is evident from allusions in the closing verses to *Lutterloh*, which was not granted until June 1781, and to *Schaghticoke*, which was not annexed until the same month. The verses are as follows:

From far Michiscoui's wild valley to where
Poosoomsuck steals down from his wood-circled lair,
From *Shocticook river* to *Lutterloh* town,—
Ho—all to the rescue! Vermonters, come down!

Come *York* or come *Hampshire*—come traitors and knaves,
If ye rule o'er our land, ye shall rule o'er our graves;
Our vow is recorded—our banner unfurled;
In the name of Vermont we defy all the world!

[2] See letter of Gov. Clinton to Gen. McDougall, *ante*, p. 269.

[3] *Ante*, p. 320.

[4] *Clinton Papers*, No. 2444.

Col. Samuel Robinson, of Vermont Militia, to Gen. Stark.[1]

BENNINGTON, Oct. 16, 1781.

Dear General:—I am surprised to learn that the militia of Albany county have no other business upon their hands, at this time of general alarm and danger, than to distress the inhabitants of Vermont, as if they considered the British from Canada not sufficient for our destruction, at a time when all our militia are under marching orders, and most of them have already marched. This they [the New York authorities] think a proper time to manifest their spite and malice. Part of my regiment has marched to Castleton. I shall this morning follow with the remainder. If your honor cannot find the militia of Albany some other employment, I shall march my regiment to that quarter, and try powder and ball with them, which I have as well as they. I pray your honor to check them if possible.

I am, dear general, your very humble servant,

Hon. General Stark, Saratoga. SAM'L ROBINSON.

Gen. Safford, of Vermont Militia, to Gen. Stark.[2]

BENNINGTON, October 17, 1781.

To Brigadier General Stark: Sir:—In consequence of your request to me of the 11th, I sent orders to the militia, now considered in this state, in the neighborhood of the New City [Lansingburgh.] Lieutenant-colonel Fairbanks is present with me, and informs that, in obedience to my orders, he had mustered a number of men to march to your assistance on Sunday morning. Saturday evening, colonel Van Rensselaer came with a party of men from Albany, and its vicinity, and took them prisoners, broke open their houses, and much distressed their families. Such conduct appears very extraordinary at this time, when every man ought rather to be employed in the defense of his country, than in destroying his neighbor's property. What colonel Van Rensselaer designs, is best known to himself: but it has the appearance of preventing men going to defend the frontier at this critical moment. I have ordered one half of our militia to the north, and the remainder I expect must shortly follow. The inhabitants of this western territory are willing to do their duty under Vermont, but are prevented by York. And now, sir, if you judge it lies within your province to quiet those disorders, I must entreat you to do it. That we may be united is my sincere desire. The dispute of jurisdiction must be settled between the states; but if such conduct is persisted in before [such settlement by the states,] I must repel force by force, and the hardest fend off.

I am, with sentiments of esteem, your obed't serv't,

SAM. SAFFORD.

Oct. 18 Gov. Clinton wrote to Gen. Gansevoort as follows:

Governor Clinton to General Gansevoort.[3]

POUGHKEEPSIE, Oct. 18, 1781.

Dear Sir:——Your letter of the 15th instant was delivered to me on the evening of the 16th. I have delayed answering it, in hopes that the Legislature would ere this have formed a quorum, and that I might have availed myself of their advice on the subject to which it relates; but as this is not yet the case, and it is uncertain when I shall be enabled to

---

[1] *Memoir of Stark*, p. 275; *Vt. Hist. Soc. Collections*, Vol. II, p. 184.

[2] *Memoir of Stark*, p. 277; *Vt. Hist. Soc. Collections*, Vol. II, p. 185.

[3] *Clinton Papers*, No. 2445.

lay the matter before them, I conceive it might be improper longer to defer expressing my own sentiments to you on this subject.

The different unwarrantable attempts, during the Summer, of the people on the Grants to establish their usurped jurisdiction, even beyond their former claim, and the repetition of it (alluded to in your letter,)[1] in direct opposition to a resolution of Congress injurious to this State and favorable to their project of independence,[2] and at a time when the coming enemy are advancing, can only be accounted for by what other parts of their conduct have given us too much reason to expect—disaffection to the common cause.[3] On my part, I have hitherto shown a disposition to evade entering into any altercation with them, that might, in its most remote consequence, give encouragement to the enemy, and expose the frontier settlements to their ravages; and from these considerations alone I have submitted to insults which otherwise would not have been borne with; and I could have wished to have continued this kind of conduct until the approaching season would have secured us against the incursions of the coming enemy. But as from accounts contained in Colonel Van Rensselaer's letter, it would appear that the militia embodying under Mr. Chittenden's orders are for the service of the enemy, and that their first object was to make you a prisoner, it would be unjustifiable to suffer them to proceed.[4] It is therefore my desire that you maintain your authority throughout every part of your brigade, and for this purpose, that you carry the laws of this State into execution against those who shall presume to disobey your lawful orders. I would only observe that these sentiments are founded on an idea that the accounts given by Col. Van Rensselaer in his letter may be relied on; it being still my earnest desire, for the reasons above explained, not to do anything that will bring matters to extremities, at least before the close of the campaign, if it can consistently be avoided.

In my last, I should have mentioned to you that it was not in my power to send you a supply of ammunition; but, as I had reason to believe you had gone to Saratoga, I conceived it improper to say any thing on the subject lest my letter might miscarry. You may recollect that of the whole supply ordered by General Washington, last spring, for the use of the militia, five hundred pounds is all that has been received in the state magazine, which you will easily conceive to be far short of what was necessary for the other exposed parts of the state. With respect to provisions, it is equally out of my power to furnish you with any, but what the state agent, who is now with me, may be able to procure.

I am, with great respect and esteem, Dear Sir, your most obed't serv't,
Brig. Gen. Gansevoort.[5] GEO. CLINTON.

---

[1] Gov. Clinton referred to the East and West Unions.

[2] The Resolution of August 20 1781.

[3] The governor's interpretation of the Haldimand correspondence.

[4] On the very day before this letter was written, Gen. Safford, of the Vermont militia, wrote to Gen. Stark that in consequence of his [Stark's] request, he had on the 11th sent orders to the militia in the West Union, in obedience to which lieutenant-colonel Fairbanks had mustered men *to march to Stark's assistance* when Van Rensselaer took them prisoners. So Van Rensselaer's (or Gov. Clinton's) suspicion or conjecture in this instance was flatly contradicted by Safford.—See preceding letter of Gen. Safford; *Vt. Hist. Soc. Collections*, Vol. II, p. 371.

[5] *Life of Joseph Brant*, Vol. II, pp. 183–185.

Oct. 22, Gov. Chittenden laid before the Vermont Assembly a letter from Fairbanks, stating his arrest by Van Rensselaer, and also his escape in a skirmish in which three New Yorkers were wounded.[1] Thereupon Gov. Chittenden at once wrote to Captain [Col. John] Van Rensselaer a letter, of which the following abstract was given in WILLIAM L. STONE'S *Life of Joseph Brant*, Vol. II.

Governor Chittenden to Captain [*Col. John*] *Van Rensselaer.*[2]

Governor Chittenden wrote to officers of New York, demanding the release of the prisoners taken from the Grants—asserting their [Vermont's] determination to maintain the government they had "set up," and threatening that, in the event of an invasion of the territory of New York by the common enemy, unless those prisoners were given up, they [Vermont] would render no assistance to New York. This letter also contained an admonition that "power was not limited to New York."

Dec. 4, Col. Van Rensselaer informed Gen. Gansevoort that he had been arrested by Col. John Abbott and taken to Bennington, where he was discharged by Vermont magistrates. He also informed Gov. Clinton of the facts, and stated that he intended to defend himself and the authority of New York.[3] Of this affair Gen. Stark gave the following account:

General Stark to Major General Heath.—[Extract.][4]

SARATOGA, 12th December, 1781.

I have sent to Bennington to gain the particulars of a riot raised some time ago, and which still continues at St. Coicks. The particulars are as follows: Men, under the direction of a captain [col.] Abbott, assaulted a public house at Hoosac, seized upon colonel Rensselaer and some others, who considered themselves under the government of New York, and abused them in a most outrageous manner; after which they carried them to Bennington, and called upon the magistrates acting under the authority of Vermont for warrants to arrest them in (as they term it) a legal manner; but, upon the magistrates refusing to interfere in the matter, they were dismissed. Rensselaer, upon his liberation, represented the matter to general Gansevoort, and invited his neighbors to join him and protect him from a second abuse, with which he was severely threatened. Gansevoort approved his conduct, and ordered the militia on both sides the North river above Albany to join them. Those persons called Vermonters discovered the motion of the Yorkers, and immediately collected their forces wi hin half a mile of the quarters of the Yorkers, and in this position the two detachments have continued nearly a week. Yesterday, about twelve o'clock, the Yorkers were about two hundred strong, and the Vermonters about two hundred do. What I mean by Vermonters is those acting under Vermont within the twenty-mile line; for I cannot learn that any have joined them belonging to old Vermont.[5]

---

[1] *Vt. Hist. Soc. Collections*, Vol. II, pp. 184, 188.

[2] Ms. letter, said Mr. STONE, from Thomas Chittenden to Captain Van Rensselaer, among the Gansevoort papers.

[3] *Vt. Hist. Soc. Collections*, Vol. II, p. 209.

[4] *Memoir of Stark*, p. 296.

[5] Ira Allen stated that the force, arrayed at this time against New York, was "the militia of the [West] Union" collected by Col. Abbott.

The Governor and others met on the 7th and consulted Gen. Safford as to military matters in the "western district." Of this meeting there is no record, but the fact of the meeting and its import are shown by the following:

Colonel Ira Allen to Colonel Thomas Lee.[1]

SUNDERLAND, December 8th, 1781.

Dear Sir:—I have to inform you that the legislature of New York, at their late session, have revived their claim to the west bank of Connecticut river. They have remonstrated against the resolutions of congress of the 7th and 20th of August last, which virtually invite this state into the confederacy of the United States. In fine, their procedures will most probably for the present bar congress from any further proceedings. When this state are left to vindicate their rights to independence against all the machinations of their old adversary, every measure is taken to divide and sub-divide the citizens of our western territory, to which this state have pledged their faith to support, and which the impartial world will justify this state in, when they consider the former proceedings of the government of New York against this people, and the resolutions above referred to.

Gov. Chittenden had endeavored in writing to reconcile both parties, and had sent Gen. Safford and Col. Walbridge, who succeeded in quieting the parties somewhat, but could not effect any accommodation. Ira Allen was then sent. He counseled Col. Abbott to avoid rash measures, and then visited Gansevoort and his officers. He endeavored to settle the controversy by observing that the measures adopted by New York had compelled Vermont to extend her jurisdictional claims, but that in time of peace the dispute might be adjusted. Gen. Gansevoort said he was much opposed to civil war, but it was the duty of New York to protect those who owed and professed allegiance to New York. Allen replied that Vermont had an equal right to protect those who acknowledged her jurisdiction; but it was advisable to use lenient measures on both sides, till Congress should have settled the boundary between the states—thus preventing the horrors of civil war when the common cause required all to be united against Great Britain. Gansevoort would not consent to withdraw his force from the West Union. Col. Allen then returned to Gov. Chittenden and advised the sending of a force sufficient (by overawing the New Yorkers) to restore tranquility without bloodshed. "The plan," said Allen, "was adopted."—*Vt. Hist. Soc Coll.* Vol. II, p. 212.

[1]*Ms. Record of Board of War*, p. 27. Col. THOMAS LEE of Rutland, it is said, was a captain in Col. Warner's continental regiment, and presided at a court martial at Fort Ranger in 1779 for the trial of Maj. Hilkiah Grout.—See *ante*, p. 178; B. H. HALL's *Eastern Vermont*, p. 329. It is certain that he was a captain in Col. Gideon Warren's regiment of Vermont militia in 1780. Probably on the removal of the latter to the "western district" Lee succeeded him as colonel. He headed the attempted insurrection in Rutland county in November 1786.—See Dr. CAVERLY'S *History of Pittsford*, pp. 246-261.

It is further to be observed, that if this state are left to support themselves against various powers, the more numerous her citizens are the better; and other advantages which are very important will arise to this state by holding the western territory, which is clearly in the power of this state to support; yet it may be necessary in order to convince the government of New York that this state will support her jurisdiction, and to suppress some internal divisions to the westward, that a body of the militia should make a move to the west, which would doubtless answer similar purposes as the tour into Cumberland County did.[1] Should anything of that kind be necessary, it is expected by the governor, general Safford, and others who were in council last evening, that you will furnish such proportion of your regiment as shall be necessary. There are other cogent reasons that at this time cannot be inserted in this letter.

It is expected by those in council [last] evening, that you consult your officers and soldiers on this subject, and make these matters familiar to them. I am, Sir, with due respect,

Your humble servant,

Col. Thos. Lee. IRA ALLEN.

Dec. 8, Gen. Stark advised Col. Yates [of N. Y.] not to begin hostilities with the Vermonters, but to stand on the defensive until reinforced.[2]

Gov. Clinton to Brig. Gens. Van Rensselaer and Gansevoort.—[Extracts.]

December 11. Having enclosed papers already noted, gov. Clinton wrote:

I have therefore to request that you will, on his [Gansevoort's] application, afford him such aid from your brigade as shall be necessary for quelling the insurrection and apprehending the offenders.

On the same day gov. Clinton wrote to Gen. Gansevoort:

I perfectly approve of your conduct [in resisting the pretended authority of Vermont,] and have only to add that should the force already detached prove insufficient, you will make such additions to it as to make it effectual[3].

Dec. 12. No. 4216 of the Clinton Papers is an affidavit by Bezaleel Phelps, that he had been admitted into the council of Gen. Safford, Moses Robinson, and others, at Bennington, and the result was a determination to disperse the New York party under Col. Yates, by taking their lives or making them prisoners. Had seen writs for apprehending Cols. Yates and Van Rensselaer and others, to punish them by Vermont laws.

On the same day, colonel Yates, at St. Coick, wrote to general Gansevoort that the Vermonters appeared desperate. He had only about eighty men, the "insurrectionists" one hundred and forty-six, and he wanted aid with speed. He thought the Vermonters would only make a great show and encourage the others. The rioters taken by him were

---

[1] The "tour" was the successful armed expedition of Ethan Allen into Cumberland County in 1779.—See Vol. I.

[2] *Clinton Papers*, No. 4206. [3] *Same*, Nos. 4213 and 4217.

secured in a block-house. He wanted a field-piece and artillerymen for defense.[1]

General Stark to Colonel Yates.[2]

HEADQUARTERS, Saratoga, 14th December 1781.

Sir:—Upon anxiously examining the nature of the disputes between New York and Vermont, I am of opinion that violent measures at present would be attended with very evil consequences. If, therefore, colonel Rensselaer can be assured of protection of his person and property, together with positive assurances that his adherents shall remain in peaceable and quiet possession of their estates, and that their persons shall be preserved from indignities and insults until congress shall determine the jurisdictional boundaries—till then, I say, I should think hostilities very dangerous.

Now, Sir, considering the inconveniences of keeping men in the field at this season of the year, I imagine, if the above mentioned preliminaries are agreed to and ratified by responsible men on the part of Vermont, it would be prudent for you to withdraw your men; but if your orders are to continue in your present station, you must obey. In that case, it would be advisable to apply to general Gansevoort, or the officer who gave the orders, that they might be remanded.

I am, Sir, your most obedient servant, JOHN STARK.

General Stark to Meshech Ware.—[Extract.][3]

SARATOGA, 14th December 1781.

Dear Sir:—Notwithstanding my letters to you seem to be treated with silent contempt, yet, when any thing intervenes where I think my country or the state of New Hampshire in a particular manner deeply interested, I conceive it my duty, apart from common politeness, to inform you of it. Such I deem the late riotous conduct of the state of Vermont, in extending their pretended claim to the westward, and threatening to support it by a military force; and, indeed, those within the twenty-mile line are actually in arms, in open defiance and violation of the rules of Congress; and are actually opposing themselves to the troops raised by the state of New York to put their laws and constitution into execution. Two detachments, one acting under the authority of Vermont, and the other under officers owing allegiance to the state of New York, are assembled now at St. Coick, in opposition. For further particulars I refer you to Captain Fogg, who will have the honor of delivering this.[4]

On the 14th the Governor and Council met, and measures were agreed to in respect to the contest with both New Hampshire and New York. The two papers following as to New York resulted from this meeting:

Governor Chittenden to General Stark.[5]

ARLINGTON, December 15, 1781.

Dear Sir:—I have consulted my council on the perplexed situation of this state, and have resolved to call the legislature thereof to meet at

---

[1] *Clinton Papers*, No. 4219.

[2] *Memoir of Stark*, p. 300. [3] *Same*, p. 301.

[4] For the remainder of this letter see *post*, on the collisions in the Eastern District, under date of Dec. 14 1781.

[5] *Memoir of Stark*, p. 302. No reply from Stark to this letter is found in the *Memoirs of Stark*, but No. 4269 of the *Clinton Papers* covers several letters of this period, and among them are two from Gen. Stark, urging peace and proposing terms.

Bennington, as soon as may be; at which time they will doubtless consult such measures as may tend to the peace and tranquility of this state and the United States.

In the mean time I earnestly request that you write to the officers of New York, that are daily making depredations to the west, to suspend any farther operations of that kind until the assembly meet; and that, if they do not comply, you will not interfere with your troops. And I do assure you that if they comply with said request, and liberate the prisoners they have taken, I will suspend the exercise of jurisdiction or law over any person or persons who profess themselves subjects of New York during that time. I am, sir, with sentiments of esteem, your most obed't and most hbl. serv't, THOMAS CHITTENDEN.

Col. John Abbott of the Vermont troops to Lieut. Col. Henrg Van Rensselaer of N. Y.[1]

Sir:—I have this minute received orders from my superior which delay me from holding any further treaty with you—therefore I shall not meet you at time and place appointed. I shall not admit of three or four of your men coming into my camp to bring one letter, as they have done heretofore. I am, sir, your humble serv't,

JOHN ABBOTT, *Colonel.*

Lieut. Col. Henry V. Rensselaer. Dec. 16, 1781.

Dec. 17. Col. H. Van Rensselaer wrote to Gen. Safford, as appears from the following reply, written by the officer in command of the Vermont party:

Col. Eb'r Walbridge to Col. H. Van Rensselar.[2]

MAPLETOWN, 17 Dec'r, 1781.

Sir:—Yours of this day to gen. Safford has been duly considered, and as you are pleased to say that you are not authorized to treat with any but subjects of the state of New York, it is imagined there is none such opposed to you. Those in opposition to the authority of New York, now in arms,—inhabitants of this territory claimed by your state, who profess to owe allegiance to Vermont,—now propose for your consideration, and request your immediate answer, viz:

1. That you release all the prisoners who are in your custody, belonging to claims [territory] in dispute.
2. That you make good all damages sustained by individuals by the troops under your command.
3. That all those inhabiting said territory repectively, professing to owe allegiance to New York and Vermont, shall rest quiet and unmolested in their persons and properties until the dispute shall finally be adjusted by congress, or such other tribunal as shall be mutually agreed on by the contending powers. I am, &c.,

E. WALBRIDGE, *Colonel in command.*

Col. Henry Van Rensselaer.

General Gansevoort to Colonel Walbridge.—[Abstract.][3]

Dec. 18. In pursuance of a law of New York, he had been detached with a part of his brigade to suppress an insurrection of some of the inhabitants of Schaticook and Hoosac; that he had come to aid the

[1] *Clinton Papers*, No. 4225. [2] *Same*, No. 4230.

[3] *Williams*, Vol. II, p. 224. Ira Allen in *Vt. Hist. Soc. Coll.*, Vol. I, p. 443. *Clinton Papers*, No. 4238.

sheriff of the county to apprehend the insurgents; and was informed that a large body of troops from the Grants were marching in force, with artillery; but before he proceeded any further, he wished to be informed what was the object of their movements into the interior parts of New York, and by what authority.

Colonel Walbridge, at Bennington, to General Gansevoort.—[Abstract.][1]

Dec. 19. The object of the movement from Vermont was to protect those of the inhabitants who, in consequence of the union, preferred allegiance to the state of Vermont. If the New York forces will release prisoners and cease to exercise jurisdiction over men claiming to be under Vermont, that state will cease to do the same over men professing allegiance to New York. He wished conciliatory methods might be adopted, but if those persons who professed to be citizens of Vermont should be imprisoned and their property destroyed, he was not to be held answerable for the consequences.

It will be observed that though Col. Walbridge twice proposed terms in the conciliatory spirit of Gov. Chittenden's letter to Stark of the 15th —terms that would have restored peace without dishonor to either party or prejudice to their rights,—Gen. Gansevoort neither responded in the like spirit, nor remained on the field to assert the authority of New York. Of his retreat, and the end of the *quasi* war, a New York author has given the following account:

On the 16th (Dec.) Gen. Gansevoort took the field himself, repairing in the first instance to the head-quarters of Gen. Stark at Saratoga, in order to obtain a detachment of troops and field-pieces. But the troops of Stark were too naked to move from their quarters; and it was thought improper for him to interfere without an order from Gen. Heath. Gansevoort then crossed over to the east side of the river, in order to place himself at the head of such militia as he could muster in Schaghticoke and Hoosick; but was soon met by Col. Yates in full retreat from the house of Col. John Van Rensselaer. He had been able to raise but eighty men of Col. John Van Rensselaer's regiment to put down the insurgents; and on arriving at San Coick he discovered a force of five hundred men advancing from the Grants to the assistance of the rebels. Gansevoort retired five miles further, in order to find comfortable quarters for his men, and then attempted, but without success, to open a correspondence with the leaders of the insurgents.[2] Calls had been made upon four regiments, viz: those of Col. Yates, and Henry K. Van Rensselaer, as before stated, and upon Col. Van Vechten, and Major Taylor. But from the whole no greater force than eighty men could be raised. Of Col. Van Vechten's regiment, only himself, a few officers and one private could be brought into the field. Under these discouraging circumstances, the general was compelled to relinquish the expedition, and the insurgents remained the victors, to the no small terror of those of the inhabitants who were well disposed [to New York] inasmuch as they were apprehensive of being taken prisoners and

---

[1] *Williams*, Vol. II, 224. Ira Allen in *Vt. Hist. Soc. Coll.*, Vol. I, p. 444; *Clinton Papers*, No. 4246.

[2] This seems to ignore Gansevoort's letter to Walbridge of the 18th, and Walbridge's reply of the 19th of December.

carried away, as had been the case with others, should they refuse taking the oath of allegiance to the government of Vermont.[1]

COLLISIONS IN THE EASTERN DISTRICT.

Chesterfield was one of the New Hampshire towns which assented to the union with Vermont and elected two representatives in the Vermont Assembly in April 1781; nevertheless it appears that some of its citizens were zealously loyal to New Hampshire. Nov. 5 1781, Samuel Davis, constable of that town under Vermont, was prevented from serving a precept by John Grandy jr. and Nathaniel Bingham; for which, on the 12th, these men were arrested and committed to the jail at Charlestown. Nov. 16, they petitioned the Council and Assembly of New Hampshire for relief.[2]

Under date of Nov. 15, Gen. Benjamin Bellows of Walpole in a confidential letter informed President Weare that Vermont had determined to exercise jurisdiction east of Connecticut river and had imposed a land tax. He feared the consequences would be violent if not sanguinary, and waited with impatience for action by New Hampshire. He wrote that officers and *posses* should be sent "from off the Grants"—that is, from the section of the state which was loyal to the government—"as it would be more likely to settle us in peace than the Employing any among us for this Purpose, where we are so intermixed and near Equally divided." He suggested the propriety of arresting "some of the Leaders of the revolt," and thought it could be done safely if it were secretly and prudently attempted.[3]

Col. Enoch Hale, sheriff of Cheshire county under New Hampshire, was ordered to release Grandy and Bingham, but in attempting to execute the order he was himself arrested. On the 27th of November he was arraigned before Benjamin Giles and Nathaniel S. Prentice, magistrates for Vermont, on the charge of attempting to break the jail; and on the 29th he was committed to the same jail.[4]

---

[1] WM. L. STONE'S *Life of Brant*, Vol. II, pp. 205-207. *Early History*, pp. 379-380. It is remarkable that ETHAN ALLEN is no where named in connection with the promised fight with New York. Nobody, certainly, could have entered into that business with a sharper appetite; and he was there. In his account against the state, settled in 1785, and recorded in *Ethan Allen Papers*, pp. 407-408, are the following items:

To my attending on the Militia at the seige of Vallumcock the last of Decr. 1781, 1£ 10|.

To Cash paid for my Expenses and for the Militia at the same time, 9£ 2|.

[2] *N. H. State Papers on the Vermont Controversy*, pp. 269-271, 275.

[3] *Same*, p. 261. [4] *Same*, p. 279.

Act of New Hampshire for the enforcement of its authority in Cheshire and Grafton counties.[1]

STATE OF NEW-HAMPSHIRE.

In the Year of our LORD *One Thousand Seven Hundred and Eighty one.*

AN ACT

For impowering the Sheriff of the County of Cheshire to release from Prison sundry of the good Subjects of this State, imprisoned by certain evilminded Persons, assuming Authority for so doing under the People inhabiting a Territory commonly called Vermont; and for apprehending the Persons so offending.

WHEREAS the People inhabiting a Tract of Country on the West Side of Connecticut River, originally granted by this State, and afterwards claimed by the State of New York, have erected themselves into a separate and independent Jurisdiction by the Name of the State of Vermont; And whereas, sundry Persons have, by Colour of Authority under the said pretended State of Vermont, acted as civil Officers, passed Judgment and committed to Prison sundry of the good Subjects of this State, and have seduced many of the Inhabitants of the Counties of Cheshire and Grafton to submit to the Jurisdiction of the said pretended State of Vermont, by Means whereof the proper Officers of the said Counties may be unable to release the good Subjects of this State from Such illegal Imprisonment, and to apprehend the Persons so offending, without the special Aid of this Assembly; and inasmuch as an impartial Trial of the said Offenders cannot probably be had within the said Counties where the Offences have or may be committed:

THEREFORE,

BE IT THEREFORE ENACTED BY THE COUNCIL AND HOUSE OF REPRESENTATIVES, *in General Assembly convened, and by the Authority of the same, it is hereby enacted,* That the Committee of Safety be, and hereby is impowered and authorized to issue their Order to the Sheriff of the County of Cheshire to release from Prison all Persons confined, or who may hereafter be confined in either of the said Counties by Order, Process or Authority of any pretended Court, Magistrate, Officer, or other Persons claiming Authority from the said pretended State of Vermont, and to apprehend the Persons, who heretofore have exercised, or who hereafter shall attempt to exercise any Office, Power or Authority within the said Counties of Cheshire or Grafton from, by or under the said pretended Authority of Vermont, and to convey said Offenders to the common Goal in the County of Rockingham, or such other County in this State as the said Committee may order, there to remain until released by Order of the General Assembly, the Committee, or by due course of Law.

And be it further enacted by the Authority aforesaid, That the said Committee of Safety be, and hereby are impowered to authorize the Sheriff of the said County of Cheshire to call upon the Sheriffs of any or either of the other Counties in this State, to raise the Body of their respective Counties to aid and assist him in executing the Order of the Committee of Safety, either to release Persons imprisoned as aforesaid, or to apprehend the Person or Persons imprisoning them, and to convey the said Offenders to any Prison within this State, and also to command the Aid of any Officer or Officers of the Militia or Troops of this State, which may at the Time be within the limits thereof, and commanded by

[1] *N. H. Papers on the Vermont Controversy*, p. 281.

an officer commissioned by this State, and all officers and other Subjects of this State shall yield due Obedience to such command.

And be it further enacted by the Authority aforesaid, That the several and respective Courts of Judicature in the County or Counties where the said Offenders may be confined, be and they are hereby respectively impowered to hear, try and determine any Process or Processes against the said Offenders, and to give Judgment and award Execution thereon in the same Manner as though the offence had been committed within the Body of the County where such Trial is had; any Law, Usage or Custom to the contrary in any wise notwithstanding.

STATE OF NEW-HAMPSHIRE, } *In the House of REPRESENTATIVES, November 27th*, 1781.

THE foregoing BILL having been read a third Time, Voted, That it pass to be enacted.

Sent up for Concurrence. WM. WHIPPLE, *Speaker P. T.*

In COUNCIL, November 28th, 1781.

THIS was read a third Time, and voted, that the same be enacted.

M. WEARE, *President.*

Copy examined by JOSEPH PEARSON, *D. Sec'ry.*

Gen. Benjamin Bellows to President Weare.[1]

WALPOLE, Novm. 29th. 1781.

Sir,—The methods taken by the General Assembly for Liberating Messrs. Bingham and Grandy are so far from being Effectual for that Purpose that the Authority of Vermont have imprisoned the Sheriff of the County of Cheshire who was sent here for the Purpose aforesaid; the Authority of said Vermont are Determined to keep the Goal and their Prisoners, and also to withstand and oppose (by Force of Arms) all the Sheriffs and their Posses who may be imployed by New Hampshire to Counteract any of their Purposes or Designs; it is said that they can raise (by their Account) Six Hundred men at the shortest notice, who will resolutely dispute the Ground Inch by Inch: That the Posse should be raised to carry the Orders of this State into Execution now, is absolutely necessary, something effectual must be done, dallying will not answer, and unless some force can be obtained from without the County of Cheshire, it will not be advisable to Dispute the Ground any longer. You cant but be Sensible of the ill Consequences of such an Attempt from within ourselves within this County and Especially within the Grants, for should the Friends of New Hampshire Generally Exert themselves at this Time it would Universally alarm the Vermonters, and many who would not otherwise arm in this Quarrel would Exert themselves to the utmost to oppose the Orders of the Assembly and all the New Hampshire Authority. I should think that if New Hampshire are Determined to Support and Protect their Friends in this Quarter and to maintain their Jurisdiction it will be Absolutely Necessary that a Sufficient force should be collected from without the Grants be sure, if not from without the County of Cheshire; You will put yourself in our Circumstances and Especially in those of the Sheriff and the other Prisoners, aud I think you cant Hesitate a moment respecting what is necessary to be done and how it should be done.

I am with Esteem Your Honor's
most Obdt. Humle. Servt. BENJA. BELLOWS.

Honble M. Weare.

---

[1] *N. H. State Papers on the Vermont Controversy*, p. 283.

Dec. 1, Doct. William Page, of Charlestown, sheriff under Vermont, informed Col. Samuel King of the imprisonment of Col. Hale and the prospect of an attempt by New Hampshire to release him. In that event he notified Col. King that he should call on him for military aid. On the 3d, Col. King issued orders to Col. Chamberlain, Capt. Franklin, Capt. Cole, and Capt. Butterfield to be ready to march to Charlestown on the shortest notice.[1] Sheriff Page sent a like notice to Col. Wm. Heywood, who ordered Capt. Hooper and Lieut. Bundy to be ready with arms and ammunition complete, with two or three days' provisions for each man, to march to Charlestown on the shortest notice.[2] Dec. 5, Michael Cresey of Chesterfield notified Gen. Bellows of the foregoing call for military aid.[3] Dec. 12, sheriff Page sent a messenger to Gov. Chittenden, notifying him of events which had occurred in the district, and of the probability that New Hampshire would attempt coercion. This messenger reached Gov. Chittenden on the evening of the 13th, when the Governor and Council were in session.

Colonel Enoch Hale to Mesheck Weare.[1]

CHARLESTOWN GOAL, December 12th, 1781.

I have to inform your honors that I wait the pleasure of the honorable Committee of Safety, whom, I trust, well know my situation. Sir, I have given bonds for the liberty of the yard, but could not give bonds to appear at an unknown court, for the honor of the state that sent me to this place. However, I was prevented doing the business that I was sent upon, yet I found the people to be much disappointed when they see that I refused to recognize [to Vermont,] and said that it would immediately bring on a quarrel; and many said they never would take up arms for the sake of jurisdiction, and could only wish to know the pleasure of Congress on the matter, which I think has been much kept from them by designing persons.

Sir, even those that are leading in the insurrection were panic-struck on hearing that two thousand men was on their march, but have since been much encouraged by hearing that the state of New Hampshire did not know what to do with them.

Sir, I think now is the time to put the laws in execution, more especially the state ones.

Sir, the wisdom of the honorable Committee is sufficient to direct them. I am, Sir, with much respect,

Your honor's most obedient, humble servant, ENOCH HALE.

Honorable Mesheck Weare, Esq., President, &c.

---

[1] *N. H. State Papers on the Vermont Controversy*, p. 285.

[2] *Same*, p. 287. Of the officers named above, Col. Samuel King resided in Chesterfield, and Capt. James Butterfield in Westmoreland. It is presumed that all were residents of that part of New Hampshire which was embraced in the union.

[3] *Same*, p. 289.

[1] *Same*, printed in the *Burlington Free Press & Times*, March 4 1871.

Gov. Chittenden to William Page.[1]

ARLINGTON, December 14th, 1781.

Sir,—I received your dispatches of the 9th and 12th instant, last evening by Capt. Watherbe, have considered the same and do approve of your conduct in every particular.

I have wrote to Major Genl. Payne in which I have given him particular orders with the advice of certain gentlemen therein named to give you such assistance as shall be necessary in the support of Government in your Quarter. I am Sir with Respect

your Hble Servant, THOS. CHITTENDEN.

William Page Esq.

True Copy. Test, WILLIAM PAGE.

Letter and orders of Gov. Chittenden to Maj. Gen. Elisha Payne.[2]

ARLINGTON, 14th December, 1781.

Sir:—I have received dispatches from William Page, Esq., Sheriff of Washington County, which give me to understand that there is a high probability that the government of New Hampshire are about taking coercive measures to compel the peaceable citizens of this state to submit to the laws and authority of New Hampshire. The sheriff further desires my special orders in matters relating to the premises, and as my remote situation renders it impracticable that I should have the knowledge of the particular occurrences which may take place should such an attempt be made [by] New Hampshire, therefore I can only give you several orders in the matter, viz: provided that New Hampshire reject the proposals of the Legislature of this state and insist upon hostile measures, you are hereby directed to call on such of the members of the Council and the Generals Fletcher and Olcott, and such of the field officers of the militia on the east side of the mountain as you may think proper, and after having consulted matters, if need be, you are directed to call on any or all of the militia of this state to the eastward of the range of Green Mountains to your assistance, and to assist the sheriff in carrying into execution the laws of this state, and to defend its citizens against any insult; and provided New Hampshire makes an attack with an armed force, you are hereby ordered to repel force by force; and in the meantime you will use every means in your power consistent with the peace, happiness, or dignity of this state, to prevent the effusion of human blood, which at this time might be more or less injurious to the common cause of America, as well as attended with many other serious considerations, and which I pray God may never take place.

I am, Sir, your ob't and humble serv't,

THOMAS CHITTENDEN, *Capt. General.*

Elisha Payne, Esq., Major General.

N. B. Provided a force from New Hampshire precipitate any measure, you must act with that expedition which their manœuvers may require, with such counsel as you can in haste collect. T. C.

A true copy, Attest, WILLIAM PAGE, *Sheriff.*

General Stark to President Weare.—[Extract.][3]

[SARATOGA, Dec. 14, 1781.]

I have been favored with a perusal of the proceedings of the legislature of Vermont state, on the subject of their being received into the union

---

[1] *N. H. State Papers on the Vermont Controversy*, p. 301.

[2] *Same*, published in the *Burlington Free Press & Times*, March 4 1871.

[3] *Memoir of Stark*, p. 300.

of the United States, and find that they have not only rejected the resolutions of Congress, but in reality have disavowed their authority; and I farther perceive that, in their great wisdom, they have thought proper to appoint a committee to determine whether New Hampshire shall exercise jurisdiction to Connecticut river or not. This proceeding appears too weak and frivolous. For men of sense to suppose that New Hampshire would ever consent to an indignity so flagrant, and an abuse so pointed as this seems to be, is what I own surprises me. However, I hope, and indeed have no doubt, that New Hampshire will be more politic than to take notice of this daring insolence. What I mean by notice is, to think of treating with them upon this or any other subject until Congress shall come to a final determination with respect to these people. I am, sir, with high respect,

Your most obedient serv't, JOHN STARK.

Lieut. Gov. Payne, of Vermont, to President Weare.[1]

CHARLESTOWN, Dec. 21st, 1781.

Sir,—I herewith transmit to your honor a copy of orders received from the commander-in-chief of the state of Vermont, issued in consequence of coercive measures pursuing by New Hampshire, from which you will learn my situation.

Inclination and duty conspire to induce my compliance with any measures which reason and justice may point out to avert threatening hostilities, pregnant not only with the horrors of civil war, but also the greatest injury to the United States, whose interest it is our desire as well as yours to support—have, therefore, by advice of sundry members of the Council of this state, and other gentlemen of influence and consideration now present, appointed Brigadier General [Roger] Enos and William Page, Esq., in conjunction with Col. Ira Allen, (already appointed by the Governor to wait on your Assembly,) to state before the said Assembly the reasonableness of the late proposals of the legislature of Vermont, transmitted to your honor by a committee appointed by said legislature for that purpose, for the settlement of disputes between New Hampshire and Vermont.

You must be sensible it has ever been our idea to have justice and equity take place in the decision; and, therefore, by the advice aforesaid, [I] renew proposals that the controversy, in respect to the territory the jurisdiction of which is in dispute between the said states, be decided by an impartial tribunal on principles of right and equity, in the mode congress have pointed out by articles of confederation of the United States in cases where disputes arise between two or more states in respect to boundary, jurisdiction, &c.,—Vermont being allowed equal privileges as the other party in support of their claim—and that hostilities between the said states be suspended till such trial can be had.

We doubt not a compliance on the part of Vermont with the foregoing proposals, which appear to us equitable and just; and are persuaded that New Hampshire are so possessed of principles of justice and equity as shall induce a compliance on their part, and hope for their favorable answer to lay before the assembly of Vermont for their concurrence at their meeting on the last Thursday in January next.

In case New Hampshire refuses compliance with equitable terms (as we view the foregoing,) and are determined on hostilities previous to attempts for an amicable settlement, [I] shall find myself under the disagreeable necessity to execute the orders I have received in raising the

---

[1] From the *N. H. State Papers on the Vermont Controversy;* published in the *Burlington Free Press & Times*, March 4 1871.

force of Vermont, to repel encroachments on its jurisdiction exercised by consent of the people, and which I doubt not their most spirited exertions to support till the dispute is decided, confident that New Hampshire, in case they commence hostilities, must be accountable for the consequences.

I have the honor to be, with esteem and respect, sir,

Your honor's most obedient and most humble servant,

ELISHA PAYNE, *Lieut. Gov.*

His Honor Mesheck Weare, Esq., President of the Council of New Hampshire.

Immediately following the foregoing document in the lost *Stevens Papers* was a letter from Gen. Samuel Fletcher to Lieut. Gov. Payne, informing that he had issued orders to call out the [Vermont] militia east of the mountains to defend the East Union.[1]

Dec. 22, Col. Enoch Hale wrote to President Weare, by sheriff Page, commending the attempt, which was to be made by Enos, Page, and Allen, to obtain an honorable settlement between the two states. Hale wrote: "I have been used well as a Prisoner, have had the liberty of the yard, and they Now begin to Desier me to depart out of their Course" [coasts.][2]

Dec. 27, by a concurrent vote of the House of Representatives and Council of New Hampshire, it was ordered that Dr. William Page be committed to jail at Exeter, to await a trial for accepting the office of sheriff "under the usurped authority of Vermont;" and on the same day bail was refused.[3]

Arrests ordered by New Hampshire in the Eastern Union.[4]

STATE OF NEW HAMPSHIRE. } IN COMMITTEE OF SAFETY, Exeter, 27th Decr. 1781.

To Robert Smith of Londonderry, Greeting:

Whereas information hath been given to this Committee, that Samuel King gentleman, Moses Smith yeoman, both [of] Chesterfield, Isaac Griswold of Keene yeoman, and Nathaniel Sartel Prentice of Alstead esquire, all in the county of Cheshire and state aforesaid, have been guilty of sundry practices inimical to this state: therefore

You are hereby required, in the name of the government and people of said state, forthwith to apprehend the bodies of the said Samuel King,[5] Moses Smith, Isaac Griswold, and Nathaniel Sartel Prentice,[5] if they may be found within this state, and bring them, as soon as may be, before the Committee of Safety to be examined touching the matters alleged against them, that they may be dealt with as to justice shall ap-

---

[1] *Index to Stevens Papers*, pp. 45, 97.

[2] *N. H. State Papers on the Vermont Controversy*, p. 357.

[3] *Same*, pp. 309, 312.

[4] *Same*, published in the *Burlington Free Press & Times*, March 25 1871.

[5] Mr. King represented Chesterfield, and Mr. Prentice Alstead, N. H., in the General Assembly of Vermont.

pertain; and all officers, civil and military, and other subjects of this state, are hereby required to be aiding and assisting you in the premises.

Hereof fail not, and make return of this warrant with your doings thereon.

Given under my hand and seal, on the day and date above mentioned.

JOSIAH BARTLETT, *Chairman.*

STATE OF NEW HAMPSHIRE, }
ROCKINGHAM, SS. }

Pursuant to the within warrant, I have apprehended the body of the within named Nathaniel Sartel Prentice, Esq., and have him before the Committee of Safety for said state this seventh day of January, 1782.

ROBERT SMITH, *Special Sheriff.*

Pursuant to the within warrant I have apprehended the body of the within named Samuel King gentleman, who was rescued: the others are not found.

ROBT. SMITH, *Special Sheriff.*

ADVERTISEMENT.

Four hundred silver dollars reward to any person or persons that brings Samuel King of Chesterfield to Exeter in the state of New Hampshire and there confine him in goal, or have him the said King before the Committee of Safety of said state, as said Samuel King was taken prisoner, by virtue of a warrant unto the subscriber directed, and conducted under a proper guard twenty miles. Said King at the town of Keene by a number of men armed with clubs, swords and staves, vizt. captains Fairbanks, Davis, Pratt, Pomeroy and Harvey of Chesterfield at their head and captain Carlise of Westmoreland with a small party, which parties did, on the morning of the first day of January, 1782, by violence rescue the said Samuel King, prisoner, from

ROBERT SMITH, *Special Sheriff.*

Mr. Ephraim Witherell—Sir:—If possible apprehend the bodies of Isaac Griswold and Moses Smith and bring them before the Committee of Safety at Exeter and you shall have an adequate reward from

ROBT. SMITH, } *Special*
JONATHAN MARTIN, } *Sheriffs.*

Joseph Burt to President Weare.[1]

Honored Sir:—This moment two men from Chesterfield, who made their escape from the mob, who after they had rescued Samuel King from the officer, returned to Chesterfield, and apprehended Lieutenant Roberson and two others, who they seemed determined to treat according to the custom of Vermont, that is by whipping them. Whether they will really venture upon this business is very uncertain to me. But they have actually driven many of the good subjects of the state from their homes in this cold night. Mr. Bingham's son is one of the men that have come to my house for shelter, who I have this account from, who expected to have found his father here with another man, who made their escape. They have not been here, and I am some concerned for them. The triumphs of the Vermonters are great, and say that New Hampshire dare not come like men in the day-time, but like a thief, and steal a man or two away. Your honor cannot be insensible of our situation. I would not wish to dictate, but pray that something may be done that shall be for the relief of the good subjects in this part of the

---

[1]From the *N. H. State Papers on the Vermont Controversy;* published in the *Burlington Free Press and Times*, March 25, 1871.

state, and for the good of the state. I thought it my duty to inform your honor, as it is not likely that any other person will be informed that will write to your honor by the post. I am, sir,

Your honor's most obedient and humble servant,

JOSEPH BURT.

Westmoreland, Jan. 1st, 1782, at 12 o'clock at night.

Hon. President Weare, Esq.

N. B. You will excuse the writing, being called out of bed in a cold night.

Benjamin Bellows to President Weare.[1]

WALPOLE, Jan. 2d, 1782.

Sir,—I have often troubled you with a narrative of our distresses and difficulties in this part of the state. Notwithstanding, I presume you and the rest of the honorable committee of safety will exercise your wonted indulgence while I give an account of some new difficulties arising upon the officers attempting to convey one Samuel King of Chesterfield to Exeter, which rescue you will have an account of before this reaches you. Upon the return of the mob, after proper refreshment at said King's, they sought for all those persons who were any way concerned in assisting the aforesaid officer, some of whom they got into their hands, and have abused in a shameful and barbarous manner, by striking, kicking, and all the indignities which such a hellish pack can be guilty of, obliging them to promise and engage never to appear against the new state again; and that is not all, they swear they will extirpate all the adherents to New Hampshire, threatening to kill, burn and destroy the persons and property of all who oppose them; that the friends to this state cannot continue at said Chesterfield with their families, but are obliged to seek an asylum in other towns among the Hampshire people. I have two respectable inhabitants of said Chesterfield now sheltering themselves under my roof, who I have the greatest reason to think would be treated by them in a barbarous manner were they in their power, as they have stove the doors and broke up houses in search of them. I am credibly informed that there is in said Chesterfield about one hundred persons who support said King, who damn New Hampshire and all their authority to hell, and say they (New Hampshire) can do nothing only in a mean and underhanded way; in short, they defy all the authority and force of the state, and are determined to support and maintain their usurped authority, maugre all attempts that have or shall be made to curb or restrain their usurpations. The wrath of man and the raging of the sea are in scripture put together, and it is He alone who can rule the latter and restrain the former. I hope and trust the Author of Wisdom will direct the honorable committee to such measures as will ultimately tend to the peace and happiness of this part of the state, and more especially those adherents to New Hampshire who are in a sense suffering for righteousness sake.

I am, with all esteem and respect,

Your most obedient humble servant, BENJ. BELLOWS.

Hon. Meshech Weare, Esq.

Jan. 4, by vote of the New Hampshire Assembly, Doct. Page was referred to the judges of the superior court on the question of bail.[2]

---

[1] From the *N. H. State Papers on the Vermont Controversy;* published in the *Burlington Free Press & Times*, March 25, 1871.

[2] *N. H. Papers on the Vermont Controversy*, p. 311.

Jan. 8, Doct. Page at Exeter wrote a long letter to Lieut. Gov. Payne, in which he deplored the state of affairs, and asserted that the people of western New Hampshire, who were friendly to Vermont, were greatly misunderstood or misrepresented. The following are extracts from this letter:

"The General Court have Ordered Two Thousand men to be Raised Immediately in the Counties of Rockingham and Strafford & March them to Subjugate the People in the Counties of Cheshire and Grafton."

"P. S. The whole State of New Hampshire are to hold themselves in Readiness to march if Required." [1]

Resolve of New Hampshire to raise Troops.[2]

STATE OF NEW HAMPSHIRE. } IN THE HOUSE OF REPRESENTATIVES, Jan^{ry} 8th 1782.

The Committee of the whole reported as their opinion "that an armed Force be immediately raised, and sent into the western part of this State for the defence and protection of the Inhabitants there, & to enable the civil officers to exercise their authority in that Quarter. That the said armed force consist of one thousand Men, including Officers—that a proclamation be issued & forwarded to the several Towns & places in the Western parts of this State, setting forth the reasons for raising said armed force—that Woodbury Langdon Esq$^{r.}$ or some other Delegate be immediately sent on to Congress to make a true representation of our present proceedings.

The foregoing report having been read & considered Voted that the same be received & accepted.

Sent up for Concurrence. JOHN DUDLEY, *Speaker P. T.*

In Council the same day read and Concurred.

E. THOMPSON, *Secr'y.*

Jan. 10, Col. Bellows wrote to President Weare against the release of Doct. Page, on the ground that, while it might quiet the people of western New Hampshire somewhat, it would encourage hostility in Vermont. He closed with a statement that Esq. Giles [Benjamin, of Newport, representative and magistrate under Vermont,] had been arrested by sheriff Hale, but had been rescued.[3]

Jan. 10, Ira Allen reported to the Governor and Council the failure of the attempt to negotiate with New Hampshire.

Jan. 11, Col. Hale informed President Weare of the arrest and release of Giles, and added the following humorous account of his own misfortune on the occasion, prefacing it with a statement that the Vermont party had a force of forty men:

For a frunt Gard they Raised some of their most ablest women and sent forward with some men dressed in woman's apparril which had the Good luck to Take me Prisoner Put me aboard one of their Slays and filled the same with some of the Principal women and drove off Nine

---

[1] *N. H. State Papers on the Vermont Controversy*, pp. 329-331.

[2] *Same*, p. 333.

[3] *Same*, p. 339. This indicates that Col. Hale had been released by the Vermont authorities; probably in return for Page's release by New Hampshire.—See BELKNAP'S account, *post*, p. 346.

miles to Wellan Tavern in Walpole the main body following after with aclimation of Joy where they Re:gailed themselves and then set me at liberty Nothing Doubting but that they had intirely subdued New Hampshire.[1]

From the fact that Col. Hale represented the people of Charlestown to be very zealous for Vermont, the inference is that the party which arrested him was raised in that town. On the next day, according to the *Index to the Stevens Papers*, p. 81, Col. Hale again wrote that he had concluded to stay at home and let the Vermonters in the East Union alone. Probably this was a condition of his release on the 11th.

Jan. 12, President Weare issued "a proclamation giving Vermonters forty days to leave the east union, or subscribe an oath &c."[2] Feb. 21 1782, in precisely forty days from the date of this proclamation, the General Assembly of Vermont resolved to dissolve both the eastern and western unions. This result was largely due to the intervention of Gen. WASHINGTON, whose letter, and the resolutions of Congress of August 1781, were accepted as pledges that, on the withdrawal of Vermont to its former boundaries, the state would be admitted to the Union.[3]

BELKNAP'S ACCOUNT OF THE SECOND EASTERN UNION—1781-2.[4]

The state of society within the seceding towns [of New Hampshire] at this time, was very unhappy. The majorities attempted to control the minorities; and these were disposed not to submit, but to seek protection of the government with which they had been connected. At the same time and in the same place, Justices, Sheriffs and Constables, appointed by the authority of both states, were exercising jurisdiction over the same persons. Party rage, high words and deep resentment, were the effect of these clashing interests. An affray which began in the town of Chesterfield, threatened a scene of open hostility, between the states of New Hampshire and Vermont.

A Constable, appointed by the authority of Vermont, had a writ, in an action of debt against a man who was in the interest of New-Hamp-

---

[1] *N. H. State Papers on the Vermont Controversy*, pp. 343-345.

[2] *Index to the Stevens Papers*, p. 81. This document is not in the New Hampshire volume of state papers on the controversy. Dr. BELKNAP, under date of Jan. 12 1782, wrote: "The assembly issued a proclamation, allowing forty days for the people in the revolted towns to repair to some Magistrate of New-Hampshire, and subscribe a declaration that they acknowledged the extent of New-Hampshire to Connecticut river; and that they would demean themselves peaceably as good citizens of the State. They also ordered the militia of all the counties to hold themselves in readiness to march against the revolters."—See BELKNAP'S *History of New Hampshire*, Vol. II, p. 348.

[3] See correspondence of Washington and Chittenden; and resolutions of the Vermont Assembly, Feb. 21, 1782, *post.*

[4] From JEREMY BELKNAP'S *Hist. of N. Hampshire*, Vol. II, pp. 346-351.

shire. He found the man in company with a number of people of his own party, and attempted to arrest him. The owner of the house interposed. The Constable produced a book which he said contained the laws of Vermont, and began to read. The owner of the house forbad him. Threatening words were used; and the officer was compelled to retreat. By a warrant from a Vermont Justice, the householder, and another of the company, were committed to prison in Charlestown. They sent a petition to the Assembly of New-Hampshire for relief. The Assembly empowered the committee of safety to direct the Sheriff of Cheshire to release the prisoners; they farther empowered the committee to cause to be apprehended and committed to prison, in any of the counties, all persons acting under the pretended authority of the State of Vermont, to be tried by the Courts of those counties where they might be confined; and for this purpose the Sheriffs were empowered to raise the *posse Comitatus.*

In attempting to release the two prisoners from Charlestown gaol, the Sheriff himself [Col. Enoch Hale] was imprisoned by the Vermont Sheriff [Doct. Wm. Page,] under the authority of a warrant from three Justices. The imprisoned [N. H.] Sheriff applied to a Brigadier General of New Hampshire,[1] to raise the militia for his liberation. This alarmed the Vermonters; and orders were issued by the Governor for their militia to oppose force with force. A committee of Vermont was sent to Exeter, 'to agree on measures to prevent hostilities.' One of this committee was the Vermont Sheriff; he was immediately arrested and thrown into prison at Exeter, and there held as a hostage for the release of the Sheriff of Cheshire. The assembly issued a proclamation, allowing forty days for the people in the revolted towns to repair to some Magistrate of New Hampshire, and subscribe a declaration that they acknowledged the extent of New Hampshire to Connecticut river; and that they would demean themselves peaceably as good citizens of the State. They also ordered the militia of all the counties to hold themselves in readiness to march against the revolters.

While affairs wore such a threatening aspect between the two States, means were used at Congress to take up the controversy on more general ground. A committee, who had under consideration the affair of admitting Vermont into the union and determining its boundaries, prevailed on General Washington, then at Philadelphia, to write to the Governor of Vermont, advising to a relinquishment of their late extension, as an 'indispensable preliminary' to their admission into the union; intimating also, that upon their non-compliance, they must be considered as having a hostile disposition toward the United States, in which case *coercion* on the part of Congress, however disagreeable, would be necessary.

This letter had the desired effect. The Assembly of Vermont, taking advantage of the absence of the members from the eastern side of the river, obtained a majority for complying with the preliminary, and resolved, 'that the western bank of Connecticut river on the one part, and 'a line drawn from the north-west corner of Massachusetts, northward, 'to Lake Champlain on the other part, be the eastern and western 'boundaries of the State of Vermont, and that they relinquished all

---

[1] Possibly Gen. Moses Nichols, of Amherst, N. H., who commanded a part of Stark's men at the battle of Bennington. In a letter to Prest. Weare by Samuel Livermore, in Congress, Jan. 1 1782, he said: "I am anxious to hear the event of Gen. Nichols' expedition."—See *Vt. Hist. Soc. Collections*, Vol. II, p. 227.

'claim of jurisdiction without those limits.' When the members from the eastern side of Connecticut river arrived, they found themselves excluded from a seat in the Assembly, and took their leave with some expressions of bitterness.

After this compliance, it was expected that Vermont would be admitted into the union, and the question was solemnly put in Congress; but a majority decided against it; to the no small disappointment of many persons, beside the inhabitants of the disputed territory. The pretence for this decision was, that they had exceeded the limited time; but they had complied with the 'indispensable preliminary;' and the order of Congress, requiring it, stood unrepealed.

Ira Allen's Account of the Collisions in the Eastern and Western Districts—1781-2.[1]

In December new scenes of difficulty and danger presented themselves, and the affairs of Vermont appeared fast approaching to an alarming crisis, assailed as she was, at the same time, and threatened by an armed force from New York and New Hampshire.

General Gansevoort, in pursuance of a law of the State of New York, and conformable to the orders of Governor Clinton, was detached with a part of his brigade of militia to assist the Sheriff of the county of Albany to suppress an insurrection in said county, alias the west union of Vermont; Colonel Abbot collected the militia in the union to oppose him; they encamped against each other, and remained in this situation for some time; the horrors of civil war seemed to moderate both parties.

In the mean time Governor Chittenden tried to reconcile both parties by writing, and he also appointed General Safford and Colonel Walbridge to repair there, and, if possible, to settle the controversy in some way, and by all means prevent the shedding of blood. They repaired to the contending parties, and were the means of keeping them more quiet, but could not effect an accommodation.

The Governor then directed Colonel Allen to see if he could devise any means to accommodate matters; for, said the Governor, a civil war is much to be dreaded. Colonel Allen repaired to Colonel Abbot's camp, held a conference with him and his officers, admonishing them against any rash measures; that some way would be found to settle the dispute without an appeal to arms, engaging them not to commence hostilities till the further order of the Governor. He then proceeded to General Gansevoort's camp, had an interview with him and his officers, endeavoured to settle the controversy, observing, that the measures pursued by New York had necessitated Vermont to extend her claims, that in time of peace the dispute might be adjusted, &c.

General Gansevoort was very much opposed to a civil war, yet thought it a duty incumbent on the State of New York to protect her inhabitants, who owed and professed allegiance to that Government. Colonel Allen observed, that the State of Vermont had an equal right to protect those who had acknowledged her jurisdiction, which was a great majority of the people; that it would be advisable to use lenient measures on both sides, till a boundary line could be settled by Congress between the States, thereby to prevent the horrors of a civil war, when the united efforts of all were necessary in the common cause against Great Britain; but no measures could be suggested to induce General Gansevoort to withdraw from said union.

---

[1] From I. Allen's *History*, in *Vt. Hist. Soc. Coll.*, Vol. I, pp. 442-446.

Colonel Allen returned to the Governor and Council, advised that the Governor, as Captain General, should direct a sufficient military force to march, from within the old bounds of Vermont, against General Gansevoort, as the only means to restore tranquility without bloodshed; for in that case General Gansevoort would, in his opinion, retreat, and not otherwise. The plan was adopted; and while the Governor was making out his orders, directing Colonel Ira Allen, with a detachment of militia, to prosecute said plan, an express arrived from William Page, Esq; Sheriff of the county of Washington,[1] announcing the prospects of hostilities in the east union from New Hampshire. This intelligence made a serious impression on the minds of the Governor and Council for a few moments (as it appeared like an agreement between the claiming States to commence hostilities at one and the same time.) When they resumed business, Colonel Walbridge was directed to march with a detachment of militia against General Gansevoort. In his way he received a letter from General Gansevoort.

At the same time the troops of New York were in motion to suppress the proceedings of their citizens, who had formed an union with Vermont. On December 18, their Commander, Brigadier General Gansevoort, wrote to the commanding officer of the troops from Vermont, that in pursuance of a law of New York, he had been detached with a part of his brigade to suppress an insurrection of some of the inhabitants of Schaticook and Housac; that he was arrived to aid the Sheriff of the County, to apprehend the insurgents; and was informed that a large body of troops from the grants, were marching in force, with artillery; but before he proceeded any further, he wished to be informed what was the object of their movement into the interior parts of that State, and by what authority. Colonel Walbridge, commandant of the troops from Vermont, wrote in answer, that the object of their movement was to protect those of the inhabitants, who, in consequence of the union, professed allegiance to the State of Vermont; that he wished conciliatory methods might be adopted, but if those persons who professed to be citizens of Vermont should be imprisoned, and their property destroyed, he was not to be answerable for the consequences. General Gansevoort retreated, and peace was restored.

The Governor and Council attended to the said dispatches from William Page, Esq; and appointed Colonel Ira Allen, and instructed him to repair to the General Court of New Hampshire, then in session at Exeter, with full powers to concert measures for an amicable adjustment of all disputes with that State. On the 14th Governor Chittenden issued orders to Lieutenant Governor Payne (who lived in the east union) to raise the militia east of the Green Mountains to protect the civil authority and inhabitants against the menacing insults of New Hampshire, and if attacked, to repel force by force.

Colonel Allen took these orders, and proceeded to Charlestown, and on conferring with William Page, Esq; found a prospect of hostilities on the eve of commencement, on the part of New Hampshire, for the protection of some persons who professed allegiance to that State. Colonel Allen immediately made out several copies of said orders to Governor Payne, ostensibly to encourage the people in the east union to remain firm to Vermont, but found means for one copy to fall into the hands of a staunch friend to New Hampshire, who eagerly seized the prize, and sent it by express night and day to the Governor of New Hampshire. Colonel Allen then proceeded to Exeter. On his way through the State, he found the people extremely enraged against Vermont, both on ac-

[1] Now Sullivan and Cheshire counties, N. H.

count of her supposed connexions with the British in Canada, and for extending her claims, so much to the injury of that State, that, in fact, very little stimulus would raise the people to a civil war, which was his duty and inclination, if possible, to prevent. These circumstances made him apprehensive it might be difficult to gain the necessary information. When he arrived, and being acquainted with the late Major General Fulsom,[1] who was Commandant of all the militia of that State, and had been friendly to Vermont, Colonel Allen, on his arrival, found means immediately to have a private interview with him, by which he learnt, that two days before the court had determined to raise a sufficient military force to assist the civil power to carry into effect the laws of the State to Connecticut River; that the day before a copy of Governor Chittenden's orders to Lieutenant Governor Payne had been delivered to Mr. Weare, purporting a determination to repel force by force; this had occasioned a delay in issuing said orders; for if the militia to the west of Connecticut River were to cross and oppose the authority of New Hampshire, it would provoke a civil war. Under these circumstances, what further order the Court would take was yet undetermined. This interview was agreed to be kept a profound secret till all disputes were settled between the contending States.

Colonel Allen waited on the President and Council, and delivered his credentials, but the President and Council received him coolly; appeared not inclined to make any stipulations whatever respecting Vermont. Indeed their countenance, &c. seemed to whisper, this is the man that has carried on the negociations with the British in Canada, that produced Lord George Germain's instructions to Sir Henry Clinton, &c. purporting an intention of Vermont's being a British colony; he has before learned our secrets and profited thereby; he is a dangerous man, and we must unite and guard against him. No information could be obtained from any member of the Legislature, notwithstanding Mr. Allen was intimately acquainted with many of them.

While Colonel Allen was thus endeavouring to reconcile matters, General Enos and William Page, Esq; arrived with a letter from Lieutenant Governor Payne to President Weare, enclosing the copy of Governor Chittenden's orders to him, informing Mr. Weare that it was his wish to avoid the horrors of civil war, but before the people who had united with Vermont, and were under her protection, should be subjected by any hostile operation of New Hampshire, they would spiritedly oppose her, and that New Hampshire must be responsible for the consequences.

These gentlemen were authorized to assist Colonel Allen in his laudable endeavours to restore harmony. Mr. Page, who had been active in opposing the laws of New Hampshire, and lived on the east side of Connecticut river, was immediately arrested and confined in gaol, as might have been reasonably expected; thus, spirited measures were pursuing on all sides, while no negociation could be entered into by the united exertions of the Agents of Vermont, nor could they learn what determination the Court had, or would probably come to; all was a profound secret.

---

[1] Gen. NATHANIEL FOLSOM was born at Exeter, N. H., and died there May 26 1790. He distinguished himself in the French war, was Brig. General of the New Hampshire forces at the siege of Boston in 1775, and subsequently Maj. Gen. of New Hampshire militia. He was a member of the Continental Congress in 1774–5 and 1777–80, and president of the convention which adopted the constitution of New Hampshire.—Drake's *Dictionary of American Biography.*

In this situation, Colonel Allen engaged a lady to gain for him the requisite information, which she effected, and informed him of the time when the business would finally be discussed and determined in the general Court, by both houses in grand Committee.

When the Court convened on this subject, Colonel Allen went into the lobby, and began to write a memorial to the Legislature of New Hampshire. In the mean time he heard the debates, and that the Court determined on appointing an Agent to take the advice of Congress previous to any hostile measures. Colonel Allen took his leave of General Enos and Mr. Page; on his return he wrote to Lieutenant-Governor Payne and the Members of Council on the east side of the mountain, requesting them to attend in Council at Arlington, [on the 10th of January 1782,] to hear his report, and take such further steps as might be thought proper.

CORRESPONDENCE BETWEEN GOV. CHITTENDEN AND GEN. WASHINGTON ON VERMONT AFFAIRS—NOV. 1781 AND JAN. 1782.

Gov. Chittenden to Gen. Washington.[1]

STATE OF VERMONT, Arlington, 14th November, 1781.

Sir:—The peculiar situation and circumstances with which this state for several years last past has been attended, induce me to address your excellency on a subject, which nearly concerns her interest, and may have its influence on the common cause of the states of America.

Placing the highest confidence in your excellency's patriotism in the cause of Liberty, and disposition to do equal right and justice to every part of America, who have by arms supported their rights against the lawless power of Great Britain, I herein transmit the measures by which this state has conducted her policy for the security of her frontiers; and as the design and end of it were set on foot, and have ever since been prosecuted on an honorable principle (as the consequences will fully evince,) I do it with full confidence that your excellency will not improve it to the disadvantage of this truly patriotic, suffering state; although the substance has already been communicated by Captain Ezra Heacock, employed by Major-Gen. Lincoln, by your excellency's particular direction, and who arrived here with the resolutions of Congress of the 7th of August last, which appeared in some measure favorable to this state.

I then disclosed to him the measures this state had adopted for her security, which I make no doubt have by him been delivered to your excellency; and, though I do not hesitate that you are well satisfied of the real attachment of the government of this state to the common cause, I esteem it nevertheless my duty to this state, and to the common cause at large, to lay before your excellency, in writing, the heretofore critical situation of this state, and the management of its policy, that it may operate in your excellency's mind as a barrier against the clamorous aspersions of its numerous, and in many instances, potent adversaries.

It is the misfortune of this state to join on the province of Quebec and the waters of the Lake Champlain, which affords an easy passage for the enemy to make a descent with a formidable army on its frontiers, and into the neighborhood of the several states of New York, New Hampshire, and Massachusetts, who have severally laid claims in part or in whole, to this state, and who have used every art which they could

---

[1] *Correspondence of the Revolution, Letters to Washington*, Vol. III, p. 440; *Early History*, pp. 500–503; *Life of Chipman*, p. 384.

devise to divide her citizens, to set congress against her, and finally to overturn the government and share its territory among them. The repeated applications of this state to the Congress of the United States to be admitted into the federal union with them, upon the liberal principles of paying a just proportion of the expenses of the war with Great Britain, have been rejected, and resolutions passed *ex parte* tending to create schisms in the state, and thereby embarrass its efforts in raising men and money for the defense of her frontiers, and discountenancing the very existence of the state. Every article belonging to the United States, even to pickaxes and spades, has been by continental commissaries ordered out of this state, at a time when she was erecting a line of forts on her frontiers. At the same time the state of New York evacuated the post of Skenesborough for the avowed purpose of exposing this state to the ravages of the common enemy.

The British officers in New York, being acquainted with the public disputes between this and the claiming states, and between Congress and this state, made overtures to Gen. Allen, in a letter, projecting that Vermont should be a colony under the crown of England, endeavouring, at the same time, to draw the people of Vermont into their interest. The same day Gen. Allen received this letter (which was in August [or last of July] 1780,) he laid it before me and my council, who, under the critical circumstances of the state, advised that no answer, either oral or written, should be returned, and that the letter should be safely deposited till further consideration, to which Gen. Allen consented. A few months after, he received a second letter from the enemy, and the same council advised that Gen. Allen should send both letters to Congress inclosed in a letter under his signature; which he did, in hopes that Congress would admit Vermont into the Union; but they had not the desired effect.

In the fall of the year 1780, the British made a descent up the Lake Champlain, and captured the Forts George and Anne, and appeared in force on the lake. This occasioned the militia of this state, most generally, to go forth to defend it. Thus the militia were encamped against the enemy near six weeks, when Gen. Allen received a flag from them, with an answer to my letter dated the preceding July to Gen. Haldimand, on the subject of an exchange of prisoners. The flag delivered a letter to Gen. Allen, from the commanding officer of the enemy, who were then at Crown Point, with proposals for a truce with the state of Vermont, during the negotiating the exchange of prisoners. General Allen sent back a flag of his to the commanding officer of the British, agreeing to the truce, provided he would extend the same to the frontier posts of the state of New York, which was complied with, and a truce took place, which lasted about three weeks. It was chiefly owing to the military prowess of the militia of this state, and the including the state of New York in the truce, that Albany and Schenectady did not fall a sacrifice to the ambition of the enemy that campaign.

Previous to the retiring of the enemy into winter quarters, Col. Allen and Major Fay were commissioned to negotiate the proposed exchange of prisoners. They proceeded so far as to treat with the British commissioners on the subject of their mission, during which time they were interchangeably entertained with politics, which they treated in an affable manner, as I have been told. But no cartel was settled, and the campaign ended without the effusion of blood.

The cabinet council, in the course of the succeeding winter, finding that the enemy in Canada were about seven thousand strong, and that Vermont must needs be their object the ensuing campaign, circular letters were therefore sent from the supreme executive authority of this state to the claiming states before mentioned, demanding of them to relinquish their claims to this state, and inviting them to join in a solid union and confederation against the common enemy. Letters were also sent to your excellency and to the states of Connecticut and Rhode Island. Each of these letters stated the extreme circumstances of this state, and implored their aid and alliance, giving them withal to understand, that it was out of the power of this state, to lay in magazines, and support a body of men, sufficient to defend this state against the force of the enemy. But to these letters there has been no manner of answer returned.

From all which it appeared that this state was devoted to destruction by the sword of the common enemy. It appeared to be the more unjustifiable, that the state of Vermont should be thus forsook, inasmuch as her citizens struck the first offensive blow against British usurpation, by putting the continent in possession of Ticonderoga, and more than two hundred pieces of cannon; with Crown Point, St. Johns, and all Lake Champlain; their exertions in defeating Gen. Carleton in his attempt to raise the siege of St. Johns; their assisting in penetrating Canada; their valor in the battles of Hubbardton, Bennington, and at the landing near Ticonderoga; assisting in the capture of Gen. Burgoyne; and by being the principal barrier against the power of the enemy in Canada ever since.

That the citizens of this state have by nature an equal right to liberty and independency with the citizens of America in general, cannot be disputed. And that they have merited it from the United States by their exertions with them in bringing about the present glorious revolution, is as evident a truth as any other, which respects the acquired right of any community.

Generosity, merit, and gratitude, all conspire in vindicating the independence of Vermont. But notwithstanding the arguments, which have been exhibited in sundry pamphlets in favor of Vermont, and which have been abundantly satisfactory to the impartial part of mankind, it has been in the power of her external enemies to deprive her of union, confederation, or any equal advantage in defending themselves against the common enemy.

The winter was thus spent in fruitless attempts to form alliances, but no advantages were procured in favor of this state, except that Massachusetts withdrew her claim, on condition that the United States would concede the independence of Vermont; but that if they would not, they would have their snack at the south end of its territory. Still New York and New Hampshire are strenuously opposed to the independence of Vermont: and every stratagem in their power, to divide and subdivide her citizens, are exerted, imagining that their influence in Congress and the certain destruction, as they supposed, of the inhabitants of this state by the common enemy, could not fail of finally accomplishing their wishes.

In this juncture of affairs, the cabinet of Vermont projected the extension of their claim of jurisdiction upon the states of New Hampshire and New York, as well to quiet some of her own internal divisions occasioned by the machinations of those two governments, as to make them experience the evils of intestine broils, and strengthen this state against insult. The legislature, accordingly, extended their jurisdiction to the eastward of Connecticut river to the old Mason line, and to the westward to Hudson's river; but, in the articles of Union, referred the determination of the boundary lines of Vermont, and the respective claiming states, to the final decision of Congress, or such other tribunal as might be mutually agreed on by the contending governments.[1] These were the principal political movements of the last winter.

The last campaign opening with a gloomy aspect to discerning citizens of this state, being destitute of adequate resources, and without any alliance, and from its local situation to Canada, obliged to encounter the whole force of that province, or give up its claim to independence and run away, Vermont being thus driven to desperation by the injustice of those who should have been her friends, was obliged to adopt policy in the room of power. And on the first day of May last, Col. Ira Allen was sent to Canada to further negotiate the business of the exchange of prisoners, who agreed on a time, place, and other particulars relating to an exchange. While he was transacting that business, he was treated with great politeness and entertained with political matters, which necessity obliged him to humor in that easy manner that might save the interest of this state in its extreme critical situation, and that its consequences might not be injurious to the United States. The plan succeeded, the frontiers of this state were not invaded; and Lord George Germaine's letter wrought upon Congress and procured that from them, which the public virtue of this people could not.

In the month of July last, Maj. Joseph Fay was sent to the British shipping, on Lake Champlain, who completed an exchange of a number of prisoners, who were delivered at Skenesborough in September last; at which time and place Col. Allen and Maj. Fay had a conference with the British commissioners. And no damage, as yet, had accrued to this, or the United States from this quarter. And in the month of October last, the enemy appeared in force at Crown Point, and Ticonderoga; but were manœuvred out of their expedition, and are returned into winter quarters in Canada, with great safety, that it might be fulfilled which was spoken by the prophet, 'I will put my hook in their nose and turn them back by the way which they came, and they shall not come into this city (alias Vermont) saith the Lord.'

It remains that I congratulate your excellency, and participate with you in the joy of your capturing the haughty Cornwallis and his army; and assure your excellency that there are no gentlemen in America, who enjoy the glorious victory more than the gentlemen of this state, and him who has the honor to subscribe himself your excellency's devoted and most humble servant, THOMAS CHITTENDEN.

Gen. Washington to Thomas Chittenden.[2]

PHILADELPHIA, 1 January, 1782.

Sir:—I received your favor of the 14th of November, by Mr. Brownson. You cannot be at a loss to know why I have not heretofore, and why I cannot now, address you in your public character, or answer you in mine; but the confidence, which you have been pleased to repose in me, gives me an opportunity of offering you my sentiments, as an individual wishing most ardently to see the peace and union of his country preserved, and the just rights of the people of every part of it fully and firmly established. It is not my business, neither do I think it necessary

[1] As Vermont utterly refused to submit the question of her independence to Congress, she really had nothing to submit, under the resolution of Sept. 24 1779, until the East and West Unions had been effected. By these, questions of boundary were *created*, which Vermont was willing to refer to Congress.

[2] *Life and Writings*, Vol. VIII, p. 220.

now, to discuss the origin of the right of a number of inhabitants to that tract of country, formerly distinguished by the name of the New Hampshire Grants, and now known by the name of Vermont. I will take it for granted that their right was good, because Congress by their resolve of the 7th of August imply it, and by that of the 21st[1] are willing to confirm it, provided the new state is confined to certain prescribed bounds. It appears therefore to me, that the dispute of boundary is the only one which exists, and that, this being removed, all further difficulties would be removed also, and the matter terminated to the satisfaction of all parties. Now I would ask you candidly whether the claim of the people of Vermont was not for a long time confined solely, or very nearly, to that tract of country which is described in the resolve of Congress of the 21st of August last, and whether, agreeably to the tenor of your own letter to me, the late extension of your claim upon New Hampshire and New York, was not more of a political manœuver, than one in which you conceived yourselves justifiable. If my first question be answered in the affirmative, it certainly bars your new claim; and, if my second be well founded, your end is answered, and you have nothing to do but withdraw your jurisdiction to your old limits, and obtain an acknowledgment of independence and sovereignty, under the resolve of the 21st of August, for so much territory as does not interfere with the ancient established boundaries of New York, New Hampshire, and Massachusetts. I persuade myself you will see and acquiesce in the reason, the justice, and indeed the necessity of such a decision. You must consider, sir, that the point now in dispute is of the utmost political importance to the future union and peace of this great country. The State of Vermont, if acknowledged, will be the first new one admitted into the confederacy, and, if suffered to encroach upon the ancient established boundaries of adjacent ones, will serve as a precedent for others, which it may hereafter be expedient to set off, to make the same unjustifiable demands. Thus, in my private opinion, while it behoves the delegates of the states now confederated to do ample justice to a body of people sufficiently respectable by their numbers, and entitled by other claims to be admitted into that confederation, it becomes them also to attend to the interests of their constituents, and see, that, under the appearance of justice to one, they do not materially injure the rights of others. I am apt to think this is the prevailing opinion of Congress, and that your late extension of claim has, upon the principles I have above mentioned, rather diminished than increased the number of your friends, and that, if such extension should be persisted in, it will be made a common cause, and not considered as only affecting the rights of the states immediately interested in the loss of territory, a loss of too serious a nature not to claim the attention of any people. There is no calamity within the compass of my foresight, which is more to be dreaded, than a necessity of coercion on the part of congress; and consequently every endeavor should be used to prevent the execution of so disagreeable a measure. It must involve the ruin of that state against which the resentment of the others is pointed.

I will only add a few words upon the subject of the negotiations which have been carried on between you and the enemy in Canada and in New York. I will take it for granted, as you assert it, that they were so far innocent, that there never was any serious intention of joining Great Britain in their attempts to subjugate your country; but it has this certain bad tendency: it has served to give some ground to that delusive opinion of the enemy, upon which they in a great measure

[1] Commonly styled the resolutions of August 20.

found their hopes of success. They have numerous friends among us, who only want a proper opportunity to show themselves openly, and that internal disputes and feuds will soon break us in pieces; at the same time the seeds of distrust and jealousy are scattered among ourselves by a conduct of this kind. If you are sincere in your professions, these will be additional motives for accepting the terms, which have been offered, and which appear to me equitable, and thereby convincing the common enemy that all their expectations of disunion are vain, and that they have been worsted in the use of their own weapon,—deception.

As you unbosomed yourself to me, I thought I had the greater right of speaking my sentiments openly and candidly to you. I have done so; and if they should produce the effects which I sincerely wish, that of an honorable and amicable adjustment of a matter, which, if carried to hostile length, may destroy the future happiness of my country, I shall have attained my end, while the enemy will be defeated in theirs.

Believe me to be, with gr't resp't, sir, &c., GEO. WASHINGTON.

Gen. Washington to Gen. Schuyler.—[Extract.]

Jan. 8, 1782. Enclosing his letter to Chittenden of the 1st, and requesting Schuyler to have it carefully transmitted, Washington added:

This letter I have shown to a number of my friends, members of Congress and others, and they have advised me to write to Mr. Chittenden in my private character, give him my opinion upon the unjustifiableness of the extension of their claim, and advise them to accept the terms offered by the resolve of last August. This I have done fully and forcibly, and perhaps it may have some effect upon Mr. Chittenden and the leaders in Vermont. I would wish you to keep the purport of this to yourself, as I do not wish to have my sentiments publicly known.[1]

DEFENSE OF THE EASTERN AND WESTERN UNIONS.

Jan. 11 1782, Lieut. Gov. Payne, Bezaleel Woodward, Ethan Allen, John Fassett jr. and Matthew Lyon were appointed by a resolution of the Governor and Council "to make a draft of the political affairs of this state to be published;" which resulted in the following pamphlet:[1]

THE PRESENT STATE OF THE CONTROVERSY between the STATES OF NEW-YORK and NEW-HAMPSHIRE on the one part, and the STATE OF VERMONT on the other. Hartford [Conn.] Printed by Hudson & Goodwin. M.DCC.LXXXII.

IT has ever been the practice of the people of Vermont from their first settlement of this disputed territory, to appeal to the impartial judgment of the public as to the justice of their cause, against the claims and

---

[1] *Washington's Letters*, in State Department.

[1] The original draft of this pamphlet was printed, from the manuscript *Ethan Allen Papers*, in the second volume of *Vt. Hist. Soc. Collections*, pp. 231–239. The argument was re-written and enlarged for the press. Though the committee consisted of five, the authorship is doubtless to be assigned to ETHAN ALLEN. It will be observed, on p. 362, that the writer used the first person singular: "*but I advize them,*" &c.

demands of contiguous governments to the jurisdiction and right of soil of this territory, and their natural and inherent right to form into a political society, and emancipate into a regular constituted government, as well to rid themselves from the inconveniences and evils inseparable from a state of nature and anarchy which they had long laboured under, as, to exempt themselves from the usurpation and iron rod of the government of New-York. In those matters the public have most generally favored Vermont with their approbation, but how comes it to pass that Vermont has laid claim to the New-Hampshire Grants East of Connecticut River, to the old Mason line, and to a district of territory to the westward of the New-Hampshire Grants (which had been granted and settled by the former government of New-York) as far to the west as the centre of Hudson's river.

The reasons which induced Vermont to thus extend her jurisdiction, are too prolix to be particularly given in this small publication, and therefore, the bulky part of them, are proposed to be shortly printed in a larger pamphlet; however to observe briefly, it is well known that the government of New-York, both before and since the late revolution, have claimed the jurisdiction and soil of the land comprehended in the territory over which Vermont first erected and extended its governmental jurisdiction, viz. from within about twenty miles east from Hudson's River, to Connecticut River, bounding Northerly on the 45th degree of latitude, and Southerly on the north line of the Commonwealth of Massachusetts.

For the space of near fifteen years previous to the commencement of the present war, the inhabitants of that territory, for a variety of reasons heretofore published, were in opposition to the jurisdiction of New-York, and great part of the time in arms, against the oppressions, laws and authority of that government, within the said territory; for the subsequent grantees under New-York at law challenged the lands and labours of the inhabitants who had previously purchased and settled the lands under the government of New-Hampshire.

During those conflicts with the government of New-York, a great plurality of proclamations were at different periods given out by the respective Governors of New-York, for the express purpose of apprehending, and (as they phrased it) to bring to condign punishment, those delinquent inhabitants, and large rewards were therein offered for that purpose, so that great part of the inhabitants had, at one time or other, become obnoxious to those proclamations, either as original actors or as accomplices.

The last memorable transactions of the government of New-York, prior to its revolution (from a province to a State) towards those inhabitants, was the passing twelve acts of outlawry against them which had the sanction of their legislative body, which wholly precluded them from the privilege of governmental protection, and amounted to a positive declaration of war against them; upon which the inhabitants of the said district (then called the New-Hampshire Grants) by the authority of their then leaders, published a declaration of a defensive war against the government of New-York, but the present revolution commencing procrastinated the decision of the dispute at arms, as both parties entered the list of opposition to the assumed prerogative of the parliament of Britain over the then colonies.

The United States declared their independence the 4th day of July 1776, and Vermont announced theirs the 15th day of January next following.

The 22d day of August 1778, the State of New-Hampshire made a demand on the State of Vermont of a relinquishment of the jurisdiction of the New-Hampshire Grants to the eastward of Connecticut river and to the westward of the old Mason line,[1] over which, at that time, Vermont had begun to exercise jurisdiction, supposing that the whole of these Grants, on both sides of Connecticut river, had a right to unite in one entire State, in consequeuce of the annihilation of Kingly power, which alone had connected the Grants east of Connecticut river and west of the Mason line to New-Hampshire, and the Grants west of Connecticut river to New-York, as by the royal adjudication of their boundary line on Connecticut river in 1764, in the determination of which the inhabitants of those Grants were unknowing and wholly passive; and all the pretensions which the Governors of New-York and New-Hampshire ever had from the crown of England, to any jurisdiction over those Grants, were derived in their commissions pointing out their boundaries of jurisdiction, or to some regal decree of the King, as that of 1764; which the State of New-Hampshire principally urged, as a reason why Vermont should recede from their claim of jurisdiction to the east of Connecticut river, for there was no other way of ascertaining the bounds of any of the United States but by the lines formerly established by the English government; their words are these,

"Were not those towns" east of Connecticut river "settled and cultivated under grants from the Governor of New-Hampshire; are they "not in the lines thereof as settled by the King of Great Britain, prior "to the present æra? Is there any ascertaining the boundaries of any "of the United States of America, but by the lines formerly established "by Great Britain? I am sure there is not."

Though this reasoning was not fully satisfactory to Vermont, viewing the whole matter on a large scale, yet as they were previously engaged in a spirited controversy with the State of New-York, the legislature of Vermont complied with the demand of New-Hampshire, and on the 12th day of February 1779 relinquished their claim of jurisdiction to the New Hampshire Grants to the eastward of Connecticut river.

The prolixity of the transactions between the respective States of New-Hampshire and Vermont, in the settlement of their boundary line on Connecticut river, will not admit it a place in this, but may be seen at large in a pamphlet entitled "A concise Refutation of the claims of New-Hampshire and Massachusetts-Bay to the Territory of Vermont."[2]

In March, 1779, the legislature of New-Hampshire proposed the laying of their jurisdictional claim to the whole of the New-Hampshire Grants, which included the State of Vermont, against which Vermont strenuously remonstrated at the General Court of New-Hampshire, but to no purpose. They violated their settlement of the boundary line, which a few months before had been amicably settled between them and the State of Vermont (as before mentioned) and laid claim to the State of Vermont, breaking over the royal line of 1764 aforesaid, although that line had been the principle predicate of their arguments with Vermont, to relinquish their claim to the Grants east of Connecticut river, and by which they enforced their right of jurisdiction to the same, and which, upon their own principle, operates with equal weight against their claim to the Grants to the westward of the same river, alias, of the said royal line. But it seems that New-Hampshire will make something, any thing, or nothing, not only with the line of 1764, but with the line which (previous to their claim of the jurisdiction to the territory of Vermont)

[1] See Vol. I, p. 276; *Vt. Hist. Soc. Collections*, Vol. II, p. xxvii, and authorities there cited.

[2] See *Appendix E.*

their government had adjusted with that of Vermont, just as their fancy and ambition may prompt them.

New-Hampshire having laid claim to the State of Vermont, united her efforts with the State of New-York to ruin and overturn the jurisdiction thereof, and began to sow discord and make divisions, on the east side of the Green Mountains and west of Connecticut river; inveigling some of the inhabitants to renounce their allegiance to Vermont and connect with New-Hampshire, while New-York were as industrious in seducing others on the west side of the mountains, to unite with them, but met with less success than their eastern ally. Their joint influence in the Congress of the United States was so great, that they procured from them, on the 24th day of September, 1779, a resolve, appointing the first day of February then next, to adjust the claims of those States to the territory of Vermont, with a proviso that they would enact laws impowering Congress to do it, which they accordingly did, and the inhabitants of the New-Hampshire Grants (in the language in that case adopted) were served with a copy of that resolution. But Vermont remonstrated against the jurisdictional right of Congress to determine their independence which had been previously established by the authority of the people of the territory of Vermont, whose right it was to constitute and organize government, and though those claiming States did not succeed, in procuring of Congress a recognizance of their said jurisdictional claims, or either of them, over the said territory, they nevertheless prevented this State from a fœderal union with the United States to this day, in consequence whereof this State has been exposed to the whole force of the enemy in Canada, without any alliances [with the neighboring states.]

In December, 1780, Vermont, with written proposals from its supreme executive authority, accompanied by a special agent, solicited those claiming States, and each and every of the New England States, for an alliance against the common enemy, but no answer was returned from any or either of them: In this critical situation Vermont was solicited, by two respectable districts of inhabitants, one from each of those claiming States which lay contiguous to the east and west side of it, to be admitted into union and governmental connection with them, as well to enjoy the privileges of their constitution and laws as by them together with their own mutual assistance to be protected from the common enemy. The legislature of Vermont, taking into their serious consideration the perplexed and embarrassed circumstances of the State, occasioned partly from its local situation to Canada, and partly by the designs and influence of those claiming States, and perceiving it was through their united efforts that this State were precluded a union with the United States, and that they made and fomented schisms among her citizens, and as their numbers and resources were inadequate to oppose the enemy's force in Canada, with a rational prospect of success, and that a union with those contiguous districts would augment their strength, and enable them to make a much better defence against the enemy, and heal those internal divisions among themselves, and give those litigious claiming States to experience the evils of intestine broils, which they had prepared for Vermont: Further considering that these districts, now called the east and west unions, had been principally defended by this State ever since the surrendery of the British army by Gen. Burgoyne, and that those districts had been neglected as to their defence from the common enemy, by the States to which they had previously yielded allegiance, more particularly the western district, which this State have reason to conclude was done by New-York, partly with design to lay them more exposed to the common enemy. That the inhabitants of those districts were, by natural situation to the waters of the northern lakes, and exposedness with the inhabitants of the old territory of Vermont to the incursions of the enemy from Canada, which in this or in future wars would render it expedient and best that they should belong to this State, as well as more remotely so to the United States, as it will make a strong barrier against Canada. But be it in future as it will, at present, self-preservation and mutual defence rendered it indispensably necessary, that the inhabitants of those districts, with those of the old territory, should unite in one entire State, and accordingly, on the 14th day of February 1781, the legislature of Vermont laid a jurisdictional claim to them, in consequence of which they became incorporated into this State.

Nor have the States of New-York or New-Hampshire, or either of them, upon the stating of their own claims, any more right of complaint against Vermont for forming the late Unions than in forming government within its first limits; forasmuch as they denominate the whole of Vermont, unions and all, a usurped government, and call its inhabitants their revolted subjects, and threaten the subjugation of them. However, it is in no ways probable that Vermont would have laid a jurisdictional claim to any part of the jurisdiction of those claiming states, had they not persisted in the prosecution of their unreasonable claims against the independence of this state. Though it is observable, that neither the old territory, or either of its unions, were ever included in any grant or charter from the crown of England, to either of the governments or people of New-Hampshire or New-York, or to their predecessors; but were extra provincial land, without the limits of any original jurisdiction whatever, but was altered from one jurisdiction to another by the sovereign mandates of the king of Great Britain. But if those royal mandates are admitted at this day to be binding, as giving validity to jurisdictional lines; that to his Excellency Governor Philip Skeen, from the same authority, [should be,] which was the best of the sort which affected the old disputed territory of Vermont and its western union, over which it vested him with jurisdictional authority, and which on the position of the validity of royal traditions and boundaries, would fatally operate against the claim of the State of New-York, and wholly frustrate the arguments deduced from the kingly settlement of their boundary line with New-Hampshire of 1764 aforesaid.

The written express condition upon which Vermont admitted those unions was, that provided that Vermont should be admitted into the fœderal union with the United States, Congress should determine its boundaries (alias its unions) agreeable to the mode prescribed by the Articles of Confederation of the United States.

On the 22d of August last, Congress proposed that Vermont should exclude or nullify their said unions, and then be admitted into the fœderal union of the United States. But why did not the legislature of Vermont at their sessions in October last dissolve their said unions and end the controversy as Congress proposed? It was not in their power to do it; the previous conditions of dissolving the unions were impossible, as the inhabitants of those unions were in the most solemn manner admitted to all and singular of the privileges and protections of government, in common with those other citizens who first erected it. The faith of government was pledged for their security, and they became incorporated into the same political body, and composed a respectable part of its legislature. Previous to the forming of those unions, had Congress proposed a union of Vermont with the United States, bonfires and public rejoicings would have been displayed as testimonies of their gratitude to Congress, and its legislative body would have unitedly complied with it.[1] Notwithstanding the good intention of Congress, had Vermont abandoned their unions to the vindictive rage of New-York and New-Hampshire, had it been in their power, would have been to their indellible and eternal reproach. Had the legislature of Vermont attempted a dissolution of their unions, it would have flung them, and consequently the whole state, into such intestine broils, that they would have fell an easy prey to their watchful competitors, viz. New-York & New-Hampshire, and not only be damn'd and tantaliz'd over by them, but spurn'd and derided by the New-England States, to whom they have granted a large quantity of land, and incorporated it into townships.

The legislature of the State of New-York, at their late session, renewed their claim to the property and sovereignty of the lands of Vermont, as far to the Eastward as Connecticut river, and to latitude forty-five degrees north; and remonstrated against the said resolution of Congress of the 22d [20th] of August last—and also against the authority of Congress to determine the Independence of Vermont, which they predicate on the articles of their confederation. So that what effect this peremptory remonstrance, grounded on former compacts, would have had with Congress, relative to the admittance of this State into the union of the United States, provided Vermont were disencumbered of its unions, is uncertain, though most probable it would have prevented it. Congress may now, if they think proper, admit Vermont into union, and then determine its boundaries, or which is the same thing, its unions, agreeable to the condition upon which the unions took place, so that it is in the power of Congress, by taking Vermont into union with the United States, legally to dissolve the unions if they think best; but not in the power of the legislature of Vermont to do it. The legislative body of Vermont at their session in October last, proposed to the legislatures of the States of New-York and New-Hampshire, to refer the disputes relative to their respective boundary lines, to the final arbitrament and decision of indifferent men, and pledged the faith of government to abide their determination; which proposals were officially transmitted to both of those States, but no manner of answer has been returned to this State —And why? the cause is very obvious; for had those States complied with the proposals of this [State], they must have necessarily surceased their respective claims to the old territory of Vermont (an object too dear to them to part with) for there could be no arbitration without parties, and no parties without Vermont was admitted to be a state, which would have been implicitly acknowledged by those states, by arbitrating on its boundaries. But queries may arise in the minds of the reader, Was it honest in Vermont to extend their jurisdiction upon the States of New-York and New-Hampshire? Previous to the solution of this question, it is requisite to determine whether honesty is trumps or not. *Sharp is the word.* Each of those states had in the first place laid their respective claims to the old territory of Vermont; and though Vermont, prior to extending its claims, had earnestly solicited them to surcease their claim to Vermont—accede to their independence, and make an alliance with them against the common enemy, which proposals were officially transmitted to those States: But no; they would return no answer to revolted subjects—Let them struggle in their insignificant

---

[1] These statements may be taken in the sense that a majority of the Assembly could not at the time be obtained. In BELKNAP'S *History of New Hampshire* it was asserted that the dissolution of the unions was finally secured by taking advantage of the absence of the representatives in the eastern [New Hampshire] district.—See *ante*, p. 346.

notions of independence, they will answer as a forlorn hope to secure the liege subjects of New-York and New-Hampshire; they are nicely situated to Canada, and when the war is terminated, if any of them remain alive, we old confederated States can easily subject them; but if we think it most prudent, we have a right to call on the whole confederacy of the United States to crush them; so that at most they are but our vassals, and cheag'd [cheated] with imaginary prospects of liberty (a thing greatly talked of in this world and but little enjoyed) will go through the hazards and fatigues of that exposed part of our frontiers better than as though they had some time past been subjugated, which we old and politic states can do any time when it best serves our purposes; we know the length of the tether and can shorten it when we please, and have some time since divided their territory between us; we have them snug enough, and scorn to answer any of their proposals. This is the language of their silence and of their claims; so that the question concerning Vermont's unions, is not so much whether it accords with old homespun honesty, as whether it is politically so; or in fine, whether it was honest for Vermont in their trying circumstances to make any accessions of power against the avowed coercive designs of those states, or the common enemy. Before we leave this subject, we will query whether it was not as honest in this state to lay a jurisdictional claim to the grants east of Connecticut river, as it was for New-Hampshire previously to break over the mutual settlement of their boundary line with Vermont on Connecticut river, and lay claim to the then whole territory of Vermont. So much for honesty.

But, say the enemies to the independence of Vermont, why was there but little or no fighting between them and the enemy in Canada last campaign? Surely there is some negotiation taking place between them inimical to the United States of America—Rouse the whole confederacy and destroy Vermont. But why, what evil have they sustained from the northward? Have the enemy been permitted to pass through Vermont to invade the United States? No, not yet: but it is going to be done—So is the last trumpet going to sound, but not yet, and it is more than probable that neither of these events will take place in our days. But how came all this jealousy and talk in America? It was undoubtedly first promoted by those who were impatient that the inhabitants of this State should have been destroyed by the common enemy (or by weak and self-conceited politicians which are apt to swarm in republican governments.)—To the former it is a mystery that Vermont yet lives; they think that having prevented its union with the United States it must have terminated in their destruction: and inasmuch as they are at a loss about these and those things, it may be best that they remain so: This publication is by no means meant to open their eyes, but leaves them to grope in the dark, conjecturing what to their depraved ideas of politics appears most eligible.[1] However, there are murmurs circulated that the whole confederacy of the United States will join and extirpate Vermont,

---

[1] The policy, which had been adopted in self-defense, would have been defeated by the people of Vermont had the proposals of Gen. Haldimand been submitted for their approval. Hence in this pamphlet, and in the conference of the Vermont agents with the committee of Congress, that subject was ignored as far as possible. Nevertheless it should be observed that Gov. Chittenden had at an earlier date informed Washington what the purposes of Vermont really were.—See letter of Chittenden to Washington, Nov. 14 1781, *ante*, p. 350.

which is as unlikely as that the tail of the next comet will set the world on fire. What eminent services have Vermont done in the common cause in the course of this war, even to those claiming States who are devoting it to destruction, in order to take possession of the fertile territory; but as it is merely interested views which unite those claiming States to endeavour the ruin of Vermont, which cannot be an inducement to the other eleven United States; it is not supposable that they will be duped to espouse their cause, the reward of which could be nothing but infamy and disgrace. How inglorious would the victorious Continental Troops, just returned from the capture of a proud and haughty army, with a Cornwallis, the pride of England, at their head, appear in arms, puissantly trampling on the rights of a brave and meritorious people, and sacrificing the liberties which they have been valiantly supporting; and all to corroberate the venal and ambitious designs of controverting States; Heavens forbid it! Preserve their laurels, and smile propitiously on Vermont, who want nothing but justice should take place between them and their competitors. Did not Vermont strike a respectable part of the mortal blow towards capturing General Burgoyne, which produced the alliance with France, and in the chain of causes brought the French fleet to Chesapeake, and brought about a second memorable æra in America. But notwithstanding what has been said on this subject, we will premise, for it is probable, that New-York and New-Hampshire will urge the confederacy at large to suppress Vermont, and subject it to their jurisdiction; but it is observable, that both of those claiming States claim this territory against each other; so that it will be pre-requisitely necessary for Congress to ascertain and establish the boundary line between those States, prior to any supposed subjugation of Vermont to those jurisdictions, or to either of them; for otherwise there could be no object in view in a supposed conquest of Vermont: But after all, it would still remain a dispute who should share the conquest, whether New-York or New-Hampshire, or whether either of them should extend jurisdiction over the disputed premises; or if over any part, how far either the one or the other, or either of them, should extend jurisdiction: So that the States of New-York and New-Hampshire, previous to the conquest of Vermont, by the confederacy of the United States, must go through a tryal at law, agreeable to the articles of confederation or otherwise, in order to settle their boundary line, or else pull off the mask and publicly own the fact, with which they stand indicted by Vermont, viz. That they have some time past clandestinely agreed upon the line of the division of that State, and so produce it to Congress as a line mutually agreed on between themselves; but I advize them to pretend to Congress, and to the world, that it was but very recently agreed upon between them.

But why does not Vermont call on the eleven United and disinterested States to espouse their cause against the oppressions of the other two; because she does not belong to the confederacy of the United States. But how came those claiming States to have a right to challenge assistance from the United States, as predicated on the guarantee of their confederation, to espouse their quarrel with the state of Vermont, which had unremittingly existed many years with New-York and some considerable time with New-Hampshire, before the confederacy of the United States took place, which was on the first day of March, 1781, and in the fourth year of the governmental independence of Vermont, and fourteen days after Vermont had formed the before mentioned unions, which was on the fourteenth day of February, 1781. Will any advocates for the confederacy of the United States be so hardy as to pretend that it could be in force before it existed, or that it could possibly have a retrospective obligatory nature, any more than a law before it is enacted? Every one will determine in the negative; and consequently the State of Vermont, including its unions, cannot come within the reach of the guarantee of the confederation of the eleven United States, to those other claiming United States; nor is there any manner of propriety in any supposable demand of any one, or both of the States of New-York and New-Hampshire, on the guarantee of their confederacy, to interfere with or espouse their controversy with Vermont, previous to the first day of March last, when their confederacy took place.[1]

Furthermore, those claiming States, previous to Vermont's extending their jurisdictional claims upon them, were the aggressors, in that they unitedly and spiritedly persisted in prosecuting their respective claims to the territory of Vermont, and made use of any and every indirect measure in their power, to accomplish their designs and frustrate the independence of Vermont, and thereby necessitated her to lay claim to those unions, to preserve herself, so that if there be any wrong in Vermont in laying claim to them, in itself, simply considered, New-York and New-Hampshire were the procuring cause of it, and therefore cannot take advantage of their own wrong to blame Vermont, or have any rightful demand on the confederacy to assist them, so as with or without them to ruin Vermont, who would never have made those claims on them, had not their previous unwarrantable claims against her, occasioned the laying of them.

It seems that those claiming States chuse to be at liberty to claim and vex Vermont, and make what reprisals they can upon her, yet, if Vermont return the compliment, as we vulgarly say *tit for tat*, they complain of abuse and injustice; and she is threatened with awful desolation from the confederacy at large, if we may credit the reports of the sticklers of those claiming States. Vermont does not mean to be so overrighteous as by that means to die before her time; but for the States of New-York and New-Hampshire, to stand griping their respective claims fast hold of Vermont, and at the same time make such a hedious outcry against the gripe of Vermont upon them, is altogether romantic and laughable.

State of Vermont, January 17, 1782.

Proceedings in Congress on Vermont—Dec. 1781 to March 1782.[2]

Wednesday, December 5, 1781.

A letter, of the 24th of November last, from the governor of the state of New-York, was read, together with concurrent resolutions of the senate and assembly of the said state, declarative of their sense on the acts of Congress of the 7th and 20th of August last, respecting the people residing on the New-Hampshire Grants, on the west side of Connecticut river:

---

[1] Jan. 22 1782—contemporaneous with this pamphlet—Mr. Madison, writing in Congress, declared that "the power of Congress, either to use force or admit her [Vermont] into the confederacy, was doubted by many States."—See *Madison Papers*, Vol. I, p. 109; *Vt. Hist. Soc. Collections*, Vol. II, p. 241.

[2] *Journals of Congress*, Folwell's edition, 1781–82, Vol. VII, p. 189.

Ordered, That the concurrent resolutions be filed in the Secretary's office among the archives of Congress.

On the next day Mr. Floyd of New York, seconded by Mr. Middleton of S. C., moved to amend the foregoing record, by adding the words "And protesting against any attempt made by Congress to carry into execution their said acts of the 7th and 20th of August last." Five states voted aye, and only one, Rhode Island, no; but as a majority of the states did not vote in the affirmative the motion was lost.

The resolutions were as follows:

[From Slade's *State Papers*, pp. 163-166.]

STATE OF NEW-YORK.

In Senate and Assembly, the fifteenth and nineteenth days of November, in the sixth year of the independence of the said state, one thousand seven hundred and eighty one:

Resolved, That it appears, from sufficient evidence, that Congress did, by their act of the 24th of September, 1779, inter alia, earnestly recommend to the states of New-Hampshire, Massachusetts-Bay and New-York, to pass laws, expressly authorising Congress to hear and determine all differences between them, relative to their respective boundaries, in the mode prescribed by the articles of confederation; and also, by express laws for the purpose, to refer to the decision of Congress all differences or disputes between them, relative to jurisdiction, which they might, respectively, have with the people of the district. called the New-Hampshire grants; and, also, to authorise Congress to proceed to hear and determine all disputes subsisting between the grantees of the said states, respecting titles to lands lying within the said district; and also, that Congress did, thereby, pledge their faith, after a full and fair hearing of all the said differences and disputes, to decide and determine the same, according to equity, and carry into execution and support their determinations and decisions in the premises.

Resolved, That it appears from the like evidence, that, at the time of passing the said act, and for above a century and an half before, to wit, from the first settlement of the colony of New-York, now the state of New-York, the said colony and this state included, by most indubitable right and title, both of jurisdiction and property, all the lands, among others to the westward therof, lying north of the north bounds of the Massachusetts-Bay, up to the latitude of forty-five degrees north, and extending between those boundaries, from Hudson's river to Connecticut river, including the waters of the northern lakes, and other waters within those boundaries: that the above extent of territory, which includes the district, called the New-Hampshire grants, was, by a decree of the British King, to whom the sovereignty thereof, as parcel of the colony of New-York, belonged, made in his Privy Council, the twentieth day of July, one thousand seven hundred and sixty-four, between the colonies of New-York and New-Hampshire, declared to be parcel of the said colony of New-York: that, in consequence thereof, the government of the colony of New-Hampshire, expressly ceded and relinquished all claim and title of jurisdiction of the above territory: that, thereupon, the same was, by acts of legislation of the colony of New-York, formed into counties, and such parts thereof as were settled, were represented in the Legislature of that colony: that they were also represented in the Provincial Congress and Convention of this State of New-York; received aids from them, as parcel of this State, both before and after the declaration of the independence of these United States; assisted, by their representatives, in forming the constitution of this state, and fully submitted to the jurisdiction thereof, till in the year one thousand seven hundred and seventy-seven.

Resolved, That it appears of record, that, notwithstanding the above clear and conclusive evidence of right, on the part of this state of New-York, to the territory above described, including, as aforesaid, the New-Hampshire grants, and though the Legislature of this state might, therefore, consistently with the strictest justice, have asserted their dignity and sovereignty over the district of the New-Hampshire grants; yet they, respectfully adopting the sentiments of Congress, that it was essential to the interest of the whole confederacy, carefully to avoid all intestine dissensions and maintain domestic peace and good order, acquiesced in the submission recommended by the said act of Congress, and, accordingly, on the 21st day of October, one thousand seven hundred and seventy nine, passed a law of this state for that purpose.

Resolved, That it satisfactorily appears that, in consequence of said law, the agents, thereby appointed to manage the controversy on the part of this state, at very great public expence, collected the necessary evidence to support the facts asserted in the second above mentioned resolution; and that, after many and repeated delays, they were, at length, on the nineteenth day of September, one thousand seven hundred and eighty, in the presence of all the parties interested (except the state of Massachusetts-Bay, who had not passed the necessary act of submission) indulged with an hearing before Congress; in the course of which, such evidence as above mentioned, was produced on the part of this state, as, in the opinion of the agents of this state, fully proved to Congress, the several facts contained in the said second above mentioned resolution; and that, on the twenty-seventh day of the same month, all parties being present, (except the state of Massachusetts-Bay, and Messrs. Allen and Bradley, agents for the people of the New-Hampshire grants, claiming to be a separate independent jurisdiction, who, though duly notified, then declined any further attendance) the state of New-Hampshire, who had also submitted by their legislative act, had an hearing in Congress, in support of their claim to the jurisdiction over the district, called the New-Hampshire grants; that this state has, on their part, fully complied with every requisite contained in the said act of Congress, of the twenty-fourth day of September, one thousand seven hundred and seventy-nine, and has, accordingly, from that day to this, abstained from the grant of any lands within the said district, and also from the exercise of jurisdiction over any of the inhabitants of the said district, who had not acknowledged the same; that, on the contrary, the revolted inhabitants of the said district having arbitrarily erected themselves into a separate and independent state, unrecognized as such, until this day, by this state, or the other United States, and, having framed a government, they have passed laws, granted lands, and exercised civil and military authority over the persons and property of those inhabitants, who profess themselves to be subjects of this state, in manifest subversion of the right of sovereignty and property of this state, and in direct contempt and infringement of several acts of Congress: that, although they had contented themselves with the exercise of jurisdiction principally up to a line running nearly parallel to Hudson's river, at twenty miles distant therefrom, until the month of June last: yet, at that time, notwithstanding the censure and prohibition of Congress, and in contempt of their recommendation and authority, by an act of their usurped government, they extended a jurisdictional claim over all the lands situate north of the north line of the state of Massachusetts, and extending the same to Hudson's river, then east of the centre of the deepest channel of said river, to the head thereof, from thence east of a north line, being extended to latitude forty-five degrees, and south of the same line, including all the lands and waters to the place where the said pretended state then assumed to exercise jurisdiction; inserting, at the same time, in their said act, a clause not to exercise jurisdiction within their jurisdictional claims, for the time being: that, of all these matters Congress have been fully apprized, and though repeatedly solicited thereto, by the delegates of this state, have not, hitherto, made any decision and determination of the said controversy, according to equity, as by their said act of the 24th day of September, one thousand seven hundred and seventy-nine, they pledged themselves, and by the law of this state they were authorized to do: that, to put an end to this delay, so injurious to the jurisdiction of this state, so subversive of its interests, peace and policy, so promotive of a repetition of those violent acts of usurped civil and military authority, which, in the judgment of Congress, declared in their resolution of the second of October, one thousand seven hundred and eighty, were highly unwarrantable and subversive of the peace and welfare of the United States, and from which they require the people inhabiting the said grants to desist, until the decision and determination of Congress in the premises, they have actually presumed to exercise sovereign authority and jurisdiction, to the full extent of their said jurisdictional claim, by appointing civil and military officers, making levies of men and money, rescuing delinquents from the hands of justice of this state, at the expence of the blood and the loss of the life of one of the subjects of this state, in the execution of his lawful duty, and forbidding the officers of justice of this state to execute their offices, as appears from the papers attendant on his Excellency the Governor's speech, and other due information; that, among these, to shew the actual exercise of jurisdiction by the usurped government of the said grants, by the stile and title of the state of Vermont, over the territory contained within the said jurisdictional claim, is the copy of a certain proclamation, bearing date the eighteenth day of July, one thousand seven hundred and eighty-one, purporting to be under the seal of the said pretended state, signed by Thomas Chittenden, who stiles himself their governor, which, after divers falsities and absurdities therein contained, asserts that commissions, both civil and military, had then been lately issued by the supreme authority of the said pretended state, to persons chosen agreeable to the laws and customs thereof, in the several districts and corporations within the limits of the above mentioned western or jurisdictional claim; strictly requires, charges and commands all persons, of whatsoever quality or denomination, residing within the said western claim of jurisdiction, to take due notice of the laws and orders of the said pretended state, and to govern themselves accordingly, on the pain of incurring the penalties therein contained; and strictly requires, charges and commands all magistrates, justices of the peace, sheriffs, constables, and all other civil and all military officers, to be active and vigilant in executing the laws aforesaid, without partiality.

Resolved, That the Legislature of this state is greatly alarmed at the evident intention of Congress, from *political expedience*, as it is expressed in a letter from his Excellency the President of Congress, to his Excellency the Governor of this state, of the 8th of August last, and as is evinced in their acts of the 7th and 20th of the same month, enclosed therein, to establish an *arbitrary* boundary, whereby to exclude out of this state the greatest part of territory described in the second resolution above mentioned, belonging, most unquestionably, to this state, as part, parcel and member thereof, and to erect such dismemberment, possessed by the revolted subjects of this state, into an independent state, and, as such, to admit them into the federal union of these United States; especially as the two last mentioned acts seem to express the sense of Congress, that the territories of this state, by the articles of confederation are, and, as in fact and truth they are, by the second and third articles thereof, guaranteed, and still more especially, as by a proviso in the ninth article, it is provided that no state shall be deprived of territory for the benefit of the United States.

Resolved, That it is the sense of the Legislature, that Congress have not any authority, by the articles of confederation, in any wise, to intermeddle with the former territorial extent of jurisdiction or property of either of these United States, except in cases of disputes concerning the same, between two or more states in the union, nor to admit into the union, even any British colony, except Canada, without the consent of nine states, nor any other state whatsoever, nor, above all, to create a new state, by dismembering one of the thirteen United States, without their universal consent.

Resolved, That in case of any attempt by Congress to carry into execution their said acts of the seventh and twentieth of August last, this Legislature, with all due deference to Congress, are bound, in duty to their constituents, to declare the same an assumption of power, in the face of the said act of submission of this state, and against the clear letter and spirit of the second, third, ninth and eleventh articles of the confederation, and a manifest infraction of the same; and do, therefore, hereby solemnly *protest* against the same.

Resolved, That a copy of these resolutions be forthwith made and certified by the President of the Senate, and the Speaker of the Assembly, in presence of his Excellency the Governor, who is hereby requested to attest the same with the great seal of this state, and transmit it, without delay, to Congress, to the end that the same may be entered on their journals, or filed in their archives, *in perpetuam rei memoriam;* and that another copy, so certified as aforesaid, be delivered to the delegates of this state, for their use and guidance, and that they be, and hereby are, expressly directed and required to enter their dissent on every step which may be taken in, and towards, carrying the said two last mentioned acts of Congress into execution.

Dec. 20, the committee on Gov. Clinton's letter of Nov. 24 reported in part and Congress ordered that two tons of gun-powder be furnished and charged to the state of New York.[1]

FRIDAY, January 25, 1782.[2]

The committee, consisting of Mr. Ellery, Mr. Randolph, Mr. Law, Mr. N. W. Jones and Mr. Clymer, to whom was recommitted the report of a committee, on sundry letters and papers respecting the district of country, commonly known by the name of the New-Hampshire Grants, delivered in their report; which was taken into consideration and debated.

---

[1] In October 1781, when preparing to suppress Vermont authority in the "western district" by force, Gen. Gansevoort wrote to Gov. Clinton for powder. On the 18th of that month the Governor replied, saying that compliance with this request was out of his power, as, out of the whole supply ordered by Washington for New York in the previous spring, only five hundred pounds had been received.—See *ante*, p. 328.

[2] *Journals of Congress*, Folwell's edition, 1781–82, Vol. VII, p. 208.

MONDAY, Jan. 28, 1782.[1]

The report of the committee respecting the New-Hampshire Grants, was debated and referred to a grand committee.

On the 1st, 5th, 7th, 12th, 13th and 16th of Feb. the following letters from the Vermont Delegates were sent to Congress—part of them to the President, and others to the chairman of the committee which had Vermont matters in charge. These papers, with the exception of the first, are not named in the journal of Congress.

Jonas Fay and Ira Allen to the President of Congress.[2]

PHILADELPHIA 30th Jan. 1782.

Sir—On the fourteenth day of August last, we had the satisfaction to communicate to Congress, a duplicate of our commission to attend on that Honble. body for the purposes therein named. We have now the honor to enclose a duplicate of our reappointment together with instructions to further negotiate the business of our appointment.[3]

Our colleague, who was expected in town before this time, has occasioned the delay of this amount. Whenever he arrives (who is hourly expected) we shall then be ready to lay before Congress such papers and matters as we are, or may be furnished with on his arrival.

We have the honor to be with great respect
Your Excellency's most Obednt Humble Servants,
JONAS FAY &
IRA ALLEN.

To His Excellency, the President of Congress.

[Endorsed] Read Feb. 1st.

Jonas Fay and Ira Allen to Samuel Livermore.[4]

PHILADELPHIA, Feb. 5, 1782.

Sir,—We have the honor to transmit herewith (for the perusal of the honble. committee) copies of the several papers following vizt.

Governor Chittenden orders to Majr. General Payne dated 14th Dec. 1782.

Major General Payne's letter to the Honble. Meshech Weare Esqr 21st Decr. 1781.

Lt. Governor Payne's appointment and instructions to General Enos and William Page Esq. December 21, 1781, and a letter from General Enos & Ira Allen Esq. to the Honble. Elisha [Ichabod] Bartlet Esq. 29th Dec. 1781.

Copy of a letter under the signature of Peter Gansevoort B. Genl. dated 18th December 1781, together with an answer thereto under the signature of Col. Ebenr. Walbridge dated Dec. 19th 1781, which together with Vermont's proposals of October last on the subject of settling boundary lines, contain the principal proceedings between N. Hampshire, N. York

[1] *Journals of Congress*, Folwell's edition, 1781–82, Vol. VII, p. 210.

[2] *N. H. Grants*, Vol. 2, No. 40, p. 207, in the State Department at Washington.

[3] For the commission referred to, see *ante*, p. 316. The "re-appointment" was on the 10th of January 1782, when Elisha Payne, Jonas Fay, Ira Allen, and Abel Curtis were appointed.—See *ante*, p. 132.

[4] *N. H. Grants*, Vol. 2, No. 40, p. 211, in the State Department, Washington.

& Vermont since August last, and as our colleague (Mr. Curtis) is not yet arrived, we have nothing further to add at present, but that we propose to proceed on the business of our mission whenever it may be agreeable to the Honble Committee.

We are sir, your honors most obedient
and very humble servants,

JONAS FAY &
IRA ALLEN.

Honble Saml. Livermore, Esq. [*Chairman.*]

Memorial of Jonas Fay and Ira Allen.[1]

The Honble Committee of Congress,—The undersigned, Delegates for the State of Vermont by virtue of their appointment and Commission, to repair to the American Congress for the purposes therein named, and in pursuance of their special instructions by the Governor and Council of said State, have the honor to represent,

That, the citizens of that part of America formerly known by the name of the N. Hampshire Grants, did in consequence of certain disputes subsisting between them and some of the British Colonies in America, form themselves into Committees of Safety and Conventions for the preservation of their just rights against lawless power, soon after the edict of G. Britain in July 1764.

That, this kind of Government was continued by adjournments and new elections until after the Grand Era of American Independence, and until the twelfth day of March, A. D. 1778, when it emerged into a Constitutional Legislature.

That immediately after the Battle of the 19th day of April A. D. 1775 at Lexington, those Inhabitants took an offensive part against British usurpation; and have since exerted themselves in common with their brethren in America in the suport of the rights, liberties and independence of the United States.

That the existence of the State of Vermont, (upon revolution principles) is at least coeval with any other of the free states of America and founded on the same grand basis of Liberty and therefore (in our opinion) entitled of every blessing and privilege which the united states do or may in the future enjoy by virtue of their stipulated union and convention each with the other.

We therefore take this method to express our wishes, and do in behalf of the said State of Vermont solicit and most earnestly request that the United States in Congress assembled would recognize her independence, admit her into the federal Union of the United States of America and to a seat in Congress—that She may yield and receive mutual aid in the general defense and obtain an equitable settlement of her boundary lines.

Done in Philadelphia, in obedience to the instructions aforesaid, this 7th day of Feby 1782.

JONAS FAY,
IRA ALLEN.

Hon. Saml Livermore, [*Chairman.*]

Jonas Fay, Ira Allen and Abel Curtis to Samuel Livermore.[2]

To the Honorable Committee of Congress.

The undersigned delegates of the State of Vermont beg leave to observe by way of addition that in royal governments in America when

---

[1] *N. H. Grants*, Vol. 2, No. 40, p. 227, in State Department, Washington.

[2] *Same*, p. 231.

regal power ceased the people were then left at full liberty to institute such government as might appear to them to be most conducive to their peace and happiness. In this situation a respectable number of the now citizens of the State of Vermont in the eastern union (so called) formed themselves into Committees of Safety and Conventions; the other part connected with New Hampshire in a temporary compact *only* which they have since rejected and united with the aforesaid Convention by which they have been since governed, except when in connection with Vermont. And in this situation were those inhabitants when the Convention aforesaid was formed that united the grants east of the river Connecticut to Vermont by which they were admitted into union with her on the two following conditions, viz$^{t.}$: first, that the existence of Vermont should be held sacred; and secondly that in case of any dispute respecting border lines and jurisdiction, to be settled agreeably to the modes prescribed by the articles of confederation or by such other way as should be mutually agreed upon.

That N. Hampshire by extending her claim west of Connecticut river have extinguished or rendered uncertain her west boundary line by the royal determination in A. D. 1764 which affords a strong plea in support of the right to a fair hearing in the settlement of said line so earnestly to be wished for in order to give satisfaction to so large number and respectable body of people, three fourths part of whom (at least) are firmly attached to the government of Vermont and among whom officers civil and military are duly elected and qualified as the law directs.

That they have many arguments and records (which we are not at present possessed of) to justify their right to a union with Vermont or at least a hearing in the settlement of the dispute, not to mention their universal rejection of the requisition of N. Hampshire to meet in convention in order to form a permanent plan of government, or the late extraordinary act of N. Hampshire which explicitly acknowledges the above assertion, and in its effects particularly tends to alienate the affections of those people from that government, and its neglect of the frontier exclusive of the act of Hon'ble Congress of twenty fourth day of Sept. A. D. 1779 recommending to N. Hampshire not to exercise jurisdiction over them etc.

That about the year 1773 a plan was set on foot by some of the inhabitants of the N. Hampshire grants together with Phillip Skeen Esq. for forming a new Colony in such wise as to include the Grants and to extend at least to Hudson river on the West and to the forty fifth degree north latitude on the north and to Massachusetts on the south. And in consequence of this plan application was made to the court of Great Britain by Mr. Skeen for that purpose, who has since been well known among the British by the title of *Governor Skeen.*

That there are papers now in the state of Vermont under the signature of the said Phillip Skeen on the subject of his appointment to government dated about the month of December A. D. 1774 mentioning among other things that he should soon call on this people to show their loyalty to the king. These papers might reflect much light on this subject and perhaps amount to a satisfactory proof that the said Phillip Skeen did actually succeed in the aforesaid plan. And then on the principle [of] royal lines overturn the pretensions of the claiming States even on their own stating. With respect to what action may have been between the people on the Western union and the state of New York we further observe that as allegiance and protection are reciprocal, when the latter is refused the former is of course void and a people left to provide new guards for their future safety and this is consonant with the declaration of independence of the United States and the constitution of the State of New York. And,

That there is at least eight tenths of the people in this [western] union who are in favor of the government of Vermont and officers civil and military elected and duly qualified.

That many of the leading gentlemen in both the aforesaid unions who are opposed to Vermont have been repeatedly heard to say that they have no objection to unite with Vermont if it were agreeable to the honorable the Congress. And that a vindication of the rights of the people both in the eastern and western Unions, thus to unite with Vermont, is preparing more fully by a committee appointed by authority for that purpose, and will undoubtedly be soon published.

We have the honor to be Gentlemen
your most obedient and humble servants,

JONAS FAY,
IRA ALLEN,
ABEL CURTIS.

Philadelphia, 12 Feby 1782.
The Honble Saml. Livermore, Chairman &c.

Messrs. Fay, Allen, and Curtis, to the President of Congress.[1]

PHILADELPHIA, 13 Feb. 1782.

Sir,—Understanding there are several official papers, lodged in the Secretary's office of Congress since August last from the States of New York and New Hampshire, which respect their dispute with the State of Vermont, We beg the favour of their respective copies, as they may be essentially necessary at this time,

And have the honor to be your Excellency's
most obedient humble servants,

JONAS FAY,
IRA ALLEN,
ABEL CURTIS,
Delegates of the State of Vermont.

His Excellency John Hanson Esqr. Pres. &c.

Same to Same.[2]

PHILADELPHIA, Feb. 16, 1782.

Sir,—As it is clearly reasonable (in our opinion) that we should be indulged with copies of any act or resolution of the States of New Hampshire or New York which respect the dispute between those States and the State of Vermont which we have the honor to represent, We therefore wish to be favored with the copies of any such papers as are lodged in the Secretary's office and which bear date since August last, in particular an act of the Legislature of the State of New York bearing date about the middle of the month of October last,

And are with great respect Your Excellency's
most obedient Humble Servants,

JONAS FAY,
IRA ALLEN,
ABEL CURTIS.

His Excellency John Hanson Esq.

IN CONGRESS, TUESDAY, February 19, 1782.[3]

The committee, consisting of Mr. Livermore, Mr. Patridge, Mr. Cornell, Mr. Law, Mr. Floyd, Mr. Boudinot, Mr. Clymer, Mr. Rodney, Mr.

---

[1] *N. H. Grants*, Vol. 2, No. 40, p. 235, in the State Department, Washington.

[2] *Same*, p. 257.

[3] *Journals of Congress*, Folwell's edition, 1781–82, Vol. VII, p. 216.

Carroll, Mr. Randolph, Mr. Hawkins, Mr. Middleton, Mr. Telfair, [one from each state,] to whom was referred the report of a committee on sundry papers relative to the people inhabiting the district of country known by the name of the New-Hampshire Grants, together with a representation of Seth Smith,[1] and a letter of the 20th [30th] of January,

---

[1] SETH SMITH appeared as the agent of the towns of Guilford and Brattleborough, with the approval of Gov. Clinton. Smith presented his "Representation" to Congress on the 28th of January, and it was referred to a committee, though the facts are not in the printed journal. Of this document the following account is given in B. H. HALL'S *Eastern Vermont*, pp. 416, 417:

To excite, if possible, an additional interest in their situation, the New York party in the townships of Guilford and Brattleborough drew up a "Representation" as it was called, of their situation, and committed it to Seth Smith their agent, with orders to present it to the Legislature of New York, and to the Congress of the United States. In this document, which was composed with much care and apparent truthfulness, Smith, as representant, declared that a "very great majority" of the inhabitants of Brattleborough and Guilford, and "at least three fourths" of the people living within the "usurped jurisdiction of Vermont, on the east side of the Green Mountains and west side of Connecticut river," were desirous of returning to the "rightful jurisdiction of the State of New York," from which by the violent measures of the new state government, and the want of necessary protection and assistance from Congress and New York, they had "much against their inclinations, been obliged to appear to depart;" that the towns which he represented, and a majority of the inhabitants of the New Hampshire Grants, were, as he believed, firmly determined to oppose by arms the "usurped jurisdiction of Vermont;" and that there was full evidence of the disaffection of "the leaders and abettors in the assumed government of Vermont" towards the United States, and of a "league of amity" between them and the enemy in Canada. In support of the last statement, he alluded to the fact that Vermont commissioners had held frequent interviews with commissioners from Canada, both in the latter province and on the "Grants;" that the leading men in Vermont had established a neutrality with Canada, publicly disavowed the authority of Congress, and authorized the transmission into Canada of prisoners belonging to Gen. Burgoyne's army, without receiving any in exchange;* that the "staunch whigs and those well affected to the true interests of the United States" were exceedingly alarmed at this friendly intercourse which they could not prevent unless by force of arms, since, as supporters of New York, they were not eligible to office under Vermont; and that the "ill-gotten powers" of the supporters of the new state "were wantonly and arbitrarily" exercised, to the "inconceivable oppression of the best friends of the American cause" in that portion of the nation.

In addition to these charges, he stated that the Vermonters had committed many acts of violence, under color of law, against the well-affected subjects of the state of New York; that they had proceeded so far against him, as to cause him to be charged—in an indictment for high treason against "their assumed government"—with an attempt to introduce a "foreign power" into Vermont, meaning undoubtedly by these words the government of New York and the authority of Congress; that

*This is improbable. In May 1782, three months later than this statement, Vermont exacted from Gen. Haldimand forty Americans in exchange for seventeen British prisoners released by Vermont.—See *ante*, p. 153, note 1.

from Jonas Fay and Ira Allen, having delivered in a report, the same was taken into consideration, and some time spent thereon.

Feb. 21, the delegates for Vermont addressed the following letter to the President of Congress, and it was read on the same day. It is not noted, however, in Folwell's printed journal.

Messrs. Fay, Allen, and Curtis to the President of Congress.[1]

PHILADELPHIA Feb. 21 1782.

Sir:—In pursuance of our appointment and instructions we have had the honor of transmitting to your Excellency and of laying before a Committee of the hon[ble] Congress sundry official papers which we are informed have been taken into consideration. But when we consider that a multiplicity of business must unavoidably engross the attention of Congress, who are esteemed the guardians of the rights of a numerous and free people, we are not urgent for a hasty determination relative to the State of Vermont. We however cannot doubt but, in due time, that State will be admitted as an additional gem in that Crown which of late, rising from obscurity, has been the peçuliar favorite of Heaven and become the astonishment of the world.

Permit us, sir, to mention that as we have no additional matters to lay before Congress at present—as it is probable another campaign is approaching, and as the legislature of Vermont expected our return previous to completing the estimates for the current year, it is necessary we should soon take our leave of this city, inasmuch as no time ought to be lost in attending to that business; and persuaded at the same time that no measures destructive to the peace and tranquility of Vermont

---

they had "debauched" into a union with themselves, portions of New York and New-Hampshire; that, although exempt from the "common burthens of the American war," they still exercised an "exorbitant power in taxation and arbitrary drafts, to support their usurpations against two of the states in the American confederacy;" and that this latter proceeding was intolerably grievous to the great body of the true friends of America, who were compelled to endure, since they were not able to resist. To support these declarations, the representant offered to adduce the "most regular and conclusive proofs," provided he and his friends should be protected while collecting the evidence. He also suggested the propriety of sending congressional commissioners to make inquiries and return a full report, and added his assurance that they would be upheld and respected by the majority of the people. In conclusion, he gave as his firm opinion "that unless Congress seasonably and vigorously interpose, the well-affected to the state of New York and the United States will fly to arms in opposition to the usurpation of Vermont."

Smith's "Representation" was presented to Congress on the 28th of January; on the 11th of February, he asked the interposition of New York to supersede the necessity of a resort to force by the New York party in Vermont; and in just twelve days thereafter, Feb. 23, he petitioned the General Assembly of Vermont for a pardon for his violation of the laws of Vermont, and it was granted on the 26th, on condition of his taking the oath of allegiance to Vermont.—See p. 147.

[1] *N. H. Grants*, No. 40, Vol. 2, p. 261, in the State Department, Washington.

will be pursued in the absence of the delegates,—that we have the fullest reason to believe the most vigorous exertions will be made by the legislature for a spirited defense of her extensive frontiers and that by the interposition of Heaven and the friendly aid of the Congress she will be able to repel any force which the enemy may send against her. In the mean time every prudent measure will be pursued to cultivate peace and harmony with her neighboring States which may be conducive to the tranquility of the rising empire of America.

We have the honor to be your Excellency's most obedient
and Humble servants,
JONAS FAY,
IRA ALLEN,
ABEL CURTIS.

His Excellency John Hanson Esq. Pres. &c.

[Endorsed]—Read same day.

IN CONGRESS, FRIDAY, March 1, 1782.[1]

The grand committee, consisting of Mr. Livermore, Mr. Patridge, Mr. Cornell, Mr. Law, Mr. Floyd, Mr. Boudinot, Mr. Clymer, Mr. Rodney, Mr. Carroll, Mr. Randolph, Mr. Hawkins, Mr. Middleton and Mr. Telfair, to whom was re-committed their report on sundry papers respecting the inhabitants of a district of country known by the name of the New-Hampshire Grants, together with a representation of Seth Smith, and a letter of the 30th of January from Jonas Fay and Ira Allen, having delivered in a report, and the following paragraph [resolution] being under consideration, viz.

"That in case the inhabitants residing within the limits aforesaid, within one calendar month from the delivery of a certified copy of these resolutions by the commissioner hereinafter mentioned, to Thomas Chittenden, Esq; of the town of Bennington, within the limits aforesaid, or from the time of the said commissioner's leaving such certified copy at the usual place of residence of the said Thomas Chittenden, Esq; shall by some authenticated act recognize the last above described boundaries to be the limits and extent of their claim, both of jurisdiction and territory, and shall accede to the articles of confederation and perpetual union between the states of New-Hampshire, Massachusetts, Rhode-Island and Providence Plantations, Connecticut, New-York, New-Jersey, Pennsylvania, Delaware, Maryland, Virginia, North Carolina, South Carolina and Georgia, as agreed to in Congress on the 15th day of November, 1777; and shall thereupon appoint delegates in their behalf, with full powers, instructions and positive orders immediately to repair to Congress, and to sign the said articles of confederation, and afterwards to represent them in the United States in Congress assembled, their said delegates shall be admitted to sign the same, and thereupon the inhabitants of the above described district shall be acknowledged a free, sovereign and independent state, and shall be considered as a component part of the federal union, and entitled to the advantages thereof."

A motion was made by Mr. Wolcott [of Connecticut,] seconded by Mr. Ellery [of Rhode Island,] to strike out the words between the words "inhabitants residing within," and the word "accede;" and in lieu thereof to insert "or belonging to the territory commonly known by the name of the New-Hampshire Grants, or by whatsoever name it may be called, west of Connecticut river, and to the eastward of the boundary conditionally guaranteed by the resolution of the 20th of August last, in favour of the state of New-York."

---

[1] *Journals of Congress*, Folwell's edition, Vol. VII, 1781–2, p. 228.

This motion was lost on the following vote: *Yeas*—Massachusetts, Rhode-Island, Connecticut, and New-Jersey. *Nays*—New-York, Pennsylvania, Delaware, Maryland, Virginia, South Carolina, and Georgia. One member each from New Hampshire and North Carolina voted in the negative, but these votes were not counted.

A motion was then made by Mr. Scott, seconded by Mr. Floyd, [both of New York,] to strike out the whole resolution.

On the question, Shall the resolution stand? the votes were as follows: *Yeas*—Massachusetts, Rhode Island, New Jersey, Pennsylvania, Delaware, and Maryland. *Nays*—New York, Virginia, South Carolina, and Georgia. One member each from New Hampshire and North Carolina voted in the negative. As a majority of the states did not vote in the affirmative, the resolution was stricken out.

A motion was then made by Mr. Clark [of New Jersey,] seconded by Mr. Atlee [of Pennsylvania,] that the rest of the report be committed; which is as follows:

Congress having resolved on the 7th day of August last, that in case they should recognize the independence of the people of Vermont, they would consider all the lands belonging to New Hampshire and New York, respectively, lying without the limits aforesaid, as coming within the mutual guarantee of territory contained in the articles of confederation; and that the United States will accordingly guarantee such lands and the jurisdiction over the same, against any claim or encroachments from the inhabitants of Vermont aforesaid: and Congress having, on the 20th day of the same month required as an indispensable preliminary to their recognition of the independence of the people inhabiting the territory aforesaid, and their admission into the federal union, the explicit relinquishment of all demands of lands or jurisdiction on the east side of the west bank of Connecticut river and on the west side of a line beginning at the north-west corner of the state of Massachusetts, thence running twenty miles east of Hudson's river so far as the said river runs north-easterly in its general course; thence by the west bounds of the townships granted by the late government of New-Hampshire, to the river running from South-bay to Lake-Champlain; thence along the said river to Lake-Champlain; thence along the waters of Lake-Champlain to the latitude of forty-five degrees north, excepting a neck of land between Missiskoy-Bay and the waters of Lake-Champlain. And the people inhabiting the territory aforesaid, not having as yet made the relinquishment aforesaid as above required, and attempting since the date of the above resolutions to extend and establish their jurisdiction over part of the lands guaranteed to the states of New-York and New-Hampshire abovesaid; and it being indispensably necessary to bring all disputes respecting the jurisdiction of the people residing within the territory aforesaid to a speedy issue:

Resolved, That the district of territory, commonly known by the name of the New-Hampshire Grants, by whatsoever name it may be called, is and shall be bounded westward by a line beginning at the northwest corner of the state of Massachusetts, thence running northward twenty miles east of Hudson's river, so far as the said river runs northeasterly in its general course, thence to the west boundary-line of the townships granted by the late government of New-Hampshire; thence northward along the said west boundary-line, to the river running from South-bay to Lake-Champlain, thence along the said river to Lake-Champlain;

thence along the waters of Lake-Champlain to latitude forty-five degrees north, including a neck of land between the Missiskoy-Bay and the waters of Lake-Champlain; thence it shall be bounded north by latitude forty-five degrees north, and eastward by the west bank of Connecticut river, from forty-five degrees north to the northern boundary-line of the state of Massachusetts, and southward by the said northern boundary of the state of Massachusetts from the said west bank of Connecticut river, to the nothwest corner of Massachusetts above-mentioned.

Resolved, [Here followed the resolution which was stricken out on motion of the delegates of New York.]

Resolved, That in case the said inhabitants, within the above-described district do not desist from attempting to exercise jurisdiction over the lands guaranteed to New-Hampshire and New-York as aforesaid, and shall not, within the time limited as aforesaid, comply with the terms specified in the foregoing resolutions, Congress will consider such neglect or refusal as a manifest indication of designs hostile to these United States, and that all the pretensions and applications of the said inhabitants, heretofore made for admission into the federal union, were fallacious and delusive; and that thereupon the forces of these states shall be employed against the said inhabitants within the district aforesaid, and Congress will consider all the lands within the said territory to the eastward of a line drawn along the summit of a ridge of mountains or heights of land, extending from south to north, throughout the said territory, between Connecticut river on the east, and Hudson's river and Lake-Champlain on the west, as guaranteed to New-Hampshire under the articles of confederation, and all the lands within the said territory to the westward of the said line as guaranteed to New-York under the articles of confederation: provided always, that Congress will consider any other partition, which shall, hereafter, by an agreement between the legislatures of New-Hampshire and New-York, be made between their respective states, concerning the territory aforesaid, as guaranteed to them according to such agreement, saving, in either case, all rights accruing to the state of Massachusetts, or any other state under the articles of confederation aforesaid: and provided always, that for the more effectually quieting the minds of the inhabitants aforesaid, the said states of New-Hampshire and New-York respectively, shall pass acts of indemnity and oblivion, in favour of all such persons as have at any time previous to the passing such acts, acted under the authority of Vermont so called, in any manner whatsoever, upon such persons submitting to the jurisdiction of the said states respectively: and provided always, that the said states of New-York and New-Hampshire, respectively, do pass acts confirming and establishing the titles of all persons whatever, to such lands as they do now actually occupy and possess within the limits of the district aforesaid, under whatever title the same may be held, either from New-York, New-Hampshire or Vermont so called: and also for confirming and establishing the titles of all persons whatever, to such lands within the district aforesaid, as they may be entitled to under grants from New-York, New-Hampshire or Vermont so called, according to the propriety [priority] of such grants in point of time, excepting in such cases where the lands are in the actual occupancy and possession of the claimants, as mentioned in the proviso abovesaid. But inasmuch as some persons claiming in right of grants made under the authority of the district or territory called Vermont, and not actually occupying the same, may be deprived thereof by the interference of other prior grants:

Resolved, That in case the partition aforesaid shall take place, any person claiming and deprived as aforesaid, his or her assignee or representative shall receive full compensation in lands or otherwise, to be provided by Congress.

Resolved, That it be, and it is hereby earnestly recommended to the states of New-Hampshire and New-York respectively, to pass acts of oblivion and indemnity, in favour of all such persons, residing without the limits of the district above described, who shall heretofore have taken part with the inhabitants residing within the same, against the governments of either of those states, upon such persons quietly and peaceably submitting themselves to the government, and jurisdiction of such state respectively, to which they belong.

Resolved, That in case of the neglect or refusal of the inhabitants residing within the district aforesaid, to comply with the terms prescribed in the resolutions aforesaid, the commander in chief of the armies of these United States, do without delay or further order carry these resolutions as far as they respect his department into full execution.

Resolved, That a commissioner be appointed on the part of these United States, whose duty it shall be immediately to repair to the district aforesaid, and deliver a certified copy of these resolutions to Thomas Chittenden, Esq; of the town of Bennington aforesaid, or leave such copy at his usual place of residence; and also to enforce on the inhabitants of the said district, the necessity of their complying without delay with the terms above prescribed by Congress, or submitting themselves peaceably to the jurisdiction of the states of New-Hampshire and New-York, agreeably to the above resolutions.

On the question for committing, the yeas and nays being required by Mr. Boudinot,

The vote was as follows: *Yeas*—Connecticut, New-Jersey, Pennsylvania, Delaware, Maryland, and Virginia. *Nays*—New-York, South Carolina, and Georgia. *Divided*—Rhode Island. One member each from New-Hampshire, Massachusetts, and North Carolina voted no. So the question was lost.

It will be observed that in the journal of Congress, above quoted, no mention is made of the attendance of the Agents of Vermont; of course because they appeared before the committee only. The following is IRA ALLEN's account, from his history in *Vt. Hist. Soc. Collections*, Vol. I, pp. 446–448.

The Agents of Vermont exhibited their credentials to Congress, and had repeated interviews with Committees and Members of that body, who appeared very much dissatisfied with the Legislature of Vermont, in not complying with their resolves of the 7th and 20th of August. The Agents of Vermont represented, in justification, that having been deprived of continental aid, while acts and resolutions of Congress were passed in favour of the claiming and neighbouring States; and those States, assisted by said acts and resolves, were taking every measure in their power to divide and sub-divide her citizens; that the Legislature of New Hampshire had, against the will of Vermont, laid a jurisdictional claim, prefaced with friendship, when subsequent transactions shewed that the object was to overturn her jurisdiction, and connect the whole territory of Vermont to New Hampshire, for the members of her General Court had, by circular letters, convened a Convention for the ostensible purpose of connecting the New Hampshire Grants on both sides of Connecticut river, into one entire State; then, on the 16th day of January, 1781, at Charlestown, where forty-three towns were represented, procured a vote to unite the whole to New Hampshire; that this was, in fact, to annihilate the existence of Vermont.

In this Convention were twelve Members of the Council and Assembly of New Hampshire; surely Congress could not blame the friends of Vermont, who had been silent spectators of these bare-faced intrigues, in exerting themselves next day, and obtaining a resolution of the Convention to unite that part of New Hampshire, west of the Mason line, to Vermont; this was turning the same trouble on New Hampshire that she had contemplated for Vermont, and was the more justifiable, as it united her citizens, and made her more formidable against her enemies, which was essential, considering the extent of her frontiers. That the claims and intrigues of New York, and self-preservation, had induced the Legislature of Vermont to claim a part of the State of New York; that the people of these territories had, by articles of union, confederated with Vermont, and became citizens thereof; her conduct might be further justified by the articles of union with said districts; in them it was stipulated, that whenever Vermont was acknowledged as a State by Congress, and admitted to a seat in that body, any dispute that might exist respecting boundary lines should be submitted to Congress for decision; that Vermont then was, and ever had been ready and willing to comply with the aforesaid principles, or any other equitable mode that might be agreed upon to settle boundary lines with either of the claiming States; but that she will not, under existing circumstances, dissolve her unions, agreeable to the late resolves of Congress, thereby weakening her strength without gaining an equivalent by a confederation; that if the United States were serious in admitting Vermont into the union, they could not see why it might not be done in the first instance, and then settle the boundary lines on principles that might be equitable and consistent with the articles of the confederacy of the United States, and articles of the unions which necessity had compelled her to make; and further that the Legislature of Vermont, in October last, passed an act, appointing Commissioners, with full powers to agree with like Commissioners from New Hampshire and New York, and they to appoint three or more Commissioners, to hear and determine on boundary lines between the respective States, which line or lines so determined on, should be boundaries between said States, which act was sent to the Legislatures of New Hampshire and New York, with a request that they would respectively pass similar acts, and attend to a settlement of boundary lines. Now had either of these States seriously wished for a settlement of boundary lines, and to admit Vermont into the confederacy, why did they not pass acts similar to that of Vermont, or, at least, withdraw their jurisdictional claim from the ancient territory of Vermont, instead of menacing a State with military operations, who, of all others, were most exposed to the common enemy, and recently deprived of continental aid.

With respect to a civil war, at a time when the liberty of America would thereby be endangered, no people were or could be more averse to it than those of Vermont, who had been eight years longer struggling for their liberties than their brethren of the United States. As to Governor Chittenden's orders to Lieutenant Governor Payne and Colonel Walbridge, so much complained of, extraordinary cases required extraordinary remedies, and these orders, like sovereign balsams, had a salutary effect, as the consequences evince; for at least they prevented the effusion of blood and civil war, as they caused General Gansevoort to retreat, when he saw a force was advancing to reinforce those he was menacing; and the Government of New Hampshire suspended their military operations on discovering the determination of Vermont, while peace was restored without bloodshed, which otherwise, in all probability, would not have taken place. This also evinces the sagacity and independence of the Governor; and unquestionably such a suggestion of facts and cogent arguments had a very powerful effect upon Congress; for on March 1st it was proposed in Congress to pass a resolve, that if within one month from the time in which the resolve should be communicated to Thomas Chittenden, the inhabitants of Vermont should comply with the resolves of August 7th and 20th, 1781, they should be immediately admitted into the union; but if they should refuse this, and did not desist from attempting to exercise jurisdiction over the lands guaranteed to New Hampshire and New York, Congress would consider such neglect or refusal, as a manifest indication of designs hostile to the United States, and that all the pretensions and applications of the said inhabitants, heretofore made for admission into the federal union, were fallacious and delusive; and that thereupon the forces of the United States should be employed against the inhabitants, and Congress would consider all the lands within the territory to the eastward of the ridge of mountains as guaranteed to New Hampshire; and all the lands to the westward of said line, as guaranteed to New York; and that the Commander in Chief of the armies of the United States do without delay or further order carry these resolutions into full execution. But after warm debates, and repeated trials, a vote could not be obtained to adopt these resolutions, and the matter subsided.

Dissolution of the Eastern and Western Unions—February, 1782.[1]

In General Assembly, Feby. 11th 1782.

His Excellency the Governor laid before the House a letter from Genl. Washington dated Philadelphia Jany. 1st 1782—a letter from Genl. Woolcut[2] dated Philadelphia Jany. 18th 1782—one from Benja. Henry[3] dated Hallifax Jany. 21st 1782—one from Simeon Olcott dated Charlestown Jany. 28, 1782[4]—which letters were directed to the Govr.—One from Govr. Chittenden directed to Colo. Yates [of New York militia in the "western district,"] dated Arlington 24th Augt. 1781.—One from Colo. Yates dated Chcheticoke Augt. 27th 1781.—One from Colo. Saml. King[5] to Govr. Chittenden dated Jany. 5th 1782—the Govrs. answer to Colo. King dated Jany. 10th 1782.—One from Wm. Page Esqr. [of Charlestown, N. H.] to Govr. Chittenden dated Decr. 9th 1781 enclosing a copy of a letter to Colo. Wm. Haywood and a copy of a letter to Brigd. Genl. Olcot.—One from Govr. Chittenden to Lieut. Govr. Payne dated Dec. 14th 1781.[6] One from

---

[1] From the manuscript *Assembly Journal*, Vol. 2.

[2] See *ante*, p. 135, note 3.

[3] A member of the Convention of Oct. 31 1780.—See *ante*, p. 278.

[4] Probably his resignation of the office of judge of the superior court.

[5] Of Chesterfield, N. H. The warrant for his arrest had been issued by New Hampshire a few days previous to the date of this letter.—See *ante*, p. 341.

[6] Dr. Page's letter announced the prospect of hostilities by New Hampshire. It was received Dec. 13, and on the 14th Gov. Chittenden ordered Lieut. Gov. Payne to repel force by force.—See *ante*, p. 339.

Elijah Parker constable dated Chester 28th Jany. 1782—one from Nathl. Brown to Govr. Chittenden dated Winhall Jany. 21st 1782. One from Nathl. Brush Esqr. [of Bennington,] to Govr. Chittenden dated December 5th 1781. One from Joseph Wait to the Govr. dated Maidstone Jany. 22d 1782. Copy of a letter from Genl. Safford to Colo. Yates dated Hoosack Dec. 8th 1781—with Colo. Yates answer. One from Isaac Sherman Lieut. Colo. Comd. Thos. Grosvenor Lieut. Colo. Willis Clift Majr. Committee to Govr. Chittenden dated Camp, near Dobbs Ferry Augt. 2d. 1781[1]—and three letters from Genl. Hazen to the Governor—were read.

MONDAY, Feby. 18th. 1782.

Ordered that Mr. Chandler be requested to wait on his Excellency the Govr. and desire him to lay before this House a copy of the letter that produced the one from Genl. Washington of Jany. 1st 1782—Likewise the original letter from Genl. Washington, with the resolution of Congress of the 21st. of Augt. 1781.[2]

On motion made, Resolved that the Governor and Council be requested to join this House in a Committee of the whole at two o-clock in the afternoon to take under consideration the above mentioned letters and resolution and the letter from Genl. Wolcott &c.

The honble Moses Robinson Esqr. informed the House that it was the request of the Govr. & Council that the meeting of the Committee of the whole be referred until tomorrow morning—which was agreed to.

TUESDAY, Feby. 19th. 1782.

Agreeable to the Order of the day the Govr. and Council and House of Representatives formed themselves into a Committee of the whole to take under consideration the Resolution of Congress of the 21st of Augt. the Letters from Generals Washington & Wolcott &c. and continued on that business from day to day until,

THURSDAY, Feby. 21st. 1782, when the Committee of the whole having dissolved the House formed and the Speaker resumed the Chair.

Ordered that the Report of the Committee of the whole be referred for further consideration until the meeting of the House in the afternoon.

2 °CLOCK P. M.

Agreeable to the order of the day the following Report of the Committee of the whole was read viz—

"STATE OF VERMONT, *Bennington, Feb. 19th*, 1782.

The Governor and Council having joined the General Assembly, in a committee of the whole, to take into consideration the resolutions of Congress of the 7th and 21st of August last,

His Excellency THOMAS CHITTENDEN, Esquire, in the Chair.

The following papers were read by the Secrety in their order, viz.

1st. The said resolutions of the 7th and 21st of August, and a letter from his Excellency the President of Congress, to his Excellency the Governor, enclosing them.

2d. A private letter from his Excellency General Washington, to his Excellency the Governor, dated, Philadelphia, January 1st, 1782.

3d. A letter from General Oliver Woolcott, to his Excellency the Governor, dated January 18th, 1782.

---

[1] These were all Connecticut officers in the continental army.

[2] Most often called the resolution of Aug. 20. It was adopted on the 20th, was reconsidered and finally adopted on the 21st, though the printed journal of Congress records it as of the 20th.

4th. A letter from Revd. Jonathan Edwards, to Noah Smith.

5th. The articles of Union with the eastern and western districts.

Adjourned until 2 oClock P. M.

Met, according to adjournment.

6th. The Proceedings of the Legislature, in October last, upon the said resolutions of Congress, were read.

After some debate, adjourned until to-morrow morning, 9 oClock.

20th *Feby.* 9 *o'clock.*

Met agreeable to adjournment.

7th. A letter from Colo. Lutterloh, to Majr. Fay, was read; and after some debate on the business, adjourned until 2 oClock, P. M.

2 oClock, P. M. met according to adjournment.

8th. A letter from Genl. Pattison to Majr. Fay, was read.

A motion was made by Mr. Chandler, that the sense of the Committee be taken upon the following question, vizt:—whether Congress, in their resolutions of the 7th and 21st of August last, in guaranteeing, to the respective States of New-York and New-Hampshire, all the territory without certain limits, therein expressed, has not eventually determined the boundaries of this State?

Which question being put, was carried in the affirmative: whereupon,

Resolved, That, in the opinion of this committee, Congress, in their resolutions of the 7th and 21st of August last, in guaranteeing to the respective States of New-York and New-Hampshire, all territory without certain limits therein expressed, have eventually determined the boundaries of this State.

And whereas, it appears to this committee consistent with the spirit, true intent and meaning of the articles of union, entered into by this State with the Inhabitants of a certain district of country, on the East side of the West bank of Connecticut river, and on the west side of a line twenty miles East of Hudson's river, (which articles of union were executed on the 23d day of Feby. and the 15th day of June last past,) that Congress should consider, and determine, the Boundary lines of this State—Therefore, this committee recommend to the Assembly of this State, to pass Resolutions declaring their acquiescence in, and accession to, the determination made by Congress of the said boundary lines, between the States of New-Hampshire and New-York, respectively, and this State, as they are, in said resolutions, defined and described, and also, expressly relinquishing all claim to, and jurisdiction of, and over, the said Districts of territory, without said boundary lines, and the Inhabitants thereon residing.

Confiding in the faith and wisdom of Congress, that they will, immediately, enter on measures to carry into effect the other matters in said resolutions contained, and settle on equitable terms, whereby this State may be received into, and have and enjoy all the protection, rights and advantages of a federal union with the United States of America, as a free, Independent and Sovereign State, as is held forth to us in and by said resolutions—

And this committee do further recommend to the Assembly, that they cause official information of their resolutions to be immediately transmitted to the Congress of the United States, and the States of New-York and New-Hampshire."

The aforesaid Report of the Committee of the Whole was read and accepted & thereupon

Resolved that a Committee of three to join a Committee from the Council[1] be appointed to prepare a Bill or Bills agreeable to said report,

---

[1] Councillor Spooner was committee for the Council.

and lay the same before this House. The members chosen Mr. Tichenor, Mr. Chandler, and Mr. Knight.

On motion made by Mr. Tichenor, Resolved that a Committee of five to join a Committee from the Council [1] be appointed to point out some mode of redress relative to the injuries the people of the Eastern and Western unions have sustained in consequence of their alliance to this State. The members chosen Mr. Jacob, Mr. Harris, Mr. Powell, Mr. Dana, and Mr. Styles.

On motion made by Mr. Styles, Resolved that this House do Judge that the Articles of Union are completely dissolved—

Ordered that the Clerk of this Assembly be & is hereby directed to make up the Debenture of the members belonging to the late unions, and lay the same before this House to-morrow morning.

FRIDAY, Feby. 22d 1782.

The Clerk requested to be directed particularly respecting making up the Debenture of Mr. Page [of Charlestown, N. H.] and Mr. [Daniel] Jones [of Hinsdale, N. H.]—therefore,

Ordered that the Debenture of Mr. Page and Mr. Jones be made up for the days only that they answered to their respective names.

A Debenture of the Members belonging to the Eastern and Western Unions that have attended this Assembly the present session, was read & passed the House and Ordered that the Treasurer be and is hereby directed to pay the same.

An Act entitled "An Act to relinquish the claims to territories therein mentioned" was read and passed the House.

The Governor and Council waited on the House and requested that they would proceed to public business of importance to the State, &c.

On motion made, Resolved that this House proceed to choose by joint ballot with the Governor and Council three persons to transact the public business of this State at Congress. The ballots being taken, the honble Moses Robinson, Paul Spooner Esquires, and Isaac Tichenor Esqr. were elected.

The Committee to whom was referred the mode for redressing the people in the Eastern and Western Unions, &c. brought in the following report, viz—

"That it is the opinion of your Comtee that some proper persons be immediately sent to those officers who are now arresting and making prisoners every person they can find, who have heretofore been active in joining this state, requesting and entreating them to suspend the execution of Law until the aforementioned persons can have time to petition the Assembly of N. York to be restored, and shewing their willingness to return to their allegiance to said State—provided the Legislature should pass an act of grace—And also that a petition be presented by our Agents to the Congress of the United States praying them to interpose by recommending to the States of New-Hampshire and New-York to pass acts of oblivion in their behalf.

JOSEPH BOWKER, *for Comtee.*"

The above report was read and accepted so far as it relates to the people of the late Western Union, & ordered that a Bill be brought in accordingly.

Resolved that Genl. Saml. Safford, Ezra Styles [Stiles,] Esqr. and Genl. Roger Enos be and they are hereby requested forthwith to repair with

---

[1] Councillors Bowker and Robinson were committee for the Council.

suitable Instructions from the Council to the Western District to prosecute the intentions of the aforesaid report.[1]

SATURDAY, Feby. 23^d 1782.

Resolved that a Committee of five to join a Committee from the Council[2] be appointed to prepare instructions for the agents that are appointed to wait on Congress—and make report. The members chosen M^r. Chandler, M^r. Townshend,[3] M^r. Strong, M^r. Knight, and M^r. Lyon.

The Committee appointed to prepare a Bill agreeable to the Report of the Committee of the whole brought in the following Resolutions which were read and passed into Resolutions of this House, viz—

Here follow the resolution and recommendation embraced in the report of the committee of the whole of Feb. 20, on page 380–'81, and also the following:

Resolved that the same be complied with.

And thereupon,

Resolved, That the west bank of Connecticut river & a line beginning at the northwest corner of the Massachusetts state, from thence northward twenty miles east of Hudsons River, as specified in the Resolutions of August last shall be considered as the east and west boundaries of this State; and that this Assembly do hereby relinquish all claim and demand to and right of Jurisdiction in and over any and every district of territory without said boundary lines; and that authenticated copies of this Resolution be forthwith officially transmitted to Congress and the States of New-Hampshire and New-York, respectively.

TUESDAY, Feby. 26th. 1782.

Resolved that this House will proceed, at the meeting in the afternoon, to choose three persons to represent this State in Congress, if articles of union can be agreed on between the Agents appointed by this State and the Congress of the United States.

The Committee appointed to prepare Private Instructions for the Agents appointed to negotiate the business of this State at Congress brought in the following Instructions viz—

Private instructions to the honourable Moses Robinson and Paul Spooner, Esq^rs., Agents Elected to negociate the admission of the state

---

[1] That this committee immediately undertook the task assigned them appears from the following extract from a letter of Judge Robert Yates to Gov. Clinton, dated Albany, Feb. 24, 1782:

I had with me this morning Generals Enox [Enos] & Safford, and M^r. Ezra Stiles, who were directed by the Legislature of Vermont, by a Resolution (a copy whereof I herewith enclose) to endeavor to get an Indemnity for those people [citizens of New-York under arrest for serving Vermont.] I told them, that I conceived, the Legislature of this State, who consider their assumption of Legislative power in Vermont as an usurpation, would not upon the grounds of such Resolutions admit of their application. For these reasons, to which they assented, they intend to return home.—*Doc. History of New York*, quarto, Vol. 4, p. 604.

[2] Councillors Robinson and Fletcher were the committee for the Council.

[3] MICAH TOWNSHEND, Secretary of State, and not a member of the Assembly; an instance, like that previously noted in the case of Ethan Allen, of the appointment upon a committee of a person who was not a member of the body.

of Vermont into the confederation of the United States, and Delegates in Congress, in case of such admission—[1]

GENTLEMEN,

You will repair without loss of time to Philadelphia and are to consider yourselves as Plenipotentiaries invested with full power to agree on terms upon which this State shall come into an union with the United States of North America; and in case of such agreement, in behalf of this State, to sign and ratify articles of fœderal union with the Confederated States of America, and thereupon to take seats in Congress; but that it is not expected that more than one of you will remain in Philadelphia at a time.

In your negotiations it is expected that you will so conduct as to induce the persons you negociate with to believe that your constituents expect to be admitted free from arrears of the Continental debt already accrued and to discharge their own. If this cannot be obtained it is expected that you will reduce that part of the Continental debt which this state shall have to pay, to as small a sum as possible,—And that you make return to his Excellency the Governor, as soon as may be, of the certain sum which you shall Covenant that this state shall pay.

SAML. FLETCHER, *for the Committee.*

The above Instructions were read and passed as Instructions for the purpose aforesaid.

2 oClock afternoon.

Agreeable to the order of the day, proceeded to choose three persons as Delegates to represent this State in Congress &c. The ballots being taken the honble Moses Robinson & Paul Spooner Esquires and Isaac Tichenor Esqr. were Elected.

WEDNESDAY, Feby. 27th. 1782.

Resolved that the Treasurer be and is hereby specially directed to lay by for the Delegates to Congress £100.

THURSDAY, Feby. 28th. 1782.

Resolved that his Excellency the Governor be and is hereby requested to Commissionate the Agents appointed with Plenipotentiary powers to negociate the admission of this State into Confederation with the United States three of whom are hereby authorised to transact said business, & if this State is admitted into Confederation any one or two of said Agents are hereby empowered to take their seats and represent this State in Congress.

Resolved that one person be added to the Agents and Delegates appointed to transact the business of this State at Congress. The ballots being taken the honble Jonas Fay Esqr. was Elected.

Resolved that the honble Paul Spooner, Moses Robinson, & Jonas Fay Esqrs. and Isaac Tichenor, Esqr. be and are hereby requested to repair to Congress without delay on the business of their appointment.

---

[1] ISAAC TICHENOR'S name was omitted on the journal, doubtless by accident. The instructions given officially embraced Mr. Tichenor and Jonas Fay with the above-named.

COMMISSION TO THE DELEGATES TO CONGRESS—MARCH 3, 1782.[1]

{STATE SEAL.} His Excellency THOMAS CHITTENDEN, Esquire; Captain General, Governor and Commander in Chief in and over the State of VERMONT,

To the Honble JONAS FAY, MOSES ROBINSON, and PAUL SPOONER, Esquires; and to ISAAC TICHENOR, Esquire, **Greeting.**

AGREEABLE to Resolutions of the Governor, Council and General Assembly of this State, passed at their Session at Bennington in February last, electing you *Agents* and *Delegates* in behalf of this State to attend the Congress of the *United States* with plenary powers to agree upon, and ratify Terms of *Confederation* and perpetual *Union* with them, and to represent this State in *Congress* as *Delegates* for the *Year* ensuing, or until recalled by act of Legislature—

I DO, in the name and by the Authority of the Freemen of the State of *Vermont*, fully authorise and amply empower you the said JONAS FAY, MOSES ROBINSON, PAUL SPOONER and ISAAC TICHENOR, Esqrs; or either three of you, to negociate and complete, on the part of this State, the *Admission thereof* into a *fœderal Union* with the UNITED STATES OF NORTH AMERICA—And in behalf of this State, to subscribe to *Articles of perpetual Union and Confederation* therewith.

Given under my Hand, and the Seal of this State, In Council, this Thirteenth Day of March Anno Domini One Thousand seven Hundred and Eighty two, and in the 6th Year of the INDEPENDENCE of this State.

THOS. CHITTENDEN.

By His Excellency's Command.

(Duplicate.) THOS. TOLMAN, *Dep. Secr'y.*

GOVERNOR CHITTENDEN TO GENERAL WASHINGTON.[2]

ARLINGTON, March 16, 1782.

Sir,—I had the honor to receive your Excellency's favor of the 1st of January by express. I am not insensible that the delicacy of your station in the empire renders it ineligible for you to address me in my public character. Your noticing us, therefore, in your private capacity, under our circumstances, I beg leave to esteem as the strongest mark of your magnanimity and friendship. While we receive with gratitude the resolves of Congress, of the 7th and 21st of August last, it affords us great satisfaction that your Excellency is willing to consider them as implying the right, which Vermont claims, to be a state, within certain described bounds. And, as the dispute of boundary is the only one that hath prevented our union with the Confederacy, I am very happy in being able to acquaint your Excellency that that is now removed on our part, by our withdrawing our claims upon New Hampshire and New York, and by confining ourselves solely, or very nearly, to that tract of country which is described in the resolve of Congress of the 21st of August last. Since, therefore, we have withdrawn our jurisdiction to the confines of our old limits, we entertain the highest expectations that we shall soon obtain what we have so long been seeking after, an acknowledgement of independence and sovereignty. For this we have appointed Commissioners, with plenary powers, to negotiate an alliance with the

[1] From one of the original commissions, now in the state library, elegantly written by Thomas Tolman.

[2] *Revolutionary Correspondence, Letters to Washington*, Vol. III, p. 492.

Confederated States, and, if they succeed, to take seats in Congress. Should Heaven prosper the designs of their negotiation, we please ourselves much that we, who are of one sentiment in the common cause, and who have but one common interest, shall yet become one nation, and yet be great and happy. The glory of America is our glory, and with our country we mean to live or die, as her fate shall be. I have no need to acquaint your Excellency, that our local as well as our military (not to say political) situation, as an extended frontier, awfully exposed these infant plantations to the power and fury of the common enemy. Might we be so happy as to draw the attention of our country, we hope to be favored with your particular exertion. I have the honor to be, Sir, with great respect,

Your most obed't and humble serv't,

THOMAS CHITTENDEN.

P. S.—This will be delivered by one of our agents, to whom I beg leave to refer your Excellency for the more particular situation of this State, with regard to military preparations and state of defence.

PROCEEDINGS IN CONGRESS ON VERMONT--APRIL 1 TO MAY 21 1782.

MONDAY, April 1, 1782.[1]

A letter, of the 31st of March, from Jonas Fay, Moses Robinson, Paul Spooner and Isaac Tichenor, was read, informing, that in consequence of the resolution of Congress of the 20th of August last, the state of Vermont have invariably pursued every measure in order to comply with the said resolution, in a manner that was consistent with the obligations she was under to the people inhabiting the east and west unions, and maintaining the peace and harmony of her citizens with those inhabitants: and enclosing several resolutions of the legislature of Vermont, announcing their compliance with the preliminary required in the said resolution of Congress of the 20th of August last; together with a duplicate of a commission to them, under the great seal of the state, empowering them in behalf of the state of Vermont to subscribe the articles of confederation.[2]

---

[1] *Journals of Congress*, Folwell's edition, 1781–82, Vol. VII, p. 244.

[2] The letter was as follows:

[From *N. H. Grants*, Vol. 2, No. 40, p. 273, in the State Department, Washington.]

Delegates for Vermont to the President of Congress.

PHILADELPHIA, 31st March 1782.

Sir,—We have the honor to inform Congress that, in consequence of their resolution of the 20th of August last, reciting vizt.

" By the United States in Congress assembled 20th August 1781.

" On a reconsideration of the resolution respecting the people inhabiting the New Hampshire Grants, it was altered and agreed to as follows.

" It being the fixed purpose of Congress to adhere to the guarantee to the States of New Hampshire and New York contained in the resolutions of the 7th instant,

" Resolved that it be an indispensable preliminary to the recognition of the independence of the people inhabiting the Territory called Vermont, and their admission into the federal Union, that they explicitly relinquish all demands of Lands or jurisdiction on the east side of the west bank of Connecticut river, and on the west side of a line beginning at

A motion was made by Mr. Clark, seconded by Mr. Scott,

"That the letter of Jonas Fay, &c. with the papers accompanying the same, together with the several papers on the files of Congress relating to the same subject, and received since the 20th of August last, be referred to a committee."

This motion was agreed to by the following vote: *Yeas*—Massachusetts, Rhode Island, Connecticut, New Jersey, Pennsylvania, Delaware, and Maryland—7 states. Mr. Livermore of N. H. voted in the affirmative, but his vote could not be counted as the vote of the state. *Nays*—New York, Virginia, and Georgia—3 states. *Divided*—South Carolina. On the 3d of April Mr. Madison moved that the proceedings of Vermont in Oct. 1781 rejecting the conditions required by the resolutions of Congress of August 20 1781, and the resolutions of New York of the 15th and 19th of November 1781, be entered on the journals.

---

the north west corner of the State of Massachusetts thence running twenty miles east of Hudson river so far as the said river runs north easterly in its general Course, then by the west bounds of the townships granted by the late Government of N. Hampshire to the river running from South Bay to Lake Champlain, thence along said river to Lake Champlain, thence along the waters of Lake Champlain to latitude forty five degrees north; excepting a neck of Land between Missisque bay and the waters of Lake Champlain."

The state of Vermont have invariably pursued every measure in order to comply with the resolution above recited, in a manner that was consistent with the obligations she was under to the people inhabiting the East and West Unions and maintaining the peace and harmony of her citizens with those inhabitants.

By the earliest opportunity we enclose several resolutions of the Legislature of Vermont, announcing their compliance with the *Preliminary* required in the *resolution of Congress*, together with a duplicate of our Commission, impowering us in behalf of the State of Vermont to subscribe Articles of confederation.

Reposing the highest confidence in the wisdom and Honor of Congress; We assure ourselves that not the least obstacle remains to our admission into a federal Union with [the] United States of America.

As we expect the enemy will make their appearance in force on the frontiers of Vermont, as soon as the Lakes will permit, which time we view to be not far distant, and as the union of the United States with the State we have the honor to represent would animate its inhabitants in support of the Confederacy, we therefore wish to be made acquainted that Congress enter on the business as soon as they may find it convenient, that we may transmit the result to our Constituents.

We are, sir, with esteem,

Your most obedient Humble servants,

JONAS FAY,
MOSES ROBINSON,
PAUL SPOONER,
ISAAC TICHENOR.

To His Excellency John Hanson Esqr.
President Congress.

[Endorsed,]

April 1, Referred with the papers on the files relating to the same subject and rec'd since 20th Aug. last, to Mr. Clymer, Mr. Law, Mr. Carroll, Mr. Clarke, Mr. Livermore.

This motion was rejected, six states to four; but on the next day Mr. Livermore moved that the papers be entered on the journals as a part of the motion made by Mr. Madison, which was agreed to.[1]

WEDNESDAY, April 17, 1782.

The committee, consisting of Mr. Clymer, Mr. Carroll, Mr. Clark, Mr. Livermore, and Mr. Law, to whom was referred the letter of the 31st of March, from Jonas Fay and others, together with other papers relating to the same subject, received since the 20th day of August last, delivered in a report, which being read,

A motion was made by Mr. Scott [of New York,] seconded by Mr. Livermore [of N. H.,] that the first Tuesday in October next be assigned for the consideration of the report.[2]

And on the question the yeas and nays were required by Mr. Scott, the report being as follows:

That Congress, on the 20th of August last, by the votes of nine states, resolved as follows: on a reconsideration of the resolution respecting the people inhabiting the New Hampshire grants, it was altered and agreed to as follows:

"It being the fixed purpose of Congress to adhere to the guarantee to the states of New Hampshire and New York, contained in the resolutions of the seventh instant:

"*Resolved*, That it be an indispensable preliminary to the recognition of the independence of the people inhabiting the territory, called Vermont, and their admission into the federal union, that they explicitly relinquish all demands of lands or jurisdiction on the east side of the west bank of Connecticut river, and on the west side of a line beginning at the northwest corner of the state of Massachusetts, thence running twenty miles east of Hudson's river, so far as the said river runs northeasterly in its general course; then by the west bounds of the townships granted by the late government of New Hampshire, to the river running from South Bay to Lake Champlain, thence along said river to Lake Champlain, thence along the waters of Lake Champlain to latitude forty-five degrees north, excepting a neck of land between Missiskoy Bay and

---

[1] See *ante*, pp. 321–323, 364–367.

[2] This motion was made in the interest of the two states which were claiming Vermont; probably in anticipation that Congress would by that time accept the cession of western lands claimed by New York, and change the votes of some states that were, at the above date, favoring Vermont. The cession of New York was accepted on the 29th of October 1782. On this event Mr. MADISON wrote to EDMUND PENDLETON as follows:

Besides the effect which may be expected from the coalition [of sundry states] with New York, on territorial questions in Congress, it will, I surmise, prove very unfriendly to the pretensions of Vermont. Duane [of New York,] seems not unapprised of the advantage which New York has gained, and is already taking measures for a speedy vote on that question. Upon the whole, New York has, by a fortunate coincidence of circumstances, or by skillful management, or by both, succeeded in a very important object; by ceding a claim, which was tenable neither by force nor by right, she has acquired with Congress the merit of liberality, rendered the title to her reservation more respectable, and at least damped the ardor with which Vermont has been abetted.—See *Madison Papers*, Vol. I, p. 470, cited in *Vt. Hist. Soc. Coll.*, Vol. II, p. 304.

the waters of Lake Champlain;" which resolution was reconsidered and confirmed on the succeeding day, to wit, the 21st of the same month:

That, in the opinion of your committee, the competency of Congress to enter into the above resolutions, was full and complete,—the concurrent resolutions of the Senate and Assembly of the State of New York, of the fifteenth and nineteenth of November last, containing a protest against the authority of Congress in the matter, notwithstanding; these concurrent resolutions, in letter and in spirit, being, undeniably, incompatible with a legislative act of the said state of a preceding day, to wit, the twenty-first of October, 1779, wherein there is an absolute reference of the dispute between that state and the people of Vermont, respecting jurisdiction, to the final arbitrament and decision of Congress: and from which alone would result to Congress all the necessary authority herein:

That on the —— day of ——, the people residing in the district, called Vermont, in considering the said acts of Congress of the 20th and 21st of August, did reject the propositions therein made to them, as preliminary to an acknowledgment of their sovereignty and independence, and admission into the federal union, as appears by their proceedings on the files of Congress: but that, on a subsequent day, the aforementioned resolutions of the 20th and 21st of August being unaltered and unrepealed, and the proposition therein contained, in the opinion of your committee, still open to be acceded to, the said people did, in their general assembly, on the 22d of February last enter into the following resolution:

" That the west bank of Connecticut river, and a line beginning at the northwest corner of the commonwealth of Massachusetts, from thence northward twenty miles east of Hudson's river, as specified in the resolutions of Congress in August last, shall be considered as the east and west boundaries of this state.

" And that this Assembly do, hereby, relinquish all claims and demands to, and right of jurisdiction in and over, any and every district of territory without said boundary lines:"

That, in the sense of your committee, the people of the said district, by the last recited act, have fully complied with the stipulation, made and required of them, in the resolutions of the 20th and 21st of August, as preliminary to a recognition of their sovereignty and independence, and admission into the federal union of the states, and that the *conditional* promise and engagment of Congress, of such recognition and admission, is thereby become *absolute*, and necessary to be performed; your committee therefore submit the following resolution:

That the district of territory, called Vermont, as defined and limited in the resolutions of Congress of the 20th and 21st of August, 1781, be and it is hereby recognized and acknowledged by the name of the State of Vermont, as free, sovereign and independent; and that a committee be appointed to treat and confer with the agents and delegates from said state, upon the terms and mode of the admission of the said state, into the federal union.

Mr. Livermore of N. H., and the states of New-York and Virginia voted for this motion; Delaware was divided; and Mr. Carroll of Maryland, and the states of Massachusetts, Rhode Island, Connecticut, New Jersey, Pennsylvania, South Carolina, and Georgia voted in the negative. Mr. Montgomery of Pennsylvania, seconded by Mr. Ellery of Rhode Island, proposed the third Tuesday of the next June; which was voted for by those two states only. Mr. Middleton, seconded by Mr

Bee, [both of South Carolina,] then proposed the next Monday; for which only the states of South Carolina and Georgia voted.[1]

SATURDAY, April 20, 1782.

A letter of the 19th, from Jonas Fay, Moses Robinson, and Isaac Tichenor, was read; whereupon a motion was made by Mr. Jones, seconded by Mr. Madison, [both of Virginia,] in the words following:

Jonas Fay, Moses Robinson, and Isaac Tichenor, stiling themselves agents and delegates from the state of Vermont, having in their letter of the 19th inst. informed Congress, "that in consequence of the faith of Congress. pledged to them in and by a resolution of the 20th of August last, and by official advice from sundry gentlemen of the first character in America, the legislature of Vermont have been prevailed upon to comply in the most ample manner with the resolution aforesaid:"

Resolved, That the secretary be directed to apply to the said Jonas Fay, Moses Robinson, and Isaac Tichenor, and request them to communicate to him the said official advice, together with the names of the gentlemen from whom the same was received.

New York, Virginia, and North Carolina only voted for this resolution, and it was therefore rejected.[2]

---

[1]Mr. MADISON explained these votes thus:

The consideration of the report will not be called for, however, until the pulse of nine states beats favorably for it. This is so uncertain that the agents (of Vermont) have returned.—See *Madison Papers*, Vol. I, p. 121, cited in *Vt. Hist. Soc. Collections*, Vol. II, p. 261.

[2] The letter of the Vermont agents and delegates was as follows:

PHILADELPHIA, April 19th, 1782.

Sir,—The situation in which Congress has been pleased to leave the business of our mission, as agents and delegates from the state of Vermont, renders our attendance, at present, unnecessary.

As the representatives of an independent and virtuous people, we esteem it our duty to inform Congress that, in consequence of their faith, pledged to us, in and by a resolution of the 20th of August last, and by official advice from sundry gentlemen of the first character in America, the Legislature of Vermont have been prevailed upon to comply, in the most ample manner, with the resolution aforesaid.

On the 31st ult. we, officially, acquainted Congress with the said compliance, together with the powers vested in us, in full confidence that, from the integrity and wisdom of that honorable body, no obstacle could prevent our confederation and union with them.

We are disappointed with the unexpected delay of Congress, in executing, on their part, the intent and spirit of the resolve above cited.

We would not wish to urge the attention of the Grand Council of America from matters of more consequence than merely the happiness of a state: but the critical situation Vermont is reduced to, by casting off a considerable part of her strength, in being exposed, as a forlorn hope, to the main force of the enemy in Canada, and destitute of the aid of the United States, in whose cause, at an early period, she freely fought and suffered, will, we presume, sufficiently apologize for being thus urgent, that unnecessary delay may not deprive us of the benefits of the confederation.

We purpose to leave this city to-morrow morning, and expect to be

TUESDAY, May 21, 1782.

Mr. Scott, a delegate for the state of New-York, delivered at the table two papers which he desired to have read; and the same being read, a motion was made by Mr. Scott, seconded by Mr. Middleton, in the following words:

That two papers which have been this day read in Congress, purporting to be certified by Robert Harpur, deputy secretary of the state of New-York, as true copies of two certain original acts of the legislature of the said state lodged in the secretary's office of the said state: the one is in the words and figures following, to wit:

"*An act for pardoning certain offences committed in the northeastern part of this state. Passed the* 14*th April* 1782.

Whereas, divers inhabitants, residing in the northeastern part of this state, who have, heretofore, denied the sovereignty and jurisdiction of the people of this state, in and over that part of this state, and, by their unwarrantable combinations, created commotions, to the great disturbance of the peace and tranquility of this state, have, by their humble petition to the Legislature, represented that they were seduced and misled, by artful and designing men, from their duty and allegiance to this state; and have, moreover, professed a sincere repentance of their crimes and misdemeanors, and implored the clemency of government, and humbly entreated the passing of an act of indemnity, oblivion and pardon: and this Legislature being disposed to extend mercy:

Be it therefore enacted by the people of the state of New-York, represented in senate and assembly, and it is hereby enacted, by the authority of the same, That all such of the inhabitants of this state, who dwell and reside north of the north bounds of the state of Massachusetts continued to Hudson's river, east of Hudson's river, south of the latitude forty-five degrees north, and west of Connecticut river, are hereby acquitted, pardoned, released and discharged from all treasons, felonies and conspiracies, whatsoever, at any time heretofore done and committed by them or

---

officially acquainted when our attendance will be necessary and have the honor to be, sir, your most obedient and humble servants.

JONAS FAY,
MOSES ROBINSON,
ISAAC TICHENOR.

His Excellency the President of Congress.

The letters of WASHINGTON and OLIVER WOLCOTT were of course the letters referred to by the Vermont agents, both of which had been read in the Vermont Assembly, and were very influential in procuring the assent of Vermont to the terms imposed by Congress. The words "official advice" were liable to criticism, though their meaning is apparent. Vermont *was* advised by the commander of the continental army, and a delegate in Congress. They held "official" positions certainly, though their letters were private. But more: a copy of Washington's letter to Gov. Chittenden was subsequently sent to the President of Congress by Washington himself, with this statement: "If it should be necessary, *a committee of Congress*, with whom I was in conference on these matters in the course of last winter, [winter of 1781-2,] can give such further information on this subject as I doubt not will be satisfactory."—See *Vt. Hist. Soc. Collections*, Vol. II, p. 224. A committee of Congress in those days ranked very near to "official" authority.

any of them, against the people of the state of New-York, as sovereign thereof, or against the government and authority derived from, or established by, the said people; all capital, corporal or pecuniary punishment, fines and forfeitures, judgments and executions, to which they severally were liable, in consequence of the crimes and offences aforesaid, are hereby remitted and discharged; and all and every the said persons shall be, and hereby are, fully and wholly restored, in person and estate, to the same state and condition wherein they severally were, at any time before the said crimes and offences were committed or perpetrated.

And be it further enacted by the authority aforesaid, That no person or persons whatsoever, shall have the benefit of the said pardon, for the purpose of pleading the same against any charge of treason or other offence already found, or hereafter to be found, against them or any of them, for adhering to the King of Great-Britain, the enemy of this state, or for any murder; or that such pardon shall be a bar to a conviction, judgment or execution for the said treason or other offence, last mentioned, or for murder as aforesaid."

And the other of the said papers in the words and figures following, to wit:

"*An act for quieting the minds of the inhabitants in the northeastern parts of this state. Passed the* 14*th April*, 1782.

Be it enacted by the people of the state of New-York, represented in senate and assembly, and it is hereby enacted by the authority of the same, That all charters, patents or grants, for lands within this state, lying within the following bounds, to wit: Beginning at a certain point in the west bank of Connecticut river, where the boundary line between the states of Massachusetts and New-Hampshire, if continued across the said river, would intersect the said west bank, and running from the said point, along the west bank of Connecticut river to the latitude of forty five degrees north, thence westerly, in the said latitude, to the west side of Missisqua Bay, in Lake Champlain, thence westerly, in the said latitude, to the east bank of the waters of the said lake, thence southerly, along the east bank of the said lake and the waters thereof, to the most southerly point where any of the grants, heretofore issued or made, by the late government of the late colony of New-Hampshire, come to the said lake, thence along the south and west bounds of the said grants, or as the said grants are now held or possessed under such grants, so far south, as to meet with a line continued from the first mentioned boundary between the states of Massachusetts and New-Hampshire, through the said place or point of beginning, thence easterly, by the said continued line as aforesaid, to the said place or point of beginning, made or issued by the government of the late colony, now state of New-Hampshire, and which were made or issued, prior to any charter, patent or grant for the same lands, heretofore made or issued by the government of the late colony, now state of New-York, or by the government of any other colony, shall be, and hereby are, ratified and confirmed to the respective grantees, their heirs and assigns forever; and every such prior charter, patent or grant, is hereby declared to be as legal and valid, to all intents, constructions and purposes whatsoever, as if the same had been made or issued under the great seal of the said late colony of New-York, or had been made or issued under the great seal of this state, and as such, may be given, and shall be allowed, in evidence, in every court of record within this state; and no such charter, patent or grant, hereby ratified and confirmed as aforesaid, shall be deemed void, or in any wise injured, by reason of the non-performance of any condition or provision therein contained, or by reason of the non-payment of any quit-rent therein reserved; any law, usage or custom to the contrary thereof, notwithstanding; provided always, that any person or persons who, heretofore, held or claimed lands under grants from the late colony of New-Hampshire, who have, afterwards, obtained grants for the same lands, either to themselves or to others, in trust for them, under the late colony of New-York, operating as a confirmation thereof,—in such case or cases, such person or persons, or their assignees, shall be deemed forever hereafter, to hold the said lands by the latter title.

And whereas, many of the inhabitants residing within the district of country above described, did, in or about the year one thousand seven hundred and seventy-seven, declare themselves an independent people, and did assume a government under the name, style or title of the government of the state of Vermont, or of the state of Vermont; and the said assumed government hath made grants of lands within the said territory:

Be it further enacted by the authority aforesaid, That all charters, patents or grants of lands, so made or issued, before the passing of this act, and which were made or issued prior to any charter, patent or grant for the same lands, heretofore made or issued, by the government of the late colony of New-York, shall be, and hereby are, ratified and confirmed to the respective grantees, their heirs and assigns forever; and such charters, patents or grants, are hereby declared to be as legal and valid, to all intents, constructions and purposes whatsoever, as if the same had been made or issued by the government of this state; and as such may be given, and shall be allowed, in evidence, in any court of record within this state; and no such charter, patent or grant, so ratified and confirmed, as last aforesaid, shall be deemed void, or in any wise injured, by reason of the non-performance of any condition or proviso therein contained, or by reason of the non-payment of any quit-rent therein reserved; any law, usage or custom, to the contrary notwithstanding.

And be it further enacted by the authority aforesaid, That all persons now actually occupying, possessing and improving, lands within the said district of country, or who did, at any time, before the passing of this act, actually occupy, possess and improve lands therein, not heretofore granted by any late colony, shall be, and they, and their legal representatives, respectively, are hereby confirmed in such their respective possessions and improvements, and shall have, and receive, patents therefor, from the government of this state, without paying for such patent any fee or reward, the expence of surveying such lands excepted; provided, that no such patent as last aforesaid, shall issue, for more than the quantity of five hundred acres of land; and where such occupant, possessor or improver, or legal representatives, shall not have possessed the said quantity of five hundred acres of land, he or she shall, respectively, be allowed and granted such additional quantity of land, out of any vacant, unappropriated lands, lying contiguous to such possession, as shall be equal to the deficiency.

And whereas, it is the intention of the Legislature, that such parts of this act as relate to quieting or confirming titles and possessions, within the district of country, as aforesaid, shall not take effect, and that the inhabitants residing within the said district of country, should not have the benefits thereby intended, unless they should agree to renounce the said assumed government, and return to their allegiance to the government of this state:

Be it, therefore, further enacted by the authority aforesaid, That, upon application of commissioners or agents, authorised and appointed by the inhabitants residing in the said district of country, or by the inhabitants of any town or towns, or district or districts therein, to the person administring the government of this state, for the time being, touching or concerning the ratifying, confirming and quieting any titles to, or possessions of, lands within the district aforesaid, in cases not provided for by this act, and of and concerning the mode, manner, terms and conditions, agreeable to, and on which, the inhabitants within the district of country aforesaid, shall agree to renounce the said assumed government, and acknowledge allegiance to the government of this state, it shall and may be lawful for the person administring the government of this state, for the time being, by and with the advice and consent of the council of appointment, to appoint and commissionate, under the great seal of this state, three commissioners to meet, confer and agree with such commissioners or agents, authorised and appointed by the said inhabitants of the said district of country, or by the inhabitants of any town or towns, or district or districts therein, on all and singular the matters and things above mentioned; and all compacts, agreements and acts, entered into, made or done by the said commissioners to be appointed on behalf of this state, or any two of them, of or concerning the premises, shall be finally conclusive and binding on the government of this state: provided nevertheless, that nothing in this act contained, shall be construed to authorise the said commissioners to agree to cede or relinquish the jurisdiction of this state over the district of country aforesaid, or any part thereof, to any people, assemblies of people, or person or persons whatsoever, or to consent or agree that any part of the constitution of this state, shall be altered or changed.

And be it further enacted by the authority aforesaid, That nothing in this act contained, shall be deemed, construed or taken, to restore any person or persons, or his or their heirs, to his or their estate, within the said district of country, who now stand attainted by the government of this state, for adherence to the king of Great-Britain, or whose estate or estates, have, or shall, become confiscate for such adherence, by virtue of any law of this state."

Be committed to a special committee to report thereon:

On this motion the vote was as follows: *Yeas*—Pennsylvania, Delaware, South Carolina, and Georgia—4 states. Mr. Scott of N. Y. voted aye, but could not cast the vote of the state. *Nays*—Massachusetts, Rhode Island, and Maryland—3 states. Mr. Root of Connecticut voted no, but could not cast the vote of the state. Virginia was divided. So the question was lost. This closes the record of Congress on Vermont affairs in the period embraced in this volume.

Observations relating to the influence of Vermont, and the Territorial Claims, on the politics of Congress. By James Madison.[1]

May 1, 1782.

The two great objects, which predominate in the politics of Congress at this juncture, are *Vermont* and the *Western Territory.*

I. The independence of Vermont and its admission into the confederacy are patronized by the eastern states (New Hampshire excepted) first, from an ancient prejudice against New York; secondly, the inter-

---

[1] *Madison Papers*, Vol. I, p. 122; *Life and Writings of Washington*, Vol. VIII, p. 547. Mr. Sparks in a note states that a copy of this important and interesting paper was given to him by Mr. Madison. In *Early History*, pp. 406 to 408, Hiland Hall gives various references on this paper.

Copy of the paper named "the enclosed Letter."

BRATTLEBOROUGH March y^e $4^{th.}$ 1778.

Gentlemen,—At the annual meeting of this town held yesterday it was unanimously agreed to send a Protest to the Assembly of the pretended State of Vermont against disavowing their allegiance to New York—A step in their opinion tending to disunite the friends of America in the present important contest with Great Britain. The town was of opinion that it would add great weight to the protest if the Towns and Districts in this County who join with us in thinking the manner and time of erecting this part of America into a new State is of bad consequence would unite in the Protest. They thereupon chose us the subscribers a Committee to confer with Committees from such Towns in this County as are inclinable to bear public Testimony against unjustifiable proceedings of a multitude.

We therefore call upon you in the most earnest manner as you value the blessings of good order and Just Government to unite with us in concerting and executing such measures as will be most efficacious for procuring those blessings and frustrating the Designs of those who are opposed to them: And we would request you to appoint a Committee to confer with us and such others as shall meet us at the house of Capt Sergeants of this Town on the 18 instant at 10 o'clock in the forenoon, authorizing them to agree to such measures as the majority of the Committees then convened shall think most expedient.

We are Gentlemen with great respect
Your most Obed Servants

BENJ. BUTTERFIELD
SAM^L KNIGHT
ISRAEL SMITH
JAMES BLAKSLEE
MICAH TOWNSEND

To the Freeholders and
Inhabitants of Springfield.

P. S. If a Majority are disinclined to choose a Committee for the purposes above mentioned we think it most advisable for as many as are willing to elect the Committee and for them to come able to ascertain the number of persons who chose them.[1]

Accordingly a Convention met at Brattleborough on the day named, and appointed a committee to draft a protest to be presented to the legislature of Vermont, and a letter to Gov. Clinton. This Convention adjourned to the same place on the 15th of April, when representatives of Guilford, Brattleborough, Putney, Newfane, Hinsdale, [Vernon,] and Rockingham attended. The protest was then adopted by this Convention, which had the approval of adherents to New York in Westminster and Weathersfield also. B. H. HALL gave the substance of this document thus:

It was in the form of an address, and was directed "To the gentlemen convened at Windsor, under the style of the General Assembly of the state of Vermont." In it the objections to the formation of a new state were strongly put, and old arguments in a regenerated form, and new ones also, were urged in opposition to the plans of the patrons and citizens of Vermont. In view of the principles adduced, the protesters announced their determination in these words:—

"We conceive that endeavoring at present to establish a separate "state here, is not only a violation of the Continental Union, but is im- "prudent, and to the last degree impolitic and dangerous, tending in the

[1] Furnished by Hon. JAMES H. PHELPS, of West Townshend.

"present important crisis to weaken the authority of the Continental "Congress, disunite the friends of America, and stimulate a spirit of "separation and sedition which may end in the ruin of the United "States; and we esteem it not only our duty, but the duty of all who are "friends to the liberty of America, to bear open testimony against it. "Therefore, on behalf of ourselves and those who delegated us for that "purpose, we publicly declare that as we have not in any way assisted "in, or consented to, the forming of a separate and independent govern- "ment, we shall not consider ourselves bound by any acts of the Legis- "lature thereof, but shall, as in duty bound, continue to yield our allegi- "ance to the state of New York, until otherwise directed by the Honor- "able the Continental Congress. And we do hereby solemnly protest "against the right of any persons to govern us and the other inhabitants "of the New Hampshire Grants, except that of the Continental Con- "gress and the Legislature of New York, and against all measures which "shall be used to enforce the pretended rights of any other person or "body of men, and against all the bad consequences which may arise "from attempting at present to establish an independent government in "the 'Grants' before mentioned."[1]

The opposition at that period culminated in the enforcement of the authority of Vermont by ETHAN ALLEN in May 1779.—See Vol. I, pp. 298-9, 442-3, and 518-520.

ORIGIN OF THE CHARLESTOWN CONVENTION OF JAN. 16, 1781.

In Convention of Committees from several Towns in the County of Cumberland 31st. October 1780.

Resolved, That Luke Knoulton Esqr. Hilkiah Grout Esqr. Oliver Lovell Esqr. Colo. John Sergeants, Micah Townsend Esqr. Major Jonathan Hunt Simon Stevens Esqr. Charles Phelps Esqr. Mr. Benjamin Henry, James Clay Esqr. Major Elkanah Day, Mr. Thomas Cutler and Mr. Barzillai Rice be and hereby (are) nominated and appointed a Committee to meet such Persons as shall be authorized for the Purpose by a Convention or Committee of Gloucester County on the West and Grafton County on the East side of Connecticut River to devise and carry into Execution such Measures as they shall deem best calculated to unite in one Political Body all the Inhabitants from Mason's Grant on the East, to the Heighth of Land on the West side of said River. And that a Majority of the Persons above named or of such of them as shall meet at Charlestown on Wednesday the Eighth day of November next be empowered to act in the Premises.

By order, MATTHEW CUSHING.[1]

NOTE BY HON. J. H. PHELPS.—The foregoing paper, except the signature, is in the hand writing of MICAH TOWNSEND.

---

[1] *Eastern Vermont*, pp. 311, 312.

[1] From the *Pingry Papers*.—See *ante*, pp. 277-285.

ADDITIONS OT AND CORRECTIONS OF VOLS. I. AND II.

COVENANT, COMPACT, AND RESOLUTIONS,

ADOPTED BY A CONVENTION OF THE REPRESENTATIVES OF THE SETTLERS ON THE NEW HAMPSHIRE GRANTS WEST OF THE GREEN MOUNTAINS—IN 1775.

IT is probable that the following document is now re-printed for the first time since the original publication in 1775. It was found in what will doubtless be known hereafter as the *Haswell Papers*, comprising pamphlets, newspapers, and books belonging to the late NATHAN B. HASWELL of Burlington,[1] which have been purchased by the State Librarian since the first volume of the Council Records was printed: otherwise this document would have been given in that volume, as the first known act of a Convention in the New Hampshire Grants having, in a degree, the form and authority of an independent civil government.

The place and date of the meeting of the Convention and the names of the town representatives who signed the "Covenant and Compact" are not given. Thus it may fairly be asked: was this document simply a form prepared, printed, and circulated for the consideration of the people, and never adopted? or, was it actually adopted? The fact that blank spaces were left, as above stated, strongly favors the theory that the document was printed previous to its formal adoption; and it is obvious that this might have been done by a committee appointed by a Convention and instructed to report at an adjourned session. That such a document was actually *adopted* by a Convention holden at Manchester, is inferred from a statement by IRA ALLEN, in his history of Vermont, in terms which do not apply to any other known document but this. After referring to the out-lawry act of New York, of March 9 1774; to a "meeting of the committees of the several towns on the west side of the Green Mountain," called in consequence thereof, "to convene in Manchester, *April* 1774;" and to the answer of Ethan Allen and others to the New York act,—IRA ALLEN added these words:

> At this Convention, *a printed constitution*, or more properly *rules* for the future government of the district of the grants were published, as a general defence became necessary to guard against the usurpations of the colony of New York.[2]

This language favors the theory above suggested.

---

[1] The most valuable formerly belonged to ANTHONY HASWELL of Bennington.—See *ante*, p. 13.

[2] *Vt. Hist. Soc. Collections*, Vol. I, p. 359.

On referring to the "Covenant" in the following document, it will be seen that it embraces such "equal *Rules*, Injunctions, *Constitution* and Officers as are judged necessaay and expedient, for the best Good of the Inhabitants of this District aforesaid."

It is to be observed, however, that ALLEN refers this "constitution" or "rules" to a convention holden at Manchester in *April* 1774, while the copy herewith given refers to events which occurred at later dates: so either he did not refer to *this* document, or he mistook the date. The last is most probably the case, for the fact is, that the pamphlet, which begins with the "Compact" in question, closes with the answer to the out-lawry act, that answer bearing date *April* 26 1774. Even if Allen wrote with a copy of this pamphlet before him, he would naturally take the date with which it closes, inasmuch as there is none to the "Compact" with which it begins; while if he wrote from memory, more than twenty years after the event, his statement as to the date is by no means conclusive. The answer to the out-lawry act was printed in 1774. The copy attached to the document in question bears the imprint of 1775,—thus showing that the answer was reprinted with the New York act as a justification for the "compact" made in 1775.

It has already been stated that this document could not have been adopted in April 1774. The reasons are the following:

1. The *year* is stated to have been "the fifteenth year of his Majesty's Reign." That year began Oct. 25 1774, and ended with Oct. 24 1775.

2. The document refers to a visit by two New York gentlemen, "in the Month of *September* 1774."

3. It also refers to the removal of the New York sheriff Lansingh of Charlotte county, and the appointment of sheriff Parker. Jonathan Parker succeeded Philip P. Lansingh November 12 1774.[1]

In fixing the date of the Convention, it is evident that it must be subsequent to Nov. 12 1774. Now noting the fact that the "Compact" was *contingent upon the pleasure of the king*, it is safe to say that it must have been adopted previous to the capture of Ticonderoga and Crown Point in May 1775, as at that time the leading Green Mountain Boys had drawn the sword against the king. Looking now for some known Convention of towns west of the Green Mountains, which met between November 1774 and May 1775, one only is to be found, to wit:

On January 31, 1775, a convention was holden at Manchester, in which the following towns were represented, viz:

Bennington, Shaftsbury, Arlington, Sunderland, Manchester, Dorset, Rupert, Pawlet, Wells, Poultney, Castleton, Danby, Tinmouth, Clarendon, Rutland, Pittsford, Neshobe, [Brandon,] Shoreham, Bridport, Addison, Panton, Ferrisburgh, Colchester, Wallingford, and Georgia—twenty-five in number.[2]

---

[1] *New York Civil List*, 1869, p. 57.

[2] *Vermont Historical Society Collections*, Vol. I, p. 8.

Gov. Hall stated that the only information in regard to this Convention, that had been found up to 1870, was derived from a petition of Peleg Sunderland to the General Assembly, and report thereon, in 1787. It can hardly be doubted that in the following document we now have every thing of public importance that was done at that Convention. The time meets every statement in the document, and every contingency in the history of the State at the period. Comparing the above list of towns represented in the Convention of January 31 1775, with the description in the following document of the district represented, the two will be found to agree. In fact, no other Convention answers so well to the description, as in no other was the district represented which is described as "the Lands contiguous to Lake Champlain, which large Tract of Land to the Forty-Fifth Degree of Northern Latitude, is comprehended in those Townships." The town of *Georgia* represented the section north of Colchester in that Convention, and *in no other*. Sunderland stated in his petition that his claim was allowed Feb. 3 1775, which shows that the Convention was in session at least four days;[1] and this proves that the business was of more than usual importance. The document is not a journal of all the proceedings of the Convention, but a proclamation to the public of very important resolutions and orders, which for a time had all the force of laws with the people of western Vermont. Probably Ethan Allen was its author.

The acquisition of the *Haswell Papers* by Hiram A. Huse, Esq., the State Librarian, was made specially on account of files of the Bennington and Windsor newspapers from their origin in 1783, which are excedingly valuable as repositories of the early history of the State; but the most rare document is the following "Covenant, Compact, and Resolutions." Probably it is the only copy in existence.

The PROCEEDINGS of the CONVENTION of the NEW HAMPSHIRE SETTLERS; containing their COVENANT, COMPACT, and RESOLUTIONS; and also Twelve Acts of OUT-LAWRY, Passed by the Legislature of the Province of *NEW YORK*, against those Settlers, and their ANSWER to the same. *HARTFORD:* [Conn.] Printed by Ebenezer Watson, near the Great-Bridge. 1775.

At a General Convention, held at [Manchester] *by the Representatives of the Inhabitants of the several Townships granted by the Government of New-Hampshire, and situate to the Westward of the Range of*

---

[1] *Vermont State Papers*, Mss., *Petitions*, Vol. 17, p. 304. The report of the committee on this petition states that the Convention met on the 31st of January 1775, and also that the committee had a record of its proceedings.

Green Mountains, and Northerly from the Province of the Massachusetts-Bay, and on the Rivers Otter Creek, *and* Onion River, *and the Lands contiguous to Lake Champlain, which large Tract of Land to the Forty-Fifth Degree of Northern Latitude, is comprehended in those Townships.*

THIS Convention taking into their most serious Consideration the several progressive Facts and Circumstances which have occurred in the Controversy, which hath for many years subsisted between the *New-Hampshire* Settlers that are seated on those Townships, and the Government of *New-York*, proceed to a short Narration thereof.

WHEREAS the governmental Authority of the Province of *New-York*, ever since his Majesty extended their Jurisdiction to the West Banks of Connecticut River, on the East, and to Latitude Forty-Five Degrees North, which was in A. D. 1764, which includes about one Hundred and Thirty-Six Townships, Six Miles square, which had been granted by the Government of *New-Hampshire*, antecedent to the aforesaid Extention of the Jurisdiction of *New-York*. And

WHEREAS the Government of *New-York*, not satisfied with exercising merely Jurisdiction over those Settlers, they re-granted (in Prejudice to them) tó certain over-bearing Attornies, and other favourite Gentlemen that were enterprizing, and which bear great Sway in the Government, large Patents interfering with those Townships, and actual Settlements aforesaid, which hath occasioned great Difficulties, Cost and Disturbances to those Settlers. And a Representation of the Conduct of the Government in the Premises being laid before his Majesty, in Privy Council, who, pursuant to their Advice, was graciously pleased to order the Government of *New-York*, not to make any Grants interfering with those of *New-Hampshire*, till his Majesty's Pleasure should be further signified concerning the same. And,

WHEREAS the Government of *New-York*, have repeatedly violated his Majesty's express Order in re-granting sundry large Tracts of Land contained in and belonging to the prohibited Premises, and have in almost every Instance exercised the Power of Jurisdiction which was delegated to them from the Crown for the Safety and Protection of its Subjects, to ravage from them (the aforesaid Settlers) their Lands and Labours, treating us, those Inhabitants, as Rioters, nay, as Felons, in Consequence of such Tumults, of which themselves were primarily the efficient Cause. And,

WHEREAS, on the 9th Day of March, A. D. 1774, the Legislature of the Province of *New-York*, did enact twelve particular Acts of OUT-LAWRY against us, his Majesty's loyal Subjects, the Inhabitants aforesaid, in Consequence of which mercenary and oppressive Administration, and tyrannical Legislature, those Inhabitants are reduced to a State of Anarchy, and not only so, but are obliged to stand on their Defence; for they are not only denied the civil Privileges of English Subjects, but by the Tenure of the Laws aforesaid, they are liable to be attainted of Felony, and to suffer Death, or Loss of Property, without a Trial. This is repugnant to the most essential Part of the English Constitution, and subversive of its greatest Privilege, namely, that of Trial by Jury. Furthermore, the Consequences resulting from such Legislation, and Administration, hath in great Measure deprived these Inhabitants of the great and inestimable Privileges of Christianity; and if not timely prevented, must inevitably sink their Posterity into a State of Barbarism and Ignorance well fitted for Tenants to the *New-York* Patentees.[1] And,

WHEREAS this Convention evidently perceive that those Inhabitants cannot any longer subsist in such anarchial Circumstances, and at the same Time hold such a Connection, and maintain such Regulation as is necessary to defend their Persons and Property against the arbitrary and avaricious Designs, and subtle Intrigues of Oppressors, therefore find it necessary to concert some effectual Measures among Ourselves and Constituents, whereby this salutary End may be practicable. Merely Anarchy, with its usual Concomitants, is a difficult and unhappy Condition for so large a Number of People; but add to these *negative* Evils under which we have so sensibly suffered, for Want of Government, the *positive* Evils of venal Legislation and Administration, with their usual Concomitants; and take into one complex View, those twelve Acts of Out-Lawry, and the several Proclamations which have been issued from Government,[2] with large Sums of Money therein offer'd, for the purpose of apprehending our Inhabitants; and that for no other Cause but for their virtuous and public spirited Zeal in manfully ascertaining and defending the natural and legal Rights of the Inhabitants of this District. This Reflection must convince all capable Judges, that both the Lives and Property of our Inhabitants are exposed, and that in the most superlative Degree. This Convention, from these cogent Reasons, and from many others too prolix to be here inserted, are fully persuaded that the extreme Circumstances of our Settlements, lay our Inhabitants under the strongest Necessity of forming in some Measure, into a civil and political Body, for the better ordering and regulating the Community.

THEREFORE, WE, HIS MAJESTY'S LOYAL SUBJECTS, the Representatives aforesaid, in Convention assembled, Do, for Ourselves, and in Behalf of our Constituents, that are settled in those Townships, which were granted by the Government of *New-Hampshire*, and which are situate to the Westward of the Heighth of Land called the *Green Mountains*, and to the Northward of the Province of the *Massachusetts-Bay*, and on the Rivers *Otter-Creek* and *Onion River*, and the Lands contiguous to *Lake Champlain*, to the Forty-Fifth Degree of Northern Latitude, which are comprehended in those Townships——Do Covenant, and upon the Principles of Honor, Virtue, and Self-Preservation, Enter into a temporary Compact, and on the good Faith of each other, and by Virtue of the Compact thus established, this Convention proceed to make such just and equal Rules, Injunctions, Constitution and Officers as are judged necessary and expedient, for the best Good of the Inhabitants of this District aforesaid.

Always provided, nevertheless, and it is the true Intent and Meaning of this Convention, That provided this, our temporary Compact, (which is solely calculated for the Purpose of present Safety, and to ward off

---

[1] The charters granted by New Hampshire reserved shares or lots in each town for the support of the gospel and schools; while the charters granted by New York contained no reservations for these purposes. Hence the above objection to the New York system.

[2] Gov. Colden's of Dec. 12 1769, for the arrest of James Breakenridge and others; Gov. Dunmore's of Nov. 1 1770, for the arrest of Simon Hathaway and others; and Gov. Tryon's of Dec. 9 1771, for the arrest of Robert Cochran and others, and of March 9 1774, for the arrest of Ethan Allen and others.—See *Documentary History of New York*, Vol. IV, pp. 379, 405, 456, 526.

impending Ruin, in so critical a Situation, till his Majesty shall determine our Controversy with the Government of *New-York)* shall be disagreeable to his Majesty's Pleasure, upon the least Notice thereof, this Convention will immediately desist from upholding the same, and conform to his Majesty's Determination, in all Things. In Witness that this is the temporary Compact of this Convention, with the Condition of the cessation of the same, the Members thereof have hereunto subscribed their Names, the [here blank for the date] and in the Fifteenth Year of his Majesty's Reign. [Here was a blank sufficient for many signatures.]

THE Government of *New-York*, by their appointment of Men to the Magistracy who inhabit in sundry of those Townships, that are inimical to the Country, evinces that it was not for its Good that they were commissionated, but, on the Contrary, that they might be instrumental of its Distruction; their baneful Influence hath been conspicuous, the Schisms and Divisions they are perpetually making and fomenting among the People, with the help of sundry other sordid Wretches among us, that are still gaping after Titles from *New-York*, portrait their malevolent Designs against their Country, which is to divide and conquer. This is the Merit they expect will ingratiate them into the Favour of a Government that have devoted this Country to Ruin; and let any Persons of common Discerning, only reflect on the Nature and Design of those Acts of Out-Lawry before spoken of, and compare them with the Appointment of these vile Wretches into the Office of Magistrates, and they will discover a premeditated Harmony of Design to run through the Whole. No Effect whatsoever can be more justly ascribed to its Cause, than the Appointment of such Pests of Society to the Rank of Magistrates, by a Government whose Design in framing the Laws, as well as in that of appointing Magistrates, were the same with those of *Ahab*, King of *Israel*, who conspired against *Naboth* the *Jezreelite*, to kill him, to take Possession of his Vineyard.

It is therefore the resolution of this Convention, That all Officers, of whatsoever Denomination or Rank, more particularly Magistrates that have been commissioned, or any Way authorised by the Government of *New-York*, which inhabit in any of those Townships which are comprehended in this District, forthwith to surcease such Commission, and wholly renounce such Authority; and they are accordingly, by this Convention, forbid to officiate in the same, on the Penalty of the Resentment of their injured Countrymen.[1] And,

WHEREAS several designing and treacherous Men that inhabit this

---

[1] The following certified copy of a similar resolution, adopted by a Convention holden at Manchester, March 12 and 13 1774, is found in an affidavit of Benjamin Hough of Socialborough [part of Clarendon,] dated Aug. 24 1774.—See *Documentary History of New York*, Vol. IV, p. 532. This resolution is the only part of the record of that Convention which the editor has been able to find:

Gentlemen the following is proposed whether it be to your minds that any person or persons in the New-Hampshire Grants under the present situation of affairs that have or shall presume to take commission or commissions of the peace shall by the Grantees in general be deemed an Enemy to their Country & Common cause untill his Majesty's pleasure in the premises be further known: passed in the Affirmative all yeas & No Nays at a general meeting holden at Manchester 12th Day of April A. D. 1774 and by adjournment to the 13th.

per JONAS FAY Clerk of the said Meeting.

District, have of late been very assiduous in prosecuting and endeavouring to carry into Execution the Design of the Government of *New-York*, and its Land-Jobbers, in Prejudice to their Fellow-Settlers, thereby to ingratiate themselves into the Favour of that Government, in Order to partake with its Honors, and with them, and their Train of Land-monopolizers, to share a Division of their Neighbour's Possessions and Labours: Therefore, in order to prevent their baneful Influence, this Convention have thought it Expedient to lay an Injunction on every Inhabitant comprehended in this District, not to receive any Commission or Post of Honour or Profit under the Government of *New-York*, till such Time as that Government obey his Majesty's Orders relative to their Conduct towards the Inhabitants of this District, and till his Majesty shall fully settle the Controversy between those Inhabitants and that Government.[1]

AND accordingly, this Convention doth strictly prohibit any Person or Persons whatsoever, that inhabit in any of those Townships comprehended in this District, from receiving any Commission or Commissions, or Post or Posts of either Profit or Honour under the Government of *New-York*, during such Time as is in the Preamble specified; and the Inhabitants of this District are directed and ordered by this Convention to govern themselves accordingly. And,

WHEREAS Mr. *Goldsbrow Banyar* and Mr. *John Kelley*, of the City of *New York*, in the Month of *September* 1774, did make a Tour through a considerable Part of this District, with a Design as is supposed, to divert the People from their true Interest, by propagating Divisions, and deluding the ignorant and unwarry by falacious and groundless Representations, and it being conjectured from the highest Ground of probability, that the old Adversaries of those Inhabitants, viz. Mr. *James Duane* and Mr. *John* [Taber] *Kemp*, of the same City were privy to, and assistant Schemers of the aforesaid Intrigues of *Banyar* and *Kelley*.[2] And provided the aforesaid *James Duane, John Kemp, Goldsbrow Banyar*, and *John Kelley*, or either of them, shall in future presume to come within this District, it is earnestly recommended by this Convention to any and every of the said Inhabitants, to apprehend

[1] The words "the Design of the Government of *New-York, and its Land-Jobbers*," and "*their Train of Land-monopolizers*," in the above preamble, furnish Gov. HALL additional evidence pertinent to his controversy with HENRY B. DAWSON, as to the phrase "Land-Traders of New York" in the Vermont petition to Congress of 1776.—See *Vermont Historical Society Collections*, Vol. II, pp. xi-xiii.

[2] All these persons were officers or favorites of the New York government; all, also, except Duane, were subsequently tories, though Banyar and Kelly seem to have escaped attainder; and all of them held enormous grants of Vermont land from New York, to wit: Deputy Secretary Banyar, 144,600 acres ; Deputy Attorney General Duane, 52,500 ; John Kelly, 115,119; and Attorney General Kempe a very large amount, though how much is not known. The property of the latter was confiscated by the Whigs, and his name does not appear in the list of claimants to the $30,000 paid by Vermont; nor does Kelly's, as his claim was rejected, partly for the reason that he had compromised with Vermont and received grants of land by its authority.—See H. Hall's *Early History of Vermont;* and Sabine's *Loyalists of the American Revolution*, Vol. I.

them or either of them, and safely conduct them or either of them to *Bennington*, and bring any of them so taken before the Elders of the People, and principal Officers of the GREEN MOUNTAIN BOYS, that they or either of them may be interrogated concerning such Misdemeanors, and be further dealt with as to Justice may appertain. It is furthermore advised that our Inhabitants be much on their Guard, and be wary of Spies and Deceivers. And,

WHEREAS sundry Proclamations have been issued from the Commander in Chief of the Province of *New-York*, for the Purpose of apprehending sundry of the Inhabitants of this District for no other Cause but for their indefatigable Zeal in defending and maintaining the natural and legal Rights of the Inhabitants thereof, from the Usurpation of the overgrown Land Monopolizers of *New-York*, who corrupt and sway the Government. And Whereas in the same Proclamations there are large Sums of Money offered for the Purpose aforesaid, together with a special Injunction on all Magistrates, Justices of the Peace, Sheriffs, and other Civil Officers of the Counties of *Albany* and *Charlotte*, (which District is included in these Counties,) to be active and vigilant in apprehending those Men;[1] which Injunction they are under the solemnity of an Oath obliged to exert themselves to obey, and as such Magistrates and other Civil Officers which dwell among us have a much better Opportunity to apprehend them than those other Magistrates and Officers in the same Counties who inhabit to the Westward of this District, and not only so, but shew a far greater Propensity for so doing—this being an essential Condition of their Appointment to Office.

THESE Considerations may serve as a further Reason why this Convention have deposed them; for it is their fixed Resolution to defend those Men, though it should be at the Hazard of the Blood and Treasure of the Inhabitants of this District, and by these Presents further certify the Public, that provided any Person or Persons whatsoever, but more particularly the Magistrates and other Civil Officers of the Counties aforesaid presume to apprehend them, they do it on their Peril.—It is nevertheless the Resolution of this Convention, and they earnestly recommend it to the Inhabitants of this District, that they pay Defference and Submission to the Courts as by Law established in both of the Counties of *Albany* and *Charlotte*, in which they respectively belong, and to all and singular of the Magistrates in these Counties, which inhabit to the Westward of this District, excepting in such Cases only, wherein the Title of Lands within this District, or Persons indicted as Rioters for defending the Possession thereof are concerned.

AND WHEREAS there hath been received authentic Intelligence that Complaint hath been made against Mr. *Lonsingh*, Sheriff of the County of *Charlotte* to the Lieutenant Governor of the Province that he is a Coward, and that Captain [Robert] *Cochran* frighted him with the Present of an Ink-Horn, (nevertheless it was instead thereof a loaded Pistol.) Mr. *Parker* at the same time boasting of his Courage, Mr. *Lonsingh* was dismissed, and Mr. *Parker* succeeded to the Office of Sheriff, on his great Encouragement to take the Persons aforesaid, pursuant to the Proclamations. And, inasmuch as Mr. *Parker* hath stipulated to take these Men, and hath succeeded Mr. *Lonsingh* on this very Condition, and hath thereby declared himself an avowed Enemy not only to them, but also to the Inhabitants of this District in general, who place much Confidence in them. Therefore this Convention advise,

---

[1] Ethan Allen and others named in Gov. Tryon's proclamation of March 9 1774.

provided the said *Parker* shall presume to come within this District in the character of Sheriff or otherways, that the Inhabitants thereof treat him as an Enemy to the Lives of their best Friends, and to their Property in general, and that in like Manner they would treat any Person or Persons deputed by him, to the End that his Courage in the Premises may be manifested, and the Governor disappointed.

Always provided nevertheless, and it is the true Intent and Meaning of this Convention, Not to hinder, or any Ways molest or impede the Sheriff of the County of *Albany* or any of his Deputies, or any of the Constables of either of the Counties of *Albany* or *Charlotte*, which inhabit to the Westward of this District, in the due Exercise of their Office in the same, except in Cases of Land Disputes, or taking of Rioters, as is before excepted: But on the contrary, it is hereby Resolved, that the Inhabitants aforesaid afford them all the Assistance in their Power when by them requested, as it is presumed they will not attempt to officiate in those Cases excepted to them as aforesaid; in which Cases they are by these Presents absolutely prohibited from officiating in their respective Offices on their Peril.

IT is lastly the Resolution of this Convention, that the three principal Officers in each respective Company in the Regiment of GREEN MOUNTAIN BOYS, forthwith muster their Companies, and see that each Soldier be furnished with a good Firelock, and Ball or Buck-Shot answerable, and a good Tomahawk, and hold themselves in Readiness at a Minute's Warning, to maintain inviolable the foregoing Compact and Resolutions of this Convention, until such Time that his Majesty's Pleasure be known concerning the same, or till he shall so exert his Royal Authority as to determine the Controversy, and bring the Government of *New-York* to a Compliance therewith. And it is the Advice of this Convention that the Laws of Outlawry before eluded [alluded] to should be here inserted, with their Answer, and that sundry of these Pamphlets be distributed to each Town in this District, that the Inhabitants may know and practice agreeable to the Covenant and Resolutions herein specified, and that not only our Inhabitants, but all impartial Readers may perceive that it is not a licentious and riotous Spirit which hath dictated this Convention in their Proceedings: But on the contrary, that Wisdom hath been their Guide, and Self-Preservation their Motive.

Here follow the New York act of out-lawry, of March 9 1774, and the reply thereto by Ethan Allen and the other persons out-lawed, James Breakenridge excepted; for which see Vol. I, pp. 472–482. To the reply, as printed in 1775, was added a *nota bene*, which was not given in Ethan Allen's *Vindication*. This was for the benefit of Mr. Breakenridge. It was as follows:

N. B. WHEREAS Mr. *James Breakenridge*, hath the Honour to be enroled a Rioter with us we can assure the Public that this worthy Gentleman hath never been concerned with us in any Mob whatsoever; but that he hath relied on a good Providence, and the regal Authority of *Great-Britain* for the Confirmation of the *New-Hampshire* Charter: exclusive of all forcible Measures whatsoever.

There are other differences in the two copies, but none of importance.

Maj. Stephen Royce, Vol. I, pp. 15, 23, 26, 287.—Maj. ROYCE came to Tinmouth in 1774, from Cornwall, Conn. Mrs. B. H. SMALLEY, in a memoir of the Royce family, states that he was an officer in the army of the revolution. He was the father of Stephen Royce, one of the first settlers of Franklin and Berkshire; grandfather of the late Gov. Stephen Royce, and Elihu Marvin Royce, both of Berkshire, and of Hon. Rodney C. Royce of Rutland,—all of whom were brothers; and great grandfather of Hon. Homer E. Royce, formerly of Berkshire, and now of St. Albans, who is a son of Elihu Marvin Royce.—See *Vt. Historical Magazine*, Vol. II, article "Berkshire."

Ira Allen, Vol. I, p. 111.—His birth was there given, on the authority of Hon. DAVID READ of Burlington, as of April 21 1751. Mr. ALLEN himself stated the date to be *the first day of May.*—See his *History* in *Vt. Hist. Soc. Collections*, Vol. I, p. 421. The new style of the calendar was adopted by the British parliament in the year Allen was born, but the act did not go into effect until 1752. One of these different dates must have been of the old style, and the other of the new. The year 1752 being leap year, eleven days were dropped from the old style by order of parliament; whereas if the change had been in the year of Allen's birth, ten days only would have been dropped, as ordered by Pope Gregory XIII. in 1582. The dropping ten days from April 21 1751 made the 21st of April old style identical with May 1 of the new.

Moses Robinson, Vol. I, p. 128.—The date of his birth should be March 26 1741, instead of 1744.

Doct. Paul Spooner, Vol. I, p. 129.—The statements that Lieut. Gov. SPOONER removed from Hartland to Hardwick and was the first town clerk in 1795, and the first representative in 1797, 1798, and 1799, were made on the authority of B. H. and Hiland Hall's histories, and were *apparently* confirmed by the *Vt. Historical Magazine*, Vol. I, article "Hardwick," and by Deming's *Catalogue.* Lieut. Gov. SPOONER died at Hartland, Sept. 5 1789; and PAUL SPOONER of Hardwick was his second son. This correction is made on the authority of Whipple Spooner, son of the late Paul Spooner of Brandon, who was a nephew of Doct. Paul Spooner.

Doct. Jacob Roback is written *Roback*, *Rhuback*, and *Ruback* in the journals of the Council.—See Vol. I; also Vol. II, p. 21. In one instance his own signature is copied as ROBACK; in another RUBACK. Like variations occur in the Vermont military pay-rolls. He was born near Lubeck, Prussia, about 1740, was of Swedish descent, and graduated as a doctor of medicine. He volunteered with the Hessian troops who joined Burgoyne's army at Quebec; but being greatly disappointed at the position assigned to him, the Doctor deserted on the first opportunity and made his way to Connecticut; and from thence as early as August 15 1777 to Vermont, as on that day he was employed as surgeon to the Vermont troops under Gen. Stark. He served as such at the battle of Bennington, and at the subsequent battles with Burgoyne; and March 20 1778,[1] he was appointed surgeon in the service of Vermont, and served as oc-

[1] Erroneously printed 1776 in Vol. I, p. 143.

casion required until the close of the war. From about 1784 he resided in Shelburne, or in Essex or Clinton counties, N. Y., until 1792, when he settled in Grand Isle, and there remained until his death in April 1809. He was eminently skillful in his profession, had many virtues, and one vice, which, the Doctor said, prevailed among the surgeons in both the American and British armies. Rev. Asa Lyon preached the funeral sermon from the text—"Physician, heal thyself," and in allusion to the Doctor's vice exclaimed, in the words of Shakspeare, "O, that men should put an enemy into their mouths, to steal away their brains!"—See *Vt. Historical Magazine*, Vol. II, pp. 541, 548.

Col. Seth Warner, Vol. I, p. 160.—The date of his death is Dec. 26 1784. The fact that he was appointed Brigadier General by the Vermont Assembly, March 20 1778, was omitted from the biographical note. Warner was then and afterward in the Continental service, and the design of the Assembly probably was to give him the command of the Vermont troops whenever they acted in conjunction with his Continental regiment.

Rev. Dr. Samuel Williams, Vol. I, pp. 177, 178.—The editor was in doubt whether the pass issued by the Council of Safety, Sept. 22 1777, applied to the Rev. Dr. Williams, inasmuch as it does not appear that he came to Vermont previous to 1788. The pass was probably issued to HON. SAMUEL WILLIAMS, another gentleman of the same name, who came to Rutland as early as 1777; and he it was who held all the civil offices which were assigned to the Rev. Dr. Williams in the biographical note. A biographical notice of the HON. SAMUEL WILLIAMS, by CHAUNCEY K. WILLIAMS, Esq., of Rutland, is reserved for use in the appropriate place.

Joseph Bowker, Vol. I, p. 190.—The date of his death is July 11 1784.

The *Lieut. Governor as Maj. General*, Vol. I, p. 257.– The note on this subject is correct as far as it goes; but the fact should be added that, by the militia act of Feb. 1779, the post of "Major General of and over all the military forces within" Vermont, was given to the Lieutenant Governor, *ex officio*.—See Slade's *State Papers*, p. 305.

Elisha Payne, Vol. I, p. 278.—Lieut. Gov. Payne was not the *Capt. Paine* referred to. Lieut. Gov. Payne came to New Hampshire from Canterbury, Conn.

Rev. Drs. Samuel and Samuel A. Peters, Vol. I, pp. 403, 404.—The date of the publication of the American edition of Samuel A. Peters's History of Connecticut should be 1829. CHAUNCEY K. WILLIAMS, Esq., of Rutland, in a private letter to the editor, has cited many authorities which apparently prove that the author of the life of Rev. Hugh Peters, and of a History of Connecticut, was the Rev. Dr. SAMUEL PETERS, of Hebron, Conn., and not the *Rev. Dr. Samuel A. Peters*, the younger, of the same place. Several other authorities might be cited to the same point; yet the editor is persuaded by the latest biographers, DRAKE and ALLIBONE, that *Samuel A. Peters* of Hebron, Conn., was the author of the books named, and was also the Bishop elect of Vermont; but he is inclined to the opinion that it was the *Rev. Dr. Samuel Peters* (the eldest of the two reverend doctors of Hebron,) for whom the younger claimed the honor of christening Vermont.—See Vol. I, p. 403. In Samuel A. Peters's history of Connecticut, the Rev. Dr. *Samuel Peters* is spoken of in terms highly complimentary, and it must be concluded either that the author of the book was a monstrous egotist in so writing of himself, or that his compliments were intended for another—by the Rev. Dr. Samuel A. the younger, for the Rev. Dr. Samuel the elder—both of Hebron, Conn., both clergymen in the Church of England, both Tories in America, and both refugees in England at the same time. The two persons have been doubtless confounded by the extraordnary parallelism in their names, birth-place, residence, profession, and history.

Dartmouth College, Vol. I, pp. 278, 428.—The suggestions as to the interest and influence of the officers and corporators of the college in the union of Western New Hampshire and Vermont, are confirmed by the following unique document:

LANDAFF October 3: 1781.[1]

We the inhabitants of s[d] Landaff having a Laudebel atachment to the State of Newhampshier and Likewise to the thirteen united States of America and as We Live wheir Vermont Claims Jurisdiction have Received so maney insults from that Quarter and are Now in Verry Grate feear of Being insulted by them and Especially from the Emesseries of the Colledge Do humbly Petition to the Honourabel Court of New: hampisher for ade and Protection Against the insults and abuses of the Vermont, and especely the Emeserries of the Coledg Which your Petitioners in Duty Bound Shall ever Pray

JOHN CLARK, Jur.
JOHN CLARK
JAMES CRISSSY
EBENEZER CLARK
JONATHAN CLARK
WILLIAM CHURCHILL
NATHANIEL RIX

Vol. I, p. 477.—"James Smith" should be *John Smith.*

Vol. II, p. 10.—The last remark on the page applies to the resolution of Oct. 25 1779 only.

Vol. II, p. 27.—"Mr. Speaker" in the list of Yeas was THOMAS CHANDLER, jr.

Vol. II, p. 38.—"Capt. J. [probably Jesse] Safford" should be *Capt. Joseph Safford.*

Vol. II, p. 52.—The grantees of *Gilead* [now *Brighton*] were *Elihu Marvin* and Company. The grant in blank to "Rossettee Griffin & Company" was of the town of *Walden*, to *Capt. Rossiter Griffin and Company.*

---

[1] *N. H. State Papers*, Ms., *Vermont Controversy*, 1764–91, p. 239.

Vol. II, p. 54.—The grant to "Gatesborough" was of the town now named *Salem.*

Vol. II, p. 55.—For "Major Elijah Buel" in the grant to Coventry, read Major *Elias* Buel.

Vol. II, p. 76.—"William Cotter" should be *Willard Cotter.*

Vol. II, p. 81.—In the list of relieved proprietors of Royalton "Peleg Parkhurst" should be *Tilly Parkhurst.*

Hon. Jonathan Freeman, Vol. II, pp. 96, 295, 299, 302. JONATHAN FREEMAN, of Hanover, N. H., was prominent in the Vermont councils in 1781, and afterward equally so in New Hampshire, where he was a member of the Council from 1789 to 1797, member of Congress, from 1797 to 1801, and one of the trustees and overseers of Dartmouth College. He died in 1808, aged 63 years.

Vol. II, p. 295.—"Mr. John Dunton, Acworth, N. H.," should be *John Duncan.*

Vol. II, p. 296, note 1.—"Ebenezer Dewey" should be *Ebenezer Dewey jr.*

Vol. II, p. 302, fifth line from the top.—"B. Smith" should be *Samuel Smith.*

Vol. II, p. 323, note 1.—The date of the proceedings referred to should be Oct. 16–19 1781.

Vol. II, p. 368.—"Ichabod Bartlett" should be *Josiah Bartlett.*

Vol. II, p. 375.—Add to the statement of the second vote in Congress the words *Connecticut divided.*

ACKNOWLEDGMENTS.

THE editor is obliged to the officers of the State Department at Washington, on the request of Hon. JUSTIN S. MORRILL, for the use of original documents touching Vermont which had never been printed, copies of which have been carefully made by C. L. DANA ; to the officers of the State Department of New Hampshire for copies of several original documents on the Second Union of New Hampshire towns with Vermont, and the consequent collisions of authority; to HENRY L. LAMB, Esq., of Albany, N. Y., for a copy of Gov. Chittenden's Proclamation of July 18 1781; to CHAUNCEY K. WILLIAMS, Esq., of Rutland, and WHIPPLE SPOONER of Burlington, for the correction of errors in the first volume; to the publishers of Miss ABBY MARIA HEMENWAY'S *Vermont Historical Magazine*, for the use of the engraved plate of IRA ALLEN, and to the historian, BENSON J. LOSSING, for liberty to copy Gov. Hall's history and description of the Catamount Tavern and Vermont Council Chamber, from *The American Historical Record.*

GENERAL INDEX.

A

C

D

G

H

Q

R

S

Towns—Continued.

Towns—Continued.

Towns—Continued.

U

V

Y

www.ingramcontent.com/pod-product-compliance
Lightning Source LLC
LaVergne TN
LVHW021132110826
845150LV00005B/1009

* 9 7 8 1 4 2 5 5 4 9 4 2 8 *